# Parents' Beliefs About Children

# Parents' Beliefs About Children

SCOTT A. MILLER

*University of Florida*

*Gainesville, FL*

OXFORD

UNIVERSITY PRESS

# OXFORD
### UNIVERSITY PRESS

Oxford University Press is a department of the University of Oxford. It furthers
the University's objective of excellence in research, scholarship, and education
by publishing worldwide. Oxford is a registered trade mark of Oxford University
Press in the UK and certain other countries.

Published in the United States of America by Oxford University Press
198 Madison Avenue, New York, NY 10016, United States of America.

© Oxford University Press 2020

Library of Congress Control Number: 2019949796
ISBN 978-0-19-087451-3

1 3 5 7 9 8 6 4 2

Printed by Integrated Books International, United States of America

*To my children and grandchildren.*

# Contents

*Acknowledgments*                                           ix

1. Why Study Parents' Beliefs?                               1

2. Theories and Methods                                     14

3. General Processes of Development                         52

4. Parenting and Family                                     88

5. Infancy                                                 128

6. Childhood: Cognitive Development                        164

7. Childhood: Social Development                           202

8. Adolescence                                             239

9. Atypical Development                                    276

*References*                                               311
*Name Index*                                               385
*Subject Index*                                            409

# Acknowledgments

I am grateful to many people for various kinds of help during the writing of this book. General support was provided by the Department of Psychology, University of Florida. Specific and much needed help came from the Interlibrary Loan Division of the University Library, which tracked down so many sources that I needed. Of the colleagues who were kind enough to share materials or to clarify aspects of their research, I owe a special thanks to David MacPhee, whose work is an important contribution to any account of parents' beliefs. This book benefitted greatly from the comments offered by reviewers of the prepublication version: Christy Buchanan, Joan Grusec, and George Holden. Finally, I am grateful for the excellent help and support provided by the editorial teams at Oxford University Press and Newgen Knowledge Works: Andrea Zekus, Abby Gross, Katie Pratt, and Sujitha Logaganesan.

# 1

# Why Study Parents' Beliefs?

Well, the most important things for her are to play, spend time out-side, move around, and stay with other kids . . . because children have their own language, they understand each other very well, they are direct, and help each other to grow up.

—(Harkness et al., 2006, p. 77)

He is occupying himself and has an incredible imagination and inventing things and talking about things. I just think that if little teeny kids are with other kids all day long, they just don't develop that kind of original self-reliant mind if they have a tendency in that direction.

—(Harkness & Super, 1992, p. 388)

Independence. I think that everyone must be independent. And I have the idea myself that you don't have to push them to be that way. Playing alone outside is independent. Doing a puzzle by your-self is independent. Making a mess and cleaning it up by yourself is independent. So it all belongs together.

—(Harkness Super, & van Tijen., 2000, p. 35)

I think that a child can do with all the affection a parent has to spare. . . . It's very vital to the emotional and physical health of the being that a parent should give him love.

—(Stolz, 1967, p. 32)

Very definitely the difference is a question of temperament, what they've been born with, because I think these traits have shown up within a few months after they were born.

—(Stolz, 1967, p. 136)

*Parents' Beliefs About Children.* Scott A. Miller, Oxford University Press (2020). © Oxford University Press.
DOI: 10.1093/oso/9780190874513.001.0001

She enjoys spending time with people and talking with people. She loves books. She's got a load of energy that just doesn't seem to quit. Um, she's a mother hen. Things have got to be just so and she knows the right way for them to be. And if they're not the right way, she gets concerned about it. She's a responsible child.

　　　　　　　　　　　—(Bond, Belenky, Weinstock, & Cook, 1996, p. 490)

The passages just quoted come from research in developmental psychology directed to the question of what parents believe about children. Most of the remaining chapters in this book will open with further passages relevant to the chapters' contents. The examples will be just a small sampling from what has become a very large research literature. Parents' beliefs about children is one of the venerable topics in developmental psychology, with research dating back more than a century, and relevant publications now number in the thousands.

Of course, one does not need research in developmental psychology to know that parents form beliefs about their children. All that is necessary is to talk to a parent. Or to be a parent oneself.

This book is devoted to the topic of what parents think about children. Two of the general conclusions for which it will argue will be illustrated in the quoted passages. One is that parents form beliefs about a wide variety of topics. A second is that there are often marked differences among parents in the beliefs they form.

A third general conclusion cannot be gleaned simply from a sampling of beliefs, but it is the central thesis of this book. It is that parents' beliefs make a difference. They make a difference in the development of the child, and they make a difference in the life of the parent.

## Definitional Issues

A book entitled *Parents' Beliefs About Children* must begin by defining the terms in its title. Such a discussion will serve to indicate what will and will not be included in the chapters to follow.

Two of the three nouns in the title are relatively easy. The *Parents'* part is straightforward. Not all research on adults' beliefs about children has focused on parents; in some cases, the subjects have consisted of adults in general. This book, however, is concerned with parents; nonparents are brought in only when they provide a comparison with some sample of parents. In most instances such comparisons are between-subject—that is, separate groups of parents and nonparents. Occasionally, however, they are within-subject, something that occurs when the same people are studied before and after the onset of parenthood.

The *Children* part of the title is also relatively easy. This is not a book about parents' thinking in general; it is a book about what parents think about children. Two points should be made, however, about the extension of the term "children." First, the term is used here in its genealogical rather than chronological sense, in that research with parents of adult children is included. Such research, however, constitutes a small proportion of the overall literature; in most cases "children" also applies in its minor-person, not-yet-an-adult sense.

The second point concerns the scope of the beliefs at issue. Not all of the studies reviewed have asked explicitly about children. Also included are two other kinds of study: those with a focus on beliefs about parenting and those with a focus on beliefs about the family. The rationale for including this work is that one could hardly penetrate very far in thinking about either parenting or family without thinking about children; beliefs about children are intrinsic to these topics. And as we will see, some of the most informative work in the beliefs literature has come from studies whose focus was on either parenting or family.

It is, of course, the third element in the title, the *Beliefs* part, that requires the most discussion. The question of exactly what sorts of parental thinking should be examined and what terms should be used for whatever *is* examined is a frequently addressed topic in the parents' beliefs literature; among the sources for discussion are Goodnow and Collins (1990), Hirsjarvi and Perala-Littunen (2001), Holden and Edwards (1989), Okagaki and Bingham (2005), and Sigel and Kim (1996). More generally, the question of exactly what is meant by "belief" and how beliefs differ from other forms of mental content is a long-standing issue in both the psychology (e.g., Sigel, 1985a) and philosophy literatures (e.g., Bogdan, 1986).

Why select "beliefs" as the generic term? Goodnow and Collins (1990) provide a good summary of arguments in support of such a choice (even though they themselves go on to use "ideas" rather than "beliefs").

It is now in fairly wide usage (e.g., Sigel, 1985b). It captures the sense of parents' ideas as constructions, as "statements of truth" from the parents' viewpoint. . . . It avoids the unhappy connotation of ideas as consisting of some "inert mental state" (Bogdan, 1986, p. 8). It also has the appeal of suggesting some of the features we wish to see acknowledged in research on parents' ideas: namely, the recognition that parents' ideas are often marked by a touch of myth, are linked to action, have a possible "executive function," are suffused with affect, and are often accompanied by a sense of attachment and ownership on the part of the believer. (p. 12)

Although I agree with all of the points made, it is the first two that mainly guided my choice of terminology. "Beliefs" is by far the most commonly used generic term in the literatures to be reviewed here. Furthermore, "beliefs" (unlike, for example, "ideas") is also an established term in the psychology literature more generally. Second, and more substantively, "beliefs" designates the types of cognitions on which I wish to concentrate—namely those that (at least from the parent's perspective) are directed to aspects of the world that have a factual status, things that can be true or false and about which the parent can be right or wrong (thus the "statements of truth" to which Goodnow and Collins refer). Several such "statements of truth" are evident in the quotations at the start of the chapter (e.g., children have their own language, parental love is vital, inborn temperament is important), and we will see many more in the pages to follow.

Having noted this delimiting of the book's target, I will add that my rule when in doubt has been to be inclusive rather than exclusive. Thus work presented under a number of labels in addition to "beliefs" ("ideas," "cognitions," "attitudes," "expectations," "perceptions") is included, and the factual status of the mental state in question is no doubt clearer in some cases than in others. The one consistent omission is research under the headings of "values" or "goals." This is not, of course, because parents' values and goals are unimportant for their children's development. Because they have no truth status, however, values and goals are a fundamentally different kind of cognition than are beliefs, and their inclusion would have stretched both the focus and the length of the book. I *do* consider such work when it appears with and helps illuminate the study of beliefs; otherwise, however, values and goals are outside the scope of coverage.

## Why Study Parents' Beliefs?

Why study parents' beliefs about children? In what follows I suggest eight reasons.

## Parents' Beliefs Are an Important Form of Adult Social Cognition

All of us have beliefs about many things—ourselves, other people, the world in general. To my knowledge, there has never been an attempt to tabulate the frequency with which different beliefs are activated in the course of a day. For any parent, however, beliefs about one's child must rank high on any such list. Rearing a child involves multiple interactions and parental decisions every day, and in many instances the process extends for 18 or more years.

Of course, the fact that parents' beliefs are frequent components of many adults' thoughts does not mean that such beliefs require some separate line of study. A century or so of research in cognitive psychology and social psychology has taught us much about adult cognition, including adult social cognition. The strategies, biases, heuristics, and so forth identified in such research clearly apply when parents try to make sense of their children. As Goodnow and Collins (1990) note, "Parental cognition is not some strange new form of thought, for which we need to invent totally new principles, or which tells us only about parents" (pp. 7–8).

On the other hand—and as Goodnow and Collins' (1990) entire book makes clear—parental cognition has a number of features that suggest that a simple application of findings from the basic adult literature will not be sufficient. In most research on adult social cognition, the targets being judged are generic ones presented in standard scenarios; in studies of parents' beliefs, the targets are highly, indeed maximally, familiar. In most studies of adult social cognition, there is no relationship between perceiver and target; in studies of parents' beliefs, there is a long-term and intense relationship. Most studies of adult social cognition do not evoke strong or perhaps any emotional responses in their participants; emotions, including strong emotions in both directions, are a frequent occurrence when parents think about their children. In most basic research, the judgments to be made are fairly circumscribed and situation-specific; parents may need to make sense of dozens of different child behaviors in the course of a single day. Finally, in most basic research, the target does not change its nature across the course of study; parents, however, must adjust to a continually changing target as the child develops from infant to toddler to preschooler and so on up to adulthood.

These points are not meant to suggest that the basic research literature is not a fruitful starting point for generating and interpreting studies of parents' beliefs. It is only a starting point, however. In addition, the relation between the two literatures definitely goes in both directions. Because of the distinctive qualities just noted, and because of their importance in the life of a parent, the study of parents' beliefs adds significantly to what we know about adult cognition. As I will argue, such study also adds to each of the general theories that have been invoked to explain parents' beliefs.

## Parents' Beliefs Affect Parents' Behavior

This point, too, has a grounding in the basic psychology literature. One of the classic issues in psychology has to do with the relation between what people believe and how they behave—an issue typically referred to as the *attitude–behavior relation* (e.g., Ajzen & Fishbein, 2005). This *is* a classic issue not only because of its importance but also because of its intractability, for it has often proved difficult to identify clear links between beliefs and behavior. This does not mean that no links exist—just that they are often weaker or less obvious or more complicated than we might have assumed. A reasonable conclusion is that most behaviors are multiply determined, beliefs are typically just one of the determinants, and the specific beliefs under study may not always be the relevant ones for the behavior in question.

Studies of parents' beliefs form an important component of the attitude–behavior literature, not only because of the sheer volume of such studies but also because of the significance of the beliefs and behaviors at issue. As we will see, the results from these studies in general mirror those from the broader literature. Not all studies find relations, and when relations are found they are typically modest in size. Nevertheless, the general conclusion, emerging from several hundred studies, is clear: Parents' beliefs do affect parents' behavior. They affect behavior in a short-term sense, in that parents' interpretation of a child's behavior may guide their response to that behavior. They also affect behavior in a long-term sense, in that general approaches to child-rearing follow out of and are maintained over time by what parents believe. Thus such studies also speak to one of the central questions in developmental psychology: What are the origins of parents' child-rearing practices?

## Parents' Beliefs Affect Children's Development

The theme of this section of the chapter is that there are many reasons to study parents' beliefs. If forced to choose one justification, however, most researchers would probably opt for the reason to be considered now: the effects of parents' beliefs on children's development. As I have already indicated, that there are such effects is the main thesis of this book. The challenges are to specify exactly what they are and how they come about.

Much of what follows is devoted to these two questions. I will, however, make one point now. It applies to the studies in the beliefs literature that include all three components of interest: parents' beliefs, parents' behaviors, and child outcomes. Such studies therefore provide information about two possible predictors of children's development: what parents believe about the child and how parents behave toward the child.

In many studies both predictors show significant relations. In a subset of studies, however, only the beliefs measure is predictive; parents' behaviors show no relation to their children's development. Clearly, this finding does not mean that parents' beliefs somehow exert their effects in the absence of any parental behavior that mediates those effects. But it does mean that the relevant behaviors may be somewhat different from those that are the typical focus of child-rearing research. It also means that it may sometimes be more informative to know what parents believe than to know how they behave. Information about beliefs may guide the search for relevant parenting behaviors. It may also provide an avenue for change in instances in which change is needed. In fact, a focus on parents' beliefs is the central component of many parent training and intervention programs.

## Parents' Beliefs Affect Parents

Parents' beliefs not only affect children; they affect the parents themselves. They do so in various ways. One way is through effects on parents' emotional responses in interactions with their children. Parents form expectations about how their children will behave, and a violated expectation will at the least produce surprise and perhaps also dismay if the violation is in a negative direction. Parents also form explanations for why their children behave as they do, and their emotional response to a child's behavior may depend on the explanation that they generate for it. An undesirable behavior that is believed to be under the child's control, for example, will elicit a more negative response than will one for which the child is believed not to be responsible. Parents form explanations as well for their own behaviors in interaction with their children, and these explanations, too, can have emotional consequences. A belief that one is responsible for a good child-rearing outcome will obviously elicit a more positive set of emotions than will a belief that one has failed at an important and potentially doable task.

The consequences of parents' beliefs for parents themselves are not only short-term. Over time a history of parenting successes or failures can lead to a generalized set of beliefs about one's competence as a parent. As we will see, predominantly negative beliefs about parental competence are associated with a variety of negative outcomes: maladaptive child-rearing behaviors, socioemotional difficulties for the parent, adverse developmental outcomes for the child.

Perhaps the most long-term consequence of parents' beliefs for parents comes from research discussed in Chapter 4 under the heading of "Value of Children." A subset of this literature focuses on parents of adult children, and a basic question directed to such parents is how well their children have turned out. For many parents the answer to this question is one of the most important determinants of how well they believe that their own life has turned out.

## Parents' Beliefs Are of Interest to Many Disciplines

This, in fact, is a point with which Goodnow and Collins (1990) begin their book. Among the students of parents' beliefs whom they cite, in addition to psychologists, are clinicians, family therapists, parent educators, anthropologists, and sociologists. A glance through the References sections of this book will confirm the multidisciplinary nature of the topic; close to 250 journals, spanning many different disciplines, are sources for the work reviewed here. Among the disciplines that contribute, in addition to those mentioned by Goodnow and Collins, are pediatrics, nursing, education, business, linguistics, and psychiatry.

To some extent, of course, practitioners of different disciplines have different reasons for an interest in parents' beliefs; the marketing researcher will seek out different sorts of information than will the clinical psychologist. But what this divergence of interests means is that a full appreciation of the nature and the importance of parents' beliefs requires a multidisciplinary perspective that encompasses all of the varied topics that have been objects of study. It also means that research in any one discipline is enriched by knowledge of the approaches taken by other disciplines. We will see a number of examples of this point as we go.

## Parents' Beliefs Are Central to the Study of Culture and Cultural Differences

One aspect of any culture is a set of belief systems that embody fundamental tenets of the culture and that are transmitted from one generation to the next. And among the important belief systems in any culture are those held by parents—beliefs about children, beliefs about parenting, beliefs about family. In the words of Harkness and Super (2006, p. 62), such belief systems serve as "the nexus through which elements of the larger culture are filtered, and as an important source of parenting practices and the organization of daily life for children and families." In the discipline that is typically labeled *cultural psychology* parents' belief systems serve as one way to characterize the nature of the culture under study. In the discipline that is typically labeled *cross-cultural psychology* parents' beliefs systems serve as one way to characterize similarities and differences between cultures. The study of parents' beliefs thus speaks to both the emic and etic aspects of cultural study.

When comparisons are made across time, such studies also speak to issues of cultural transmission and cultural change (Goodnow, 2006). By this point, comparisons *have* been made across time for many cultures, and we will see examples of both continuity and discontinuity in parental beliefs in the chapters to come.

## Parents' Beliefs Are the Basis for Parent-Report Measures of Child Characteristics

Like most outcomes of interest in psychological research, children's charac-teristics can be measured in various ways, including (for at least some char-acteristics) naturalistic observations and experimental tests. Probably the most commonly used measurement option, however, is verbal report from some informant who knows the child well enough to provide the necessary information. For school-aged children, reports from teachers may be an option. When children grow old enough, peer reports and self-reports be-come possibilities. By far the most commonly used informants, however, are children's parents. Thus much of what we know about children's development comes from what parents tell us about their children. How accurately parents can judge their children therefore becomes a critical question.

In some studies parent-report measures are limited-focus assessments created for the purposes of the study. Often, however, the measures take the form of standardized assessment instruments that are intended for wide-spread use. This is especially the case for measures of children' social devel-opment and for measures that have clinical conditions as their targets. In no instance are parent reports the only possible source of evidence. But they are often an important source.

The chapters to come will include discussions of the parent-report meas-ures relevant to the topics in question. In most instances the sampling will be a partial one because often there are too many such measures to attempt an exhaustive coverage. I will, however, provide some description of the most frequently used instruments. I will also discuss the psychometric proper-ties of such measures—in particular, the question of validity. Parent-report measures depend on parents' ability to judge their children, and the valida-tion data for such measures provide the most rigorous test of how accurately parents can do so.

## Parents' Beliefs Are of Pragmatic Importance

Many uses of the parent-report measures just described occur as part of basic research with regard to the developments in question. Much of what we know about both attachment and temperament, for example, comes from the use of parent-report measures. Such a basic science orientation also applies to most uses of parent-report measures in the cognitive domain. We will see some examples in Chapter 6.

Although the kinds of research uses just noted are important, they do not constitute the main context in which parent-report measures are found. The main context is a pragmatic one: instances of problems or of perceived problems in the development of the child. Again, parent-report measures are unlikely to be the only source of information. But they often are an important source with regard to three decisions: Are problems serious enough to warrant an intervention? If so, what form should the intervention take? And how should the results of the intervention be evaluated?

The importance of parents' beliefs in cases of possible developmental problems extends beyond the use of formal parent-report measures. A parent's belief that something is amiss in her child's development may lead her to seek help, even in the absence of a formal assessment. Conversely, a parent's belief that an apparent problem is not serious or will resolve on its own may lead to a decision not to seek help. Clearly, it is critical to be right in either case.

This section has stressed the pragmatic importance of parents' beliefs. But as the earlier discussion should have made clear, the importance of parents' beliefs is not limited to cases of potential problems in development. Parents' beliefs are important in the development of every child.

## Organization of the Book

There are various ways to organize the material on parents' beliefs. One possibility, for example, is to organize in terms of the nature of the belief—thus a section on attributions, a section on expectations, a section on beliefs about the timing of different developments, and so forth. Another possibility is to organize in terms of the general issues that underlie such research. In this case there would be a section devoted to the origins of beliefs, another devoted to the relations between beliefs and behavior, and another devoted to the relations between beliefs and children's development.

My coverage will, of course, encompass both of the substantive groupings just sketched—thus the different types of beliefs that parents form and the general issues that guide the study of beliefs. My presentation, however, will follow a third organizational strategy: an organization in terms of the child characteristics that are the targets for the beliefs. Like any of the possible organizational schemes, this approach does not capture every point of interest, and thus I will occasionally deviate from it (most markedly in Chapter 4). In general, however, the book's focus will mirror the parent's focus in most of the research reviewed: What is it about the child that we are attempting to understand?

More specifically, the organization of the book is as follows. The next chapter discusses two topics that are necessary preludes to the review of research: the theories that underlie the study of parents' beliefs and the methodological possibilities and methodological issues that arise in such research. The discussion of theories will introduce a basic theme to which I will return periodically: namely, the reciprocal relation between theories and research. Theories help to guide research on parents' beliefs, but such research also feeds back on and broadens all of the theories to be discussed. The discussion of methods will consider not only methods for studying beliefs but also the methods that underlie study of the three further questions of interest: the origins of beliefs, the relation between beliefs and parents' behavior, and the relation between beliefs and children's development.

The first of the review chapters focuses on parents' beliefs about general processes of development. Of interest are beliefs of various sorts, all of which tie in to central questions in developmental psychology. A basic issue is that of nature and nurture: To what extent is development under biological control, and to what extent does it derive from experience? Assuming that experience plays a role, who are the important social agents in the child's life? Of particular interest, of course, are beliefs about the importance of parents. A further question concerns the nature of learning. Are children active or passive as they take in information from the world around them, and what is the relative importance of formal and informal forms of learning?

Chapter 4 focuses on beliefs about the child as part of a larger social context. The first half of the chapter discusses beliefs about parenting, and the second half discusses beliefs about the family. A central question will be the agreement between parents' beliefs and children's beliefs, as well as what happens when (as is often the case) the two parties do not agree.

The organization of the next four chapters is chronological. This set of chapters begins very early in development with a discussion of infancy in Chapter 5, and it concludes a dozen or so years later with a discussion of adolescence in Chapter 8. As any parent knows, both periods are times of dramatic change across a broad range of developments, and they therefore can present special challenges for parents' attempts to understand their children.

Chapters 6 and 7 are devoted to the childhood years that span the period between infancy and adolescence. The division between the two chapters is a topical one. Chapter 6 discusses parents' beliefs about children's cognitive development, and Chapter 7 adds a complementary treatment of parents' beliefs about children's social development. In both instances the focus is broad, reflecting the wealth of developments that fall under the cognitive and social headings. Among the targets for questioning in the Cognitive chapter are intelligence, language, memory, and theory of mind. Among the targets in the Social chapter are morality, aggression, emotional development, and gender differences.

As the earlier discussion indicated, one of the reasons for an interest in parents' beliefs is their pragmatic importance in instances in which development departs from its typical course. Chapter 9, "Atypical Development," considers departures of two sorts. One is at the child end, and thus includes clinical conditions such as Down syndrome, autism spectrum disorder, and attention deficit hyperactivity disorder (ADHD). The other is at the parent end, with a focus on both clinical conditions (e.g., depression, anxiety) and maladaptive parental practices—in particular, abuse and neglect.

As this overview suggests, this book's coverage is broad, encompassing not only a wide range of different beliefs but also what we know about the origins and effects of such beliefs. In two respects, however, the coverage falls short of being exhaustive. First, some topics that appear in the beliefs literature are both too removed from my organizational structure and too limited in their literatures to be included; examples include food preferences (Russell & Worsley, 2013), music training (Dai & Schader, 2002), and farm work (Pickett, Marlenga, & Berg, 2003). Second, for many of the topics that are discussed the number of relevant sources is too great (in some instances numbering in the hundreds) to permit a full coverage. My goal has been to select studies for discussion that are either representative of the literature as a whole or in some way especially informative and, of course, to offer conclusions that follow from the literature as a whole.

# 2

# Theories and Methods

Relevant theories and methods will be discussed in each of the chapters to come. The purpose of this chapter is to provide an initial overview, a set of possibilities and issues that can be returned to and expanded as needed. As would be expected, the main focus in what follows is on parents' beliefs: Thus theories of the form that beliefs take in the section on "Theories" and methods to study such beliefs in the section on "Methods." As we saw in Chapter 1, however, the nature of parents' beliefs is just one of the issues to which to this literature speaks. We also want to know where the beliefs come from, and we want to know how they relate to parental behavior and to child development. Consequently, this chapter also considers theories and methods relevant to these further issues.

## Theories

A first point about theories is that much of the literature on parents' beliefs is not very theoretically driven. Some studies are primarily pragmatic in origin—attempts to identify, and in some cases to change, forms of parental thought that may make a difference in the lives of children. In other instances there *is* a theoretical framework, but it remains at a general, almost common-sensical, level. Thus, the basic reasoning behind much research appears to be of the following sort: People form beliefs about the important aspects of their lives; therefore parents form beliefs about their children. Beliefs are one determinant of how people behave; therefore parents' beliefs are one deter-minant of how they treat their children. Parents' treatment of children is one determinant of how children develop; therefore parents' beliefs contribute to children's development. It is hard to disagree with this general framework; still, a truly theoretical account requires both more specificity and more grounding in established psychological theories.

This chapter discusses eight positions that provide at least some of the needed grounding. Each of the positions will be returned to at various points

*Parents' Beliefs About Children.* Scott A. Miller, Oxford University Press (2020). © Oxford University Press.
DOI: 10.1093/oso/9780190874513.001.0001

throughout the book. In addition, other, more narrowly focused theories will be added as they become relevant.

I will begin with two preliminary points. Often, when multiple theories are discussed, the emphasis is on contrasts and choice among the competing positions. The theories to be considered now are much more complementary than contradictory. In part they address different aspects of the belief-behavior-outcome nexus, and in part they use different terminology for what seem to be essentially the same conclusions. In addition, elements of one approach may be incorporated by advocates of a different approach. Dix and Grusec (1985), for example, situate attribution theory within a more general information-processing perspective. Bugental and Happaney (2002) discuss working models as a component within an attribution theory framework. A reasonable expectation—and, as we will see, a reasonable conclusion—is that all of the approaches have something to offer.

The second point is a reiteration of a point made in Chapter 1. It is that the relation between theory and research is very much a reciprocal one. An appropriate theoretical framework can guide and illuminate research on parents' beliefs. At the same time, the study of parents' beliefs provides a valuable broadening of each of the theories to be considered.

## Attribution Theory

Attributions have to do with the causal explanations that people offer for behavior, both their own behavior and the behavior of others. It is the position that deals most directly and most fully with the nature and effects of parents' beliefs about children. Not coincidentally, it is also the position that has exerted the most influence in research to date. Interim reviews of this literature include Bugental and Happaney (2002) and Miller (1995). I am not aware of any more recent review, but I will, of course, provide one across the relevant chapters here.

Attribution theory is a long-standing position within social psychology, with a number of theoretical progenitors of what remains very much an ongoing research literature (Heider, 1958; Jones & Davis, 1965; Kelley, 1967; Weiner, 1986). Although there are some differences among the various guiding theories (see Malle, 2011), for the most part they emphasize different aspects of the attributional process and thus are more complementary than contradictory.

**Table 2.1**  Factors That Govern Attributions

| Factor | Description |
|---|---|
| Covariation principle | Attribute an outcome to the cause with which it covaries over time |
| Consistency information | Extent to which an individual responds to a given situation in the same way over time |
| Distinctiveness information | Extent to which an individual responds in the same way to different situations (similar response equals low distinctiveness) |
| Consensus information | Extent to which others respond to the same situation in the same way as the individual being judged |
| Augmenting principle | Attach greater importance to a potential cause if the behavior occurs despite the presence of other, inhibitory causes |
| Discounting principle | Attach less importance to a potential cause if other potential causes are also present |

What factors govern how people reason about the causes of behavior? Tables 2.1 and 2.2 summarize some of the core principles that are stressed in attributional accounts. The first table is based mainly on the theorizing of Kelley, and the second is based mainly on the theorizing of Weiner.

The principles in Table 2.1 address the basic question of how attributions are formed. The most fundamental of the entries is the covariation principle: attribute an outcome to a cause with which it covaries. If, for example, a child cleans his room always and only when promised a reward for doing so, a reasonable attribution is that the reward is the cause of the behavior. Or if a child falters in school only when she has failed to study, a natural inference is that the failure to study is the cause of her problems.

**Table 2.2**  Dimensions Along Which Attributions Vary

| | Dimension | | |
|---|---|---|---|
| | **Internal–External** | **Stable–Unstable** | **Controllable–Uncontrollable** |
| Causal factor | | | |
| Ability | Internal | Stable | Uncontrollable |
| Effort | Internal | Unstable | Controllable |
| Task difficulty | External | Stable | Uncontrollable |
| Luck | External | Unstable | Uncontrollable |

The remaining entries in the table are particular forms of covariation information that may apply in different situations. Suppose, for instance, that the child in the first example wants very much to play with friends but nevertheless stays inside and cleans his room. In this case the augmenting principle suggests that we should attribute even more causal power to the reward, given that it produced the behavior even in the face of an opposing force. Or suppose that the girl in the second example claims that bad luck led to her low test score, even though her parents know that she failed to study. The discounting principle suggests that the parents will be dubious about the role of luck given that they are aware of an alternative and sufficient cause.

The entries in Table 2.2 pick up on a somewhat different aspect of the attributional process; namely, the underlying dimensions along which attributions vary. In the parents' beliefs literature this model has been applied most often to attributions for academic performance, and academic performance is therefore taken as the example here; clearly, however, the same principles could apply to reasoning about other domains as well.

Suppose that parents have just received news of a disappointing test score from their child's school. If they attribute the score to a lack of ability on their child's part, then they will expect similar results in the future (ability being stable over time) and they will not expect their child to be able to do anything to change the situation (ability being uncontrollable). If, on the other hand, they attribute the low score to a lack of effort on the child's part, then they will be less pessimistic about the future (effort being unstable), but they will expect, and probably work to achieve, change on their child's part (effort being controllable). Attributions to task difficulty or luck will lead to their own reactions and expectations.

Note that the qualities ascribed to the various attributions in the table (effort controllable, ability uncontrollable, etc.) are modal ones that most people make most of the time. They are not inevitable; a particular parent, for example, may believe that ability can change. Nor are they necessarily accurate. To continue with the ability example, we know (most obviously from Carol Dweck's work, e.g., Dweck, 1999) that aspects of ability are not fixed but rather can change with experience.

The attributional dimensions in Table 2.2 are relevant to the effects that an attribution has on the person who makes it. Most immediately, the particular attribution drawn can influence the perceiver's emotional response. A mother who believes that some negative outcome was under her child's control will be more upset with the child than one who believes that the outcome was uncontrollable; conversely, a mother who believes that effort led to a good test score will be more pleased than one who assumes that the test was easy or the child got lucky. The particular attribution drawn can also influence the perceiver's future behavior. The mother distressed by a controllable negative outcome is likely to work to change the controllable behavior that produced the outcome, just as the mother pleased by the positive test score will work to maintain the effort that produced the good result.

Parents make attributions not only for children's behavior but also for their own behavior, and these attributions too can affect subsequent emotions and behaviors. Mothers vary, for example, in their perceived ability to control events, both in an absolute sense and relative to the power they ascribe to their child. As we will see, low perceived control on the mother's part is associated both with difficulties in parenting and with various unfavorable outcomes for both child and mother.

The reference to low-control mothers raises a further point about attributions. Attributions are always at least partly the result of the immediately available information about the behavior in question. But they can also be a result of the memories, biases, expectations, or whatever that the perceiver brings to the situation—can be a result of what is referred to as *attributional style*. Parents differ in the attributions that they are most likely to make. This, too, is an issue to which we will return.

I will draw two more points from the general attribution literature. We have seen that attributions are not always accurate. Basic attribution research has identified a number of common errors or biases that people show when making attributions. Three, in particular, are worth noting.

One is the *fundamental attribution error*. The fundamental attribution error refers to the tendency to overrate the internal, dispositional bases for behavior and to underrate the external, situational contributors. A parent, for example, may judge a behavioral lapse on her child's part as evidence for lack of self-control without taking into account the peer pressure that led to the behavior. Or a parent may attribute a low test score to lack of sufficient effort on the child's part while neglecting the fact that a bad night's sleep left the child unready to perform at his best.

A second kind of error provides a qualifier to the point just made about dispositional versus situational. Let us suppose now that we are attempting to explain our own behavior. In this case the direction of the bias reverses. The *actor-observer bias* refers to the tendency to emphasize situational rather than dispositional factors when making judgments about the self. Thus, the same parent who ignores the lack of sleep factor when reasoning about her child may be quite ready to cite situational determinants for her own behavior.

The third type of error reflects a general bias that is by no means limited to attributions. The *self-serving bias* refers to the tendency to make attributions that reflect favorably on the self. Because one's children are an important source of accomplishment and validation for most parents, the self-serving bias suggests that parents will tend to make positive attributions about their children—in particular, attributions that stress internal causes for good outcomes and external causes for bad ones. It also suggests that the attributions that they make for their own behavior will be ones that reflect positively on themselves. We will see that research generally supports both of these predictions. But we will also see that a subset of parents tend to make negative attributions about their children, a pattern that is predictive of both parenting difficulties and negative child outcomes.

The final point drawn from the general literature concerns the conditions under which attributions are most likely to occur. Among the factors that heighten the probability of attributional activity are expectation of continued interaction between perceiver and target;, desire for control on the part of the perceiver;, and the occurrence, at least sometimes, of unexpected and perhaps undesired outcomes (Hewstone, 1989). Clearly, all of these factors apply to the parent–child relationship.

## Information Processing

None of the theories discussed in this chapter takes a single form that is agreed on by all of its proponents. For no position, however, does this point apply more strongly than for information processing. The information-processing perspective has never reduced to a single theory; rather, it is a general framework within which a number of specific theories have been developed. Information processing emerged as an important position in cognitive psychology in roughly the last third of the past century, and it soon became an important position in the study of cognitive development as well.

As an example of an information-processing approach to parents' beliefs, I will take a program of research by Azar and colleagues (Azar, Okado, Stevenson, & Robinson, 2013; Azar, Reitz, & Goslin, 2008). Other examples include Rubin and Mills (1992b; Mills & Rubin, 1993), Crittenden (1993, 2016), and Milner (1993, 2003).

The Azar research is grounded in the social information processing (SIP) theory developed by Dodge and Crick (Crick & Dodge, 1994; Dodge, 1986). Figure 2.1 presents a schematic model of the approach. To anyone with some acquaintance with information processing, the general form of the figure will be familiar. Flowchart depictions are part of the common language of the information-processing approach. Such depictions capture several elements that are intrinsic to the approach. Most generally, they capture the computer metaphor that has long served both as a framework for theorizing and as a means to convey what is meant by information processing. Both humans and computers are information-processing systems: systems that take input of various sorts, use stored knowledge to operate on the input in various ways, and generate a response that is, at least usually, adaptive and appropriate. In this perspective, the external stimulus and external response, the traditional concerns of learning theory approaches, are no longer all-important. It is what goes on between stimulus and response that requires specification and explanation.

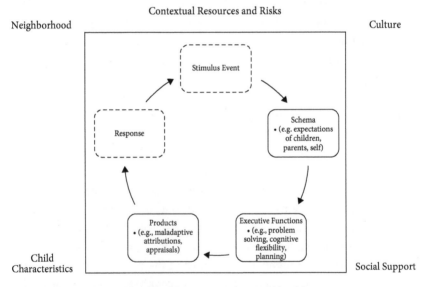

**Figure 2.1**  Azar's Social Information Processing Theory. From "Mothering: Thinking Is Part of the Job Description: Application of Cognitive Views to Understanding Maladaptive Parenting and Doing Intervention and Prevention Work," by S. T. Azar, E. B. Reitz, and M. C. Goslin, 2008, *Journal of Applied Developmental Psychology, 29*, p. 297. Copyright 2008 by Elsevier. Reprinted with permission.

As the figure suggests, quite a bit may be going on. In presenting the SIP account, I will use the same example as do Azar and colleagues in one summary
of their position (Azar et al., 2008). The example is of a mother whose child is
throwing a tantrum in the grocery store while she stands in the checkout line.
What sort of thinking might this mother engage in?

Azar's theory emphasizes two sequentially activated forms of cognitive activity. The term *schema* refers to "knowledge structures in memory that help
people organize past experiences and respond to stimulus events" (Azar et al.,
2008, p. 297). All of us possess numerous schemas that span various content
areas. If one is a parent, these schemas will include child schemas—beliefs
about what one's child is and is not capable of, beliefs about what incentives
or threats the child responds most readily to, beliefs about how the child
compares to other children of the same age, and many other schemas as well.
The schemas will also include parent schemas—beliefs about one's ability to
soothe or redirect an upset child; beliefs about one's ability to cope with multiple tasks simultaneously (e.g., comfort child and pay for groceries); beliefs
about one's susceptibility to criticism from others when parenting occurs in a
public space; and, again, many other schemas as well.

Activation of relevant schemas is the starting point in the problem-solving
process, but it must be joined by *executive function*—Azar's term for the
problem-solving resources that underlie eventual response. In the case of the
tantrum, the executive functions might include perspective taking to understand the child's point of view, planning a sequence of actions, and evaluating
possible solutions before acting.

Note that immediate output from these two steps is not the external response; rather, it is a further cognition or set of cognitions. Attributions are
one likely form of cognition. In the case of the tantrum example, the mother
might attribute the child's behavior to the fact that he missed his nap and is
very tired. Alternatively, she might attribute the behavior to the child's recent
tendency to test and embarrass her whenever possible. These two attributions
are likely to lead to different responses, both immediately and over time.

I should add a clarification to the account just given. With its multiple cognitive components, the Azar model might seem to suggest that the mother
will stand for several minutes lost in thought before finally responding to
her child's behavior. This, of course, does not happen. Many of the situations
with which parents deal are simpler than the tantrum in the store example
and require little in the way of cognitive processing. Other situations are re-
current, familiar ones for which responses have become largely automatized.

And even when on-the-spot problem solving is required, as would be true for the tantrum episode, the underlying processes are rapid, often simultaneous, and often unconscious.

The model in Figure 2.1 illustrates the general flow of information processing that is believed to underlie much of human cognition. Clearly, however, the formulation also allows for individual differences among parents. Other mothers faced with the grocery store tantrum may recruit different schemas and different problem-solving resources and may therefore respond differently. In addition, schemas differ not only in content but also in structure. For some parents schemas are relatively rigid and permit little deviation, whereas for other parents schemas are more flexible and adaptive. Some schemas are relatively complex and elaborate, whereas others are overly simplistic and thus limit the intake and processing of information. These dimensions, too, are sources of individual differences.

Such differences among parents are not only of theoretical interest; they also have pragmatic implications. At the extreme, distorted parental cognitions contribute to various forms of maladaptive parenting, including abuse and neglect. As we will see in Chapter 9, a major goal of Azar's work has been to identify the cognitive bases for parenting problems and to structure interventions that can alter the relevant cognitions.

## Vygotsky's Sociocultural Theory

The theory to be considered next has its origins in the writings of the Russian psychologist Lev Vygotsky, especially as these writings were translated and made available to Western readers in the 1960s and 1970s (Vygotsky, 1962, 1978). Numerous explications of Vygotsky's theory have appeared since (e.g., Damianova & Sullivan, 2011; Fernyhough, 2008), and various researchers have built on and extended the Vygotskian beginnings to develop contemporary versions of sociocultural theory (e.g., Nelson, 2007; Rogoff, 2003; Tomasello, 1999).

The sociocultural approach has relatively little to say about the starting point in the study of parents' beliefs: the nature of the beliefs that parents form. Its emphases, rather, are on two other questions: Where do beliefs come from, and how are beliefs translated into behavior?

The answer to the first question is implied by the name of the approach. For Vygotsky and those inspired by him, much of human thought and human knowledge has its origins in the social world and the general culture within which the child develops—a view that is sometimes referred to as "development from the outside in." An often quoted passage from Vygotsky (1978) expresses this idea: "Every function in the child's cultural development appears twice: first, on the social level, and later, on the individual level" (p. 57). This position does not mean that children are passive recipients of whatever the social world offers; they still must act on and make sense of their experiences. For sociocultural theorists, however, the critical experiences on which they act are primarily social in nature.

The idea that social experience is important for development might seem obvious. At the time at which translations of Vygotsky's writings began to appear, however, the zeitgeist was quite different. The dominant theory of cognitive development was Piaget's, and the Piagetian emphasis was on the child's own action and self-construction of knowledge, not on what the social world taught. The information processing approach, which was then emerging as a challenge to Piaget, also had little to say about social experience. Undoubtedly one of the reasons that Vygotsky's writings proved so attractive was that they seemed to redress an important limitation in the theories that were then dominant.

Vygotsky's theorizing was not limited to the assertion that social experience is important; rather, he also offered a number of suggestions as to how such experience affects the developing child. A particular emphasis was on the intellectual "tools" that a culture makes available to its members. Of these tools the most important is language. Language plays two, related roles in Vygotsky's theory. First, language is a source of information; it is primarily through language that cultural knowledge is embodied and that parents and other adults teach things to children. Second, language is a means of thinking. As children develop, they gradually become capable of using language not only for communication with others but also to guide their own thinking—they become capable of what is labeled *speech-for-self*. It is the transformation of thought by language that constitutes the main difference between animal intelligence and human intelligence, as well as the main difference between intelligence early in life and intelligence in maturity.

The discussion to this point has concerned children. But our focus, of course, is on parents. Do parents' beliefs have a similar sociocultural grounding? The answer for theorists in this tradition is yes. The importance of the social world does not disappear in adulthood; rather adults also learn from those around them and from the various resources that culture makes available. Indeed, adults in general have more access to such resources and more readiness to benefit from them than do children. One clear conclusion that will emerge across the coming chapters is that cultural teachings are an important contributor to parental thinking, a conclusion that is compatible with every version of the sociocultural approach.

There is a second reason that a model formulated to explain child development remains relevant when we consider adults. As we will see, one of the striking findings from research on parents' beliefs is that parents' own childhood experiences are often an important source for how they think about children. Thus what is internalized in childhood does not necessarily disappear in maturity. Some childhood developments remain an important basis for adult thought.

As noted, the second question with which sociocultural theory deals concerns the relation between parental beliefs and parental behavior. The key construct in this case is what is probably the best known aspect of Vygotsky's theory: the *zone of proximal development*. The zone of proximal development refers to the difference between what a child can do on his or her own and what the child can do with help from others, or—to make the same point in more Vygotskian language—to the difference between the actual level of development and the potential level of development. Both Vygotsky's studies and subsequent research make clear that for any aspect of development children differ in their zones or readiness to benefit from help and that instruction within the child's zone—that is, beyond the child's current level but not too far beyond—is most beneficial. The theory therefore offers a clear role for the importance of parental knowledge: Parents who know their children best can teach things and structure the child's environment in optimal ways, thus promoting positive development.

## Working Models

If Vygotsky is one of the giants among developmental theorists, John Bowlby certainly ranks as another. It was Bowlby, along with Mary Ainsworth, who is largely responsible for our modern conception of the attachment relationship between parent and child: its nature, its origins, and its effects.

It is to Ainsworth and colleagues (Ainsworth, Blehar, Waters, & Wall, 1978) that we owe both the invention of the most influential way to measure

Table 2.3  Attachment Classifications

| Classification | Description |
| --- | --- |
| Secure attachment | On reunion after brief separation from parent, child seeks physical contact, proximity, interaction; often tries to maintain physical contact. Readily soothed by parent and returns to exploration and play. |
| Insecure-avoidant attachment | Child actively avoids and ignores parent on reunion, looking away and remaining occupied with toys. May move away from parent and ignore parent's efforts to communicate. |
| Insecure-ambivalent attachment | Although infant seems to want closeness and contact, parent is not able to effectively alleviate the child's distress after brief separation. Child may show subtle or overt signs of anger, seeking proximity and then resisting it. |
| Insecure-disorganized attachment | Child shows signs of disorganization (e.g., crying for parent at door and then running quickly away when the door opens; approaching parent with head down) or disorientation (e.g., seeming to "freeze" for a few seconds) |

Adapted from *Social Development* (2nd ed., p. 106), by R. D. Parke and A. Clarke-Stewart, 2014, Hoboken, NJ: Wiley. Copyright 2014 by John Wiley & Sons. Adapted with permission.

attachment, the Strange Situation procedure, and the now well-accepted typology of different forms of attachment that the Strange Situation reveals. Table 2.3 summarizes the four attachment patterns that the Strange Situation identifies. As can be seen from the description in the table, the procedure places a special emphasis on the infant's ability to separate from and reunite with the caregiver.

One of the most influential aspects of Bowlby's theorizing about attachment was a move beyond the behavioral level to the notion that children form representations, or *internal working models*, of the attachment relationship (Bowlby, 1969, 1973). A working model represents the belief system that the child has developed, based on a history of experience with the caregiver, of the caregiver, of the self, and of the relation between the two. A child with a history of satisfactory experience, for example, will develop positive beliefs about both the caregiver and the self and will be confident that his or her needs will continue to be met. Such a child is likely to show a secure attachment. In contrast, a child with a history of unsatisfactory experience will develop a more negative set of beliefs and is likely to fall into one of the insecure categories. Although the initial working model is specific to the attachment relationship, its effects can be more widespread because, as a first belief system about the social world, it can affect, for better or worse, the child's subsequent social endeavors.

What is the relevance of this conception for the study of parents' beliefs? The relevance lies in the fact that adults also possess working models of their childhood attachment relationships, a conclusion that comes from research with an instrument labeled the Adult Attachment Interview (AAI), developed by Mary Main and colleagues (George, Kaplan, & Main, 1985). The AAI is a semistructured interview that consists of a series of questions that probe the adult's memories and feelings about his or her early relationship with the parents. A starting point question is "I'd like you to try to describe your relationship with your parents as a young child if you could start from as far back as you can remember?" Subsequent questions include a request to list five adjectives that describe the participant's mother and five that describe the father, a question about which parent the participant felt closer to, questions about instances of separation from the parents and about whether the participant ever felt rejected by the parents, and a request to identify any early experiences that the participant believes had an adverse effect on subsequent development.

The AAI yields four general types of working model. Table 2.4 lists and describes the types. The similarity to the Ainsworth childhood attachment categories should be evident. The secure/autonomous type, for example, has

Table 2.4  Categories of Adult Attachment Measured by the Adult Attachment Interview

| Category | Description |
| --- | --- |
| Secure/ Autonomous | Secure/autonomous individuals value attachment, they have access to detailed childhood memories, and they provide coherent, consistent, and objective accounts of their attachment experiences. |
| Dismissing | Dismissing individuals minimize the importance of attachment, their childhood memories are often either idealized or inaccessible, and they attempt to project a picture of strength and independence. |
| Preoccupied | Preoccupied individuals show excessive attention to past and current attachment experiences, their accounts are nonobjective and inconsistent, and they often express current anger. |
| Unresolved | Unresolved individuals are dealing unsuccessfully with the loss of an attachment figure or some other trauma, and their accounts of attachment experience are disoriented and confused. |

its parallel in the secure attachment of infancy, and each of the other types has a counterpart in the various forms of insecure attachment.

It is important to stress that the purpose of the AAI is to measure adults' *current* conceptions of their childhood attachment relationships. There is no claim that the attachment relationship first developed in infancy persists unchanged into adulthood and is revealed by the AAI; rather, it is an empirical question whether the infant form and the adult form relate. The answer is that they do relate—not strongly, however, and with a number of qualifications and exceptions. Relations may vary, for example, across different forms of attachment and across different samples (e.g., typical vs. high-risk). Both Sroufe and colleagues (Sroufe, Egeland, Carlson, & Collins, 2005) and Groh and colleagues (Groh et al., 2014) provide helpful summaries of what has been found.

Although the issue of the continuity of attachment is an intriguing one, it is not important for the question to be considered now. The question is whether adults' current thinking about their early attachment relationships, as measured by the AAI, affects how they think about and treat their own children.

The answer is that it does (Verhage et al., 2016). I will consider the bases for this conclusion more fully throughout the book, but I will mention two key findings now. One is that parents' responses to the AAI relate to their children's attachment classifications. Parents who fall in the secure/autonomous category, for example, are likely to have children who are securely attached, and similar parallels exist for the other adult and child categories. The second finding is that parents' responses to the AAI relate to their childrearing practices with their children. In particular, they relate to the sensitivity with which the parent interacts with the child. And it has been clear since the original Ainsworth research (Ainsworth et al., 1978) that parental sensitivity is the main predictor of a secure attachment.

I noted in the previous section that a variety of kinds of evidence tell us that childhood experiences contribute to how parents think about children. The study of working models is one of the clearest and most important demonstrations of this point.

## Self-Efficacy

Although social learning theory is one of the long-standing theoretical positions in developmental psychology, the contemporary version of the theory is in some respects quite different from the version that emerged in the 1930s and 1940s. It is different largely because of the work of one researcher and theorist: Albert Bandura.

The most general change that Bandura brought to social learning theory was a greatly increased cognitive emphasis, an emphasis reflected in the name given his approach: *social cognitive theory* (Bandura, 1986). Rather than simply responding to links between stimuli and responses and rewards and punishments, people are seen as processing the available environmental information and recruiting various cognitive resources to generate a response. If this description sounds similar to that given for the information-processing approach, the similarity is not accidental. Although there are both terminological and substantive differences between the approaches, both share the belief that cognitive processes underlie behavior, as well as the goal of identifying what the relevant processes are.

In what specific ways is Bandura's theory more cognitive than its predecessors? One of the major ways, as well as one of the most important components of the theory, comes in the concept of *self-efficacy*. Bandura (1997) defines self-efficacy as "beliefs in one's capabilities to organize and execute the courses of action required to produce given attainments" (p. 3). Self-efficacy, in short, has to do with what we believe we are capable of doing.

Self-efficacy, it is important to note, is a domain-specific rather than across-the-board set of beliefs. People do not have one general sense of self-efficacy; rather, they have different degrees of self-efficacy across different tasks or domains. Depending on relevant experience, someone might have high self-efficacy for academic tasks or chess or gardening, but considerably lower self-efficacy for car mechanics or tennis or playing the piano. For someone else, the pattern of strengths and weaknesses might be the reverse.

Where does self-efficacy come from? Various sources contribute. The most obvious source is performance at a given task. If we have been consistently successful at a particular task, then our self-efficacy for that task is likely to be high. Performance, however, is not the only determinant of self-efficacy. Vicarious experience can also be important. Observing others' successes and failures can affect conclusions about our own likely ability to succeed. What others convey about our abilities may also contribute. Such verbal input may be especially important for children, who have many new tasks to master as well as many adults to offer guidance as to what they can and cannot do. Finally, physiological responses can also play a role. Failure at a task may produce various forms of emotional arousal, and the experience of similar emotions when confronting the same task in the future may lower self-efficacy.

I noted earlier that the concept of self-efficacy is similar to aspects of the information-processing approach. There is a similarity to attribution theory as well. In particular, people with high-self efficacy attribute successful outcomes to their own behaviors, and they regard the relevant behaviors as both controllable and stable.

If self-efficacy were simply another set of beliefs about the self, the concept might be of limited interest. But both Bandura's research and the research of others make clear that self-efficacy is not only an outcome of performance; it also contributes to performance. When self-efficacy is high, people are more likely to attempt a task, they are more likely to persist at the task, and they are more likely to succeed at the task.

The conclusion just stated raises an obvious question. We know that good performance leads to higher self-efficacy; perhaps this effect alone is sufficient to explain the relation between self-efficacy and performance. Further evidence, however, makes clear that the causality runs in both directions. For example, experimental manipulations of self-efficacy affect subsequent performance, and they do so in both possible directions—better performance when self-efficacy is raised, poorer performance when self-efficacy is lowered. Across-time relations also support a causal role for self-efficacy, in that self-efficacy at an earlier time is often predictive of performance at some later time.

By this point, hundreds of studies have documented effects of self-efficacy across numerous different outcome measures. Among the domains for which effects have been clearly established are academic performance, athletic performance, organizational functioning, career choice, memory and aging, health behaviors and exercise, and response to therapy. As some of these entries make clear, the concept is of pragmatic as well as theoretical importance.

Self-efficacy also applies to the domain of parenting. As we will see in Chapter 4, parents form self-efficacy beliefs with respect to their parenting behaviors. The particular beliefs differ among parents, however, and these differences make a difference, both for the life of the parent and for the development of the child.

## Ecological Systems Theory

Unlike the other positions discussed in this chapter, the theory to be considered now does not focus on either adult cognition or parent–child relations. What it does focus on, however, has implications for what we conclude about both of these topics.

The theory in question is Urie Bronfenbrenner's *ecological systems theory* (Bronfenbrenner, 1979, 1989, 2005). As the name of the approach indicates, the focus of the theory is on the ecological systems, or contexts, within which development occurs. Bronfenbrenner envisions a series of interrelated systems, ranging from maximally proximal to the child to maximally distal. Figure 2.2 provides a pictorial depiction of the various systems that the theory identifies.

The most familiar of the layers is the *microsystem*. The microsystem is the layer that is closest to the child and that acts most directly on the child. Parents' beliefs and related behaviors are part of the microsystem. So, too, are interactions with friends, or watching TV, or talking to a teacher at school, or listening to a pastor at church.

Most research in psychology focuses on the microsystem, and this concentration is not hard to understand. The microsystem is the layer of the environment within which causal forces operate and the child's development takes place. The real question is why we should be concerned with anything else—that is, why are the other systems necessary?

Bronfenbrenner's answer is that they are necessary because microsystem processes can be understood only once the other systems are taken into account. Consider first the *mesosystem*, which is defined as the relations among the child's microsystems. Both parents and peers constitute microsystems for any child, and the beliefs and related behaviors of the two groups may or may not be in accord. It perhaps goes without saying that parenting is easier when the former is the case. Similarly, both home and school are important microsystems for any child, and again the parent's role is likely to be both easier and more successful if there is agreement on important issues (e.g., amount of homework, the role of standardized testing) than if home and school diverge.

The *exosystem* is Bronfenbrenner's term for social systems that can affect children but in which they do not participate directly. To continue with the education example, a school board that sets educational policies relevant to the child would be an example of the exosystem. So, too, would be an employer who either grants or fails to grant a maternity or paternity leave.

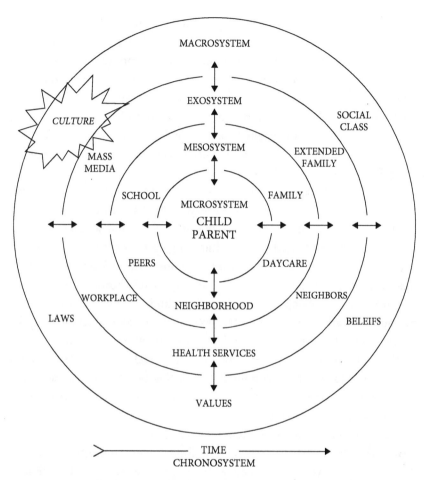

**Figure 2.2** Bronfenbrenner's Ecological Systems Theory. From "The Place of 'Culture and Parenting' in the Ecological Contextual Perspective on Developmental Science," by M. H. Bornstein & C, L. S. Cheah. In K. H. Rubin & O. B. Chung (Eds.), *Parenting Beliefs, Behavior, and Parent-Child Relations: A Cross-Cultural Perspective*, p.18. Copyright 2006 by Psychology Press. Reproduced by permission of Taylor and Francis Group, LLC, a division of Informa plc.

The broadest of the layers pictured in Figure 2.2 is the *macrosystem*, which refers to the culture or subculture in which the child develops. The macrosystem affects parents' beliefs and related behaviors in two ways. First, it affects what the beliefs are. As I have already said—and as we will see repeatedly in the coming chapters—different cultures promote different parental beliefs or *ethnotheories* about children. To take just one example for now: Many Asian cultures promote a belief in the importance of obedience and respect for authority, and many Asian parents adopt child-rearing practices that are in line with this belief, that is, firm control with relatively little discussion or overt expressions of affection. Western cultures, in contrast, tend to place an emphasis on autonomy and self-direction, and Western child-rearing practices typically take a more democratic and overtly affectionate form. (Obviously, these are broad characterizations with a number of exceptions.)

The same contrast can serve as an example of the second way in which the macrosystem can exert effects: namely, that the same beliefs and related behaviors may have different effects in different cultural settings. A child-rearing style characterized by imposition of parental power and absence of reasoning (the so-called *authoritarian style*) does not work out very happily in studies with Western samples; the same approach, however, often yields positive results for Asian or Asian American children. What seems to be important is the embedding of the style within a more general set of culturally approved beliefs and behaviors. And note that the child's beliefs about appropriateness are also important. Bronfenbrenner (1993, p. 39) quotes an Asian American student whose comment makes this point. When asked what Asians thought about such strict parental control, the student replied, "That's how we know our parents love us."

The final component of Bronfenbrenner's model is a relatively recent addition. The *chronosystem* adds a temporal dimension to the theory in that it encompasses events associated with the passage of time. The child, of course, changes with time, and so do various sociohistorical conditions. To take again just one example—both the Great Depression of the 1930s and the Great Recession of 2007–2010 led to straitened economic conditions that adversely affected millions of families. For many, the changes in financial circumstances led to changes in family life (e.g., a decline in marital relations, nonoptimal child-rearing practices), and these changes negatively impacted various aspects of the children's development (Elder, 1999; Schneider, Waldfogel, & Brooks-Gunn, 2015). Here, then, we have the interplay of three ecological systems: a historical change (the chronosystem) that affects conditions relevant to children (the exosystem) that in turn affect the parent–child relationship and children's development (the microsystem).

The discussions of context in the chapters to come will not always refer to ecological systems theory. Nevertheless, Bronfenbrenner's formulation remains the field's most influential approach to the question of how contexts shape behavior and development.

## Theory of Mind

*Theory of mind* has to do with thoughts and beliefs about the mental world, both one's own mental world and the mental worlds of others (Wellman, 2014). It has been perhaps the most often studied topic in cognitive development for close to 30 years now. The question now is how theory of mind applies to the study of parents' beliefs. Can such beliefs be usefully interpreted within a theory-of-mind perspective?

Not all the beliefs that parents form about their children fall under the theory-of-mind heading. A belief that one's child is good at soccer, for example, does not require theory of mind because such a belief need not involve any attempt to understand the child's mental life. Similarly, a belief that one's child is on the honor roll does not require any mentalistic reasoning; rather, all that is necessary is to note and remember an empirical fact. On the other hand, a belief that one's child is on the honor roll because of inborn ability or that a desire to impress friends underlies a child's soccer prowess *does* require theory of mind because such beliefs go beyond the observed behavior to posit an underlying mental substrate for what is observed.

Despite its popularity in the developmental literature, and despite what could be argued to be its by-definition relevance, theory of mind has not been an important contributor to the study of parents' beliefs. As we will see in Chapter 6, it does appear as one of the large number of child outcomes that have been explored as possible effects of parents' beliefs. There is also some intriguing recent work at the independent variable end—that is, parents' theory of mind regarding their children as a contributor to parental behavior and to child development (Meins, 2012). This work will be considered in both Chapter 5 and Chapter 6. But research to date is limited.

Why has theory of mind not played a more prominent role in the parents' beliefs literature? Two factors are probably important. A first is that theory of mind has been very much a childhood literature. Indeed, it has been mostly an *early* childhood literature, given that the bulk of studies concentrate on developments in the first 5 years of life. The developments in question are basic ones (e.g., understanding of false belief, mastery of the appearance/reality distinction) that have long ceased to be an issue by adulthood. And this means that they are not a locus for possible individual differences among parents.

Of course, no researcher of theory of mind believes that development is actually complete by age 5. The second generation of theory-of-mind research saw the creation of a number of measures of higher order theory-of-mind understanding (Miller, 2012). These measures show continued development throughout the span of childhood, and, in some instances adult samples are not at ceiling. In addition, a burgeoning literature on adult theory of mind has begun to emerge (e.g., Bernstein, Thornton, & Sommerville, 2011; Low, Apperly, Butterfill, & Rakoczy, 2016). This work, too, reveals individual differences among adults as well as evidence about situations that make application of theory-of-mind skills either more or less easy. In Chapter 6 I discuss both actual and potential contributions of the work on more advanced theory of mind to the understanding of parents' beliefs.

As noted, there is a second possible explanation for the limited role of theory of mind in parents' beliefs research. It concerns a distinction first proposed by Tory Higgins in a discussion of the perspective-taking literature (Higgins, 1981). As Higgins noted, the challenges in perspective taking are of two general sorts. In some cases the differences between self and other are *situational* in origin. This is the case, for example, when a child attempts to describe a referent to a peer who does not share his or her visual perspective. In other cases the differences between self and other reflect what Higgins labels the *individual* dimension, that is, general status differences that cut across different situations. This would be the case, for example, when an older child attempts to explain the rules of a game to a younger child.

As I have argued elsewhere (Miller, 2000, 2016; see also Achim, Guitton, Jackson, Boutin, & Monetta, 2013), theory-of-mind research has been heavily skewed toward the situational bases for mental ascriptions. In a standard false belief task, for example, the nature of the protagonist (adult–child, familiar–unfamiliar, etc.) does not matter; given the available information, *anyone* should form a false belief. Other basic theory-of-mind tasks show a similar situational focus. Because they do, they provide limited insight into many real-life social judgments in which the task is to employ knowledge about a person, not about a situation. Arguably, most judgments that parents make about their children fall in the person, or individual, category.

As with the variable of age, there are exceptions to this characterization of the theory-of-mind literature—in this case, studies in which accurate judgment requires taking into account the characteristics of the target being judged. This work, too, will be discussed in Chapter 6. In general, however, there are limits on the extent to which a theory-of-mind approach to parents' beliefs can build on the existing theory-of-mind literature because only a small part of that literature is directly relevant to the tasks that face parents. Most of the contributions from the approach are therefore at present prospective rather than actual. But note that because of the gaps in the theory-of-mind literature, there is already a clear contribution in the other direction, that is, from studies of parents' beliefs to our understanding of theory of mind. Indeed, theory of mind serves as a prime example of one of this book's themes: that the study of parents' beliefs can enrich the theoretical positions for which it is relevant.

## Ethnotheories

Many researchers and theorists have contributed work under this heading, but two have been most prominent: Sara Harkness and Charles Super. The following summary is drawn mainly from their writings (Harkness, Mavridis, Liu, & Super, 2015; Harkness & Super, 1996, 2006).

The definition of ethnotheories is prefigured by the two parts of the word. *Ethnotheories* are cultural belief systems—the shared beliefs about a range of topics that characterize all of the world's cultures. The focus now is on what is arguably the most important of these shared belief systems, the beliefs held by parents. Such parental ethnotheories encompass "the nature of children, development, parenting, and the family" (Harkness, Super, & van Tijen, 2000, p. 24)—in short, all of the topics to which this book is addressed.

As we will see at various places throughout the book, aspects of parental ethnotheories often show marked variations across cultural settings, variations that affect both parents' behavior and children's development. The variations, moreover, are not limited to comparisons between obviously distinct cultures; research by Harkness and Super reveals interesting differences even within Western, industrialized nations (e.g., Harkness et al., 2011). Their research and theorizing, however, also identify some basic similarities in parental ethnotheories, and it is these similarities on which I concentrate now.

One similarity concerns the form or structure that ethnotheories take. Harkness and Super argue that ethnotheories are organized in a hierarchical fashion, ranging from abstract and general and often implicit beliefs at the highest level to more specific and narrow and conscious beliefs at lower levels. As an example, consider parents in a society in which rearing of live-stock is an important source of subsistence. Such parents may assume that a son will grow up to take care of the family's stock, a taken-for-granted assumption that may require little conscious reflection or decision-making. Also required, however, are ways to prepare the son for this role, and in this case specific beliefs of a variety of sorts may guide parents' actions. A likely progression, for example, is a gradual increase in the complexity of demands on the child: begin with care of the family pet, move next to relatively simple chores with the farm animals, and so forth. Middle-class parents in the United States might show a similar division between general and specific but with different content—an eventual college education may be a taken-for-granted assumption, and the specific beliefs will concern ways to make this happen.

A second similarity among ethnotheories is that they are characterized by pervasive themes, themes that cut across different domains of family life. In the United States, for example, a belief in the importance of independence and autonomy is an important theme for many segments of the population, and this belief finds expression in numerous contexts from infancy through adolescence—discouragement of what is perceived as overly dependent behavior in a toddler, insistence on independent completion of homework by a grade schooler, encouragement of civic and political engagement by a high schooler. In cultures with a more interdependent, communal emphasis—as has been argued to be true of many Asian societies—the dominant themes will be at least somewhat different and so, therefore, will be parental behaviors across these and other developmental contexts. The themes that characterize a culture function to provide a unifying link between what otherwise might be disparate and unrelated developments.

A third aspect of Harkness and Super's theorizing concerns what they label the *developmental niche*, or "the cultural context of child development" (Harkness & Super, 1986, p. 552). The developmental niche is made up of three interrelated subsystems. One subsystem consists of the physical and social settings in which the child develops, settings that provide the places and people that shape the child's learning. A second subsystem consists of culturally regulated forms of child care and child-rearing, experiences that may (depending on the culture) include going to preschool, learning to read, or caring for a younger sibling. Finally, the third subsystem is the psychology of the caretakers. Parental ethnotheories fall within the last of these subsystems.

As this formulation indicates, ethnotheories are not the only ways in which culture shapes development; the "cultural context" consists of all three components of the developmental niche. In addition to their direct effects, however, ethnotheories also influence the other two subsystems. The parent's beliefs, for example, may determine the neighborhood in which the family lives, or how early the child is sent to school, or which of the culturally provided forms of experience are sought out and which are ignored. It is important to add, however, that parents' beliefs and related actions are never all-important. As do other positions, work on ethnotheories recognizes that characteristics of the particular child are always a major contributor to how development proceeds.

Harkness and Super (2002, p. 272) summarize the niche formulation as "a theoretical framework for studying how the child's microenvironment of daily life is culturally shaped." A slight rewording makes clear the compatibility with Bronfenbrenner's ecological systems theory: "a theoretical framework for studying how the child's microsystem is shaped by the surrounding macrosystem."

The theme of this section has been that parental ethnotheories show both similarities and differences across the world's cultures. This conclusion should not be surprising. The specific content of parents' beliefs varies with cultural history and cultural needs, and these differences in content can produce important differences in how children develop. But as products of human cognition and human communication, such beliefs necessarily share aspects common to all human thought. This notion of both similarity and difference is captured in the title of one prominent review of the research literature: "The Cultural Psychology of Development: One Mind, Many Mentalities" (Shweder et al., 2006). Most research focuses on the "Many," but it is important not to lose track of the "One." And not yet mentioned is what is perhaps the most basic similarity across cultures: However much they may differ in specifics, all parental ethnotheories have the goal of optimizing development within the cultural setting and preparing the child to be a successful and productive member of the culture.

## Methods

Even more than is true for theories, methods is a topic that will be reappear throughout the book. The purpose of the present discussion is to provide a preliminary framing—an overview of issues and possibilities that will be returned to as we go.

## Measuring Beliefs: Questions of Who

Any researcher of parents' beliefs must make various decisions about what to study and how to study it. Table 2.5 provides a rough flowchart of the decisions that must be made and the options available at each point.

Clearly, a starting point decision is whom to study. Because this book is about parents, parents either constitute or form part of the subject group for every study reviewed. As is true for the parenting literature in general, mothers appear more often than do fathers, for a substantial majority of studies include mothers only. An obvious prescription for future research is that more attention be paid to fathers—a prescription that applies, of course, not just to the study of parents' beliefs but more generally (Cabrerra, Volling, & Barr, 2018).

When studies do include both mothers and fathers, two questions can be asked. One question concerns possible mean differences: Do mothers and fathers differ, on the average, in their beliefs about children? Any differences,

Table 2.5  Methodological Decisions in the Measurement of Parents' Beliefs

| Decision | Possibilities |
| --- | --- |
| Who is being asked | Mother, father, child, nonparent, grandparent |
| Who is being asked about | Own child, children in general, parent, family |
| What is being asked about | Processes of development, cognitive development, social development, atypical development, some combination of outcomes |
| Specific focus of questioning | Attribute or ability of child or of children in general, explanation for attribute or ability, other aspects of the development in question (e.g., importance, desirability, stability), role of parenting |
| Presentation of target | Actual own child behavior, hypothetical own child behavior, behavior or characteristics of children in general |
| Elicitation of response | Open-ended questioning about child in general, open-ended questioning about specific behavior or attribute, closed-choice selection among response alternatives |

of course, need not be across-the-board ones; rather, gender differences may occur for some sorts of beliefs but not for others. As we will see, such variability across topics is in fact the case. We will also see that when differences of an evaluative sort occur (e.g., greater parental knowledge, greater accuracy in judging the child), it is usually, although not always, mothers who score more positively.

The second question that can be asked when both parents appear in research concerns concordance between spouses: How similar are mother–father pairs in the beliefs they hold? The concordance question is of interest for various reasons: It provides evidence relevant to the issue of the origins of parents' beliefs; it speaks to the question of the consistency of the messages that the child receives; and it provides additional and instructive data on the relations among beliefs, behaviors, and child outcomes. Unfortunately, only a minority of studies with both parents include analyses for concordance, even though the necessary data are readily available. Another prescription, therefore, is for a more consistent use of an available and valuable piece of information.

In some studies parents are not the only participants. A basic comparison is between parents and a comparable group of nonparents. Nonparents, of course, cannot be expected to hold beliefs about the particular children represented in the parent segment of the sample; thus such comparisons necessarily involve beliefs about children in general (the only exception being when parents and teachers are compared). The most obvious issue to which such studies speak concerns the experiential bases for parental beliefs. Does experience as a parent alter how adults think about children? In particular, are parents in general more knowledgeable, more insightful, or more sophisticated than are nonparents in their beliefs about children? As we will see, this is another question for which the answer is "usually but not always."

As Table 2.5 indicates, two other subject groups appear in some parents' beliefs studies. Although grandparents are not a frequent entry, their occasional inclusion (e.g., Civitas Initiative, Zero to Three, & Brio Corporation, 2000; Sistler & Gottfried, 1990) addresses two issues of interest: possible effects of their own parent on how parents think about children and possible changes in beliefs about children across generations.

Not all studies of parents' beliefs also collect data from the parents' children. When children do appear, the data they provide take various forms. In some instances the child assessments serve as outcome measures to which the parents' beliefs can be related. In a study of beliefs about homework, for example (e.g., Silinskas, Kiuru, Aunola, Lerkkanen, & Nurmi, 2015), children's school performance might serve as evidence with respect to which beliefs are relatively helpful ones for parents to hold. Or in a study of self-concept development (e.g., Pesu, Viljaranta, & Aunola, 2016), children's self-concept might be examined as a function of how their parents judge their academic abilities.

In some studies the child assessments serve not only as outcome measures but also as targets for parents' judgments. The children might respond to a series of IQ items, for example, and the parents are then asked to predict their children's responses (e.g., Miller, 1986). Such studies provide evidence with respect to an important question: How accurately can parents judge their children's attributes? Furthermore, in many such studies the interest is not simply in parental accuracy but also in possible effects of such accuracy. In the IQ study, for example, we can ask whether more accurate parents have children with higher IQs, an expectable outcome if parental knowledge leads to optimal parenting techniques. The answer, as we will see, is yes, although the explanation for this outcome is still not totally clear.

A third possibility when children serve as participants is that the children respond to the same measures as do their parents. A study by Cashmore and Goodnow (1985) provides an example. In this study parents rated the importance of various qualities (e.g., "Tries hard," "Concentrates well," "Is organized") for an "ideal student," and their 12- to 14-year-old children in-dependently completed an identical set of ratings. This approach, clearly, addresses the same general issue as do the studies of spouse concord-ance: How similar are parents and children in the beliefs they hold?

There is still one more possibility, and it too was represented in the Cashmore and Goodnow (1985) study. The child participants in this study not only offered their own ratings of the importance of the various qualities; they also indicated how they thought that their parents had responded. Here, then, the measure of actual agreement is supplemented by a measure of per-ceived agreement. How accurately can children judge their parents' beliefs? And do they know when they are agreeing or disagreeing with their parents?

The discussion to this point has focused on the participants for research. A second methodological decision concerns the target for these participants' beliefs, that is, whom will they be asked about? Given this book's agenda, the answer, of course, is children, but this decision still leaves open various pos-sibilities. As I noted in Chapter 1, in some studies the target is not children alone but rather children as part of some larger unit, either the parent–child dyad or the family as a whole. These studies are the subject matter for Chapter 4.

When the focus is on individual children, the most frequent target is the parent's own child. This was the case, for example, in the IQ and self-concept studies sketched earlier, and it is also the case when parent-report measures are used to identify characteristics in some sample of children. The other possibility is to elicit beliefs about children in general. This is the case, for example, when the questions concern timetables for mastery of various achievements (e.g., Roopnarine, Logie, Davidson, Krishnakumar, & Narine, 2015) or when general processes of development are the target (e.g. McGillicuddy-DeLisi & Subramanian, 1996). As noted, comparisons between parents and nonparents necessarily focus on children in general.

The own child-children in general decision is not a matter of either-or. Some studies include both targets. As we will see, the comparative information provided by the own-other comparison adds significantly to what can be learned from a focus on the child in isolation.

## Measuring Beliefs: Questions of What

We have considered the two forms of the who question: Who will be studied, and who will be asked about? We turn now to the question of what will be asked about: that is, what attribute or attributes of the target population will be the focus of the questioning?

A first point is that in some studies there is no specific focus; rather, an open-ended question (e.g., "Tell me what your child is like") is used to elicit the parent's description of her child. Such is often the case in research on ethnotheories, and many of the quotations with which the chapters in this book open come from the study of parental ethnotheories. Open-ended, nondirective questioning is also often a prelude to the development of more standardized measures (e.g., Bugental, Blue, & Cruzcosa, 1989; Mugny & Carugati, 1989). In this case the open-ended phase serves to identify issues and response options of interest, thus helping to guide the subsequent construction of a standardized instrument. Finally, although the majority of studies of parents' beliefs fit the familiar quantitative psychology mold, research under the qualitative psychology heading also contributes (e.g., Chen, Flores, & Shetgiri, 2016), and, in such cases exploratory, nondirective methods of study are the norm.

Despite the exceptions just noted, most studies concentrate on specific aspects of children's development. As Table 2.5 suggests, the range of possibilities is broad—essentially anything that developmental psychologists have studied is a possible target for parents' beliefs about their children. And indeed, almost everything that psychologists have studied does appear in studies of parents' beliefs, although some topics have received more attention than have others.

Selection of a particular content area still leaves several methodological decisions to be made. There are too many options and complexities at each of these steps for me to attempt a full discussion here. But I can make some general points, with specifics to be added as we go.

One decision concerns exactly what will be asked about the aspect of development under study. What sorts of beliefs might parents hold about their children's intelligence, or about their relations with peers, or about their acts of aggression? The answer, as we will see, is quite a number of different beliefs, but three general categories are most often examined. One is a judgment of the child's status on the attribute in question. How many IQ items can the child solve, or how satisfactory are the child's friendships? A second category concerns explanations for the child's status. If the child is having difficulties with peers, what are the bases for the difficulties, or what are the causes of the child's aggressive behavior? Finally, a third general category concerns the role of parenting. How much has parenting contributed or could parenting contribute to the outcomes in question, and how satisfied or confident does the parent feel about his or her parenting efforts?

A second decision concerns how the child behavior or attribute will be presented to the parent. Clearly, what we would like to be able to do is present an actual behavior or set of behaviors for the parent to judge. And a number of studies in fact do this. Beliefs about academic performance clearly qualify; the grades, test scores, or whatever that are the target for questioning reflect the child's naturally occurring behavior. When a specific measure has been administered to the child, the parent can be asked to predict response to it— for example, response to a series of IQ items (e.g., Hunt & Paraskevopoulos, 1980). Although this approach is most common in the cognitive domain, it is also found for some social outcomes—for example, parents' prediction of responses to a test of emotion understanding (Karstad, Kvello, Wichstom, & Berg-Nielsen, 2014).

Asking about naturally occurring rather than experimentally elicited behavior is more challenging. Several approaches have been tried. Parents may be asked to offer explanations for their children's behavior or their own behavior immediately after an experimentally arranged interaction session with their child (e.g., Russell & Russell, 1988). Videotaped instances of the child's behavior may be presented for judgment, thus minimizing the memory demands when questions concern some past event (e.g., Johnston & Freeman, 1997). In some research parents keep a diary in which they record their children's behaviors and their reactions to and explanations for the behaviors (e.g., Enlund, Aunola, Tolvanen, & Nurmi, 2015). Or parents may simply be asked to recall some past instance or instances of the targeted behavior (e.g., Gretarsson & Gelfand, 1988). Parent-report measures, it should be noted, always rely on parents' memory for their children's behaviors.

Actual child behavior is not always the starting point for assessment. Instead, many studies present standardized vignettes that illustrate the situations and behaviors of interest. We will see several examples of such vignettes in the chapters to come. In some instances the parent is asked to imagine that her child is the protagonist in the vignette (e.g., Mills & Rubin, 1990). In other instances the questions concern the story protagonist, but the assumption, at least usually (not all authors are explicit on this point), is that the parent answers as she would for her own child (e.g., Dix, Ruble, & Zambarano, 1989).

A final methodological decision concerns how the parental responses will be elicited. In the great majority of studies the measures are explicit self-report measures—that is, we learn what parents believe by asking them what they believe. The predominance of this approach is, of course, not a surprise. Beliefs are internal, personal, subjective phenomena—how else could we learn about them other than by directly asking the holder of the belief? Still, all of the cautions that apply in general to the use of self-report measures must be considered when evaluating the beliefs literature.

There are a handful of exceptions to the point just made. In the work on mind-mindedness to be considered in Chapters 5 and 6, parents are not asked for their beliefs about their children's mental lives; rather, such beliefs are inferred either from the way they describe the child or from the way they talk to the child. An instrument labeled the Leeds Attributional Coding System, developed by Peter Stratton (1997), permits a similar inferential approach in the study of attributions: Some segment of naturally occurring behavior is recorded, and trained judges subsequently code the transcript to identify attributions. Other researchers have also inferred attributions from parents' conversations with or about the child (e.g., Goodvin & Rolfson, 2014).

When beliefs are explicitly elicited—which, again, is the norm—response formats vary along a continuum from maximally open to maximally closed. The most open-ended approach is the describe-your-child method described earlier because in this case neither the attributes of the child nor the nature of the parents' responses is constrained. An open-ended approach is also possible when there is a specific target to be judged. The parent might be asked, for example, to offer explanations for her child's successes or failures in school. A good deal more common, however, is use of some closed-choice format in which the parent chooses among rather than generates the response options. In a study of attributions, for example, the parent may be asked to rate the importance of various factors for the behavior in question. At the extreme end of the open-closed continuum, the parent may be required to select a single explanation as most important.

There are, of course, good reasons for the methodological decisions that researchers have made. The use of standard scenarios and questions provides a degree of control and comparability across participants that would be hard to achieve otherwise. In addition, the situations asked about in such research (good performance on a test, aggression toward a peer, etc.) are both familiar to any parent and easy to convey verbally.

Once these points are made, it is still important to acknowledge a basic caution with respect to the beliefs literature. What we are interested in when we study parents' beliefs are parents' spontaneous beliefs about aspects of children's development for which they in fact hold beliefs. What the great majority of studies measure is elicited beliefs about aspects of development that researchers present.

This section has concentrated on ways to measure the content of parents' beliefs—thus, what parents believe their child is capable of, how they explain their child's behaviors, and so forth. As Goodnow and Collins (1990; see also Goodnow, 2006) point out, the content question is not the only question we can ask about parents' beliefs, or, indeed, beliefs of any sort. These authors identify six characteristics of beliefs that cut across different content areas and that they place under the heading of *quality of beliefs*. Table 2.6 lists and briefly describes these characteristics.

We will encounter two of these characteristics most often in the chapters to come. The accuracy with which parents can judge their children is a basic issue in the parents' beliefs literature; it appears frequently in studies of cognitive abilities, and it is a central question whenever parent-report

**Table 2.6**  Characteristics of Parents' Beliefs (from Goodnow & Collins, 1990)

| Characteristic | Description |
| --- | --- |
| Accuracy | The accuracy with which parents can judge attributes of their children or of children in general. |
| Differentiation | The degree to which beliefs are multidimensional and encompass various possibilities, as opposed to an undifferentiated, unidimensional view. Can apply to beliefs about children, about causal factors, or about the self. |
| Agreement or shared meaning | The degree to which a belief is held by others as well as the self. Can apply at the individual level (e.g., mother–father, parent–child) or the societal or cultural level. |
| Awareness and accessibility | The degree to which a belief either is or can be made accessible to conscious awareness. |
| Intensity or attachment | The degree of firmness and commitment with which a belief is held. |
| Structure or connectedness | The degree to which beliefs are interrelated in larger structures or hierarchies. |

measures are used. As we will see in Chapter 4, the issue of agreement or shared meaning also figures prominently in several programs of research. In most instances, however, the agreement at issue is between family members (parent and child, mother and father); other forms of agreement (e.g., between a parent and society more generally) have been little explored. "Little explored" is also an accurate description for the other characteristics described in the table. Here too, then, are some further entries for the needed future research list.

## Origins of Beliefs

Evidence with respect to the origins of parental beliefs divides into two general categories. The parent–nonparent contrast is an example of the first category: compare naturally occurring groups that are assumed to differ in their experience with children. The studies that compare mothers and fathers also fall in this category. And so do studies that use either number of children or (more commonly) age of children as a proxy for amount of experience with children (e.g., Bornstein, Cote, Haynes, Hahn, & Park, 2010).

The other possibility is to measure relevant experience directly. The most often used instrument that does so was an early entry in the parents' beliefs literature, a measure labeled the Catalog of Previous Experience with Infants (COPE), developed by David MacPhee (1983). Table 2.7 presents a sampling of items from the COPE (specifically, 18 of the 25 items). As can be seen, the measure assesses various forms of experience that might contribute to parental knowledge, including direct experience with children both before and after becoming a parent and indirect sources of information such as the

**Table 2.7** Examples of Items From the Catalog of Previous Experience (COPE)

If you have ever taken care of an infant brother or sister, how much time did it take, per month?

_____ Never have.

_____ An hour or so a month.

_____ Once a week for several hours at a time.

_____ Regularly—every day for several hours at a time.

How much time have you spent babysitting other infants (before becoming a parent)?

_____ Never have.

_____ One or two times.

_____ More than twice but never regularly.

_____ Have been a regular babysitter—several times a month.

How many classes in infant care have you taken?

_____ None.

_____ One.

_____ More than one.

How often do (did) you do the following for or with your baby?

|  | Never | Sometimes | Fairly Often | Regularly |
|---|---|---|---|---|
| Give baths. | 0 | 1 | 2 | 3 |
| Change diapers. | 0 | 1 | 2 | 3 |
| Dress him or her. | 0 | 1 | 2 | 3 |
| Take charge of feeding. | 0 | 1 | 2 | 3 |
| Play with him or her. | 0 | 1 | 2 | 3 |
| Put him or her to bed. | 0 | 1 | 2 | 3 |
| Read or sing to him or her. | 0 | 1 | 2 | 3 |

**Table 2.7** Continued

Circle *one number* for each question below.

| How much have you learned about infants from: | Very little | Some but not much | A fair amount | A lot |
|---|---|---|---|---|
| the mass media—radio, movies, television, or newspapers. | 1 | 2 | 3 | 4 |
| reading magazine articles or books about infants or toddlers. | 1 | 2 | 3 | 4 |
| watching infants and their parents when you were younger. | 1 | 2 | 3 | 4 |
| talking to your own family (mother, father, sister, grandparent). | 1 | 2 | 3 | 4 |
| talking to friends or other adults who have babies of their own. | 1 | 2 | 3 | 4 |
| comparing your baby or child to others whom you see or know. | 1 | 2 | 3 | 4 |
| talking to doctors or nurses before and after your baby was born. | 1 | 2 | 3 | 4 |
| talking to your husband (wife). | 1 | 2 | 3 | 4 |

Adapted from "Catalog of Previous Experience," by D. MacPhee, 1983. Copyright 1983 by David MacPhee. Adapted by permission. For further information, contact David MacPhee (David. Macphee@ColoState.EDU).

mass media and conversations with others. I will add that the latter category has grown considerably in the years since the COPE was developed, as both Internet sites (e.g., Niela-Vilen, Axelin, Salantera, & Melender, 2014) and social media (e.g., Bartholomew, Schoppe-Sullivan, Glassman, & Kamp Dush, 2012) have emerged as important sources of information for parents.

The emphasis so far has been on experience during adulthood. But not all of the experiences that contribute to parents' beliefs about children occur in adulthood. As I have already noted at various points, a variety of kinds of evidence tell us that the effects of childhood experience can persist into adulthood and affect the way that parents think about and treat their children. The chapters to come will discuss the various bases for this conclusion.

The emphasis in this discussion of origins has been on what might be labeled rational sources for parents' beliefs—that is, forms of information about children and about parenting to which parents are exposed and from which they form beliefs. As any parent probably realizes, however, not all thinking about children is rational in origin. Parents' emotional state can affect their reasoning; mothers who are angry, for example, make more negative judgments about their children's behavior than do mothers who are in a better mood (Dix, Reinhold, & Zambarano, 1990). Across a longer time span, various psychological characteristics of the parent can influence how she thinks about her child, including clinical conditions such as depression. We will consider this work in Chapter 9.

## Effects of Beliefs

Not all research on parents' beliefs attempts to establish the effects of the beliefs. In some studies the main goal is a descriptive/exploratory one: to identify the nature of beliefs, perhaps especially in groups that are seldom the focus of research. In other studies the main interest is in the issue just discussed: the origins of beliefs. Questions of the effects of the beliefs may be left for other research to tackle.

Research that attempts to do so faces several challenges. A first challenge is that of measurement. If the interest is in effects on parental practices, then we must be able to measure the parental behaviors of interest; if the interest is in effects on children's development, then we must be able to measure the child outcomes of interest. Many studies are directed to both possible effects, and thus face both challenges. And every study, of course, has the challenge of measuring the relevant parental beliefs.

Much of developmental psychology is directed to the measurement of children's characteristics and to the determination of factors, such as parents' child-rearing, that affect those characteristics. I will settle here for one point about the measurement challenges. As I have already indicated, one common way to measure children's characteristics is via parents' reports about their children. I will add now that one common way to measure parents' child-rearing practices—indeed, the most common way—is via parents' reports about their typical practices. The measurement of the third component of the triad, parents' beliefs, is, of course, almost always accomplished through some form of parental report.

A considerable amount of evidence testifies to the validity of parent-report measures for all three of these general targets. Nevertheless, problems can arise when the same measurement option is used for two or more outcomes in the same study—when, for example (to take the extreme case), an interview with the parent is the source for not only for the measure of parental beliefs but also for the measures of parental behaviors and child outcomes. The danger in such a case is that any relations among the measures may lie more in the mind of the informant than in the developmental reality. Bias of this form is referred to as *single-reporter bias*, a construct that falls under the more general heading of *shared methods variance*, that is, aspects of measurement that are common across different targets and therefore may inflate relations among the targets (Podsakoff, MacKenzie, & Podsakoff, 2012). Although I will not do so on a study-by-study basis, I will try to make clear as we go the extent to which single-reporter bias is a possible problem in the research reviewed.

Measurement is the first general challenge in determining the effects of parents' beliefs. The second general challenge is establishing causality. This *is* a challenge because research on parents' beliefs is (with a few exceptions) correlational research. Because it is correlational, it can identify relations among variables, but it cannot establish what, if any, causal relations hold among the variables.

The issue of correlation and causality is, of course, a familiar one in the general child-rearing literature. Most discussions of the issue identify four possible bases for correlations between parental practices and child outcomes. The first three possibilities speak to what is referred to as the *directionality issue*: Assuming a causal relation between parent and child measures, which variable is the cause and which is the effect? The explanation that is generally of greatest interest—and the one that was the common assumption in early generations of child-rearing research—is that parents' child-rearing practices cause developmental outcomes in their children. A second possibility, however, is that the causal direction is the reverse: that aspects of children elicit particular practices from their parents. Finally, a third possibility with respect to directionality is that the causality flows in both directions: that, over time, parents and children influence each other in a reciprocal, back-and-forth fashion. Such a bidirectional causal relation is referred to as the *transactional model* of development (Sameroff, 2009).

There is still one more possible explanation for parent–child correlations. The fourth possibility is that there is no causal relation at all between the parent and child measures; rather, both parental practices and child outcomes are caused by some third factor or set of factors. The genes that parents and children share may be the most general and commonly evoked possibility under the third factor heading.

Of course, the basic child-rearing literature does not stop with a discussion of these complexities; rather, much effort has been devoted to techniques that can surmount the difficulties and make causal inferences more plausible. Three general approaches are most common (for discussion of other possibilities, see Bornstein, 2015; Collins, Maccoby, Steinberg, Hetherington, & Bornstein, 2000; and Miller, Henry, & Votruba-Drzal, 2016). One is the use of statistical controls to test for and potentially rule out third-factor explanations. Such techniques vary from simple partial correlations to path analysis and structural equation modeling. A second approach is longitudinal study, in which relations between hypothesized cause and effect can be traced over time. Because causes must precede their effects, the across-time relations can help determine which variable is affecting which—in particular, whether variations in parenting at time 1 relate to variations in child outcomes at time 2. Finally, the third possibility is experimental study, in which the hypothesized causal factor can be experimentally manipulated. A well-executed experimental study can establish causality with certainty, and the convergence of experimental and correlational evidence on the same conclusion—which, in fact, is often the case in the child-rearing literature—makes inferences about causality a good deal more certain.

What about the parents' beliefs literature? Clearly, a complex issue becomes more complex when parents' beliefs are added to the mix because now there is no longer just one but three possible sets of correlations to interpret: not just relations between parents' behaviors and child outcomes but also between parents' beliefs and parents' behaviors and between parents' beliefs and child outcomes. All three relations are, in fact, found frequently in the literature, often in the same study. The challenge is to figure out why.

As we will see in the coming chapters, the same three approaches found in the general child-rearing literature appear in the parents' beliefs literature. Statistical controls are common, including the use of structural equation modeling and other so-called causal modeling techniques (e.g., Aunola, Nurmi, Lerkkanen, & Rasku-Puttonen, 2003; Simpkins, Fredricks, & Eccles, 2015). Such approaches are not merely statistical; instead, they posit and test particular theoretical formulations. Nor are they limited to the elimination of third-factor explanations because in some uses they also speak to the directionality issue. An article by Paschall and Mastergeorge (2016) provides a helpful discussion of the possibilities.

Longitudinal studies also appear with some frequency in the beliefs literature, although they are more common for some topics and some age periods than for others. Because of their across-time nature, such studies can provide evidence for beliefs as both causes and consequences of children's development. In addition, the question of the stability of parents' beliefs is an important issue in its own right, and longitudinal study provides the only way to address this issue.

Finally, experimental studies of two sorts are found in the beliefs literature. Some studies employ short-term manipulations of parental beliefs to determine whether changes in behavior follow from a change in beliefs (e.g., Moorman & Pomerantz, 2010; Stein et al., 2012). Changes typically do follow, and the experimental control establishes beliefs as a causal contributor to behavior. The second approach is intervention research—that is, large-scale attempts to alter parents' beliefs and parents' behaviors, usually for pragmatic purposes. Intervention studies will be addressed at various places throughout the book, but I can note three general conclusions from such research here. First, it *is* possible to change parents' beliefs through experimental intervention. Second, changes in parents' behavior often follow from changes in their beliefs. Finally, changes in child outcomes often follow from changes in parents' behaviors.

This section concludes with two points concerning how the directionality issue applies in research on parents' beliefs. The first concerns relations between parents' beliefs and parents' behaviors. The usual explanation when such relations are found is the one that I have presented to this point: that parents' beliefs are a cause of how they behave. As a number of authors (e.g., Goodnow, 1988; Murphey, 1992; Weary, Stanley, & Harvey, 1989) have pointed out, however, it is possible that the causality at least sometimes runs in the other direction—parents may act first and only later formulate a belief to justify their action (e.g., "I spanked him, so he must have done it on purpose"). Such effects, moreover, are not necessarily only short-term. Over time, belief systems may build up to justify habitual parental practices.

The second point concerns relations between parents' beliefs and child outcomes. The idea that children's characteristics affect their parents' behaviors was late in coming to the general child-rearing literature; a paper by Bell (1968) is often credited with sparking the interest in children's effects on parents. In contrast, the notion of child effects is central to the beliefs literature—whatever other sources there may be for parents' beliefs about their children, characteristics of the child are clearly one source. The challenge in this case is to demonstrate that causality also flows in the other direction—that parents' beliefs not only reflect but also contribute to children's development. This challenge will be a topic in each of the chapters to come.

# 3

# General Processes of Development

I'd say that some combination of different heredity and different environment, in the sense that out of their basic selves they select certain things to respond to out of their environments. We tried to keep this as near as possible alike for all of them but they make a different selection of what they respond to.

—(Stolz, 1967, pp. 135–136)

Those that are happy will probably stay happy; those that are pensive will probably stay pensive; those that are extraordinary will always have that in them in some form or another. There are some things about them that won't change.

—(Seifert, 2000, p. 81)

Well, children learn a lot by playing. I play memory games with cards with X, that is to help him to learn figures and the amounts they express. He also learns to memorize. He likes very much to turn the cards and to remember the figures he saw. Well things like this, they learn a lot just by playing.

—(Moussaoui & Braster, 2011, p. 376)

All kids are like little monkeys, they like to "ape" adults in just about every respect. This is how they learn.

—(Stolz, 1967, p. 138)

Parents form beliefs about numerous specific aspects of their children's development—how well the child plays with others, how good the child is at arithmetic, what activities the child enjoys or does not enjoy doing. But as the passages just quoted indicate, parents also form beliefs about how these various outcomes come about—that is, the processes that led to playing well

*Parents' Beliefs About Children.* Scott A. Miller, Oxford University Press (2020). © Oxford University Press.
DOI: 10.1093/oso/9780190874513.001.0001

with others, being good at arithmetic, or whatever. It is beliefs of this sort that form the subject of this chapter.

Parents, of course, are not the only ones who form beliefs about processes of development—the question of how development comes about is *the* central question with which developmental psychology deals. The various sections of the chapter are organized with respect to the particular issues that psychologists address under the overall *how* question. In each case we can see how well parents' beliefs about developmental processes map onto relevant theorizing and research in developmental psychology. And, as always, the interest will be not simply in the nature of the beliefs but also in their effects— are some beliefs more adaptive than others?

## Nature–Nurture

Although terminology and emphases may vary some across different presentations, developmental psychologists are in substantial agreement with regard to the basic questions that define their field (even if they do not always agree on the answers to those questions). Table 3.1 provides a brief overview of the issues that are most often discussed. Some of the points in the table will be elaborated as we go.

The first issue to be discussed appears under various labels: nature– nurture, heredity–environment, maturation–learning, innate–learned. Whatever the label, the question is the most general one with which developmental psychology deals: To what extent does development result from biology, and to what extent does it result from experience?

A starting point answer is easy enough to give, and that is that development always results from both factors—there would not be an organism without a biological foundation and an environment in which to develop. As some authors like to state, development is 100% nature and 100% nurture. As we will see, most parents appear to appreciate this point. It is less clear whether they appreciate two further points that govern more specific answers to the nature–nurture question.

One is that the answer varies across different aspects of development. Although all developments (as just noted) have a biological basis, some developments are more biologically prepared than are others; conversely, some developments are more dependent on specific experiences than are others. An example from the cognitive realm concerns the distinction

Table 3.1  Issues in Developmental Psychology

| Issue | Description |
|---|---|
| Nature–nurture | To what extent is development governed by biological factors and to what extent does it derive from experience? |
| Nurture: social agents | What is the relative importance of the various social agents with whom children interact (e.g., parents, teachers, siblings, peers), and do different social agents affect different aspects of development? |
| Nurture: processes | What are the processes through which nurture exerts effects (e.g., direct tuition, observational learning, self-discovery)? To what extent are children active or passive learners, and what is the relative importance of formal and informal learning experiences? |
| Continuity–discontinuity | Do children's characteristics remain stable as they develop or can characteristics change? Is development in general a matter of quantitative increments or do qualitative changes also occur? |
| Holistic-separate | Are children consistent in their attributes and ability levels across different aspect of development or is performance variable? Are different contexts or types of functioning governed by the same or different rules and processes? |

between language and reading (Bjorklund, 2007). Language is a species-wide behavior pattern, found in every typically developing member of the species and not dependent on specific tuition for its emergence. Humans have evolved to master language. Reading, in contrast, is not a species-wide accomplishment, people differ markedly in their degree of mastery, and success is almost always dependent on some degree of explicit teaching. Both developments, to be sure, require both nature and nurture, but the balance and the form of the two contributors differ.

The second point is that the answer to the nature–nurture question depends on what we are trying to explain with respect to a particular development. In some instances the goal is to explain similarities in development—why, for example, virtually all children master a complex language system, or why aggression is part of the human behavioral repertoire. In other instances the goal is to explain differences in development—why, for example, some children master linguistic milestones more quickly than do others, or why some children are more aggressive than are others. The particular forms of biology or experience that are important are not necessarily identical across these two questions, nor are the kinds of evidence that can be gathered, nor are the kinds of conclusions that can be offered. In particular, questions about differences lend themselves to quantitative conclusions about the relative importance of nature and nurture (although with many qualifications and many disputes; see Neisser et al., 1996), something that is impossible in the case of similarities.

The distinctions just discussed are complex ones that remain, after a century or so of concentrated attention, the subject of much research, discussion, and controversy in developmental psychology. It is perhaps not surprising that researchers of parents' beliefs have foregone these complexities and opted for a relatively simple, basic-level approach to the nature–nurture issue. Table 3.2 provides a sampling of the questions that have been used to explore what parents believe. The particular examples ask about nature, but in most instances they are accompanied

Table 3.2  Examples of Items Used in Studies of the Nature–Nurture Issue

| Source | Item |
| --- | --- |
| Civitas Initiative (2000) | "Children's capacity for learning is pretty much set from birth and cannot be greatly increased or decreased by how their parents interact with them." (degree of agreement on a 4-point rating scale) |
| McGillicuddy-DeLisi (1992) | "Some children are more sociable than others by nature." "Personality is largely inborn." (degree of agreement on a 6-point rating scale) |
| McGillicuddy-DeLisi and Subramanian (1996) | "Some children are born smarter than others." "Children with different natures seek out different experiences." (degree of agreement on a 6-point rating scale) |
| Muenks, Miele, Ramani, Stapleton, and Rowe (2015) | "My child's math ability is innate and will never change." (degree of agreement on a 6-point rating scale) |
| Mugny and Carugati (1989) | "The child spontaneously develops his innate capacity for intelligence." "Intelligence does not develop; it is a hereditary gift." (degree of agreement on a 7-point rating scale) |
| Palacios (1990) | "What do you think is the reason why differences in intelligence exist between normal children?" (open-ended responses coded for different beliefs) |
| Tazouti, Malarde, and Michea (2010) | "The development of a child's intelligence depends mostly on genetic factors." (degree of agreement on a 5-point rating scale) |

by comparable questions directed to various forms of nurture. As can be seen, some questions focus on differences among children, whereas others leave the similarities–differences option open. Many ask explicitly about intelligence, and this is in fact representative, for intelligence has been the most frequently explored outcome with respect to beliefs about nature and nurture.

What has such questioning shown? I begin with some findings from the first entry in the table, the Civitas project (Civitas Initiative, Zero to Three, & Brio Corporation, 2000). This work is worth singling out for two reasons. First, its sample was both the largest and the most representative (of the United States population) of any study reviewed in this chapter. Second, its single nature–nurture question (the one given in the table) lends itself to a clear, right-or-wrong interpretation. The statement is false. Do parents realize that it is false?

Most do. Judgments of "definitely false" or "probably false" were given by 85% of the parents in the sample, with no differences between mothers and fathers. Nonparents and grandparents achieved a slightly lower success rate. Performance, then, was good. Still, 15% of parents apparently believe that their children's intellectual development is totally under biological control. On another question from the survey, 25% of parents failed to realize that what parents do can impact a baby's brain development from birth. As Bornstein (2015, p. 67) notes, "Such a statistic incites some wonder about investment in children's parenting in that 25% of the population." Unfortunately, the Civitas study included no measures of parental behavior; thus the belief–behavior relation could not be explored.

As noted, most studies ask about both nature and nurture, and most parents ascribe some importance to both factors. When differences occur, experiential factors are usually rated as more important than biological ones, although exceptions exist (e.g., McGillicuddy-DeLisi & Subramanian, 1996). Whether the weighing of nature and nurture makes a difference is not clear from research to date. A relatively strong belief in biology is sometimes associated with negative child outcomes (e.g., Johnson & Martin, 1983; McGillicuddy-DeLisi, 1992), an expectable finding if such a belief reduces the chances of helpful parental behaviors. Such negative findings are scattered, however, and null results are more common. What emerges as more important than the nature–nurture split are the particular beliefs that parents hold about nurture, and that is the topic to which we turn next.

## Nurture: Agents

The discussion of nurture begins with parents' beliefs about the importance of different social agents in children's lives. Of particular interest, of course, are beliefs about the importance of parents.

Perhaps not surprisingly, most parents believe that parents are important contributors to their children's development, a conclusion that holds whether the questioning concerns parents in general (e.g., Miller, 1986) or whether it concerns the participating parents themselves (e.g., Knight & Goodnow, 1988). Beliefs about the relative importance of parents compared to other social agents vary some depending on the development in question. In the Knight and Goodnow (1988) study, parents rated themselves as more important than teachers for socioemotional developments (e.g., "expresses love and affection," "has strong moral values"), whereas only minimal differences emerged for outcomes in the cognitive realm ("is able to work things out, to think, reason, and solve problems"; "understands easily or catches on quickly"). Parents judged their own influence as greater for socioemotional than for cognitive outcomes, whereas the reverse pattern was seen as true for teachers.

Two studies by Miller and associates (Miller, 1986; Miller, White, & Delgado, 1980) suggest that the particular cognitive outcome may be important for parents' judgments. In the Miller (1986) study, mothers rated their influence as greater for IQ-type abilities (e.g., vocabulary, memory) than for Piagetian concepts (e.g., conservation, class inclusion). In the Miller et al. study (1980), parents judged self-discovery as a more important contributor to mastery of Piagetian concepts than either parental teaching or school teaching. Although it is difficult to verify the accuracy of these judgments, both beliefs fit with both Piagetian theory and common sense.

Beliefs may also vary as a function of cultural setting. For example, both American and Tanzanian mothers regard themselves as important contributors to their children's success in school, but beliefs about particular school subjects vary in predictable ways as a function of cultural emphases (McGillicuddy-DeLisi & Subramanian, 1994). American mothers, for example, regard themselves as more important for sociopolitical knowledge than do Tanzanian mothers, a finding in keeping with the American emphasis on the autonomy of the family in such matters. In contrast, Tanzanian mothers regard themselves as more important for historical knowledge than do American mothers, a finding explicable in terms of the importance of such knowledge for kinship and tribal connections. Beliefs about the relative importance of parents and teachers for different subjects show similar cultural variation. Chapter 6 will take up the issue of cultural differences in beliefs about schooling more fully.

Kochanska and colleagues provide a group comparison of a different sort, a comparison of depressed mothers, both unipolar and bipolar, with normally functioning mothers (Kochanska, Radke-Yarrow, Kucyniski, & Friedman, 1987). The targets for judgment were 20 child outcomes drawn from the cognitive, social, and affective domains, and maternal influence was one of seven contributors that were examined. For the sample as a whole, maternal influence was rated as the most important contributor. Depressed mothers, however, placed more weight on uncontrollable factors ("other people," "luck") than did well mothers, and mothers with bipolar depression placed more emphasis on genetics than did other mothers. Depression, then, appears to be accompanied by a reduced sense of control over how one's children develop. We will return to this work in Chapter 9 in the context of a general discussion of clinical disorders and parental beliefs.

An obvious comparison of interest is that between mothers and fathers. Somewhat surprisingly, the Knight and Goodnow (1988) study reported only slight and nonsignificant differences between mothers and fathers in their beliefs about parental influence. In contrast, Becker and Hall (1989) found that mothers rated themselves as more important for mastery of pragmatic skills (e.g., learning to use polite speech forms) than did fathers. And working with a wider array of outcomes, Russell and Russell (1982) found gender differences in 7 of 22 possible instances. Mothers reported greater influence in six cases, all involving various child characteristics (e.g., getting along with children; well-mannered, neat, and tidy; doing well in school). Fathers claimed greater influence in only one case: financial security in the future. It is difficult to know, of course, whether this pattern reflects mother–father differences in beliefs or simply developmental reality, given that mothers probably are the more influential parent in most cases. In none of the studies just discussed were the parents asked to judge the other parent's importance.

What happens when they are? Two findings emerged in a study by Favez and associates (Favez, Tissot, Frascarolo, Stiefel, & Despland, 2016). First, mothers and fathers of 18-month-olds often disagreed in their beliefs, especially when judging the mother's importance. Second, such disagreements were predictive of conflicts in coparenting when both parents were interacting with the child. Interestingly, it did not seem to matter which parent held which belief; it was the clash of beliefs that proved maladaptive.

## Nurture: Processes

The previous section considered nurture from the point of view of the social agents who contribute to children's development. The subject of this section is beliefs about the child's part in the process: How do children take in and learn from the environmental sources around them? I begin the discussion with two of the pioneering approaches to this question, research projects carried out by Irving Sigel and Ann McGillicuddy-DeLisi at the Educational Testing Service (ETS) (McGillicuddy-DeLisi, 1992; Sigel, 1992; Sigel & McGillicuddy-DeLisi, 2002) and by Arnold Sameroff and associates as part of the Rochester Longitudinal Study (Sameroff & Feil, 1985; Sameroff & Fiese, 1992).

## The Sigel and McGillicuddy-DeLisi Approach

Two methods of studying beliefs about developmental processes were used in the ETS research. The initial approach was to interview parents of 3- and 4-year-olds. The Construction of the Child Interview presents 12 vignettes, most of which describe some form of cognitive understanding that children must come to master. One vignette, for example, has to do with how children learn which things float. Another has to do with how they learn about time. The initial question poses the issue for discussion (e.g. "Does a 4-year-old understand time?"), and a series of standardized probes then elicit beliefs about how such understanding comes about.

Chapter 2 discussed the challenge of identifying parents' naturally occurring beliefs, as opposed to responses to experimenter-defined issues and distinctions. The ETS group's adoption of an interview approach was an attempt to meet this challenge, and it appears, at least for the most part, to have been successful. Although there clearly were exceptions, most parents seemed to possess already formed beliefs about most of developments that were explored, beliefs that they were happy to share with the researchers. In McGillicuddy-DeLisi's (1982a) words, "parents seemed to have complex belief systems about how children develop," beliefs which were "nearly always presented as truth statements or obvious facts about children" (p. 193). They had, moreover, a variety of beliefs; the researchers were able to identify 27 at least somewhat distinct beliefs about developmental processes. Table 3.3 lists the beliefs that were identified.

The entries in the table convey a rich picture of parental thinking, but such a tabulation does not lend itself readily either to statistical comparisons or to summary conclusions. Further analyses, however, demonstrated that beliefs did not occur in isolation; rather, there was an underlying coherence to parents' thinking. Principal component scores derived from factor analysis indicated that the beliefs could be ordered in terms of the degree to which the child was regarded as an "active constructivist" in his or her development. Parents who held a constructivist view made frequent reference to constructs such as experimentation, stages, and readiness. For those at the other end of the continuum, it was categories such as dependency, accumulation, and absorption that provided the most common answers.

I noted that the ETS group has taken two approaches to the measurement of beliefs. The Child Development Questionnaire (McGillicuddy-DeLisi & Subramanian, 1996) is a reworking of informative aspects of the interview into a questionnaire format. An example of a constructivist item on the questionnaire is "Children figure ideas out on their own" (responses are made on a 6-point degree of agreement scale). An example of a more passive view of learning is "Copying other people is the way that children learn." Note—to revisit a point from Chapter 2—that the questionnaire was constructed only after an interview had been used to identify the response options of interest.

Two findings from the ETS research have already been noted: Parents do hold organized beliefs about how their children take in experience and benefit from it, and parents vary in the beliefs they hold. The original ETS studies explored three possible contributors to such variations. One was socioeconomic status (SES; as defined by both income and education), and this proved to be important: Middle-SES parents were more likely to hold constructivist views than were lower-SES parents (McGillicuddy-DeLisi, 1982b). A second factor was family size (one child vs. three), and this too, had an effect: Parents of three children were more likely to emphasize internal factors (e.g., self-regulation, impulsivity) than were parents of one child; they also showed more awareness of individual differences among children than did parents of one child. These findings suggest that one result of experience with children may be a heightened awareness of forces that are in a sense inside the child,

**Table 3.3** Parental Beliefs Identified in the ETS Research

| Belief | Description |
| --- | --- |
| Innate factors | Child's natural growth |
| Readiness | Child's mental or physical preparedness |
| Empathy/contagion/projection | Child's fusion of own inner state with that of another person |
| Negative feedback | Unpleasant state produced in child serving to change child's behavior |
| Dependency | Child's reliance on others for support, guidance, etc. |
| Rigidity | Child's thinking/behavior unyielding |
| Impulsivity | Child's tendency toward spontaneous action |
| Conflict | Child's internal struggle between external and internal demands |
| Logic/reasoning | Child's ability to think logically |
| Structure of environment | External influences acting upon child |
| Accumulation | Child's growth in knowledge/behavior by passive accumulation |
| Creativity/imagination | Child's ability to form original ideas |
| Cognitive restructuring | Child's ability to reintegrate ideas, reflect, and restructure them into a logical whole |
| Self-regulation | Child's ability to exercise control over own actions |
| Absorption | Child's incorporation of material/ideas without transformation |
| Modeling/identification | Child's tendency to incorporate traits of another person |
| Direct instruction | External information presented directly to child |
| Proximity/exposure | External information occurs in presence of child |
| Observation/perception | Child's awareness of an event and making a judgment about it |
| Stage | Progressive step in child's life |
| Generalization | Child's ability to apply knowledge to another situation |
| Infusion | Injection of material from environment into child |
| Positive feedback | Pleasant state produced in child serving to change child's behavior |
| Positive affect | Child's possession of a positive internal state |
| Negative affect | Child's internal state marked by anxiety |
| Balance | Child's tendency toward harmonious resolution of personal and nonpersonal material |
| Experimentation | Child's application of a new idea/behavior to a situation, receipt of feedback, and modification of his behavior |

Adapted from "A Conceptual Analysis of Beliefs" (pp. 353–355), by I. E. Sigel. 1985. In I. E. Sigel (Ed.), *Parental Belief Systems* (pp. 83–105). 1985. Hillsdale, NJ: Erlbaum. Copyright 1985 by Laurence Erlbaum Associates. Adapted with permission of Taylor and Francis Group, LLC, a division of Informa pic.

as opposed to simple environmental explanations for development. This is a point that is probably familiar to any parent of two children who has been struck by how different the children are.

Comparisons of mothers and fathers provided the third approach to the origins question. Although the specific conclusions vary some across different reports (cf. McGillicuddy-DeLisi, 1982b, and Sigel, 1986), the dominant impression is one of similarities rather than differences. In the McGilluddy-DeLisi (1982b) report, for example, mothers and fathers differed in only 4 of the 26 beliefs that were scored. Despite this overall similarity, the degree of concordance between spouses was modest at best (correlations in the .40s). The conclusion is one that we will see again: Even when mothers and fathers are similar on the average in what they believe, spouses may still differ in their beliefs.

Most of the research with the ETS approach has been with White samples from the United States. To my knowledge, the only extension to another cultural setting comes in a study of Tanzanian mothers by McGillicuddy-DeLisi and Subramanian (1996). All of the mothers had at least one child between 5 and 12 years of age, as did the American mothers who were included for purposes of comparison. Data were collected via the Child Development Questionnaire, which measures beliefs about seven potential contributors to development: biological processes, absorption, didactic instruction, reinforcement, cognitive processing, experimentation/discovery, and observation. Interestingly, biological processes earned the highest rating for both groups, but the ordering of the other contributors differed. American mothers placed more emphasis on cognitive processing, experimentation, and observation than did their Tanzanian counterparts, whereas Tanzanian mothers placed more emphasis on direct instruction than did American mothers. Although these contrasts do not align perfectly with the constructivist–nonconstructivist continuum, they do suggest a more constructivist orientation on the part of the American sample.

In one other—and important—respect, beliefs for the two groups proved similar. Measures were taken of the children's school performance, and in both cultures mothers' beliefs proved predictive of how well their children were doing in school. Indeed, some of the same beliefs proved predictive in the two settings. Specifically, in both Tanzania and America, beliefs in learning through cognitive processing and observation were associated with relatively good school performance.

The finding just described brings us to one of the general issues in the study of parents' beliefs: Do parents' beliefs relate to the quality of their children's development? The answer from the ETS studies is yes. Furthermore, it is yes in a consistent, theoretically predicted direction: namely, that relatively constructivist beliefs are associated with relatively positive developmental outcomes. This conclusion has been demonstrated across a range of child measures. As just noted, parents' beliefs relate to children's performance in school. In the original ETS studies, the children responded to a variety of cognitive and social tasks, including conservation, classification, spatial imagery, and interpersonal problem solving. Again, constructivist beliefs on the parent's part were predictive of relatively good child performance. A report by McGillicuddy-DeLisi (1992) provides an extension to social outcomes more generally, and one by Sigel and Kim (1996) extends the approach to academic performance in grade-school children. I should add that the beliefs–outcomes relations that are demonstrated in these studies are never strong, and, in some instances, they are scattered among a large number of nonsignificant outcomes (something that is especially true of the last two reports cited). Nevertheless, on balance, the research program has been successful at identifying forms of parental thinking that are apparently beneficial for children's development.

Determining exactly how and why such thinking is beneficial requires that we identify the intermediate step: namely, the parental behaviors that mediate between what parents believe and how their children develop. We need to know how beliefs lead to parent behaviors, and we need to know how parent behaviors lead to child outcomes.

Here, despite what can accurately be described as prodigious effort, the ETS group has been only partially successful. As their main measure of parent behavior they have opted for a common approach in the child-rearing literature: parental teaching tasks on which the parent attempts to teach some concept or some activity to the child. The original research included two such tasks: a storytelling task on the theme of imagining different uses for an object and a paper-folding task with the goal of creating either a plane or a boat. Note, with respect to a point discussed in Chapter 2, that this approach avoids the problem of single-reporter bias that can occur when parental report is the source for both the beliefs measure and the parenting measure. It also provides a direct measure of behavior, rather than a verbal report about behavior.

The main interest in analyzing the teaching behavior has been in what Sigel (1982) calls *distancing strategies*: parental behaviors that help the child to separate ("distance") from the immediate environment and thus promote the development of representational thinking. Encouraging anticipation of the future or reconstruction of the past is a form of distancing strategy. So, too, is encouraging use of imagination to solve problems or helping the child to generalize a discovery or to reach cause-and-effect conclusions. The expectation has been that parents who hold constructivist beliefs will be most likely to engage in practices that promote distancing.

Such is, in fact, the case (Sigel, 1992; Sigel & Kim, 1996). This conclusion, however, comes with the same qualifiers that were discussed with respect to the beliefs–development relation. Relations between beliefs and behaviors are only sometimes found, and significant effects are often accompanied by a larger number of nonsignificant ones. Relations, when they do occur, are not large; correlations average about .25, and path coefficients are similarly small. Relations, moreover, are not across the board but rather vary as a function of a number of factors. They vary as a function of task, with somewhat different findings for the storytelling and paper-folding tasks. They vary as a function of the method of measuring behavior, appearing more consistently for self-report than for observational measures. And they vary as a function of whether the mother or father is the focus of study. Although the research program as a whole identifies effects for both parents, belief–behavior relations emerge more consistently for fathers than they do for mothers. This, as we will see across the chapters to come, is just one of a number of instances in which fathers' beliefs prove to be more predictive of behavior than do mothers' beliefs. McGillicuddy-DeLisi (1982b) offers an interesting explanation for this difference between parents. She suggests that mothers have more experience with their children and more knowledge of which child-rearing practices work best in which situations. The mother's behavior, therefore, can be guided by her knowledge of her child and does not necessarily reflect her beliefs about children in general. Fathers, in contrast, have a less intimate knowledge of the moment-by-moment specifics of their child's behavior and are therefore more dependent on their general beliefs about how children learn.

Whatever the validity of the argument just offered, the notion that parents' beliefs and practices are often context-specific is both a theoretical and a methodological emphasis in contemporary child-rearing research. Theoretically, the emphasis on context reflects a growing consensus that parental "consistency," an often studied variable in early child-rearing research, is not always a virtue; rather, optimal parenting practices often vary across different contexts, and the most effective parents are those who can adapt their behavior to their child's immediate needs (Bornstein, 2015; Grusec & Goodnow, 1994). Methodologically, the emphasis on context implies that researchers interested in belief–behavior relations must select beliefs that match as closely as possible to the behaviors under study—or, of course, select behaviors that match as closely as possible to the beliefs of interest. Indeed, this is the main conclusion in Sigel's various discussions of the belief–behavior issue (Sigel, 1986, 1992; Sigel & Kim, 1996). In his words, "the greater the overlap between the knowledge domain of the belief and the task to be taught or learned, the greater will be the relationship" (Sigel, 1992, p. 453). The same point has been made in general discussions of the belief–behavior issue (Ajzen & Fishbein, 2005).

What about the relation between parent behaviors and child outcomes? As with the belief–behavior issue, the ETS approach makes a clear prediction: behaviors that promote distancing should relate to positive child outcomes. And, as with the belief–behavior issue, tests of the prediction are mixed: enough positive results to support the value of distancing as a parenting practice, but enough negative results to indicate that distancing is a far from sufficient explanation for the outcomes in question. In some instances the results take the form discussed in Chapter 1: a positive relation between beliefs and outcomes, but no relation for the behaviors (distancing or otherwise) that were hypothesized to mediate the effect of beliefs. As various authors have discussed, the relevant behaviors in such cases may take a less direct and more cumulative form than the behaviors that are the typical focus of research (McGillicuddy-DeLisi, 1985; Miller, 1988; Murphey, 1992). Here, I reproduce my own summary of this argument.

> Not all important parental beliefs are likely to be expressed in direct interaction with the child. The parent's structuring of the early physical environment, purchasing of toys or books, general expectations concerning household responsibilities—all are examples of potentially important parental decisions that are not clearly captured in discrete behaviors. Furthermore, some beliefs may be conveyed to the child only through a cumulative history of interaction with the parent. The child may come to realize, for example, that the parent values curiosity and exploration, even though no single parental behavior is sufficient to convey this message. (Miller, 1988, p. 277)

## The Sameroff Approach

We turn now to the second of the pioneering research programs mentioned at the start of this section, the work by Sameroff and associates (Sameroff & Feil, 1985; Sameroff & Fiese, 1992).

In several respects the Sameroff research program is similar to the ETS work just discussed. Again, the goal has been to identify differences in the sophistication or quality of parental thinking, as well as the effects of such differences on how children develop. Again, both interviews and questionnaires have been used in this attempt, and again the two approaches lead to similar conclusions. Finally, again, there is a definite theoretical grounding for the research, and the grounding is in fact the same for the two projects: namely, a starting point in Piagetian theory. The notion of the child as an active constructivist, a central component of the ETS approach, has a clear basis in Piaget's work. The Piagetian underpinnings are if anything even greater for the Sameroff research, for its goal has been to determine whether Piaget's stages of development have analogs in parental thinking. Piaget's childhood stages provided us with our fullest model of developmentally ordered, qualitatively distinct forms of thinking. Can we identify parallel differences in how parents think about children?

The answer turns out to be yes, but only in part. Attempts to identify four distinct levels of adult thought, parallel to the four Piagetian stages, proved unsuccessful. The final model therefore consists of just two levels: categorical and compensating/perspectivist. Table 3.4, which reproduces one of the questionnaires used in the research, shows the kinds of thinking that define the two levels. Reasoning at the categorical level interprets development as caused by a single biological or environmental factor, and it regards the labels that can be applied to development (e.g., a "good child") as reflections of intrinsic qualities that are unlikely to change. Such reasoning shows a limited ability to take into account context and possible variations in behavior across settings or across time. Reasoning at the compensating/perspectivist level, in contrast, recognizes that development typically has multiple rather than single causes and that the developmental course might have been different—and still could be different—if the determining factors were different. Rather than focusing on causes in isolation, perspectivist reasoning demonstrates an appreciation of how multiple contributors act together to produce developmental outcomes. We can see here a rough parallel to the developmental progression described by Piaget: movement from a relatively simple focus on

Table 3.4  Concepts of Development Questionnaire

**Perspectivist/Compensating Items**

1. Children have to be treated differently as they grow older.
2. It is not easy to define a good home because it is made up of many different things.
3. The mischief that 2-year-olds get into is part of a passing stage they'll grow out of.
4. Parents need to be sensitive to the needs of their children.
5. Difficult babies will grow out of it.
6. Children's problems seldom have a single cause.
7. Parents can be turned off by a fussy child so that they are unable to be as nice as they would like.
8. There is no one right way to raise children.
9. Firstborn children are usually treated differently than are later-born children.
10. Parents change in response to their children.

**Categorical Items**

1. Parents must keep to their standards and rules no matter what their child is like.
2. Fathers cannot raise their children as well as mothers.
3. A child who isn't toilet trained by 3 years of age must have something wrong with him.
4. Girls tend to be easier babies than are boys.
5. There's not much anyone can do to help emotionally disturbed children.
6. The father's role is to provide the discipline in the family and the mother's role is to give love and attention to the children.
7. A child's success at school depends on how much his mother taught him at home.
8. Boy babies are less affectionate than girl babies.
9. An easy baby will grow up to be a good child.
10. Babies have to be taught to behave themselves or they will be bad later on.

Responses are made on a 4-point scale ranging from "strongly agree" to "strongly disagree." From "Parental Concepts of Development" (p. 91), by A. J. Sameroff and L. A. Feil. In I. E. Sigel (Ed.), *Parental belief systems* (pp. 83–105). 1985. Hillsdale, NJ: Erlbaum. Copyright 1985 by Laurence Erlbaum Associates. Adapted with permission of Taylor and Francis Group, LLC, a division of Informa plc.

readily available causal factors (the preoperational response) to a more complex weighing of multiple, often less obvious contributors (the concrete- or formal-operational response).

Where do such differences in reasoning come from? The sample for the original Sameroff studies was mothers only, something that is also true of almost all of the follow-up studies to date; the one exception (Siller, Reyes, Hotez, Hutman, & Sigman, 2014) does not analyze for possible mother–father differences. This work, therefore, provides no information with respect to one common entry under the question of origins of beliefs: How do mothers and fathers compare? It does provide information with respect to another common entry: social class. As in the ETS research, a clear difference is evident: Middle-SES mothers espouse more perspectivist beliefs than do lower-SES mothers. There is, however, one interesting exception to this conclusion: No SES differences emerged in the one English sample included in the research, a finding attributed to "a cultural tradition of inherited social position and an accompanying belief that individuals should 'stay in their place'" (Sameroff & Feil, 1985, p. 96), a tradition that apparently outweighed the capacity for advanced reasoning that would otherwise accompany higher SES status.

Two studies by Gutierrez and colleagues with Mexican American mothers add some further wrinkles to the SES picture (Gutierrez & Sameroff, 1990; Gutierrez, Sameroff, & Karrer, 1988). In both studies, degree of acculturation—that is, extent of successful adaptation to the United States culture—proved to be a more important determinant of level of reasoning than the limited effects attributable to SES. More highly acculturated mothers showed higher levels of reasoning than did less acculturated ones, and SES differences were found only when degree of acculturation was high. Indeed, not only did highly acculturated mothers outperform their less acculturated counterparts; they also outperformed a comparison sample of Anglo mothers of comparable SES. The researchers suggest that the cognitive challenges involved in living simultaneously in two cultures promote perspective-taking skills, skills that subsequently enhance mothers' ability to reason about their children.

The Rochester Longitudinal Study, the original locus for the Concepts of Development measures, had the goal of identifying early risk factors that adversely affect later development. Low scores on the categorical–perspectivist dimension were one of 10 potential risks that were examined. The potential risks did, in fact, prove predictive across a range of developmental outcomes. For example, children who experienced eight or more risk factors averaged 30 points lower in IQ than did those who had experienced no risks (Sameroff, Seifer, Barocas, Zax, & Greenspan, 1987). When the Concept of Development scores were considered individually, it was in fact IQ for which they proved most predictive. Other research, however, makes clear that social development can also be affected. Preschoolers' social responsiveness, for example, has been shown to relate positively to the complexity of their mothers' reasoning as measured by the Sameroff approach (Miller-Loncar, Landry, Smith, & Swank, 2000). In the other direction, behavior problems of a variety of sorts have been shown to relate negatively to the level of mothers' reasoning (Benasich & Brooks-Gunn, 1996).

Parents' child-rearing behaviors also relate to Concept of Development scores, and they do so in predictable ways. Parental warmth, sensitivity, and responsiveness have all been shown to relate positively to level of maternal reasoning (Miller-Loncar, Landry, Smith, & Swank, 1997; Miller-Loncar et al., 2000; Pratt, Hunsberger, Pancer, Roth, & Santolupa, 1993). Low reasoning scores, in contrast, are predictive of various forms of maternal maltreatment (Berger & Brooks-Gunn, 2005).

The Benasich and Brooks-Gunn study (1996) adds two further points. One of their behavioral measures was the Home Observation for Measurement of the Environment (HOME; Caldwell & Bradley, 1979), an often-used instrument in the study of parenting. The HOME is divided into six subscales, some of which measure face-to-face interaction between parent and child (e.g., mother is responsive to child's vocalizations; mother structures child's play periods) and some of which measure more general qualities of the early environment (e.g., child is taken regularly to doctor's office or clinic; child gets out of house at least four times a week). The HOME therefore speaks to the point noted earlier: that parenting involves not only what is done with the child but also what is done for the child—for example, purchase of books or selection of a safe neighborhood (both of which are, in fact, items on the HOME). Benasich and Brooks-Gunn reported a positive relation between Concept of Development scores and HOME scores; thus mothers whose reasoning was relatively advanced provided a more positive early environment.

The Benasich and Brooks-Gunn study (1996) also included one of the measures that will be discussed in Chapter 4: the Knowledge of Infant Development Inventory (KIDI; MacPhee, 1981). As its name indicates, the KIDI assesses parental knowledge, including knowledge of parenting practices and knowledge of infant development. KIDI scores correlated positively with Concept of Development scores; thus more knowledgeable parents tended to show higher levels of reasoning. As we will see, such interrelations among beliefs are a common finding; parents who are relatively accurate or sophisticated on one measure tend to be accurate or sophisticated on other measures as well. Such coherence in parents' thinking is both an expectable and an important finding. Note, though, that the interrelations among beliefs complicate the task of identifying the effects of any one form of belief.

I conclude this section with a final point about the Sameroff research. As we will see across the coming chapters, we still know relatively little about the stability of parents' beliefs—whether, for example, a mode of thinking that is present when the child is 2 is still present when the child is 4 or 6 or 8. In the Rochester Longitudinal study, mothers responded to the Concepts of Development Questionnaire twice, once when their child was 4 and again when the child was 13. The correlation between the two measures was .65, a remarkable degree of stability across a 9-year period (Sameroff & Fiese, 1992). It is interesting to note, however, that scores were slightly lower at the second testing point (Sameroff, Seifer, Baldwin, & Baldwin, 1993). Thus 9 additional years of experience as a parent apparently did not enhance mothers' ability to reason about children.

## Other General Approaches

The ETS and Rochester projects do not exhaust the attempts to identify differences in how parents think about processes of development. This section adds two other examples.

One is research by Palacios and colleagues with Spanish mothers and fathers (Palacios, 1990; Palacios, Gonzalez, & Moreno, 1992; Palacios & Moreno, 1996). The instrument for the research was the Parents' Ideas Questionnaire, a wide-ranging measure that includes, among other topics, questions directed to developmental processes. One of the nature–nurture questions from the measure is reproduced in Table 3.2.

Three distinct patterns were evident in parents' responses to the Questionnaire. Parents whom the Palacios group labeled as *modern* responded in ways that were generally consistent with contemporary scientific views about how development occurs. Such parents were in general well-educated and well-informed about child development, they realized that both nature and nurture are involved in every developmental outcome, they believed that children's characteristics are not necessarily fixed but can change, and they were optimistic about their ability to nurture positive development in their children. In contrast, parents labeled as *traditional* tended to give answers at the opposite end of the various dimensions. These parents had made little attempt to learn about children, they emphasized innate bases for development and minimized their own potential contribution, they held stereotyped views with regard to differences between the sexes, and they favored authoritarian forms of child-rearing. Finally, the third group, labeled *paradoxical*, showed a mixture of the characteristics of the first two groups.

On the positive side, these parents had made attempts to read about child development, they realized that environmental factors were important, and they held optimistic (at times overly optimistic) views of what children were capable of. On the negative side, many of their responses suggested that they had retained little of what they had read; they showed a mixture of stereotyped and more modern beliefs; and they had little faith, despite their generally environmentalist views, in their ability to influence their children's development.

Both parent behaviors and child outcomes were examined as possible consequences of these differences in beliefs (Palacios et al., 1992). In both cases the comparisons of modern and traditional parents yielded expectable results. Modern parents engaged in more distancing behaviors (ala the Sigel approach) during teaching tasks than did traditional parents, they had higher HOME scores, and their children scored close to 20 points higher on the Bayley Scales of Mental Development. As befits their label, the results for paradoxical parents were less predictable. In keeping with the mixed, in-between nature of this group's beliefs, both their HOME scores and their children's Bayley scores fell between those for the modern and traditional groups. By some measures, however, their distancing scores were the highest of the three sets of parents. Why, then, did their children not show more cognitive benefit? Palacios et al. (1992) invoke the Vygotskian concept of the *zone of proximal development*, suggesting that many of the distancing behaviors produced by these parents were beyond what their children were ready for. Modern parents, in contrast, apparently judged their children more accurately, they produced simpler and more appropriate forms of distancing, and these forms did relate to their children's cognitive performance.

The remaining approach to be considered in this section is a longstanding theoretical and empirical effort by Mary Belenky, Lynne Bond, and colleagues (Belenky, Clinchy, Goldberger, & Tarule, 1986; Bond, Belensky, Weinstock, & Cook, 1996). The general heading under which the work falls is *epistemology*, a standard definition of which is "reflection on the nature of knowledge and relation between knowledge and reality" (Pillow, 2008, p. 299). Epistemology has been a central topic in philosophy ever since the dawn of philosophy thousands of years ago. The topic is not limited to philosophers, however; rather, all of us have beliefs, albeit often implicit ones, about knowledge—where it comes from, what forms it takes, how it relates to the world around us. Indeed, epistemological conceptions are among the broadest belief systems that people form. Among the researchers, in addition to Belenky and Bond, who have addressed this topic are Perry (1970), Kuhn (1991), and Mansfield and Clinchy (2002).

The particular focus of the Belenky/Bond approach is given in the title of a book devoted to the work: *Women's Ways of Knowing* (Belenky et al., 1986). The goal has been to identify the beliefs that women form about knowledge and about themselves as knowers, including differences in the level or sophistication of the beliefs. A particular interest has been in the beliefs of poor, rural, minimally educated women, a vulnerable group that is seldom a focus for research. The method consists of an extensive, semistructured interview that probes various beliefs about knowledge; sample items from the interview are "Can you say that some answers are better than others?" and "How do you know what's right or true?" Responses to such questions are coded into five increasingly complex levels of reasoning. At the lowest levels women express powerlessness with respect to affecting or even understanding forms of knowledge; the best that can be hoped for is to memorize what others convey and to transmit such knowledge unchanged. At higher levels there is increasing realization of the subjective, personal contribution to knowledge, a progression that culminates in a conception of the self as a creator and not just transmitter of what is known.

What are the implications of such beliefs for parenting practices? The relation is argued to be a close one, with epistemological level as a prime determinant of what mothers think and what they do. In the words of Bond et al. (1996, p. 467): "The premise . . . is that mothers' beliefs about child development and mothers' actual parenting strategies are strongly linked to their own broad epistemological perspectives (i.e., their conceptualization of the general nature of knowledge and of how they themselves come to know and understand themselves and their world)."

Research to date supports this argument. Some of the work has been grounded in the ETS approach, with an attempt to identify parental distancing strategies, as measured through both parental teaching tasks and self-reported parental practices. By both measures, relatively advanced epistemological conceptions predicted relatively advanced parenting (Bond et al., 1996). Other research has shown that epistemological level relates to contingent, responsive turn-taking in interactions with one's child (Jimerson & Bond, 2001) and to mothers' use of mental state language—a contributor to theory of mind—when talking to the child (Hutchins, Bond, Silliman, & Bryant, 2009). The latter study also showed a relation to children's own use of mental state language and thus effects on an important developmental outcome. We will see another example of effects on both maternal behavior and child outcomes in Chapter 8 on adolescence.

## Play

One particular form of experience is important enough to single out under the "Processes" heading. Play is a universal feature of children's development. It is also, not coincidentally, the subject of one of the largest research literatures in developmental psychology, one subsection of which is devoted to what parents believe about play. This section discusses what parents believe about the importance of play.

Before asking what parents believe about play, we can ask what psychologists believe. Here, to be sure, there is less than perfect agreement when the discussion turns to specifics (e.g., effects of different forms of play). At a general level, however, the field converges on one quite broadly accepted conclusion, and that is that play is an important contributor to children's development. Such has long been argued by major theorists in the field (Piaget, Vygotsky, Erikson), and a substantial research literature can be marshalled in support of the conclusion (Ginsburg, 2007; Hirsh-Pasek, Golinkoff, Berk, & Singer, 2009; St. George, Wroe, & Cashin, 2018; though see Lillard, 2015, for a more cautious summary). In recent years the long-standing basic-science approach to the topic has been supplemented by a strong applied focus, as a number of authors have decried the loss of playtime entailed by an earlier and earlier focus on academic skills (e.g., Golinkoff & Hirsh-Pasek, 2016; Miller & Almon, 2009; Warash, Root, & Doris, 2017).

Most parents also believe that play is important for children's development. In the Civitas study, for example, 89% of parents judged that play was "very important" for 5-year-olds (Civitas Initiative, Zero to Three, & Brio Corporation, 2000). Similarly high values emerge in most other examinations of the issue (with one important exception that I will discuss shortly). Table 3.5 presents one of the instruments from which this conclusion derives. As can be seen, the measure includes an explicit contrast between beliefs about play and beliefs about academic skills. Other measures of parents' beliefs about play include Mothers' Perceptions of Their Children's Play (Morris, 2013), Parents' Perception of Child's Play (Lin & Yawkey, 2014), and Toddler and Play Scale (Mantz & Bracaliello, 2016).

**Table 3.5** Examples of Items from the Parent Play Beliefs Scale

---

<u>Play Support</u>

Play can help my child develop better thinking abilities.
Playing at home will help my child get ready for kindergarten.
I teach my child social skills during play.
Play helps my child to express his or her feelings.
Play can improve my child's language and communication abilities.
Playing together helps me build a good relationship with my child.
My child has a lot of fun when we play together.
It is important to me to participate in play with my child.

<u>Academic Focus</u>

I do not think my child learns important skills by playing.
I would rather read to my child than play together.
Playtime is not a high priority in my home.
It is more important for my child to have good academic skills than to play well with others.
Play does not help my child learn academic skills.

---

Responses are made on a 5-point scale ranging from "Disagree" to "Strongly Agree." Adapted from "Assessing the Play Beliefs of African American Mothers with Preschool Children," by L. M. Fogle and J. L. Mendez, 2006, *Early Childhood Research Quarterly, 21*, p. 510. Copyright 2006 by Elsevier. Reprinted with permission.

Despite the generally high endorsement of play, some differences do emerge across samples or across forms of play. Relatively well-educated parents typically ascribe greater importance to play than do less well-educated ones (LaForett & Mendez, 2017b; Mantz & Bracaliello, 2016). Income level is also a predictor, with more positive ratings by relatively affluent parents than by those with lower incomes (Ivrendi & Isikoglu, 2010; Lin & Yawkey, 2013). Differences between mothers and fathers are sometimes but not always found; when differences do occur, it is usually mothers who believe more strongly in the value of play, perhaps especially pretend play (Lin & Yawkey, 2013; Warash et al., 2017). As is true for many types of beliefs, spouse concordance in beliefs about play is moderate but far from perfect; typical correlations are in the .40s (Warash et al., 2017). Finally—and as a caution to the generally positive conclusions to this point—there is evidence that parents may overvalue some forms of play, such as use of flash cards or playing computer games (Civitas Initiative, Zero to Three, & Brio Corporation, 2000; Fisher, Hirsh-Pasek, Golinkoff, & Gryfe, 2008).

Of course, a belief that play is important does not answer the question: Important for what? Most examinations of the issue offer parents three broad alternatives: cognitive development, language development, and social development. All three outcomes receive endorsements, with no clear ordering in research to date. In the Civitas study, play was judged as most important for social outcomes, followed by cognitive outcomes and then language (Civitas Initiative, Zero to Three, & Brio Corporation, 2000). In other studies, cognitive development, including performance in school, has been judged as the primary benefit of play experience (Farver & Howes, 1993; Shiakou & Belsky, 2013). Two studies that focused on pretend play reveal further differences in parents' beliefs: in one, cognitive development, especially creativity, was judged the most important outcome (Haight, Parke, & Black, 1997); in the other, social development and language development emerged as most important (Gleason, 2005).

As we saw in the discussion of the ETS research—and as we will see again at various places throughout the book—specifying exactly what parental behaviors should follow from a set of beliefs can be challenging. In the case of play, however, the prediction seems straightforward: Parents who believe in the importance of play should do various things to encourage and support play in their children. And such is, in fact, the case. Parents' beliefs about the value of play relate positively to their involvement in their children's play and in their children's early learning more generally (Ivrendi & Isikoglu, 2010; Mantz & Bracaliello, 2016). Beliefs about the value of play also relate positively to parental warmth and responsiveness in interaction with the child (LaForett & Mendez, 2017b) and to the adoption of an authoritative rather than authoritarian style of child-rearing (Morris, 2013).

What about effects on children's development? Again, one predicted relation seems straightforward. The most obvious developmental outcome that would be expected to follow from parents' beliefs and practices regarding play is play itself. And such is, in fact, the case. Children whose parents believe in the value of play and are supportive of play show greater competence in play with peers than do children who lack such support (Fogle & Mendez, 2006; LaForett & Mendez, 2017a). More generally, ratings of children's social competence, as provided by both parents and teachers, relate positively to parents' beliefs about the value of play (Lin & Yawkey, 2014).

A further finding is worth noting here. Morris (2013) took the unusual step of determining whether children (8- to 10-year-olds in her study) were aware of their parents' beliefs about play. Most were; indeed, many of the correlations between the parent and child scales were in the .70s and .80s. Of course, the fact that children are aware of their parents' beliefs does not mean that they will be positively affected by those beliefs. But in most instances it probably does, and such appears to be the case for play.

I noted earlier that there is one important qualifier to the conclusion that parents believe that play is important for children's development. It is a point that was prefigured in the discussion of ethnotheories in Chapter 2. The qualifier comes when we expand the focus of study beyond the Western industrialized samples that have been the source for most of the conclusions to this point. Beliefs about play vary across cultures, as well as across subcultures or ethnic groups within a culture. Here are a few examples. In a study by Farver and Howes (1993), American mothers believed more strongly in the value of play than did Mexican mothers, and the two groups also differed in what they saw as the prime benefits that children take away from play: educational benefits for American mothers, amusement for Mexican mothers. A study by Farver and colleagues reported a similar result in a comparison of Anglo American and Korean American mothers: an emphasis on learning by the Anglo mothers, an emphasis on amusement by the Korean mothers (Farver, Kim, & Lee, 1995). In research by LaForett and Mendez (2017a), Latino parents expressed stronger beliefs in the value of play than did African America parents. Finally, two studies have reported lower beliefs in the value of play for Chinese American than for Euro American parents; conversely, Chinese American parents place more stress on early educational opportunities than do their Euro American counterparts (Jiang & Myse, 2016; Parmar, Harkness, & Super, 2004).

Findings such as those just summarized are only the tip of the proverbial iceberg. A more comprehensive sampling of the world's cultures, including cultures more distinct from the Western industrialized mode, reveals striking differences in both children's play and parents' beliefs about play (Gaskins, 2015; Roopnarine, 2011; Roopnarine & Davidson, 2015). The amount of time that children spend in play varies markedly across cultures, with Western industrialized cultures toward the high end of the continuum. The nature of the play also varies; although some elements may be universal (e.g., some degree of pretense), other aspects vary as a function of the physical and social settings in which children find themselves. The materials used for play vary; it probably goes without saying that shelves lined with toys are not a starting point for children's play in many of the world's cultures. The partners with whom children play vary. Involvement of parents in children's play tends to be highest in Western industrialized nations; in many other settings, parents seldom participate, and siblings and peers take on more important roles.

Finally—and related to these other differences—the reasons for play and the perceived benefits of play vary across cultures. As we have seen, in some cultures play is seen more as a source of amusement than of learning. In some cultures, especially those in which children stay close to adults' workplaces, play functions as a distractor that allows adults to carry on without interruption. Finally, in some cultures play serves as training for the child's eventual entry into the workplace and as a contributor to the family economy. In such instances forms of play (e.g., playing with a family pet) may gradually transform into a work responsibility (e.g., tending the family's cattle). This is a point to which we will return in Chapter 4.

The foregoing does not negate the role of play and of parents' beliefs about play in cultures in which play is accorded a central role in children's development. Nor, of course, does it mean that forms of play that may be less familiar to Western observers do not fulfill intended roles within their cultural settings, just as activities that take the place of play may fulfill intended roles. As we saw in Chapter 2, ethnotheories may differ in their specifics (e.g., beliefs about play), but they have the common goal of nurturing optimal development within the cultural setting.

## Continuity–Discontinuity

As Table 3.1 indicates, the continuity–discontinuity issue has to do with consistency or change across the course of development. As applied to similarities among children, the issue concerns the overall nature and shape of development. Is development primarily a matter of adding on, of expansion, of incremental growth (the continuity position), or does development also involve reworking of the psychological system and thus qualitative and not only quantitative change (the discontinuity position)? As applied to individual differences, the issue is that of individual stability. If a child is relatively high in IQ or aggression or empathy early in life, will that child remain relatively high on these dimensions later in life? The work to be considered now addresses aspects of both of these questions, but its primary concern is with the stability of individual differences.

Recall from Chapter 2 that beliefs about the stability of behavior are an important component of attribution theory (Weiner, 1986). The discussion begins with research that examines the continuity issue from an attributional perspective. It then moves on to a recent body of work, based on Carol

Dweck's research and theorizing, that addresses beliefs about the "fixedness" of intelligence and other traits.

## Attribution Approaches

Although all of the studies to be considered in this section have the same goal—namely, to assess parents' beliefs about the stability of some behavior or trait—they vary in how they go about pursuing this goal. In some studies, actual instances of behavior from the participants' children serve as the target for judgment (e.g., Gretarrson & Gelfand, 1988), whereas in other studies parents respond to standardized vignettes that present the behaviors of interest (e.g., Dix, Ruble, Grusec, & Nixon, 1986). When standardized vignettes are used, parents are sometimes asked to imagine that the child in the vignette is their own (e.g., Mills & Rubin, 1990); in other studies, no such instruction is provided, but the usual assumption is that parents will respond in terms of their own child. The content area for the child behavior or characteristic varies; behaviors in the social realm are most common (e.g., Ozdemir & Cheah, 2015), but some studies present either cognitive outcomes or a mixture of cognitive and social (e.g., Becker & Hall, 1989; Knight, 1986). The age of the target child varies between and sometimes within studies, as does the span across which stability or change is predicted (although many studies refer to "some time" or the "future" without specifying the span). Possible sex differences at either the child or the parent level are sometimes a focus (e.g., Gretarsson & Gelfand, 1986; Knight, 1986); examinations of the latter question, however, are limited by the fact that most studies, like the beliefs literature in general, include mothers only. Although Western samples make up most of the literature, Korean (Cheah & Park, 2006), Lebanese (Goodnow, Cashmore, Cotton, & Knight, 1984), Taiwanese (Chiang, Barrett, & Nunez, 2000), and Turkish (Ozdemir & Cheah, 2015) families also contribute. Finally, some studies have a clinical focus, with a concentration on either children or parents who are experiencing difficulties (e.g., Sobol, Ashbourne, Earn, & Cunningham, 1989). This work will be discussed in Chapter 9.

The preceding overview is based on studies that ask explicitly about stability. As we saw in the discussion of attribution theory, the continuity-discontinuity question can also be examined indirectly, for stability is assumed to be a property of some, but not all, of the causal attributions that can be invoked to explain behavior. Table 2.2 presents the standard mapping between attributions and associated properties, including stability. The entries in the table are directed to cognitive outcomes, but the same argument applies to outcomes in the social domain; in this case "ability" is typically replaced by "disposition" (i.e., internal personality attributes that are assumed to remain stable over time). Although my focus is on direct measures of beliefs about stability, I will occasionally bring in this more indirect evidence as well.

What do we know about parents' beliefs about stability? A reasonable starting point is to ask what we know about stability: That is, what has research shown with respect to consistency or change as children develop? We can then see how well what parents believe fits with the research evidence.

A first thing we know is that every psychological characteristic that develops across a span of time (as do IQ and aggression and empathy, among many others) shows moderate but not perfect stability as children grow. Thus some children (usually most children) stay essentially the same, but some children change. In itself, therefore, a parent's prediction of stability or change cannot be evaluated for accuracy because either outcome is possible. Potentially, accuracy could be tested through longitudinal study, in which parents' predictions of stability or change at some early developmental point are compared to actual stability or change at some later developmental point. To my knowledge, no study has provided such a test.

Beyond documenting typical degrees of stability, research has also identified some of the factors that contribute to stability or change. One is the age of the child. In general, stability increases as children grow older; conversely, the younger the child at the initial assessment, the greater is the likelihood of change. Another determinant is the time span between the assessments. The shorter the span, the greater the average stability. Both of these findings fit common sense, and we might expect that parents' beliefs would reflect them. As noted, however, many studies do not make clear the span across which stability is to be judged, and no study has provided a within-study comparison of different spans. Examinations of possible age-of-child effects that ask specifically about stability have produced some evidence, with qualifications, that perceived stability increases with age (Dix et al., 1986; Fincham & Grynch, 1991; Gretarsson & Gelfand, 1988). More clearly, attributions to internal factors such as ability or disposition increase with age, and such factors are generally regarded as stable determinants of behavior. Sensibly, then, most parents appear to expect greater stability in their adolescent than they do in their toddler.

Gender differences are not a prominent part of the stability literature; by most measures boys and girls show equivalent stability as they develop. Gender differences are also not a prominent part of most parents' beliefs about stability, at least for the outcomes that have been examined to date. Although there are occasional exceptions (e.g., Gretarrson & Gelfand, 1988), the majority of studies report no effect of sex of child on what parents believe about stability.

Effects of the particular behavior or attribute under consideration are also rare in the (admittedly limited) examinations of the issue in the beliefs literature. One interesting effect has emerged, however. It concerns beliefs about two problematic behaviors in preschool children: social withdrawal and aggression. Parents (mothers only in most research to date) predict greater stability for social withdrawal than they do for aggression. This finding has been reported in Canadian (Mills & Rubin, 1990), Korean (Cheah & Park, 2006), and Turkish (Ozdemir & Cheah, 2015) samples, and it emerged as a trend in a Taiwanese sample (Cheah & Rubin, 2004). Presumably, the difference reflects a belief that aggression, more than social withdrawal, is a developmentally normative phase that children will eventually outgrow. I return to this argument shortly.

Not yet mentioned is the most consistent finding to emerge from the literature on parents' beliefs about stability. The finding is of a valence effect: Positive aspects of the child's development are expected to remain stable; negative aspects are expected to improve. Among the studies that demonstrate such an effect with respect to beliefs about stability are Becker and Hall (1989); Dix et al. (1986); Goodnow et al. (1984); Gretarrson and Gelfand (1988); Knight (1986); and Melson, Ladd, and Hsu (1993). The demonstrations include both within-parent comparisons, in which parents predict greater stability for desirable attributes than for undesirable ones, and between-parent comparisons, in which parents whose children are doing well predict greater stability than do parents whose children are having difficulties.

The valence effect is not limited to beliefs about stability; rather, it applies more generally to the explanations and expectations that parents offer for positive as opposed to negative child behaviors or child attributes. Thus positive behaviors are judged as more internal in origin than are negative ones, they are judged as broader in scope and more general than are negative ones, and they are judged as more under the child's control than are negative ones. They are also judged as more under the parent's control—that is, parents claim greater responsibility for positive than for negative outcomes in their children.

Why does the valence effect occur? Chapter 2 discussed the *self-serving bias*: the tendency to make judgments that reflect positively on the self. The usual explanation for the valence effect is that it is a form of self-serving bias. Knight (1986, p. 194) summarizes the argument: "Parents operate as developmental optimists. Believing that the good things will remain stable or that the bad things will improve is useful; it makes sense of the task of parenting and allows one to continue."

Does self-serving bias provide a complete explanation for the valence effect? Or are undesirable behaviors or characteristics in fact more likely than positive ones to change as children develop—that is, is there some accuracy to parents' developmental optimism? We know that there is no general or at all strong tendency for difficulties to disappear with development—early problems are predictive of continuing problems across just about every aspect of psychological functioning. Still, two considerations suggest that parents' optimism may have some justification.

The first concerns the distinction between a focus on individual differences and a focus on similarities or commonalities among children. Stability studies address individual differences. They do so, moreover, in a relative sense, asking how a child compares to his or her agemates. If, for example, a child is relatively high in aggression at age 4, will that child still be relatively high in aggression at age 12? The answer, for aggression and many other attributes, is yes. As numerous authors (e.g., Bornstein, Putnick, & Esposito, 2017) have pointed out, however, stability in this sense may apply, even though the nature or the amount of the behavior has changed greatly with development—as, indeed, is true of aggression between 4 and 12. Many parents, as we saw, appear to think about aggression in this way—as a typical problem of early childhood that lessens as children develop. Aggression is just one of a number of early behavior problems (e.g., tantrums, sleep problems, language delays) that tend to take their strongest form early in development. This argument does not mean, of course, that older children do not present their own set of challenges. But it does suggest that there may be some merit to the belief that "things will get better."

The second argument in support of parental optimism ties in to one of the clearest findings from the general stability literature. Research consistently shows that a major contributor to the stability of children's characteristics is the stability of the environment. When important aspects of children's environments remain stable as they develop, then children's characteristics, positive or negative, also tend to remain stable. When important aspects of the environment change, then children often change as well. Parents, of course, are among the important aspects of children's environments and thus among the contributors to stability or change. Parents who hold a positive set of beliefs (my child is doing well, I am an important contributor to my child's success, I can continue to parent well) are likely to do things that maintain the positive course of the child's development. Although they face a greater challenge, parents whose children are experiencing difficulties can also affect the future course of development, assuming they believe, as we have seen that many parents do, that early problems can be overcome and that they themselves are important agents in this regard. Success, to be sure, is by no means guaranteed. In some cases, however, developmental optimism can become a self-fulfilling prophecy.

## Fixedness of Intelligence

The title for this section reflects the original focus for the research to be considered now. As we will see, however, recent research has extended the approach to a number of other outcomes in addition to intelligence.

The work on fixedness of intelligence began as a study of motivation in childhood (Dweck, 2017). Carol Dweck was struck by the fact that the children she studied had very different reactions to experiences of success and failure. For some, success at a task was clearly not the major goal, and they were not fazed when their efforts sometimes fell short. For these children, challenging tasks were a learning opportunity—a chance to develop new skills. Such children were said to possess a *mastery orientation*. For other children, success seemed to be the only goal when they were faced with some problem to solve. These children preferred easy or familiar problems to hard or novel ones, and they found failure very upsetting. Children in this category were said to possess a *performance orientation*.

A natural question was what underlay these very different reactions to success and failure. Further study revealed that the critical determinant was what children believed about the nature of intelligence. Children with a performance orientation believe that intelligence is something that people have to varying degrees, that it is unchanging, and that it is revealed by one's successes and failures. Such children are said to hold an *entity theory* of intelligence. It is because of their beliefs about intelligence that failure is so devastating to such children because failure signals, to both others and the self, that intelligence is not only lacking but always will be lacking. In contrast, children with a mastery orientation believe that intelligence is not fixed but rather is malleable (i.e., it can grow with effort and experience). They regard tasks to be solved as a chance to develop rather than to demonstrate their abilities, something that may be especially likely when a task is initially beyond what they know how to do. Such children are said to hold an *incremental theory* of intelligence.

I should note that *entity* and *incremental* were the original labels for the two contrasting sets of beliefs. The currently preferred term is *mindsets*— thus either a *fixed mindset* (the entity view) or a *growth mindset* (the incremental view).

Not yet discussed is how mindsets are measured. The answer is through simple rating scales on which participants indicate their extent of agreement with various statements about fixedness or malleability. Examples from studies of children's beliefs about intelligence are "You have a certain amount of intelligence, and you really can't do much to change it," and "No matter how much intelligence you have, you can always change it quite a bit."

As noted, work on beliefs about fixedness or malleability has extended well beyond the initial focus on intelligence, although intelligence and academic achievement remain the most often studied topics (Burnette, O'Boyle, VanEpps, Pollack, & Finkel, 2013; Dweck, 2017). Table 3.6 provides a sampling of the behaviors and characteristics that have been the targets for research. As can be seen, the focus of study has expanded to encompass social and personality outcomes of a variety of sorts. It has also expanded beyond its childhood origins to grow into a large literature with adults.

What has such research shown? Although there are, of course, exceptions and qualifications, the general conclusions are easy to state. Across a range of samples and a range of outcome measures, most people (there are some in-the-middle exceptions) hold either fixed or growth mindsets. Furthermore— and much like children's beliefs about intelligence—the mindsets that people hold affect their response to various tasks or situations and their reactions to success or failure (Dweck, 1999, 2006, 2017). Mindsets, in short, make a difference.

Our interest, of course, is in parents and the possible contribution of parents' beliefs and related behaviors to what children believe and how children develop. We might expect that the relations would be straightforward.

**Table 3.6** Targets for Studies of Beliefs About Fixedness or Malleability

| Behavior or attribute | Source |
| --- | --- |
| Academic abilities | Karkkainen, Raty, and Kasanen (2010) |
| Aggression | Yeager, Trzesniewski, and Dweck (2013) |
| Athletic abilities | Biddle, Wang, Chatzisarantis, and Spray (2003) |
| Conflict resolution | Halperin, Russell, Trzesniewski, Gross, and Dweck (2011) |
| Morality | Dweck, Chiu, and Hong (1995) |
| Personality | Erdley, Cain, Loomis, Dumas-Hines, and Dweck (1997) |
| Romantic relationships | Knee (1998) |
| Self-regulation | Job, Dweck, and Walton (2010) |
| Shyness | Beer (2002) |
| Weight management | Burnette (2010) |

Parents who hold a growth mindset, for example, would convey to children the importance of effort and mastery and would help them to see failures as learning opportunities rather than as condemnations of the self. Parents who hold a fixed mindset would convey a different, less adaptive set of beliefs. And this sort of pattern is in fact an occasional outcome, emerging in both correlational and experimental examinations of the issue. As an example of the former, Muenks et al. (2015) reported that parents with a fixed mindset emphasized performance-oriented strategies (e.g., telling the correct answer) more than mastery-oriented ones as ways to help their children with academic tasks. As an example of the latter, Moorman and Pomerantz (2010) found that experimentally inducing either a growth mindset or a fixed mindset moved mothers' teaching behaviors in the expected direction, for example, more directed teaching and rote learning with a fixed mindset.

The difficulty in interpreting the literature is that these positive outcomes are accompanied by at least as many negative ones (Dweck, 2017). Indeed, in some instances, the relations are opposite to what might have been predicted. For example, in a study of Finnish school children and their parents, parents' beliefs in a growth mindset, the presumably positive parental orientation, related negatively to how well their children were doing in school (Rautianen, Raty, & Kasanen, 2016). The authors suggest that this result reflects a child-to-parent effect grounded in the self-serving bias: When one's children are doing well, it is rewarding to believe that things will continue unchanged;

when one's children are doing poorly, it is rewarding to believe that things will change.

The preceding argument does not mean that all parent–child relations in this domain reflect children's effects on parents. A recent study by Haimovitz and Dweck (2016) suggests a new perspective on exactly how parents' beliefs—in this case beliefs about intelligence—may affect their children. In addition to analyzing the effects of parents' mindsets in general, these researchers added a special focus on parents' failure mindsets—specifically, whether they viewed failures as opportunities for learning and growth (a failure-is-enhancing mindset) or as situations of inhibition and loss (a failure-is-debilitating mindset). The rationale for concentrating on failure mindsets was that such beliefs might be more visible to children than are parental mindsets in general, a plausible assumption given the salience of failure experiences in most families. The 10- and 11-year-old children in the research did in fact show an above-average knowledge of what their parents believed about failure. Furthermore, the parents' failure mindsets related to both their parenting behavior (e.g., more concern and less helpful support with a failure-is-debilitating mindset) and their children's development (e.g., more belief in fixed intelligence when parents held a debilitating mindset). Clearly, the generality of these conclusions awaits further study, but the work suggests a promising direction for future research.

I conclude this section with a brief consideration of the fit between the two issues that have occupied us to this point in the chapter: nature–nurture and continuity–discontinuity. Is there a relation between the two sets of beliefs? In particular, does a fixed mindset imply a belief in nature, whereas a growth mindset implies a belief in nurture? Some assessment instruments (although none of the measures devised by Dweck) use the word "innate" when presenting fixedness alternatives, an approach that confounds the two issues. In any case—and even when the assessments are not confounded—there is in fact an on-the-average relation in people's belief systems: Beliefs about fixedness tend to covary with beliefs about innateness (Dweck, 1999). But the relation is far from perfect. And conceptually, of course, the two dimensions are separable. A strong biological basis for some development need not imply a lack of change; puberty is just one of the obvious counterexamples. Nor does a strong environmental basis imply that change will continue forever; many early, experience-based developments reach an eventual final level, and stability rather than change then characterizes the developmental course.

## Holistic–Separate

Not yet discussed is the final issue presented in Table 3.1: holistic versus separate. As the brief description in the table indicates, the question at issue is how developmental outcomes fit together: whether they constitute a tightly knit, interrelated whole (the holistic view) or whether the developmental course is characterized by numerous separate, largely independent developments (the separate view). If, for example, a child has mastered competency X or possesses attribute X, can we assume that competencies Y and Z or attributes Y and Z will also be found? Or are children—and indeed the rest of us—more variable than the holistic model predicts?

The general answer to this question is the usual answer whenever either-or alternatives are posed and that is that there is some truth to both positions. This, of course, is what we saw with regard to the nature–nurture issue. As with nature–nurture, however, this general answer leaves many more specific questions unanswered, which is why the holistic–separate contrast remains a central issue in developmental psychology.

Historically, the holistic view of development first arose in association with general stage theories such as Piaget's. If (as Piaget claimed) the same cognitive structures govern a wide range of cognitive outcomes, then children should be consistent in their performance across a wide range of tasks. Such homogeneity is one of the two main criteria for a stage model, the other being that development consists of qualitative and not merely quantitative changes.

In contemporary writings, the holistic–separate issue is often talked about in terms of domain-generality (holistic) versus domain-specificity (separate). The term *domain* refers to some distinct area of psychological development or psychological functioning. It may be relatively narrow (e.g., logical reasoning) or relatively broad (e.g., problem solving in general). In either case, the holistic view argues that the same rules or processes govern performance across a range of contexts and that children should therefore be consistent in their responses; the separate view argues for contextual diversity and possible inconsistency. The resolution to this debate is important because the question at issue is whether we know exactly what is developing as children change. And knowing what is developing is a necessary prelude to explaining exactly how it develops.

What do parents believe about the holistic–separate issue? We really do not know. As we saw in the discussion of the ETS research, parents sometimes talk about "stages" in describing their children's development, but no researcher has probed exactly what this term means or how general such reasoning is. As we will see in the coming chapters, parents certainly have beliefs about when various competencies emerge, as well as about consistencies or inconsistencies in their children's attributes or behaviors. No researcher, however, has probed explicitly to determine the extent to which such thinking reflects a holistic or separate view of development. Admittedly, the practical implications of such a belief system, in terms of possible effects on parents' behavior and thus on children's development, are less obvious than is the case for many parental beliefs. Still, a (holistic) belief that everything hangs together might have different effects in the case of a developmental problem than does a (separate) belief that different behaviors follow their own course. Such possible effects remain to be explored.

# 4

# Parenting and Family

How should you discipline your children and should you spank them? When I was raised, not only could you spank and not be frowned upon, but you were supposed to, you really were. I mean, there is, was no question. The common phrase at that time was "Spare the rod, spoil the child." . . . Now, what do you do now? . . . You don't do that kind of discipline as much as people used to, and is it right or wrong? I'm still not convinced. I know it's fashionable to not be very forceful physically but I'm still not sure that there shouldn't be some role for it.

—(Bretherton, Lambert, and Golby, 2006, p. 197)

The most frustrating part of being a mother has been the idea that I should know what to do. My husband assumes I know what to do and when to do it because I'm the mother, like I have had a child before or something.

—(Roy, Schumm, and Brit, 2014, p. 117)

Everybody has to do his or her part. I work. I come home. I'm tired. I can't stand it when Henry doesn't pick up. He walks in the door, drops his backpack and his jacket. Then he leaves a trail of paper and books up the stairs. He needs to pick up. He has to do his part as a member of the family and do his chores. Henry just doesn't want to do it.

—(Smetana, 2011a, p. 61)

I'm thinking of another, more important value, and it's that they progress in their autonomy, in their capacity for organization, knowing where things are. For me, more important than order in

*Parents' Beliefs About Children.* Scott A. Miller, Oxford University Press (2020). © Oxford University Press.
DOI: 10.1093/oso/9780190874513.001.0001

itself, more than that is their capacity for independence, for organizing themselves, for knowing what their space is, because that will help them in the future.

—(Pena, Menendez, and Torio, 2010, p. 143)

There is at best a thin dividing line between the two topics to which this chapter is devoted. In both cases the beliefs at issue extend beyond those concerning the child to focus on a larger unit, in one case the parent–child dyad and in the other case the family as a whole.

## Parenting

There is also often a thin dividing line between the subject of this part of the chapter—namely, beliefs about parenting—and an even more often studied topic, parenting practices. With some measures it is not clear whether the parent is reporting what she does (thus practices), or what she thinks should be done (thus beliefs), or, of course, both. As far as possible, the present concentration will be on parental beliefs and not parental behaviors.

The discussion of beliefs about parenting is divided into five sections. It begins with research directed to knowledge of parenting—that is, response to questions about parenting that have, at least according to a consensus of experts, right or wrong answers. The discussion moves next to applications of one of the theoretical approaches discussed in Chapter 2: Bandura's concept of self-efficacy. Parental self-efficacy is one of the most often-studied forms of beliefs about parenting and also, as we will see, one of the most important. The next section is devoted to attributions, that is, the explanations that parents offer for the success or failure of their parenting behaviors. The fourth section discusses a potpourri of beliefs about parenting that do not fit under any of the first three headings. Finally, the first half of the chapter concludes with work on the transition to parenting and thus possible effects of becoming a parent on how one thinks about being a parent.

## Knowledge of Parenting

Some studies under this heading have created their own instruments to measure knowledge of parenting (e.g., Reich, 2005; Sommer et al., 1993); most, however, have used one of the standardized instruments designed for this purpose. There are a number of such instruments, including the Knowledge of Child Development Inventory (KCDI; Larsen & Juhasz, 1986), the Knowledge of Effective Parenting Scale (KEPS; Morawska, Sanders, & Winter, 2007), the Caregiver Knowledge of Child Development Inventory (CKDI; Ertem et al., 2007), the Parent Behavior Importance Questionnaire-R (PBIQ-R; Mowder & Shamah, 2011), and the Knowledge of Parenting Strategies Scale (KOPSS; Kirkman, Dadds, & Hawes, 2018). The most often used such instrument, however, is the Knowledge of Infant Development Inventory (KIDI; MacPhee, 1981). Table 4.1 presents a sampling of the 75 items that make up the KIDI.

**Table 4.1** Examples of Items from the Knowledge of Infant Development Inventory (KIDI)

Please mark for each of the following whether:
   (A) you agree;   (B) you disagree;   (C) you are not sure of the answer

The parent just needs to feed, clean, and clothe the baby for it to turn out fine.
The baby should not be held when he (she) is fed because this will make the baby want to be held all of the time.
You must stay in the bathroom when your baby is in the tub.
In general, babies cannot see or hear at birth.
Talking to the baby about things he (she) is doing helps the baby's development and later competence.
Taking care of a baby can leave the parent feeling tired, frustrated, or overwhelmed.
Putting a soft pillow in the crib is a good, safe way to help the baby sleep better.
The baby's personality (individuality) is set by 6 months of age.

Each of the following asks you about the age at which infants can do something. If you think the age is about right, check "Agree." If you don't agree, then decide whether a *Younger* or *Older* infant could do it. If you aren't sure of the age, check "Not Sure."

Most babies can sit on the floor without falling over by 7 months.
A baby of 6 months will respond to someone differently depending on whether the person is happy, sad, or upset.
An 8-month-old acts differently with a familiar person than with someone not seen before.
A 2-year-old is able to reason logically, much as an adult would.
A 1-year-old knows right from wrong.

Adapted from "Knowledge of Infant Development Inventory," by D. MacPhee, 1981. Copyright 1981 by David MacPhee. Adapted by permission. For further information, contact David MacPhee (David.Macphee@ColoState.EDU).

The examples in the table suggest two points about the KIDI, points that apply as well to most of the other instruments listed in the preceding paragraph. First, and as the name of the measure indicates, the focus is on developments early in life—specifically, developments in the first 3 years. Second, although beliefs about parenting are an explicit component of the measure, they are not the only component; rather, the test items constitute four subscales: norms and milestones, principles of development, parenting, and health and safety. It is possible to analyze the subscales separately, but few studies do so. Thus what most of the studies to be reviewed examine might be labeled *parenting knowledge*, a construct that includes but is not limited to knowledge about parenting practices.

Two further points about the KIDI can be noted. First, many studies use a shortened version of the full test; because there is no standard short form, however, different researchers select different items for their abbreviated measures. In most instances approximately 20 items are used, a degree of shortening that precludes the possibility of analyzing separately by subscale. Second, the original instrument was designed to yield two scores: number of items attempted and accuracy in response to the items that *are* attempted. The two scores show somewhat different correlational patterns, and the manual for the measure recommends using both. Most studies, however, analyze only accuracy and not attempts.

Three questions are of interest in research with the KIDI and similar measures. The first is the descriptive question: How accurately can parents make judgments about children and about parenting? The second is the origins question: What are the sources of individual differences in parental knowledge? Finally, the third is the effects question: What are the relations between parental knowledge and both parental behavior and child outcomes?

The standardization data for the KIDI provide a starting point for the descriptive question. The mothers in the standardization sample were correct on 72% of their judgments. This performance was better than that of college students (62% correct) but not as good as that of pediatricians (87%) or developmental psychologists (86%).

Not all of the subsequent studies that have used the KIDI report descriptive information, and interpretation of what *is* reported is complicated by the fact that different studies use different subsets of items. In any case, the range of reported values spans the performance of the normative sample, with some samples averaging around 50% correct and others coming in at 80% or slightly higher. Most studies report total scores only, with no breakdown by subscale. It is interesting to note, however, that the parenting subscale emerges as relatively easy in the handful of studies that provide relevant information. In one instance, for example, mothers averaged 92% correct on the parenting items (Bornstein, Cote, Haynes, Hahn, & Park, 2010).

The descriptive data speak to the origins question because the range of performance suggests that the nature of the sample is an important predictor of parenting knowledge. Various aspects of the sample are in fact predictive although, of course, far from perfectly so. Income level is one predictor: Middle-income parents typically score higher on the KIDI than do lower income parents (e.g., Berger & Brooks-Gunn, 2005). Educational level is another predictor: Relatively well-educated parents typically outperform those with less education (e.g., Huang, O'Brien Caughy, Genevro, & Miller, 2005). Maternal age is a predictor: Older mothers score higher than younger ones, and adolescent mothers are especially likely to perform poorly (e.g., Bornstein et al., 2010). Age of child is also a predictor, with better performance by parents of older children, an expectable finding if greater caregiving experience leads to greater knowledge (e.g., Cote & Bornstein, 2003). Another expectable finding is that performance tends to be worse in samples that qualify as high-risk, for example, mothers of infants with low birthweight or mothers with a history as victims of abuse (Benasich & Brooks-Gunn, 1996; Zand et al., 2015). Finally, differences are sometimes found as a function of race, ethnicity, or nationality, with better performance by predominantly White Western samples than by other groups (e.g., Al-Maadadi & Ikhief, 2015; Bornstein & Cote, 2004; Jahromi, Guimond, Umana-Taylor, Updegraff, & Toomey, 2014). The bases for such differences are not yet clear, however, given both the limited available research and the presence of various confounding factors (e.g., income level, age of mother) in the group comparisons.

Most of what has been said to this point has concerned mothers, for the good reason that mothers are the only parents included in most studies with the KIDI. To date, however, the limited work with fathers suggests more similarities than differences between the two parents (Nobre-Lima, da Luz Vale-Dias, Mendes, Monico, & MacPhee, 2014; Roggman, Benson, & Boyce, 1999; Scarzello, Arace, & Prino, 2016).

Chapter 2 distinguished between indirect and direct sources of evidence with respect to the effects of experience on parents' beliefs. The comparisons of different groups just discussed fall in the indirect category. The main direct evidence comes from the COPE measure that was introduced in Chapter 2. As would be expected, higher scores on the COPE (i.e., greater experience with children) are associated with better performance on the KIDI (Al-Maadadi & Ikhief, 2015; MacPhee, 1983). The relations, however, are modest.

As noted, the KIDI is just one of a number of approaches to assessing what parents know about parenting. Although results from the other measures add some wrinkles to the descriptive picture, they do not change the basic conclusions: Parents show moderate but far from perfect knowledge of aspects of parenting and early development, there are marked individual differences in knowledge both within and between samples, and such differences show expectable relations to various demographic characteristics of the samples. I will return to several of the measures, as well as the KIDI, in Chapter 5 on Infancy. Most of the measures, in fact, concentrate more on knowledge of infancy than on knowledge of parenting.

Possible effects of parents' knowledge about parenting are of two sorts: effects on parents' behavior and effects on children's development. That both sorts of effects occur is a clear conclusion from the literature, found for both the KIDI and a number of the other measures that have been used. In general, greater parental knowledge is associated with more effective parenting practices and more positive child outcomes. Once this conclusion is stated, the same qualifiers that applied at various points in Chapter 3 are important to add. Not all studies find significant effects, the effects that do occur are modest in size, the magnitude of the effects is sometimes reduced when other factors (e.g., demographics) are taken into account, and significant outcomes are often embedded within a larger array of nonsignificant results. In what follows, I single out several studies that add in various ways to these general conclusions.

Relations between the KIDI and other measures are, of course, correlational in nature. As I discussed in Chapter 2, causal explanations for correlational relations can be offered with more confidence when relations are charted across time and not just within a single time period. Several studies have taken such a longitudinal approach, administering the KIDI during the first year of life and then measuring either parental practices or child outcomes at some later point (Benasich & Brooks-Gunn, 1996; Huang et al., 2005; Jahromi et al., 2014; Nuttall, Valentino, Wang, Lefever, & Borkowski, 2015). Although exceptions and qualifications occurred in all of the studies, each did succeed in identifying some relations between early knowledge and the later measures. In Benasich and Brooks-Gunn (1996), KIDI scores obtained at 12 months related to Home Observation for Measurement of the Environment (HOME) scores at age 3, and they related to IQ for the White children in the sample when they were 3. In Huang et al. (2005), early KIDI scores also related to later HOME scores as well as to other parenting measures, although results again varied across groups, with more consistent relations for Black and Hispanic parents than for White parents. Working with a sample of Mexican American adolescent mothers, Jahromi et al. (2014) reported a positive relation between early KIDI scores and performance on the Bayley Scales of Infant Development when the child was 2. Finally, the focus of the Nuttal et al. (2015) study was on parentification, or the extent to which the parent had been required to take on a parental role while still a child (and thus another way in which childhood experience might affect parents' beliefs). KIDI scores mediated the relation between parentification and warm responsiveness as a parent; specifically, parentification was associated with lower parental knowledge, which in turn was associated with less responsive parenting.

The work just considered suggests that the KIDI may be differentially predictive for different ethnic groups. A study by Scarzello et al. (2016) suggests that it may also be differentially predictive for mothers and fathers. The outcome measure they examined was the Parenting Scale (Arnold, O'Leary, Wolff, & Acker, 1993), a self-report measure that assesses a broad range of parenting practices. The KIDI showed only scattered and modest-sized relations to the subscales of the Parenting Scale; the relations that did emerge, however, were more consistent for fathers than for mothers. This finding is reminiscent of that from the McGillicuddy-DeLisi (1982b) study discussed in Chapter 3. In both cases the results suggest different bases for fathers' and mothers' behavior: general beliefs about children for fathers, beliefs about one's own child for mothers.

As noted, the conclusions just summarized come from assessments of parenting knowledge in general, assessments in which knowledge of parenting practices is only one component. The literature does include several recently developed instruments that, unlike the KIDI and similar measures, focus exclusively on knowledge of parenting practices: Kirkman et al. (2018), Morawska et al. (2007), and Mowder and Shamah (2011). Of these, only one has had research applications to date, and that is the Knowledge of Effective Parenting Scale (KEPS), developed by Morawska et al. (2007) and since used in several studies (Morawska, Winter, & Sanders, 2009; Winter, Morawska, & Sanders, 2012a, 2012b). The KEPS addresses four aspects of parenting: promotion of development, principles of effective parenting, use of assertive discipline, and causes of behavior problems. Table 4.2 shows a sampling of the 28 items that make up the test.

**Table 4.2** Examples of Items from the Knowledge of Effective Parenting Scale (KEPS)

---

An environment which facilitates children's independent play is one where:

  a. There are lots of fun and interesting things to do.
  b. The parents sets up a number of structured activities.
  c. Parents spend a lot of time playing with children.
  d. Children are expected to play independently.

When disciplining a child, it important that a parent:

  a. Is consistent in their reaction to the child's misbehavior.
  b. Makes sure their child feels a bit of pain or discomfort so they will remember what they have done wrong.
  c. Speaks firmly to their child so they know who is the boss and that they mean business.
  d. Encourages their child to express their negative or angry feelings openly.

Parenting is less stressful when:

  a. The parent strives to be a better parent than their own parents.
  b. A parent expects that children will sometimes break rules and not do as they are asked.
  c. There are too many rules in life; let children be children.
  d. A parent expects that their child should always do as they are told.

It is Saturday morning and a mother is ironing. Her 4-year-old son comes up to show her something. What is the best way for her to respond?

  a. Tell him she is busy and not to interrupt.
  b. Ignore his interrupting.
  c. Stop what she is doing, give him her attention, and then continue ironing.
  d. Tell him that she'll look when she has finished the ironing.

A 6-year-old child has refused to put her toys away when her mother asked her to, and when she repeated the instruction, the child started screaming and throwing the toys around the room. What should the mother do?

  a. Give her a smack on the bottom, and let her know that there will be no dessert tonight.
  b. Pack the toys away herself, but let her child know that she will not be able to play with them for the rest of the week.
  c. Give the child a cuddle to help settle her down and then assist with packing the toys away.
  d. Take her child to time out and wait until she (the child. has calmed down before letting her out and reinstating the instruction to put the toys away.

---

Adapted from "The Knowledge of Effective Parenting Scale," by A. Morawska, M. R. Sanders, and L. Winter, 2005. Copyright 2005 by Parenting and Family Support Centre, The University of Queensland, Brisbane, Australia. Adapted with permission.

As with the KIDI, research with the KEPS does not always show expected relations to parental practices and child outcomes (Morawska et al., 2009). In the one comparative study, however, the KEPS related positively to an observational measure of parental competence and negatively to problematic child outcomes, whereas no relations were found for the KIDI (Winter et al., 2012b). The KEPS has also been productively used as an outcome measure in intervention research, as indeed have other measures of parental knowledge.

## Parental Self-Efficacy

Chapter 2 defined self-efficacy as "beliefs in one's capabilities to organize and execute the courses of action required to produce given attainments." Parental self-efficacy, therefore, is belief in one's capabilities to be successful as a parent.

As I noted in Chapter 2, self-efficacy is a domain-specific concept—that is, self-efficacy is always efficacy *for* something. Chapter 2, however, did not address the question of how broad this something is. Researchers disagree on this issue. Some, including Bandura, prefer a relatively narrow, task-specific focus. Thus (to return to one of the examples in Chapter 2), rather than self-efficacy for academic performance, such researchers might examine self-efficacy for math or reading or science. Other researchers cast a broader net—thus academic performance in general or perhaps even cognitive activities in general.

The same issue of degree of specificity applies to work on parental self-efficacy (Coleman & Karraker, 1998; Jones & Prinz, 2005). Some approaches focus on parenting in general; others target specific aspects of parenting. Similarly, some approaches are applicable to children of any age, whereas others focus on a particular part of the developmental span (most commonly, infancy). Table 4.3 presents a sampling of items from one often-used measure that falls in the relatively specific rather than general category. Crncec and colleagues (Crncec, Barnett, & Matthey, 2010) provide a fuller overview of the (literally dozens of) available measures.

Whatever their standing on the specific to general continuum, all of the approaches to measuring parental self-efficacy reveal individual differences among parents. Some parents are more confident about their parenting than are others. As always, therefore, the origins question arises: Where do these differences come from?

**Table 4.3** Examples of Items from the Self-Efficacy for Parents Task Index

*Discipline*

> I have trouble deciding on appropriate rules for my child.
> I have more trouble with discipline than with any other aspect of parenting.
> I really don't have much trouble disciplining my child.

*Achievement*

> I am probably more helpful to my child when it comes to homework than other parents.
> Helping my child with school work is very frustrating.
> I am good at helping my child work through school problems.

*Recreation*

> I don't do enough to make sure my child has fun.
> I am satisfied with my ability to provide recreation for my child.
> I do a good job in the area of seeing to it that my child has a variety of recreational experiences.

*Nurturance*

> I am definitely an adequately nurturing parent.
> I have trouble expressing my affection for my child.
> I know that I'm not there enough emotionally for my child.

*Health*

> I am a good person when it comes to taking care of my child's physical health.
> I know I am not concerned enough about my child's health.
> I always see to it that my child receives prompt medical attention as needed.

Responses are made on a 6-point scale ranging from *strongly agree* to *strongly disagree*.

Adapted from "Parenting Self-Efficacy Among Mothers of School-Age Children: Conceptualization, Measurement, and Correlates," by P. K. Coleman and K. H. Karraker, 2000, *Family Relations, 49*, p. 24. Copyright 2000 by John Wiley and Sons. Reprinted with permission.

The discussion of self-efficacy in Chapter 2 identified four sources of self-efficacy: direct experience with the task in question, vicarious experience through observations of others, verbal input from others, and emotional arousal. The literature on parental self-efficacy provides some evidence that each of these factors contributes (De Montigny & Lacharite, 2005). By far the most important contributor, however, is the first: experience in the parenting role. A history of perceived success as a parent is associated with relatively high self-efficacy; a history of problems and disappointing outcomes is associated with relatively low self-efficacy.

Various factors influence the likelihood of success or failure in the parenting role. Some infants or children present more difficult challenges than do others. The extreme example of this point comes in cases of clinical syndromes or developmental disabilities, which is work that I consider in Chapter 9. Within a normal range of variation, the most often studied contributor is child temperament. Some children possess more difficult temperaments (e.g., more irritable, more reactive, less predictable) than do others, differences that may be evident in some form from birth and that may persist throughout childhood. Not surprisingly, difficult child temperament is a predictor of relatively low parental self-efficacy (e.g., Coleman & Karraker, 2000; Jahromi, Umana-Taylor, Updegraff, & Lara, 2012).

Characteristics of the parent and the parent's life circumstances may also be important. Social support can help buttress against difficult conditions; conversely, an absence of social support is associated with relatively low self-efficacy (e.g., Shorey, Chan, Chong, & He, 2015). So, too, are conditions of fatigue, stress, and anxiety (Chau & Giallo, 2015; Leahy-Warren & McCarthy, 2011). And so, as I discuss in Chapter 9, is depression. In most instances the relations in question appear to be reciprocal ones. Thus stress or anxiety or depression may result in lower self-efficacy, but the problems attendant on low self-efficacy may make the stress or anxiety or depression even worse.

Mother–father comparisons are always relevant to the origins question, given the on-average differences in parental experience between spouses. Chapter 2 noted that fathers are underrepresented in the parents' beliefs literature. The study of parental self-efficacy provides a partial exception to this statement because fathers, although less often studied than mothers, do appear in several dozen studies, and thus in a higher proportion of the literature than for any other topic under the parents' beliefs heading. Indeed, a number of studies focus on fathers only (e.g., Hudson, Campbell-Grossman, Fleck, Elek, & Shipman, 2003; Rominov, Giallo, & Whelan, 2016; Secer, Ogelman, & Onder, 2013), and a measure specifically designed for fathers, the Fathering Self-Efficacy Scale, was recently added to the literature (Sevigny, Loutzenhiser, & McAuslan, 2016).

Given both the size and the inconsistency of the available literature, it is difficult to summarize the mother–father comparisons briefly. Three general conclusions appear valid. First, when differences in self-efficacy emerge, mothers typically have higher self-efficacy than do fathers (e.g., Hudson, Elek, & Fleck, 2001; Juntilla, Aromaa, Rautava, Piha, & Raiha, 2015). This difference is compatible with other mother–father differences in the beliefs literature, and it presumably reflects mothers' greater parenting experience. Another possible contributor, however, is the nature of the measuring instruments, at least some of which may not adequately sample the parenting tasks that fathers typically perform (Murdoch, 2013; Sevigny et al., 2016).

A second set of conclusions concerns relations between parents. In the studies that provide the relevant data (which are not very many), mothers' self-efficacy and fathers' self-efficacy turn out to be moderately correlated, with values in the .30s and .40s (de Haan, Prinzie, & Dekovic, 2009; Juntilla et al., 2015). Self-efficacy for both parents relates positively to both marital satisfaction (Sevigny & Loutzenhiser, 2010) and successful coparenting, that is, a balanced and harmonious division of parental roles (Merrifield & Gamble, 2013). In addition, fathers' self-efficacy relates positively to parenting support provided by the mother (Bogenschneider, Small, & Tsay, 1997).

The final set of conclusions from the mother–father comparisons concerns the effects of self-efficacy that is, relations to either parental behaviors or child outcomes. Here, in particular, results diverge across studies. In some studies maternal and paternal self-efficacy show similar relations to the outcomes of interest (e.g., Giallo, Wood, Jellett, & Porter, 2013, in some studies different patterns of relations characterize the two sexes (e.g., Glatz & Buchanan, 2015), and in other studies there is a mixture of similarities and differences (e.g., Murdoch, 2013). What does seem clear, however the specifics may vary, is that self-efficacy is an important component of parenting for both mothers and fathers.

The findings just discussed provide a start on the final general question: the effects of parental self-efficacy. Does it make a difference how confident parents are about their parenting? The answer to this question must begin with the usual qualifiers: Not all studies or analyses within studies report effects, and the effects that do occur are generally modest in size and sometimes reduced when other factors are taken into account. Once these points are acknowledged, the general conclusion is clear, and that is that self-efficacy relates in expected ways to a wide range of both parental practices and child behaviors. High self-efficacy is associated with desirable forms of parenting, and it is associated with positive developmental outcomes. Table 4.4 provides a partial list of the relations that have been demonstrated. Note that, in some instances (e.g., maltreatment, conduct problems), the relations in question are negative ones.

With a few exceptions, the relations summarized in the table, as well as those in the literature in general, are correlational and thus do not establish

**Table 4.4** Relations of Parenting Self-Efficacy to Parenting Practices and Child Outcomes

| Parenting practice | Source |
|---|---|
| Sensitivity | Gondoli and Silverberg (1997) |
| Involvement | Hoover-Dempsey, Bassler, and Brissie (1992) |
| Warmth | Izzo, Weiss, Shanahan, and Rodriguez-Brown (2000) |
| Consistency | Rominov et al. (2016) |
| Control | Dumka, Gonzales, Wheeler, and Millsap (2010) |
| Discipline | Sanders and Woolley (2005) |
| Monitoring | Shumow and Lomax (2002) |
| Maltreatment | Mash, Johnston, and Kovitz (1983) |

| Child outcome | Source |
|---|---|
| Academic achievement | Bandura, Barbaranelli, Caprara, and Pastorelli (1996) |
| Bayley Mental Scale performance | Coleman and Karraker (2003) |
| Language | Albarran and Reich (2014) |
| Social competence | Juntilla and Vauras (2014) |
| Self-efficacy | Ardelt and Eccles (2001) |
| Anxiety | Hill and Bush (2001) |
| Aggression | Roskam, Brassart, Loop, Mouton, and Schelstraete (2015) |
| Peer victimization | Secer et al. (2013) |
| Adolescent self-disclosure | Rangnathan and Montemayor (2014) |
| Adolescent conduct problems | Dumka et al. (2010) |
| Adolescent substance use | Chang et al. (2015) |

causality. Although almost all studies attempt to do so, it is difficult to rule out all the third factors that might be contributing to the relations. In addition, the issue of causal direction could be argued to apply with special force in the case of self-efficacy. We know that successful parenting leads to self-efficacy; how do we know that self-efficacy leads to successful parenting?

The answer is that the kinds of evidence discussed with respect to self-efficacy in general in Chapter 2 are also available in the case of parental self-efficacy. Longitudinal studies often show that self-efficacy assessed early in the child's development is associated with various outcomes assessed later in development, a cross-time relation that supports the inference that self-efficacy is the causal factor in the relation (e.g., Dumka, Gonzales, Wheeler, & Millsap, 2010; Rominov et al., 2016). In addition, experimental studies in which self-efficacy is manipulated demonstrate that improvements in self-efficacy can lead to changes in both parental practices and child outcomes. I should add, however, that evidence on this point is still limited (Wittkowski, Dowling, & Smith, 2016).

Some of the most interesting findings with respect to self-efficacy come when it is examined in conjunction with other variables. In a number of studies self-efficacy has proved to be a mediator of a demonstrated correlational relation, that is, a causal factor that at least partly and in some instances totally accounts for a significant relation between two other variables. For example, in a study by Giallo et al. (2013), a negative relation between difficult child temperament and parental involvement was reduced significantly when self-efficacy was considered, indicating that low self-efficacy accounted for much of the effect of temperament. In a study by de Haan et al. (2009), relations between measures of parents' personality and their parenting practices either disappeared or were reduced when self-efficacy was considered, again indicating that self-efficacy played a causal role. MacPhee and colleagues (MacPhee, Fritz, & Miller-Heyl, 1996) obtained a similar result for relations between social support and parenting; again, self-efficacy was the main causal force underlying the relations. And, as one final example, Gondoli and Silverberg (1997) reported a negative relation between mothers' emotional distress and their parenting responsiveness, a relation that disappeared, however, when self-efficacy was added to the analyses.

In some studies self-efficacy has been examined along with other measures of parents' beliefs, in particular, measures of parental knowledge. Doing so has proved informative. I will single out two studies with the KIDI to illustrate this point (for a similar result with the KEPS, see Morawska et al., 2009). Conrad and colleagues (Conrad, Gross, Fogg, & Ruchala, 1992) included both maternal self-efficacy and maternal knowledge as possible predictors of quality of parenting. When considered separately, neither variable showed any relation to parenting. When they were considered together, however, an interaction emerged: High self-efficacy related positively to quality of parenting, but only when knowledge was also high; when knowledge was low, self-efficacy had no effect. An even more striking interaction occurred in a study by Hess, Teti, and Hussey-Gardner (2004). Again, self-efficacy and knowledge, considered alone, showed no relation to parenting, and again, self-efficacy related to quality of parenting when knowledge was high. In this case, however, self-efficacy related *negatively* to parenting when knowledge was low. These parents, in the authors' words, appeared to be "naïvely confident about their parenting abilities" (Hess et al., 2004, p. 423), and the confidence apparently sustained practices that were far from optimal.

These findings make sense. Confidence in one's parenting is generally a good thing. But confidence is most likely to be beneficial when it is accompanied by relevant knowledge.

## Attributions

As noted in Chapter 2, attributions are causal explanations for behavior. Parents make attributions for numerous aspects of their children's behavior, and such attributions will be topics in most of the chapters to come. The focus of the current discussion is on how parents reason about their own behavior—in particular, how they explain successes and failures in the caregiving process.

I concentrate on what is undoubtedly the most influential work directed to this question, research by Daphne Bugental and colleagues (Bugental, 1992; Bugental, Blue, & Cruzcosa, 1989; Bugental et al., 1993). The principal measure used in the Bugental research is the Parent Attribution Test (PAT). Table 4.5 presents a sampling of items from the PAT. As can be seen, the items vary along three dimensions. Half of the items address successful outcomes of the caregiving process, and half address unsuccessful outcomes. In half the cases, the basis for the outcome is controllable (e.g., selection of a particular parenting approach), and in half the cases, it is uncontrollable (e.g., good or bad luck). Finally, half the items present the parent as the cause of the outcome, and half present the child as the cause. The focus is thus a dyadic or relative one—not the parent in isolation but the parent in comparison to the child.

In the Bugental research, it is response to the unsuccessful outcomes that turns out to be informative, and it is therefore this component of the measure on which I concentrate. The group of greatest interest is the subset of mothers (most of the research is with mothers or other adult females) who attribute greater power to the child than to the self when caregiving goes awry. Such mothers are said to possess low perceived control over failure—that is, they believe that they can do little or nothing to avoid failure because it is the child who has the power to determine the outcome. Note (to return to a point

**Table 4.5** Examples of Items from the Parent Attribution Test

Suppose you took care of a neighbor's child one afternoon, and the two of you had a really good time together. How important do you believe the following factors would be as reasons for such an experience?

|  | Not at all Important |  |  |  |  |  | Very Important |
|---|---|---|---|---|---|---|---|
| How well you get along with children in general | /____/ | ____/ | ____/ | ____/ | ____/ | ____/ | ____/ |
| How pleasant a disposition the child has | /____/ | ____/ | ____/ | ____/ | ____/ | ____/ | ____/ |
| Whether the child was rested | /____/ | ____/ | ____/ | ____/ | ____/ | ____/ | ____/ |
| How good a mood you were in that day | /____/ | ____/ | ____/ | ____/ | ____/ | ____/ | ____/ |

Suppose you took care of a neighbor's child one afternoon, and the two of you did *not* get along well. How important do you believe the following factors would be as possible reasons for such an experience?

How unlucky you were in having

| Everything just worked out wrong | /____/ | ____/ | ____/ | ____/ | ____/ | ____/ | ____/ |
|---|---|---|---|---|---|---|---|
| Whether you used the wrong approach for this child | /____/ | ____/ | ____/ | ____/ | ____/ | ____/ | ____/ |
| Whether the child doesn't like other people taking care of him (or her) | /____/ | ____/ | ____/ | ____/ | ____/ | ____/ | ____/ |
| How little effort the child made to take an interest in what you said or did | /____/ | ____/ | ____/ | ____/ | ____/ | ____/ | ____/ |

Reprinted courtesy of Daphne Bugental.

made in Chapter 2) that such a characteristic mode of response constitutes an attributional style, a habitual way of thinking that colors response to a wide range of situations.

Believing that one can do little or nothing to avoid failure does not sound like a promising approach to parenting, and low perceived control is in fact associated with a number of negative outcomes. Such effects are not inevitable, however, but rather depend on the context. In particular, negative effects are most likely if the child being dealt with is in some way difficult or if the situation is ambiguous and therefore challenging. Mothers with low perceived control typically do fine when dealing with easy children and familiar situations.

When they do not do fine, various problems can occur (Bugental & Happaney, 2002; Bugental & Johnston, 2000). Mothers with low control tend to send inconsistent and confusing messages, both verbally and nonverbally, when interacting with a difficult child, the result being that the child is often unsure what the mother wants. Such mothers are likely to show deficits in information processing, failing to read cues from the child and failing to match their approach to the situation at hand. In the absence of better alternatives, mothers with low perceived control often resort to harsh, power-assertive techniques of discipline, techniques that are unlikely to promote lasting behavioral compliance. At the extreme, such techniques may shade into forms of maltreatment and abuse. As I discuss in Chapter 9, the prevention and remediation of abuse has always been a major goal of the Bugental research program.

A perception of low control affects mothers' emotional responses as well as their behaviors. Mothers with low control show heightened stress, heightened negative affect, and physiological reactivity of various forms (increased heart rate, increased skin conductance, increased cortisol levels) when interacting with difficult children (Bugental & Cortez, 1988; Martorell & Bugental, 2006). Because such interactions are often unsuccessful, these negative reactions may worsen over time. The result is that child-rearing is often an anxiety-arousing and unhappy experience for such mothers. We can see here an example of a point made in Chapter 1: Children are not the only ones affected by parents' beliefs; parents are also affected.

A methodological point is worth noting here. In many of the Bugental studies, mothers interact with children other than their own, including children who are known to be difficult or who have been trained to act in difficult ways (e.g., Bugental, Brown, & Reiss, 1996; Bugental & Shennum, 1984). This means, of course, that some children interact with mothers other than their own, including mothers who are low in perceived control. Such a crossing of mother–child pairs is rare in the child-rearing literature, and it provides an opportunity to disentangle the contributions of mother and child to the nature and success of the interactions.

Most of the Bugental research has been with American mothers. A research team headed by Bornstein and Lansford provides a cross-cultural extension of the PAT approach to eight countries in addition to the United States: China, Colombia, Italy, Jordan, Kenya, the Philippines, Sweden, and Thailand (Bornstein, Putnick, & Lansford, 2011; Lansford & Bornstein, 2011). Such a rich dataset defies brief summary, but I will note that differences among countries were common and often showed sensible relations to ways in which the cultures are known to vary. I will note also that US mothers fell toward the favorable end of the low perceived control dimension, along with those from Colombia and the Philippines.

The Bornstein and Lansford project included fathers as well as mothers, and it therefore provides a rare gender comparison of responses to the PAT. The similarities between mothers and fathers proved to be more marked than the few differences, and this point held across all of the countries studied. Despite this mean-level similarity, however, the degree of concordance between spouses, although significant, was low (average $r$ of .21). Thus mothers and fathers in general think alike, but mother–father pairs often do not do so.

Similarities between mothers and fathers, including similarity not just in the level but in the effects of low perceived control, have also emerged in the Bugental research program (Bugental & Happaney, 2000). There is also the suggestion, however, that the origins of the low-control attributional style may be in part different for the two sexes. The sample in a study by Bugental and Shennum (2002) consisted of mothers and fathers who had reported a history of abuse as a child. For mothers, this history was predictive of low perceived control; for fathers, however, there was no relation. Although the basis for this gender difference is not yet clear, a similar contrast is evident at the child level: Girls who have been abused tend to show low perceived control, but no such effect is evident for boys who have been abused.

The Bugental and Shennum (2002) study is not the only evidence that attributional styles may have childhood origins. Grusec and colleagues (Grusec, Hastings, & Mammone, 1994) administered both the PAT and the Adult Attachment Interview to a sample of mothers and fathers. Parents whose recollections of childhood attachment placed them in the dismissive

category had lower perceived control than any of the other groups. This difference had been predicted—just as dismissive adults deny their parents' influence on them, so too do they deny responsibility for negative outcomes
in interaction with their own children. In both instances such adults adopt
a self-protective stance that stresses their independence from others in their
social worlds.

I will mention one more indication that parents' attributional styles may
at least partly predate their experience with a particular child. Bugental and
Happaney (2004) administered the PAT to women who were either in the last
trimester of pregnancy or had just given birth. Low perceived control on the
PAT related to harsh parenting when the infant was 1-year-old—and did so
even though the mother had no knowledge of her child at the time when the
attributions were measured.

## Other Beliefs About Parenting

This section adds several kinds of parenting beliefs not captured in the
first three sections of the chapter. To do so I draw from two measures: Self-
Perceptions of the Parental Role (SPPR), developed by MacPhee, Benson,
and Bullock (1986), and the Meta-Parenting Profile Questionnaire (MPQ),
developed by Holden and Hawk (2003).

The SPPR assesses beliefs about four dimensions of parenting: competence, satisfaction, investment, and balance or integration. Of these, I focus
on the last two. The competence subscale is a measure of self-efficacy, a topic
already discussed, and parental satisfaction will be discussed in the "Value of
Children" section with which the chapter concludes.

The format for the SPPR is based on Susan Harter's Perceived Competence
Scale for Children (Harter, 1982; note that the measure is now labeled the
Self-Perception Profile for Children). Each item offers a pair of contrasting
statements of the form "Some parents. . . . But other parents. . . ." For example,
one item on the investment subscale is "Some parents do a lot of reading
about how to be a good parent. But other parents don't spend much time
reading about parenting." One item on the balance subscale is "Some parents
resent the fact that having children means less time to do the things they like.
But other parents don't mind having less free time for themselves." The respondent first chooses which of the alternatives is true of him or her and then
indicates whether it is "Really true" or "Sort of true."

As the example items suggest, the investment subscale assesses the commitment and effort devoted to the parenting role. The balance subscale assesses the fit between the demands of parenting and other aspects of the parent's life. The descriptive data from the normative sample for the measure produced three main findings (MacPhee et al., 1986). First, mothers (the only parents included in the normative sample) feel moderately positive about both aspects of parenting, although somewhat more so for balance (mean of 3.82 on a 5-point scale) than for investment (mean of 2.98). Second, there are marked individual differences among mothers in both sorts of belief. Finally, three of the four subscales show moderate positive correlations among themselves, indicating that there is a tendency for mothers to be generally positive or negative across these dimensions of parenting. The exception to this conclusion is the investment subscale, which is unrelated to the other three measures. Two studies by Bornstein and colleagues (Bornstein et al., 1998; Bornstein et al., 2003) replicated each of these findings.

To date, more work has been directed to the origins question than to the effects of the beliefs tapped by the SPPR. The competence subscale provides a partial exception to this statement for beliefs about competence have been shown to relate in expectable ways to both parental practices and child outcomes (MacPhee et al., 1996; MacPhee, Miller-Heyl, & Carroll, 2014; Miller-Heyl, MacPhee, & Fritz, 1998). The SPPR thus provides further evidence for the importance of parental self-efficacy.

Several studies speak to the origins question. In the normative sample, investment showed a positive relation to education, and balance showed a negative relation to number of children (MacPhee et al., 1986). Two further findings are expectable: Investment relates positively to parental knowledge as assessed by the KIDI (Bornstein et al., 2003), and both investment and balance relate positively to social support (Bornstein et al., 2003; Seybold, Fritz, & MacPhee, 1991). Finally, Bornstein and colleagues provide cross-cultural comparisons of response to the SPRR across seven nations: Argentina, Belgium, France, Israel, Italy, Japan, and the United States (Bornstein et al., 1998). As in the cross-cultural work on attributions discussed in the previous section (Bornstein et al., 2003), differences among nations were common; in the authors' words, "Mothers in these seven cultural groups shared remarkably few patterns of self-evaluation. . . . Cultural differences reigned pervasively" (pp. 670–671). Again, the richness of the dataset defies a brief summary, but I will note some of the findings for the two dimensions under consideration here. On the investment subscale, Italian and Japanese mothers emerged as highest, followed by mothers from the United States. On the balance subscale, mothers from France, Italy, and the United States emerged as highest.

The MPQ (Hawk & Holden, 2006; Holden & Hawk, 2003) is in some respects different from most of the measures considered to this point. Many approaches to parents' beliefs concentrate on online, rapid, often implicit cognitive processes that are activated in the course of parent–child interactions. As we saw in Chapter 2, this is the case with information-processing approaches, and it is also true of the Bugental concept of attributional style. As the "meta" suggests, the MPQ addresses more deliberate, conscious, and evaluative forms of parental thought, thoughts that typically occur not while face to face with the child but rather before or after parent–child interactions. It addresses, in short, how parents think about parenting when they are not actively parenting.

Hawk and Holden (2006) identify four components of meta-parenting. *Anticipating* refers to thoughts and often related plans about the future, in some instances short-term (e.g., how to avoid a tantrum when the TV is turned off) and in some cases more long-term (e.g., how to childproof the home for a soon to be mobile baby). *Assessing* has to do with evaluation of ongoing or recent events, with a focus sometimes on the child (e.g., "Why did my child produce that behavior?"), sometimes on the self (e.g., "Why did I react that way?"), and sometimes on external factors (e.g., "Is day care proving to be a bad influence?"). *Reflecting* involves a return to and reassessment of behaviors and characteristics of either parent or child, typically across a longer time frame than is true of assessing. It might involve wondering whether the child is taking on characteristics of the parent or whether one's parenting techniques mirror those of one's own parents. Finally, *problem solving*, as the label indicates, involves the generation and evaluation of solutions to some parenting problem—for example, deciding whether day care would be good for a shy child or seeking expert advice with respect to a child's slow language development. Table 4.6 shows a sampling of the 24 items that assess the four dimensions.

The mothers in the Hawk and Holden (2006) study reported that they engaged in all four forms of thought fairly often, with assessing occurring most frequently and reflecting least often. Attempts to identify the bases for individual differences in such thinking have had mixed results. Parental education is sometimes (Nicholson, Howard, & Borkowski, 2008) but not always (Hawk & Holden, 2006) a predictor, with more meta-parenting by relatively

**Table 4.6** Examples of Items from the Meta-Parenting Profile Questionnaire

---

**Assessing**

---

In general. How often do you consider, or think about what, is occurring with you and your child?

| Never/Rarely | Sometimes | Usually | Often | Constantly |

How often do you think about how your child is developing compared with her/his peers?

| Never/Rarely | Sometimes | Usually | Often | Constantly |

How often do you think about how well your parenting meets your child's needs?

| Never/Rarely | Sometimes | Usually | Often | Constantly |

---

**Anticipating**

---

In general, how often do you think ahead about things related to your child or your parenting?

| Never/Rarely | Sometimes | Usually | Often | Constantly |

To what extent do you plan ahead for situations in which your child might get bored (for example, bring toys or book for use in the car while you're running errands)?

| Never/Rarely | Sometimes | Usually | Often | Constantly |

To what extent do you think about activities that will happen the next day?

| Never/Rarely | Sometimes | Usually | Often | Constantly |

---

**Reflecting**

---

In general, how often do you have concerns, worry, or think about things that have already happened with your child?

| Never/Rarely | Sometimes | Usually | Often | Constantly |

How often do you have concerns about your parenting behaviors or the decisions you've made as a parent?

| Never/Rarely | Sometimes | Usually | Often | Constantly |

How often have you changed your mind about a parenting decision after thinking about it for a while?

---

**Problem solving**

---

In general, how often have you identified and attempted to solve a problem you're having with your child or with your parenting?

| Never/Rarely | Sometimes | Usually | Often | Constantly |

How often do you talk with your friends about things that are happening with your child?

| Never/Rarely | Sometimes | Usually | Often | Constantly |

When you're having a problem with your child, how often do you develop a strategy to deal with the problem?

| Never/Rarely | Sometimes | Usually | Often | Constantly |

---

Adapted from "Meta-Parenting: An Initial Investigation into a New Social Cognition Construct," by C. K. Hawk and G. W. Holden, 2006, *Parenting: Science and Practice, 6*, pp. 339–341. Copyright 2006 by Taylor & Francis Ltd. Adapted with permission.

well-educated parents. Child age was a predictor in the Hawk and Holden (2006) study, with more meta-parenting by parents of younger children; other studies, however, have found no effect of age of child (Holden, Hawk, Smith, Singh, & Ashraf, 2017; Merrifield, Gamble, & Yu, 2015). Finally, Holden et al. (2017) reported a racial/ethnic difference: more meta-parenting by African American mothers than by European American mothers. They suggest, reasonably, that this difference reflects the "extra socialization burden" of rearing a minority child while coping with issues of race oneself.

Results with regard to possible effects of meta-parenting are also mixed. The original study by Hawk and Holden identified an effect of the problem-solving dimension: A relatively low level of problem solving was associated with both laxness and overreactivity in parenting behaviors. Nicholson et al. (2008) reported a more general effect: Relatively high meta-parenting was associated with authoritative child-rearing, the most positive of the parenting styles identified by the Baumrind approach to parenting (Baumrind, 1971). Two other studies, however, found little evidence of links between meta-parenting and parental behavior (Holden et al., 2017; Tamm et al., 2012). The Holden et al. (2017) study also reported an unexpected link with another outcome measure: The quality of the mother–child relationship, as reported by the mother, related negatively to meta-parenting; that is, the mothers who were most satisfied with the relationship engaged the least in meta-parenting. The authors suggest a child-to-parent explanation for this finding: Mothers who are dissatisfied with the relationship work to correct the situation, whereas "there is less need to expend cognitive energy . . . when the relationship is positive and cooperative" (Holden et al., 2017, p. 487). Clearly, this explanation requires further study, as do the more general questions of how and why meta-parenting relates to other measures.

## Transition to Parenthood

Chapter 1 made the point that parents' beliefs are of interest to many disciplines. Such is certainly the case for the topic to be considered now. Sociologists, for example, have long studied effects of the transition to parenthood (Belsky, Ward, & Rovine, 1986). So, with somewhat different emphases, have doctors and nurses, anthropologists, and, of course, psychologists.

Not all research on the transition to parenting addresses effects on parents' beliefs (Heinicke, 2002; Roy et al., 2014). The studies that do address beliefs focus on one or more of three topics: effects on beliefs about parenthood, effects on beliefs about the infant, and effects on beliefs about the marital relationship. The first of these topics is the subject of this section, and the second will be discussed in Chapter 5 on Infancy. Although the marital relationship per se is not a topic for this book, the quality of the relationship affects how parents think about children and about family, and it will therefore receive some consideration both in the present discussion and in the later "Family" section.

In contrast to the other topics covered in this chapter, the transition to parenthood falls at the independent variable end of research—that is, it is of interest not as a type of belief but rather as a possible determinant of whatever beliefs parents may hold. Determining possible effects of the transition requires longitudinal study with at least two time points: assessment of beliefs either during the prenatal period or at birth and assessment of beliefs at some point after the child has joined the family. Three general questions are of interest. How stable are parents' beliefs about parenting as they move from anticipating parenthood to actually being parents? To the extent that change in beliefs occurs, what is the direction and the magnitude of the change? Finally, what are the factors that contribute to either stability or change?

The most often studied belief in this literature is self-efficacy, and I therefore begin with research on self-efficacy. Here and in general, the stability question takes two forms. One form concerns stability at the group level: Does the overall level of self-efficacy remain the same across the transition to parenthood, or does self-efficacy either increase or decrease following the arrival of the child? The second form is stability at the individual level: Are individual parents consistent in their level of self-efficacy across the transition? Note, of course, that the answers to these two questions are not necessarily the same.

The studies of self-efficacy provide fairly clear answers to both questions. Although dips are occasionally found, in the great majority of instances the means for self-efficacy either remain stable or increase from the prenatal period to time points during infancy. Becoming a parent, therefore, is associated, on the average, with greater confidence in one's parenting abilities. Specifying the extent of the increase is made difficult both by the variable measures that have been used and by the absence of effect sizes; most gains, however, are in the 6–12% range. Mothers are more likely to show gains than are fathers, and, as in the literature in general, mothers often have higher self-efficacy than do fathers (e.g., Biehle & Mickelson, 2011; Leerkes & Burney, 2007).

The degree of within-person stability varies some across studies. Virtually every across-time analysis reports significant relations, however, and, in many instances, the correlations reach the .70s (e.g., Kunseler, Willemen, Oosterman, & Schuengel, 2014; Verhage, Oosterman, & Schuengel, 2013). Similarly high values are found when self-efficacy is assessed at several points across the prenatal period (Wernand, Kunseler, Oosterman, Beekman, & Schuengel, 2014). Early self-efficacy is hardly set in stone (to borrow a phrase from research on another part of the life span), but it does show considerable stability.

What accounts for either maintenance of good self-efficacy or improvements in self-efficacy across the transition to parenthood? The answer is the same factors that were discussed earlier with respect to self-efficacy at any point in the developmental span, factors that are important because they make successful parenting either more or less likely. Social support is again a predictor of relatively good self-efficacy. Anxiety and depression are again predictors of relatively poor self-efficacy, and again the relations appear to be reciprocal ones, with anxiety or depression leading to lower self-efficacy, which in turn leads to greater anxiety or depression (e.g., Kunseler et al., 2014). Difficult child temperament is again predictive of low self-efficacy, and there is some evidence here also that relations may run in both directions—specifically, that low self-efficacy contributes to mothers' perception that their infant is temperamentally difficult (Verhage et al., 2013). At present it is not clear whether low self-efficacy affects temperament itself and not just maternal perceptions of temperament.

We turn next to another approach discussed earlier in the chapter: the Bugental PAT. We saw that the Bugental team has administered the PAT to parents during the prenatal period and has shown that prenatal parental attributions predict postnatal parental behaviors. The Bugental team, however, has not included a further administration of the PAT as a measure of stability or change in attributions across the transition to parenthood. To my knowledge, the only researchers to do so are Bernstein and colleagues, who administered the PAT to expectant mothers during the third trimester of pregnancy and then readministered the measure at 5 and 7 months following birth (Bernstein, Laurent, Measelle, Hailey, & Ablow, 2013). Although response to some of the components of the measure changed over time, the perceived control over failure—which, recall, is the critical concept in the

Bugental approach—did not. Despite this mean-level stability, however, the within-person stability was modest (correlations in the .20s). Thus the overall level of perceived control over failure did not change with time, but many mothers did change.

I consider one more body of work in this section. It is work that addresses a basic belief about parenting: Who should do what when a child joins the family? What do expectant mothers and expectant fathers believe that each partner will contribute to the care of the infant, and how do these beliefs fit with the eventual developmental reality?

A general answer to the "how do beliefs fit reality" question is easy to give: not very well. In particular, it is mothers' expectations about parenthood that often do not work out happily. They do not work out happily because expectant mothers tend to believe that their spouses will assume more of the child care duties—and that they themselves will therefore need to do less—than in fact proves to be the case. Among the many studies that demonstrate this pattern are Biehle and Mickelson (2012); Khazan, McHale, and Decourcey (2008); and Ruble, Fleming, Hackel, and Stangor (1988). Why the pattern occurs is an interesting question, given that the nonegalitarian nature of child care is a familiar and long-established feature of the culture. Why should new mothers expect that their situation will be different from the norm? Ruble et al. (1988) suggest (although are unable to test) two possible explanations. One is that most information-seeking about a new baby, including social comparison of maternal and paternal roles, occurs after birth, and thus too late to affect prenatal expectations. The other is that pregnancy is typically a time of increased closeness and marital support, and expectant mothers may therefore believe that their situation will be different from what is typically the case.

Fathers appear less often in this literature than do mothers. When fathers do appear, however, their prebirth expectations are generally similar to those of mothers; that is, they expect a more egalitarian division of child care than what eventually occurs. Despite this overall similarity, within-spouse concordance in beliefs is modest at best (Rodriguez & Adamsons, 2012).

What are the consequences of violated expectations? The major consequence is not surprising. Faced with the challenges of a new baby and a less helpful than expected spouse, many mothers show a decline in marital satisfaction in the months following the birth of the child. Such declines are neither inevitable (see, e.g., Green & Kaftersios, 1997) nor necessarily long-lasting, but they are a common finding across a range of studies. Fathers' marital satisfaction also occasionally declines in the months following birth, but less consistently and less strongly than does that of mothers (Roy et al., 2014). Indeed, in some instances, fathers have been found to show at least a temporary increase in satisfaction, a result that has been attributed to the fact that the expectations in their case are not unmet (as for the mother) but overmet—the mother is doing more than expected, and the demands on the father are therefore less (Biehle & Mickelson, 2012).

The fact that most studies in the transition literature do not extend for more than a few months following birth limits the opportunity to identify more general effects on either parent behaviors or child outcomes. There is some evidence, however, that lowered marital satisfaction in the months following birth is associated with nonoptimal forms of early parenting, for example, decreases in harmonious coparenting (Khazan et al., 2008; Van Egeren, 2004). If we expand the time frame beyond infancy to childhood in general, then effects of the marital relationship are clear: Low marital satisfaction is associated with both nonoptimal forms of parenting and a variety of negative child outcomes (Grych, 2002). Beliefs about the marital relationship and beliefs about the child are also related; for example, negative attributions about one's spouse are associated with negative attributions about the child (Fincham & Hall, 2005).

## Family

One of the many strengths of Goodnow and Collins's (1990) *Development According to Parents* was the wealth of suggestions they offered with respect to needed directions for future research. Their first such suggestion was for more work on beliefs about the family. As we will see, 30 years of subsequent research have certainly not answered all the questions of interest. Nevertheless, we know more than we did when the Goodnow and Collins book appeared. And Goodnow and Collins have themselves been major contributors to what we know.

The research by Collins and associates has focused on the parents of adolescents, and I therefore defer its coverage to Chapter 8 on Adolescence. This chapter's discussion of beliefs about the family begins with the research by Goodnow and colleagues on household responsibilities, that is, who should do what around the home. The special interest, of course, is in beliefs about what children should do, both parents' beliefs and those of the children themselves.

A joint focus on parents and children is also a theme in the second section under the "Family" heading. The question at issue now is who should have the decision-making power over different aspects of the child's life. As with household responsibilities, this is a matter for which both parents and children have some definite beliefs, and, as with household responsibilities, the beliefs often differ.

The final section of the chapter addresses what is perhaps the broadest and most important belief about the family: what parents believe about the value of children. As we will see, in addition to assessing beliefs about the developing child, research has also addressed what might be considered an end point of parenting: parents' satisfaction with their adult children.

## Household Responsibilities

As I noted in Chapter 2, the starting point for most research on parents' beliefs is not parents; rather, it is some topic from the research literature that psychologists believe is important to study. In many instances we simply do not know whether parents spontaneously hold the beliefs that researchers ask about. In the present case, however, there can be no doubt. The question at issue is one that any parent must eventually address as his or her children develop: What should be the child's responsibility for the myriad of tasks that must be performed to keep a household functioning? The answer to this question lies at the core of what it means to be a member of a family.

What factors might influence parents' thinking about household responsibilities? The following are among the factors that emerge as important in the research directed to this topic by Goodnow and colleagues (Goodnow, 1996, 2004).

One, certainly, is the nature of the task. No one expects a 4-year-old to prepare the family meals or to fix a leaky pipe—some things are clearly outside the province of early childhood. On the other hand, children do not remain 4 forever, and, by adolescence, cooking or home repair *may* be an expectation. In general, parents expect children to do more as they grow older, and they expect children to handle more complicated tasks as they grow older. If circumstances add special challenges to what must be done (e.g., life on a farm, life in a one-parent home), then the expectations may be even greater.

The gender of the child may also be a factor. If parents hold gender-stereotypical views, then the tasks just sketched are not likely to be randomly assigned; rather, cooking is a more likely responsibility for daughters and home repair a more likely responsibility for sons. Although there are of course exceptions, many parents do hold gender-stereotypical views and distribute household tasks accordingly (Antill, Goodnow, Russell, & Cotton, 1996). And although again there are exceptions, many children also hold gender-stereotypical views with respect to who should do what around the house (Schuette & Killen, 2009).

A further consideration is the extent to which the child "owns" the task in question. Cleaning up a mess one has made oneself seems a reasonable expectation for most parents; picking up after a sibling is less likely to be expected. More generally, Goodnow and Delaney (1989) draw a distinction between self-care tasks, such as cleaning one's room and making one's bed, and family-work tasks, such as setting the table and doing the dishes. Although most parents eventually expect both sorts of contribution, they typically introduce self-care tasks earlier in development than they do family-work tasks, and they are more likely to press for completion of self-care tasks. Family-work tasks, in contrast, are seen as more "movable," that is, more transferable from one person to another, a view held by both parents and children. Asking a sibling, at least occasionally, to take one's place in setting the table is likely to be seen as reasonable by both generations. Asking a sibling to clean one's room is likely to elicit an opposite response.

Parents, of course, not only form beliefs about household responsibilities; they adopt parenting practices that they believe will produce the desired outcomes. Virtually all parents explicitly delegate some tasks to their children, but they vary in how forcefully and consistently they do so. They vary also in how often and how explicitly they model the desired behaviors. And they vary in their use of external incentives to elicit the behaviors–in particular, whether they pay children for the completion of chores. The issue of payment is one with which many parents struggle, and it is one for which parents differ markedly in what they believe (Warton & Goodnow, 1995).

The issue of payment raises an important point about the goals that underlie the assignment of household responsibilities. An immediate goal, of course, is completion of the task in question, and thus the child's compliance with the parent's wishes. For many parents, however, more basic and long-term goals also enter in. Such parents hope not just for compliance but for *willingness*—for the child to complete the task not in response to parental pressure but rather because it is something that he or she has come to want to do. Such willingness is important because it signals a basic realization about families: that members of a family are part of an important unit, that members of a family help each other and help the family as a whole, and that as a member of the family the child needs to contribute as well. In addition, many parents see household responsibilities as not only immediately beneficial for the functioning of the family but also as a way to build future competencies: learning how to function harmoniously in groups and relationships more generally, for example, or developing skills that will contribute to future self-direction and autonomy. This view that household chores help to nurture positive developmental outcomes is expressed clearly in the last of the quotations given at the beginning of the chapter.

The preceding account is based largely on Australian parents, these being the only participants in most of the Goodnow studies (although the quotation just referred to was from a Spanish father). As always, if we expand the cultural range we expand what we can conclude. Indeed, this point holds even within the Goodnow research program. In one early study, Australian-born mothers were compared with mothers who had immigrated to Australia from Lebanon (Goodnow, Cashmore, Cotton, & Knight, 1984). When asked about possible household tasks for a 5-year-old, the Australian-born mothers had no difficulty generating various possibilities. The Lebanese-born mothers, in contrast, "regarded it as laughable that one would expect any regular task of 5-year-olds," with many going on to explain "they're still babies" (Goodnow, 1996, p. 319). Other, more wide-ranging cultural comparisons have revealed further differences in both parental and child beliefs about household responsibilities, along, to be sure, with a bedrock of similarity in beliefs at both the parent and child levels (Bowes, Chen, San, & Yuan, 2004; Bowes, Flanagan, & Taylor, 2001; Lansford et al., 2016).

I conclude this section with a basic point not yet addressed, one that will lead to a further consideration of cultural comparisons. The emphasis thus far has been on the child's willingness to perform the tasks that are asked of him or her. But to complete a particular task the child must not only be willing: the child must be *able*, and, in most instances it is the parent who is responsible for instilling the necessary competence. Household tasks, therefore, constitute a prime target for parental teaching, as well as a prime topic for examining the relation between parents' beliefs and parents' behaviors.

It is true, of course, that in early childhood the teaching demands are likely to be fairly minimal. Putting toys away in a toy box does not require much instruction. As children develop, however, the complexity of the tasks facing them, and thus the need for some sort of guidance, increases. In addition, early forms of child engagement and parental teaching become more evident once we expand our focus beyond the Western, industrialized nations that are the usual targets for research. In many cultures children participate in and learn from adult activities from early in life (Gaskins, 2015). In Mali, for example, boys who will eventually be camel herders begin to care for goats at age 4, graduating to a baby camel by age 8 or 9 (Spittler, 1998). In villages in rural Bolivia, young children perform a variety of tasks, ranging from fetching firewood to washing clothes to feeding and milking the animals (Punch, 2003). In Cameroon, girls whose mothers are potters begin to learn pottery-making skills as early as age 7 (Wallat-Petre, 2001). Finally and more generally, children, including some as young as age 5, serve as caregivers for younger siblings in a large number of the world's cultures (Zukow-Goldring, 2002). In all of these instances, some instruction and guidance is necessary from early childhood on.

Although all of the theories introduced in Chapter 2 are relevant to the question of how such guidance comes about, two speak to the issue most directly: the work on parental ethnotheories and the Vygotskian sociocultural perspective. I draw from the latter for the present discussion.

As we saw, the social/cultural embedding of development—the notion of development from the outside in—is a central thesis of the Vygotskian approach. So, too, is an emphasis on the social agents, especially parents, who make cultural knowledge and practices available to the developing child. To do so optimally, parents must be able to judge what the child is ready for, which means that parental knowledge of the child, as embodied in the Vygotskian concept of the zone of proximal development, plays a critical role. Finally, and as noted in Chapter 2, an emphasis on the social bases for development does not imply a passive child recipient. Indeed, just the reverse is the case. In large measure, the forms of learning sketched in the preceding paragraph occur not through direct, explicit instruction but rather through the parent's involvement of the child in ongoing activities, activities such as animal care or pottery making or child care. The traditional label for the learning that occurs through such involvement, *guided participation*, captures the contributions of both partners: a child who is not merely a passive onlooker but a participant (hence *participation*) and a parent who is not merely an actor but also a teacher (hence *guided*) (Rogoff, 1990). Another, more recent label places even more emphasis on the active nature of the child's contribution: *learning by observing and pitching in* (Rogoff, 2014).

# Autonomy

The previous section addressed the question of who should do various activities. This section addresses the question of who should make decisions about who does various activities. In particular, when in development does the initial decision-making power of the parent give way, at least at times, to the wishes of the child or adolescent?

The answer to this question depends on what the activities are. The relevant research is grounded in theorizing by Elliot Turiel concerning different domains of behavior and development, theorizing since built on and elaborated by others, most notably Judith Smetana (e.g., 2011a; Turiel, 2002). Table 4.7 lists the domains that are distinguished in contemporary research, along with examples of behaviors that fall under each domain.

In what follows I concentrate on the personal and multifaceted domains. I concentrate on these domains for the same reason that most of the research on parents' beliefs has done so: namely, that it is in these cases that we find variability in beliefs and thus can search for concordance or lack of concordance in what parents believe and what children believe. In contrast, parents show substantial uniformity in their beliefs about the moral, conventional, and prudential domains: namely, that these are distinct aspects of behavior,

Table 4.7  Domains of Development

| Domain | Description | Examples of violations,_____ |
|---|---|---|
| Moral | Acts that affect others' rights or from a store welfare | Hitting a playmate, stealing |
| Conventional | Arbitrary, agreed-on norms that structure social interactions in different contexts | Wearing pajamas to school, calling teachers by their first names |
| Prudential | Acts that pertain to safety, comfort, health, and harm to the self | Playing with matches, running into the street |
| | | Examples_____ |
| Personal | Acts that have consequences only to the actor and are therefore viewed as beyond societal regulation and moral concern | Decorating one's room Deciding what music to listen to |
| Multifaceted | Issues that involve overlap between conventional or prudential and personal issues | Selection of friends or romantic partners, staying out late at night |

each governed by its own set of rules, and that, as parents, they have the right to regulate their children's moral, conventional, and prudential behaviors (we will encounter some exceptions to this conclusion shortly). A similar uniformity is evident at the child level. Children, to be sure, require time to develop knowledge about the various domains—not necessarily very much time, however. Indeed, a major conclusion from early research on domains was that children can distinguish moral and conventional issues by age 4 or 5, a finding that offered a valuable corrective to the theories of moral development that were then dominant (Turiel, 1979).

Smetana (2011a) notes a further point with respect to beliefs about the first three domains. Parents not only believe that they have the right to set and enforce rules with regard to moral, conventional, and prudential issues; they also believe that they have an *obligation* to do so—that doing so is part of being a parent. And again, this is a belief that children eventually come to share (Smetana & Asquith, 1994).

The examples in Table 4.7 signal an important difference once we move to the personal and multifaceted domains. Now any examples that can be cited do not constitute clear violations of the rules governing the domain; rather, whether a behavior is a violation is an "it depends" question—it depends on context, and it depends, critically, on who is doing the judging. In particular, matters that children or adolescents regard as personal may be regarded as conventional or prudential by their parents. Such conflicts do not arise because parents fail to recognize a personal domain; indeed, many parents encourage children to make decisions about personal issues (e.g., foods, games, playmates) from early in life, the belief being that such decision-making helps to nurture competence and autonomy (Nucci & Smetana, 1996). The conflicts come when children exercise their autonomy in ways with which the parents disagree.

Let me say a word about the methods used in the studies by Smetana and colleagues before turning to findings. Some of the studies include parents only, some (a larger number) include adolescents only, and some include both parents and adolescents. In some studies the participants respond to standardized vignettes that present the situations of interest (e.g., Smetana & Asquith, 1994), in some studies the participants provide real-life examples of conflicts to which the subsequent questioning is then directed (e.g., Yau & Smetana, 2003), and in some studies both hypothetical and actual conflicts are explored (e.g., Smetana, 1988). In some studies, possible developmental changes are examined cross-sectionally across the span of adolescence (e.g.,

Yau & Smetana, 1996); in other studies, such changes are examined longitudinally, an approach that permits an examination of individual stability in beliefs over time (e.g., Smetana, 2000). Finally, although most of the studies are limited to the occurrence and nature of conflicts, a subset of studies provide evidence with respect to possible effects of parents' beliefs about control and autonomy—in particular, relations to parents' child-rearing practices (e.g., Smetana, 1995).

I have already previewed one general conclusion from the research program, and that is that parent–child conflicts are a frequent, perhaps inevitable, part of family life. As Smetana (2011b) emphasizes, however, such conflicts, especially if they are moderate in intensity, are not necessarily detrimental; some may present valuable learning opportunities, and few seem to have long-lasting negative effects. Occasional conflicts are, in her words, "a temporary perturbation in adolescent–parent relationships" (Smetana, 2011b, p. 183). In addition, although conflicts may sometimes involve potentially dangerous forms of behavior (e.g., drug use, premarital sex), most, at least in the samples studied, do not. In the words of one summary, conflicts "were primarily over every-day, mundane details of family life, such as doing the chores, getting along with siblings (and others), doing homework and getting good grades, and teenagers' choice of friends and activities" (Smetana, 2011a, p. 36). Chores were the most frequent topic, thus reinforcing a point made in the previous section: that children do not always agree with their parents' views of who should do what around the house.

Possible developmental changes across the span of adolescence are always of interest whenever adolescents are the targets of study, and such is certainly the case for the topic of parent–child conflicts. Changes do in fact occur as children move through the teenage years: changes in what parents believe, changes in what children believe, and changes in the fit between the two sets of beliefs. In general, parents cede more authority and grant more autonomy as children grow older, especially with regard to the personal domain but also to some extent with regard to the prudential domain. As they grow older, children expect more autonomy, again especially with regard to issues that they regard as personal. We have, then, a compatible developmental progression for the two generations. The problem is that in many instances parents' rate of change lags behind adolescents' rate of change—that is, adolescents expect autonomy before parents are ready to grant it. The result is that parent–child conflicts tend to peak in early adolescence, when the two sets of beliefs are most discrepant, and to decline, although not disappear, by late adolescence, when the beliefs are most concordant. The same conclusions about developmental change emerge from both cross-sectional and longitudinal examinations of the issue (Smetana, 2011a).

Longitudinal research is necessary for examination of a further issue. Analyses of group-level stability or change cannot tell us whether individual parents are stable in what they believe over time. If, for example, a mother grants a relatively high level of autonomy when her child is 12, will she continue to do so when the child is 14, 16, or 18? The answer is the usual one for longitudinal studies of stability: probably, but not necessarily (Smetana, 2000). Across-time correlations vary some across parents and across issues, but most are in the .4 to .6 range.

The initial phase of the Smetana research program focused on middle-class White American families. The range soon expanded, however, to include African American families in the United States (Smetana, 2000) and Chinese families in Hong Kong and Shenzen (Yau & Smetana, 1996, 2003). Recent years have seen further expansion, with studies of mothers of adolescents in Iran (Assadi, Smetana, Shahmansouri, & Mohannadi, 2011) and studies of refugee youth in Jordan, Iraq, Syria, and Palestine (Smetana, Ahmad, & Wray-Lake, 2015, 2016). Two general conclusions emerge from these studies. First, some variations are evident across ethnicities, races, and cultural settings. The frequency of conflicts may vary across groups (it is relatively low in Chinese samples, for example), and the specific content areas that provoke conflict may also vary—most obviously, when cultures with marked differences in customs and values are compared. Second, such differences among groups are accompanied by some basic and arguably more fundamental similarities. Thus parent–child conflicts are an aspect of every culture that has been studied; parents and children in every culture distinguish among the different domains of development; and the developmental course and developmental implications of conflicts appear similar across groups and across settings.

Not yet addressed are possible long-term effects of parents' beliefs about autonomy. Despite the basic similarities discussed earlier, parents are not identical in what they believe, especially when behaviors concern the personal and multifaceted domains. Some parents grant autonomy more readily than do others. Does this difference make a difference?

The main attempt by the Smetana research team to address this question has been to explore possible links with the Baumind parenting styles

(Baumrind, 1971). Their focus has been on the first three styles identified by the Baumrind research: authoritative (characterized by high warmth and high control), authoritarian (characterized by low warmth and high control), and permissive (characterized by high warmth and low control). Their research reveals that there are in fact links between parents' beliefs and their parenting styles (Smetana, 1995, 2011a). Furthermore, the links are expectable ones. Permissive parents grant more autonomy than do parents in the other two groups, especially for behaviors in the personal and multifaceted domains. They also show a tendency to treat moral issues as conventional ones, and thus as less subject to parental control. Authoritarian parents, in contrast, grant less autonomy than do the parents in the other two groups, again especially with regard to the personal and multifaceted domains. They also show a tendency to conflate conventional issues with moral ones, thus treating such issues as subject to especially strict parental control. Only authoritative parents behave in ways that consistently maintain distinctions among domains and that convey clearly to their children why autonomy is or is not possible.

A large body of research has shown that the authoritative parenting style is associated with the most positive developmental outcomes, a conclusion that holds across a range of populations and a range of outcomes (Larzelere, Morris, & Harrist, 2013). The Smetana research program suggests that the beliefs parents hold may be important contributors to their adoption of a particular parenting style.

## Value of Children

The discussion of the value of children is divided into three sections. It begins with beliefs about the plusses and minuses of having children, both the beliefs of parents and those of prospective parents. Such beliefs have to do with the value of children in general, although, of course, responses may also reflect the respondent's personal experiences or expectations. The remaining two sections focus on beliefs about one's own children and the question of how satisfied parents are with their children and thus with the experience of being a parent. The first of these sections is directed to parents whose children are still children, whereas the second focuses on parents whose children have grown. The latter provides the book's main coverage of the parents of adult children.

Historically, much of the research on the value of having children has been motivated by an attempt to understand fertility decisions and population trends, work begun several decades ago (Arnold et al., 1975; Fawcett, 1972) and built on and expanded since (Kagitcibasi & Ataca, 2015; Trommsdorff & Nauck, 2010). Three general reasons for having children emerge from such research. One is economic/utilitarian: Once they are old enough, children can contribute to the economic welfare of the family, and they can support their parents in the parents' old age. A second reason is social/traditional: Parenthood is a strong expectation in many cultures, and parenthood provides a way to keep alive one's accomplishments and family name. Finally, a third reason is psychological: Perhaps more than any other experience, children are a potential source of joy, love, companionship, and accomplishment for any parent.

Research from the population perspective has identified two general determinants of the extent to which each of these factors contributes to decisions about parenthood. Because of its concern with population trends, such research has always had a strong cross-national emphasis, and the nature of the society is in fact important. In general, an emphasis on economic or social factors is most common in traditional, nonindustrialized cultures, and an emphasis on psychological factors is most common in wealthier, industrialized settings. Societies change over time, however, and thus historical time emerges as the second general determinant. Across a range of nations, economic factors are less important and psychological factors more important now than was true 40 or so years ago (Kagitcibasi & Ataca, 2015).

I turn now to the question of how well these beliefs about the value of children are borne out once children arrive—that is, how satisfied are parents about the experience of parenthood? As noted, we begin with parents whose children are not yet grown. Like many topics in this book, the question of parental satisfaction is a difficult one to address at all briefly, not only because of the size of the relevant literature but also because of the profusion of concepts, terms, and measures that appear in it. Thus the outcome of interest is sometimes talked about as "parenting satisfaction," sometimes as "life satisfaction," sometimes as "well-being," sometimes as "adjustment," and sometimes as "happiness," and the overlaps and distinctions among the terms are not always clear. In addition, each of the constructs is operationalized in multiple ways—a review by Nelson, Kushlev, and Lyubomirsky (2014) lists 38 measures that appear in the literature, and in many instances the listed measure is simply an example of a larger category of options.

The answer to the "how satisfied" question is, in any case, not a simple one. The usual approach to the issue is to compare parents and nonparents. Such comparisons take two forms: examinations across the transition to parenthood (and thus a within-subject form) and comparisons between groups of parents and nonparents (and thus a between-subject form). In both cases greater well-being or happiness for parents is an occasional but far from inevitable outcome; indeed, the opposite result is a frequent enough occurrence for one review to conclude (with qualifications) that "people are better off without having children" (Hansen, 2012, p. 29). Another review (Nelson et al., 2014) offers a more mixed conclusion; parents *are* sometimes happier than nonparents, but null results or opposite results are also common.

Of course, the fact that there is no across-the-board answer to the parent versus nonparent question should not come as a surprise. Both everyday observation and a large research literature tell us there are marked individual differences among parents in how satisfied or happy they are with their parenting efforts. Thus whether parents are happier than nonparents depends on which parents we are talking about. A central question is what determines these differences among parents.

Many of the contributors are familiar ones that we have seen in other contexts. Parenting knowledge, as assessed by the KIDI, relates positively to parental satisfaction (Bornstein et al., 2003). Social support also relates positively to satisfaction (Luthar & Ciciolla, 2015). In the other direction, having a child who presents challenges, such as a difficult temperament, relates negatively to satisfaction (Nelson et al., 2014). Child age shows a relation, with both infancy and adolescence sometimes associated with relatively low satisfaction, a finding that presumably reflects the challenges posed by these developmental periods (Luthar & Ciciolla, 2016; Nelson et al., 2014). Parental age also contributes; older parents are generally more satisfied than are younger ones, and this finding holds even when child age is controlled (Nelson et al., 2014).

Aspects of the marriage can be important. One contributor is whether there *is* a marriage, for satisfaction is lower on the average for single parents than for married ones (Aassve, Goisis, & Sironi, 2012). As is often the case, marital satisfaction is a predictor; happiness in the marriage relates to happiness as a parent, a relation that presumably reflects a two-way causal direction between the two sets of experiences (Erel & Burman, 1995). Finally—and as any mother could probably predict—positive effects of parenthood are more likely for fathers than for mothers, and thus for the parent who is less likely to experience most of the negative aspects of being a parent (Nelson, Kushlev, English, Dunn, & Lyubomirsky, 2013).

As one of the reviews of this literature notes, the limited and often qualified benefits of parenthood come as a surprise to many—such findings contradict the common belief or folk theory "that children make people happier; that childless persons lead empty and lonely lives" (Hansen, 2012, p. 30). Perhaps the overall, lasting benefits of parenthood are obscured when the research focus is primarily on the ups and downs of daily life. Research that adopts a more global, macro approach provides some support for this possibility. In a survey of nationally representative United States parents, 94% indicated that having children was worth it despite the costs (Martinez, Chandra, Abma, Jones, & Mosher, 2006). When adults in a study of long-term memory were asked to indicate the most positive event of their lives, birth of a child was by far the most common response (Bernstein, Rubin, & Siegler, 2011).

Possible long-term benefits of parenthood are a central issue for the final topic to be considered: What do parents of adult children believe about how well their children have turned out? And how do these beliefs affect their own well-being?

Three general dimensions enter into most parents' answers to the "how well" question (Brackbill, Kitch, & Noffsinger, 1988; Cichy, Lefkowitz, Davis, & Fingerman, 2013; Ryff, Lee, Essex, & Schmutte, 1994). One is objective success in the educational/occupational realm. Children who have done well in school, who hold good jobs, and who are well-off financially are evaluated more positively than are children whose attainments fall short in one or more of these aspects of life. A second dimension is success in the social, interpersonal realm. A satisfactory marriage, parenthood, and an absence of socioemotional problems constitute the positive end of this dimension; divorce and various problems of adjustment constitute the negative end. Finally, a third dimension is the quality of the relationship with the parent. Maintenance of contact, positive interactions when contact does occur, mutual care and support—again, there is a clear positive end to the dimension, as well as clear ways in which children may fall short of the parent's desires.

These determinants of how parents evaluate their children are, of course, predictable. Children who have done well are evaluated more positively than are children who have struggled. In general, the effects of such beliefs on parents' well-being are also predictable. Well-being and happiness are most likely when one's children are perceived as successful; conversely, problems for the children often mean problems for the parents as well. In what follows, I add a few specific points to this general conclusion.

Relations between children's successes and failures and parents' well-being are, of course, correlational, which means that causality cannot be established with certainty. As I have discussed at various points, longitudinal research can add to the plausibility of causal inferences, and a study by Kalmijn and de Graff (2012) provides such data for the topic of well-being. The dependent measure was depressive symptoms in the parents of adult children, with measures taken twice at a 3- to 4-year interval. Such symptoms decreased following both the children's marriage and the birth of a grandchild and increased following a divorce—exactly the pattern that would be predicted if children's ups and downs impact parents' well-being.

Both mothers and fathers show effects of their children's successes or failures, but the specific effects sometimes vary. They varied, in fact, in the Kalmijn and de Graff (2012) study: Fathers were more positively affected by parenthood, and mothers were more negatively affected by divorce. Here is one more example. In a study by Cichy et al. (2013), children's lack of career success was associated with negative emotions for both parents but somewhat different ones: disappointment and worry for mothers, disappointment and anger and guilt for fathers. Children's lack of relationship success related only to mothers' emotions (disappointment, worry, guilt); fathers showed no apparent effects.

As the Kalmijn and de Graff (2012) study (among many others) shows, both positive and negative aspects of their children's lives can affect parents' well-being. In some instances, however, negative events have been found to produce stronger effects (e.g., Fingerman, Cheng, Birditt, & Zarit, 2012; Umberson, 1992). These effects, moreover, are not necessarily only short-term. In one study, children's problems during the teen years continued to affect parental anger and depression decades later and did so even when problems during the intervening years were controlled for (Milkie, Norris, & Bierman, 2011).

The study by Fingerman et al. (2012) adds one final point. These researchers took the rare step of examining beliefs about several children in the same family. In many instances, parents offered different evaluations of successes and failures for their different children, and these mixed-outcome instances proved especially informative. Having one successful child was not sufficient to ensure parental well-being; rather, boosts were found only if all children were perceived as successful. In contrast, having one perceived failure was enough to lower well-being even when other children were deemed a success. This differential impact of bad compared to good is captured in the article's title: "Only as Happy as the Least Happy Child."

# 5

# Infancy

I have this vivid memory when she was born of them taking her to clean her off and put the blanket around her and all that. And she was looking all around. She was looking at us. She was looking around the delivery room. She was alert from the very first second. Even when I would take her out—I took her out when she was six weeks old to a shopping mall to have her picture taken—people would stop me and say, "What an alert baby." . . . And it was just something about her. She was very engaging and very with the program, very observant. She's still fabulously observant.

—(Harkness, Super, and van Tijen, 2000, p. 26)

My child is just beginning to walk and he's gotten to the stage where he wants me around all the time. But I have the feeling he needs me, that he needs somebody there to reassure him and help him. So I just try to use the free time I have when he sleeps for doing things around the house. Then when he's awake I'll have nothing else on my mind but being a companion to him.

—(Bettelheim, 1962, p. 201)

I think he needs to be warm, to be fed, to be clean, dry, that kind of thing, but I also think he definitely needs some stimulation. There are times when he is in a chair and we're not paying attention to him or, you know . . . he needs some stimulation, something of interest to look at, something to, you know, just for him to play with.

—(Harkness et al., 2010, p. 69)

My baby looks at new things very intensively for a long time. I think he recognizes things and he is thinking . . . .I like it. It is his brain development. I would like to show him lots of things to help and encourage his brain development.

—(Harkness et al., 2010, p. 70).

*Parents' Beliefs About Children.* Scott A. Miller, Oxford University Press (2020). © Oxford University Press.
DOI: 10.1093/oso/9780190874513.001.0001

The next four chapters address parents' beliefs about specific aspects of children's development. The organization is chronological. This chapter discusses what parents believe about infancy. The next two chapters concentrate on the childhood years, that is, the age period from roughly 2 to 12. Chapter 6 discusses beliefs about cognitive development, and Chapter 7 adds beliefs about social development. Finally, Chapter 8 rounds off the developmental span with a consideration of what parents believe about adolescence.

We have already had some coverage of work relevant to beliefs about infancy. The discussion of beliefs about parenting in Chapter 4 included two bodies of research that also speak to beliefs about infant development. One is research on the transition to parenthood and the possible effects of becoming a parent on how parents think. The other is parental knowledge as assessed by measures such as the Knowledge of Infant Development Inventory (KIDI), most of which, as we saw, tap not only knowledge about parenting but also knowledge about infancy. The earlier coverage of these literatures concentrated as far as possible on beliefs about parenting. This chapter picks up on the infancy aspect of such research.

The organization of the chapter is as follows. The first section addresses parents' general knowledge about infancy. It revisits the KIDI and similar measures, and it also reviews so-called *milestones* or *timetable studies*—that is, studies in which parents are asked to estimate ages of attainment for various developmental achievements. This chapter addresses milestones within the span of infancy; Chapter 6 adds studies of later development.

The second section of the chapter considers a variety of developments that, although not confined to infancy, typically receive special attention from both parents and researchers during the infant years. Three such developments are discussed: crying, sleeping, and eating.

The final section of the chapter addresses two of the most important topics under the heading of children's social development: attachment and temperament. Neither development, to be sure, is an infancy-only topic; I have already discussed the life-long relevance of the attachment construct, and temperament also applies throughout the life span. Both developments, however, have their origins in infancy, and both have been studied most with respect to infancy. In addition, both, as we will see, have been important topics for parents' beliefs about infants.

## General Knowledge of Infancy

Two sorts of assessments provide the basis for the findings to be discussed now. One basis is the KIDI and similar measures of general knowledge about infancy. As I noted in Chapter 4, there are many such measures, only a subset of which were cited in that chapter. A review by Orme and Hamilton (1987) identified 18 such measures, and that was the tally some 30 years ago.

The second source of data comes from the milestones studies that focus on infancy. The knowledge in question is a basic one for our understanding of infant development: At what age do various competencies emerge, and therefore what can infants do or not do at various points in development? As Super and Harkness (2011) point out, questions of this sort have been central to child psychology since the inception of the discipline. Many of the classic studies in the field were directed to milestones; Arnold Gesell's work is probably the best-known example (e.g., Gesell & Ilg, 1949). In addition, childhood IQ tests are built around milestones, for such tests assess the extent to which a child's development either outstrips or lags behind the rate of development that has been found to be typical for children in general.

As with the KIDI-like measures, milestones measures have proliferated in the literature. Some focus on specific aspects of infant functioning, most commonly cognitive development (e.g., Ninio, 1988). Others encompass infant development more generally. The example I use, an instrument devised by Tamis-LeMonda and colleagues (Tamis-LeMonda, Shannon, & Spellman, 2002), falls in the latter category. Table 5.1 presents a sampling of items from the measure. As can be seen, the assessment comprises five aspects of infant functioning: cognitive development, language development, motor development, social development, and play. The table reproduces 24 of the 52 items that make up the assessment.

The breadth of coverage is one strength of the Tamis-Lemonda et al. (2002) measure. Another strength is the specificity with which the target accomplishments are described. Little if any inference or interpretation is required on the parent's part; rather, the referents are overt behaviors that the parent has either seen or not seen. Such specificity was not always true of the initial attempts to measure knowledge of milestones. Some early measures, for example (e.g., Keller, Miranda, & Gauda, 1984; Ninio, 1979), asked about the age at which babies begin to "think," an answerable question only if there is some clear criterion for "think," and even then a question on which experts

**Table 5.1** Examples of Items from the Tamis-LeMonda et al. (2002) Study of Beliefs About Developmental Milestones

| Cognitive milestones | Estimated age of onset (range in months) |
| --- | --- |
| Turns head when he or she hears a sound. | 2–4 |
| Reaches for objects held in front of him or her. | 3–5 |
| Looks at pictures in books or magazines. | 6–14 |
| Put small objects or toys in a container. | 11–16 |
| Builds a tower of 8 or more blocks. | 20–31 |
| **Language milestones** | |
| Look around the room and then look in air and make "aaah, oooh" noises over and over. | 1–4 |
| Look over to caretaker and respond to that person talking to them with sounds such as "gagaga, bababa." | 4–10 |
| Look at a person leaving a room and say "bye-bye," imitating that person saying "bye-bye." | 9–13 |
| Look over to juice, reach to juice, and say "more ju" to request juice. | 18–24 |
| Look at a picture of a boy crying, point to the picture, and say "boy sad" or "boy cry." | 30–36 |
| **Motor milestones** | |
| Supports own head upright and with good control. | 1–3 |
| Rolls over from back to stomach. | 5–7 |
| Crawls across floor on hands and knees. | 7–10 |
| Walks up stairs with help from an adult. | 14–19 |
| Can run easily and with good coordination. | 18–25 |
| **Social milestones** | |
| Makes sound in response to another person's voice. | 3–5 |
| Becomes upset when caregiver leaves the room or home. | 6–9 |
| Looks at an object or person when an adult points. | 9–14 |
| Shows interest in other children besides brothers or sisters. | 18–24 |
| Shows a desire to please mother or caregiver. | 24–36 |
| **Play milestones** | |
| Reach for a small nesting cup, hold on to it, and look at it. | 3–6 |
| Grab a toy telephone, touch the buttons on it, and push one of the buttons. | 7–12 |
| Find a baby doll, hold it in arms, and kiss its face. | 12–16 |
| Hold out finger, stir in frying pan, and eat from finger. | 18–27 |

Adapted from "Low-Income Adolescent Mothers' Knowledge About Domains of Child Development," by C. S. Tamis-LeMonda, J. Shannon, and M. Spellman, 2002, *Infant Mental Health Journal, 23*, pp. 93–94. Copyright 2002 by Michigan Association for Infant Mental Health. Adapted with permission by John Wiley and Sons.

are likely to disagree. And, of course, some degree of expert consensus is a necessary basis for determining how accurate parents are.

## Accuracy and Its Determinants

Parental accuracy is, in fact, the central question that is addressed in this research. Its measurement takes two forms, forms that correspond to the two ways in which beliefs about ages of mastery are elicited. Some measuring instruments present either a target age with which parents can agree or disagree or a set of ages among which they can choose. In such cases the determination of accuracy is straightforward: Either the response matches the empirically determined correct answer or it does not. The KIDI is one of many examples that fall in this category. Other instruments require parents to provide an age of emergence for each of the items that are presented. The Tamis-LeMonda et al. (2002) measure is one of the examples in this category. In the case of measures of the latter sort, an acceptable range of responses must be determined; that is, how close to the target age is close enough to be considered accurate? Table 5.1 shows the range of acceptable responses for the items given in the table. In each instance, the range is based on what research shows is a normal range of variation for the development in question.

A tally of correct and incorrect responses is not the only information that measures of this sort yield. Also of interest are the types of errors that parents make. When parents are incorrect, they may be incorrect in either of two directions: They may overestimate what infants are capable of, or they may underestimate what infants are capable of. The distinction is an important one. It is easy to imagine that expecting too little of a child will lead to different parental behaviors than will expecting too much, and also that the consequences for the child will be different for the two sorts of errors. As we will see, research bears out these expectations, both for infancy and for later development.

Before discussing what research shows, I should make a point about terminology. The terms "overestimation" and "underestimation" are not used consistently in the studies to be reviewed. Some authors define "over" and "under" with respect to the fit between estimated age and actual age; thus, an estimate that is earlier than the actual age is labeled an underestimation. This is the case, for example, in the Tamis-LeMonda et al. (2002) report from which Table 5.1 is drawn. More commonly, however, the terms are used to refer to the beliefs about child competence that the two sorts of errors reveal. By this definition, a predicted age of mastery earlier than the actual age is an overestimation because it imputes greater competence than the infant possesses. Similarly, a predicted age later than the actual age is an underestimation. It is the latter use of "over" and "under" that I adopt in what follows.

We can begin the summary of findings with the Tamis-LeMonda et al. (2002) study. The mothers in their study showed some but far from perfect accuracy in judging age of emergence for the various milestones; their mean estimates fell within the accepted range for only 13 of the 52 items. Accuracy did vary some across the different items. It varied as a function of the developmental level of the item, with greater accuracy for developments in the first year of life than for those that emerged later. It varied also as a function of the domain of development, with greater accuracy for cognitive, language, and motor items than for social and play items. It is important to note, however, that domain comparisons based on other measures have yielded somewhat different orders of difficulty, a finding that suggests, not surprisingly, that the particular exemplars sampled are an important determinant of relative difficulty (Jahromi et al., 2014; Keller et al., 1984).

The predominant error in the Tamis-LeMonda et al. (2002) study was overestimation of infant abilities. To give a few examples—the build-a-tower item described in the table was placed at 12 months, the label-the-boy-crying item was placed at 18 months, and the please-mother-or-caregiver item was placed at 10 months. All of these estimates, as well as a number of others, were a year or so earlier than the actual age of mastery. An exception to the tendency to overestimate was provided by the developmentally earliest abilities because on these items mothers tended to underestimate what infants can do (of course, the earlier a competency emerges, the more difficult it is to overestimate ability). The result of the two kinds of error was a severe truncating of the developmental range: Developments that are in fact spread across 3 or more years were seen as emerging within the span of about 1 year. We will see a similar phenomenon in Chapter 6, in the discussion of parents' beliefs about more advanced abilities.

Two qualifiers should be noted with respect to these generally negative conclusions. First, Tamis-LeMonda et al. (2002) not only examined beliefs about the timing of abilities; they also examined beliefs about the order in which abilities emerge. The mothers' performance was a good deal more impressive by this second criterion. Indeed, the orderings were close to perfect for the cognitive, language, and motor domains; the correlations between

predicted sequence and actual sequence were .91, .98, and .93. The social and play domains again proved more difficult; even here, however, the
correlations between predicted and actual were .68 and .66. The message
is a general one: How accurate parents are depends on what they are asked
to judge.

The second qualifier concerns the sample. The sample for the Tamis-
LeMonda et al. (2002) study was low-income adolescent mothers. As we will
see, this is not a group that fares well in comparisons of parental knowledge.
To my knowledge, the Tamis-Lemonda et al. measure has yet to be used with
any other sample; almost certainly, however, performance would be more
impressive if the mothers were either older or more affluent or both.

Broad as it is, the Tamis-LeMonda et al. (2002) approach does have one
omission, and that is a sampling of very early-emerging abilities, including
those (e.g., seeing, hearing) that are present at birth. Other studies (e.g.,
Ertem et al., 2007; Ninio, 1988; van Beek, Genta, Constabile, & Sansavini,
2006) fill in this gap. The general conclusion is again one of some underestimation of early competencies. For example, mean estimates for when babies
can first see are typically between 1 and 2 months, and in some studies more
than half of the sample fail to give the correct "at birth" answer. Performance
is only slightly better with respect to questions about when infants can hear.

As we saw in the discussion of the Civitas study in Chapter 3 (Civitas
Initiative, Zero to Three, & Brio Corporation, 2000), these beliefs about infant competence have implications for how parents think about possible
effects of early experience, including the experiences that they themselves
provide. In a follow-up of the Civitas work with African American mothers,
Combs-Orme, Orme, and Lefmann (2013) reported that only slightly more
than half of the mothers believed that their behaviors could impact the baby's
brain development from birth. Nearly a third thought that any such effects
would occur only at 6 months or later, and 15% believed that any effects
would have to wait until 1 year or later.

Shortly, the discussion turns to what we know about the origins of such
beliefs. First, I add one more piece of descriptive information. It concerns
a contrast between the infancy studies and studies directed to beliefs about
older children. As we will see in Chapter 6, many studies with parents of
older children ask not only about milestones or development in general but
also about the development of the parent's own child. Such studies thus provide an own versus in-general comparison that can be informative. In fact,
such comparisons *are* informative for they provide another instance of the

valence effect: Parents tend to give more positive evaluations of their own child than they do of children in general.

Whether such an effect occurs among parents of infants is not clear. As the quotations at the start of the chapter indicate, research on ethnotheories often includes open-ended questioning about the participant's own child. Parent-report measures will be discussed at various points later in the chapter, and such measures always concern the parent's own child. The research on knowledge of infant development, however, has almost all been directed to beliefs about infants in general. This is what the KIDI and similar measures address, and it is also the focus of milestone measures. Parents may, of course, draw from experiences with their own infants when responding to such instruments. But the questions are not about their own infants.

The limited available evidence suggests that some own-child valence effect may occur in parents' beliefs about infants. Pharis and Manosevitz (1980) asked first time parents-to-be about babies' capacities at birth and about the timetable for various infant achievements. In both cases the parents-to-be overestimated infants' capacities, and they did so to a greater extent than did a comparison group of nonpregnant adults. The tendency to overestimate, however, was modest when the questions concerned children in general; it was greater when expectant parents were thinking about their own future child.

Karraker and Evans (1996) elicited beliefs about both infants in general (judgments of various milestones) and the parents' own infants (predictions of performance on the Bayley test) in samples of adolescent and adult mothers. Because different measures were used, it is difficult to compare accuracy for the own- and in-general judgments (although means were higher for the own-child judgments). In both instances the older mothers outperformed the adolescent mothers, which, as we will see, is a typical finding. More interesting were the patterns of errors made by the two groups. The older mothers overestimated infants' abilities on both the milestones and Bayley measures, and the tendency to do so was correlated across the two tasks. The adolescent mothers also overestimated performance on the milestones measure, indeed even more strongly than did the older mothers. At the same time, many *under*estimated what their own babies could do. What occurred, therefore, was a kind of reverse valence effect: especially negative judgments with respect to one's own child. It is an outcome that we will encounter again, especially in Chapter 9 in the discussion of various forms of atypical development or disturbed parenting.

The discussion of adolescent mothers brings us to the most often studied determinant of parents' beliefs about infant abilities, namely the age of the mother. Dozens of studies have examined what adolescent mothers know about infancy, usually in comparison with a sample of older mothers. A consistent finding, across a range of outcome measures, is that adolescent mothers know less than do older mothers (e.g., Bornstein, Cote, Haynes, Hahn, & Park, 2010; Jahromi et al., 2014; Kliman & Vukelich, 1985; Sommer et al., 1993). Age differences are evident even within the span of adolescence, with younger adolescent mothers showing less knowledge than older ones (Fry, 1985; Reis, 1988). They are also evident prior to the arrival of the baby, with pregnant adolescents showing less knowledge than older mothers-to-be (Sommer et al., 1993).

Whether type of error (i.e., overestimation or underestimation) varies with maternal age is difficult to determine, given that most studies do not report type of error. The available evidence suggests that the general pattern identified earlier holds for both younger and older mothers, that is, a tendency to underestimate early abilities and to overestimate later ones. When differences occur, it is adolescent mothers who are more likely to overestimate what babies can do. As noted, it is not clear whether this conclusion holds not only for beliefs about infants in general (the usual target for study) but also for beliefs about the adolescent mothers' own babies.

The other common group comparison in this literature is that between mothers and fathers. The general conclusion is the usual one for mother–father comparisons: Differences are not always found, but when they do occur they favor mothers. In some instances mothers have been found to be more accurate than fathers (Kliman & Vukelich, 1985; Stevens, 1988). More commonly, mothers have been found to be more optimistic than fathers, that is, to offer earlier age estimates for the mastery of various milestones (Mansbach & Greenbaum, 1999; Ninio, 1987, 1988; Ninio & Rinott, 1988). In the Ninio (1987) study, for example, mothers offered earlier estimates for all 15 of the milestones that were asked about. Although no formal determination of accuracy was reported, the mothers' responses appear closer to what is known about the development of the milestones in question, most of which emerge in the early months. This, in fact, is a point that the author makes.

The Ninio research program adds another important finding. Presumably, fathers are less knowledgeable than mothers because fathers typically have less experience with their infants than do mothers. Ninio and Rinott (1988) measured caregiving experiences of a variety of sorts in a sample of fathers of infants. The greater the fathers' experience, the more positive were their assessments of infant competence and the closer were their age estimates to those of their spouses. Overall, mothers and fathers correlated .48 in their age-of-mastery estimates. Other studies have reported similar mother–father correlations when accuracy rather than age estimates is the measure (Scarzello, Arace, & Prino, 2016; Stevens, 1988).

Why might fathers and mothers be similar in their beliefs? One basis for similarity (though certainly not the only one) is revealed by studies that have asked parents about the sources for their beliefs—that is, how have they learned, or how might they learn, about aspects of infant develop-ment (Kliman & Vukelich, 1985; Scarzello et al., 2016; Stevens, 1988)? Both mothers and fathers typically identify a range of sources, including family members and books and magazines for parents. For many, however, an im-portant source is one's spouse, and this is especially true for fathers. In one study, fathers (although not mothers) chose their spouse as their most im-portant source of information, outranking family, friends, teachers, doctors, books, and mass media (Scarzello et al., 2016). Clearly, if one parent turns to the other for expertise and advice, it is not surprising if their beliefs eventu-ally converge.

The source of beliefs is also an important issue in the study of adolescent mothers. Adolescent mothers typically seek out fewer sources of informa-tion than do older mothers, and they place less reliance on expert sources of information (books, magazines, doctors, nurses) than do older mothers (Vukelich & Kliman, 1985). Furthermore, a common source of help for older parents—namely, reliance on a spouse for support and advice—is not an op-tion for many adolescents. For many, however, reliance on their mother *is* an option, and most adolescent mothers list their own mother as their most important source of parenting advice and help (Stevens, 1984a; Vukelich & Kliman, 1985). The quality of support from the mother is in fact a pre-dictor of parenting knowledge for adolescents (Jahromi et al., 2014). And adolescents' knowledge of infancy correlates with that of their mothers—the more knowledgeable the mother, the more knowledgeable the adolescent (Jahromi et al., 2014; Stevens, 1984a). Nevertheless, the daughters, on the av-erage, still lag behind their mothers.

As I noted, the work on knowledge of infancy includes both prenatal assessments of prospective mothers and postnatal assessments of actual mothers. An obvious question is what changes between pre and post. We saw in Chapter 4 that experience as a parent can bring about various changes, most obviously (although not only) in beliefs about the marital relationship. We will see some further effects of the transition to parenthood both later in this chapter and in the chapters to come. Presumably, what parents know about infancy should be one of the outcomes that is affected by the transition from prospective parent to actual parent.

Potentially, this question could be addressed by a between-subject comparison of mean knowledge scores before and after the transition to parenthood. If experience is beneficial, then the latter should be higher. At present, however, the samples and measures are too diverse and the available data too limited to permit even tentative conclusions from such an approach. And, of course, the preferred method of study is to follow the same people over time.

To my knowledge, only one study has done so, and that is research by Sommer and colleagues (Sommer et al., 1993). Their sample consisted of both adolescent and older mothers, and their knowledge measure, which was created for the study, asked about age of emergence for 40 milestone items. The initial assessment occurred during the last trimester of pregnancy, and the follow-up assessment was given when the infants were 6 months old.

Several findings emerged. As is generally true, the older mothers outperformed the adolescents, and this difference held at both assessment points. Both groups improved from the first assessment to the second, but the improvement was greater for the older mothers (17%) than for the adolescents (4%). Finally, the adolescent mothers showed moderate stability in performance from first assessment to second ($r = .62$), but the value for older mothers ($r = .25$) fell short of significance.

Perhaps the most interesting, and also the most sobering, of these findings is the minimal gain for the adolescent mothers. Six months of parenting experience apparently had little effect on what these mothers knew about babies. Clearly, however, we need more research directed to the effects of becoming a parent on parental knowledge, research with a variety of samples (including fathers) and across a variety of time periods. Of interest are both potential gains in knowledge as a result of experience and stability in relative standing over time—that is, do relatively knowledgeable parents remain relatively knowledgeable as their children develop? At present, we have almost no evidence on this question.

## Effects of Parental Knowledge

Chapter 4 addressed the question of effects of parental knowledge as assessed by general knowledge measures such as the KIDI. In this section I add results from measures that provide a more exclusive focus on what parents know about infancy, including the various milestones measures. As always, two outcomes are of interest: effects on parental behavior and effects on child development. And, as always, various qualifiers apply to the summary of conclusions: Expected relations are not always found; when they do occur, they tend to be small in magnitude and the correlational nature of the data does not allow definite cause-and-effect conclusions.

Once these points are acknowledged, some relation between what parents know about infancy and how they behave with their infants is the outcome in almost every study that has examined the issue. In the Sommer et al. (1993) study just described, observational assessments were made of the quality of parent–child interactions, including dimensions such as positiveness, stimulation, flexibility, and affectional match. More positive scores on the knowledge measure were associated with more positive parenting behaviors. Other studies with various measures of parenting quality have reported similar knowledge–behavior relations (Fry, 1985; Miller, Miceli, Whitman, & Borkowski, 1996; O'Callaghan, Borkowski, Whitman, Maxwell, & Keogh, 1999). In addition, several studies have documented positive relations between parental knowledge and scores on the Home Observation for Measurement of the Environment (HOME), which, as we saw, is perhaps the most general measure of the quality of the early environment (Parks & Smeriglio, 1986; Stevens, 1984b, 1988). Here, and in general, the relations are what we would expect: the more knowledgeable the parent, the better the early environment and the more optimal the child-rearing practices.

Effects are also what we would expect with regard to child outcomes. Relations have been shown, for example, with children's IQs, as measured during infancy with the Bayley and during childhood with the Stanford-Binet (Farris, Lefever, Borkowski, & Whitman, 2013; Miller et al., 1996). There is some evidence that parents' underestimation errors are especially detrimental with regard to their children's intellectual development (Jahromi et al., 2014). Within the social realm, parental knowledge has been shown to relate to adaptive behavior as measured by the Vineland Scales (Sommer et al., 2000), to relatively low levels of problem behaviors as measured by the Child Behavior Checklist (Miller et al., 1996), and to academic achievement and behavioral adjustment (Farris et al., 2013). The last of these findings is an impressively long-term relation: Parental knowledge measured during the prenatal period predicted academic achievement and behavioral adjustment when the children were 10 years old.

## Parent-Report Measures

Chapter 1 discussed eight reasons for an interest parents' beliefs. One was that parents' reports about their children constitute one of the major ways to measure children's characteristics, and parents' beliefs are at the core of such assessments. The validity of parent-report measures—and there are literally hundreds of such measures spanning dozens of topics—depends on the accuracy with which parents can judge their children.

Given the nature of the topics under consideration, parent-report measures were not a subject in Chapters 3 and 4. But they are a subject for this chapter, and they will be as well for the chapters that follow.

Parent-report measures—both for infancy and for other age periods—vary along two dimensions. One variation is in scope, that is, in how broad a range of children's characteristics they attempt to capture. Several measures with a relatively specific focus will be discussed in later sections of the chapter. This section addresses more general assessments, that is, those directed either to infancy in general or to some broad area of infant development. Among the entries in this category are Baker, Schafer, Alcock, and Bartlett (2013); Glascoe (1997); Ireton (1994); Saudino et al. (1998); and Squires, Twombley, Bricker, and Potter (2009).

The second dimension along which measures vary is purpose. In some instances the goal is a basic-science one: to use the measure as part of the examination of some topic of current research interest. In such instances, the parent-report measure serves either as a replacement for or as a complement to other ways to measure the development in question, such as observational assessments or laboratory tests. We will see some examples of such research uses later in the chapter, in the discussions of both temperament and attachment.

The other goal that underlies such measures is a pragmatic one: to identify children who are experiencing problems or who are at risk for developing problems. Such assessments are often a prelude to some form of intervention designed to ameliorate the problems and perhaps to prevent further difficulties. The measures listed earlier all fall under the pragmatic heading, their general goal being to identify delays or problems in infant development. I will use the Infant Development Inventory (Ireton, 1994) as an example.

The Infant Development Inventory spans the period from birth to 18 months. It assesses five broad categories of infant development: social, self-help, gross motor, fine motor, and language. Table 5.2 presents a sampling of the items that make up the Inventory, drawn from 4 of the 18 age periods into which the test is divided. As can be seen, for each age period (with a few exceptions), one or two emerging competencies are described. The parent is instructed to begin at the age that is half her child's current age (e.g., 3 months if she has a 6-month-old infant) and to indicate Yes or No for each of the items—her child demonstrates the ability in question or does not yet demonstrate the ability. The sum of the Yes responses constitutes the child's score for that domain.

It is important to note two differences between the presentation of items given here and what a parent who responds to the Inventory actually encounters. First, the items are randomly ordered when the test is administered (thus not ordered by age of mastery, as in the table). Second, no age labels accompany the items. In short, there are no obvious cues as to what infants of different ages can do.

The basic question with regard to this and similar measures is whether parents' reports accurately reflect the child's developmental level, including identifying delays or gaps in development. Before discussing the relevant evidence, I will note that there are certainly reasons to be doubtful that they will (as, indeed, many professionals were when such measures first began to appear; Ireton, 1992). We saw in the discussion of the Tamis-LeMonda et al. (2002) research that parents were correct on only 25% of their milestones judgments, and, in many instances, their age estimates were off by at least a year. The instruments being considered now, however, make fewer demands on their respondents than does the Tamis-LeMonda approach. In particular, there is no need to specify general ages of mastery for a wide range of infant developments. All that is necessary is to indicate accurately whether one's infant does or does not demonstrate the development in question.

There is a further difference between parent-report measures and the other measures considered to this point in the chapter. With instruments such as the KIDI or the various milestones tests, it is an open question how accurate parents are—that is what the measures are designed to tell us. Furthermore, some variability in parental accuracy is a goal in the creation of such

**Table 5.2** Examples of Items from the Infant Development Inventory

| Age | Domain | | | | |
|---|---|---|---|---|---|
| | Social | Self-help | Gross motor | Fine motor | Language |
| Birth | Quiets when fed and Comforted Makes eye contact. | Alert: Interested in sights and sounds. | Wiggles and kicks. Thrusts arms and legs in play. | Looks at objects or faces. | Cries. Makes small throaty sounds. |
| 6 months | Reaches for familiar persons. | Looks for object after it disappears from sight—for toy after it falls off tray. | Rolls over from back to stomach. | Transfers objects from one hand to the other. | Babbles. Responds to his/her name: turns and looks. |
| 12 months | | Helps a little when being dressed. | Stands alone, steady. | Turns pages of books a few at a time. | Says Mama or Dada for parent. Hands you a toy when asked. |
| 18 months | Wants a doll, teddy bear or blanket in bed with him/her. Sometimes says No when interfered with. | Eats with a fork. | Kicks a ball forward. Good balance and coordination. | Builds tower of 4 or more blocks. | Uses at least 10 words. Asks for a drink or food using words or sounds. |

Copyright 1992, 2005, by Harold Ireton. Adapted with permission from Behavioral Science Systems, Inc. DBA Child Development Review, Box 19512. MPLS, MN 55419.

instruments for variability is a necessary starting point for examinations of both the origins and the effects of parents' beliefs. For parent-report measures, in contrast, accuracy is not an outcome to be studied; rather, it is *the* criterion against which the measures are validated. Items and questions are selected and, if necessary, refined in an attempt to maximize the accuracy with which parents respond, and any item that proves too difficult will not make it into the final instrument. Of course, variability in the outcomes assessed remains of interest; such instruments would be of no use if all children received the same score. The goal, however, is to measure variability that resides in the child, not variability that resides in the parent's beliefs about the child.

Whether an instrument succeeds in doing so is the question of validity: Does the test measure what it is intended to measure? For tests used for pragmatic purposes, such as the Infant Development Inventory, two kinds of error can threaten the validity of an assessment. A test with an overly broad criterion for identifying problems or delays might succeed in identifying all of the truly problematic cases, but it would also mislabel some children who are not experiencing any difficulties at all. Conversely, a more conservative approach to defining problems might avoid such "false positives," but it would do so at the cost of "false negatives," failing to identify some children who are experiencing genuine problems. Successful measures are both *sensitive*—they identify all problem cases—and *specific*—they identify *only* problem cases.

No measure does so perfectly. But the validity evidence—not just for the Infant Development Inventory but for such measures in general—is generally positive, which, of course, is why such measures continue to be used. The evidence takes various forms, of which I will discuss two (see Macy, 2012, for a fuller treatment). One form is positive correlations with other, conceptually related measures of infant development, measures that use methods other than parent-report to obtain their data. A frequently studied correlate is the Bayley Scales of Infant Development, probably the most often used measure of infant functioning (Bayley, 2006). The second form of evidence concerns diagnostic accuracy in identifying problems in development. A common validation step for any new measure is to apply it to a sample that is known to have difficulties, the question being whether the measure succeeds in identifying known problems. A common next step is to apply the measure to a new sample along with other, already established diagnostic tests. The question in this case is whether results from the new measure agree with those from the established measures.

The need for further diagnostic tests does not necessarily disappear once a parent-report measure has been validated. In their most common uses, parent-report measures function as "screening" devices, as an initial source of evidence with respect to possible problems in development. Because they are an imperfect source of evidence (as, of course, are most psychological measures), it is usually important to acquire further information about the child before deciding how to proceed.

## Specific Infant Developments

Each of the three topics to be considered in this section receives some attention in the instruments discussed to this point in the chapter. The KIDI, for example, includes items directed to all three developments, as do several similar measures. My concentration now is on studies whose sole focus is the development in question.

## Crying

Crying is a biologically prepared behavior that is present, literally, from birth. Its adaptive value is clear: Without means, such as the cry, to summon caregivers and to keep them near, the newborn infant could not survive.

Of course, the newborn will survive only if adults respond appropriately to his or her cries. Most researchers believe that adults are also biologically prepared to play their role in early infant–caregiver interactions. Much research has had the goal of determining exactly what form this preparation takes. Among the questions of interest are the following:

Do adults have a built-in, automatic response to infant cries that is distinct from response to other kinds of stimulation?
Are there different types of infant cries (e.g., hunger vs. pain), and, if so, can adults distinguish between them?
Are parents able to recognize the cries of their own infant? More generally, are there differences between parents and nonparents in their response to infant cries? Or between mothers and fathers? Or between women and men?

Despite considerable research effort, answers to many of these questions remain tentative. As one summary puts it, "For nearly every claim made about the human infant's cry, the opposite has also been claimed" (Soltis, 2004, p. 443). Nevertheless, some evidence exists for each of the possible group differences just sketched. Thus, by some measures, women show more adaptive patterns of reactivity to infant cries than do men (Messina et al., 2015; Rigo et al., 2017), mothers show more adaptive patterns than do fathers (Esposito, Nakazawa, Venuti, & Bornstein, 2015), and parents show more adaptive patterns than do nonparents (Out, Pieper, Bakermans-Kranenburg, & van IJzendoorf, 2010). Parents can indeed recognize the cries of their own infant (at least sometimes; Soltis, 2004), and adults in general, perhaps especially parents, can sometimes distinguish among different cries, although the cues that they use to do so are not totally clear (Gustafson, Wood, & Green, 2000). Other effects of parental experience are also evident; for example, parents are better than nonparents at using cries to judge infant age (Esposito et al., 2015), and parents of several children show more differentiation among types of cry than do parents of a single child (Stallings, Fleming, Corter, Worthman, & Steiner, 2001).

The discussion so far has focused on biologically prepared, essentially automatic responses to infant cries. Clearly, however, such responses qualify as parents' beliefs only on a broad definition of "belief." What do we know about parents' more explicit thoughts about infant crying?

Some answers come from a recently developed instrument labeled the Infant Crying Questionnaire (Haltigan et al., 2012; Leerkes, Parade, & Burney, 2010). The Questionnaire is designed to reveal beliefs of two sorts concerning infant crying. Infant-directed beliefs "indicate a prioritization of infant needs, desires, and well-being . . . the notion that crying . . . serves adaptive functions and provides an opportunity for closeness" (Haltigan et al., 2012, p. 881). Examples of items from the Questionnaire that fit this category are "I want my baby to feel safe" and "I think that my baby is trying to tell me something." Parent-oriented beliefs, in contrast, assume that "crying serves little purpose and efforts should be made to ignore, minimize, or control crying" (Haltigan et al., 2012, p. 882). Examples in this category are "I want my baby to stop because crying doesn't accomplish anything" and "I let my baby cry it out so he/she doesn't get spoiled."

Not surprisingly, infant-oriented beliefs appear to be more adaptive. Relatively strong infant-oriented beliefs relate positively to maternal sensitivity in interacting with the infant at 6 months and negatively to infant behavior problems at 12 months (Haltigan et al., 2012). Other research with different approaches to measuring beliefs confirms the value of an infant-oriented approach (e.g., Zeifman, 2003). Two other findings from such research will sound familiar. On the average, mothers are higher in infant-oriented beliefs than are fathers. And there is evidence that each spouse's beliefs affect those of the other (Leerkes et al., 2010).

Not yet addressed is a problem that confronts roughly 15–20% of parents in the early weeks of the infant's life: infant colic. *Colic* is defined as inconsolable crying, primarily in the first 3 months, that begins and ends without warning. It is often discussed in terms of "Wessel's rule of 3's": an infant cries for more than 3 hours a day, for more than 3 days a week, for more than 3 weeks (Wessel, Cobb, Jackson, Harris, & Detwiler, 1954). A colicky baby adds considerable stress to a parent's life, stress that increases the likelihood of negative consequences for both the parent (e.g., guilt, depression) and the infant (e.g., abuse). Shaken baby syndrome is a particular concern (Peterson et al., 2014).

At present, there is no agreement about the causes of colic nor about the best ways to treat it, other than a general agreement that no treatment method has more than limited success (Kaley, Reid, & Flynn, 2011; Twomey, High, & Lester, 2012). Fortunately, there is evidence that attempts to educate parents about colic *can* have positive effects, not necessarily on amount of crying but on both parental well-being and the parent–child relationship (Fujiwara et al., 2012; Twomey et al., 2012). The focus of such approaches is on parents' beliefs and an attempt to make parents aware of several generally accepted conclusions that apply to most (although admittedly not all) cases of colic: that the parents did not cause the problem, that the parents' behaviors are not to blame for the continuation of the problem, and that the condition will soon resolve on its own with no lasting negative effects. Also important is the "walk away" principle: the realization that at times it is best simply to walk away from a crying baby rather than risk the harmful responses that may follow from yet more frustration and anger.

## Sleeping

This section addresses three topics. In this case, I begin with problems—the difficulties that some infants have with sleep and the parental beliefs that accompany, and in some cases precede, such difficulties.

The second and third topics have to do with where and how infant sleep occurs. The main issue under the where heading is *bed-sharing*: Should the infant share the parents' bed, or should such sharing be avoided? The main issue under the how heading is how the infant should be laid down to sleep: on the back, on the side, or on the stomach. In this case there is little dispute among experts about the correct answer: on the back. The question is whether parents realize this.

The sleep difficulty that parents identify most often is waking during the night, followed by problems at bed time and establishing a regular sleep schedule (Mindell, Leichman, Puzino, Walters, & Bhullar, 2015). Night waking is also a common target for intervention programs whose goal is to improve infant sleep (Field, 2017). And it is a focus of standardized instruments designed to measure parents' beliefs about sleep (e.g., Bessey, Coulombe, Smith, & Corkum, 2013; Morrell, 1999; Sadeh, Flint-Ofir, Tirosh, & Tikotzky, 2007). Table 5.3 provides a sampling of items from one such measure. As can be seen, the assessment includes the mother's beliefs not just about the infant but also about herself—in particular, how she should respond to nighttime awakening.

The mother's beliefs turn out to be important. A number of studies have demonstrated that beliefs that emphasize the infant's distress and the need for the parent to intervene are associated with a relatively high number of sleep problems (Morrell, 1999; Sadeh et al., 2007; Tikotzky & Sadeh, 2009).

Table 5.3  Examples of Items from the Maternal Cognitions About Infant Sleep Questionnaire

When my child cries at night, I think something awful may have happened to him/her.
When my child wakes at night, I think I might not have fed him/her enough during the day.
It is all right to allow my child to cry at night.
I should be getting up during the night to check that my child is still all right.
When my child wakes crying, I always know what he/she needs.
If I try to resist my child's demands at night, then he/she will get even more upset.
When my child doesn't sleep at night, I doubt my competence as a parent.
I am able to let my child sleep on his/her own.
When my child cries at night, I can find myself thinking I wish I had never had a child.
If I give up feeding at night, then he/she will never sleep.

Responses are made on a 6-point scale ranging from *strongly agree* to *strongly disagree*. Adapted from "The Role of Maternal Cognitions in Infant Sleep Problems as Assessed by a New Instrument, the Maternal Cognitions About Infant Sleep Questionnaire," by J. M. B. Morrell, 1999, *Journal of Child Psychology and Psychiatry, 40*, pp. 257–258. Copyright 1999 by John Wiley and Sons. Adapted with permission.

Thus an overly involved, protective approach apparently exacerbates rather than reduces the infant's difficulties.

Because these data are correlational, the issue of causal direction arises: Perhaps mothers are responding to rather than creating sleep problems in their children. Although such child-to-parent effects probably occur, longitudinal studies indicate that at least part of the causal direction is from mother to child and not the reverse. Indeed, mothers' beliefs about sleep assessed during the prenatal period are predictive of children's later sleep difficulties (Tikotzky & Sadeh, 2009).

What about fathers? The handful of studies that have included fathers suggest three conclusions (Reader, Teti, & Cleveland, 2017; Sadeh et al., 2007). First, fathers typically express less concern about sleep difficulties and indicate less need to intervene than do mothers. Second, despite this average difference, mothers' beliefs and fathers' beliefs about sleep are moderately related (correlations in the .30s and .40s). Finally, discrepancies between spouses in their beliefs are associated with difficulties in coparenting, that is, in the ability to maintain a balanced and harmonious relationship in parenting the child.

The work discussed so far has been primarily with Western samples, and this is a limitation. It has long been clear that beliefs about sleep vary across cultures; indeed, one of the chapters by Harkness and Super uses beliefs about sleep to introduce the notion of ethnotheories (Harkness & Super, 2002). Differences with respect to bed-sharing are especially marked. Bed-sharing is relatively uncommon (although far from nonexistent) in Western industrialized nations but is close to universal in many African and Asian societies. A tally by Mileva-Seitz and colleagues encompassing 45 countries reported a range from 6% in Israel to 100% in one Asian and four African countries (Mileva-Seitz, Bakermans-Kranenburg, Battaini, & Luijk, 2017). The value for the United States was intermediate (23%); it is important to note, however, that the rate varied substantially (from 5% to 88%) across the 30 US samples that were included.

The Mileva-Seitz et al. (2017) article also summarized results from 659 studies of bed-sharing (a fraction of the total literature—many studies did not meet their inclusion criteria). A sentence in their opening paragraph previews their conclusions: "The literature is often polarized, filled with interesting questions, creative designs, and, ultimately, insufficient evidence" (Mileva-Seitz et al., 2017, p. 4). Part of the reason for the uncertainty, despite such a massive research effort, is the nonexperimental nature of almost all of the relevant evidence. Researchers do not randomly assign parents to bed-share; rather, parents self-assign themselves to the groups being compared. Because of this lack of control, it is difficult to determine whether bed-sharing is the causal basis for any differences that are observed, as opposed to other ways in which the groups being compared may differ. It is also difficult, assuming that bed-sharing *is* a causal factor, to specify exactly what it is about bed-sharing that is important. Note that these same points apply to the main topic in the next section of the chapter: breastfeeding versus bottle feeding.

Of the many questions examined with respect to bed-sharing, three have been most prominent. One is method of feeding. In this case the conclusions are both relatively clear and relatively positive. Breastfeeding is more likely when infant and mother share a bed than it is when the infant sleeps separately, and breastfeeding bouts are typically more frequent, longer, and more productive when bed-sharing is in effect. When mothers are asked about the decision to bed-share, ease of breastfeeding is the most often cited reason (Ward, 2015). Other reasons that receive frequent endorsements include comfort for both mother and infant, ability to monitor the infant, and better sleep for infant or mother or both.

Quality of sleep is, in fact, another often examined outcome. Although the hoped-for improvements in sleep with bed-sharing are occasionally reported, difficulties in sleep are a more common finding (Mileva-Seitz et al., 2017). Whether such difficulties are a result or a cause of bed-sharing, however, remains controversial and may hinge on a distinction between two types of bed-sharing (Ramos, 2003). Some bed-sharing is intentional, in the sense that the parents have made a willing commitment to the process, often from the birth of the child. Other bed-sharing, however, is reactive, in the sense that parents feel compelled by circumstances to attempt bed-sharing, even though this was not their original intention. Infant sleep difficulties may be one of the unanticipated factors that lead to reactive bed-sharing. One theme of the Mileva-Seitz et al. (2017) review is that the intentional–reactive distinction remains understudied, not only with regard to sleep problems but with regard to correlates of bed-sharing more generally.

The third often studied topic with respect to bed-sharing is *sudden infant death syndrome* (SIDS): a sudden and unexpected infant death, almost always in the first few months, for which a cause cannot be determined (Task Force on Sudden Infant Death Syndrome, 2016). SIDS is one entry under the more general category of *sudden unexpected death in infancy* (SUDI), which includes not only unexplained deaths but those for which a cause can be identified (e.g., suffocation, asphyxia). As with almost every topic in the bed-sharing literature, results with respect to bed-sharing and infant death are mixed (Mileva-Seitz et al., 2017). Many studies report no relation, and other risk factors (e.g., maternal smoking, drug or alcohol use) are often present when relations do emerge. Nevertheless, the preponderance of evidence supporting a link with bed-sharing (more than half of the studies in the Mileva-Seitz et al. review reported a relation) has led the American Academy of Pediatricians to recommend against the practice (Task Force on Sudden Infant Death Syndrome, 2016). Their recommendation is that the infant sleep in the same room with the parents, not, however, in the same bed.

This recommendation, to put it mildly, is controversial. As the figures cited earlier indicate, millions of parents do not follow it, including virtually all parents in some countries and many parents in Western countries who are aware of the recommendation but choose to act otherwise. As Ward's (2015) review makes clear, parents have various reasons for the decision to bed-share, including presumed and in some cases actual benefits of the practice (e.g., ease of breastfeeding), distrust of expert opinion, belief that their specific approach can counter any dangers, and long-standing cultural tradition. Despite the position of the American Academy of Pediatricians, this is a view that is shared by many professionals who believe that their role should be to help make bed-sharing as safe and productive as possible, rather than to argue against a practice that is widespread, that carries clear benefits, and that is often deeply culturally ingrained (McKenna & Gettler, 2016, 2017).

Less controversial is the final topic to be considered: infant sleep position. That placing the infant in the supine or on-the-back position reduces the chances of SIDS has long been clear, and implementation of this knowledge in campaigns directed to parents (e.g., Back to Sleep) has resulted in clear effects: In the United States, deaths due to SIDS declined from 130 per 100,000 live births in 1990 to 38 per 100,000 live births in 2016 (Centers for Disease Control, 2018b). In contrast to the issue of bed-sharing, beliefs about sleep position are not widely embedded in cultural tradition, and, in contrast to bed-sharing, few arguments exist for an approach other than the recommended one. It is true that aspects of early motor development are slowed down when infants spend most of their time in the supine position, but this effect is easily countered by the provision of "tummy time," as current advice for parents recommends (Adolph & Robinson, 2015).

The issue, then, is one of education and compliance. Various principles, all expectable, emerge from educational efforts to date (Aitken et al., 2016;

Gaydos et al., 2015; Herman, Adkins, & Moon, 2015). First, it is important, especially when working with parents who are not part of the dominant culture, to be aware of any preexisting beliefs or practices that may need to be respected and addressed. Second, it is important to convey not only what should be done but also why it should be done, that is, to provide parents with a clear rationale for the on-the-back position. Finally, it is important to remember that parents may not be the only ones responsible for infant sleep; other socialization agents, perhaps grandparents in particular, should also be targets of educational efforts.

I will conclude this section with a point that is familiar to many parents. Although I do not attempt to address later time periods, children's sleep, including possible problems with sleep, is not an issue that necessarily disappears with the end of infancy (Nevsimalova & Bruni, 2017). Nor, of course, is the topic to be considered next confined to infancy. In most instances parents remain important determinants of their children's diets throughout much of childhood. In addition, older children and adolescents are at risk for eating problems not found in infancy, and such problems may be targets for considerable parental thought, emotion, and effort (Doyle & Le Grange, 2015). Again, however, the present coverage will be limited to the infant years.

## Eating

Just as consideration of a range of cultures enriches our understanding of beliefs about sleep, so does a cultural perspective add to what we know about feeding beliefs and practices. Perhaps the most striking example of this point comes from study of the !Kung people of southern Africa (Barr, 2011). !Kung mothers carry their infants with them wherever they go, they engage in frequent feeding (an average of four times per hour), and they typically respond immediately to frets and cries, usually through breastfeeding. Clearly, this example demonstrates not only beliefs about feeding but also beliefs about crying and how to calm a crying baby.

The !Kung example illustrates the two questions about feeding that have long been central to both parents and researchers: When should infants be fed, and how should they be fed? The !Kung answer to the when question is perhaps the most extreme example of an on-demand schedule: whenever the infant fusses, and up to four times or more per hour. The answer to the how question is the one that was once universal to the species: at the mother's breast. Now, of course, bottle feeding provides a possible alternative to the traditional approach.

The breast versus bottle, or breast milk versus formula milk, issue is easily the most often addressed question with regard to infant feeding. As with the issue of the safest position for infant sleep, there is expert consensus on the correct answer: Breast feeding is preferable to bottle feeding. Breast milk is nutritionally superior to formula milk, and breast milk reduces the likelihood of numerous early diseases and disorders, including several potentially fatal conditions. It has been estimated that universal or close to universal breastfeeding would result in 823,000 fewer child deaths every year (Victora et al., 2016). Breastfeeding has health benefits for the mother as well as for the baby; in particular, the probabilities of both breast cancer and ovarian cancer are substantially reduced when women breastfeed.

Benefits of breastfeeding extend beyond infancy and beyond effects on physical health. A large research literature indicates that children who were breastfed as infants have higher IQs than do children who were bottle-fed (Boutwell, Young, Young, & Meldrum, 2018; Kanazawa, 2015); there is also evidence that breastfeeding relates positively to later academic learning abilities (Kim et al., 2017). Breastfeeding is associated with various structural changes in the brain, and these changes provide a possible neurological basis for the behavioral differences that are observed (Ruby, Belden, Whalen, Harms, & Barch, 2016). I should add, however, that the breast versus bottle difference in IQ is not large (typically 2 to 4 points), it is not found in all studies (cf. Girard, Doyle, & Tremblay, 2017; von Stumm & Plomin, 2015), and it is sometimes reduced when various potential confounding factors (e.g., maternal IQ, family income) are statistically controlled. As noted, it is important to remember that almost all of the relevant evidence on the breast–bottle issue is correlational rather than experimental in nature.

Despite the qualifications just noted, the overall benefits of breastfeeding are unquestioned, yet breastfeeding remains a minority choice in the great majority of the world's cultures (Rollins et al., 2016). Extended breastfeeding—that is, continuation to at least 12 months—is especially unlikely, and this conclusion holds most strongly in wealthier nations. As Victora and colleagues note, this finding provides a rare instance in which poorer countries rank higher on a health-related practice than do wealthier ones (Victora et al., 2016).

As with safe sleep, various professional organizations have mounted efforts to increase the frequency and duration of breastfeeding (Arts, Taqi, & Begin, 2017; Bradford et al., 2017; Rollins et al., 2016). Important to such efforts is not only transmission of information about the value of breastfeeding but also the creation of conditions (e.g., maternal leave time, usable public spaces) that make breastfeeding possible. Possession of the relevant knowledge is a starting point, but it must be joined by the belief that one can act successfully upon the knowledge. The notion of beliefs about the ability to act successfully should sound familiar for it is a way of summarizing Bandura's concept of self-efficacy. And self-efficacy—specifically, breastfeeding self-efficacy—is in fact one of the determinants of successful breastfeeding (Bartle & Harvey, 2017; Martinez-Brockman, Shebl, Harari, & Perez-Escamilla, 2017).

## Temperament

The pioneering work on infant temperament was carried out by Thomas, Chess, and Birch (1968; Thomas & Chess, 1977), and these authors provided a definition of the concept that still applies.

> Temperament may best be viewed as a general term referring to the *how* of behavior. It differs from ability, which is concerned with the *what* and *how well* of behaving, and from motivation, which accounts for *why* a person does what he is doing. Temperament, by contrast, concerns the *way* in which an individual behaves. Temperament can be equated to the term *behavioral style.* (Thomas & Chess, 1977, p. 9)

Thomas and colleagues also provided a first instance of what has become the most common way to measure infant temperament: namely, parent report. Their conclusions about temperament were based on extensive interviews with the babies' mothers, interviews that asked about the infant's typical response to various common experiences (e.g., being put down for a nap, meeting a new person, being taken to the doctor). From the maternal interviews, the researchers were able to identify nine dimensions of temperament along which infants varied; examples include activity level, rhythmicity, attention span, and intensity of reaction. They also identified three general categories of temperament: easy, difficult, and slow to warm up.

More recent work on temperament typically retains only some of the dimensions and emphases from the Thomas et al. work (Chen & Schmidt, 2015). As noted, though, the parent-report approach to measurement remains common, via not only interviews but also questionnaires that the parent can fill out. Table 5.4 presents a sampling of items from one such questionnaire, a measure drawn from one of the most influential contemporary approaches to temperament, the work of Mary Rothbart and colleagues (Rothbart, 2011). I should note that this *is* a sampling; the full instrument includes 14 scales and 191 items.

Parent reports are not the only way to measure temperament. Physiological measures (e.g., heart rate, electroencephalogram [EEG]) can pick up on some aspects of temperament; furthermore, they can do so from very early in life, including in some instances the prenatal period (DiPietro, Voegtline, Pater, & Costigan, 2018). Behavioral measures are also used, typically in laboratory settings in which a standardized set of controlled experiences can be presented to the infant and temperament can be inferred from the infant's reactions to the various events (e.g., Goldsmith & Rothbart, 1991). In addition to being valuable in their own right, these additional forms of measurement provide important validation data with regard to the parent-report approach. The value of parent reports depends on their accuracy, and the only way to determine accuracy is to see whether such reports agree with other ways to measure the same target.

The evidence is that they agree moderately well but far from perfectly (Rothbart & Bates, 2006). Of course, lack of agreement among measures does not necessarily mean that it is the parent-report component that is in error. Laboratory tests place the child in an unfamiliar setting that may not elicit the child's typical behavior (although see Lo, Vroman, & Durbin, 2015, for a counterargument), and in any case, such measures are limited in the range of situations and behaviors that they can sample. It is the scope of information they provide—essentially anything that a mother has ever seen her child do—that constitutes the greatest strength of the parent-report approach. Indeed, one could argue that this is a special strength with regard to the measurement of temperament, considering the breadth of the target that is being assessed. And temperament, not coincidentally, is among the topics in developmental psychology for which parent reports have been most important.

The preceding is not meant to imply that parent reports do not carry their own problems and uncertainties. Lo et al. (2015) provide a list of the parental

**Table 5.4** Examples of Items from the Infant Behavior Questionnaire – Revised

| | | | Response choices | | | |
|---|---|---|---|---|---|---|
| 1 | 2 | 3 | 4 | 5 | 6 | 7 |
| Never | Very rarely | Less than half the time | About half the time | More than half the time | Almost Always | Always |

| Temperament scale | Sample items |
|---|---|
| Approach | When given a new toy, how often did the baby get very excited about getting it? |
| Vocal reactivity | When being dressed/undressed how often did the baby coo or vocalize? |
| High intensity pleasure | During a peek-a-boo game, how often did the baby smile? |
| Activity level | When put into the bath water, how often did the baby splash or kick? |
| Perceptual sensitivity | How often did the baby notice fabrics with scratchy texture (e.g., wool)? |
| Distress to limitations | When placed on his or her back, how often did the baby fuss or protest? |
| Fear | How often did the baby startle to a sudden or loud noise? |
| Cuddliness | When rocked or hugged, how often did the baby seem to enjoy himself or herself? |

Adapted from "Studying Infant Temperament via the Revised Infant Behavior Questionnaire," by M. A. Garstein and M. K. Rothbart, 2003, *Infant Behavior and Development, 26*, p. 72. Copyright 2003 by Elsevier. Adapted with permission.

(usually maternal) characteristics that have been shown to affect judgments of temperament, including stress, anxiety, depression, alcoholism, and marital discord. In some instances maternal characteristics assessed during the prenatal period have proved predictive of later temperament ratings. Such findings do not mean that temperament as assessed by parent report is all maternal perception—just that some proportion of the variance may reside in the mother rather than in the child.

Parents' contribution to the temperament literature extends well beyond their role as informants for parent-report measures. A substantial proportion of the research directed to temperament, especially in infancy and early childhood, has explored relations between parenting practices and children's temperaments. That there are relations has long been clear. Furthermore, it has long been clear that the causal basis for such relations runs in both directions (Bates & Pettit, 2015). Although temperament clearly has a biological underpinning, children's experiences can affect how temperament develops, and in most instances parents are the major source of relevant experiences. In particular, parents' child-rearing practices are an important determinant of the fate of early forms of difficult temperament (e.g., high negativity, low self-control). A consistently warm, sensitive, and patient approach on the parent's part is associated with reductions in negative temperamental qualities over time; conversely, a generally harsh style of parenting is likely to exacerbate the early difficulties (Bates & Pettit, 2015).

Not only does parenting affect temperament; temperament affects parenting. Indeed, various effects of temperament are probably the most often cited examples of ways in which children affect their parents. Early negative temperament again provides an example. Parents faced with a child with a difficult temperament have been found to respond in either of two ways (Putnam, Sanson, & Rothbart, 2002). Most commonly, and perhaps predictably, such parents show lower levels of warmth and involvement in interactions with their infant than do parents whose baby provides an easier, more enjoyable interaction partner. In some instances, however, parents may make a special effort to cope with the challenges of a difficult temperament, and in these instances it may be the difficult child who receives heightened levels of parental involvement and responsiveness. In either case, the effects of the child's temperament show a clear child-to-parent causal direction. Recall also two findings discussed in Chapter 4: Difficult child temperament is associated with both lower parenting self-efficacy and lower parenting satisfaction.

A further point about child-to-parent effects is important to note. In some instances such effects are immediate ones; a tantrum, for example, may elicit an attempt at comforting, just as a distracted response may elicit a redirection of attention. Over time, however, it is the general characteristics of the child that shape parental behavior—thus, for example, not just occasional but habitual difficulties with behavioral control or maintenance of attention. Furthermore, it is the general characteristics as interpreted by the parent, the view of the child that the parent has abstracted from innumerable specific instances of tantrums, wandering attention, or whatever. Thus it is parents' beliefs that guide parents' behavior (Karraker & Coleman, 2005).

As always, conclusions about development are enriched when research moves beyond a few often-studied settings to encompass a wider range of the world's cultures. Although some basic aspects of temperament may well be universal, the frequency of different forms of temperament varies across different cultural settings (Chen & Schmidt, 2015; Super et al., 2008). These differences, moreover, show clear relations to parental beliefs and related parental practices. For example, a shy, inhibited temperamental pattern is more common among Chinese and South Korean children than it is for children in Western societies (Rubin et al., 2006). In Western cultures, such a temperamental pattern is generally regarded as problematic, and parents often work to make their timid child more confident and assertive. In China, in contrast, a reserved, nonassertive behavioral style is both culturally valued and culturally adaptive, and parents are therefore more likely to nurture than to change such characteristics in their child (Chen & French, 2008).

## Attachment

The construct of attachment was introduced in Chapter 2. Although that discussion focused on adults, it also described the most influential procedure for studying attachment in infancy: the Strange Situation procedure devised by Mary Ainsworth and colleagues (Ainsworth, Blehar, Waters, & Wall, 1978). Here I add what is undoubtedly the second most influential approach to the study of early attachment: the Attachment Q-Set (AQS) procedure developed by Everett Waters (1995; Waters & Deane, 1985).

In contrast to the Strange Situation, the AQS is grounded in behaviors observed in the natural setting. Table 5.5 presents a sampling of the 90 items that make up the measure. Note that in some cases (e.g., the first several items

**Table 5.5** Examples of Items from the Attachment Q-Set

| Item number | Description |
|---|---|
| 1 | Child readily shares with mother or lets her hold things if she asks to. |
| 11 | Child often hugs or cuddles against mother without her asking or inviting him to do so. |
| 21 | Child keeps track of mother's location when he plays around the house. Calls to her now and then; notices her go from room to room. |
| 71 | If held in mother's arms, child stops crying and quickly recovers after being frightened or upset. |
| 73 | Child has a cuddly toy or security blanket that he carries around, takes to bed, or holds when upset. |
| 76 | When given a choice, child would rather play with toys than with adults. |
| 79 | Child easily becomes angry at mother. |
| 81 | Child cries as a way of getting mother to do what he wants. |

From "The Attachment Q-Set (Version 3.0), " by E. Waters, 1995, *Monographs of the Society for Research in Child Development, 60* (2-3, Serial No. 244), pp. 236–246. Copyright 1995 by the Society for Research in Child Development. Reprinted with permission of John Wiley and Sons.

listed) a positive response is indicative of a satisfactory attachment, whereas in other cases (e.g., the last two items) it is the infrequency of the characteristic that is desirable. As with the q-sort approach in general, the person rating the child makes a series of sequential judgments about the degree to which the listed behaviors are characteristic of the child's typical behavior. It is the overall picture provided by this rich array of information that constitutes the child's attachment assessment.

Not yet indicated is who makes these judgments. There are two possibilities. In some cases trained observers visit the home for several hours and make observations of mother–infant interaction. In other cases the parent (almost always the mother) provides the ratings of her child's typical behavior. Attachment, then, is another topic for which parent reports play an important role in the literature.

How accurate are such reports? In this case there are two comparisons of interest. One is with AQS ratings made by trained observers. Waters and Deane (1985) reported an average correlation of .80 in ratings between mothers and observers, a substantial, albeit less than perfect, degree of agreement. Of course, the correlation does not tell us whose judgment is closer to the truth in cases of disagreement; the authors suggest, however, that "in many instances, the differences were clearly examples of the mother having better access to the behavior than the observers did" (p. 59).

The second comparison is with conclusions from the Strange Situation procedure. In this case maternal reports fare less well. AQS ratings by trained observers correlate moderately well with results from the Strange Situation; the relation is a good deal lower, however, when mothers are the source for the reports (Cadman, Diamond, & Fearon, 2018; van IJzendoorn, Vereijken, Bakermanns-Kraneburg, & Riksen-Walraven, 2004). As van IJzendoorn and colleagues note, such discrepancies between measures do not necessarily reflect measurement error on one or the other side for the measures may be capturing different aspects of the target construct. Still, the data do suggest caution in using maternal reports as the sole measure of attachment.

As in the study of temperament, the importance of parents in the attachment literature extends well beyond their role in the assessment of the construct. Attachment is an inherently social development—that is, not simply a set of related behaviors but rather behaviors that reflect the nature of a relationship with another person. For the great majority of babies, that other person is a parent. A central question, therefore, is what parents do that either promotes or fails to promote secure attachment.

There is no single or simple answer to this question. Research does converge, however, on the importance of one contributor, a contributor first identified in one of the pioneering studies of attachment, that by Mary Ainsworth and colleagues (Ainsworth et al., 1978). In Ainsworth et al.'s words, "The most important aspect of maternal behavior . . . is manifested in different specific ways in different situations, but in each it emerges as sensitive responsiveness to infant signals and communications" (p. 152). Important are both the willingness to respond to one's baby and the ability to do so effectively; that is, to read signals accurately and respond in a way that speaks to the child's immediate need.

What sort of parental beliefs might underlie sensitive responsiveness? Three possible contributors have received the most attention in the literature.

A first was introduced in Chapter 2: parents' working models of their own attachment relationships. As we saw in Chapter 2, research with the Adult Attachment Interview indicates that adults do have working models of important interpersonal relationships, models that have their origins in their own attachment histories. As Table 2.4 shows, these models take different forms that correspond roughly to the forms of attachment identified in childhood—thus a secure, generally satisfactory form and various types of insecure, less satisfactory forms. If these working models affect how parents treat their own children, we can make two predictions: Parents whose working models fall in the secure/autonomous category should show higher levels of sensitive responsiveness than do parents in general, and the children of such parents should be more likely to form secure attachments than are children in general.

Research confirms both of these predictions (Kondo-Ikemura, Behrens, Umemura, & Nakano, 2018); van IJzendoorn, 1995; Verhage et al., 2016). It also reveals a puzzling third finding, however, and that is that sensitivity at best accounts for only part of the effect of working models—that is, sensitivity does not fully mediate the relation between parents' working models and children's attachment. There is, then, a "transmission gap" in the evidence with regard to how attachment is passed from one generation to the next, and therefore a need to search for other beliefs and related behaviors that may contribute to the transmission.

One possibility is the recently formulated concept of *secure base scripts* (Vaughn et al., 2006; Waters & Waters, 2006). A central feature of a satisfactory attachment is a *secure base*: an attachment figure who is available when needed and who is a consistent source of comfort and support. A secure base script is a representation of the degree to which a secure base can be counted on when needed, a representation derived from the individual's history of close interpersonal relationships. As so described, a secure base script sounds similar to a working model, and, in fact, the two concepts are related. A secure base script, however, is a more focused, more specific, and more potentially testable formulation. It has the virtue of focusing on a key feature of the attachment relationship, and it also has the virtue of a grounding in cognitive psychology, within which the notion of scripts has long been an important theoretical construct.

Because a secure base script is an implicit form of knowledge, it cannot be elicited by direct questioning. The usual approach is the *prompt-word method*: A series of words is presented, and the participant is asked to create a story using the words. Table 5.6 provides an example of the method and of responses that do and do not reflect secure base scripts.

A growing research literature indicates that secure base scripts show the correlational relations that we would expect if they are an important contributor to parenting and to attachment (Hawkins, Madigan, Moran, & Pederson, 2015; Vaughn et al., 2007). Such scripts relate to (but also are distinct from) working models as assessed by the Adult Attachment Interview, they relate

**Table 5.6** Examples of Secure Base Scripts as Elicited by the Word-Prompt Method

---

*Word Prompts*

Mother hug teddy bear baby smile lost play story found blanket pretend nap

*Narrative with Clear Secure Base Script Structure*

A mother and baby were playing one morning. Mother would hide under a blanket and then jump out and the baby would smile and hug her and then do the same thing. Then they read a story. And then the baby wanted to play with his teddy bear, but it was lost and he got upset. But Mother found it and said "Here it is. He's ok." And the baby was happy and they played some more and then the baby took a nap.

*Narrative Lacking Secure Base Script Structure*

A mother was watching her baby play with a blanket in his crib. He would smile and hug the blanket. After a while, the mother wanted to read him a story. She knew he was too little to understand but she liked sitting with him and his teddy bear and pretending to read to them. But today the teddy bear was lost. And by the time she found it, the baby was already taking a nap. So they didn't have a story today.

---

From "The Attachment Working Models Concept: Among Other Things, We Build Script-Like Representations of Secure Base Experiences," by H. S. Waters and E. Waters, 2006, *Attachment and Human Development, 8,* p. 190. Copyright 2006 by Taylor and Francis Ltd. Reprinted with permission.

to the sensitivity with which parents treat their children, and they relate to the probability that the children will form secure attachments. Longitudinal research demonstrates that secure base scripts also show the developmental origins that we would expect—that they are most likely in adults who experienced sensitive parenting when they themselves were children (Waters, Ruiz, & Roisman, 2017).

Both working models and secure base scripts concentrate on parents' beliefs about close relationships, beliefs that largely predate their experiences as parents. A third approach focuses more directly on beliefs about one's child. Responsive parenting depends on the ability to read signals from the child accurately; thus, knowledge of one's child is an almost by-definition component of sensitive responsiveness. Various researchers have attempted to specify the kinds of knowledge that are important. I concentrate here on research by Elizabeth Meins and colleagues (Meins, 1997, 2013; Meins et al., 2012); for related approaches, see Fonagy and Target (1997) and Shai and Belsky (2017).

The core construct in the Meins approach is *mind-mindedness,* which Meins and colleagues define as "caregivers' proclivity to treat their young children as individuals with minds of their own" (Meins, Fernyhough, Arnott, Leekam, & de Rosnay, 2013, p. 1778). Mind-mindedness, then, is the realization that even infants are mental beings with thoughts, desires, emotions, and so forth, and that parenting requires an appreciation of the infant's current mental state. The main way in which the construct is measured in parents of infants is through mental state comments that mothers direct to their infants during free play, comments such as "You like that toy," or "You want that ball." Of interest are both the frequency of such comments and their appropriateness—that is, has the mother accurately judged her infant's mental state? Mothers who produce a high level of appropriate mental state comments rate highest in mind-mindedness.

Being high in mind-mindedness turns out to be a positive parental attribute. Mothers' mind-mindedness relates positively to security of attachment in their infants. Mothers' mind-mindedness also relates positively to the sensitivity with which they interact with their infants; indeed, even prenatal assessments of mind-mindedness predict eventual maternal sensitivity (Foley & Hughes, 2018). Consistently, however, the Meins research program finds that mind-mindedness is a stronger predictor of security of attachment than is sensitivity as it is typically measured. Meins (2013) argues, in fact, that the concept of mind-mindedness recaptures aspects of Ainsworth's original conception of sensitive responsiveness that have often been neglected in subsequent research. In particular, it highlights the importance of not just maternal behaviors but also maternal beliefs.

Attachment is not the only development for which parental mind-mindedness has proved to be important. We will see in Chapter 6 that mind-mindedness also contributes to the development of theory of mind in older children.

This discussion has concentrated on what is known about the origins of attachment—thus, attachment as a dependent variable. The other major question addressed in the literature concerns the consequences of attachment—thus, attachment as an independent variable. Does the quality of the early attachment relationship make a difference for other aspects of the child's development? A large research literature indicates that it does. In the words of one summary, attachment has been shown to relate to "a truly dizzying array of later outcomes" (Thompson, 2013, p. 205). A partial list of these outcomes includes sibling relations, peer relations, social competence, self-esteem, problem solving, academic performance, theory of mind, and romantic relationships in adulthood (Berlin, Cassidy, & Appleyard, 2008;

Bornstein, 2014). In all of these instances, children with secure attachments fare better than those whose attachments are less secure. Attachment, then, makes a difference in children's lives. And parents, as we have seen, make a difference in the development of attachment. Given the centrality of attachment to children's development, there is perhaps no topic in developmental psychology for which parental beliefs and related behaviors are more important.

# 6

# Childhood: Cognitive Development

The school should spend a lot of time helping children develop their creativity, and make them creative people. So that they can draw and paint and express themselves in different ways through dance and such, which is so much more important and worthwhile than knowing how to write and read, for that will come automatically anyway.

—(Harkness et al., 2011, p. 810)

As a parent I'm convinced of the fact you can contribute to the intelligence of your child. Reading from a good book, interacting about that to expand their intellect is a start, involving your child in a lot of interactions and answering their questions, helps constructing knowledge. It makes a remarkable difference when they enter the primary school, it makes the transfer to school much easier.

—(Moussaoui and Braster 2011), p. 374)

I think reading is one of the most important things to do. I think it's very informative for children, even though they can't read. You can read to them, it's important for them to hear stories. By reading books, they can develop knowledge about different subjects.

—(Moussaoui and Braster, 2011, p. 377)

It's a terrific time for learning. All she understands is the fun part. She has no idea that she is being taught, due to my rebelling against it. As far as she's concerned we use counting so she can come and find me in hide and seek, and that's the big part. As far as she's concerned she's just learning a new song, which she loves to sing, or she's actually curious as to how many Barbies she really has.

—(Cannon and Ginsburg, 2008, p. 251)

*Parents' Beliefs About Children.* Scott A. Miller, Oxford University Press (2020). © Oxford University Press.
DOI: 10.1093/oso/9780190874513.001.0001

This chapter and the next address parents' beliefs about development during the childhood years, that is, the time period between the end of infancy and the onset of adolescence. This chapter discusses beliefs about children's cognitive development, and the next chapter adds a comparable treatment of beliefs about children's social development.

What aspects of cognitive development might be targets for parents' thinking? Any child psychology textbook provides a starting point for this question. A textbook—or a survey of relevant journals—will reveal the topics that child psychologists have believed are important to study. Are these the topics that appear in the parents' beliefs literature?

The answer for the most part is yes. As we will see, however, some topics have been relatively neglected in comparison to others. Also, although the topics studied are sometimes those spontaneously brought up by parents, more often it is the researcher who decides what will be discussed. And it is, of course, not surprising that researchers ask parents about the things that researchers believe are important.

## Academic Performance

Work under this heading constitutes the largest literature to be covered in this chapter, with the relevant studies numbering in the hundreds. It is also arguably the most pragmatically important literature. I begin, therefore, with parents' beliefs about their children's academic performance.

Four features of this literature distinguish it from much of the research discussed in this book. The first is that parents receive explicit feedback about their child's academic performance. This feedback takes various forms (test scores, achievement test results, grades), and it comes on many occasions across many years. There is no other aspect of development for which such frequent and explicit feedback is available.

The second feature is related. As we will see, a common dependent variable in studies under the "Cognitive" heading is judgment of the child's ability—how many problems of a particular sort can the child solve, what score will be earned on an IQ test, and so forth. Such judgments are sometimes elicited in the academic realm, especially predictions of future performance. Judgments of current performance are not very common, however.

They are not very common for the obvious reason that the parent already knows how the child performs having received multiple forms of relevant feedback. The interest, rather, is in *why* the child performs as he or she does. Explanations for the why of behavior are at the core of attribution theory, and this literature therefore provides one of the major applications of attribution theory to the study of parents' beliefs.

A third distinguishing feature of this work is a focus on possible gender differences between children. The variable of gender takes two forms in the parents' beliefs literature, just as it does in the developmental psychology literature in general. In some instances gender comparisons are incidental to the main purpose of the research but are included simply as a further, easy-to-provide piece of information, given that the great majority of studies include both sexes. In other instances possible gender differences are the primary focus of the research. The latter is the case for much of the research to be considered now. In particular, the possible contribution of parents' beliefs to gender differences in math and science has been the impetus for several dozen studies.

The final distinguishing feature is the cross-cultural nature of much of the research. In particular, Asian countries, especially Japan (e.g., Holloway, Kashiwagi, Hess, & Azuma, 1986) and China (e.g., Stevenson & Lee, 1990), have long been the subject of concentrated research attention. As we will see, the studies of academic performance provide some of the clearest evidence for cultural differences in what parents believe and in the effects that their beliefs have.

The discussion of beliefs about academic performance is divided into three sections. It opens with studies directed to parents' attributions for their children's successes or failures in school. After a consideration of the issues involved in the study of attributions, the discussion moves on to various group comparisons (mothers–fathers, parents–teachers, different cultures) that provide evidence about the origins of attributional beliefs. The discussion of attributions also includes work directed to the two other major issues in the study of parents' beliefs in addition to origins: effects of beliefs on parents' behavior and effects of beliefs on children's development.

Important though they are, attributions do not exhaust the ways in which parents think about their children's lives in school. The second section adds coverage of another important and frequently studied topic: parents' expectations for their children's academic performance and future development. As we will see, expectations play an important role with respect to both of the

**Table 6.1** Further Topics in the Study of Parents' Beliefs About Academic Performance

| Topic | Example |
| --- | --- |
| Atypical development | Skibbe, Justice, Zucker, and McGinty (2008) |
| School-related anxiety | Karing, Dorfler, and Artelt (2015) |
| School readiness | Belfield and Garcia (2014) |
| School fit | Bahena, Schueler, McIntyre, and Gehlbach (2016) |
| School climate | Schueler, Capotosto, Bahena, McIntyre, and Gehlbach (2014) |
| School satisfaction | Chen (2001) |

issues singled out for special attention: effects of culture and effects of child gender.

Relations between beliefs and parental behavior will be addressed at various points in the first two sections. The final section under the "Academic" heading provides a fuller coverage of the issue. Of interest are both parents' involvement with their children's school and the outside-of-school activities that prepare for and support school learning.

The literature on academic beliefs is easily the most diverse and multifaceted literature encountered in this chapter—indeed, perhaps in the book as a whole. Both its size and its diversity preclude an exhaustive coverage of every issue and related body of research. Table 6.1 provides a list of other topics that make up the larger literature, along with an example source for each.

## Attributions

As the "Methods" section of Chapter 2 noted, presenting actual instances of children's behavior as targets for parents' beliefs can often be a challenge. The present topic, however, is relatively easy in this regard. Performance in school is both a familiar and an easily conveyed form of child behavior, and it lends itself to questions of a variety of sorts.

The most often-asked question is why the child performs as he or she does—that is, what are the parent's attributions for the child's performance? We saw in Chapter 2 that studies of attributions tend to focus either on specific causes (e.g., ability, effort) or on underlying dimensions (e.g., stability, controllability). Research on academic performance has primarily taken the former approach. As Table 2.4 indicates, however, causes are generally regarded as providing information about underlying dimensions as well. Thus an attribution to effort, for example, is typically assumed to imply several further beliefs: that the behavior was under the child's control; that the child therefore bears responsibility for the behavior; and that effort, and therefore the behavior, might change in the future.

Methods of eliciting attributions fall on a continuum from completely open-ended (e.g., "Why do you think that your child got that grade?") to maximally closed-choice (e.g., "Pick one of the following as the explanation for your child's grade"). Most studies employ closed-choice methods that offer the parent the possibility of rating or ranking several possible causes. The preponderance of closed-choice measures mirrors what we have seen is the typical approach in the parents' beliefs literature as a whole.

Most commonly, the causes offered for rating or ranking are some version of the four causes shown in Table 2.2. In fact, for most respondents, the options reduce to ability and effort, for task difficulty and luck typically receive few endorsements. Two other possible causes, however, are offered in a number of studies, and both are accorded some importance in parental thinking. One is parental help. The other is school teaching.

However attributions are elicited, parents differ in the explanations they offer for their children's academic performance. As always, a basic question is where these differences come from. We will consider two forms of evidence: comparisons among different judges and comparisons among different child targets—specifically, boys versus girls.

Although mothers, as usual, are the more often studied parent, fathers appear in a relatively high proportion of the studies of attributions for academic outcomes. Teachers have also been included in several studies. Comparisons among these three judges speak to two general issues. One is the issue just identified, that of the origins of beliefs. Mothers, fathers, and teachers have different amounts and kinds of experience with children, and they may also bring different biases to the task of judging children. The second issue is that of the consistency of the attributional messages that the child receives, a factor that is known to influence the effect that attributions have.

An earlier review of these issues offered several general conclusions (Miller, 1995). The first was that similarities between parents are a more common outcome than are differences. More recent research has not changed this conclusion. Scattered differences between mothers and fathers do appear, of course, but the differences do not seem to follow any consistent pattern.

A second conclusion from the earlier review was a null one. At that time, no conclusions could be drawn about concordance between spouses because no study had reported the relevant information. Although such analyses remain infrequent, the most extensive examination of the issue—a longitudinal study with close to 3,000 parents—reported substantial degrees of spouse concordance in beliefs about the contribution of ability to the child's performance in math and reading, a finding that held both within time periods and in longitudinal patterns over time (Enlund, Aunola, Tolvanen, Lerkkanen, & Nurmi, 2017). Mothers' and fathers' general attributional styles—that is, not just child-specific attributions but attributions more generally— also show moderately strong concordance (Khodayarifard, Brinthaupt, & Anshel, 2010).

A third conclusion concerned the parent–teacher comparison. To my knowledge, no further studies of the issue have joined those available at the time of the original review (Bar-Tal & Guttmann, 1981; Beckman, 1976; Holloway & Hess, 1985), and I therefore reiterate the points made there. A first point mirrors one of the conclusions from the mother–father comparisons, and it is that the similarities between judges are more common than are differences. In the Holloway and Hess (1985) study, none of the parent-teacher comparisons reached significance, and nonsignificant comparisons outweighed significant ones in the other two reports. Despite this general similarity, the one examination of concordance, that by Holloway and Hess, found little agreement in parents' and teachers' judgments for particular children. When differences between judges do occur, there is some, although not strong, evidence for self-serving biases, in that both parents and teachers tend to make judgments that reflect positively on the self. There is also some evidence, although again limited, that differences may arise from parents' and teachers' use of the different kinds of evidence available to them. Beckman (1976) provides a discussion of this possibility.

A further comparison of judges addressed in the original review came from cross-cultural research—in particular, comparisons between parents from Asian countries (primarily China and Japan) and parents from Western countries (primarily the United States). In this case a clear pattern of differences emerged, albeit with some exceptions and qualifications. The pattern was most clearly illustrated by attributions for success or failure in math during the late grade-school years. Parents in both Asian and Western countries judged effort as a more important contributor than ability, especially when judging their children's failures. In general, attributions of lack of ability seem to be a difficult evaluation for parents in any culture to make. The emphasis on effort, however, was considerably stronger for Asian parents than it was for Western parents, a conclusion that is supported by more recent examinations of the issue (e.g., Kinlaw, Kurtz-Coster, & Goldman-Fraser, 2001; Phillipson (2006). The review summarized this conclusion as follows:

> Asian parents, more than American parents, are likely to believe that children are born with the same amount of ability, that differences in achievement are therefore determined primarily by the effort expended, and that any child should be able to do well if he or she simply tries hard enough. (Miller, 1995, p. 1570)

What are the possible effects of such an attributional pattern on children's development? There are two outcomes of interest. One is an effect on the children's own attributions. If, for example, a child's parents believe strongly in the role of effort, will the child adopt a similar belief? A number of studies, both the cultural comparisons just discussed and studies of attributions more generally, have examined this question. At the level of group comparisons there is evidence for both similarities and differences. The cultural comparisons provide evidence for similarities across generations, in that Asian children are more likely to stress effort than are Western children. But there are also generational differences that suggest a self-serving bias on the part of children. Specifically, children are more likely than parents to credit success to effort and to blame failure on lack of ability—thus a factor that they can control when they do well and a factor that is beyond their control when they do poorly.

The group-level analyses, of course, do not tell us about within-family similarity. Results with respect to parent–child concordance are mixed—fairly strong similarity in some studies (e.g., Bird & Berman, 1985; O'Sullivan & Howe, 1996), very little similarity in other studies (e.g., Georgiou, 1999; Phillipson, 2006). There is some evidence that the similarity is greater when the attributions concern a single target (e.g., performance in math) than when they concern school achievement in general. The evidence is not perfectly consistent, however, and the question of the basis for variations in parent–child concordance remains to be resolved.

The second possible effect of parents' attributions is on children's academic performance. In fact, it was differences in academic performance—specifically, superior performance in math by children in Asian countries—that sparked the interest in the Asian–Western cross-cultural comparisons. The results from such comparisons are certainly compatible with a causal role for parental attributions: Asian parents make more adaptive, development-enhancing attributions than do Western parents; Asian parents are more likely to behave in ways that support school achievement (e.g., help with homework, outside-of-school tuition) than are Western parents; and Asian children perform better in school than do Western children. As I noted in my earlier review (Miller, 1995), however, a weakness of the early literature was that the demonstrated relations remained at the group rather than within-individual, within-family levels. Thus there was no demonstration that a particular parent's attributions related to *that parent's* behavior and to the development of *that parent's* child. Although the evidence on this point is still not all that might be wished in terms of either quantity or consistency, more recent studies do provide some evidence for expected within-family relations, a finding that holds for both Asian and Western families (e.g., Chen, 2001; Phillipson, 2006).

As is true of most of the parents' beliefs literature, the findings just noted are correlational, which means that the issue of causal direction arises. Perhaps the attributions that parents make are responses to rather than causes of how their children perform in school. As we have seen at various points, longitudinal research provides a way to disentangle these possibilities through the examination of across-time relations between the variables in question. If attributions are the causal factor, then we would expect attributions at time 1 to relate to academic performance at time 2; if the causal direction is the reverse, then the pattern of relations will also be reversed.

In fact, both relations are found. Attributions early in the child's school life relate to later academic performance, but early academic performance also predicts later attributions (Enlund, Aunola, & Nurmi, 2015; Natale, Aunola, & Nurmi, 2009). We have, then, a prime example of the transactional model discussed in Chapter 2. Parents affect their children, but children also affect their parents.

Longitudinal research also speaks to another question of interest: namely, the stability of parents' attributions. As we have just seen, attributions are not perfectly stable, for they may change in response to the child's school performance. Beyond the early grade-school years, however, the degree of stability is substantial, including across an 8-year span in one study (Enlund et al., 2015). As I suggested earlier (Miller, 1995), most parents apparently decide early on about the bases for their child's school performance, and most maintain their beliefs over time.

The final issue to be considered in this section concerns the target for attributions: boy or girl. Most of the research on gender as a determinant of parents' beliefs has concentrated on math, a domain in which gender-stereotypical beliefs suggest that differences exist (boys more interested, more talented, etc.). But math is not the only academic domain that is subject to stereotypes, and thus science (stereotypically masculine) and reading, music, and art (stereotypically feminine) also appear in some studies.

If a parent subscribes to the stereotype for math, an attributional pattern is easy to predict. Because boys are good at math, their successes in that domain should be attributed to ability and their failures should be attributed to lack of effort. For girls the pattern should be the reverse: success as a result of effort, and failure as a result of lack of ability.

As both my earlier review (Miller, 1995) and more recent reviews (e.g., Simpkins, Fredericks, & Eccles, 2015) indicate, this pattern is sometimes found (e.g., Raty, Vanska, Kasanen, & Karkkainen, 2002) but is by no means always found (e.g., Cote & Azar, 1997). Adherence to the stereotypes clearly varies among parents, and thus the messages that children receive also vary. Expected relations between parents' attributions and children's academic performance are also sometimes but not always found, that is, increased interest and success over time when the domain of study matches the stereotype for the child's gender and parents support the stereotype, decreased interest and success over time when success is counterstereotypical.

The message from the preceding should not be surprising. Academic performance is multiply determined, and parents' stereotypic attributions and related behaviors are at best one of the determinants. In addition, attributions are not the only potentially important parental belief. The expectations that parents hold for their children's academic performance also play an important role in the gender differences literature, especially through the work of Jacquelynne Eccles and colleagues (e.g., Simpkins et al., 2015). It is to this work that I turn next.

## Expectations

"Expectations" are in a sense a straightforward object of study, for the term has the same meaning in research as it has in the language: namely, beliefs about what will occur—in the present case, a parent's belief about what will occur in her child's future academic life. As operationalized, however, the construct takes various forms, with the most obvious variation coming in the time scale involved. In some instances the expectation is a short-term one, such as predictions of upcoming grades (e.g., Entwisle & Hayduck, 1978); in other instances it is considerably more long-term, such as expectations for the most advanced degree that the child will eventually attain (e.g., Briley, Harden, & Tucker-Drob, 2014) or the occupation that the child will eventually hold (e.g., Shipman, McKee, & Bridgeman, 1976). The form of the question may also vary. Although most studies ask only about the highest level of expected achievement, parents may also be asked about the minimum level that they would find acceptable or about both a maximum and minimum (e.g., Okagaki & Frensch, 1998).

Whatever the specific target for judgment, most parental expectations reflect the weighting of two contributing factors. One is the parent's objective evaluation of the child's ability to perform a particular task or to achieve a certain outcome. Central, then, is the question that recurs throughout this book: How accurately can parents judge their children? Particularly when the target is a short-term and circumscribed one (e.g., a grade on next week's test), parents' expectations may be a direct reflection of such judgments of competence. Suppose, however, that the target is both larger and more delayed, such as a belief about the highest level of education that the child will attain. In such instances objective evaluations are likely to be joined by values and goals—thus not just what is likely to occur but what is hoped to occur. They may also be joined by intentions: a commitment on the parent's part to work toward the hoped-for outcome. Some authors use the term *aspiration* to refer to hoped-for rather than objectively expected outcomes (e.g., Murayama, Pekrun, Suzuki, Marsh, & Lichtenfeld, 2015); most, however, do not distinguish between the two concepts.

In what follows I first discuss what we know about the objective component; that is, parents' ability to judge their children's academic competence. The rest of the chapter will add to the points made in this section, given that parental knowledge will be a recurring theme across all of the topics considered.

Studies of beliefs about academic competence support several conclusions (e.g., Aunola, Nurmi, Lerkkanen, & Rasku-Puttonen, 2003; Korat, 2011; Pezdek, Berry, & Renno, 2002). Parents are moderately accurate in judging their children's academic abilities, a conclusion that holds for both mothers and fathers and for a range of academic subjects. Typical correlations between parental estimates and objective measures are in the .5 to .7 range, although lower values are sometimes reported (e.g., Sonnenschein, Metzger, & Stapleton, 2014). When parents err, they tend to overestimate what their children can do. In one study, for example, parents' estimates of their children's math performance were 30% higher than the actual performance (Pezdek et al., 2002). Most studies have focused on parents of kindergarten and first-grade children, and thus a time period before parents have received extensive school feedback. When families are followed longitudinally across the school years, parents' expectations, like parents' attributions, show fairly strong stability, although there may eventually be a dip when initially overly optimistic beliefs are not fulfilled (Raty & Kasanen, 2013).

The central question in the study of parents' expectations is whether expectations relate to children's school performance. A large body of research makes clear that the answer is yes: the more positive the parents' expectations, the better the child's performance (Child Trends, 2015c; Elliott & Bachman, 2018; Simpkins et al., 2015). This finding holds for different cultures, for different ethnic or socioeconomic groups within a culture, for high-risk samples, for different ages, and for both boys and girls. It also holds for the cultural comparisons discussed earlier. Asian parents hold higher expectations, on the average, than do Western parents, and Asian children, on the average, outperform Western children.

As with many developments, the relation between expectations and performance is a reciprocal, transactional one. As longitudinal studies show, children's early school performance can affect later parental expectations, and there is also evidence from twin research that children's genetically given characteristics can affect expectations (Briley et al., 2014). Longitudinal research, however, also supports a causal role for expectations for a consistent finding is that what parents expect early in development relates to how their children perform later in development. There is also experimental evidence for an effect: Increasing parents' expectations leads to beneficial changes in parental behavior (e.g., in how they read with their children) and to improvements in children's academic performance (Loughlin-Presnal & Bierman, 2017).

What do the studies of expectations tell us about the issue of gender differences? As with attributions, the expected pattern for parents with gender-stereotypical beliefs is easy to predict: high expectations when the stereotype for the domain matches the child's gender (e.g., math for boys, reading for girls), lower expectations when there is a mismatch. And as with attributions, tests of the predictions turn out to be mixed—not all parents hold stereotypic beliefs, and expected effects from such beliefs are sometimes but not always found. It is interesting to note, in fact, that in a recent report of the Eccles research (Simpkins et al., 2015), effects are stronger for the nonacademic domains of sports and music than they are for math and reading. Nevertheless, in balance a large research literature leaves little doubt that parents' expectations are one of the contributors to how boys and girls perform in school. Expectations affect children's motivation to pursue and to work hard at different academic subjects. They also affect children's concepts of their ability to do well at different subjects. Indeed, parents' expectations are a stronger determinant of children's self-concepts than is past academic performance (Frome & Eccles, 1998).

The discussion to this point indicates that high parental expectations are a positive contributor to academic performance, in part because they foster high expectations in children. Does this mean that higher is always better, or can there be (to echo the title of one of the first examinations of the issue) Entwisle and Alexander's 1978 *Too Great Expectations*? The answer is that higher is not always better (see also Murayama et al., 2015). As we will see later in the chapter, and indeed throughout the book, it is accurate beliefs about one's child, and not errors of either overestimation or underestimation, that are associated with optimal parental behaviors and positive child development. It is true that it in most instances it is probably better, if one is going to err, to do so in a positive, overly optimistic direction. The research on parent expectations and school achievement supports this conclusion, and so (with some controversy) does the work on teacher expectancy effects (Rosenthal, 2002). But there must still be some grounding in reality and possibility, some relation between what is expected and what is doable. This is a point that we saw in Chapter 4 in the discussion of self-efficacy. High self-efficacy is an adaptive belief for many outcomes, including children's performance in school. But high self-efficacy is most likely to be helpful when it is accompanied by an accurate conception of what one can and cannot do. Thus great expectations, but not too great.

## Parental Involvement and Support

So far there has been only limited discussion of the parent behaviors that mediate between parents' beliefs on the one hand and children's school performance on the other. This section takes up this issue more fully.

As any teacher knows, parents vary in how much involvement they have in their children's school lives. For some, discussion of the day's activities and help with homework may be a daily occurrence; for others, involvement may not extend beyond signing a report card a few times a year. Figure 6.1 present an influential model of the contributors to such differences among parents.

All three of the contributors identified in the model are in fact important (Green, Walker, Hoover-Dempsey, & Sandler, 2007). As can be seen, the parents' beliefs component encompasses both beliefs about the proper role for parents in children's schooling and beliefs about one's own ability to fulfill this role. The key construct with regard to the latter question is self-efficacy, and school involvement is another topic for which parental self-efficacy turns out to be important (Hoover-Dempsey, Bassler, & Brissie, 1992). The relation is a reciprocal one: Over time, successful involvement nurtures self-efficacy, and self-efficacy in turn nurtures further involvement.

Not all parent–school contact is at the parent's initiative. Invitations from the school come at various times in various forms, and parents vary in how responsive they are to such requests. The form of involvement that Figure 6.1 labels School Involvement (e.g., parent–teacher conferences, visits to the child's classroom) is especially dependent on invitations. Although general school announcements may sometimes be sufficient, specific requests from teachers or from children are generally a more effective way to elicit participation (Green et al., 2007).

| Parents' Involvement Forms | | | | | | |
|---|---|---|---|---|---|---|
| Home Involvement | | | School Involvement | | | |

↑

| Parents' Motivational Beliefs | | Parents' Perceptions of Invitations for Involvement from Others | | | Parents' Perceived Life Context | |
|---|---|---|---|---|---|---|
| Parental Role Construction | Parental Self-Efficacy | General School Invitations | Specific Teacher Invitations | Specific Child Invitations | Skills and Knowledge | Time and Energy |

Figure 6.1 Hoover-Dempsey and Sandler model of parental involvement. From "Parents' Motivation for Involvement in Children's Education: An Empirical Test of a Theoretical Model of Parental Involvement," by C. L. Green, J. M. T. Walker, K. V. Hoover-Dempsey, and H. M. Sandler, 2007, *Journal of Educational Psychology*, *99*, p. 533. Copyright 2007 by the American Psychological Association. Reprinted with permission.

Finally, whatever a parent's beliefs and goals may be, more general life circumstances may constrain the possibility for involvement. A parent with a full-time job may find it difficult to participate in school activities, and a parent with several children may have less time to help with homework than a parent with just one child.

As would be expected, the topic just mentioned—help with homework— is a major entry under the Home Involvement heading shown in the figure (i.e., activities whose locus is the home rather than the school). Homework has also long been the subject of a concentrated research effort directed to both the value of homework in general (Cooper, Steenbergen-Hu, & Dent, 2012) and the value of parental involvement in homework in particular (Patall, Cooper, & Robinson, 2008). I concentrate on the latter issue, basing my conclusions mainly on the Patall et al. (2008) review. Other helpful sources include Jeynes (2005); Moroni, Dumont, Trautwein, Niggli, and Baeriswyl (2015); and Wilder (2014).

A first finding is that most parents believe that helping with home- work is important, and most parents help in some way with homework. The results of such help are mixed: sometimes positive, sometimes neg- ative, and sometimes null. Positive effects are more likely for homework itself (e.g., successful completion, absence of problems) than they are for measures of academic achievement, although effects on the latter are also sometimes found. Positive effects are more likely for elementary school students than for older students, and parents in fact typically offer more help to younger than to older children. Effects may vary across different academic subjects; in particular, help with math shows limited posi- tive effects, especially by the high school years, a finding that may re- flect parents' own difficulties with the subject matter. Finally, whether would-be parental help actually helps depends on the form that the help takes (probably a safe conclusion with respect to parents' contribution to any aspect of development). Setting clear rules for homework is ben- eficial; so, too, is creation of a supportive environment that is responsive to the child's needs. In the other direction, forcing help on the child may be regarded as intrusive and may therefore be counterproductive, and simply monitoring the situation rather than actively helping is likely to have limited effects at best.

Most of the research just summarized is correlational, which means that issues of causal direction arise. Rather than parental involvement af- fecting child performance, it may be child performance that affects parental involvement. In particular, children who are struggling in school may elicit more help from their parents, a situation that might obscure any positive effects of the help. Fortunately, the literature also includes a number of experimental studies in which parental help is experimentally manipulated, and the results from these studies are in general agreement with those from the correlational research. Help, to be sure, is not always beneficial, and the benefits that do occur may vary across outcome measures, age groups, and academic subjects. In balance, however, the overall conclusion is clear: Help with homework, if appropriately provided, is a positive contributor to children's academic development.

Homework hardly exhausts the ways in which parents may contribute to their child's success in school. In some instances a contribution may begin very early, before the child has even begun school. A basic question for both educators and parents of young children is that of school readiness: What competencies and attributes must a child possess to be ready for formal schooling? Most parents have beliefs about school readiness, although the beliefs do not always align perfectly with those of educators (e.g., Barbarin et al., 2008). Many parents, moreover, act on their beliefs—that is, engage in activities at home that are intended (perhaps among other benefits) to boost readiness for school (Belfield & Garcia, 2014; Prendergast & MacPhee, 2018). Prominent among such activities is reading with the child and thus an early introduction to the challenges and rewards of literacy (Cottone, 2012; DeBaryshe, 1995).

Surveys indicate that indices of school readiness, at least in the United States, have improved across the past 25 years (Child Trends, 2015b). Part of the improvement can be traced to increased enrollment in preschool programs prior to formal schooling. Part, however, may well reflect changes in parental practices, both in the selection of good preschools and in the provision of development-enhancing activities at home.

## Intelligence

We move now from one large literature to another large and clearly related one: parents' beliefs about their children's intelligence. The studies under this heading divide into two groups. In some studies, intelligence is equated to IQ: performance on standard intelligence tests. In other studies, there is no experimenter-defined notion of the concept; rather, the goal is to discover how parents define and reason about intelligence. I begin with work under the standardized test heading.

## Intelligence as IQ

The first set of studies to be discussed follow the same general format (e.g., Hunt & Paraskevoupolos, 1980; Miller, 1986). The children of the parents being studied are administered either a complete IQ test or a subset of items from a test, and the parents are subsequently shown the same items and asked to predict their children's performance. In some cases, parents make item-by-item predictions (e.g., Miller, 1986); in other cases, they provide a global estimate of overall performance (e.g., Furnham & Bunclark, 2006). In either case, the measure of child performance permits a determination of how accurately parents can judge their children.

Three main findings emerge. The first is that parents show an above-average but far from perfect ability to predict how their children have done or will do. Correlations between child performance and parental prediction cluster around .5 to .6. Accuracy does vary, however, with the nature of the questioning. Not surprisingly, parents do better when all that is required is a global estimate, with no need to make item-by-item judgments. They also do better when the questions are directed to percentile standing, and thus rank order, rather than to absolute level of performance (Delgado-Hachey & Miller, 1993).

The second finding is that most parents overestimate what their children can do. Parents also overestimate what children in general can do, in the subset of studies that elicit such judgments; the overestimation is greater, however, when one's own child is the target. For example, in the Miller (1986) study, overestimations occurred on 54% of the possible occasions (i.e., instances in which the child had failed an item); the comparable figure for underestimations was 9%. We have, then, another example of the valence effect: unrealistically positive expectations when judging one's own child.

The third finding concerns the relation between parental accuracy and children's performance. Do more knowledgeable parents have brighter children? Not all examinations of the issue have reported a relation (Delgado-Hachey & Miller, 1993; Sattler, Feldman, & Bohanan, 1985). Most, however, have, and the relation is often a substantial one. In the Hunt and Paraskevoupolos (1980) study, the correlation between parents' inaccuracy in predicting their child's performance and the child's actual performance was −.80, that is, the less accurate the parent, the worse the performance. Other studies have also reported correlations in the .80 range (Cotler & Shoemaker, 1969; Stoiber, 1992). The relation holds not just for global measures of IQ but also for subtests of larger measures considered separately (Miller & Davis, 1992; Miller, Manhal, & Mee, 1991).

Why does parental accuracy relate positively to child performance? The most interesting explanation is what Hunt and Paraskevoupolos (1980) labeled the *match hypothesis*. The "match" refers to the fit between the parent's beliefs about the child's ability and the child's actual ability. When the match is good—that is, when parents hold accurate beliefs—parents can teach things to the child in optimal ways and can structure the child's environment in optimal ways, the result being enhanced cognitive development. Thus parental accuracy nurtures child intelligence.

The match hypothesis has much to recommend it. It fits with common sense—in any domain, we would expect that relevant knowledge will lead to more effective behaviors. It also fits with major theoretical positions in developmental psychology that stress the importance of the fit between children's current level and their ability to benefit from new experience; examples include Piaget, Vygotsky, and information processing. And as we have seen—and will see again in subsequent chapters—it is supported by numerous demonstrations that parental knowledge is associated with positive child outcomes.

Attractive though the match hypothesis is, the problem in accepting it is that it is not the only possible explanation for the parent–child correlation; there are in fact three other possibilities (Miller, 1986, 1988; see also Price & Gillingham, 1985). One is that the causal direction is the reverse of what has been posited. Perhaps bright children are easier to judge than are children in general, and it is this factor that accounts for the correlation between accuracy and performance. Clearly, this argument is a particular instance of the directionality issue that always applies in correlational research: Does A cause B, or does B cause A?

A second possibility is that the correlation results from general similarity between parent and child. Both, after all, are performing cognitive tasks, and we know that children's ability to do so correlates with their parents' ability to do so. It is true that this explanation is not necessarily incompatible with the match hypothesis—bright children may resemble their parents because their bright parents treat them in optimal ways. But the clear evidence for a genetic basis for parent–child similarity renders the need for an environmental explanation uncertain.

These first two alternative explanations are interesting possibilities in themselves, even if they do not support the match hypothesis. The third explanation is less interesting because it suggests an artifactual basis for the relation. If parents hold overly optimistic expectations about what their children can do—and this, as we saw, is the typical direction of error—then some degree of parent–child correlation is ensured because parents whose children do well will necessarily end up with more correct predictions than parents whose children do poorly. At the extreme, if all parents predicted perfect performance for their child, then parental accuracy would be perfectly predicted by how well the child actually performed, and the correlation between accuracy and child performance would be 1. The variation and correlation, however, would come completely from the children's performance.

As I have argued elsewhere (Miller, 1986, 1988), these various explanations are not incompatible; all may apply. That the overestimation bias contributes to the accuracy–performance correlation is almost certainly true; Miller (1986) provides some direct evidence for this possibility, and in any case correlations in the .80 range are, to put it mildly, suspiciously large. But such a conclusion does not mean that overestimation bias is the sole basis for the relation. Parents do vary in the accuracy with which they judge their children, these variations are not determined solely by the level of the child's performance, and in many contexts parents are more accurate than other judges and accuracy–performance correlations are greater for parents than for other judges. Furthermore, if parents who believe correctly that their children are bright treat them accordingly, it may not matter if their accuracy has a partly fortuitous basis in the tendency to overestimate—their beliefs may still lead to development-enhancing behaviors. Finally, beliefs not subject to the overestimation bias also relate to children's development; in particular, parents' accuracy in judging their children's preferences shows a positive relation to measures of children's intelligence (Miller & Davis, 1992; Miller, Davis, Wilde, & Brown, 1993). In short, both theoretical and empirical arguments attest to the value of parental knowledge, and the work on intelligence can be argued to be another example of this conclusion.

## Multiple Forms of Intelligence

The preceding studies are not the only ones in which IQ tests have served as targets for parental judgments. The remaining studies, however, do not include measures of child performance, which means that there is no possibility of determining the accuracy of the judgments. And this means that there is no possibility of determining effects of parental accuracy.

What, then, are the issues addressed in these studies? There are three main ones. One is comparison among different forms of intelligence—thus not simply a single intelligence score, such as is produced by the Stanford-Binet, but different scores for different forms of intellectual ability. A second is a comparison among different judges. Of interest are not simply parents' beliefs about their children but also judge–target links of a variety of sorts, including in some instances self-judgments. Finally, a third interest is in cultural comparisons. In particular, work by Furnham and associates has explored beliefs about intelligence in a wide range of cultures. Among the cultures studied with respect to parents' beliefs about their children are England (Furnham, 2000), China (Furnham & Wu, 2014), Japan (Furnham & Fukumoto, 2008), South Africa (Furnham & Mkhize, 2003), Portugal (Neto & Furnham, 2011), and Iceland (Furnham & Valgeirsson, 2007).

Most parents in these studies do ascribe to the notion of multiple forms of intelligence. The evidence for this conclusion is indirect, in that parents are not asked explicitly whether intelligence takes different forms. But parents often provide different estimates of their child's ability across different measures of intelligence, indicating that they do not regard intelligence as a monolithic, consistently high or low entity. This conclusion holds across various ways of conceptualizing multiple intelligences, including not only divisions common on standard tests (e.g., verbal vs. quantitative) but also the more distinct forms of intelligence proposed in theories by Gardner and Sternberg. The conclusion also holds not just for parents' beliefs about their children but also for the other kinds of judge–target pairings that are examined in the research program: self-estimates of one's own intelligence, spouses' estimates of each other's intelligence, teachers' estimate of their pupils' intelligence, and children's estimates of their parents' intelligence.

A further finding is that of gender differences in beliefs as a function of both judge and target. Males typically rate their own intelligence more highly than females rate theirs, parents rate boys' intelligence more highly than they rate girls' intelligence, and there is sometimes an interaction of sex of judge and sex of target, with fathers especially likely to indicate differences between the sexes. There are exceptions to these general conclusions, however. The type of intelligence at issue can be important. High ratings for males, whether for oneself or one's child, are most likely on measures of mathematical or spatial intelligence; females often receive higher ratings on interpersonal and emotional intelligence. We have, then, further evidence for gender-stereotypical beliefs about cognitive abilities. The culture can also be important. Parents in some cultures believe more strongly in sex differences than do parents in other cultures. Parents in some cultures also offer more optimistic estimates of intelligence, for both themselves and their children, than do those in other cultures. For example, estimates tend to be relatively low in Asian cultures, a finding that has been labeled "Asian modesty bias."

The preceding is a brief and incomplete summary of a large and multifaceted research program. A general message from the work, however, is easy to state, and it is that conclusions about parents' beliefs about intelligence will be limited as long as only one type of culture and one type of intelligence are studied.

## Parents' Conceptions of Intelligence

The work just discussed indicates that many parents believe that intelligence is a multifaceted construct that does not reduce to a single kind of competence. In the studies considered thus far, however, parents are responding to alternatives offered by researchers. The goal of the work to be considered now is to explore naturally occurring, spontaneously held beliefs about intelligence.

The relevant literature is a broad and rich one, for numerous investigators have probed in various ways for beliefs about intelligence across a range of cultures. Several articles by Sternberg (2004, 2007, 2014) provide a helpful summary of what has been found. I offer several general conclusions here.

A first conclusion is that there are indeed differences in cultural belief systems, or *ethnotheories*, about what constitutes intelligent behavior. Here are a few examples. In Kenya, parasitic diseases are a threat to every child's survival, and a child may have learned the names of as many as 100 natural herbal medicines that can combat disease. The capacity for such learning, as well as the resulting knowledge, is an important form of intelligence for a Kenyan child (Sternberg et al., 2001). In the Yup'ik Eskimo villages of Alaska, hunting and fishing are major occupations, and children who are trained to do so become proficient in the necessary skills, even though they often lag behind in traditional school-taught knowledge (Grigorenko, Meier, Lipka, Mohatt, & Sternberg, 2004). Finally, among the Baoule people of the Ivory Coast, the most readily offered attribute of childhood intelligence is the readiness and ability to carry out tasks in the service of family and community (Dasen, 1984). Interestingly, evaluations of where children stand on this dimension are always offered in the future tense, for the Baoule wish to acknowledge that a child can change.

As the preceding examples suggest, beliefs about intelligence have implications for what parents expect and encourage in children. In Kenya, for example, parents may keep their brighter children at home rather than send them to school, because the skills learned outside of school are the important ones for both the family and the community. In these and other instances, what is regarded as intelligence, and what therefore is nurtured, depends on what the culture values.

The differences discussed to this point mainly concern the content to which intelligence is directed and the context in which it is expressed. There are also differences—arguably more fundamental ones—in beliefs about the underlying nature of intelligence; that is, what intelligence *is*. In many African countries, for example, an interpersonal dimension—concern for others, good behavior toward others—is central to conceptions of what constitutes intelligent behavior or an intelligent person. The Baoule culture is one example of this point. In China, both Confucian and Taoist traditions promote a similar emphasis on benevolence and both interpersonal and intrapersonal awareness. In these and similar cases, beliefs about intelligence often encompass both a social and a pragmatic dimension that are lacking in standard Western conceptions.

Cultures may also differ in beliefs about where intelligence comes from. The belief systems of some cultures place an emphasis on maturationally paced, developmentally natural forms of development—thus a predominantly "nature" answer to the nature–nurture question. In other cultures the emphasis is on experience as a source of developmental change, often including explicit tuition in necessary skills—thus a predominantly "nurture" answer to the nature–nurture question.

The discussion thus far has been on differences among countries. Differences may also be evident among ethnic groups within a country. For example, in a sample of US mothers, both Hispanic and Asian mothers ascribed to a broader conception of intelligence than did Anglo mothers, a particular difference being a greater emphasis on social competence by the former group (Okagaki & Sternberg, 1993). In Singapore, mothers of Indian origin showed a similar social emphasis, judging a factor labeled "appropriate behavior" as more important for intelligence than did mothers of either Malaysian or Chinese origin (Nevo & Khader, 1995). Recall also that

Chapter 3 discussed one important within-country difference in beliefs concerning the malleability of intelligence: the contrast between growth mindsets and fixed mindsets.

A final conclusion is a cautionary note with regard to an exclusive focus on differences among cultures. The argument is that, in some instances, such differences may mask an underlying commonality—that the same basic intellectual components may be necessary contributors to intelligent behavior in any cultural setting, no matter how diverse the resulting behaviors may seem. Sternberg (2007, p. 152) summarizes this point as follows: "In every culture, people have to recognize when they have problems, define what the problems are, solve the problems, and then evaluate how well they have solved them. But the content of the problems to be solved is different, and what is considered a good solution differs as well."

This final point has broader applicability. That a survey of the world's cultures will reveal both similarities and differences is probably a safe conclusion for any aspect of human development.

## Piaget

We turn now from several very large literatures to a much smaller one. The limited work devoted to parents' beliefs about Piagetian concepts is my own (Miller, 1986; Miller, White, & Delgado, 1980). It was carried out at a time when the Piagetian position was a good deal more prominent than is now the case. Still, whatever the contemporary uncertainties may be concerning some aspects of the work, there is little doubt about the importance of concepts such as object permanence and conservation, which makes such concepts worthy targets for the study of parents' beliefs.

Two aspects of the sorts of developments studied by Piaget make them potentially challenging targets for parents to judge. First, many forms of cognitive development are at least sometimes visible in the parent's interactions with the child. Such is the case for academic performance and for many of the skills tapped by IQ tests. It is also true for both language and memory. Piagetian concepts, in contrast, seem less likely to be evident in the child's overt behavior. A parent could wait a long time before seeing his or her child struggle with a conservation or class inclusion task.

The reference to "struggle with" brings up the second aspect of Piagetian developments that may make them challenging to judge. One of the interests in Piaget's research has always lain in its ability to surprise us with respect to what children, at least for a while, do *not* know. Prior to Piaget, psychologists were unaware of a number of gaps in children's understanding of the world. Perhaps parents show a similar lack of awareness.

The limited research suggests that they do. Miller et al. (1980) elicited age-of-mastery judgments for 13 Piagetian concepts ranging from object permanence tasks of infancy to scientific reasoning problems typically mastered in adolescence. Both parents and nonparents were studied. Few differences were evident between the groups, and neither group performed very well. Even with a generous criterion for determining accuracy, the age estimates were correct on only slightly more than half of the 13 trials. The predominant error was to underestimate what infants can do and to overestimate what older children can do. Recall that this same truncating of the developmental range emerged in the milestones studies discussed in Chapter 5. More positively, and also similar to results from the milestones studies, the subjects showed a good awareness of the order in which the various abilities emerged despite their shakiness about exactly when they emerged.

The Miller (1986) study discussed under "Intelligence" also presented 18 Piagetian tasks for parents to judge, again with respect to both their own child and children in general. For the reasons just discussed, the Piagetian items were expected to be more difficult than the IQ items, and this proved to be the case. Mothers were correct on only slightly more than half of the own-child judgments, and their age of mastery judgments for children in general also lagged behind those for the IQ items. In other respects, findings for the two test batteries were similar. Thus the predominant error was again to overestimate what children can do. The tendency to overestimate was greater when one's own child was the target than it was for children in general. Finally, there was a positive relation between mothers' accuracy in judging their child and the level of the child's performance—indeed, an even stronger relation ($r = .85$) than held true for IQ. Clearly, the same cautions and uncertainties discussed earlier about the interpretation of such parent–child correlations apply here as well.

## Theory of Mind

Theory of mind was not a focus for the first wave of parents' beliefs studies, given that the topic had not yet emerged as a distinct area of study. Related developments, to be sure, had long been studied under other headings (e.g., perspective-taking, social cognition). But the methods, findings, and theories that define theory of mind had not yet arrived.

Now, of course, not only has theory of mind arrived; it also has emerged as one of the most active topics in the field. Although many uncertainties and controversies still characterize the literature, there is little dispute about the importance, both theoretically and pragmatically, of the developments in question. It is a good target, therefore, for parents' beliefs. As we will see, to date the beliefs literature includes one extended program of research devoted to theory of mind, along with a handful of promising beginning efforts. (The work to be considered now is discussed more fully in Miller, 2016.)

The extended program of research is by Elizabeth Meins and colleagues (e.g., Meins, 2012; Meins, Fernyhough, Arnott, Leekam, & de Rosnay, 2013). The Meins research program was introduced in Chapter 5 in the discussion of attachment, that being one of the main outcomes to which it has been directed. The other main outcome is theory of mind.

As we saw, the core concept underlying the research is *mind-mindedness*, or the tendency to attribute mental states to one's child. In parents of infants, mind-mindedness is inferred from parental speech directed to the infant. In parents of older children, the usual measurement technique is to elicit a description of the child from the parent. Again, frequent use of mental state terms constitutes relatively high mind-mindedness.

Relatively high mind-mindedness on the parent's part correlates with relatively good theory of mind on the child's part. Although there are occasional exceptions (e.g., Ereky-Stevens, 2008), positive relations between the two constructs emerge in the great majority of studies that have examined the issue (e.g., de Rosnay, Pons, Harris, & Morrell, 2004; Lundy, 2013). Relations have been shown for both of the methods of assessing mind-mindedness, and they have been shown for a variety of theory-of-mind outcomes, including false belief, appearance/reality, origins of knowledge, perspective-taking, and understanding of desire. Relations have been shown to occur in different cultures, and there is evidence that differences in parents' mind-mindedness across cultures contribute to cultural differences in children's theory-of-mind performance (Hughes, Devine, & Wang, 2018). Finally, relations have been shown not only concurrently but also prospectively—that is, mind-mindedness assessed early in development relates to theory of mind assessed later in development (e.g., Meins et al., 2013; Meins et al., 2003). As always, across-time relations strengthen the argument for causality—in this case, that mind-mindedness plays a causal role in the development of theory of mind.

What are the parental behaviors that mediate between mind-mindedness and children's theory of mind? The answer to this question is still not totally clear. Almost certainly one of the behaviors, however, is the use of mental state language in speech directed to the child. A large correlational literature indicates that parents (usually mothers) who are high in the use of mental state terms have children who do well on theory-of-mind measures (e.g., Adrian, Clemente, Villanueva, & Rieffe, 2005; Ruffman, Slade, Devitt, & Crowe, 2006). Again, relations have been shown not only concurrently but also prospectively; that is, mental state language early in development relates to children's theory of mind later in development. Also supportive of a causal role for such language are the results from training studies of theory of mind. Among the approaches that have achieved some training success is the provision of conversational input that is high in mental state terms (Guajardo & Watson, 2002; Ornaghi, Brockmeier, & Gavazzi, 2011).

The more general parenting literature suggests some further ways in which mind-mindedness may contribute. Mind-mindedness has been shown to relate to a number of aspects of parenting that are known to have positive effects on children's development, including the development of theory of mind. As we saw in Chapter 5, mind-mindedness relates to parental sensitivity, and it does so not only in infancy but during later childhood as well (e.g., Demers, Bernier, Tarabulsy, & Provost, 2010; Meins et al., 2002). Mind-mindedness also relates positively to emotional availability (Licata et al., 2014), to sensitivity while feeding the infant (Farrow & Blissett, 2014), and to lower levels of hostility in parent–child interactions (Lok & McMahon, 2006; McMahon & Meins, 2012). In short, mind-mindedness goes along with, and almost certainly contributes to, a number of beneficial parental practices.

In addition to the Meins research, a handful of other studies have explored what parents believe about their children's mental lives. Two studies by Sharp and colleagues (Ha, Sharp, & Goodyear, 2011; Sharp, Fonagy, & Goodyer, 2006) examined parents' (mostly mothers') ability to judge their children's responses to various problems in social understanding. In both studies the child's task was to make attributions for peers' probable responses to situations that might cause embarrassment or distress (e.g., sitting alone on the playground without a playmate), and the parent's task was to predict how her child would respond. The results mirrored those discussed earlier in the chapter for other kinds of parental beliefs. Parents showed moderate but above-chance levels of accuracy in judging their children; they correctly identified the child's choices on slightly less than half of the scenarios (one third would be the chance rate), and their assessment of the child's overall attributional style correlated significantly with the child's actual style. In addition, parental accuracy related in expected ways to aspects of children's development. Relatively low accuracy was associated with an unrealistic and overly positive attributional style, the least adaptive of the attributional styles. Low parental accuracy also related to the children's psychosocial adjustment—specifically, to a relatively high level of conduct problems and psychopathological symptoms

The theory-of-mind literature also includes several recently developed parent-report measures of theory of mind (Hutchins, Prelock, & Bonazinga, 2012; Peterson, Garnett, Kelly, & Attwood, 2009; Tahiroglu et al., 2014). These measures take the same basic form: description of a number of theory-of-mind competencies, accompanied by questions asking whether the parent's child has or has not mastered the abilities in question. Such instruments have several attractive features. One is the scope of the theory-of-mind developments that they encompass, a breadth of coverage that is considerably greater than is possible in a typical child assessment. Another is the grounding of many items in familiar real-life settings, in contrast to the laboratory locus that characterizes the typical child performance measures. Finally, the validation data for such measures indicate that parents do have some (although admittedly far from perfect) ability to predict their children's performance on theory-of-mind tasks, which, of course, is a prerequisite for the use of such instruments as measures of theory of mind.

To date, parent-report measures of theory of mind have had limited applications, appearing mainly in studies of autism and theory of mind (which, indeed, is the context in which two of the instruments were developed). More uses will undoubtedly be forthcoming. Note, though, that the potential value of such instruments extends beyond their use simply as another index of children's theory of mind. Such measures tap parents' beliefs about an important aspect of their children's development, and they therefore lend themselves to study of all of the issues that run through the parents' beliefs literature: Where do parents' beliefs come from? How do the beliefs affect parents' behavior? And how do the beliefs affect children's development?

# Memory

Some topics, such as Piagetian-inspired research, wax and wane in popularity across the history of the field. Memory, however, has remained a central topic in psychology since the birth of the discipline. The particular emphases, to be sure, have varied some across different time periods, but the centrality of memory as an aspect of human functioning—not just in childhood but across the life span—has never been in doubt.

The importance of memory in the psychology research literature is not matched by its prominence in the study of parents' beliefs. The beliefs literature includes several parent-report measures of children's memory, along with a handful of studies directed to parents' accuracy in judging their children's memory performance. As we will see, it also includes one line of research that provides compelling, albeit mostly indirect, evidence for the importance of parents' beliefs.

I begin with the parent reports. Table 6.2 provides a sampling of items from one such measure; others include the Modified Prospective and Retrospective Memory Questionnaire (Kliegel & Jager, 2007) and the Observer-Memory Questionnaire – Parent Form (Gonzalez et al., 2008). Levick (2010) provides a review of such measures.

We saw that parent-report measures of theory of mind have had a pragmatic grounding and a focus on clinical conditions such as autism. The same is true of the measures being considered now. The goal of such measures has not been to add to the basic memory research literature; rather, it has been

Table 6.2  Examples of Items from the Children's Memory Questionnaire – Revised

---

Forgets where she/he has put something.
Forgets the name of someone she/he met for the first time recently.
Forgets what she/he was told a few minutes ago.
Loses things.
Slow to learn new routines.
Sets off to do something, then seems to forget what it was he/she wanted to do.
Seems to forget something she/he has just said.
Forgets the names of common things or uses the wrong names for them.
Gets the details of what someone told him or her mixed up and confused.

---

Responses are made on a 5-point scale ranging from "Never or almost never happens" to "Happens more than once a day." Adapted from "The Children's Memory Questionnaire-Revised," by R. Hedges, K. Drysdale, and W. R. Levick, 2015, *Applied Neuropsychology: Child, 4,* p. 291. Copyright 2015 by Taylor & Francis Group. Adapted with permission of Taylor and Francis Ltd.

to identify memory problems that may be serious enough to require intervention. Their success to date in doing so has been modest. The Children's Memory Questionnaire – Revised, the measure shown in the table, does succeed in identifying a substantial proportion of known memory difficulties, but it also yields a number of false positives, that is, indications of problems in children who are in fact doing well (Drysdale, Shores, & Levick, 2004. Thus the measure shows—to return to the terminology introduced in Chapter 5—good sensitivity but low specificity.

Another potential form of validity evidence for such measures comes from correlations with children's memory performance as assessed on standard laboratory tasks. Here the results are clear: only low and sporadic correlations across a number of comparisons (different age groups, different forms of memory). As advocates of parent-report measures argue, however, the minimal relations between the two sets of scores do not necessarily mean that parents are inaccurate judges of their children's memory abilities (although this is certainly one possible interpretation). Another possibility is that the two kinds of measures tap different kinds of memory—in particular, that parent reports pick up on forms of everyday memory that are not captured by typical laboratory tasks. A consideration of the items in Table 6.2 suggests the plausibility of this argument, for most of the behaviors listed there have no clear analogs on standard laboratory measures.

What do we know about parental accuracy in instances (unlike those just discussed) in which judgment and criterion involve the same kind of memory, that is, studies in which parents predict performance on the tasks to which their children have responded? The limited available evidence suggests only modest accuracy at best, although perhaps somewhat greater for mothers than for fathers (Bird & Berman, 1985; Miller & Davis, 1992; Miller et al., 1991). As with other targets for judgment, parents tend to overestimate their children's memory abilities, and the few task comparisons indicate lower accuracy for memory than for other cognitive abilities.

The discussion to this point provides limited evidence for either parents' knowledge of their children' memory or parents' effects on their children's memory. Those familiar with the literature on memory development will realize that one important line of research has yet to be discussed. Several dozen studies have examined so-called *memory talk*; that is, the sorts of reminiscing about past events that parents (mothers in most studies) engage in with their children. That such talk nurtures various positive developments has long been clear (Salmon & Reese, 2016; Wang, 2013).

Most obviously, it nurtures memory development, in particular the form of memory labeled *autobiographical memory*, or personal and long-lasting memories regarding the self. Memory talk also contributes to aspects of language development, to a positive emotional bond between parent and child, to children's understanding of emotions, and to the development of a positive self-concept.

Parents vary in both how often and how they talk to their children about the past; indeed, it is these variations in parental talk that make it possible to determine the effects that such talk has. For the most part, the beliefs that underlie these differences among parents have been inferred from the nature of the talk itself rather than studied directly. If, for example, a Chinese mother's memory talk focuses on her child's transgressions and the moral lessons to be learned from them (as, in fact, is often the case in Eastern cultures; Miller, Fung, Lin, Chen, & Boldt, 2012), then it is reasonable to infer that the mother believes that such lessons are important to convey and that talk about past events is a good vehicle for doing so. Similarly, if an American mother's talk centers on her child's past successes and achievements (as, in fact, is often the case in Western cultures), then a reasonable inference is that she believes that it is important to instill a sense of self-confidence and autonomy in her child. Recently, however, several research programs have attempted to move beyond inference to measure the cognitive bases for such talk directly, in some instances through open-ended interviews (e.g., Kulkofsky, Wang, & Koh, 2009) and in some instances through questionnaires directed to beliefs about the value of memory talk (e.g., Zevenbergen, Haman, & Olszariska, 2012). Although much work remains to be done, initial results suggest several conclusions: Parents do differ in their beliefs about memory talk, including differences that divide roughly along cultural lines; these differences relate in expectable ways to how parents engage in such talk with their children; and variations in memory talk relate in expectable ways to various aspects of children's development.

## Executive Function

*Executive function* is an umbrella term for general problem-solving resources that underlie performance on a wide range of cognitive tasks. Examples include inhibition, working memory, rule switching, and planning. Although the "executive function" label is a relatively recent coinage, these are processes that have long played important roles in the study of learning, reasoning, and problem solving.

As with memory, the importance of executive function in the research literature is not yet matched in the study of parents' beliefs. It is true that the outcomes for which executive functions are important do receive attention; indeed, executive functions contribute to each of the topics discussed in this chapter. But a focus on executive functions per se is rare.

Parents do enter into one component of the executive function literature: that directed to the bases for individual differences among children. It has long been clear that part of the basis for such differences is genetic (Friedman et al., 2008). Part, however, is environmental, and parents are clearly important contributors under this heading. In general, the same aspects of parenting that have been found to be beneficial for other developmental outcomes turn out to be beneficial for executive function as well (Bernier, Carlson, Deschenes, & Matte-Gagne, 2012; Fay-Stammbach, Hawes, & Meredith, 2014). The predictors include a secure attachment relationship, sensitivity in interactions with the child, provision of appropriate stimulation, and avoidance of hostility. They also include a form of teaching known as *scaffolding*, in which the parent adjusts the level of her help in response to the child's performance, zeroing in when the child is struggling and pulling back when she judges that the child is capable of working independently (Bibok, Carpendale, & Muller, 2009; Hammond, Muller, Carpendale, Bibok, & Liebermann-Finestone, 2012). Scaffolding nurtures a number of positive developments, and executive function skills are among them.

The value of scaffolding suggests a clear role for parental knowledge—adjusting one's teaching appropriately requires both general knowledge of one's child and the ability to read immediate signals accurately. Indeed, parental knowledge is implicated in all of the contributors to executive function noted in the preceding paragraph. For the most part, however, the role of knowledge remains implicit in the executive function literature, inferred from parental behaviors rather than studied directly. As we saw, the same point applies to the memory literature.

There is one exception to this statement. In a study by Johnston (2011), mothers of 4- to 7-year-old boys were first shown the measures to which their sons would respond (various tasks testing inhibition and planning), then predicted how the child would perform. Mothers were moderately accurate in predicting their children's executive function skills, with a tendency to overestimate performance on the planning tasks and to underestimate performance on the inhibition tasks. Maternal accuracy, in turn, was negatively related to child behavior problems as assessed by the Child Behavior Checklist. We have, then, another instance in which parental knowledge appears to be beneficial for children's development. There was no attempt made, however, to identify the parental behaviors that underlay the effect.

In addition to the parenting studies, executive function has been a target for parent-report measures (McCloskey & Perkins, 2013). Table 6.3 presents a sample of items from the most often used such measure, the Behavior Rating Inventory of Executive Function (BRIEF; Roth, Isquith, & Gioia, 2014). As the sampling suggests, the measure has the same strengths that were noted for parent-report measures of theory of mind and memory: a broad scope of coverage and a grounding in real-life events, both of which are attractive alternatives to the usual laboratory approach to assessment.

Despite these virtues, the BRIEF has not been a major contributor to the basic research literature on executive function, most of which is based on children's performance on standardized laboratory tasks. The BRIEF, however, has proved quite useful as a diagnostic tool for clinical purposes;

**Table 6.3** Examples of Items from the Behavioral Rating Inventory of Executive Functioning (BRIEF)

| Scale | Item |
| --- | --- |
| Inhibit | Is unaware of how his or her behavior affects or bothers others. |
| | Is impulsive. |
| Shift | Becomes upset with new situations. |
| | Is upset by a change in plans or routines. |
| Emotional control | Becomes upset too easily. |
| | Mood changes frequently. |
| Working memory | When given two things to do, remembers only the first or last. |
| | Has trouble concentrating on games, puzzles, or play activities. |
| Plan and organize | When instructed to clean up, puts things away in a disorganized, random way. |
| | Has trouble thinking of a different way to solve a problem or complete an activity when stuck. |

Adapted from "Executive Function in Preschool Children: Examination Through Everyday Behavior," by P. K. Isquith, G. A. Gioia, and K. A. Espy, 2004, *Developmental Neuropsychology, 26,* p. 410. Copyright 2004 by Lawrence Erlbaum Associates. Adapted with permission of Taylor and Francis Ltd.

a review by Roth et al. (2014) lists 44 conditions for which the BRIEF has been part of the assessment. Interventions often follow from the detection of problems, and results from the BRIEF have also been helpful in guiding and evaluating intervention efforts (Isquith, Roth, Kenworthy, & Gioia, 2014).

## Language

As with the previous three topics, parent-report measures make up part of the literature devoted to beliefs about language. As we saw, such measures, at least to date, have had limited impact on the basic research literature in the study of theory of mind, memory, or executive function. In the case of language, however, parent-report measures have long been a major source of data. The reliance on such measures is understandable given the breadth of the target: namely, everything that the developing child has come to know about language. Observational assessments and structured laboratory tests can illuminate aspects of the developments in question, but a fuller picture requires access to the multitude of instances each day in which children express their linguistic competence. And in the typical case it is only parents who have access to this information.

In addition to their breadth of coverage, parent-report measures have other points to recommend their use, especially in comparison to the in-the-home observations by trained observers that characterized the first generation of child language research (e.g., Brown, 1973). Parent-report measures are considerably less labor-intensive than are observational assessments, or, for that matter, laboratory tests. They also make possible much larger sample sizes than are feasible with other approaches.

Of the numerous parent-report measures devoted to language, I briefly describe what is undoubtedly the best established and most influential such measure: the MacArthur-Bates Communicative Development Inventories (CDIs; Fenson et al., 1994; Fenson et al., 2007). The Inventories come in both an infant form, for children 8–18 months old, and a toddler form, for children 16–30 months old. Both forms assess a wide range of linguistic developments, including vocabulary, grammar, and use of gestures for communicative purposes, and both address both the child's comprehension of language and the child's production of language. The Inventories are available in Spanish as well as in English, and they have been adapted for use in more than 90 languages.

The format for the CDIs is a receptive one: Particular linguistic developments are presented, and the parent indicates whether his or her child demonstrates the competence in question. In the case of early word knowledge, for example, the infant form lists 396 words spanning 19 semantic categories, and the toddler form lists 680 words drawn from 22 semantic categories. As a measure of early grammatical development, the toddler form asks about the ability to add proper endings to words, for example, the "s" ending that indicates a plural or the "ed" ending that signals past tense.

The primary validation data for the MacArthur-Bates measures—and, indeed, for the many other parent-report measures of child language—come from correlations with other methods of measuring language, either naturalistic observations or laboratory tests. Although exceptions exist, the overall picture is a positive one, with the CDIs showing significant and often substantial correlations with a range of different measures in a range of different populations (Fenson et al., 1994; Fenson et al., 2007; Frank, Braginsky, Yurovsky, & Marchman, 2017). No one believes, of course, that parents are perfectly accurate reporters of their children's language; all parent reports are susceptible to problems of parental bias, misinterpretation, or lapses of memory. In balance, however, the evidence for parental knowledge is impressive.

Apart from parent-report measures, attempts to determine the accuracy of parents' beliefs about their children's language are rare. Several studies have shown that parents of preschool and grade-school children are fairly accurate at judging their children's vocabulary as measured by the Peabody Picture Vocabulary Test (Miller, 1986; Miller et al., 1991; Sattler et al., 1985), a finding that extends conclusions about knowledge of infant and toddler vocabulary to parents of older children. We will see in the next section that parents find early linguistic milestones relatively easy to judge in comparison to other sorts of milestones, again suggesting good knowledge of language development. Several studies have found that parents' general knowledge of early development, as assessed by the Knowledge of Infant Development Inventory (KIDI), relates positively to both children's language development and relevant parental practices to support language learning (Rowe, Denmark, Harden, & Stapleton, 2016; Zajicek-Farber, 2010). Finally, Suskind et al. (2018) have recently developed a KIDI-like measure oriented specifically to knowledge of early language development; sample items include "Infants learn little about language in the first six months of their life" and "Children 0 to 2 years old can learn just as many words from educational

TV as they can from their parents." The validation data for the measure are promising, but its application to the research literature remains a task for the future.

What do we know about the effects of parental knowledge? One kind of evidence comes from intervention studies in cases of language problems, one finding from which is that experimentally induced improvements in parental knowledge can have beneficial effects on both parents' behavior and children's subsequent language (e.g., Suskind et al., 2016). In most basic research, however, the relevant beliefs are not assessed directly but rather must be inferred from parents' behavior—thus, the same situation we saw with respect to both memory and executive function. Fortunately, we know quite a bit about what the behaviors are that support language learning. The following is a brief and partial overview of what has been found.

Children must have models from whom to learn language, and, in the typical case, parents are the most important models. Especially early in development, a simplified speech style when talking to the child (a style labeled either *motherese* or *infant-directed speech*) can be helpful, and some parents are more likely to use this style than are others. Recognizing the child's focus of attention can aid greatly in word learning, and again some parents are more successful at this task than are others. Finally, the sheer quantity of input can be important, and here the differences in how much parents talk to their children are staggering. It has been estimated that by age 4 a child from a high socioeconomic status (SES) home has heard 30 million more words than has one from a low SES home (Hart & Risley, 1995; Rowe, 2018).

How parents respond to their children's speech is also important. Although parents seldom explicitly correct their children's grammatical errors, other forms of response can be helpful, and some parents provide such responses more often than do others. Faced with an incomplete or incorrect utterance, parents may *expand* it into a fully formed adult equivalent, thus giving the child a model of the correct form. They may ask a *clarification question*, thus conveying to the child that something was unclear about the original utterance. And even when the original utterance was problem-free, they may *recast* it into another form, thus conveying that the same thing can be said in different ways. All of these responses give the child a chance to learn something new.

The research just summarized depends on individual differences among children—it is only if children vary in their language development that we can determine the effects of what their parents do. One of the surprising findings from early work with the CDIs was the extent of variability among children, which proved to be considerably greater than had previously been assumed. Parents' beliefs and practices undoubtedly contribute to these differences among children. But they also contribute to one of the most important commonalities in human development: the fact that whatever the differences may be, all typically developing children eventually master a complex and powerful language system.

## Milestones

Table 5.1 presented an example of a measure designed to assess parents' beliefs about various milestones of infant development. Table 6.4 provides an example of a similar measure intended for the childhood years (Roopnarine, Logie, Davidson, Krisnakumar, & Narine, 2015). The table shows 12 of the 25 items that make up the instrument.

**Table 6.4** Examples of Items from the Roopnarine et al. (2015) Study of Beliefs About Developmental Milestones

| Milestone | Correct age of onset |
| --- | --- |
| Identify body parts | 2–3 years |
| Match three to four colors | 2–3 years |
| Use short sentences | 2–3 years |
| Begin to obey requests | 2–3 years |
| Can tell a story | 3–4 years |
| Count 10 objects | 3–4 years |
| Use past tense correctly | 3–4 years |
| Identify triangle, circle, and square | 3–4 years |
| Tie shoelaces | 4–5 years |
| Distinguish left and right | 4–5 years |
| Print first and last names | 4–5 years |
| Do simple math | 4–5 years |

Adapted from "Caregivers' Knowledge about Children's Development in Three Ethnic Groups in Trinidad and Tobago," by J. L. Roopnarine, C. Logie, K. L. Davidson, A. Krishnakumar, and L. Narine, 2015, *Parenting: Science and Practice, 15*, p. 236. Copyright 2015 by Taylor and Francis Group. Adapted with permission.

As can be seen, the items in Table 6.4 concentrate on cognitive development, although there are a few exceptions (e.g., the tie-shoelaces item). Many other milestones measures are more eclectic, encompassing behaviors of a variety of sorts from a variety of domains (e.g., Hess, Kashiwagi, Azuma, Price, & Dickson, 1980). The Hess et al. (1980) measure, for example, in addition to various cognitive and social milestones, includes such items as takes care of own clothes, uses scissors, and keeps feet off furniture. To borrow a phrase from the aging literature, such all-purpose measures address "tasks of daily living," although from the perspective of a 4-year-old rather than a 70-year-old.

We saw in Chapter 5 that parents' ability to date milestones of infancy is often not very impressive. Not all of the studies of childhood milestones attempt to determine the accuracy of parents' responses; indeed, only a minority do. As the "Correct" column in Table 6.4 indicates, Roopnarine et al. (2015) is one of the studies that makes the attempt. The sample for the research consisted of mothers of preschoolers from Trinidad and Tobago, and the mothers' task was to select one of three age ranges (2–3, 3–4, or 4–5) as the time of mastery for each milestone presented. Mothers showed moderate success in doing so, achieving 50% or more correct responses on 19 of the 25 items. Performance was best on the developmentally earliest items and on the linguistic items, a finding that the authors attribute to the relative visibility of linguistic competence in the child's overt behavior.

As we saw, parents of infants tend to overestimate infant competence, indicating earlier ages of mastery than actually obtain. In the Roopnarine et al. (2015) study over- and underestimations were approximately equally likely. Note, though, that the method constrains the possibilities for two of the age ranges. It is impossible to overestimate children's mastery of developments in the 2- to 3-year range because an age earlier than the correct one is not a response option. Similarly, it is impossible to underestimate mastery of developments in the 4–5 range because in this case an age older than the correct one is not an option. This constraint holds in general whenever the response measure is selection among possible age ranges.

To my knowledge, the only other attempt to measure accuracy for dating of childhood milestones is a study by Tamis-LeMonda, Chen, and Bornstein (1998). Two kinds of milestones were examined: those for early forms of play and those for early forms of language. Mothers were more accurate in dating the language milestones, and this finding held for both estimated ages of mastery and rank ordering of different achievements. The latter performance was especially impressive: a correlation of .82 between predicted ordering and actual ordering. Maternal knowledge was not across-the-board, however, for there was no relation between accuracy for language and accuracy for play.

The relative ease of the language items fits with the argument that linguistic competence is a relatively visible aspect of young children's behavior. Tamis-LeMonda et al. (1998) suggest a further possible basis for the language–play differences. As they note, language development is characterized by the replacement of early forms by later, more mature forms, a progression that may make it relatively easy to remember or to predict which developments come when. Although play also grows more complex with development, early forms of play do not necessarily disappear as children grow older; rather, they are simply joined by more advanced possibilities. This persistence of early forms may complicate the task of specifying exactly what emerges when.

As noted, accuracy is not an issue in the majority of studies that examine beliefs about milestones during the childhood years. What, then, are such studies designed to tell us? By far the most common question that has been addressed concerns possible cultural differences in the beliefs that parents hold about when various developmental competencies emerge. And by far the most common finding is that there are in fact cultural differences in such beliefs.

In some instances early versus later expectations emerge as a general difference between the cultures being compared. For example, Lebanese-born mothers in Australia have been found to hold later expectations for developmental milestones than do Australian-born mothers (Goodnow, Cashmore, Cotton, & Knight, 1984), and the same is true for Vietnamese-born mothers in Australia (Rosenthal & Gold, 1989). Two studies with mothers in the Netherlands found that Dutch mothers hold earlier expectations than do both Turkish mothers (Durgel, van de Vijver, & Yagmurlu, 2013) and Zambian mothers (Williamsen & van de Fons, 1997). Puerto Rican mothers have been found to hold later expectations than do both European American and African American mothers (Pachter & Dworkin, 1997), and the same pattern is evident for Latina mothers of Mexican descent (Savage & Gauvain, 1998). In these and other instances, what seems to emerge is a rough Western versus non-Western, industrialized versus traditional division, with earlier expectations for countries in the former category.

Differences, however, are not necessarily across the board; rather, they may vary with the particular milestones in question. One of the earliest milestone studies, that by Hess and colleagues (Hess et al., 1980), demonstrated this point. Although the Japanese and American mothers in the study showed no overall differences in expected ages of mastery, differences did emerge when subcategories of items were considered separately. Specifically, Japanese mothers held higher expectations for the development of emotional maturity, compliance, and social courtesy, whereas American mothers expected earlier mastery of verbal assertiveness and social skills with peers. Here and in general, the cultural differences that emerge in parents' expectations appear explicable in terms of cultural values and related socialization practices. As discussed earlier, expectations for one's child may be a function not only of an objectively formed conception of reality—beliefs about what is—but also of values and goals and plans for the future—beliefs about what should be. Culture is both a source of such beliefs and a context for attempting to turn them into reality.

# 7

# Childhood: Social Development

I think any emotions can be expressed, but it's how you express it that makes the difference. All emotions are allowed, and you're going to have every single kind of emotion, but it's not okay to express it in a negative way . . . if you're angry or frustrated, you can't hit the wall or kick your sister or throw the item across the room.

—(Parker et al., 2012, p. 50)

I'm not going to encourage him to fight other youngsters to solve problems, but to think it out and see if there is another way to handle these problems, instead of violence you see. Maybe by talking things out.

—(Stolz, 1967, pp. 51–52)

He started having problems interacting with other kids because, um, his shyness, ah, prevented him from knowing how to interact and approach other kids in order to play with them and to make friends. . . . So he would do things like run up to kids and steal their pencils, and run away. Or, he would, um, walk up to them and scrunch up their work.

—(Hiebert-Murphy et al., 2012, p. 389)

She is now in a stage of trying hard to figure out what are the limits. How far can I go before Daddy will get mad? Or before I say "Hey don't do that!" Or "Now that's enough." And that is trying to push out the boundaries of what is allowed and what isn't.

—(Harkness, Super, and van Tijen. 2000, p. 26)

The topic of children's social development is at least as large and multifaceted as is the topic of children's cognitive development. The literature on parents'

*Parents' Beliefs About Children.* Scott A. Miller, Oxford University Press (2020). © Oxford University Press.
DOI: 10.1093/oso/9780190874513.001.0001

beliefs is also large and diverse. The goal of this chapter is to convey the most important conclusions from this large body of work.

Two important outcomes of children's social development have already been discussed. Both temperament and attachment are major foci for infant research, and these topics were therefore covered in Chapter 6, "Infancy." As will be seen, some of the topics to be considered now also have their origins in infancy. For the most part, however, these are aspects of social functioning that develop most fully across the childhood years and that first become important components of children's personality during those years.

Like Chapter 6, this chapter is organized in terms of major outcomes in children's development. Five outcomes are addressed: emotional development, aggression, moral development, social competence, and gender-role development.

As we will see, these topics are not neatly compartmentalized; rather, aspects of two or more often flow together as children deal with their social worlds. Controlling one's emotions, for example, may be necessary to avoid an aggressive act, which in turn may help to maintain good social relations with others. We will see various such interrelations as we proceed.

## Emotions

I begin with the topic that has its earliest manifestation in children's behavior: the expression of emotions. As the cry of the newborn conveys, a general emotion of arousal/distress is present from birth. A more positive emotion of excitement/attention is also evident at birth or soon after. Across the early years these broad starting points gradually differentiate into the more specific emotions that characterize the range of human emotional experience—thus sadness, fear anger, and disgust on the negative side, and happiness, interest, and surprise on the positive side. These later developments also include the so-called *secondary* or *social emotions*: guilt, shame, empathy, pride, embarrassment, and jealousy. Emotions of this sort depend on a cognitive underpinning that takes time to develop.

The development and expression of emotions is one of three main topics in the study of emotional development. The other two topics are related. One concerns children's understanding of emotions. The other concerns children's ability to regulate their emotions—that is, to control their emotions in adaptive ways.

Parents' beliefs and related behaviors encompass all three of these aspects of emotional development. Methodologically, most of the data concerning parents' beliefs about emotions come from standardized instruments designed to measure such beliefs. There is, in fact, a plethora of such instruments, among them are the Parent Meta-Emotion Interview (Katz & Gottman, 1986), Parents' Beliefs About Negative Emotions Questionnaire (Halberstadt, Dunsmore, McElwain, Eaton, & McCool, 2001), Maternal Emotional Styles Questionnaire (Lagace-Seguin & Coplan, 2005), Parents' Beliefs About Feelings Questionnaire (Dunsmore & Karn, 2001), Emotion-Related Parenting Styles Self-Test (Hakim-Larson, Parker, Lee, Goodwin, & Voelker, 2006), Emotion-Related Parenting Styles Short Form (Paterson et al., 2012); and Parents' Beliefs About Children's Emotions Questionnaire (Halberstadt et al., 2013). Table 7.1 provides a sample of items from the last of these measures.

As would be expected, there is considerable overlap among the measures just listed. In addition, several have the same theoretical basis: the *parental meta-emotion philosophy* (PMEP) approach to emotions and emotional development formulated by Gottman, Katz, and Hooven (1996, 1997). Gottman and colleagues define parental meta-emotion philosophy as "an organized set of feelings and thoughts about one's own emotions and one's children's emotions" (Gottman et al., 1996, p. 243). The concept is thus broad—not just thoughts about emotions but also emotions about emotions (as the term "meta-emotion" implies), and not just thoughts and feelings about the self but also thoughts and feelings about one's children.

Figure 7.1 provides an overview of the PMEP approach. As can be seen, the model addresses three of the basic questions in the study of parents' beliefs. A first question concerns the nature of the beliefs. Important in the PMEP approach are both awareness of the child's emotion, and thus some degree of parental accuracy, and acceptance of what the child is experiencing, and thus not minimization or outright dismissal. A second question concerns the relation between beliefs and parental behavior. As the figure indicates, the behavior emphasized is *coaching*, a term that encompasses a number of specific ways by which parents can help their children cope with emotions; among the 11 forms examined by Gottman et al. (1996) are comforting the child, showing respect for the child's experience, teaching the child how to express emotions, and teaching the child strategies to self-soothe in the case of negative emotions. A final question concerns how parental beliefs and behavior relate to children's development. The model includes the three outcomes of

**Table 7.1** Examples of Items from the Parents' Beliefs About Children's Emotions Questionnaire

| Scale | Item |
|---|---|
| Negative consequences | Too much joy can make it hard for a child to understand others. |
| | Children who feel emotions strongly are likely to face a lot of trouble in life. |
| Value/Acceptance | It is useful for children to feel angry sometimes. |
| | Being angry can motivate children to change or fix something in their lives. |
| Manipulation | Children use emotions to manipulate others. |
| | Children often cry just to get attention. |
| Control | Children can control their emotions. |
| | Children can control what they show on their faces. |
| Parental knowledge | Parents don't have to know about all their children's feelings. |
| | Parents should encourage their child to tell them everything they are feeling. |
| Autonomy | It is usually best to let a child work through being sad on their own. |
| | When children are angry, it is best to just let them work it through on their own. |
| Respect | Making fun of children's behavior is never a good idea. |
| | Parents should not show contempt toward their children. |
| Stability | Children's emotions tend to be long-lasting. |
| | Children's emotion styles tend to stay the same over time. |

Responses are made on a 6-point scale ranging from "strongly disagree" to "strongly agree." Adapted from "Development and Validation of the Parents' Beliefs About Children's Emotions Questionnaire," by A. G. Halberstadt, J. C. Dunsmore, A. Bryant, Jr., A. E. Parker, K. S. Beale, and J. A. Thompson, 2013, *Psychological Assessment, 25,* pp. 1200–1201. Copyright 2013 by the American Psychological Association. Reprinted with permission.

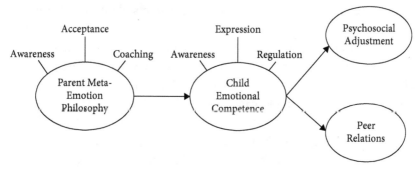

**Figure 7.1** Theoretical model of parent meta-emotion philosophy and its effects. From "Parental meta-emotion philosophy: A review of research and theoretical framework," by L. F. Katz, A. C. Maliken, & N. M. Stettler, 2012, *Child Development Perspectives, 6,* p. 418. Copyright 2012 by Wiley. Reprinted with permission.

emotional development identified earlier: expression, understanding, and regulation. It also extends to other outcomes, such as peer relations and social adjustment, for which emotions are important contributors.

Comprehensive though the model is, it does not—at least in the schematic form summarized in the figure—address one further basic question: namely, where do parents' beliefs come from? Why, for example, are some parents more aware of their children's emotions or more accepting of the emotions than are others? There is certainly relevant evidence, however—some from the PMEP perspective and some from other approaches to the study of emotions. I begin with what this research tells us about the origins of parents' beliefs.

Mother–father comparisons are again one source of evidence. At a general level, the conclusions from such comparisons mirror those that we have seen for other topics (Dunsmore, Her, Halberstadt, & Perez-Rivera, 2009; Stettler & Katz, 2014; Wong, McElwain, & Halberstadt, 2009). Differences between spouses are by no means always found; indeed, the similarities in this literature are arguably more noteworthy than the differences. When differences do occur, they typically favor mothers. Thus mothers are sometimes more supportive of their children's emotions than are fathers, they are more expressive of their own emotions than are fathers, and they believe more strongly than do fathers in the importance of coaching to help their children cope with emotions. As we have seen for other topics, concordance in beliefs between spouses is modest, with typical correlations in the .30 to .40 range.

The mother–father comparison is of interest as a proxy for variations in amount and kind of experience with children. Age of child is another proxy. By some measures, parents' knowledge of their children increases with the age of the child. We might expect, then, that parents' ability to judge and respond appropriately to their children's emotions would increase as the child grows older and parental experience grows richer. Such is sometimes the case. Any such simple relation is complicated, however, by developmental changes across childhood in the understanding and regulation of emotions. Older children, for example, can mask their emotions in ways not yet available to younger children, and their emotion regulation skills take on more varied and subtle forms. Not surprisingly then, parents' ability to recognize their children's emotions sometimes dips for a period as children grow older (Stettler & Katz, 2014), and judgments of emotion regulation skills sometimes show a similar developmental pattern (Hourigan, Goodman, & Southam-Gerow, 2011).

The research just discussed concerns parents' experience with children. Also of interest is parents' experience *as* children. We have already seen several instances in which childhood attachment experiences carry over to adulthood and affect parents' responses to their own children. The socialization of emotions provides a further example, with the clearest effects coming in response to children's negative emotions. Compared to parents in general, parents with insecure attachment representations (i.e., high in anxiety or avoidance) are often more distressed by children's negative emotions, are less supportive of their children's emotional experiences, and are harsher in the ways that they respond to their children's emotions (Jones, Brett, Ehrlich, Lejuez, & Cassidy, 2014; Morey & Gentzley, 2017).

I turn finally to what is always an important entry under the origins heading: culture or ethnicity. One basic contrast here is one that we have seen before: that between Western cultures, characterized (with the qualifications noted in Chapter 2) by an emphasis on independence and autonomy, and Eastern cultures, characterized (again with qualifications) by an emphasis on interdependence and respect for others. Several predicted differences follow from these differences in cultural emphases. One is that Western parents will be more accepting and supportive of self-focused emotions such as anger and pride than will Eastern parents. A second is that Eastern parents will promote skills, such as self-display rules, that minimize the expression of emotions such as anger or pride, emotions that might damage relations with others. Finally, a third is that Eastern parents will encourage more other-directed emotions such as sympathy and shame, emotions that prioritize others over the self. As with the Eastern–Western contrast in general, such a broad swath oversimplifies a complex reality and leaves much unexplained, including the presence of marked individual differences *within* a culture. Still, research does provide some support for all three of the predicted on-the-average contrasts between Western and Eastern cultures, including differences in both parental practices and related child outcomes (Cole & Tan, 2015; Friedlmeier, Corapci, & Cole, 2011).

Ethnic as well as cultural differences are evident, although ethnicity is often confounded with immigration status. For example, Indian immigrant mothers in the United States have been found to be lower in awareness, acceptance, and support of their children's emotions than are White mothers (Daga, Raval, & Raj, 2015; McCord & Raval, 2016). Latina immigrant mothers have been found to be more likely to hold maladaptive beliefs about emotions, such as the belief that emotions are dangerous or that children need constant guidance in dealing with emotions (Perez Rivera & Dunsmore, 2011). Degree of acculturation is important, however, because differences among groups are often reduced as acculturation proceeds. In addition, in many instances, the similarities among cultural or ethnic groups have proved at least as noteworthy as the differences (Denham, Caal, Bassett, Benga, & Geangu, 2004; Parker et al., 2012). Such findings are a valuable reminder that the task of emotion socialization is a universal one and that differences among parents may reflect varied approaches to a common goal.

The discussion to this point gives some idea of the nature of parents' beliefs about emotions. Not yet addressed, however, is a basic question that recurs throughout the book: How accurate are these beliefs? Do parents in fact know what their children are feeling or what their children understand about emotions?

Parent-report measures provide one context for examining this question, given that the validity of such measures depends on a demonstration of parental accuracy. The most often used of the available measures is the Emotion Regulation Checklist (ERC; Shields & Cicchetti, 1997). As its name indicates, the ERC concentrates on one aspect of emotional development: the ability to regulate emotions. Among the items, each of which is rated on a 4-point scale, are "is easily frustrated," "is able to delay gratification," "is prone to disruptive outbursts of energy and exuberance," and "can modulate excitement in emotionally arousing situations."

The original validation evidence for the ERC was based on responses of camp counselors rather than parents (Shields & Cicchetti, 1997). Subsequent studies with parents have shown that parental ratings do correlate significantly with other indices of emotion regulation, such as observational assessments; the relations, however, are modest at best (e.g., Nader-Grosbois & Mazzone, 2015; Reis et al., 2016). Does such divergence call the parent-report approach into question? A point made with respect to parent-report measures in Chapter 6 applies here as well, and that is that there is no "gold standard" in the measurement of children's emotions, some clearly valid assessment against which other approaches can be validated (Adrian, Zeman, & Veits, 2011). Parent reports are imperfect, but so then is every other measurement option, and divergence among measures may reflect error on either or both sides. In addition—and this is another point discussed in Chapter 6—some differences may reflect the fact that parent reports pick up on aspects of development not captured by other approaches. The fact that the ERC has been a productive contributor to a range of research questions suggests that it does capture something of importance in children's emotion regulation.

Parent reports are not the only source for a determination of parental accuracy. A number of studies have examined whether parents' beliefs about their children's emotions match what the children themselves say about their emotions. Some studies have taken the approach that we saw is common in the study of cognitive development: namely, asking parents to predict their child's response to standard assessments of the development of interest (Karstad, Kvello, Wichstom, & Berg-Nielsen, 2014; Karstad, Wichstom, Reinfjell, Belsky, & Berg-Nielsen, 2015). In other studies, there is no explicit request to predict the child's response, but parents respond to an identical or similar measure, thus permitting a determination of the degree of parent–child agreement (Hourigan et al., 2011; Lagattuta, Sayfan, & Bamford, 2012; Vinik, Almas, & Grusec, 2011).

The degree of agreement is not very great. Given the uncertainties that surround child self-reports, the discrepancies do not necessarily reflect parental inaccuracy—parents may sometimes possess insights not yet available to their children. Still, both the direction and extent of the differences suggest that parents are often unaware of how their children are feeling or thinking. In a study by Karstad and colleagues (Karstad et al., 2014), parents' ability to judge their children's emotion understanding skills barely exceeded chance ($r = .14$), and judgments were at chance level or below on six of the nine dimensions of understanding that were examined. The dominant parental error was overestimation; 91% of parents overestimated their children's performance, and the total score estimated by the parents was almost twice the actual total earned by the children. In the Lagattuta et al. (2012) study, parents' responses showed no relation to their children's responses across three studies, two directed to worry/anxiety and one directed to optimism. In each case parents' judgments were more positive than those of their children—thus fewer judgments of worry/anxiety and more judgments of optimism. Other studies have reported that parents overestimate their children's happiness (Lopez-Perez & Wilson, 2015) and underestimate their emotional problems (Michels et al., 2013). We have, then, further examples of the valence effect: parental overoptimism in judging their own children. Because the findings just summarized have to do with emotion expression and emotion understanding, I will add that parents' performance is also far from perfect in judging their children's emotion regulation (Hourigan et al., 2011).

Does parental accuracy, or its absence, make a difference? There is limited evidence on this point. In the Vinik et al. (2011) study, parents' accuracy in judging their child's distress related positively to the children's ability to cope with distress. In the Karstad et al. studies (Karstad et al., 2014, 2015), parents' accuracy in judging emotion understanding related positively to parents' emotional availability, a generally positive parental attribute across a range of child outcomes. Accuracy also related positively to improvements in children's emotion understanding between ages 4 and 6. Finally, both of the Karstad et al. studies reported substantial correlations (.67 and .81) between parental accuracy and children's understanding, a finding clearly supportive of the value of accuracy. As we saw in Chapter 6, however, such accuracy–outcome correlations typically have multiple possible interpretations.

Parental accuracy is not the only dimension of parental thinking that may impact parents' behavior and children's development. An examination of Table 7.1 is instructive in this regard. Although there are certainly better or worse answers to the questions presented in the table, the required judgments do not lend themselves to a clear right or wrong, accurate or not determination. In addition, they are not judgments about the parent's own child; rather, the items refer to emotions in general and to children in general. The goal of the measure—and indeed of all of the measures cited earlier in the chapter—is to assess individual differences in the quality of parents' thinking about emotions and not, at least directly, knowledge about their own children.

What do such measures tell us about differences in parents' thinking and how such differences impact children's development? I provide a brief summary of a large literature; fuller treatments are available in Bader and Fouts (2019); Bridgett, Burt, Edwards, and Deater-Deckard (2015); Katz, Maliken, & Stettler (2012); and Morris, Criss, Silk, and Houltber (2017).

As the PMEP model proposes, awareness and acceptance of the child's emotions are clearly beneficial. This point applies especially to negative emotions, for negative emotions present more challenges to both child and parent than do positive ones. Acknowledging the value of emotions, teaching children the language to talk about emotions, and offering helpful support in times of emotional need are all related to positive emotional development (Dunsmore & Karn, 2004; Halberstadt, Thompson, Parker, & Dunsmore, 2008; Wong et al., 2009). Parents' expressiveness with regard to their own emotions is also a positive predictor, as is a positive overall emotional climate within the home (Dunsmore & Karn, 2001; Morris et al., 2017).

On the other hand, not all parental beliefs and related behaviors are beneficial. A parent's belief that emotions are dangerous relates to relatively poor emotional development in her child, in part because parents with such a belief are likely to mask their own emotions (Dunsmore et al., 2009). A belief that children need constant guidance to cope with emotions appears to be a form of overparenting, for such a belief on parents' part predicts relatively poor emotion recognition on children's part (Castro, Halberstadt, Lozada, & Craig, 2015). As Castro et al. (2015) acknowledge, however, the relation may be a bidirectional one: Perceived problems in children's development may elicit more guidance by parents.

The results summarized to this point reflect correlational approaches to the issues of belief–behavior and behavior–outcome relations (which, of course, is why the causal direction in the Castro et al., 2015, study is uncertain). Intervention studies in which beliefs are experimentally manipulated provide a more certain basis for conclusions about causality, as well as speaking to issues of pragmatic importance. Chapter 2 identified three outcomes of interest from intervention research, and work on emotional development provides evidence of all three. First, interventions can succeed in altering parents' beliefs about emotions in a positive direction. Second, changes in parental behaviors often follow from the changes in beliefs. Finally, changes in children's development often follow from the changes in beliefs and behaviors (Havighurst et al., 2013; Havighurst, Wilson, Harley, Prior, & Kehoe, 2010; Wilson, Havighurst, Kehoe, & Harley, 2016).

There is still one further form of evidence for parents' contribution to emotional development. It comes from the memory talk paradigm discussed in Chapter 6. In some memory talk studies, parents are asked to talk about emotions, and even when no such instructions are given, emotions are a frequent topic of many families' conversations. Such studies verify a conclusion reached earlier: that parents' talk about emotions, if offered in a clear and supportive fashion, can nurture positive emotional development. They also reveal a possible gender difference in the nature and effects of such talk. Differences in speech to boys and girls are by no means always found. When differences do occur, however, it is typically daughters who receive more emotion talk than do sons (e.g., Fivush, Brotman, Buckner, & Goodman, 2000; Reese, Haden, & Fivush, 1996). Talk directed to daughters often includes both a greater number and a greater variety of emotion terms than does talk directed to sons, and it is also more likely to focus on the causes of emotions. Differences are especially pronounced with respect to discussion of negative emotions, especially sadness. Furthermore, over time, children's talk comes to reflect these differences in parental input, for eventually girls come to talk more about emotions, especially sadness, than do boys.

## Aggression

Especially when children are young, making sense of their children's emotions may be a daily task for most parents. Aggression, in contrast, is not an issue for at least the first year or so of a child's life, and it may be only an occasional and minor concern for many parents from that point on. For some, however, aggression may be a major concern because it is a major concern for their children, either in the role of perpetrator, or in the role of victim, or as both. In what follows, I first discuss parents' beliefs and related behaviors with respect to aggression that falls within a normal range of variation. I then move on to how parents cope with more extreme forms of aggression. Two forms are of interest: bullying and delinquency. Bullying can start quite early in childhood, and it therefore is considered in this chapter. Delinquency (which, of course, can take many forms in addition to aggression) is typically not a concern until the teen years, and its coverage is therefore deferred until Chapter 8 on Adolescence.

### Normative Development

We can begin by revisiting one of the findings discussed in Chapter 3: parents' beliefs about the stability of early forms of aggression. We saw there that many parents of preschoolers regard early aggression as a developmentally normative behavior that will lessen naturally as children mature, and that they hold this belief more strongly for aggression than they do for social withdrawal. Although there are some specific differences in beliefs across the cultural groups that have been studied, this general conclusion has emerged in a range of settings, including Canada (Mills & Rubin, 1990), China (Cheah & Rubin, 2004), South Korea (Cheah & Park, 2006), Turkey (Bayram Ozdemir & Cheah, 2015), and the United States (Cheah & Rubin 2004). It also emerged for fathers in the one study to make a mother–father comparison (Mills & Rubin, 1990).

A belief that aggression is age-related and therefore somewhat transient does not mean that parents are happy to see it. The dominant emotional responses to aggression in the studies just cited are concern, anger, and disappointment, and anticipated socialization strategies to correct the problem often take a strong, power-assertive form. We will return shortly to the issue of how parents' beliefs relate to their parenting practices.

The studies just discussed suggest that children's age is one contributor to how parents think about aggression, but they do not establish this point definitively, given that age of child is not a variable in any of the studies. Rubin and Mills (1992a) added the age dimension by following up a subset of the Mills and Rubin (1990) sample 2 years later. As expected, attributions to age-related factors were less common for 6-year-olds than for 4-year-olds, a finding that held for both aggression (a drop from 23% of the attributions to 9%) and social withdrawal (a drop from 10% to 3%). Other studies have reported compatible results—for example, that aggression is perceived as more intentional and more blameworthy as children grow older (Del Vecchio & O'Leary, 2008). In most other respects, however, the follow-up findings to the Mills and Rubin study were similar to the original ones, including (as the means just given indicate) more emphasis on age-related factors for aggression than for withdrawal. Despite this similarity at a group level, mothers' beliefs showed only moderate consistency (correlations of .27 to .56) across the 2-year span.

Not yet discussed is the type of aggression to which parents are responding in these studies. The following is one of the vignettes devised by Mills and Rubin (1990, p. 141) and used in a number of subsequent studies.

> The last three times a mother arrives to pick up her child from an activity group, she sees her 4-year-old child playing in a group. Each time, the mother notices that whenever her child wants a toy that another child is playing with, her child grabs the toy and pushes the other child down.

The act described in the vignette is a form of *proactive aggression*— proactive because the aggressor initiates the action in an attempt to achieve a goal. Suppose, however, that the aggressed-upon child does not meekly give in but rather fights back. Such aggression in response to a clear provocation would be an example of *reactive aggression*.

As we might expect, parents respond differently to these two forms of aggression (Bayram Ozdemir & Cheah, 2017; Cheah & Sheperd, 2011). They are more upset by proactive than reactive aggression, and they advocate more power-assertive socialization strategies for controlling proactive aggression. They also draw different attributions for the two types of aggression: internal/dispositional factors for proactive aggression, external/situational factors for reactive aggression.

Despite the differences just noted, proactive and reactive aggression share a basic similarity, and that is that both are forms of physical aggression. In very early childhood all aggression is physical. Eventually, however, children become capable of using not just their actions but their words to inflict harm—become capable of verbal aggression. Of the various forms that verbal aggression can take, the form labeled *relational aggression* has been of special interest. Relational aggression refers to the use of language to manipulate the social situation in ways detrimental to the target of the aggression. "I won't be your friend unless you give me that toy" might be a simple early example. With development, relational aggression increases in proportion relative to physical aggression. The two forms also show a clear gender difference. Whereas boys are consistently higher than girls in physical aggression, most studies report no gender differences in relational aggression, and in occasional samples girls score higher than do boys (Dodge, Coie, & Lynam, 2006).

As with the proactive–reactive contrast, parents in some ways respond differently to relational than to physical aggression (Hurd & Gettinger, 2011; Swit, McMaugh, & Warburton, 2017). Relational aggression is seen as more normative and thus less problematic than is physical aggression, parents show less empathy for the targets of relational aggression than they do for the targets of physical aggression, and they are less likely to intervene in instances of relational aggression. It is interesting to note that teachers make the same sorts of physical–relational distinctions.

This section began with some similarities across cultures in beliefs about the age-related nature of aggression. Such similarities, however, are often accompanied by marked cultural differences in other kinds of belief, as well as by differences in amount of aggression across cultures (Eisner & Malti, 2015). Once again, the collectivist–individualist distinction has been one focus of study. We might expect that both methods of socializing aggression and resulting levels of aggression will be lower in collectivist than in individualist societies, given the focus of the former on concern for others and the prioritization of the group over the individual. A large research literature makes clear that this is in fact the case, although, as always, such broad

Eastern–Western comparisons leave many differences both between and within cultures still to be explained (Bergeron & Schneider, 2005; Bergmuller, 2013; Shuster, Li, & Shi, 2012).

Differences among ethnic groups are also common in the aggression literature. Although no ethnic group consistently values or encourages high levels of aggression, African American parents tend to be more accepting of aggression than are White parents and also more likely to endorse physical punishment as a technique of discipline, not only with respect to aggression but as a socialization tool more generally (Blake, Lease, Olejnik, & Turner, 2010; Child Trends, 2015a; Solomon, Bradshaw, Wright, & Cheng, 2008). As numerous authors have pointed out, difficult environmental circumstances may account for at least some of these differences among groups. Parents whose children are growing up in a dangerous neighborhood may feel a need both to exert tight control over their children's behavior (thus the use of punishment) and to prepare the child for aversive encounters with others (hence the tolerance of aggression).

The discussion of physical punishment can serve as a transition to what we know about the effects of parental practices on children's aggression. Perhaps the clearest thing we know is that physical punishment does not work well in controlling aggression—or, indeed, in producing any desirable outcome in children's development (Gershoff, 2002; Gershoff & Grogan-Kaylor, 2016). A large body of research demonstrates that relatively high use of physical punishment by parents is associated with relatively high levels of aggression in their children. This does not mean that physical punishment cannot sometimes be effective in inducing immediate compliance. But physical punishment as a preferred technique of discipline is associated with a range of negative outcomes, heightened aggression being just one among them.

We have encountered the directionality issue with respect to parent–child correlations at various points, and the issue certainly applies to the present topic. Perhaps the causal basis for the punishment–aggression relation lies in the child rather than the parent. Aggressive children may elicit physical punishment from their parents, other, milder tactics having been tried and failed. Although longitudinal research provides some evidence for such a child-to-parent effect, the bulk of the evidence goes in the opposite direction—that is, punishment early in childhood relates to aggression later in childhood, the outcome we would expect if punishment is the causal factor in the relation (Dodge et al., 2006). Intervention programs designed to prevent or reduce physical punishment are a further source of evidence. Many programs have been successful in doing so, and reductions in children's aggression often follow from the reduction in parental punishment (Santini & Williams, 2016).

Why do parents resort to physical punishment? Some instances are no doubt heat-of-the moment reactions with little or no cognitive underpinning. For many parents, however, the practice follows from a firmly held belief that physical punishment is both an effective and a legitimate practice in disciplining one's children (Child Trends, 2015a; Chiocca, 2016). Table 7.2 provides a sampling of the justifications that parents offer in support of physical punishment (see also Kish & Newcombe, 2015). Note, with respect to some of the examples, that this is another instance in which childhood experiences contribute to adult beliefs and behavior (Chung et al., 2009).

A belief in the value of punishment is not the only cognitive contributor to how parents respond to their children's aggressive behaviors. We saw in Chapter 4 that parents bring different attributional styles to the task of making sense of their children's behavior, and this point clearly applies to the interpretation of children's aggression. Parents of aggressive children tend to make negative, child-blaming attributions for aggression and other undesired behaviors on their child's part, attributions that heighten the probability of an angry, punitive attempt to control the child (Crandall, Ghazarian, Deater-Deckard, Bell, & Riley, 2018; Dix & Lochman, 1990). Over time, children often take on the attributional biases of their parents, a development that makes future aggression even more likely.

The discussion of parenting and aggression to this point has focused on what *not* to do. More positively, the same parental qualities that underlie

Table 7.2 Reasons Offered by Parents for the Use of Physical Punishment

I was spanked and I am OK.
Spanking improves child behavior.
Other forms of discipline are not as effective as spanking.
Spanking is discipline, not abuse.
I spanked my children and they are OK.
Spanking was common in my generation and my generation is OK.

Adapted from "Beliefs and Ideologies Linked with Approval of Corporal Punishment: A Content Analysis of Online Comments, by C. A. Taylor, R. Al-Hiyari, S. J. Lee, A. Priebe, L. W. Guerrero, and A. Bales, 2016, *Health Education Research, 31,* p. 567. Copyright 2016 by Oxford University Press. Adapted with permission.

other positive developments contribute to low levels of aggression, including maintenance of a warm and supportive relationship, sensitivity in reading and responding to the child's needs, and control exerted primarily through reasoning rather than through the greater power of the parent (Eisner & Malti, 2015; Kawabata, Alink, Tseng, van IJzendoorn, & Crick, 2011). In addition, aggression is another outcome for which the attachment relationship with the parents turns out to be important, for securely attached children are less aggressive than are children with insecure attachments. The disorganized attachment pattern is especially predictive of problems with aggression and other externalizing behaviors (Fearon, Bakersman-Kranenburg, IJzendoorn, Lapsley, & Roisman, 2010).

## Bullying

In addition to its seriousness, bullying has two features that distinguish it from most instances of aggressive behavior. One is that there is an imbalance of power between the participants: The bully has power; the victim lacks it. The other is that bullying is (at least usually) not a onetime occurrence; rather, it involves repeated acts of aggression. In most cases bullies bully multiple times, victims are victimized multiple times, and the same pairing of bully and victim occurs multiple times.

Bullying is measured in various ways, the two most common of which are self-report and peer report (Hymel & Swearer, 2015). Parent reports are seldom used for the obvious reason that parents are not present for most of the actions that we wish to measure. Indeed, the same point applies to the measurement of aggression in general beyond the early childhood years. Thus most of what we know about bullying comes from the participants themselves.

We know quite a bit. The literature on bullying is a large and multifaceted one, encompassing work on the antecedents of both bullying and victimhood, the consequences of being a bully or being a victim, and intervention programs designed to reduce the frequency of bullying (Juvonen & Graham, 2014; Olweus, 2013; Salmivalli & Peets, 2018; Zych, Ortega-Ruiz, & Del Rey, 2015). It also includes a growing body of work on the relatively new phenomenon of *cyberbullying*—a verbal form of aggression in which the attack occurs not face to face but rather via electronic media (Hinduja & Patchin, 2015; Vollink, Dehue, & Mc Gunkin, 2016).

The role of parents is of interest at two points in the study of either bullies or the victims of bullies. One is as possible contributors to their child's problematic behavior. As is always true, what parents do is rarely a sufficient cause for problems in development, and in particular cases it may not be a contributor at all. Nevertheless, it is clear—as it is clear for aggression in general—that parental practices can make a difference. The childhood experiences of many bullies-to-be are characterized by lack of warmth, lack of control, poor communication, insufficient parental monitoring, and harsh parental practices that in some cases shade into abuse (Cook, Williams, Guerra, Kim, & Sadek, 2010; Kijakovic & Hunt, 2016). Not surprisingly, then, bullies tend to be low in empathy, high in need for control, and especially susceptible to peer influence, all factors that increase their tendency to bully others.

What about the victims of bullying? Although there are exceptions, such children tend to be physically weak, they are often socially isolated, they manifest internalizing difficulties (e.g., anxiety and depression), they often have fearful temperaments, and they tend to give in to and therefore reinforce aggression. Again, parental practices can contribute to these difficulties, including many of the same factors that underlie bullying, such as lack of warmth and poor communication. In addition, the home lives of victims are often characterized by an overprotective form of parenting in which the parent attempts to shield the child from problems or to correct the problems herself, an approach that leaves children poorly prepared to meet challenges on their own, including the challenges posed by bullies (Cook et al., 2010; Lereya, Samara, & Wolke, 2013).

Concerns about bullying have spurred the creation of numerous intervention programs across the past several decades, the goal of which is to reduce both the frequency and the effects of bullying. The best known and arguably most successful of these efforts is the Olweus Bullying Prevention Program (OBPP; Limber, Olweus, Wang, & Masiello, 2018; Olweus, 1993). Like most interventions, the OBPP is a school-based program, school being the locus for most acts of bullying. A central emphasis of the program, however, is the involvement of all those with a stake in the outcome—thus not only students, teachers, counselors, and administrators at school, but also parents at home. And it is clear—not just from the OBPP but from interventions more generally—that family involvement can be an important contributor to the success of interventions in reducing bullying (Bradshaw, 2015).

I noted that most bullying occurs in school. Cyberbullying, however, provides an exception to this statement because both the production and the reception of cyberbullying can occur wherever bully and victim have access to an appropriate device and the opportunity to use it. As several authors have pointed out, their closer proximity to acts of cyberbullying gives parents greater opportunity for influence than is true for physical bullying, and some evidence supports this possibility (Elsaesser, Russell, Ohanessian, & Patton, 2017; Seiler & Navarro, 2014). Clearly, however, parents can affect their children's Internet experiences only if they know what these experiences are, something that is by no means always the case. The question of what parents know about their children's activities on the Internet will be one of the topics in Chapter 8, on Adolescence.

## Morality

The topic of moral development provides a clear illustration of the earlier point about the interrelations among aspects of social development, for morality overlaps with both of the topics considered to this point in the chapter. Moral development includes a behavioral component, and aggression is a clear entry under this heading; it is typically talked about separately (as was done here) only because of its importance. Moral development also includes an emotional component—in particular, a focus on the "moral emotions" of guilt, shame, and empathy. These emotions were not singled out for specific coverage in the "Emotions" section, but they will be one of the topics in this section.

The third component of moral development is the cognitive one: how children reason about moral issues and how their reasoning changes with development. Chapter 4 presented an initial consideration of this question in its discussion of Judith Smetana's work on beliefs about domains of development. As we saw, this work addresses the basic question of what behaviors fall within the domain of morality, as well as possible parent-child differences in how behaviors are allotted to domains.

I should note that this tripartite division of the domain of morality has been challenged in recent years, with questions raised about the separability and the interplay of the different components (Haidt, 2007; Killen & Smetana, 2015; Malti & Ongley, 2014). Nevertheless, it remains a customary and useful distinction, and I therefore follow it here. The present treatment begins with a further consideration of the cognitive aspect of morality. It then moves on to discussions of moral emotions and moral behavior.

## Cognitions

Although Chapter 4 introduced the notion of domains of development (Table 4.7), it said relatively little about the moral domain. It said relatively little because the moral domain is seldom the focus for the topic that was being considered then: namely, parent–child disagreements about decision-making autonomy. By adolescence (the age period for most of the research discussed), children, at least in most instances, share their parents' beliefs about what constitutes morality. The question now is how they come to hold such beliefs. Our main interest, of course, is in the contribution of parents.

Parents are by no means all-important to their children's ability to distinguish different domains of social functioning. Other social agents (peers, siblings, teachers) also play a role. In addition, whatever the source, children are not passive recipients of environmental input; they must be cognitively ready to take in and benefit from their experiences. Nevertheless, that parents do contribute to learning about domains has long been clear (Smetana, 1999). Observational studies indicate that parents respond differently to moral and social-conventional transgressions from early in the child's life, even to some extent in interactions with 1-year-olds (Dahl & Campos, 2013; Smetana, 1989). Parents, at least usually, tailor their responses to the domain in question: thus an emphasis on the consequences for others when responding to moral transgressions and an emphasis on the social order when a social convention is violated. The parent's tone of voice can also provide helpful cues. Moral transgressions elicit more intense and angry-sounding vocalizations than do other forms of transgression; conversely, a worried and comforting tone is more common for prudential (i.e., safety-endangering) violations (Dahl, Sherlock, Campos, & Theunissen, 2014).

Interviews that explicitly probe for parents' beliefs provide further evidence that many parents hold definite beliefs that guide their socialization efforts (Nucci & Smetana, 1996). Table 7.3 presents a summary of the justifications that mothers of 5- and 7- year-olds offer for their parenting practices across different domains. Note that the parental goals include general developmental achievements (e.g., develop competence, develop autonomy) in addition to instilling domain-specific knowledge.

More general child-rearing characteristics can also be important. Children whose parents adopt an authoritative style of parenting (establishment of a warm and supportive relationship, firm but nonpunitive control,

**Table 7.3**  Mothers' Justifications for Socializing Understanding of Different Domains

| Justification | Description |
|---|---|
| Foster competence | Action serves to increase child s mastery or competence (e.g., "It helps her develop decision making") |
| Develop autonomy | Action serves to establish the child's control, allows the child to develop a sense of individuality and independence, permits the child to separate from parents, or helps establish the child's uniqueness |
| Fosters self-development | Control over act allows child to develop a sense of self-mastery, positive self-esteem, or sense of self |
| Conventional | Action serves to coordinate the social interactions of individuals in the family, maintains social order, or is prohibited or restricted by rules, norms, or the commands of those in authority |
| Moral | Act affects others' well-being, is harmful, violates others' rights, is unfair, results in an imbalance in rights between persons, or violates parents' religious beliefs or values |
| Prudential | Act has nonsocial, negative consequences to the child, such as, it is unsafe, uncomfortable, or unhealthy |
| Pragmatic | References to practical needs and consequences |
| Personal | Act is an individual choice, a private matter, the person's own business, is inconsequential, and/or is not dangerous to the self or others |

Adapted from "Mothers' Concepts of Young Children's Areas of Personal Freedom," by L. Nucci and J. G. Smetana, 1996, *Child Development, 67,* p. 1874. Copyright 1996 by the Society for Research in Child Development. Adapted with permission from John Wiley and Sons.

frequent use of reasoning) arrive at an understanding of domains earlier and more firmly than do children of either authoritarian or permissive parents (Smetana, 1999). As Chapter 4 noted, part of the basis for these differences may lie in differences in the parents' own beliefs systems. Authoritarian parents show a tendency to treat conventional issues as matters of morality and thus as subject to strict control, whereas permissive parents show the opposite tendency, treating moral issues as conventional and thus less likely to require parental intervention (Smetana, 2011a). It is not surprising, therefore, that the children of such parents may be slow to master the standard distinctions among domains.

The work on domains of social functioning constitutes one basic line of research in the study of moral cognitions. A second basic line of research—one that is both historically earlier and a good deal larger—falls under the heading of *moral reasoning*. The interest now is in how the child reasons about situations that require moral evaluations and moral decisions, as well as in changes in such reasoning as the child develops.

The historically earliest approach to moral reasoning was initiated by Piaget (1932) and subsequently built on by Kohlberg (1969). Methodologically, this approach is characterized by the presentation of moral dilemmas to which children respond and from which their level of moral reasoning is determined—fairly simple dilemmas in Piaget's case, more complicated ones in the Kohlberg research. Theoretically, the approach is characterized by an emphasis on stages: an ordered progression from the first budding conceptions of morality to the developmentally highest forms found in adulthood. The main determinant of level of moral reasoning is the child's cognitive level; as children progress cognitively, their moral reasoning progresses as well.

The Piaget/Kohlberg research concentrates on what is typically labeled *justice reasoning*: rules and laws and sanctions for various forms of misbehavior (e.g., lying, cheating, stealing). What it neglects is the more positive side of morality: not just the avoidance of bad behaviors but the production of good behaviors—thus the *prosocial* behaviors of comforting, helping, cooperating, and sharing. A program of research by Nancy Eisenberg (1986; Eisenberg-Berg, 1979) redresses this limitation through the presentation of dilemmas that require decisions about when and how to act prosocially. Not coincidentally, the Eisenberg research also redresses a further limitation of the Piaget/Kohlberg approach: its almost exclusively negative picture of young children's moral reasoning abilities. A focus on prosocial reasoning provides a more positive picture of early developments than emerged in either Piaget's or Kohlberg's justice-oriented studies.

As noted, for both Piaget and Kohlberg advances in moral reasoning follow from advances in cognition more generally. Experience is also important, however, and the form stressed by both Piaget and Kohlberg is experience with peers. Unlike with parents or other adults, the peer relationship is one of equals, and this equal footing allows the kind of back-and-forth exchanges that challenge the child's thinking and eventually motivate a reorganization at a higher level.

Research provides general support for both of the claims just summarized: Children's moral reasoning does indeed relate to their general cognitive level, and interactions with peers can be an especially fruitful impetus for cognitive change (Rest, 1983). Research also makes clear, however, that parents play a more important role than envisioned by either Piaget or Kohlberg. Two studies by Walker and colleagues are especially informative in this regard (Walker, Henning, & Krettenauer, 2000; Walker & Taylor, 1991). In both studies, children (ranging in age from 6 to 17) and their parents discussed two moral dilemmas, one a standard dilemma from the Kohlberg research program and one an actual, real-life dilemma provided by the child participant. Of interest were the levels of reasoning shown by both parent and child, the types of arguments offered in an attempt to reach a resolution, and any long-term effects of the discussions on the child's level of reasoning, as followed up after 2 years in Walker and Taylor (1991) and 4 years in Walker et al. (2000). The latter study also included another comparison of interest: that between discussions with parents and discussions with peers as a source of change.

Several general conclusions emerged. First, discussions with parents were predictive of future advances in moral reasoning—only, however, when the discussions involved real-life rather than hypothetical dilemmas. Discussions with peers were also predictive of future advances, but the processes underlying the changes were in part different for peers and parents. For peers, an interactional style labeled as *interfering* (negative affect, threats, refusals) was predictive of change, a finding in general support of the Piaget/Kohlberg argument that the egalitarian nature of peer relationships permits a free and challenging exchange of different points of view. For parents, the interfering style showed minimal effects; what proved beneficial was a supportive style of interaction characterized by support for the child's emotions, helpful but nonthreatening questioning, and the presentation of reasons that were beyond, but not too far beyond, the child's current level of reasoning. These proximal-level conclusions about how parents contribute to moral reasoning fit with the more distal-level conclusions that emerge from studies of general child-rearing practices (Killen & Smetana, 2015).

One further finding is worth noting. Parents adjusted their level of reasoning (which had been assessed independently) downward when interacting with their children, and they did so more strongly the lower the level of their child's reasoning. The children, in turn, reasoned at a higher level when interacting with their parents than they had proved capable of on an independent assessment. This set of conclusions has a Vygotskian sound: Parents adjusted their input to work within the child's zone of proximal development, and children were able to perform at a higher level when they received helpful parental support.

## Emotions

Some definitions are necessary at the start for the three emotions to be considered now: guilt, shame, and empathy. As their natural language uses suggest, guilt and shame are similar in some respects; in particular, both are negative, self-punitive emotions that arise in response to some dissatisfaction with the self. But they also differ in important ways (Eisenberg, 2000). As typically used in the research literature, guilt is a more focused and less painful emotion than is shame, and it is tied to a particular action that the actor wishes could be undone. Shame, in contrast, is not tied to a particular action but rather reflects a more general dissatisfaction with the self. It also has a more salient social dimension than does guilt (i.e., a concern with what others think about the self).

Empathy refers to the tendency to share the emotions of others—to feel happy when others are happy, sad when others are sad, and so forth. It is in various ways a more complicated construct than either guilt or shame. To begin with, empathy is not a single emotion but rather varies with the target—sometimes happiness, sometimes sadness, sometimes fear, and so on. Empathy is generally considered to consist not only of an affective component but also of a cognitive component, that is, some form of interpersonal awareness that makes possible the understanding of another's emotional state. In one influential theory of moral development, empathy is not a single development but rather comprises several developmentally ordered forms that emerge sequentially across the span of childhood (Hoffman, 2000). Finally, in the case of negative emotions such as sadness, empathy can take either or both of two forms: sympathy directed toward the other or personal distress directed toward the self. Clearly, the implications for behavior differ for these two forms of empathetic arousal.

I turn next to a question that was not addressed in the section on emotions: namely, how are emotions measured? The answer, both for emotions in general and for moral emotions in particular, is in a variety of ways, none of which, given the difficult nature of the target, is free from error. Facial expressions are usable from birth, and accompanying vocalizations are often helpful as well. Although they are seldom sufficient in themselves, physiological responses can provide a valuable complement to other measures. Once they are old enough, children can provide self-reports of their emotions. Finally, parent-report measures are a potential source of information at any age; indeed, emotions are one of the targets for which parent reports have been most influential. Table 7.4 provides an example of a parent-report measure of empathy. Other examples include Rieffe, Ketelaar, and Wiefferink (2010) for empathy and Kochanska, DeVet, Goldman, Murray, and Putnam (1994) for both empathy and guilt.

The initial section of the chapter addressed parents' beliefs and socialization practices with respect to children's emotions, and the points made there apply as well to the socialization of moral emotions. Again, awareness and acceptance of the child's emotions are beneficial, as is the parent's expression of his or her own emotions, and as is help and support in times of emotional distress. In addition, parents' use of a form of reasoning labeled *induction* relates positively to the development of empathy in their children. Inductive reasons (in particular, those sometimes labeled *other-oriented inductions*) are those that point out the consequences of the child's actions for others— for example, "Billy is sad when you take his toy." Such reasons focus squarely

Table 7.4  Examples of Items from the Griffith Empathy Measure

---

**Affective Items**

My child

becomes sad when other children are sad.
gets upset when another person gets upset.
gets sad when watching sad movies on TV.
acts happy when another person is acting happy.
can continue to feel OK even if people around are upset.
Cognitive items

My child

can't understand when other people get upset.
rarely understands why other people cry.
reacts badly when they see people kiss and hug in public.
doesn't understand why other people cry out of happiness.
doesn't seem to notice when I get sad.

---

Responses are made on a 9-point scale ranging from "strongly disagree" to "strongly agree." Adapted from "A Measure of Cognitive and Affective Empathy in Children Using Parent Ratings," by M. R. Dadds, K. Hunter, D. J. Hawes, A. D. J. Frost, S. Vassalio, P. Bunn, S. Merz, and Y. E. Masry, 2008, *Child Psychiatry and Human Development, 39*, p. 116. Copyright 2007 by Springer Science & Business Media, LLC. Adapted with permission.

on the other's emotional state, and it is therefore not surprising that they promote awareness of and response to the feelings of others.

Inductive reasoning also shows some relation to both guilt and shame, but other parental practices contribute as well. One predictor of relatively strong guilt is the parent's use of *love withdrawal* techniques of discipline, that is, discipline based on the explicit anger and disappointment of the parent (Zahn-Waxler & Kochanska, 1990). Ignoring the child, turning away, and expressing dislike would all be examples of love withdrawal. One predictor of relatively strong shame is the parent's explicit attempt to induce shame in response to some misbehavior (Mills, 2005). Here are some examples from one examination of the issue (Fung & Chen, 2001, pp. 424–425). "Aren't you ashamed of yourself?' "How come you're so sissy?" "I've never seen any three year old who behaves like you."

That parents seek to nurture the development of empathy in their children is understandable. But why should parents wish to make their child feel ashamed or guilty? The answer dates back to Freud, and it is that these negative emotions are believed to govern the moral behaviors that are the ultimate goal of parents' socialization efforts. It is to the question of the origins of moral behavior that we turn next.

## Behaviors

Moral cognitions and moral emotions are of interest in themselves. As just suggested, however, they are also of interest as possible contributors to the topic to be considered now: moral behavior. The predictions are straightforward. If moral reasoning affects moral behavior, then we would expect more mature, truly moral behavioral decisions as children's reasoning abilities develop. If moral emotions affect moral behavior, then we would expect that the experience of guilt or shame will inhibit the expression of immoral behavior and that the experience of empathy and sympathy will make positive, prosocial behavior more likely.

The relevant literature to test these predictions is, to put it mildly, inconsistent, with positive results accompanied by numerous exceptions and qualifications and theoretical disputes about the separability of the three components (Eisenberg, Spinrad, & Knafo-Noam, 2015; Killen & Smetana, 2015). At best, moral cognitions and moral emotions are just two among many determinants of moral behavior. Nevertheless, the bulk of the evidence indicates that they *are* among the determinants. Level of moral reasoning relates positively to moral behavior, and moral emotions also show predicted relations to moral behavior. Thus one way in which parents affect their children's moral behavior is by nurturing the cognitions or emotions that make such behavior more likely.

How else do parents contribute? The same general parenting factors that are positive predictors of moral cognitions and moral emotions—and, indeed, of numerous other positive developmental outcomes—are also predictors of moral behavior (Grusec, Chaparro, Johnston, & Sherman, 2014; Hastings, Miller, & Troxel, 2015). These include a warm and supportive relationship, modeling of behaviors that the parent hopes to instill, and frequent use of reasoning and infrequent use of physical punishment. They also include the attributions that parents draw for their children's behavior, attributions that can affect the parent's subsequent behavior and thus the child's development (Dix, Ruble, & Zambarano, 1989).

Two other contributors are also familiar ones. As we have seen, parental talk in the context of family interactions contributes to children's learning about domains of social functioning, and such talk also contributes to their ability to reason about moral issues (Dunn, 2014). Interactions among siblings are an especially fertile ground for such learning. Finally, moral behavior is another outcome for which the attachment relationship proves to be important, with securely attached children more likely to show compliant and prosocial behavior than are children whose attachments are less secure (Kochanska, 2002; Thompson, 2014). One way in which both family talk and secure attachment promote moral behavior is through nurturing the forms of empathy that underlie such behavior (Dunn, 2014; Stern & Cassidy, 2018).

I conclude this section with a general point that applies to each of the topics considered under the "Morality" heading. Research on parents' contribution to their children's moral development is another instance in which the relevant parental beliefs are seldom explicitly elicited; rather, they must be inferred from parents' behavior. Obviously, this situation precludes examination of the beliefs–behavior issue, given that there is no independent measurement of the two constructs. On the positive side, the studies that do examine the issue generally report expectable links between what parents believe and how they behave. In addition, it does not seem difficult to infer the beliefs held by parents whose socialization efforts are relatively successful, that is, whose children rank positively on the various measures of moral development. A reasonable assumption is that such parents believe in a distinct domain of morality defined by concern for others and by the production or avoidance of certain behaviors, that they believe that it is important for their children to adopt a similar belief system and to govern their behaviors accordingly, and that they believe that particular parental practices (e.g., reasoning, modeling) will help to produce these desired outcomes. Again, the relevant beliefs are not difficult to infer. Nevertheless, both theory and application would benefit from more studies that measure rather than guess at what parents believe about moral development.

## Social Competence

I will begin by noting that social competence is another topic for which parent reports play an important role in the research literature. Such is especially the case for large national surveys, the scope of which typically makes individual testing of children not feasible. An article by Halle and Darling-Churchill (2016) provides a critical evaluation of the available parent-report measures.

The Halle and Darling-Churchill (2016) article also provides a definition of the construct at issue. Social competence is "the degree to which children are effective in their social interactions with others, including making and sustaining social connections, demonstrating cooperative skills and flexibility, and adjusting behavior to meet the demands of different social contexts" (p. 9).

Two distinct but closely related developments can be abstracted from this definition. As various phrases indicate ("cooperative skills," "adjusting behavior," etc.), success in the social world requires mastery of a set of social skills that permit positive interactions with others. The nature and origins of such skills is one central topic in the study of social competence. The effect of such skills is another central topic—in particular, the quality of the various relationships that children form as they develop. Peer relations and sibling relations have been of special interest.

### Social Withdrawal

As with the topic of aggression, we can begin with some work that was briefly considered in Chapter 3, but in this case with a focus on the social withdrawal aspect of the research. Here is one of the vignettes used in the study of beliefs about social withdrawal.

> The last few times you went to your child's school to pick her/him up, you were able to observe her/him during free play. On each occasion, you noticed that your child was not playing with anyone and spent almost the entire time alone. (Mills & Rubin, 1990, p. 141)

As we saw, parents (mothers only in most studies) regarded social withdrawal as more stable than aggression; that is, as less a transient developmental phase and more an enduring characteristic of the child. Somewhat paradoxically, however, they were less upset by withdrawal than by aggression, the dominant emotional responses being puzzlement and concern in the case of withdrawal, and concern, disappointment, and anger in the case of aggression. They also endorsed stronger socialization strategies in the case of aggression (Mills & Rubin, 1990). Note that social withdrawal was still seen as undesirable, just not (for most mothers) as undesirable as aggression.

In the work just summarized, the target being judged was hypothetical; that is, imagined rather than actual instances of child behavior. In addition, the parental beliefs and related practices were reactive ones in that they came in response to particular child behaviors. The Rubin and Mills research program also encompasses parents' proactive beliefs about how to nurture social competence in their children, and it relates such beliefs to actual rather than hypothetical child outcomes (Rubin & Mills, 1990; Rubin, Mills, & Rose-Krasnor, 1989).

Beliefs turn out to be important. Not surprisingly, a belief in the importance of nurturing social skills is beneficial, as is a low-power, child-guided method of teaching such skills. Conversely, highly directive teaching and high-power methods of control are predictive of social difficulties. Mothers of withdrawn children are also more likely than other mothers to attribute their child's difficulties to something internal to the child, and they are less likely to believe that change is possible—a pattern of attributions that we have seen before for negative outcomes. More recent research supports these general conclusions and adds a further one: social competence is another outcome for which the attachment relationship is important, with securely attached children faring better than their less secure counterparts (Booth-LaForce & Groh, 2018).

Is social withdrawal always viewed negatively by parents? The answer may depend on the culture. At various points we have seen the argument that development in Eastern cultures (China being the most often studied example) is shaped by a grounding in Confucian philosophy and by a collectivist, interpersonal orientation that values the group over the individual. In such cultures, a shy, reserved pattern of behavior may be regarded as a sign of maturity because it fits with cultural precepts, and such behavior may therefore be responded to positively by parents and by others. In fact, a program of research by Chen and colleagues has shown that for Chinese children shy and timid behavior is typically not a predictor of social difficulty and is sometimes associated with measures of social success (Chen, Chung, Lechcier-Kimel, & French, 2011). We can see again a point that we have seen before: Whether a behavior is adaptive often depends on its cultural appropriateness.

Having offered this conclusion, I should qualify it in two ways. First, although the two constructs are related, social withdrawal and shyness/timidity are not identical, and whereas shyness may sometimes be valued, it is doubtful that extreme withdrawal is adaptive in any culture (Rubin, Coplan, Bowker, & Menzer, 2014). Second, the Eastern–Western differences just noted have been smaller in more recent research, a finding that is usually taken as evidence that Eastern nations are gradually moving toward the autonomous/independent orientation typical in the West (Chen & Chen, 2010; Rubin, Cheah, & Menzer, 2010). The next section takes up more fully the question of which attributes and behaviors lead to success in the social group.

## Peer Relations

Two topics are prominent in the study of peer relations. One is the child's general standing within the peer group—so-called *sociometric status*—with the possible outcomes ranging from popular at the positive end of the continuum to neglected or rejected at the negative end. The other is friendship, with an interest not just in the existence of friendships but also in their nature—in particular, how satisfactory the child's friendships are.

As we would expect, sociometric status and friendship are related, for the same qualities that make a child a good friend also contribute to general success in the peer group. Rubin et al. (2010, p. 232) provide a summary of these qualities: "skilled at initiating and maintaining qualitatively positive relationships . . . cooperative, friendly, sociable, and sensitive." The two developments, however, are not always linked. It is possible to be generally well liked but not to have any close friends. It is also possible to be unpopular in general but to have at least one or two satisfactory friendships.

That parents contribute to their children's success with peers is clear (Furman & Rose, 2015; Ladd & Pettit, 2002). As is true for many developments, an authoritative style of parenting is associated with positive outcomes—better standing in the peer group, more probability of satisfactory friendships. The attachment relationship is also predictive of both sociometric status and friendship, with securely attached children scoring higher on both dimensions. In both instances, the positive parental factors are associated with the child's mastery of social skills, which in turn make positive relations with peers more likely. The overall quality of the relationship between the parent and child is also a predictor of success with peers, as is the quality of the marital relationship. In general, when one social world is going well others tend to go well also, and such is the case for relations with parents and peers.

The factors just discussed are distal-level predictors of children's peer relations. Also of interest are the specific contexts in which parents' behaviors play a role. Chapter 3 mentioned one such context. As we saw there, parents' belief in the value of play relates positively to their children's social competence (Lin & Yawkey, 2014). Parents' involvement in their children's play also contributes for such involvement often nurtures skills that carry over to interactions with peers, such as turn-taking and expression of positive emotions (Tamis-LeMonda, Uzgiris, & Bornstein, 2002). Parents' direct participation in their children's play with peers can also be helpful, especially when children are young and still uncertain about how best to proceed (Bhavnagri & Parke, 1991).

Some of the most informative work on parents' contribution to peer relations comes in research by Gary Ladd and colleagues (Ladd, 2005; Ladd, Profilet, & Hart, 1992). This research identifies four general ways, summarized in Table 7.5, through which parents, typically mothers more than fathers, affect their children's success with peers. Although each of the parental roles may apply at any point in development, there is a rough developmental progression, with hands-on intervention becoming less likely as children grow older and the consultant role becoming more likely. Note that

**Table 7.5** Parents' Management of Their Children's Peer Relations

| Parental role | Description |
|---|---|
| Designer | Parents make decisions that determine the nature of the child's environment, including the neighborhood in which to live, whether to place the child in early child care, and which outside-of-school activities to support. Such decisions affect the availability of peers, the nature of the peers to whom the child is exposed, and the ease of access to various peer groups. |
| Mediator | Parents play an active role in their child's involvement with peers. They arrange play dates, enroll the child in group activities, purchase toys intended for peer play, and encourage or discourage play with particular peers. |
| Supervisor | Parents oversee and regulate their child's interactions with peers, in some instances through their direct involvement and in some instances through provision of guidance and support. Parents also monitor and if necessary control activities for which they are not physically present. |
| Consultant | Parents provide advice and support outside the context of ongoing peer interactions, either in response to questions or concerns expressed by their children or as a proactive attempt to heighten the probability of social success. |

the parent-as-designer role is another example of an important point about parenting: that the ways in which parents affect their children's development are not limited to the face-to-face interactions that are the subject of most child-rearing research.

Three general conclusions emerge from the Ladd research. First, parents vary in the extent to which and the skill with which they perform each of the supportive roles. Second, parental beliefs are a contributor to these variations. For example, parents who believe in the importance of play with peers are especially likely to arrange such play opportunities (Ladd & Hart, 1992), and parents who are concerned about their child's social competence are especially likely to supervise their play (Mize, Pettit, & Brown, 1995). Finally, parents' skill as managers relates positively to various measures of their children's success with peers, including friendships and sociometric status.

This section has discussed the effect of parents on children's peer relations. I should add that the reverse causal direction also occurs; that is, relations with peers can affect the parent–child relationship (Reich & Vandell, 2014). Note that either sort of effect is an example of the mesosystem in

Bronfenbrenner's ecological systems theory, the interplay of two of the important microsystems in children's lives.

## Sibling Relations

As many know from personal experience, relations among siblings can take many different forms. Some siblings interact frequently and are important parts of each other's lives; other siblings have more distant, less involved relationships. Some sibling relationships are predominantly positive, some are predominantly negative, and some are a mixture of positive and negative.

Parents are hardly the only contributors to these differences, but they are often among the contributors. Once again, the quality of the attachment relationship is a positive predictor of other relationships, in this case relations between siblings, and the quality of the marital relationship is also a predictor (Dunn, 2015; Furman & Lanthier, 2002). The most often studied parental contributor, however, is parents' differential treatment of siblings. Although there are exceptions (as I will discuss shortly), parents' differential treatment of their children is associated with relatively poor relations between the children. Not surprisingly, it is usually the child who receives the less favorable treatment (less warmth, more discipline, etc.) who is most dissatisfied.

Why might parents treat their children differently? Some reasons are good ones. As we have seen, more experience as a parent does not always confer greater parental knowledge and skill; it does in some cases, however, and parents may therefore bring enhanced resources to the task of parenting their later-born children. At the least, greater parental experience is likely to increase awareness of a basic point: that even children within the same family are not identical, and different children may therefore require different socialization strategies. Much research in developmental psychology tells us that this is in fact the case (e.g., Kochanska, 1995).

The point just made leads to the qualifier with respect to the negative effects of differential treatment. Sometimes what is most important is not the treatment per se but siblings' *perceptions* of the treatment. When siblings believe that the differential treatment is justified, and when they agree on this point, then the sibling relationship may not be harmed at all (Kowal, Krull, & Kramer, 2006).

## Gender-Role Development

In what follows, I use the terms *sex* and *gender* interchangeably, a practice followed by some but not all authors who write about the topic (see Muelenhard & Peterson, 2011, for a discussion).

Parents' beliefs about gender differences have been discussed at various points throughout the book. We saw an example earlier in this chapter in the work directed to beliefs about how emotions should be talked about with boys and girls. Chapter 6 reviewed one of the most thoroughly examined contexts for beliefs about gender: expectations and attributions for performance in school and beyond school. Chapter 4 considered another set of beliefs with potentially broad scope: beliefs about the division of household responsibilities and about preparation for future adult roles.

In the research just noted—and indeed in research in developmental psychology more generally—gender takes an independent variable form. That is, the main focus of the research is on some other aspect of development (e.g., academic achievement, emotion understanding), and gender is examined as one possible source of individual differences.

The interest now is in gender-role development as *the* outcome of interest—thus not just individual aspects of development but all of the ways in which boys and girls are either similar or different as they develop. No study, of course, examines all the possible ways. Still, many include multiple outcomes, and numerous reviews bring together the results from the literature as a whole (Hines, 2015; Hyde, 2014; Zell, Krizan, & Teeter, 2015).

Three general questions are addressed in such research. One is the normative question just identified: What are the similarities and differences between boys and girls in their psychological development? A second question concerns individual differences: To what extent do particular children adhere to or depart from the pattern that is typical for their sex? Finally, the third question is that of causes: How do we explain the differences between sexes that have been found, and how do we explain individual differences within a sex?

As is often the case, parents play two roles in the literature. One is as informants with regard to their own children's gender-role development. Table 7.6 provides an example of a parent-report measure, one directed to the preschool age period. I should add that parent reports are by no means the only measurement option. Self-reports (once children are old enough to

Table 7.6  The Preschool Activities Inventory

---

Response options: Never, Hardly Ever, Sometimes, Often, Very Often

*Toys*
Please answer these questions according to how often the child played with the
following toys during the past month.

1. Guns (or objects used as guns)
2. Jewelry
3. Tool set
4. Dolls, doll's clothes or doll's carriage
5. Trains, cars or airplanes
6. Swords (or used objects as swords)
7. Tea set

*Activities*

Please answer these questions according to how often the child engaged in the
following activities during the past month.

1. Playing house (e.g., cleaning, cooking)
2. Playing with girls.
3. Pretending to be a female character (e.g., princess)
4. Pretending at having a male occupation (e.g., soldier)
5. Fighting
6. Pretending to be a family character (e.g., parent)
7. Sports and ball games
8. Climbing (e.g., fences, trees, gym equipment)
9. Playing at taking care of babies.
10. Showing interest in real cars, trains and airplanes
11. Dressing up in girlish clothes

*Characteristics*

Please answer these questions according to how often the child shows the following
characteristics.
1. Likes to explore new surroundings
2. Enjoys rough and tumble play
3. Shows interest in snakes, spiders, or insects
4. Avoids getting dirty
5. Likes pretty things
6. Avoids taking risks

---

Adapted from "The Pre-School Activities Inventory: A Standardized Assessment of Gender Role in
Children," by R. Golombok a J. Rust, 1993, *Psychological Assessment, 5*, pp. 135–136. Copyright 1991
by Susan Golombok and John Rust. Adapted with permission.

provide them), teacher reports, laboratory tests, and naturalistic observations
all contribute as well.

The second, and more important, role that parents play in the literature
is as possible contributors to their children's gender-role development. Two

qualifications, by now familiar, must precede any discussion of this issue. First, parents are at best one among many contributors to a set of multiply determined outcomes; a partial list of the other contributors would include biological factors, siblings, peers, teachers, and mass media. Second, any conclusions about parents' beliefs and related behaviors reflect on-the-average patterns that do not apply to every parent. Nor do they apply to every culture (Best, 2010; Leaper, 2002).

Once these points are made, it is clear that parents do contribute to gender-role development, as numerous reviews directed specifically to the role of parents have concluded (Leaper, 2002; Leaper & Farkas, 2015; Mesman, & Groeneveld, 2018; Smith Leavell & Tamis-LeMonda, 2013). In what follows, I single out some of the ways in which parents can make a difference.

A first point is that differential treatment of boys and girls can begin very early. Pink or blue clothes and matching crib sheets and wallpaper are often in place before the baby is born, and dolls or trucks may follow soon after. Parents, especially fathers, may describe their newborn sons as strong and alert and their daughters as soft and fine-featured, even though no objective differences between the sexes are apparent (Rubin, Provenzano, & Luria, 1974). Mothers have been found to overestimate their sons' crawling abilities and to underestimate their daughters' abilities, predicting marked differences at a time when no differences exist (Mondschein, Adolph, & Tamis-LeMonda, 2000). Mothers have also been found to offer more unrestricted movement opportunities to boy babies than to girl babies, a practice that relates positively to later motor development (Leavell Smith, 2013).

More opportunities for differential treatment emerge as children enter the toddler and preschool years (Hines, 2015). Differences in toy preferences are evident quite early, at a point when parents rather than children are making the toy choices. Indeed, parents' choice of different toys for boys and girls is one of the clearest and potentially most important ways in which many parents treat the two sexes differently (Brown & Stone, 2018). Differences in forms of play (more physically active for boys) are also evident from an early age, as are differences in preferred play partners, with boys preferring boys and girls preferring girls. Parental practices can contribute to both developments. Differences in physical aggression can be seen by age 2, as can parents' greater tolerance of aggression in boys than in girls (Martin & Ross, 2005). Here, and in general, gender differences are often found at both the parent and the child levels: fFthers are more likely than mothers to treat boys and girls differently, and boys are more likely than girls to receive pressure to adhere to gender-typical behaviors.

We have seen that parents talk about emotions differently with sons and daughters. Others aspects of parental talk also show on-the-average differences between the sexes (Leaper, Anderson, & Sanders, 1998). Mothers talk more to daughters than to sons, they use more supportive speech with daughters than with sons, and by grade-school age they use more directive speech with daughters than with sons—differences that may, as the authors suggest, encourage closeness in girls and independence in boys.

The role of beliefs is often implicit in the research discussed to this point. An explicit focus on beliefs comes in work on gender schemas. Different researchers define and operationalize the term somewhat differently; in general, however, a *gender schema* is an organized set of beliefs about gender, beliefs that include both the self and others and that encompass perceived gender similarities and differences across a range of attributes and behaviors. Although the relation is far from perfect, children's gender schemas relate to their tendency to engage in gender-typical behaviortets; for example, to show a preference for same-sexed peers or sex-stereotypical toys (Martin, Ruble, & Szkrybalo, 2002). And although the relation is again far from perfect, children's gender schemas relate positively to their parents' gender schemas; for example, parents with traditional gender beliefs tend to have children who possess similar beliefs (Tennenbaum & Leaper, 2002). Clearly, this is another parental effect with potentially broad scope.

The preceding is only a partial summary of the parental beliefs and practices that can lead to differences between the sexes, and parents, as noted earlier, are only one of many factors that contribute to such differences. Given all these converging forces, we might expect to find marked differences between boys and girls on a wide range of developmental outcomes. In fact, we do not. An early review by Maccoby and Jacklin (1974) identified only a handful of consistent gender differences along with many similarities, and more recent reviews, using meta-analytic procedures, have reached similar conclusions (Hyde, 2005, 2014; Zell et al., 2015). The general conclusion is summarized in the title of one of these reviews: "The Gender Similarities Hypothesis" (Hyde, 2005). Many measures of important developmental outcomes show no differences between the sexes, and when differences do emerge they are, with a few exceptions, small differences.

This conclusion does not negate the points made earlier in this section. Many parents do have beliefs about both the nature and the appropriateness of differences between the sexes, and they socialize their children accordingly. But many parents do not. And probably no parent's beliefs about differences extend to all or even most of the developmental outcomes that make up the developmental psychology literature and for which parents can be important. In fact, in one meta-analysis of the issue, no consistent socialization differences as a function of gender were found for seven of the eight aspects of development that were examined, support of gender-typical play being the lone exception (Lytton & Romney, 1991). It is true, as many authors have argued, that differences in gender-typical play may plant the seeds for various boy–girl differences later in development—a common example is early block play as a basis for boys' later superiority in spatial skills (Liben, Schroeder, Borriello, & Weisgram, 2018). The same broad-effects argument has been applied to parents' beliefs and related practices with respect to household responsibilities and academic achievement, both of which seem likely to have effects beyond the immediate target of the parents' socialization effort. Nevertheless, the "gender similarities" conclusion from the developmental literature suggests that any such effects are not as broad as many have argued.

So what can we conclude? As is usually true for difficult and contentious issues, the truth probably lies between the extremes in either direction. Boys and girls differ—on the average and usually moderately—in some aspects of development. Boys and girls do not differ in other, probably more frequent aspects of development. Parents' beliefs and related practices contribute to both outcomes.

# 8

# Adolescence

When your child hits puberty, they're gonna be disgusted and distressed and dismayed with you every five minutes, and they're gonna be raging and acting a little strange.

> —(Parker et al., 2012, pp. 74–75)

Again, it's the age thing. I think 14 is just too young to turn them loose right now. . . . I know what happens . . . I talk to students and work with students in her age group, and some kids say they don't have a curfew or that they can go and hang out and come home, and their parents don't know where they are. I can't imagine that. It's not safe.

> —(Smetana, 2011a, p. 64)

I think everyone needs some kind of guidance. They are not adults, and even some adults don't make the right decisions, so as a parent, I feel it's my responsibility to make sure she is following certain rules so that when she grows up and there are rules to follow she will already have experience with rules.

> —(Smetana, 2011a, p. 167)

It was the best of times, it was the worst of times.

> —(Dickens, 1859, p. 1)

The last of the quotations is of course a ringer. I include it because it captures the experience of adolescence for many adolescents and many parents. Adolescence is a time of wonderful, life-long accomplishments; of dramatic advances in the physical, cognitive, and social realms; of the movement from child to adult. But it also a time of uncertainty and conflict, of new challenges of a myriad of sorts, and of consequent risk of new and serious and sometimes

*Parents' Beliefs About Children.* Scott A. Miller, Oxford University Press (2020). © Oxford University Press.
DOI: 10.1093/oso/9780190874513.001.0001

lasting problems. And parents are not only spectators but also participants in both the good and the bad.

One way to convey the challenging nature of adolescence is to cite the titles of books written for parents of adolescents (I take this idea from Smetana, 2011a). Table 8.1 presents a sampling of titles. It perhaps goes without saying that the challenge of surviving one's child is not a theme of books devoted to other parts of the developmental span.

Is such a worst-of-times view of adolescence justified? Is adolescence really the time of storm and stress that it has long been depicted as being? A brief answer is mostly no—at least for most adolescents and their families most of the time (Gutman, Peck, Malanchuk, Sameroff, & Eccles, 2017; Smetana, 2011a). But it is for some. And it is at some times for many. It is not surprising that many parents, as well as many psychologists, believe that parenting adolescents is the greatest challenge that parents face.

This chapter is devoted to both the challenges and the accomplishments of adolescence and to parents' role in both. It addresses five general topics. The chapter begins with work on parental knowledge: what parents know about adolescence and about their adolescents. Parental knowledge is, of course, a recurring theme throughout this book. As we will see, however, much of the adolescent research takes a different direction from that typical in the study of earlier age periods.

The next two sections deal with the risks and problems that accompany the movement through adolescence. The second section addresses parents'

**Table 8.1** A Sampling of Books for Parents of Adolescents

| Author | Title |
|---|---|
| Caldwell (1996) | *Teenagers! A Bewildered Parent's Guide* |
| Gluck and Rosenfeld (2005) | *How to Survive Your Teenager* |
| Leman (2011) | *Have a New Teenager by Friday* |
| Levine (2013) | *When Good Kids Do Bad Things: A Survival Guide for Parents of Teenagers* |
| Phelan (1998) | *Surviving Your Adolescents: How to Manage and Let Go of Your 13-18 Year Old* |
| Ross (2017) | *How to Hug a Porcupine: Negotiating the Prickly Points of the Tween Years* |
| Wolf (2002) | *Get Out of My Life—But First Would You Drive Me and Cheryl to the Mall? A Parent's Guide to the New Teenager* |

beliefs and practices with respect to risky behaviors of several sorts, including smoking, drinking, drug use, and premarital sex. The third section revisits the issue of parent–child conflict, building on and expanding what was said about this topic in Chapter 4.

The fourth section of the chapter considers a relatively recent but clearly important topic: parents' beliefs and practices with regard to their child's use of the Internet. Both risky behaviors and parent–child conflict will receive some further attention in this context. Finally, the concluding section of the chapter is meant as a counterweight to the predominantly negative tone of much that has been said to that point. It addresses various positive developments that mark successful movement through adolescence, as well as parents' contribution to these developments.

## Parental Knowledge

### Adolescents' Activities

Like the Infancy chapter, this chapter begins with a consideration of what parents know about the age period in question. As we will see, however, most work on adolescence differs in two ways from that discussed with respect to infancy.

The first difference concerns a distinction that has arisen at various points throughout the book: that between a focus on children in general and a focus on one's own child. As we saw, research on infancy falls primarily in the first category. It is knowledge about infancy in general that the Knowledge of Infant Development Inventory (KIDI) and similar measures address, and the same is true when parents are asked to estimate age of mastery for various milestones of development. A subset of adolescent studies have a similar in-general focus, and we will of course consider this work. Such studies are the exception, however, for in the great majority of cases it is their own child, and not the generalized adolescent, about whom parents are asked.

The second difference provides a contrast not only with the infancy research but also with work discussed in both Chapter 6 and Chapter 7. In those instances the questioning—whether directed to one's own child or to children in general—had to do with general characteristics and attributes of the age group under study. In Chapter 6 the focus was on cognitive attributes (intelligence, theory of mind, memory, etc.), and in Chapter 7 the topic was social attributes (emotions, aggression, moral understanding, etc.). As I noted, the starting point for this research was the general child psychology literature—parents are asked about the developments that psychologists believe are important.

Again, a minority of adolescence studies adopt the approach used with younger age groups. Most, however, have a quite different emphasis. Table 8.2 shows what is perhaps the most often used measure of parents' knowledge of their adolescents, the Parental Knowledge Scale developed by Stattin and Kerr (2000). As can be seen, the focus is no longer on the nature of the child; rather, it is on the nature of the child's activities—in particular, what the child does when the parent is not present to supervise and control.

It is not difficult, of course, to discern why knowledge of free-time activities might be a focus for parents of adolescents. Two contrasts with early childhood account for the heightened interest. First, adolescents spend considerably more time apart from their parents than do younger children, including more time with peers (Smetana, Robinson, & Rote, 2015). Second, various forms of risky behavior that are not a concern in childhood (e.g., smoking, drinking, drug use) are definitely a concern in adolescence (Steinberg, 2014).

The version of the Parental Knowledge Scale shown in the table has a child-report format: Adolescents report what their parents know. In general, child-report measures play a larger role in the adolescent literature than they do for younger age groups, which of course is not surprising, given the greater competence of adolescents to provide the sought-after information. For many measures, however, a parallel parent-report version also exists, and

**Table 8.2**  Parental Knowledge Scale

---

*Items*
    Do your parents know what you do during your free time?
    Do your parents know who you have as friends during your free time?
    Do your parents usually know what type of homework you have?
    Do your parents know what you spend your money on?
    Do your parents usually know when you have an exam or paper due at school?
    Do your parents know how you do in different subjects at school?
    Do your parents know where you go when you are out with friends at night?
    Do your parents normally know where you go and what you do after school?
    In the last month, have your parents ever had no idea of where you were at night?

---

Responses are made on a 5-point scale ranging from "never" to "always." Adapted from "Parental Monitoring: A Reinterpretation," by H. Stattin and M. Kerr, 2000, *Child Development, 71*, p. 1074. Copyright 2000 by the Society for Research in Child Development. Adapted with permission.

such is the case for the Parental Knowledge Scale. In this case the wording shifts from "Do your parents know" to "Do you know."

The existence of both child and parent versions raises an obvious question: How well do the two sets of informants agree? The answer is moderately well. In the Stattin and Kerr (2000) study, the correlation between adolescents' reports and parents' reports was .38. Other studies have typically reported similar values—thus above chance but far from perfect agreement (Crouter & Head, 2002). Descriptively, both parents' and adolescents' ratings typically average around 4 on the 5-point scale—thus judgments that parents possess good but not complete knowledge (Kerr, Stattin, & Burk, 2010). In some studies, including Kerr et al. (2010), parents and adolescents provide equally positive estimates of parental knowledge. In some studies, however, they do not, and in most instances it is parents who give the higher ratings. Thus parents believe that they possess greater knowledge than their children believe they possess (e.g., Dotterer & Wehrspann, 2016).

As we have seen before, discrepancy between informants leaves open the question of which informant is more accurate. Data from the Parental Knowledge Scale cannot answer this question. Although the authors of the scale refer to its results as "parenting knowledge," what the scale in fact measures are *perceptions* of parenting knowledge. And there is no way to determine how accurate such perceptions are, as well as whose perceptions are more accurate in cases of disagreement, without an independent assessment of the target being judged, namely adolescents' activities.

Some studies do provide measures of actual rather than perceived parental knowledge, although none, to my knowledge, has done so in conjunction with the Parental Knowledge Scale. One approach used in a number of studies was devised by Crouter and associates (e.g., Crouter, Helms-Erikson, Updegraff, & McHale, 1999; Waizenhofer, Buchanan, & Jackson-Newsom, 2004). In these studies, parents are asked about their child's daily activities each day for a week, with different activities (e.g., school-related issues, leisure activities, relationships) the targets on different days. The adolescents are independently asked about the same activities. The assumption is that adolescents can accurately report their recent activities; thus their responses serve as a standard for determining parental accuracy.

Accuracy—at least for the samples and the activities that have been examined—turns out to be fairly good, with matches between parent report and adolescent report typically averaging around 70%. Accuracy varies, however, as a function of both the judge and the target. Although the differences are typically not large, mothers are more knowledgeable than are fathers (e.g., Waizenhofer et al., 2004), a finding that presumably reflects the fact that adolescents typically spend more time with their mothers and have closer relationships with their mothers (Steinberg & Silk, 2002). This gender difference is qualified, however, by an interaction with gender of child: Mothers typically know more about daughters than about sons, and fathers typically know more about sons than about daughters (Crouter & Head, 2002). Ordinal position is also a predictor, with greater knowledge for second born than firstborn children (Crouter & Head, 2002). The usual explanation for this finding is reflected in the title of one of the studies that demonstrate the effect: "What Parents Learn from Experience: The First Child as First Draft?" (Whiteman, McHale, & Crouter, 2003).

The activities under study in the research considered to this point are, at least for the most part, normal, nonproblematic forms of behavior. Not all adolescent behaviors fit this description. The question of what parents know about their children's engagement in risky behaviors is one of the central issues in the adolescent literature, and we will consequently return to a consideration of parental knowledge in the next section of the chapter.

Not yet addressed is the question of how parents obtain their knowledge about their children. For years the accepted answer was that parents acquire knowledge through *monitoring* their children's activities, with monitoring defined as "a set of correlated parenting behaviors involving attention to and tracking of the child's whereabouts, activities, and adaptations" (Dishion & McMahon, 1998, p. 61). Thus parents actively seek out knowledge about their child, and it is their successful information-seeking efforts that lead to parental knowledge.

The Stattin and Kerr (2000) article called this view into question. As they pointed out, most "monitoring" studies did not actually measure monitoring; rather, they measured the presumed outcome of monitoring, parental knowledge. They pointed out as well that monitoring, although certainly a plausible source of parental knowledge, was not the only possible way that parents might learn about their children. In their study they measured two forms of monitoring directly: parents' solicitation of information from their adolescents and parents' control of their adolescents' activities. They also measured a third possible source of knowledge: adolescents' self-disclosures to their parents about their activities. All three measures related significantly to both parents' and adolescents' reports of parental knowledge; the strongest predictor, however, was adolescent self-disclosure. The same conclusion has emerged in other examinations of the issue (Kerr & Stattin, 2000; Kerr et al., 2010; Stattin, Kerr, & Tilton-Weaver, 2010).

Given the importance of self-disclosure, an obvious question concerns the factors that make it likely that adolescents will self-disclose. The main predictor is an expectable one, and it is the quality of the relationship with the parents: the more positive the relationship, the greater the likelihood of self-disclosure (Racz & McMahon, 2011; Smetana, 2011a). Although most of the relevant research has been with European American families, the finding is not limited to such families; a positive parental relationship has been shown to be a predictor of disclosure across a range of cultural settings (Hunter, Barber, Olsen, McNeely, & Bose, 2011). Longitudinal studies suggest that the relation is a reciprocal one (Smetana, 2011a). A positive parent–child relationship makes disclosure more likely, but over time adolescents' willingness to share information strengthens the bond with the parents.

Several other predictors of self-disclosure have been identified. One is gender of the child: On the average, girls self-disclose more than do boys, especially in conversations with mothers (Smetana, 2011a). Another is the gender of the parent: On the average, mothers receive more disclosures than do fathers (Smetana, 2011a). This finding fits, of course, with the conclusion that mothers typically possess more knowledge than do fathers. The age of the adolescent also contributes, with self-disclosures declining, on the average, between early adolescence and mid-adolescence (Keijsers et al., 2016; Padilla-Walker, Son, & Nelson, 2018). Not surprisingly, parents' self-perceived knowledge also declines across this period (Masche, 2010).

Parents' behavior can affect the probability that an adolescent will self-disclose. Although some parental monitoring may be necessary to elicit needed information, too much monitoring may be counterproductive, for adolescents disclose less when they perceive their parents as regularly invading their privacy (Hawk et al., 2013). Negative effects are especially likely when beliefs in the legitimacy of parental knowledge are low (LaFleur, Zhao, & Zeringue, 2016). Parents' own willingness to self-disclose can be important; when parents share information, adolescents are more likely to do so also (Kil, Grusec, & Chaparro, 2018). Parenting style is, once again, a predictor of positive outcomes, with more disclosure when parents have adopted an authoritative style of parenting (Darling, Cumsille, Caldwell, & Dowdy, 2006). Finally, and as would be expected, the topic in question is important. Adolescents disclose less for topics on which they and their parents disagree than they do for topics on which they agree, and they disclose less for activities they know to be disapproved than they do for more benign behaviors (Darling et al., 2006; Smetana, Villalobos, Tasopoulous-Chan, Gettman, & Campione-Barr, 2009). I return to this last finding in the next section of the chapter.

The preceding does not mean that adolescent self-disclosure is the only way that parents learn about their children's activities. Although their effects are typically weaker, measures of monitoring behavior often do show some relation to parental knowledge; that is, monitoring, at least sometimes, does work. This point holds for the general activities that are the subject of this section; it holds also for the risky behaviors that are the subject of the next section. Table 8.3 presents a sampling of items (14 of 27) from one of the more detailed monitoring measures. The table shows the adolescent-report version of the measure; again, a comparable parent-report version also exists.

Table 8.3  Sampling of Items from the Parental Monitoring Scale

In the past 4 months, how many times has your parent done the following: (response options: 0, 1 to 2, 3 to 4, 5-plus)

| Type of monitoring | Items |
| --- | --- |
| Indirect monitoring | Asked to meet your friends |
| | Talked to other parents about your activities |
| Direct monitoring | Talked to you about what you had planned |
| | Asked about specifics of planned activities |
| School monitoring | Checked to make sure you completed homework |
| | Talked to teachers about your schoolwork |
| Health monitoring | Checked on what you ate |
| | Talked to you about changes in mood |
| Computer monitoring | Placed computer in an open area where it can be observed |
| | Checked what websites you viewed through history or other method |
| Phone monitoring | Set limits for phone calls |
| | Told you to end phone conversations |
| Restrictive monitoring | Listened to your phone conversations |
| | Looked through your drawers or closets |

Adapted from "Development and Validation of a Parental Monitoring Instrument: Measuring How Parents Monitor Adolescents' Activities and Risk Behaviors," by S. A. Cottrell, S. Branstetter, L. Cottrell, C. V. Harris, C. Rishel, and B. F. Stanton, 2007, *Family Journal, 15*, p. 332. Copyright 2007 by Sage Publisher. Adapted by permission.

In addition to self-disclosure and monitoring, Crouter and colleagues (Blocklin, Crouter, Updegraff, & McHale, 2011; Crouter, Bumpus, Davis, & McHale, 2005) identify four other possible sources of information for parents: everyday observing and listening to the child, information from one's spouse, information from siblings, and information from people outside the family (e.g., teachers). In their research each of these contributors shows some effect, although outside-the-family sources typically rank lowest. It is interesting to note that information from one's spouse is a more important source for fathers than for mothers, a finding in keeping with the conclusion that mothers typically possess greater knowledge than do fathers.

The discussion to this point has focused on the nature and origins of parents' knowledge about their adolescents' activities. Not yet considered are the effects of such knowledge. How are parents' behaviors shaped by what they believe, and how is adolescents' development shaped by what parents do? The main examinations of these questions come in two bodies of work still to be discussed: that directed to risky behaviors (the next section of the chapter) and that directed to positive developments (the last section of the chapter). I will take up the effects question in both of these contexts.

## Adolescence in General

Although beliefs about their teen's activities have dominated the research literature, such beliefs do not exhaust the ways in which parents think about adolescence. As the lead-in to the chapter suggested, parents—and, indeed, any of us—also hold beliefs about adolescence in general: what adolescents are like and how they are similar to and different from what comes before (childhood) and what comes after (adulthood).

One question that has been addressed is familiar from earlier sections of the book: timetables for mastery of developmental achievements. In this case, however, the focus has been primarily on personal-social rather than cognitive achievements (e.g., handle money, accept bodily changes, establish a romantic relationship). Two findings emerge most clearly (Dekovic, Noom, & Meeus, 1997; Feldman & Quatman, 1988; Rosenthal & Bornholt, 1988). First, adolescents, on the average, hold earlier expectations for various developments than do their parents, a difference, as we saw in Chapter 4, that paves the way for parent–child conflicts of a variety of sorts. Second—and in line with work on earlier developmental periods—expectations vary across different cultural settings. Western parents, for example, tend to hold earlier age-of-mastery expectations than do parents in Asian countries, a difference in keeping with the greater emphasis on autonomy and independence in Western culture (Collins & Steinberg, 2006).

Another approach to the study of beliefs about adolescence focuses on the attributes that characterize the adolescent period, often with a starting point in stereotypes (e.g., storm and stress conceptions) of what adolescents are like. Table 8.4 shows a sampling of items from one of the measures in this category. As is often the case, open-ended interviews were used to generate potential items for the measure (Buchanan & Holmbeck, 1998).

Descriptively, responses to the Stereotypes Scale confirm that many adults do hold stereotyped (although, of course, not necessarily incorrect) beliefs about adolescence, for items such as risk taking and rebelliousness often receive strong endorsements, and they do so more clearly for adolescent than for elementary-school targets. This finding holds for both mothers and fathers, although in some instances more strongly for mothers. It holds also for both parents and nonparents, including teachers. Indeed (and depressingly), the more experienced the teacher, the stronger the beliefs in the difficulty of adolescence (Buchanan et al., 1990; Buchanan & Holmbeck, 1998).

Clearly, a question of interest is whether parents' beliefs about adolescence in general affect how they think about and treat their own children. The answer is that they do. Although effects in both a positive and a negative direction have been demonstrated, the latter emerge more clearly in research to date. Thus parents who hold a negative, storm-and-stress view of adolescence in general tend to hold negative expectations for their own child's adolescence and negative beliefs about the child once adolescence is reached (Buchanan, 2003). Their children, in turn, also tend to hold negative expectations about their upcoming adolescence while they are preadolescents, and they are more likely to show negative behaviors (risk-taking, rebellion, alienation) once they become adolescents (Buchanan & Hughes, 2009). The general message from this research echoes a conclusion from the discussion of academic performance in Chapter 6. Parents form general belief systems and related expectations about a number of aspects of children's development, including the nature of adolescence and including gender differences in academic ability. These expectations affect how parents treat their children, they affect the expectations that children themselves form, and they affect how children develop.

Table 8.4   Items from the Stereotypes of Adolescence Scale

| Subscale | Items |
|---|---|
| Risk taking/rebellious | Takes risks |
| | Tests limits |
| | Impulsive |
| Friendly | Friendly |
| | Considerate |
| | Caring |
| Problem behaviors | Uses alcohol |
| | Sexually active |
| | Uses drugs |
| Classic adolescents behaviors | Listens to music |
| | Into clothes |
| | Materialistic |
| Social | Spends time with friends |
| | Social |
| | Sad |
| Internalizing | Awkward |
| | Anxious |
| | Insecure |
| Active | Active |
| | Adventurous |
| | Energetic |
| Conforming | Conforms to peers |
| | Easily influenced by friends |
| | Faddish |
| Upstanding/prosocial | Interested in school |
| | Inquisitive |
| | Helpful |

Responses are made on a continuous scale ranging from "0% (or definitely NO)" to "100% (or definitely YES)." Adapted from "Measuring Beliefs about Adolescent Personality and Behavior," by C. M. Buchanan and G. N. Holmbeck, 1998, *Journal of Youth and Adolescence, 27*, p. 614. Copyright 1998 by Plenum Publishing Corporation. Adapted by permission.

## Risky Behaviors

This section addresses three topics. It begins with adolescents' use of forbidden (at least for minors) substances—specifically, alcohol, tobacco, and illicit drugs. It then moves to the topic of sexual activity, and it concludes with a consideration of delinquency.

## Substance Use

It is customary for discussions of the present topic to begin with statistics, and this presentation will be no exception. Table 8.5 is taken from Monitoring the Future, a long-term longitudinal study that tracks substance use of various forms in United States teenagers (Johnston et al., 2018; http://www.monitoringthefuture.org/). The table shows the prevalence of three forms of substance use by adolescents across the last several decades.

There is certainly some positive news in the numbers. Cigarette use has declined dramatically across the span covered by the survey. Alcohol use has also declined, although primarily in the two younger age groups sampled. It is worth noting that two particular and dangerous forms of alcohol consumption, binge drinking and drunk driving, have also declined.

Once these points are made, it is clear that the picture is far from totally positive. Both illicit drug use and alcohol use remain high, especially for 12th graders, and there is some evidence that an across-time pattern of decline in usage reversed with the 2017 testing. In addition, the survey does not attempt to encompass all forms of risky behavior; reckless driving (a leading cause of adolescent deaths) is one obvious exception.

The Monitoring the Future data are limited to US adolescents. A recent report examined risk-taking behaviors across 11 Western and non-Western countries spanning five continents (Duell et al., 2018). As would be expected,

Table 8.5 Trends over Time in Percentage of Substance Use by American Adolescents (Monitoring the Future Study)

| | Type of substance | | | | | |
| | Illicit drug | | Alcohol | | Cigarettes | |
| | 1991 | 2017 | 1991 | 2017 | 1991 | 2017 |
|---|---|---|---|---|---|---|
| Grade 8 | 18.7 | 18.2 | 70.1 | 23.1 | 44.0 | 9.4 |
| Grade 10 | 30.6 | 34.3 | 83.8 | 42.2 | 55.1 | 15.9 |
| Grade 12 | 44.1 | 48.9 | 88.0 | 81.5 | 63.1 | 26.8 |
| Combined | 30.4 | 33.4 | 80.1 | 57.0 | 53.5 | 17.0 |

the frequency of specific risk-taking activities varied across countries; norms and opportunities for particular behaviors are often different in different cultural settings. Nevertheless, a basic similarity emerged: I every culture, the propensity for risk-taking behavior peaked in adolescence. Many scholars believe—with much supporting evidence—that changes in the brain across the adolescent years underlie such increases in risky behavior (Morris, Squeglia, Jacobus, & Silk, 2018; Steinberg, 2014).

Whatever the biological underpinnings for the phenomenon may be, they do not provide a complete explanation, especially for individual differences among adolescents. The contribution of parents has long been a central issue in the risk-taking literature, and parental knowledge is the starting point for most examinations of the issue. That at least most parents want to know about their adolescent's potentially dangerous behaviors is clear; in one examination of the issue, risky behaviors topped mothers' responses to a question about what they would "always want to know" about what their adolescents do (Smetana & Rote, 2015).

How much parents actually know is less clear. We saw in the previous section that adolescent self-disclosure is a main source of parental knowledge and that adolescents are reluctant to disclose information about forbidden activities that they know will displease their parents. In many instances, therefore, parents' knowledge about risky behavior is less than ideal and less than they would like to possess. Nevertheless, parents vary in how much they know, and these variations permit a determination of whether parental knowledge makes a difference.

Two lines of research speak to this question. In what follows I first discuss work using the Parental Knowledge Scale and similar measures, and thus what parents know in general about their adolescents' activities. I then consider work that focuses directly on knowledge of substance use.

In discussing research with the Parental Knowledge Scale I will follow the typical practice of referring to the results as a measure of "knowledge," even though, as I pointed out earlier, the Scale actually measure perceptions of knowledge, with no independent assessment of the accuracy of such perceptions. As we will see, however, the predictive power of responses to the Scale is substantial, which certainly suggests that what the measure captures, at least in part, is actual knowledge and not just beliefs about knowledge.

The main predictive relation is the one of greatest interest: Parental knowledge relates negatively to adolescent risk behavior; that is, the more knowledgeable the parent is about the adolescent's activities, the less likely it is that the adolescent will engage in risky behavior (Daddis & Smetana, 2014; Racz & McMahon, 2011; Ryan, Jorm, & Lubman, 2010). This conclusion holds for both boys and girls, it holds for both mothers and fathers, and it holds for the three forms of substance use considered in this section. It holds also across a number of cultural and ethnic groups (e.g., Albertos et al., 2016; Boyd-Ball, Veronneau, Dishion, & Kavanagh, 2014). Moreover, parental knowledge relates not only to the probability of substance use but also to the effects of such use, for both parental knowledge and a positive parent–child relationship serve as buffers against the typical negative effects (Branstetter & Furman, 2013).

When considered separately, the contributors to parental knowledge are also predictive of engagement in risky behavior. Adolescents' willingness to self-disclose is negatively related to risky behavior: the greater the self-disclosure, the fewer the behavioral problems (e.g., Soenens, Vansteenkiste, Luyckx, & Goossens, 2006). Parents' monitoring of their adolescent's activities is also a predictor: the more thorough the monitoring, the fewer the problems (e.g., Fletcher, Steinberg, & Williams-Wheeler, 2004). Because these various predictors (knowledge, disclosure, monitoring) are typically related, it is important to note that each makes an independent contribution (at least in some instances) when the others are controlled statistically.

As we have seen, either parent reports or adolescent reports can provide the information about parental knowledge, self-disclosure, or monitoring. As we have also seen, these reports are sometimes discrepant—parents say one thing, and adolescents say another. Parent–child discrepancy turns out to be another predictor of behavioral problems: the greater the discrepancy, the more likely it is that problems will be found (e.g., Abar, Jackson, Colby, & Barnett, 2015; Reynolds, MacPherson, Matusiewicz, Schreibers, & Lejuez, 2011). Presumably, marked discrepancies between what parents and children believe reflect problems in parent–child communication and perhaps in the parent–child relationship more generally.

Given the lack of perfect agreement between parent and child, does it matter whose report is used as the measure of knowledge or disclosure or monitoring? It does matter. Another well-established finding from the literature is that adolescent reports yield stronger and more consistent relations than do parent reports (e.g., Abar et al., 2015; Clark, Donnellan, Robins, & Conger, 2015). This finding provides a possible answer to the question posed earlier of which informant is more accurate when the two disagree. What adolescents say tells us more about the determinants of risky behavior than what parents say, which suggests that adolescents are the ones with the better grasp of what parents know and how they know it.

The research discussed to this point is correlational and thus cannot establish causality with certainty. As always, two alternatives to a parental causal model must be considered. One is any third-factor explanation for the relations, that is, some basis, other than parents' behavior, that could account for the parent–child links. In this case, as in most parenting research, there is an obvious third-factor possibility, and it is the genes that parents and children share. It is clear, in fact, that genetic similarities between parents and children do account for some of the relation between parental characteristics and children's substance use and other problem behaviors (Neiderhiser, Reiss, Hetherington, & Plomin, 1999; Prom-Wormley & Maes, 2014). Genes, however, provide only a partial explanation.

The second alternative is that the causal direction is the reverse of that typically assumed, that is, from child to parent rather than parent to child. Perhaps adolescents who refrain from risky behaviors self-disclose more often and more fully to their parents, respond more readily and informatively to parents' monitoring efforts, and in general present an emotionally close, easy-to-judge target. In this case, parental knowledge and adolescent behavior would be related because the adolescent's behavior leads to the parent's knowledge.

That such a child-to-parent causal chain exists is widely agreed to by researchers of the topic. But this conclusion does not preclude a link in the parent-to-child direction as well; the consensus, rather, is of a two-way, reciprocal process whereby each member of the pair influences the other over time. Two kinds of evidence, both familiar by now, support a causal role for parental knowledge and related behaviors. One is longitudinal study, a frequent result of which is that parenting factors measured early in development relate to adolescent outcomes measured later in development (e.g., Clark et al., 2015; Fletcher et al., 2004). The other is experimental study in the form of intervention research, a basic finding from which is that altering parents' beliefs and practices can reduce the probability of adolescent substance use (e.g., Dishion, Nelson, & Kavanagh, 2003; Van Ryzin, Roseth, Fosco, Lee, & Chen, 2016).

I turn now to the second line of research, that directed not to parental knowledge in general but to knowledge of substance use in particular. How much do parents know about their adolescent's substance use?

The answer for many parents is not very much. Two main findings emerge from comparisons of parents' beliefs about substance use and adolescents' reports of substance use (Fisher et al., 2006; Green et al., 2011; Williams, McDermitt, Bertrand, & Davis, 2003). First, the degree of agreement between parent and child, although typically statistically significant, is modest at best, and it is accounted for primarily by agreement about nonuse. Second—and as implied by this first point—parents mainly err when their adolescents have engaged in substance use, and they err by underestimating the degree of use. The underestimation, moreover, is often substantial. In one study, for example, only 39% of parents were aware of their children's smoking, only 34% were aware of their drinking, and only 11% were aware of their use of illegal drugs (Williams et al., 2003). In another study only 32% were aware of tobacco use, and only 6% were aware of alcohol use (Chang et al., 2013). Underestimation also occurs for judgments beyond simple use or nonuse, for example, judgments of daily or weekly use or of use that constitutes dependency or abuse (Fernandez-Hermida, Calafat, Secades-Villa, Juan, & Sumnall, 2013; Fisher et al., 2006). Although most of the data come from US samples, similar effects have been reported across a number of cultural settings (Chang et al., 2013; Engels, Van der Vorst, Dekovic, & Meeus, 2007; Fernandez-Hermida et al., 2013).

Various contributors to parental accuracy have been identified. As indicated by the numbers just cited, accuracy is typically greater for smoking than it is for drinking. One possible explanation for this finding (although certainly not the only one) is that smoking is more likely than drinking to leave perceptible traces that parents may notice. Accuracy is also typically greater for older children than for younger children (e.g., McGillicuddy, Rychtarik, Morsheimer, & Burke-Storer, 2007), although the opposite effect is sometimes reported (e.g., Chang et al., 2013). The latter finding may result, at least in part, from parents' overly optimistic expectations—most parents believe that their children are nonusers, and such beliefs are more likely to be accurate for younger children. More generally, it is difficult, with the current state of research, to disentangle the causal relations between parental knowledge and child outcomes. More knowledgeable parents have children who are less likely to engage in substance use, which suggests that parental knowledge is beneficial—as is, of course, the case for many aspects of development. But if parents' default assumption is of nonuse, then parents whose children abstain will necessarily be more accurate.

Although most research on substance use has focused on parental knowledge, knowledge is not the only kind of parental belief that might be important. We saw in Chapter 6 that parents' expectations about academic performance can affect both their own behaviors and their children's development, and we saw earlier in this chapter that parents' expectations about the nature of adolescence can have similar effects. Research by Madon and colleagues (Madon, Guyll, Spoth, Cross, & Hilbert, 2003; Madon, Willard, Guyll, Trudeau, & Spoth, 2006) extends this conclusion to expectations about alcohol use. Using a longitudinal approach, Madon et al. showed that mothers' expectations for their preadolescents' eventual alcohol use predicted actual use when the children reached adolescence and did so even when other early predictors were controlled. Similar self-fulfilling effects of parental expectations have been demonstrated for smoking (Simons-Morton, 2004) and for marijuana use (Lamb & Crano, 2014).

As the studies of expectations suggest, parents' general beliefs about the activity in question can be important. Although most parents undoubtedly disapprove of substance use by their adolescents, some parents are more tolerant than are others, and relative tolerance on the part of the parent relates to heightened probability of substance use by the child (Ennett et al., 2016). Not surprisingly, parents' own practices are also important. Adolescents are more likely to drink if their parents drink and more likely to smoke if their parents smoke (Prom-Wormley & Maes, 2014).

Other than modeling the behaviors in question, what other parental practices might be important? The same variations in parenting that contribute to other developmental outcomes apply also to explanations for adolescents' substance use. On the negative side the predictors include hostility, conflict, and inconsistency, and on the positive side they include warmth, responsiveness, involvement, communication, and control but not overcontrol (Mynttinen, Pietila, & Kangasniemi, 2017; Racz & McMahon, 2011; Ryan et al., 2010). At a more general level, attachment is again a predictor, with greater probability of substance use in the case of insecure attachment (Fairbairn et al., 2018). Parenting style is also again a predictor, with more positive outcomes for adolescents whose parents adopt an authoritative style (Scheir & Hensen, 2014; although see Kerr, Stattin, & Ozdemir, 2012, for a cautionary note).

## Sexual Activity

I begin again with some statistics. In the United States in 2017, 40% of high school students, responding to the Youth Risk Behavior Surveillance, indicated that they had had sexual intercourse, and 30% indicated that they were currently sexually active. Slightly less than 10% reported experience with four or more sexual partners, and 46% indicated that they had not used a condom during their most recent intercourse (Centers for Disease Control and Prevention, 2018c).

The consequences of such sexual activity are evident in another set of statistics. In the United States in 2016, women between the ages of 15 and 19 gave birth to approximately 210,000 babies, a birth rate of approximately 2 births per 100 women (National Vital Statistics Report, 2018). In that same year, reported instances of chlamydia, the most common sexually transmitted disease (STD), were approximately 2 per 100 among 15- to 19-year-old women, a figure second only to that for 20- to 24-year-olds (Centers for Disease Control and Prevention, 2017).

As with the statistics cited with respect to substance use, these numbers reflect some improvements in recent years. In particular, both sexual activity by teenagers and births by teenage mothers in the United States have shown a steady decline for several decades now. In 1991, for example, 10.2% of teenagers were sexually active before age 13; in 2017, the number was 3.4% (Centers for Disease Control and Prevention, 2018c). In 1991, the birth rate for women between 15 and 19 was 6.2 per 100 women, more than three times the rate in 2016 (Child Trends, 2018).

Once again, however, the improvements over time do not negate the genuine risks that still remain. Both adolescent birth rates and adolescent STDs remain higher in the United States than in the great majority of developed nations. In addition, the problems attendant on adolescent sexual activity fall disproportionally on different segments of the population; minority groups, especially Hispanic youth, are at particular risk.

As with the work on substance use, what parents know is a major question in the study of adolescent sexual activity. And, as with the work on substance use, what parents know is often not very much. The dominant parental error is again one of underestimation, in this case underestimation of their adolescent's sexual experience. As a few examples—in a study by Jaccard, Dittus, and Gordon (1998), 58% of adolescents reported having had sex; the reported figure by mothers was 34%. In a study by Molborn and Everett (2010), 55% of mothers whose adolescents had in fact had sex believed that they had not. Finally, O'Donnell et al. (2008) showed that parental underestimation extends to behaviors that precede intercourse: 34% of 6th-grade girls reported that they had hugged and kissed a boy "for a long time," but only 3% of parents believed that they had done so.

I will add a point here that applies also to research on substance use. Parents' knowledge of their adolescent's behaviors is measured by the fit between what the parent believes and what the adolescent reports, an approach that assumes that adolescents' reports are accurate. We know that in some instances they are not. In particular, boys tend to overestimate the extent of their sexual activity, and girls tend to underestimate the extent of their activity (Diamond & Savin-Williams, 2009). As would be expected, however, various techniques to enhance the accuracy of reports (e.g., confidentiality of responses, written rather than oral answers, tests for social desirability) are common in research, and the evidence suggests that deliberate distortions are probably minor (Jaccard et al., 1998; Siegel, Aten, & Roghmann, 1998).

Much of the research directed to parenting and adolescent sexual behavior has focused on "the talk": the conversations that parents have with their adolescents about sexual behavior and its possible consequences. Such conversations serve two purposes. First, they are a source of information for the issue just discussed: parents' knowledge of their adolescent's sexual activities. Second, and perhaps more fundamentally, they are a way for parents to influence these activities through the values, expectations, and information that they convey.

Families vary markedly in how much and in how they talk about sex, including in some instances no talk at all (Byers & Sears, 2012; Byers, Sears, & Weaver, 2008; de Looze, Constantine, Jerman, Vermeulen-Smit, & Bogt, 2015). Mothers are more likely than fathers to provide such talk, and daughters are more likely than sons to receive such talk, in part because daughters are more likely than sons to seek out information about sex (O'Sullivan & Thompson, 2014). This literature provides another instance of the importance of parental self-efficacy, for mothers who are confident in their ability to discuss sex with their children are more likely to do so (Byers & Sears, 2012). It also provides another instance of the importance of childhood experience, for parents' satisfaction with the parental teaching that they received as adolescents relates positively both to their own confidence as teachers and to the quality of the teaching that they themselves provide (Byers et al., 2008).

The extent to which having "the talk" (or perhaps versions of it over time) is beneficial is part of the general question of what parents do that affects the likelihood, the nature, and the effects of sexual activity by their adolescents. In what follows I identify three general parental contributors, drawing from several reviews devoted to the question (Dittus et al., 2015; Guilamo-Ramos et al., 2012; Kincaid, Jones, Sterret, & McKee, 2012; Markham et al., 2010). Before doing so, I will make a point that we have seen many times before: This is yet another literature that is decidedly mixed, with some discrepant results accompanying any general conclusion that might be offered.

This said, one conclusion is that parent–child communication, whether in a single "talk" session or distributed as needed over time, is beneficial. Assuming that it takes a generally accurate and supportive form, talk with parents is associated with greater sexual knowledge on the adolescent's part, delayed initiation of sexual activity, and heightened probability of using protective devices when activity *is* initiated. Although most of the research has focused on mothers, similar effects have been reported for both mothers and fathers.

A second conclusion is that monitoring is beneficial. As we have seen, "monitoring" takes two forms in the literature, in some cases referring to parents' monitoring behaviors and in other cases referring to the knowledge that presumably results from such behaviors. The major review of this work (Dittus et al., 2015) distinguishes the two forms and concludes that both are beneficial. As with communication, effects extend not only to the initiation of sexual activity but also to the use of contraceptives when sexually active.

The third predictor is the quality of the parent–child relationship. Warmth, support, closeness, involvement—none is a guarantee of satisfactory outcomes, but all make such outcomes more likely. In part they do so by affecting other contributors. The adolescent's willingness to share information with the parent, for example, is enhanced by a positive, supportive relationship, and monitoring is certainly easier when family time and family activities occupy an important part of the adolescent's day.

The conclusions just stated are ones that we have encountered before—we saw them in the section on substance use, and we saw versions of them for topics discussed earlier in the book. I will add two other points that we have also seen before. First, it is again clear that not only do parents affect their children but also that children affect their parents. In particular, signs that the child has become or is likely to become sexually active are likely to elicit heightened communication and heightened monitoring on the parent's part (de Looze et al., 2015). Second, many of the constructs of interest (e.g., communication, monitoring, closeness) can be measured via either parent report or adolescent report, and again the measurement decision makes a difference. It is the same difference that we have seen before: Adolescent reports apparently provide the truer picture for they lead to more consistent and more meaningful results than do parent reports (Jaccard et al., 1998; O'Donnell et al. (2008).

I conclude this section by acknowledging three ways in which my brief coverage of the topic has been limited. First, the focus has been on research conducted in industrialized and mostly Western nations. It has long been clear from anthropological studies that parents' socialization of their children's sexual development takes different forms in different cultures, including forms that are both more permissive and less permissive than those typical in the Western world. Schlegel and Barry (1991) remains a classic source for a discussion of these cultural differences.

A second limitation is that my focus—and the focus of most research—has been on adolescents' engagement in sexual intercourse. Sexual intercourse, however, is not the sole form of sexual activity for most adolescents, and it may not be a form at all for adolescents with a gay or lesbian or bi orientation. A chapter by Diamond and Savin-Williams (2009) is a good starting point for a broader consideration of sexual activity during adolescence. The same chapter is also a good source for acknowledgment of a third limitation in the present coverage, and it is that an exclusive focus on the risks of adolescent sexual activity provides a limited and overly negative view of the topic. The risks, to be sure, are real, but so are the achievements and the developmental advances. This is a point that applies in general to the challenges with which adolescents cope.

## Delinquency

The term "juvenile delinquent" is in a sense self-defining: some prohibited action performed by a juvenile. The meaning of "juvenile" varies, however, across different actions. Fourteen-, 16-, and 18-year-olds are all prohibited from buying alcohol; only 14-year-olds, however, are prohibited from driving, and only14-year-olds and (in some states) 16-year-olds are prohibited from leaving school before graduating.

As these examples suggest, delinquent behaviors fall into two categories. Some are actions (e.g., assault, robbery, vandalism) that are prohibited at any age. Others are actions, such as school truancy, whose status depends on the perpetrator's age.

Another division concerns the nature of the action. So-called overt forms of delinquency typically include aggression or the threat of aggression, for example, attacking someone, rape, or murder. In contrast, covert forms of delinquency take a primarily nonaggressive form, for example, shoplifting, vandalism, or selling drugs.

These two forms of delinquency have different developmental histories. Overt forms are more likely to show what is called an *early-onset pattern*, that is, deviant actions, especially high aggression, that are evident well before adolescence. Covert forms are more likely to appear in adolescence and, in most cases, to be limited to adolescence (Moffitt, 1993).

That parental practices contribute to adolescent delinquency has long been clear. Indeed, in a review by Hoeve and colleagues (2009), all nine parenting practices that were examined showed significant relations to measures of delinquency. Among the predictors were several measures that tap into parents' beliefs: parental monitoring behaviors, parental knowledge in the Stattin and Kerr (2000) sense, and child disclosure. High scores on these measures related to a relatively low probability of delinquency.

Two further findings from the review are worth noting. Negative aspects of parenting (e.g., rejection, neglect) showed stronger relations to delinquency than did positive aspects (e.g., affection, support). In addition, the review revealed a sex of parent by sex of child effect: Mothers' practices were more important for daughters, and fathers' practices were more important for sons. Relations between attachment and delinquency show a similar matched-sex effect, that is, attachment to the mother more important for girls, and attachment to the father more important for boys (Hoeve et al., 2012). In both cases the relation is what we would expect: less probability of delinquency when the attachment relationship is secure.

As always, alternative explanations exist for such correlational findings. Child-to-parent effects certainly contribute to the relations (e.g., Laird, Pettit, Bates, & Dodge, 2003), and so do genetic similarities between parent and child (e.g., Beaver, Schwartz, Connolly, Al-Ghamdi, & Kobeisy, 2015). Again, however, evidence beyond simple correlations (across-time patterns, experimental manipulations) supports a causal role for parental practices.

Two other findings that we have seen before also appear in this literature. Again, discrepancy between parent and child reports is predictive of problems, in this case a heightened risk of delinquency (De Los Reyes, Goodman, Kliewer, & Reid-Quinones, 2010; Ksinan & Vazsonyl, 2016). And again, child reports show greater predictive power than do parent reports (Augenstein et al., 2016).

I conclude the discussion of delinquency with a point about the differences in parents' beliefs that are likely to be important. The forms of evidence cited earlier (monitoring, disclosure) have to do with beliefs about one's own child, beliefs that clearly vary among parents. In contrast, general beliefs about delinquency seem likely to show a fair degree of similarity in parental thinking; at the least, most parents presumably are against actions such as robbery and vandalism, and most parents presumably wish to avoid negative encounters with the justice system. A study by Cavanaugh and Cauffman (2015), however, makes clear that not all parents are identical in how they think about legal matters (see also Walters, 2015). The focus of the study was on recidivism by male juvenile delinquents, that is, a return to offending after receiving punishment for a previous offence. Both the adolescents and their mothers responded to a series of questions concerning the legitimacy of the justice system (e.g., "Court decisions are almost always fair," "I feel people should support the police"). Negative beliefs about the justice system by the mother predicted negative beliefs by the adolescent, and negative beliefs by the adolescent predicted a heightened probability of recidivism. It is worth noting also that one of the best predictors of an adolescent's delinquency is a history of arrests by family members, with arrest of the father the best predictor for adolescent males (Farrington, Jolliffe, Loeber, Stouthamer-Loeber, & Kalb, 2001).

## Conflict

Much of the research under this heading—especially that concerned with parents' beliefs—was addressed in Chapter 4. As we saw there, conflicts between parents and adolescents often revolve around the issue of autonomy: whether parent or adolescent should have the decision-making power for various aspects of the adolescent's life. Both parties typically agree that the answer depends on the domain in question, with moral, conventional, and prudential issues being ceded (at least usually) to the parent and personal issues seen as the province of the adolescent. The conflict comes when parent and adolescent hold discrepant beliefs about which domain applies—in particular, when adolescents believe that a matter should be under their personal control and parents believe otherwise. The result is that the intensity of conflicts peaks across the early years of adolescence, as the adolescent's growing belief in a right to autonomy outpaces the parent's willingness to grant such autonomy. As we saw, however, most such conflicts center on fairly mundane matters (e.g., doing chores, keeping one's room clean), and, in most instances, they do not have lasting negative effects on either the child's development or the parent–child relationship. Indeed, a certain amount of conflict may be a normative, development-enhancing experience (Branje, 2018).

The literature on parent–child conflict during adolescence is by no means limited to work from the domain perspective (for fuller reviews, see Laursen & Collins, 1994; Laursen, Coy, & Collins, 1998). I have concentrated on the domain approach because it focuses squarely on parents' beliefs and related practices, something that is not true of much of the larger literature. Nevertheless, beliefs about domains are not the only parent cognitions that may affect the probability and the nature of parent–child conflicts. In this section I add five others.

One is the expectations that parents have for their adolescent's behavior. As we saw, most parents appear to hold general expectations about the period of adolescence, including ways in which their child will change as he or she enters the teen years. Some parents, however, hold less realistic expectations than do others, and some parents are slower to adjust to their changing child than are others. The result is frequent violations of expectation, as what the parent expects to happen does not match what actually happens. This, clearly, is a recipe for conflict. Work by Collins and colleagues verifies that violations of parents' expectations are especially likely in early adolescence; that such violations are a frequent source of conflict, especially when the issue is deemed an important one by both parent and child; and that the eventual result of such violations may be cognitive change on either the parent's part or the child's part or both (Collins, 1992, Collins & Luebker, 1994). This last finding fits with the more general literature: The idea that violation of expectations is a source of change is found in virtually every theory of how cognitive change comes about.

I will add a further point that Collins and other students of adolescence (e.g., Steinberg & Silk, 2002) make, and it is that adolescents may not be the only ones who are changing across the teenage years. Many parents may be moving from young-adult to middle-aged status, and many may be undergoing biological and social changes that present various challenges in addition to those of parenthood. The result is that adolescents too may face a changing, hard-to-predict interaction partner, and these partners may not always be optimally poised to avoid or to resolve whatever conflicts arise.

The work on expectations suggests that the accuracy with which parents can judge their children is important. This, of course, is a conclusion that we have seen at various places throughout the book. A study by Hastings and Grusec (1997) verifies that parental accuracy is indeed a contributor to parent-child conflicts and their resolution. These researchers interviewed parents and adolescents separately about recent conflicts that they had had, asking the participants about their own thoughts and feelings during the conflict and also their beliefs about what their interaction partner was thinking and feeling. Parents differed in their ability to judge their children's beliefs and emotions, and these differences proved to be important—in different ways, however, for mothers and fathers. For fathers, greater accuracy was associated with a lower probability of conflict. For mothers, greater accuracy was associated with greater satisfaction with how conflicts were resolved. It is interesting to note that there was no relation between maternal accuracy and paternal accuracy, a finding that suggests that the significant results did not reflect a child-to-parent effect (i.e., that adolescents' qualities made them both easy to judge and tractable interaction partners).

One determinant of the accuracy with which parents can judge their children—and indeed of the accuracy with which any of us can judge other people—is perspective-taking ability: the ability to break away from one's own perspective to take the point of view of someone else. Perspective taking—and its converse, egocentrism—began as a childhood literature with some of Piaget's earliest studies (Piaget, 1926). In recent years, however, it has become clear that overcoming egocentrism can be a life-long challenge, for, under some circumstances even adults struggle to understand the perspective of another (e.g., Epley, Morewedge, & Keysar, 2004).

Parents may also struggle. Lundell and colleagues (Lundell, Grusec, McShane, & Davidod, 2008) measured mothers' perspective taking through a series of questions directed to attempts to understand their child's point of view (e.g., "I try to look at my son's/daughter's side of a disagreement before I make a decision," "When I'm upset with my son/daughter, I usually try to put myself in his/her shoes for a while"). Mothers varied in their perspective-taking efforts, and these variations related in expectable ways to mother–child conflicts. Relatively high perspective-taking scores predicted less intense conflicts. They also predicted positive aspects of the adolescent's approach to conflicts: fewer attempts at dominating the interaction and more concern with maintaining a satisfactory relationship with the mother. Thus the adolescents appeared to appreciate their mothers' attempts to understand how they thought and felt.

The goal of perspective taking is often to understand the reasons for another person's behavior. A focus on the causes of behavior brings us to a construct that we have encountered in a number of different contexts: parents' attributions for their children's behavior. Parent–child conflicts provide another context in which attributions prove to be important. Negative attributions for the partner's behavior, whether offered by parents or by adolescents, are predictive of negative results of the interaction: more intense conflict, less satisfactory resolution, more probability of difficulties in the future (Heatherington, Tolejko, McDonald, & Funk, 2007; MacKinnon-Lewis, Castellino, Brody, & Fincham, 2001). Especially damaging are attributions that posit an internal locus for an undesired behavior on the partner's part—thus not "My child is having a bad day," but "My child is always like this." As we have seen before, a belief that an unwanted behavior is internal in origin and unlikely to change does not lead to the most helpful parenting practices.

The final form of belief to be considered ties back to some material discussed in Chapter 3. There we saw that mothers' epistemological beliefs— that is, their general beliefs systems about the nature of knowledge—affect how they think about their child and how they treat their child. In particular, mothers who reason at the higher levels of the epistemological hierarchy are more sensitive to their children's ways of thinking and more supportive of their children's attempts to construct their own ways of understanding the world.

The effects of mothers' epistemological beliefs extend to the domain of mother-adolescent conflicts (Holmes, Bond, & Byrne, 2008). Conflicts, to be sure, do not disappear simply because the mother possesses a relatively advanced conception of the nature of knowledge. In various ways, however, conflicts take a more favorable form in such cases: lower in intensity, lower in the proportion of negative behavior, more positive in how adolescents feel about the openness and the fairness of the communications. A statement by one of the mothers suggests a basis for this last conclusion: "The child has to understand that their opinions do matter . . . because it makes her feel that she has a say. Because the last thing I want her to do is to think she's got nothing to say and whatever she has to say is not important" (Holmes et al., 2008, p. 576).

## The Internet

I begin with two qualifiers. First, the Internet is not something that appears in children's lives for the first time at adolescence, nor do parents' beliefs and decisions about the Internet become relevant only at adolescence. Good sources for earlier periods of development include Blumberg and Brooks (2017) and Livingstone (2009). Second, my concentration is skewed toward use of social media and also skewed toward potentially negative effects of such use. Clearly, the Internet consists of more than social media, and time on the Internet—for adolescents as for any of us—carries many benefits to go along with the risks.

Still, there are risks, and they have been the focus of most research on adolescents' use of the Internet. The title of one such study succinctly summarizes the concerns: "Peers, Predators, and Porn" (Byrne, Katz, Lee, Linz, & Mcllrath, 2014). More formally, Livingstone and Haddon (2008) identify four general categories of risk. *Content* risks involve exposure to illegal or harmful content, for example, pornography or websites advocating hate or violence. *Contact* risks involve potentially dangerous online contacts, for example, cyberbullying or contact with strangers. These two categories account for the bulk of research. Also of concern, however, are *commercial* risks (e.g., advertising exploitation, illegal downloading) and *privacy* risks (e.g., giving out personal information).

As with the risks discussed earlier in the chapter, two questions are central to an examination of parents' role in adolescents' use of the Internet. The first is what parents know about their adolescent's online activities. The second is what parents do about these activities.

The answer to the "what do parents know" question will sound familiar. Most parents possess limited knowledge of what their adolescents do online, and most believe that they know more than they in fact do (with knowledge again determined by the fit between parents' beliefs and adolescents' reports). Again, the dominant error is underestimation: Parents report fewer risky online behaviors than adolescents themselves report. As an example, in a study by Byrne et al. (2014), parents (mostly mothers) identified only 33% of the instances in which their child had been cyberbullied, only 27% of the instances in which the child had cyberbullied someone else, only 51% of the instances in which the child had sought out a porn site, and only 35% of the instances in which the child had been approached by a stranger online. Similar underestimations, in some instances more marked, are a common finding across a number of studies and a number of countries (e.g., Cho & Cheon, 2005; Liau, Khoo, & Ang, 2008; Livingstone & Bober, 2004; Symons, Ponnet, Emmery, Walrave, & Heirman, 2017).

This is another literature in which gender can make a difference at both the parent and the child ends. As we have seen before, mothers are sometimes more knowledgeable than are fathers, in this case with respect to their adolescent's online activities (e.g., Liau et al., 2008), but as we have also seen before, such differences are not always found (e.g., Symons et al., 2017). Similarly, parents are sometimes more accurate in judging boys' online risky behaviors than they are in judging girls' behaviors (e.g., Symons et al., 2017), but this difference also is not always found (e.g., Byrne et al., 2014). In any case, it is difficult to know whether any boy–girl differences reflect greater parental insight into sons than daughters or simply a general belief about boys' and girls' Internet activities. Boys typically engage in more risky online behaviors than do girls (Notten & Nikken, 2016), and parents who hold this expectation may be less likely to underestimate their son's activities.

How do parents acquire their knowledge of their children's online activities, incomplete though such knowledge may be? Adolescents' self-disclosure is again one important source, especially for activities (e.g., being bullied) that the adolescent finds distressing and may therefore want to discuss (e.g., Law, Shapka, & Olson, 2010). Parental monitoring also contributes, with greater knowledge in cases in which parents have made an active effort to learn about what their child does online (Sobring & Lundin, 2012; Symons et al., 2017). As is often the case with monitoring, however, results are inconsistent, with positive results for some forms of monitoring but not others, or for some outcomes but not others. In addition, parent–child discrepancies are again evident: Parents typically report more monitoring than adolescents agree has occurred (e.g., Liau et al., 2008; Padilla-Walker, Coyne, & Collier, 2016).

Monitoring is of interest not only, or even primarily, as a source of parental knowledge. The focus of most studies of monitoring has been on monitoring as a parental practice, the goal being to determine whether monitoring serves as a protective factor against the risks of online activities. Potentially, it could do so either by reducing the exposure to risky material or by reducing the effects when such exposure occurs. Or, of course, both routes are possible.

Three forms of monitoring are distinguished. *Restrictive monitoring* refers to setting rules and limits with respect to online time and online activities; it may also include controls that block access to certain online material. In contrast, *active monitoring* involves discussion with the child about different sorts of online content, the goal being to promote critical thinking and eventual self-regulation. Finally, *co-use* refers, as the label suggests, to parent and child experiencing the online content together, either incidentally or (especially if the parent has concerns) intentionally on the parent's part. These forms of monitoring are not mutually exclusive; rather, parents may use combinations of all three (Padilla-Walker, Coyne, Kroff, & Memmoff-Elison, 2018).

Not all studies report positive effects of monitoring on adolescents' behavior, and the positive effects that do occur are typically limited and qualified in various ways (Collier et al., 2016; Elsaesser et al., 2017; Padilla-Walker, Coyne et al., 2018). Clearly, parents face many challenges in attempts to control their adolescent's online activities. As we have seen, they often have limited knowledge of what these activities are, a problem that has grown in magnitude as Internet use becomes less and less tied to a single in-the-home location. Their own online skills, or lack thereof, may be a stumbling block, Internet use being a rare instance in which children often possess greater expertise than their parents. Parents' self-efficacy with respect to the relevant technology is in fact one determinant of how successfully they monitor their children's activities (Sanders, Parent, Forehand, Sullivan, & Jones, 2016). Determining effects of monitoring requires accurate measures of monitoring; as we saw, however, parents tend to overestimate how thoroughly they monitor what their children do. In addition, establishing a causal role for monitoring may be frustrated by the directionality issue. Parents may increase their monitoring efforts when they perceive problems in their children's online activities, an effect that would undercut an expected negative relation between monitoring and problematic child outcomes.

Once these points are made, there is no doubt that monitoring *can* be effective, even if, in some instances, it falls short of its goal. All three forms of monitoring identified earlier have been shown to be beneficial, although conclusions are probably clearest and most consistent for active monitoring. Positive results extend to a range of online activities and related outcomes, including substance use, bullying, and sexual behavior. Again, however, effects are not ensured. As with other parental practices, effects of monitoring depend on the skill with which it is executed; restrictive monitoring, for example, may be ineffective or even detrimental if adolescents perceive it as a violation of their autonomy (e.g., Padilla-Walker et al., 2016). And as with other parental practices, effects depend on the general context within which monitoring occurs, with positive effects most likely in the context of a warm and supportive parent–child relationship (e.g., Fikkers, Piotrowski, & Valkenburg, 2017).

I will conclude this section by noting two features that characterize the literature on parents' contribution to their adolescents' Internet experience. First, a high proportion of studies directly measure parents' monitoring behaviors as opposed to inferring monitoring from measures of parental knowledge. Second, a high proportion of studies directly measure parental knowledge as opposed to inferring knowledge (ala the Stattin and Kerr approach) from claims of knowledge. The more general literature would benefit from a more consistent incorporation of both of these characteristics.

## Positive Developments

One definition of successful adolescence is the absence of the problems discussed to this point in the chapter. This section takes up a more ambitious conception: not just the absence of problems but the emergence of clearly positive developments. Three such developments are discussed: romantic relationships, civic engagement, and ethnic identity. (See also Lerner, Phelps, Forman, & Bowers, 2009.)

## Romantic Relationships

Although "romantic relationships" may not require a definition, I will provide one, taken from Collins, Welsh, and Furman (2009, p. 632). "The term 'romantic relationships' refers to mutually acknowledged ongoing voluntary interactions. Compared to other peer relationships, romantic ones typically have a distinctive intensity, commonly marked by expressions of affection and current or anticipated sexual behavior."

As this definition indicates, romantic relationships are similar in some respects to friendships. Both must be mutually acknowledged (one person cannot constitute a friendship or a romance), and both are predominantly positive relationships characterized by reciprocal affection. They differ, though, in developmental timing; friendships may be evident as early as the toddler years, whereas romantic relationships, with occasional exceptions (Carlson & Rose, 2007), do not appear until adolescence. They differ also in gender composition: primarily same-sex in the case of friendship, primarily other-sex in the case of romantic relationships (although, of course, not only other-sex; see Russell, Watson, & Muraco, 2012). And they differ in the ways indicated in the second sentence of the definition—in particular, the prospect or the fact of sexual activity in the case of romantic relationships.

As their inclusion in this section indicates, romantic relationships can be considered a normative task of adolescence—an expectable achievement of the adolescent years that prepares the way for various positive outcomes in adulthood. "Normative," however, does not mean "universal," and there are in fact marked individual differences among adolescents in both the existence and the quality of romantic relationships (Collins et al., 2009; Connolly & McIsaac, 2009; Furman, 2018; Furman & Rose, 2015). Some adolescents go through the teenage years without ever forming a romantic relationship, some form a single relationship, and others eventually have several romantic partners. Some relationships, especially early in adolescence, are short-lived; others may persist through the span of adolescence and perhaps into adulthood as well. Finally, some relationships are predominantly positive, supportive, and mutually enjoyable, but others, again especially those in early adolescence, are marked by uncertainty, conflict, and in some instances physical violence

These differences make a difference. To be sure, no one's eventual romantic history is fixed by what happens in adolescence. But it often is affected in either a positive or a negative direction. A history of positive romantic relationships in adolescence is associated with a heightened probability of successful romantic relationships in adulthood. It is also associated with various other measures of successful adjustment, including social competence, self-esteem, personal identity, and academic achievement (Collins et al., 2009).

Understandably, much of the research on adolescent romantic relationships has attempted to determine where the differences among adolescents come from. I concentrate here on the role of parents, beginning with the usual proviso that parents are never all-important causes of their children's development. But they are often important contributors, and such is clearly the case for romantic relationships.

One way in which parents contribute begins early in life. We have seen that the attachment relationship forged during infancy is predictive of a number of later developments, either positive ones in the case of secure attachment or negative ones in the case of the various forms of insecure attachment.

Security of attachment is also predictive of positive romantic relationships during adolescence and young adulthood (Simpson, Collins, & Salvatore, 2011; Sroufe et al., 2005). The usual explanation for this finding is the one offered in Chapter 2: As the earliest social relationship, attachment is the source for the first working model of the social world that children form, a working model that then affects, for better or worse, subsequent social relationships.

Various aspects of parents' child-rearing practices also contribute, more clearly, as is often the case, for mothers than for fathers (e.g., Seiffge-Krenke, Overbeek, & Vermulst, 2010; Walper & Wendt, 2015). A history of sensitive, involved, responsive parenting is associated with a greater likelihood of positive romantic relationships; conversely, a history of familial conflict—both parent–child conflict and mother–father conflict—predicts conflict with one's romantic partner or partners (Furman, 2018). Both concurrent (i.e., within adolescence) and across-time relations with parenting practices have been shown.

Parents are not the only social agents who affect romantic relationships. We would expect that peers will also be important, and such is in fact the case: Both satisfactory friendships and general success in the peer group are predictive of satisfactory romantic relationships (Collins et al., 2009). But note that parents contribute here as well. As we saw in Chapter 7, family and peers are not separate social worlds; rather, parents are one determinant of how successfully their children fare in their interactions with peers, which in turn affects how successful they are in their romantic endeavors.

The contributors discussed to this point do not speak directly to the more proximal ways in which parents contribute—that is, what does a parent do when faced with a child who is either already in a romantic relationship or on the cusp of entering one? The general answer to this question is the same answer that applies to all of the potentially risky adolescent behaviors discussed throughout this chapter: Parents talk to their children, both proactively and in response to particular experiences; they set rules and limits that reflect their beliefs about the domain in question, often with a special emphasis on the dangers of particular behaviors or (in this case) the dangers of particular partners; and they attempt to monitor and if need be redirect their adolescent's behavior (Kan, McHale, & Crouter, 2008; Madsen, 2008; Mounts & Kim, 2009). As with parents' management of their children's peer relations more generally (recall Table 7.5), parents vary in how skillfully they perform these various roles, differences that contribute to differences in their adolescents' romantic experiences.

I will add that this is another instance in which the parents' own developmental history may contribute to their beliefs and behaviors. Research suggests that mothers' history of adolescent romantic relationships affects the ways in which they think about and respond to their daughters' actual or potential relationships (Shulman, Scharf, & Shachar-Shapira, 2012).

Having summarized some of the main conclusions from this literature, I will conclude by noting that work on romantic relationships is very much an ongoing enterprise, with much still to be learned. A recent review by Furman and Rose (2015) makes this point. Within three pages, phrases such as "little is known" and "further work is needed" appear 21 times.

## Civic Engagement

A reasonable first question under this heading is what forms civic engagement by adolescents might take. Sherrod and colleagues (Sherrod, Flanagan, & Youniss, 2002; Sherrod & Lauckhardt, 2009) identify three general ways in which adolescents might begin to play an active and positive role in their communities. One way—and the most often studied form of civic engagement—is through political activity, for example, working for a candidate or political position, participating in a protest or demonstration, or (once the requisite age is reached) regularly voting. A second way is through community service directed to those in need, for example, raising money for charity or volunteering to help at a local soup kitchen. Finally, a third possible form of engagement comes from membership in some service-oriented organization, for example, a church, a school group, or a scouting troop.

Research on adolescents' engagement in such activities dates back to the 1950s, and it now constitutes a large literature that encompasses samples from dozens of different nations (Sherrod & Lauckhardt, 2009; Torney-Purta, Lehmen, Oswald, & Scholz, 2001; Youniss, 2014). As we might expect, the degree of civic engagement varies some across forms of engagement, across time periods, across nations, across ages, across ethnicities, and (occasionally) across genders. It is never close to universal, however, and there is little evidence for an upward trend in recent years. A basic question then, of both scientific and pragmatic importance, is what determines the differences among youth: Why do some but not others become involved in civic activities?

As always, parents are not the sole cause of differences among children. Indeed a major resource on the topic, *The Handbook of Research on Civic Engagement in Youth* (Sherrod, Torney-Purta, & Flanagan, 2010), does not include the words "parents" or "parenting" in its index. But it does make clear, as do other sources (e.g., Nuendorf, Niemi, & Smets, 2016; Rossi, Lenzi, Sharkey, Vieno, & Santinello, 2016), that a variety of outside-the-family experiences can contribute to youths' civic engagement. These experiences include the school, especially programs designed to promote civic engagement (Lin, 2015). They include peers, for adolescents are most likely to show civic engagement when they have friends who are engaged (Rossi et al., 2016). And they include social media, especially informational and expressive uses of such media (Skoric, Zhu, Goh, & Pang, 2016).

Of course, these various other contributors do not negate a role for parents. In fact, civic engagement could be argued to be one of the outcomes for which the importance of parents is least in doubt. One of the most robust findings in this literature is that parents' civic engagement predicts their adolescents' civic engagement: the more knowledgeable and involved the parent, the more knowledgeable and involved the adolescent (McIntosh, Hart, & Youniss, 2007; Pancer, 2015). Thus one way in which parents affect their children is by providing models of the desired behavior. Another way is through the messages they provide, for adolescent civic engagement is most likely when frequent conversations with parents stress both the value of helping others and ways in which to do so (Oosterhoff & Metzger, 2016; Pancer, Pratt, Hunsberger, & Alisar, 2007). Although the beliefs behind such parental practices are seldom explicitly elicited, they are not difficult to infer. A reasonable inference is that many parents believe that civic engagement is important, that one's children should become engaged, that adolescence is the appropriate time to initiate such engagement, and that various parental practices (modeling, instruction, encouragement) are effective ways to do so.

As with other outcomes, parents also contribute to their children's development through their effect on other sources of influence. Exposure to news media, for example, is most likely to have an effect if it leads to conversations with a parent about the issue in question (Boyd, Zaff, Phelps, Weiner, & Lerner, 2011). In addition, peers are not a clearly separate source; rather, parents affect both the peers with whom their children associate and their susceptibility to influence from these peers.

I will note finally that the origins of civic engagement—and of parents' contribution to such engagement—do not necessarily wait for the onset of adolescence. Successful civic engagement requires a variety of cognitive and social skills (e.g., problem solving, perspective taking, empathy, moral reasoning) that provide both the motivation and the ability to help others (Astuto & Ruck, 2015). These skills begin to develop early in life, and parents are important contributors to their development. Thus another way in which parents play a role is by nurturing the qualities that underlie an eventual commitment to civic engagement.

## Ethnic Identity

One way to convey what is meant by ethnic identity is to consider how it is measured. Table 8.6 presents the most commonly used of the available measures: the Multigroup Ethnic Identity Measure (MEIM; Phinney, 1992). Urmana-Taylor (2015) provides a description of other measurement possibilities.

As can be seen, the MEIM assesses individuals' feelings of belongingness to and satisfaction with a particular ethnic group. It includes both items directed to exploring and learning about one's ethnicity (e.g., the first item in the table) and items that reflect commitment to a specific ethnic identity (e.g., items 5 and 6). It treats ethnic identity not as a dichotomous, present or absent development but rather as a matter of degree—as something that develops with time and varies among individuals. Adolescence is seen as an especially important time for such development.

References to "identity" and "exploration" and "commitment" as tasks of adolescence may sound familiar. Much of the work on ethnic identity is grounded in the theorizing of both Erikson (1968) and Marcia (1980). As in these more general approaches to the notion of identity, a fully formed and satisfactory ethnic identity is regarded as an important developmental achievement, valuable both in itself and as a contributor to other developments. Among the developments that relate positively (at least usually) to ethnic identity are self-esteem, peer relations, and academic achievement.

Because everyone has an ethnicity, ethnic identity is potentially an issue for everyone's development. In fact, ethnic identity is most often studied in groups that are minorities within their countries of residence. Most such research has been carried out in the United States, and African Americans

**Table 8.6** The Multigroup Ethnic Identity Measure (MEIM)

In this country, people come from many different countries and cultures, and there are many different words to describe the different backgrounds or *ethnic groups* that people come from. Some examples of the names of ethnic groups are Hispanic or Latino, Black or African American, Asian American, Chinese, Filipino, American Indian, Mexican American, Caucasian or White, Italian American, and many others. These questions are about your ethnicity or your ethnic group and how you feel about it or react to it.

Please fill in: In terms of ethnic group, I consider myself to be _____

Use the numbers below to indicate how much you agree or disagree with each statement.

(4) Strongly agree   (3) Agree   (2) Disagree   (1) Strongly disagree

1. I have spent time trying to find out more about my ethnic group, such as its history, traditions, and customs.
2. I am active in organizations or social groups that include mostly members of my own ethnic group.
3. I have a clear sense of my ethnic background and what it means for me.
4. I think a lot about how my life will be affected by my ethnic group membership.
5. I am happy that I am a member of the group I belong to.
6. I have a strong sense of belonging to my own ethnic group.
7. I understand pretty well what my ethnic group membership means to me.
8. In order to learn more about my ethnic background, I have often talked to other people about my ethnic group.
9. I have a lot of pride in my ethnic group.
10. I participate in cultural practices of my own group, such as special food, music, or customs.
11. I feel a strong attachment towards my own ethnic group.
12. I feel good about my cultural or ethnic background.
13. My ethnicity is
    (1) Asian or Asian American, including Chinese, Japanese, and others
    (2) Black or African American
    (3) Hispanic or Latino, including Mexican American, Central American, and others
    (4) White, Caucasian, Anglo, European American; not Hispanic
    (5) American Indian/Native American
    (6) Mixed; Parents are from two different groups
    (7) Other (write in): _____
14. My father's ethnicity is (use numbers above)
15. My mother's ethnicity is (use numbers above)

From "The Multigroup Ethnic Identity Measure: A New Scale for Use with Diverse Groups," by J. S. Phinney, 1992, *Journal of Research in Adolescence*, 7, pp. 172–173. Copyright 2007 by Sage Publisher. Reprinted by permission.

are the most often studied minority, with growing literatures on Hispanic American and Asian American populations as well. White samples are sometimes, but rarely, included, appearing primarily for purposes of comparison with minority samples (e.g., Else-Quest & Morse, 2015). A recent call for more work with White adolescents may eventually change this conclusion (Loyd & Gaither, 2018).

Like the other developments discussed in this chapter, ethnic identity has multiple sources, including the peer group in general and friends in particular (Rivas-Drake, Urbana-Taylor, Schaefer, & Medina, 2017; Santos, Kornienko, & Rivas-Drake, 2017). Much of the research, however, has concentrated on the role of parents. Indeed, the literature on parents' contribution is large enough to have spawned four review articles to date (Hughes et al., 2006; Lesane-Brown, 2006; Priest et al., 2014; Yasui, 2015).

That parents are important contributors is clear. As with civic engagement, one piece of evidence is parent–child similarity: Parents with strong ethnic identities tend to have children with strong ethnic identities. At a more proximal level, several parental practices have been shown to affect ethnic identity. The most broadly influential practice is labeled *cultural socialization*: behaviors and messages that explicitly teach children about their ethnic heritage and promote cultural traditions and cultural pride (Hughes et al., 2006). Also influential in some instances are two practices with seemingly opposite orientations. *Egalitarianism* refers to an emphasis on individual qualities and fitting in the larger social system rather than an emphasis on group membership, whereas *preparation for bias*, as the name suggests, teaches children about possible discrimination and ways to deal with it. The latter is especially likely in African American families (Hughes et al., 2006). I will add that in many instances relevant parental beliefs are assessed along with such parental practices, thus allowing examination of the full belief-practice-outcome causal chain (Priest et al., 2014; Yasui, 2015).

Two further findings from this literature mirror conclusions offered for topics discussed earlier in the chapter. First, parents' reports and adolescents' reports of parents' ethnic socialization often differ, and when they do, adolescents' reports show stronger relations to ethnic identity (Peck, Brodish, Malanchuk, Banerjee, & Eccles, 2014). Second, parents' own history of ethnic socialization is one contributor to the ways in which they socialize their children (Hughes & Chen, 1997).

My brief coverage of ethnic identity has glossed over several issues that are the subject of much ongoing attention, including possible distinctions between ethnic identity and racial identity, the development of identity in bicultural and multicultural individuals, and contrasts between immigrant and nonimmigrant populations. Two articles in a special issue of *Child Development* are excellent further sources for discussions of these and other issues (Schwartz et al., 2014; Urmana-Taylor et al., 2014).

# 9

# Atypical Development

Well you always wonder . . . if your child acts like that, what, you know, what have you done wrong to make him be like that. Or what, what from really little . . . could we have changed so that he wouldn't be afraid. Or, you know, should we have got him babysitters sooner so that he would get used to different people? Should we . . . could we have done anything different right from the beginning, you know right from when he was a baby?

—(Hiebert-Murphy et al., 2012, p. 392)

All those normal milestones that a child has are not normal for her. They all happen at a different time, so it's not the same. You will go through months and months of her achieving all these wonderful things, you're really excited, and then you realise, hang on she's not going to be able to do that, or she can't do that, and there's triggers that will remind you of the things that aren't going to be.

—(Pillay, Girdler, Collins, & Leonard, 2012, p. 1504)

It's upsetting, and it hurts, I get hurt because of him, and I think, well, he doesn't look like a monster from outer space. I mean he's beautiful, he's got a lovely face on him. . . . He's a good wee soul. He's hard work, but he's worth it, you know, I wouldn't part with him. I keep saying that I'll look after him till every breath in my body goes.

—(Hubert, 2011, p. 219)

It's not all sadness and woe, I mean, she's a lovely little kid. . . you get used to her over the years, you know, what would be an annoyance to other people. It's like the sun comes up tomorrow, you know, it's just part of life, isn't it? It becomes part of your life.

—(Hubert, 2011, p. 221)

*Parents' Beliefs About Children.* Scott A. Miller, Oxford University Press (2020). © Oxford University Press.
DOI: 10.1093/oso/9780190874513.001.0001

Several of the preceding chapters touched on instances in which development had departed from the typical path. In some instances the departure was at the child end, for example, substance abuse or delinquent behaviors by adolescents. In other instances the departure was at the parent end, for example, maternal depression as a contributor to negative parenting, or harsh parenting that shaded into abuse or neglect.

The purpose of this chapter is to take up such instances of departure from the norm more fully. Doing so will provide a valuable expansion of what can be concluded about the nature and the effects of parents' beliefs. Doing so will also address what is clearly one of the most pragmatically important contexts for the study of what parents believe and what they do.

The chapter is divided into two sections. The first section deals with child problems of a range of sorts. As we will see, parents play two roles in the relevant literatures, just as was true for many topics discussed in earlier chapters. One role is as informants in the assessment of possible problems. The other is as potential contributors to both the problems and their eventual remediation.

The second section of the chapter focuses on problems at the parent end. Its two subsections correspond to the two examples just sketched. The first concentrates on clinical conditions, such as depression, that may impair parental thinking and parental behavior. The second discusses forms of parental behavior that clearly *are* impaired; namely, instances of abuse or neglect.

## Developmental Problems

Table 9.1 provides a (nonexhaustive) list of the childhood conditions that appear in the parents' beliefs literature, along with an example study of each.

The review that follows is necessarily selective, given both the number of conditions that have been explored and the size of some of the relevant literatures. My concentration is on conditions that have been among the most frequent targets for research. It also, as far as possible, is on the behavioral/psychological rather than purely medical implications of the child's disorder.

### Assessment

The starting point for studying some problem or attempting to ameliorate it is accurate diagnosis. As noted in Chapter 1, parents' beliefs and related behaviors

**Table 9.1** Clinical Conditions That Have Been the Subject of Studies of Parents' Beliefs

| Condition | Example |
| --- | --- |
| ADHD | DuPaul, Reid, et al. (2016) |
| Antisocial behavior | Shaw, Hyde, and Brennan (2012) |
| Anxiety | Hiebert-Murphy et al. (2012) |
| Asthma | Shepperd, Lipsey, Pachur, and Waters (2018) |
| Autism | Reyes et al. (2018) |
| Blindness | Sola-Carmona et al. (2016) |
| Callous-unemotional traits | McDonald et al. (2018) |
| Cerebral palsy | Barfoot, Meredith, Ziviani, and Whittingham (2017) |
| Cystic fibrosis | Hobbs, Schweitzer, and Cohen (2003) |
| Deafness | Young and Tattersall (2007) |
| Depression | Sheeber et al. (2009) |
| Diabetes | Chisholm et al. (2011) |
| Down syndrome | Ly (2008) |
| Eating disorders | Hibbs et al. (2015) |
| Epilepsy | Kurt (2018) |
| Fragile X syndrome | Bailey, Skinner, and Sparkman (2003) |
| Language delay | Majorano and Lavelli (2014) |
| Learning disabilities | Fernandez-Alcantara et al. (2017) |
| Obesity | Jain et al. (2001) |
| Phenylketonuria (PKU) | Antshel, Brewster, and Waisbren (2004) |
| Prader-Willi syndrome | Ly and Hodapp (2005) |
| Prematurity | Stern, Karraker, Sopko, and Norman, 2000 |
| Separation anxiety disorder | Sood, Mendez, and Kendall (2012) |
| Spina bifida | Lennon, Murray, Bechtel, and Holmbeck (2015) |
| Trauma | Quota, Punamaki, and Sarraj (2008) |
| Williams syndrome | Klein-Tasman, Lira, Li-Barber, Gallo, and Brei (2015) |

are often important in this respect, even if the parent ends up playing no role in the formal assessment. A parent's suspicion that something is amiss may start the process of assessment and eventual treatment. Conversely, a parent's belief that all is fine may delay or even prevent a needed intervention.

Although parents may not always be involved formally in the assessment process, in many instances they are. Indeed, parent-report measures play a larger role in the work to be considered now than is true for any other aspect of children's development. Parent reports are typically not the sole basis for making a diagnostic decision; they may be the starting point, however, and they often are eventually used in conjunction with other forms of evidence. Parent reports are likely to be especially important when children are young and have limited experience with people and settings outside the home (Briggs-Gowan, Godoy, Heberle, & Carter, 2016).

Many different parent-report measures contribute to the literature. These include the Child Behavior Checklist (Achenbach, 2001), the Infant-Toddler Social and Emotional Assessment (Carter, Little, Briggs-Gowan, & Kogan, 1999), the Multidimensional Anxiety Scale for Children 2 (March, 2013), the ADHD Rating Scale-5 (DuPaul, Power, Anastopoulos, & Reid, 2016), the Parent-Reported Inventory of Callous-Unemotional Traits (Frick, 2004), and the Strengths and Difficulties Questionnaire (Goodman, 1997). As an example, Table 9.2 reproduces the items from the last of these measures.

**Table 9.2** Strengths and Difficulties Questionnaire

Response options: Not True, Somewhat True, Certainly True

1. Considerate of other people's feelings
2. Restless, overactive, cannot stay still for long
3. Often complains of headaches, stomach aches, or sickness
4. Shares readily with other children; for example toys, treats, pencils
5. Often loses temper
6. Rather solitary, prefers to play alone
7. Generally well behaved, usually does what adults request
8. Many worries or often seems worried
9. Helpful if someone is hurt, upset, or feeling ill
10. Constantly fidgeting or squirming
11. Has at least one good friend
12. Often fights with other children or bullies them
13. Often unhappy, depressed or tearful
14. Generally liked by other children
15. Easily distracted, concentration wanders
16. Nervous or clingy in new situations, easily loses confidence
17. Kind to younger children
18. Often lies or cheats
19. Picked on or bullied by other children
20. Often volunteers to help others (parents, teachers, other children)
21. Thinks things out before acting
22. Steals from home, school or elsewhere
23. Gets along better with adults than with other children
24. Many fears, easily scared
25. Good attention span, sees chores or homework through to the end

Adapted from "The Strengths and Difficulties Questionnaire: A Research Note," by R. Goodman, 1997, *Journal of Child Psychology and Psychiatry, 38*, p. 586. Copyright 1997 by John Wiley and Sons. Adapted with permission.

Recall also that some of the measures discussed in Chapter 6 can help to diagnose clinical conditions. To date, the most informative of these cognitively oriented assessments has been the Behavior Rating Inventory of Executive Function (BRIEF) measure of executive function (Roth et al., 2014).

Most clinically oriented measures, including those just cited, are not designed solely for parental use; rather, with a slight rewording they are appropriate also for other informants who know the child well enough to make the necessary judgments. These other informants include teachers and (once they are old enough) the children themselves. A basic question then becomes how well these various informants agree.

The answer is the same one that we saw for various topics in Chapter 8: not very well. The opening sentence of one review states the general conclusion: "modest cross-informant agreement is one of the most robust findings in clinical child research" (Rescorla et al., 2013, p. 263). This conclusion echoed that given in earlier reviews of the issue (Achenbach, McConaughy, & Howell, 1987; De Los Reyes & Kazdin, 2005), and it emerged as well in three other recent meta-analyses of informant agreement (De Los Reyes et al., 2015; Huang, 2017; Rescorla et al., 2014). Most of the evidence, I should note, concerns the Child Behavior Checklist, which is by far the most often used instrument in this literature. But the conclusion extends to other measures as well.

The preceding does not mean that there is *no* agreement among informants—just that the agreement is not very strong. The two meta-analyses by Rescorla and colleagues are especially informative in this regard because of their cross-national focus: 25 countries in one case (Rescorla et al., 2013) and 21 countries in the other (Rescorla et al., 2014). The average correlation between parent report and youth report was .41, with a range across countries of .17 to .58. The average correlation between parent report and teacher report was .26, with a range of .09 to .49. These values are comparable to those reported in other reviews. Other reviews also add two further comparisons of interest. Correlations between teacher reports and youth reports are typically in the .2 to. 3 range, and thus lower than those for parent and child. Correlations between mothers and fathers vary some across samples and across measures, but they are generally in the neighborhood of .50.

The values just given are summed across all items of a measure. It may be, however, that some problematic behaviors are easier to see and thus to agree on than are others. In particular, both the Child Behavior Checklist and many other measures include a division between externalizing problems (e.g., aggression, rule breaking) and internalizing problems (e.g., anxiety, depression). Although the difference is not large, informant agreement is generally greater for externalizing problems, an expectable finding given the more visible nature of such behaviors (De Los Reyes et al., 2015).

The correlations between informants do not tell us the direction of the difference in cases in which the informants disagree. Which informant is more likely to report problems in the child's development? Here a fairly clear pattern emerges (although of course with exceptions in individual cases): Parents report more problems than do teachers, and children or adolescents report more problems than do parents. The latter finding is reminiscent of a recurring theme in Chapter 8: Adolescents often report more risky behaviors than their parents are aware of. Another finding also mirrors a conclusion from Chapter 8: Discrepancies between parent reports and child reports are predictive of various negative outcomes, including severity of problems and failure to treat successfully (Becker-Haimes, Jensen-Doss, Birmaher, Kendall, & Ginsburg, 2018; Bein, Petrik, Saunders, & Wojcik, 2015).

Correlations and mean differences are not the only ways in which informants can be compared. A third comparison is especially relevant to the decisions that must be made in clinical contexts. Most diagnostic measures include a cutoff score beyond which a disorder is judged to be present and intervention may be recommended. An important question, therefore, is whether the ratings of different informants agree with respect to whether a child falls above or below this cutoff. The answer is that, in most instances, they do. The Rescorla et al. meta-analyses reported a range across countries of 71% to 85% parent–child agreement and 71% to 81% parent–teacher agreement on the cutoff decision (Rescorla et al., 2013; Rescorla et al., 2014). Still, the agreement was not perfect. In addition, most agreements reflected a consensus that whatever problems existed were not in the deviant range, a predictable finding if most informants offer mostly positive evaluations. Agreements were less common for judgments that a problem existed—such judgments by one informant were matched less than half the time by the other informant. The result, clearly, is uncertainty in cases in which an accurate diagnosis may be most important (De Los Reyes & Kazdin, 2005).

The work on informant agreement speaks to a question that recurs throughout the book: How accurately can parents judge their children? Certainly, the modest levels of agreement among informants suggest that no one, including parents, is perfectly accurate in judging the attributes assessed by the various diagnostic instruments. This is another instance, however, in which there is no "gold standard" criterion for judging accuracy, and therefore no way to determine the relative accuracy of different informants. In addition—and this also is a point we have seen before—discrepancy between informants does not necessarily mean that one or the other is inaccurate; different informants may have different information to work with and may therefore acquire different knowledge about the child. The variations in agreement across different pairs of informants have been cited as evidence for such a context effect. Mother and fathers are more likely to see the child in similar contexts than are other possible pairs of informants, and mother and father agree more strongly in their evaluations than do other pairs of informants (De Los Reyes et al., 2015). Still, the agreement is far from perfect.

I turn now from parents as diagnosticians to parents as parents. How do parents cope with a child whose development departs from the norm? I will begin with some general points, followed by a discussion of work directed to three much-studied topics: intellectual disabilities, ADHD, and autism spectrum disorders.

## General Points

A first point concerns a familiar division in developmental psychology, that between cognitive development and social development. If developments in general can be classified as either cognitive or social, it may be natural to assume that disorders of development will show a similar cognitive-social division. And, indeed, some primarily do. As the label indicates, intellectual disabilities are defined by cognitive difficulties. Antisocial behavior, as its label indicates, is defined by problems in the social realm. Even in such relatively clear cases, however, problems are seldom solely cognitive or solely social. Many children, for example, have comorbid disorders; that is, they fit the diagnostic criteria for at least two different conditions (e.g., ADHD and autism). Even in the absence of comorbidity, cognitive and social problems typically co-occur, in part because each affects the other. Lowered cognitive abilities necessarily impact the child's social life, and problems in the social realm often both reflect and add to the child's cognitive struggles. Finally, both cognitive and social difficulties are central to the definition of many conditions, including two to be discussed shortly: ADHD and autism spectrum disorder.

A second point is that referring to a child as "having" a particular disorder also distorts a complex reality. Although there are of course similarities among children who receive the same diagnosis, marked individual
differences are also evident for every disorder that has been studied. The
most obvious difference is in severity. IQs, for example, may vary across 50
or more points, and the "spectrum" in autism spectrum disorder is an explicit indication that autism encompasses a range of severity. But there are
other, more subtle differences as well, for example, in which abilities or which
characteristics are either impaired or spared. A saying popular among those
who work with autism makes this point: "If you've met one child with autism,
you've met one child with autism" (Bernier & Dawson, 2016, p. 82).

Note that the differences among children with a particular disorder add to
the challenges faced by parents. Many organizations exist to help parents of
children with specific disorders; examples include Autism Speaks, National
Down Syndrome Society, and National Fragile X Foundation. Such organizations are wonderful resources, but a parent must still adapt the necessarily
general information that they provide to fit the specific situation of his or
her child.

A further challenge for parents, as well as a further way that various
disorders differ, concerns the issue with which this chapter began: diagnosis.
Many disorders, especially those of genetic or chromosomal origin, can be
diagnosed at birth or even prenatally. This does not mean, of course, that
they always are diagnosed so early. But when they are, parents have some
idea of what they are facing from early in the child's life, and an early and
accurate diagnosis is in fact helpful in various ways. Other disorders, however, may only gradually become apparent in the child's behavior and may
frustrate attempts at an agreed-upon diagnosis for years. It is in these cases,
of course, that parents and other informants may play an important role in
the diagnostic process. But both the timing and the certainty of an eventual
diagnosis may be far from optimal.

Having stressed differences among disorders and among children, I conclude this section by noting some basic similarities. Whatever the specific
condition, learning that one's child has a disorder is an unexpected event for
parents, it is a negative event for parents, it is a source of sadness and stress
for parents, and it adds to the already formidable challenges of being a parent.
But as the last two quotations at the start of the chapter make clear, positive
aspects of the parenting experience may accompany and in some cases out-
weigh the negative ones. Any child can be a source of accomplishment and

of joy for parents, and countless children with a disorder have proved to be so for their parents (Hastings & Taunt, 2002; McConnell, Savage, Sobsey, & Uditsky, 2015).

## Intellectual Disabilities

Conceptually, *intellectual disability* (or what used to be labeled *mental retardation*) is defined as a level of intelligence that is below the normal range and that is accompanied by difficulty in adapting to the demands of everyday life (Hodapp & Dykens, 2006). Operationally, what this has usually meant (with some fluctuation in definition over the years) is an IQ below 70, or two standard deviations or more below the population mean.

Intellectual disability can result from many possible sources; indeed, more than 1,000 genetic or chromosomal etiologies have been identified (Burack, Russo, Green, Landry, & Iarocci, 2016). Down syndrome, for example, has a chromosomal basis—specifically, an extra or partial copy of chromosome 21. It is among the most commonly occurring forms of intellectual disability, and also one of the most often studied forms. Other relatively common forms that have been frequent targets for research include Fragile X syndrome, Prader-Willi syndrome, and Williams syndrome.

Some of the earliest research with parents of children with intellectual disabilities examined parents' (usually mothers') ability to estimate their children's IQs; indeed, such work preceded the more basic research directed to this question by 25 or so years (e.g., Ewart & Green, 1957; Heriot & Schmickel, 1967). These early studies had a primarily pragmatic goal. Standardized testing is often difficult to arrange, and parental estimates provide quick and potentially helpful information in cases in which a problem is suspected. This rationale still exists, and so therefore does the use of parent reports as an initial index of children's developmental level (Chandler, Howlin, Simonoff, Kennedy, & Baird, 2016; Martin et al., 2012).

Of course, parents' estimates will be helpful only if parents show some accuracy in judging their children. Parents do show some accuracy, although with a good deal of variability across samples, measures, and disorders (Chandler et al., 2016; Miller, 1988). At a general level, the results with special populations are similar to those for typically developing children discussed in Chapter 6. Parents are above chance but far from perfect in judging their children's IQ or developmental level, although in some instances the fit with standard assessments is impressive (Pulsifer, Hoon, Palmer, Gopalan, & Capute, 1994; Sexton, Thompson, Perez, & Rheams, 1990). When parents err, they tend to overestimate their children's abilities, just as parents in general tend to overestimate what their children can do. There is some evidence that parental accuracy increases with the age of the child, an expectable finding given that the available evidence about the child's abilities also increases with age. A basic conclusion, however, is that even in the absence of formal feedback the great majority of parents of a child with a disability realize from early in development that their child has a problem.

Much research has examined parents' reactions to this realization. The general conclusion has already been stated, and it is that most parents react negatively—increased levels of stress, anxiety, and depression are common, especially soon after learning of the disability (Glidden, 2012). On the positive side, an early and clear diagnosis, including the cause of the disorder, generally helps parents to cope. And, as is always the case, parents' success at dealing with a difficult situation is affected by the forms of social support available to them, as well as by their own coping resources (Burack et al., 2016; Families Special Interest Research Group, 2014).

Parents' reactions may also vary across different forms of disability. As we would expect, the more severe the child's disability, the more negative the reactions tend to be (Hassall & Rose, 2005; Mori, Downs, Wong, Heyworth, & Leonard, 2018). Even when the extent of impairment (as defined by IQ) is equivalent, different syndromes may elicit different reactions. The clearest example of this point is labeled *Down syndrome advantage*: more positive reactions (less stress, more sense of reward) by parents of children with Down syndrome than by parents of children with other disabilities (Hodapp & Dykens, 2006). One possible explanation for this finding is that children with Down syndrome are typically sociable and pleasant to interact with, and these positive characteristics of the child may elicit positive responses from parents. Although this explanation is not the only possible basis for the phenomenon (Hodapp, 2000), it fits with a general theme in the disability literature, and that is the effects of children on their parents. We have seen that the idea that children affect their parents was slow to enter the general parenting literature and that the transactional nature of the parent–child relationship may still not be fully appreciated. In contrast, an emphasis on child-to-parent effects has always been central to work on disabilities.

It is not surprising, of course, that a child with a disability will affect how parents behave. The most general change is what we would expect: lower, simpler forms of input and interaction than are found for typically developing children of the same age. A partial exception to this conclusion, however (shown most clearly by parents of children with Down syndrome), is that in some instances parents provide especially high levels of explicit teaching and stimulation, almost as though they are afraid to lose any opportunity to nurture their child's development (Hodapp & Dykens, 2006). More generally, parents of children with disabilities often rank high on measures of behavioral control and interference with the child's ongoing activities, a pattern that is associated with a range of negative child outcomes (Green, Caplan, & Baker, 2014). They also often rank low on measures of sensitivity and responsiveness in interaction with the child, another less than optimal parenting pattern (Blacher, Baker, & Kaladjian, 2013; Slonims, Cox, & McConachie, 2006). And they are less likely than parents in general to adopt what we have seen is generally an optimal approach to child-rearing; namely, an authoritative style of parenting (Phillips, Connors, & Curtner-Smith, 2017).

Of course, parents of children with disabilities are not a homogenous group, and many fall at the more positive end of the dimensions just discussed. And just as with typically developing children, parents' positive behaviors can have positive effects on their children's development. Not all forms of control are detrimental; a more supportive, directive form (e.g., offering a toy of interest, joining in an ongoing game) is associated with enhanced social skills (Green et al., 2014). Similarly, not all forms of stimulation are overstimulation; interactions that are sensitive to the child's developmental level and responsive to the child's interests can nurture various positive developments (Hauser-Cram et al., 1999; Sterling, Warren, Brady, & Fleming, 2013). In addition to specific forms of interaction, the general harmony and cohesiveness of family relations is a predictor: the more positive the family environment, the better the child's development (Hauser-Cram, Warfield, Shonkoff, & Krauss, 2001; Hauser-Cram et al., 1999). In all of these instances the genetically given syndrome sets limits on what is possible, but what actually occurs depends also on the environment, including the parents (something which, of course, is true for all children).

As I noted at the start of this section, intellectual disabilities have many origins. Furthermore, different syndromes have their own patterns of strengths and weaknesses. Children with Down syndrome, for example, are relatively good at visual short-term memory but weak in expressive language. Children with Williams syndrome, in contrast, do relatively well on measures of language development (although still with some deficits) but are poor at visual-spatial tasks. Finally, children with Prader-Willi syndrome are relatively strong at simultaneous processing of information but weak at sequential processing. These cognitive differences among syndromes are accompanied by differences in social behavior and by differences in the kinds of health problems that typically form part of the syndrome.

Are parents aware of these syndrome-specific qualities? The answer is that some are, to varying degrees, and some are not (Fidler, Hodapp, & Dykens, 2002; Ly & Hodapp, 2005). Parents of children with Down syndrome are more knowledgeable than are parents in the other two categories, perhaps because information about Down syndrome is more readily available. Not surprisingly, parents tend to be most knowledgeable about relatively visible aspects of the syndrome, including problematic behaviors; this is especially true for parents of children with Williams or Prader-Willi syndrome. Sadly, many parents are less aware of the relative strengths that their child possesses.

## ADHD

The full, unabbreviated name for this condition spells out what is involved: *attention-deficit hyperactivity disorder*. Children with ADHD have difficulties in one or both of two areas of functioning. One is in focusing and maintaining attention. The other is in avoiding impulsive, overly active bursts of behavior.

All children, of course, occasionally have difficulties in focusing attention or controlling impulses. For children with ADHD, however, the problems are pervasive ones, appearing early in life, applying across a range of contexts, and often persisting into adulthood. In addition, ADHD is correlated with a number of other negative developments; a partial list includes academic difficulties, oppositional defiance, conduct problems, substance use, depression, and aggression. In some instances ADHD is clearly not just a correlate but a contributor to these further problems (Nigg, 2016).

The prevalence of ADHD has increased across the span during which the disorder has been formally assessed, although it is not clear to what extent the heightened incidence reflects a genuine increase in the condition and to what extent it reflects changes in the probability and nature of diagnosis (Safer, 2018). A 2016 survey of US children between the ages of 2 and 17 reported that 6.1 million children (9.4% of the population) had received a diagnosis of ADHD and that 5.4 million (8.4% of the population) currently had such a diagnosis (Danielson et al., 2018). Estimates of the worldwide prevalence of the disorder are somewhat lower but still substantial, with typical rates around 7% (Thomas, Sanders, Doust, Beller, & Glasziou, 2015). The rate is consistently higher in boys than in girls; in the US survey, for example, boys accounted for 70% of the cases.

ADHD clearly has a genetic basis, with reported heritability values in the .6 to .8 range; that is, 60–80% of the variance among children attributable to genetic factors (Nigg, 2016). Unlike intellectual disabilities, however, no single gene or single chromosome has been identified (or is likely to be identified) as a sufficient causal agent; rather, ADHD, like most developmental outcomes, depends on the operation of multiple genes. Although progress is being made in identifying the relevant genes, the field is far from possessing a genetic profile that can serve as an indicator of ADHD. Diagnosis, therefore, depends on behavioral rather than genetic evidence. As is always the case, diagnosis is most certain if there are multiple forms of converging evidence: parent reports, teacher reports, behavioral measures, and doctor or clinician assessments.

The most influential measurement instrument for diagnosing ADHD is presented in the 5th edition of the *Diagnostic and Statistical Manual of Mental Disorders* (DSM-5; American Psychiatric Association, 2013). Respondents (typically parents or teachers) indicate the extent to which various descriptions are characteristic of the child. Some items address problems with attention: for example, "Does not seem to listen when spoken to directly" and "Has difficulty sustaining attention in tasks or play activities" Other items are directed to impulse control: for example, "Interrupts or intrudes on others" and "Blurts out an answer before a question has been completed." As is often the case, correlations between parent and teacher assessments are moderate at best (DuPaul et al., 2016). When disagreements occur, parents typically report more problems than do teachers (Narad et al., 2015). Correlations between mothers and fathers are also moderate at best, with mothers typically reporting more problems than do fathers (Caye, Machado, & Rohde, 2017). Agreement is greater for items tapping impulsivity than for those tapping inattention, a finding that is another example of the externalizing-internalizing distinction mentioned earlier.

The fact that ADHD has a genetic basis does not mean that experience, including experience with parents, is unimportant. Indeed, earlier chapters have already talked about some of the ways in which parents can make a difference. ADHD is not separate from other outcomes discussed throughout the book; rather, the processes that underlie ADHD are components of a number of basic developments. Two such developments, in particular, are clearly relevant: temperament (recall Table 5.4) and executive function (recall Table 6.3). As we saw, parents are important contributors to both their children's executive function skills and their eventual temperaments (Bates & Pettit, 2015; Fay-Stammbach et al., 2014), and it follows that parents may also be contributors to ADHD or its absence.

Research that looks specifically at parenting and ADHD adds several further points with respect to relatively positive and relatively negative parental practices (Johnston & Chronis-Tuscano, 2015). The entries in both categories mirror conclusions discussed for other developmental outcomes. On the positive side, parental warmth, firmness, consistency, and (by adolescence) monitoring are associated with lower probability of ADHD. On the negative side, parental stress, conflict, harshness, and inconsistency are associated with a heightened probability of ADHD. As with many developments, the attachment relationship with the parents is also important. An insecure attachment is another predictor of ADHD (Storeba, Rasmussen, & Simonsen, 2016).

Parenting, then, can clearly make a difference. The Johnston and Chronis-Tuscano (2015) review, however, adds two qualifying points. One is that links with parenting are stronger for the various disruptive behaviors that are often sequelae of ADHD than they are for ADHD symptoms per se. The other is that child-to-parent effects are often clearer and stronger than are parent-to-child effects, a conclusion that emerges from both longitudinal and experimental studies.

I noted earlier that ADHD is highly heritable. This fact adds two further complexities to the issue of parenting and ADHD. First, it means that parents affect their children not only through their parenting behaviors but also through the genes they pass on. Second, it means that many parents of children with ADHD will themselves have ADHD; high heritability is an indication of similarity among genetically related individuals, including parents and children. Estimates are that approximately half of children with ADHD have at least one parent with ADHD (Johnston & Chronis-Tuscano, 2015). Although there are of course exceptions, parenting by parents with ADHD is often less than optimal, in some cases too harsh and in other cases too lax (Park, Hudec, & Johnston, 2017). The children of such parents are therefore at double risk: Both genes and environment predispose them to ADHD.

Not yet considered are the beliefs that underlie parents' behavior. Two forms of parental belief that have proved important for various topics throughout the book also play a role in the study of ADHD. One is the attributions that parents offer for their children's behavior. The most general finding is that parents of children with ADHD tend (with exceptions, of course) to offer more negative attributions for child behavior than do parents in general (Huang et al., 2014; Johnston, Hommersen, & Seipp, 2009). Thus negative behaviors on the child's part tend to be judged as internal in origin, global, and stable, whereas positive behaviors are likely to be seen as situational in origin and less under the child's control. Such negative attributions have negative effects because, over time, they are associated with increases in child oppositional behavior (e.g., loses temper, argues with others, annoys others). It is interesting to note, however, that the pattern of attributions changes some when the child is on medication for the disorder (as were 62% of the children in the Danielson et al., 2018, survey). When the child is medicated, mothers are more likely to judge positive behaviors as global and stable, and they are more likely to judge negative behaviors as external in origin and less global and stable (Johnston et al., 2000). The attributions, in short, become more positive. But there is one exception: Under medication, negative behaviors are judged as even more under the child's control, a potentially damaging attributional pattern.

Parental self-efficacy is a second form of parental belief that has received attention in the ADHD literature. Not surprisingly, self-efficacy tends to be lower in parents of children with ADHD than it is in parents of typically developing children (Johnston & Mash, 1989). Success at a task is a major determinant of self-efficacy, and the challenges of parenting a child with ADHD ensure that failure will be a frequent parenting experience. As is generally the case, however, self-efficacy is not only a result of parenting experiences but also a contributor to parenting behaviors. The contribution in the case of ADHD is an important one: Both parents' belief in the value of prescribed behavioral therapies for ADHD and their willingness to participate in such therapies are greatest when parental self-efficacy is relatively high (Johnston, Mah, & Regambal, 2010; Mah & Johnston, 2008).

Parents' role in treatment provides another instance of the importance of parents' beliefs. When children are minors, their parents must consent to treatment, and in many instances parents must agree to be part of the treatment process themselves, either as participants in behavior therapy (as just noted) or as dispensers of medication or as both. Surveys reveal that parents vary in both their knowledge of treatment options and their evaluation of different possibilities (Corcoran, Schildt, Hochbrueckner, & Abell, 2017; Hart, Ros, Gonzalez, & Graziano, 2018). Differences among parents, and reluctance to agree to treatment, are especially marked with regard to the use of stimulant medication, an approach that is generally recommended, in conjunction with behavior therapy, for children beyond preschool age. Not all parents agree to medication treatment, and not all persist with an agreed-upon treatment; treatment adherence, which one summary refers to as "notoriously low" (Lench, Levine, & Whalen, 2013, p. 141), is a general problem. It can be argued that the most important parental beliefs with respect to ADHD are those that underlie decisions about whether, how, and how long to treat.

## Autism Spectrum Disorder

From early in life, the development of children with autism spectrum disorder (ASD) diverges in various ways from the course for typically developing children. Some of the differences are social, reflecting the fact that the social world does not seem to hold either the interest or the value for children with ASD as it does for children in general. Other differences are cognitive, in some cases impacting mainly language and in some cases extending to cognitive processes in general. Table 9.3, which is adapted from a recent review by Bernier and Dawson (2016), summarizes the most typical and important differences.

Earlier, ASD was mentioned as an example of two points. One was that most disorders involve both cognitive and social difficulties, a point that is clearly illustrated by the entries in the table. The other was that no disorder takes the form of a single, same-for-all phenotype; rather, disorders vary in the form they take across children, with the most obvious variation being in the severity of the problem. In the case of ASD, approximately 25% of children never develop any language, but another 25% have language that is generally indistinguishable from that found in typical development (Bernier & Dawson, 2016). Approximately 40% of children with ASD have IQs that place them in the disabled range, but 60% do not (Bernier & Dawson, 2016). The recognition of such variations is reflected in a change over time in the commonly used label for the disorder: once "autism," now "autism spectrum disorder."

**Table 9.3** Characteristics of Autism Spectrum Disorder (ASD) (Bernier & Dawson, 2016)

| Characteristic | Description |
| --- | --- |
| Social attention | Typically developing children show preferential attention to the social world from early in life. Children with ASD show considerably less interest in social stimuli, typically preferring nonsocial objects, a preference that emerges early and persists throughout development. |
| Joint attention | From late in the first year, typically developing children share the attentional focus of others and direct the attention of others through gestures and other actions. Children with ASD show limited and delayed mastery of joint attention, especially with regard to sharing their own attentional focus. |
| Face perception | Typically developing children are interested in the human face from birth, they quickly learn to recognize familiar faces, and recognition and discrimination of faces remain strong throughout development. Children with ASD do not look preferentially at faces, and their face-processing skills lag well behind those of typically developing children. |
| Emotion perception | By middle to late in the first year, typically developing children respond appropriately to the emotional displays of others and use others' emotional displays to regulate their own emotions and behavior. Children with ASD are less attentive to emotional cues from others and less likely to respond in appropriate ways to such cues. |
| Imitation | In typically developing children, imitation of others is evident soon after birth, and imitation serves as a powerful source of social learning throughout development. Children with ASD show considerably less spontaneous imitation of others, and the imitations they do produce are often partial at best. |
| Symbolic play | In typically developing children, symbolic play emerges in the second year of life, and it serves as an important precursor to the development of language. In children with ASD, the emergence of symbolic play is delayed, and for most it remains at best limited and repetitive. |
| Language and communication | In contrast to the language learning prowess that characterizes typical development, children with ASD are often delayed in language development, and approximately one-fourth never develop any usable language. The language that does develop often has unusual features (e.g., echolalia, pronoun reversal) and is especially weak in the social/pragmatic functions of language. |
| Restrictive and repetitive interests | In comparison to typically developing children, children with ASD often show a restricted range of interests, are overresponsive to sensory stimulation, and produce unusual repetitive behaviors (e.g., hand flapping, spinning). |

From Bernier, R., & Dawson, G. (2016). Autism spectrum disorders. In D. Chicchetti (Ed.), *Developmental psychopathology: Vol. 3. Maladaptation and psychopathology* (3rd ed., pp. 81–115). Hoboken, NJ: Wiley.

Like ADHD, ASD clearly has an important genetic/chromosomal basis, but like ADHD the identification of the relevant genes remains largely a task for the future. Diagnosis, therefore, depends on behavior. In many instances parents start the diagnostic process because of concerns about how their child is developing. Such concerns are unlikely in the first year—many of the behaviors that characterize the disorder are not yet evident, and children with ASD may initially be indistinguishable from typically developing infants on other indices. By the second year, however, warning signs begin to appear, and diagnosis is typically possible by age 3 or 4 (Rogers & Talbott, 2016). As we would expect, the more severe the disorder, the earlier the diagnosis tends to occur (Zablotsky et al., 2017).

Controversy currently exists about how early to begin the diagnostic process—in particular, whether some form of screening should be universal during the second year of life (Robins et al., 2016). Although not yet universal, screening is becoming more common, the goal being not to arrive at a final diagnosis but to identify children in need of a more thorough assessment. Parent reports play an important role in the screening process; a few examples from the many measures designed for this purpose include the First Year Inventory (Reznick, Baranek, Reavis, Watson, & Crais, 2007), the Parent's Observations of Social Interactions (Smith, Sheldrick, & Perrin, 2013), the Modified Checklist for Autism in Toddlers (Robins et al., 2014), and the Autism Parent Screen for Infants (Sacrey et al., 2018).

In addition to its partly (but not totally) genetic basis, ASD shows two other similarities to ADHD. One is that the disorder is more common in boys than in girls—approximately four times more common. The other is that is that the prevalence of the disorder has increased markedly in recent years. In the 1980s, estimates were that only 1 child in 2,500 had autism (Ritvo et al., 1989). By 2016, the figure had risen to 1 child in 59, or 1.7% of the child population (Centers for Disease Control and Prevention, 2018a). As with ADHD, it is not clear to what extent the increase in prevalence reflects a genuine increase in the disorder and to what extent it reflects changes in diagnosis (Rice et al., 2012). Probably both factors contribute.

The importance of genes in the etiology of autism does not mean that there is no environmental contribution. Although the conclusions in many cases remain tentative, a variety of both prenatal conditions (e.g., maternal infections, maternal obesity, exposure to pesticides) and perinatal conditions (e.g., maternal hemorrhage, umbilical cord complications, feeding difficulties) have been associated with increased risk of autism (Bernier & Dawson,

2016). Thus there are things that parents (primarily mothers) either do or experience that can make autism more likely. What has long been clear, however (in contrast to the "refrigerator mothers" theory of the '50s and '60s), is that parents do not cause autism with their parenting practices.

Parents can, however, influence the development of children with ASD, just as they can influence the development of children with any of the conditions listed in Table 9.1. And parents' beliefs clearly play a role in the process. Parental self-efficacy can be important. As with other disabilities, self-efficacy tends to be lower in parents of children with ASD than in parents of typically developing children (e.g., Meirsschaut, Roeyers, & Warreyn, 2010), just as stress tends to be higher (Hayes & Watson, 2013). Relatively high self-efficacy, however, is associated with various positive outcomes for both child and parent. Maternal self-efficacy relates positively to mothers' attempts to take an active role in their child's development (Kuhn & Carter, 2006). Maternal self-efficacy also relates positively to the child's ability to function independently, as shown by participation in a range of everyday activities (Bar, Shelef, & Bart, 2016). Finally, both maternal and paternal self-efficacy relate positively to the intensity of intervention that parents seek for their child (Siller, Reyes, Hotez, Hutman, & Sigman, 2014). The Siller et al. (2014) study identifies one other cognitive predictor of decisions about intervention: Parents' categorical thinking (recall the discussion of the Sameroff research in Chapter 3) relates negatively to intensity of intervention.

The attributions that parents draw for their children's behavior also contribute. In many cases the attributions are less than optimal. For example, many parents appear to judge any misbehavior on the child's part as an inevitable result of the child's ASD, as shown by attributions of internality, stability, and (at least when the disorder is severe) uncontrollability for such behaviors (Hartley, Schaidie, & Burson, 2013; Whittingham, Sofronoff, Sheffield, & Sanders, 2008). Parents' attributions also relate, again less than optimally, to decisions about treatment. For example, parents are less likely to agree to a parent-focused intervention when they believe that stable aspects of their own behavior are a contributor to the child's problems (Choi & Kovshoff, 2013).

Several studies have explored what parents of children with ASD understand about their children's mental states, using either the mind-mindedness approach described in Chapters 5 and 6 or one of the other, related approaches cited in those chapters. Kirk and Sharma (2017) reported no differences in maternal mind-mindedness for a child with ASD compared to a typically developing sibling, an interesting finding given the presumably greater challenge posed by a child with ASD. They did find, however, that mothers used more negative attributes when talking about the child with ASD. In research by Hutman and colleagues (Hutman, Siller, & Sigman, 2009), mothers' insightfulness in talking about their child with ASD related positively to their use of synchronous communications during mother–child play, a characteristic that has been found to be a positive predictor of children's language development. Finally, Oppenheim and colleagues (Oppenheim, Koren-Karie, Dolev, & Yirmiya, 2009), using a similar insightfulness measure, reported that maternal insightfulness predicted a clearly important developmental outcome: namely, the security of the attachment between mother and child.

We saw that the high heritability of ADHD ensures that many parents of a child with ADHD will themselves either have the disorder or will show some characteristics of the disorder. ASD also has a strong genetic basis and therefore is also a locus of parent–child similarity—parents of children with ASD have a heightened probability of falling somewhere on the autism spectrum themselves, an outcome that is labeled the *broader autism phenotype* (Cruz, Camargos-Junior, & Rocha, 2013; Ingersoll & Wainer, 2014). To date, only limited attempts have been made to explore how parental thinking and behavior might be affected by vestiges of ASD—the kind of theory-of-mind reasoning discussed in the preceding paragraph would be an especially interesting target of study. One conclusion, however, is clear. The high heritability of ASD means that ASD poses the same interpretive challenge as does ADHD: namely, determining whether parent–child relations are genetic or environmental in origin.

The most thoroughly studied parental belief about ASD concerns the disorder itself—what parents know about autism. Some studies have examined what they know about their own child; others, what they know about ASD in general.

As we have already seen, parents' beliefs about their own child can play an important role in the diagnostic process. Comparisons between parents' beliefs and standard assessments confirm that parents can often be quite accurate in judging their child's autism-related behaviors (Mayes & Lockridge, 2018; Miller, Perkins, Dai, & Fein, 2017). When parents and clinicians diverge, it is generally parents who offer a more positive assessment—fewer autism-related symptoms, greater mastery of basic skills.

Studies of beliefs about ASD in general also provide a generally positive picture of what parents know, especially when some time has passed since their child's diagnosis (Chaidez et al., 2018; Dardennes et al., 2011; Fischbach, Harris, Ballan, Fischbach, & Link, 2016; Kuhn & Carter, 2006). Such studies have concentrated mainly on two questions: the etiology of the disorder and the best treatment for it. As is true of professionals who work with ASD, most parents rate genetics as the most likely cause of the disorder, although not as consistently as do professionals. The great majority realize that parenting did not cause the disorder, and—at least in the samples studied—only a small minority endorse vaccines as a cause. Still, some do. And some endorse non-standard treatments (e.g., vitamins, special diets) not generally advocated by professionals. On the whole, however, both the degree of parental knowledge about ASD and the resulting parental behaviors present a generally positive picture.

One final point about parents and autism is worth making. It is a point that I draw from an historical overview of work on the disorder by Silverman and Brosco (2007). Perhaps more than is true for any other disorder, parents have long played an influential role with respect to how the field thinks about and responds to the phenomenon of autism. Parent advocacy groups have helped to set priorities for research, have contributed in major ways to fund-raising efforts, have sometimes been the first to suggest new directions of study, and have offered valuable input to decisions about conceptualization, diagnosis, and treatment. In Silverman and Brosco's words, "parents have often been at the vanguard of critical changes in expert understanding of autism" (p. 393).

## Parenting Problems

The discussion of parenting problems is divided into two sections. The first addresses clinical conditions that may adversely affect parents' beliefs and related behaviors. The second discusses the most maladaptive forms of parental behavior: child abuse and neglect.

## Clinical Conditions

Of the various possibilities, I focus on two conditions. The first is depression, which is both the most common and the most often studied parental clinical disorder. The second is schizophrenia, which is among the most serious of the possible disorders. Other conditions that appear in the parenting literature include bipolar disorder (e.g., Mowbray, Oyserman, Bybee, & MacFarlane, 2002), eating disorders (e.g., Astrachan-Fletcher, Veldhuis, Lively, Fowler, & Marcks, 2008), anxiety disorders (e.g., Kaitz & Maytal, 2005), and personality disorders (e.g., Newman, Stevenson, Bergman, & Boyce, 2007). Both of the latter conditions can take multiple forms. In addition, and as we saw is true of childhood disorders, comorbidity is common; in particular, depression and anxiety often occur together.

Depression

The study of depression raises a measurement issue. In some instances the mothers being studied (this literature is heavily skewed toward mothers) have received a clinical diagnosis of depression. In other, and more common, instances, depression is determined by a self-report measure completed by the mothers. Although cautions always apply with regard to self-report measures, the instruments in this case (most often, the Center for Epidemiological Study Depression Scale and the Beck Depression Inventory) are well established ones, and conclusions about both parenting and child outcomes generally do not vary across the two methods of identifying depression (Dix & Meunier, 2009).

The most general conclusions are that depression is associated with both negative parental behaviors of a range of sorts and negative child outcomes of a range of sorts. Table 9.4 provides a sampling of the entries in both categories. As is always the case, not all studies fit the general pattern, and not all parents or children within a study fit the general pattern. Still, there is little doubt that depression is a predictor of problems for both parent and child.

Various factors can moderate the effects summarized in the table, that is, make the negative outcomes more or less likely. The gender of the child often proves to be important, with either stronger effects or different effects for one gender compared to the other (e.g., Gartstein, Bridgett, Dishion, & Kaufman, 2009; Gruhn et al., 2016). The child's temperament may also contribute; in some instances, for example, negative effects are magnified for children with difficult temperaments (Jessee, Mangelsdorf, Shigeto, & Wong, 2012). When the effects are associated with the mother's depression (as is the case in most studies), the father's' role in the family may either lessen their impact (if the father is positively involved with the child) or add to the difficulties (if involvement is less positive or if the father himself is depressed; Mezulis, Hyde, & Clark, 2004). I will add that paternal depression, although less studied than maternal depression, has been shown to exert its own independent effects on

**Table 9.4** Relations of Parental Depression to Parenting Practices and Child Outcomes

| Parenting practice | Source |
| --- | --- |
| Hostility and rejection | Epkins and Harper (2016) |
| Lower sensitivity | Bernard, Nissim, Vaccaro, Harris, and Lindhiem (2018) |
| Lax, withdrawn parenting | Wang and Dix (2013) |
| Intrusive, overly reactive parenting | Gruhn et al. (2016) |
| Negative emotional expression | Cummings, Cheung, and Davies (2013) |
| Family conflict and disorganization | Cummings, Keller, and Davies (2005) |

| Child outcome | Source |
| --- | --- |
| Psychopathology | Goodman et al. (2011) |
| Internalizing problems (e.g., anxiety, depression) | Chen, Johnston, Sheeber, and Leve (2009) |
| Externalizing problems (e.g., aggression, delinquency) | McCullough and Shaffer (2014) |
| Insecure attachment | Martins and Gaffan (2000) |
| Delayed mastery of infant milestones | Black et al. (2007) |
| Lower social competence | Wang and Dix (2015) |
| Lower executive function | Hughes, Roman, Hart, and Ensor (2013) |

both parenting behaviors and child outcomes (Connell & Goodman, 2002; Wilson & Durbin, 2010).

One potential moderator that has received considerable attention is the method of measuring the child outcomes of interest. As with developmental research in general, use of parent reports, especially maternal reports, is common. The concern in this case stems from a form of bias labeled the *depression distortion hypothesis*: the possibility that depressed parents will provide overly negative evaluations of their children's behavior. If so, links between depression and child problems might have more to do with parents' beliefs than with developmental reality.

The status of the depression distortion hypothesis has long been controversial. An influential review of the first wave of studies concluded that methodological weaknesses called into question the apparently supportive results (Richters, 1992), and more recent reviews are also cautious in the conclusions they draw (De Los Reyes et al., 2015). Distorted beliefs about one's child are clearly not an inevitable result of depression. But they are an occasional result, as a number of more recent, methodologically sound studies make clear (e.g., Chi & Hinshaw, 2002; Gartstein et al., 2009; Youngstrom, Izard, & Ackerman, 1999). As the authors of these studies stress, this conclusion does not mean that all of the links between depression and child outcomes reflect reporter bias—just that some subset may.

Let us return to Table 9.4. A basic question is what causes the two sets of maladaptive outcomes shown in the table. Why do parents behave as they do, and why do children develop as they do? A general answer, of course, is that parental depression is responsible. Such an answer, however, does not tell us the proximal, causal processes through which depression exerts its effects.

Parents' beliefs clearly play a role in the link between depression and parental behavior. In various ways, depressed parents tend to hold more negative beliefs about their children than do parents in general. The work on the depression distortion hypothesis is one basis for this conclusion because, in many instances, parents provide more negative evaluations than do others who know the child. Furthermore, the beliefs at issue in the distortion studies—the child's typical behaviors, the child's general characteristics—are hardly minor ones; rather, they reflect central ways in which parents think about their children. Two more specific forms of belief that recur throughout the parents' beliefs literature are also susceptible to effects of depression. Depressed parents' attributions for their children's behavior tend to take the child-blaming pattern that we have seen is often maladaptive—thus a belief that problems are internal to the child, controllable by the child, and unlikely to change in the future (e.g., Bolton et al., 2003; White & Barrowclough, 1998). In some instances depressed parents' attributions also take a self-blaming form, with parents feeling both responsible for the child's problems and unable to do anything to make things better (e.g., Leung & Slep Smith, 2006). As this last finding suggests, parental self-efficacy is another belief impacted by depression, with depressed parents typically feeling less confident about their parenting abilities than do parents in general (e.g., Heerman, Taylor, Wallstaon, & Barkin, 2017; Kohlhoff & Barnett, 2013).

As we have seen, parents' beliefs are seldom the sole explanation for how they behave. In the case of depression, Dix and Meunier (2009) identify 13 processes that may mediate the transition from parental depression to parental behavior, including goals of various sorts and emotions of various sorts. Beliefs are a prominent part of their model, however, and their review makes clear that beliefs are major contributors. Evidence is especially strong for negative attributions and low self-efficacy as contributors to each of the forms of maladaptive behavior listed in Table 9.4.

What about the negative child outcomes summarized in the table? Just as there is never a one-to-one relation between parental beliefs and parental behavior, so there is never a one-to-one relation between parental behavior and child outcome. Parents are at best one contributor among many to developments that have multiple sources. In addition, the correlational nature of most of the evidence leaves open alternatives to the parents-as-causal factor interpretation. Perhaps parent–child links reflect effects of children on their parents, or perhaps they reflect genetic similarities between parent and child. There is, in fact, no doubt that both factors contribute (Zahn-Waxler, Duggal, & Gruber, 2002).

Once these points are acknowledged, there is also no doubt that depressed parents' behavior contributes to their children's developmental difficulties. Evidence exists for deleterious effects, in some cases spanning a range of outcomes, for all of the parenting practices listed in Table 9.4. Critically, the evidence is not limited to one-point-in-time correlations between parental practice and child outcome. A number of longitudinal studies have demonstrated that forms of maladaptive parenting early in development relate to problems in children's development later in development (e.g., Cummings, Cheung, & Davies, 2013; Wang & Dix, 2013, 2015). Intervention studies provide another form of evidence that parenting plays a causal role through their demonstration that experimentally altering parents' behavior can lead to improvements in child outcomes (Boyd & Gillham, 2009; Nylen, Moran, Franklin, & O'Hara, 2006). And, of course, such studies are of clear pragmatic as well as scientific value.

As the discussion to this point should make clear, effects of parental depression are not tied to any single age period; effects are evident across the span of development and indeed even into adulthood. The period of infancy, however, has been of special interest because of a form of depression that is specific to parents (primarily mothers) of infants. *Postpartum depression* refers to depression that has its onset at or soon after birth, although the definition of "soon after" has varied over time; the DSM-5 extends the range to 6 months. Estimates of the prevalence of postpartum depression vary across the postbirth time period used to define the term, across samples, and across methods of measurement, but by any tabulation it is frequent. One recent review gives a figure of 13–19% (O'Hara & McCabe, 2013), whereas another cites a figure of 20–40% (Field, 2010).

As with depression in general, postpartum depression is associated with the negative effects for both parent (usually the mother) and child. Compared to mothers in general, depressed mothers are less engaged with and attuned to their infant, they play less with the infant, they show less warmth and positive emotion in interactions with the infant, and they often are either passive and withdrawn or intrusive and overstimulating (Field, 2010). Over time, various problems become evident in children exposed to such nonoptimal parenting, including impaired attachment, slower language development, lower IQ, and health problems of a variety of sorts (O'Hara & McCabe, 2013).

Two other parental practices discussed in Chapter 5 are also affected by postpartum depression. One is breastfeeding. Compared to mothers in general, mothers with postpartum depression are less likely to initiate breastfeeding, more likely to terminate breastfeeding, and more likely to have breastfeeding difficulties (Dennis & McQueen, 2009). The other is safe-sleep practices. Mothers with postpartum depression are less likely than mothers in general to place their infants in the recommended supine position for sleep. More generally, depressed mothers are less likely to engage in a number of safety practices, including well-child health visits and completion of immunizations (Zajicek-Farber, 2009).

Although most of the research on both postpartum depression and depression in general has been in Western industrialized nations, the problem is certainly not confined to such settings. Indeed, evidence suggests that both the prevalence of maternal depression and its negative effects may be even greater in poorer, developing countries (Parsons, Young, Rochat, Kringelbach, & Stein, 2012; Wachs, Black, & Engle, 2009). As the title of one commentary indicates, the human and economic costs of maternal depression constitute "A Global Threat to Children's Health, Development, and Behavior and to Human Rights" (Wachs et al., 2009, p. 51).

Schizophrenia

I turn now to schizophrenia. For various reasons, general conclusions are harder to draw for schizophrenia than they are for depression. To begin with, the literature on schizophrenia is considerably smaller than that for depression. In addition, the sample sizes for the groups with schizophrenia are often quite small (7 in one instance, 8 in another, 13 in another). In many studies the comparison groups are limited to parents with other disorders; that is, there is no typically functioning comparison group to serve as a baseline. In some studies the focus is on serious mental illness in general, comprising various disorders, and there is no separate consideration of schizophrenia. Finally, schizophrenia is not a unitary disorder but takes various forms, including variations in the severity of the disorder, in the balance of positive symptoms (e.g., delusions, hallucinations, disorganized speech) to negative symptoms (e.g., flat affect, difficulty in sustaining behavior), and in whether symptoms are currently active or whether the disorder is in at least partial remission. All of these differences can make a difference.

Once these points are made, it is clear that schizophrenia can have serious effects on both the parent (usually the mother) and the child, beginning in infancy and extending to adulthood (Davidsen, Harder, MacBeth, Lundy, & Gumley, 2015; Wan, Abel, & Green, 2008). Furthermore, the effects are, at least in most instances, more severe than those found for other clinical disorders, including depression and including various conditions that, like schizophrenia, constitute the most serious forms of mental disorder (e.g., Goodman & Brumley, 1990; Riordan, Appleby, & Faragher, 1999; Wan et al., 2007). From early infancy on, mothers with schizophrenia are often more remote and less involved with their infant than are mothers in general, they are less sensitive and less warm when they do attempt involvement, and their parenting efforts are often intrusive and disruptive rather than comforting and enjoyable. The infants, in turn, are less attentive to the mother, show less affect in interaction with the mother, and are more likely to avoid the mother. Across time, they are at heightened risk of developing insecure attachment (Davidsen et al., 2015). And across more time, parental schizophrenia is associated with a range of negative outcomes in both the cognitive and social realms, as well as with a heightened risk of psychopathology (Wan, Abel, et al., 2008).

In many of the studies just summarized, the measures are limited to either parenting problems or child outcomes, a situation that precludes a determination of whether the first is a cause of the second. Studies that examine both parent and child do typically report expectable links between parental practices and child outcomes—for example, a link between maternal insensitivity and infant avoidance (Wan et al., 2007), or between parental involvement and responsiveness and child IQ (Goodman & Brumley, 1990). As is typically the case, such relations are modest in magnitude, and they do not rule out other contributors to the parent-child links. Given the substantial heritability of schizophrenia, these other contributors clearly include genetics: Parents with schizophrenia affect their children not only through their parenting practices but also through the genes they pass on.

Given the negative tenor of the discussion to this point, I should add that the picture is not totally bleak. In some studies, mothers with schizophrenia have proved equivalent to or even better than other clinical samples in their parenting behavior (e.g., Pawlby et al., 2010). In addition, conclusions about negative effects may vary depending on whether symptoms of the disorder are active at the time of the study. The variation is what we would expect: When symptoms are in abeyance, parenting is typically less disturbed, and infants and children generally fare better (Kahng, Oyserman, Bybee, & Mowbray, 2008; Snellen, Mack, & Trauer, 1999).

The preceding account suggests that the parenting deficits in schizophrenia may often be a matter of degree, that is, the same kinds of problems that are found in other populations (low warmth, low sensitivity, etc.) but simply present to a greater, and more damaging, extent. In addition to such quantitative differences, are there any qualitative differences that distinguish parenting with schizophrenia from what is seen in other populations? A study by Wan and colleagues (Wan, Warren, Salmon, & Abel, 2008) suggests that there are (see also Chandra, Bhargavaraman, Raghunandan, & Shaligram, 2006). Their comparison was between mothers with schizophrenia and mothers with affective disorders, and their interest was in forms of abnormal behavior not seen in typical mother–infant interaction. Among the behaviors of interest were negative responses to positive infant behaviors (very rare in typical samples), psychological withdrawal from interaction with the infant (as opposed to the typical behavioral withdrawal because of distraction), and bizarre responses such as fear in reaction to infant gaze. Such behaviors were infrequent whatever the sample; all the instances that occurred, however, were provided by the mothers with schizophrenia.

Not yet addressed is the central question of this book: What sorts of beliefs underlie parents' behavior, in this case the behaviors shown by parents with schizophrenia? For the most part, beliefs have not been an explicit target of study in this literature but rather must be inferred from the behavioral evidence. There is one interesting exception, however, and it concerns a form of belief discussed at various places throughout the book: namely, theory of mind. Theory of mind is in fact a long-standing topic in the study of schizophrenia; indeed, the literature is large enough to have spawned several review articles (e.g., Bora, Yucel, & Pantelis, 2009; Brune, 2005; Sprong, Schothorst, Vos, Hox, & Van Egeland, 2007). The reason for interest is straightforward. Distorted cognitions are an intrinsic component of schizophrenia, and many of the distortions (e.g., feelings of persecution, delusions of control, auditory hallucinations) seem to reflect a difficulty in understanding the mental states of other people (Frith, 1992). Perhaps impaired theory of mind can account for much of what is seen in schizophrenia.

As the reviews cited make clear, theory of mind *is* impaired in schizophrenia. Moreover, it is seriously impaired—meta-analyses of the available evidence consistently yield large effect sizes. The effect sizes are reduced somewhat when the disorder is in remission, but they remain substantial. Similarly, they are reduced somewhat when general cognitive ability is controlled, but again they remain substantial. Theory-of-mind deficits clearly do not reduce to general cognitive difficulties for people with schizophrenia.

Two predictions follow for work on parenting and schizophrenia. One is that theory-of-mind deficits will account for at least some of the differences in parenting between parents with schizophrenia and other samples. The other is that individual differences in theory of mind will account for at least some of the differences in parenting within samples of parents with schizophrenia. The latter prediction, of course, is just a specific version of a prediction that we have encountered at various points: Theory of mind should make a difference in how people parent.

The limited evidence to date provides some support for the second of these predictions. In research by Mehta and colleagues (Mehta, Bhagyavathi, Kumar, Thirthalli, & Gangadhar, 2014), deficits in higher order forms of theory of mind were predictive of dysfunctional parenting in a sample of parents with schizophrenia. In research by Rigby and colleagues (Rigby, Conroy, Miele-Norton, Pawlby, & Happe, 2016), performance on a battery of theory-of-mind tasks predicted the sensitivity that mothers with schizophrenia showed in interacting with their infants. Finally, Pawlby et al. (2010) reported that a sample of mothers with schizophrenia were equivalent to a typically functioning comparison sample in mind-mindedness (a form of theory of mind) and in the quality of their interactions with their infants—an encouraging finding, but one that does not help to explain the usual problems in schizophrenia.

Clearly, parental beliefs—both theory of mind and other forms of belief—deserve more attention than they have received in the schizophrenia and parenting literature. An earlier review concluded that "the extent to which children are affected by specific cognitive impairments and biases associated with schizophrenia has not been studied" (Wan, Abel, et al., 2008, p. 620). This conclusion remains valid.

## Abuse and Neglect

Most discussions under this heading identify four forms of maltreatment: physical abuse, emotional abuse, sexual abuse, and neglect (Cicchetti, 2016). The Child Abuse Prevention and Treatment Act provides a typical definition that encompasses these forms: "any recent act or failure to act on the part of a parent or caretaker which results in death, serious physical or emotional harm, sexual abuse or exploitation; or an act or failure to act, which presents an imminent risk of serious harm."

Statistics about the prevalence of abuse and neglect vary across countries, across samples within countries, and across criteria for defining the various forms (Cicchetti & Toth, 2016). By any measure, however, the statistics are depressing. In the United States in 2016, an estimated 676,000 children were victims of abuse or neglect, which equates to a rate of 9.1 victims per 1,000 children (US Department of Health & Human Services, Administration for Children and Families, Administration on Children, Youth and Families, Children's Bureau, 2018). Neglect was a good deal more common than abuse, accounting for approximately 75% of the cases.

Several qualifiers should be noted with regard to these figures. First, not all abuse is perpetrated by parents, although most is—approximately 90% of instances in the 2016 survey. Second, the survey, like most attempts to determine the prevalence of abuse, was based on reported cases that had reached legal authorities. Not all cases do, and therefore the actual prevalence is undoubtedly greater—by some estimates, at least twice as great (Cicchetti, 2013). Finally, the prevalence is also greater for groups of children whose characteristics place them at heightened risk for abuse or neglect. Among these groups are the populations discussed in the first section of this chapter: children with disabilities or clinical syndromes (Perrigo, Berkovits, Cederbaum, Williams, & Hurlburt, 2018). Such children account for approximately one-fourth of reported cases of abuse or neglect (Lightfoot, Hill, & LaLiberte, 2011).

Just as certain children are at risk to become victims of abuse or neglect, so certain parents are at risk to become perpetrators of abuse or neglect. Among the predictors are low socioeconomic status, low or borderline IQ, high levels of stress, and alcohol or drug abuse (Azar, 2002; US Department of Health & Human Services, Administration for Children and Families, Administration on Children, Youth and Families, Children's Bureau, 2018). Also predictive is a history of having been abused or neglected as a child. Compared to parents in general, parents who were maltreated as children are almost three times more likely to mistreat their own children (Assink et al., 2018). When the abuse was severe, transfer to the next generation is even more likely (Babcok Fenerci & Allen, 2018).

One hardly needs research to know that abuse or neglect is bad for children's development. But a large body of research verifies that there are, in fact, widespread detrimental effects. A review by Cicchetti and Toth (2015) discusses negative outcomes under the following headings: emotion regulation, emotion recognition, attachment, self-development, peer relationships, adaptation to school, memory, personality, psychopathology, and physical health. Many of these topics, of course, encompass numerous more specific outcomes. And extensive though the Cicchetti and Toth review is, it does not attempt to discuss all of the adverse effects that have been demonstrated. Other examples include social understanding (Luke & Banerjee, 2013), bullying and victimization (Shields & Cicchetti, 2001), risk taking (Azar, 2002), age of menarche (Boynton-Jarrett et al., 2013), and alcohol and drug use (Widom & White, 1997). In short, virtually everything in a child's development can be affected by abuse or neglect.

For most of the topics considered in this book, a major goal is to identify the relevant parental behaviors. In the present case, the topic is defined by the behaviors; the goal is to figure out why parents behave the way they do. This question is summarized in the title of one of the articles devoted to the issue: "Parents Who Abuse: What Are They Thinking?" (Seng & Prinz, 2008, p. 163).

The answer is that such parents are often thinking in a variety of nontypical and nonoptimal ways. Seng and Prinz (2008) divide their discussion of such thoughts into child-oriented cognitions and parent-oriented cognitions—thus maladaptive beliefs about the child and maladaptive beliefs about the self.

One entry under the first of these headings is a form of belief that we have encountered at various points throughout the book: the expectations that parents hold for what their child is and is not capable of doing. In work by Azar and colleagues (Azar, Robinson, Hekimian, & Twentyman, 1984; Azar & Rohrbeck, 1986), the emphasis is on potentially unrealistic expectations that might push parenting in a wrong direction—thus beliefs such as "There is nothing wrong with punishing a 9-month-old for crying too much," or "A 5-year-old can be expected to help by feeding, dressing, and changing diapers for an infant." Although there are occasional exceptions (Haskett,

Scott, Willoughby, Ahern, & Nears, 2006), in most studies parents who have maltreated their children are more likely to express such beliefs than are parents in general. This conclusion holds for neglect as well as abuse (Azar, McGuier, Miller, Hernandez-Mekonnen, & Johnson, 2017).

Another child-oriented cognition concerns not the nature but the valence of the beliefs. How do parents feel about their children? The finding here is not a surprise: Parents with a history of maltreatment hold more negative beliefs about their children than do parents in general (Haskett, Scott, Grant, Ward, & Robinson, 2003; Young et al., 2018). They are more likely, for example, to endorse items such as "cries easily," "steals," and "lies," and they do so even when other measures do not support such a negative view of the child (a finding reminiscent of the depression distortion effect). The Young et al. (2018) study demonstrates that such negative perceptions are apparent as early as infancy.

A third child-oriented cognition is a familiar one: the attributions that parents offer for their children's behavior. The general conclusion is also a familiar one: As with other forms of maladaptive parenting, negative, child-blaming attributions are predictive of parenting problems—in this case, abuse or neglect (Azar et al., 2016; Haskett et al., 2006). Parents who abuse or neglect are more likely than parents in general to believe that negative behaviors from their children are internal in origin, stable, global, and controllable. Two conclusions follow from such a belief. One is that the child can be blamed for the behavior. The second is that the parent can legitimately punish the behavior.

Attributions can also be a form of parent-oriented cognition. As we saw in Chapter 4, research by Bugental and colleagues (e.g., Bugental & Happaney, 2002) has focused on parents' attributions for successes and failures in the parenting role. Of particular interest has been the perceived relative power of parent and child in determining outcomes, especially negative outcomes. Who has control when things go wrong? As we saw, a consistent belief on the parent's part that the child has control is associated with both maladaptive parenting practices of a variety of sorts and negative parental emotions. It is also associated with a heightened probability of abuse as the powerless-feeling parent resorts to violence as the only way to control a deliberately provocative child. As Bugental (2009, p. 99) writes, "such parents appeared to think of themselves as victims of their children."

The work on perceived control overlaps with another form of parent-oriented belief that we have encountered frequently: parental self-efficacy.

Not surprisingly, parents who abuse or neglect tend to be low in self-efficacy. Furthermore—and as is typically the case—the low self-efficacy is both a result of parenting failures and a contributor to further failures, in this case either the tendency to withdraw from the parenting role (as in neglect) or to turn to overly harsh techniques as the only way to control the child (as in abuse—Seng & Prinz, 2008).

Although I have discussed these various forms of parental cognition separately, they do not operate separately when parents interact with their children. In general, various forms of problematic thinking (unrealistic expectations, negative attributions, low self-efficacy, etc.) tend to co-occur, making the risk of maladaptive parental behavior, including abuse or neglect, even greater (Azar, 2002; Haskett et al., 2003).

This section has revisited the work of Azar and of Bugental that was discussed in earlier chapters of the book. As I noted in those earlier discussions, the work of these two research teams is important not only for its attempt to explicate the contribution of parental beliefs to how parents behave and how their children develop. It is important also because it includes attempts to *change* beliefs and behaviors as a way to change development— that is, includes interventions directed to families that are having difficulties or at risk for having difficulties (Azar et al., 2008; Bugental, 2009; Bugental et al., 2002). In this attempt the two research programs join a large and long-standing literature whose goal is to prevent or redress child maltreatment by altering how parents behave (Temcheff, Letarte, Boutin, & Marcil, 2018; Toth, Petrenko, Gravener-Davis, & Handley, 2016).

Such efforts take many forms. Some interventions have the goal of correcting current problems, some have the goal of preventing future problems, and some have both goals. Some work with parents only, some work with children only, and some work with both parents and children. Some are directed to parents of infants, some to parents of adolescents, and some to every age period in between. Finally, some—including the programs developed by Azar and Bugental—place their emphasis on parents' beliefs, whereas others work more directly with the parental behaviors of interest. I will note, however, that the value of a focus on beliefs is clear, for some of the most successful programs achieve their effects by altering beliefs as a way to alter behaviors (Azar et al., 2008).

A more general conclusion follows from the point just made, and that is that such programs *are* successful. Not in every instance, of course, and clearly not every family in need of help receives help. Still, interventions designed to move parenting in a more positive, more child-enhancing direction have had a positive impact for thousands of families, both in forestalling abuse or neglect in families at risk and in lessening and repairing the damage when maltreatment has already occurred. Such programs—and the capacity for change that they demonstrate—constitute a clear ray of hope in what is otherwise the most negative of the parenting literatures.

They are not the only ray of hope. Although no child is immune from the damaging effects of abuse or neglect, some children somehow emerge relatively unscathed in comparison to peers who have undergone similar adversity. Such children are a small minority of those who have experienced maltreatment, and their developmental course is not necessarily problem-free. Still, they demonstrate a capacity for resilience and recovery that tells us that early adversity need not determine permanent destiny. This is a conclusion, it is important to note, that is not limited to maltreatment; such resilience has been demonstrated across a wide range of early adverse experiences (Masten, 2014). Some examples among the many such experiences are natural disasters, terrorism, homelessness, poverty, parental divorce, parental mental illness, and death of a parent.

Clearly, a critical question is what determines these individual differences in resilience. Why do some children fare so much better than others? Researchers agree that three general factors are important (Luthar, Grossman, & Small, 2015; Masten & Cicchetti, 2016).

One is characteristics of the child. High IQ and related cognitive skills are predictors of resilience, as are certain aspects of temperament and personality. In general, attributes that relate positively to other aspects of the child's development also relate positively to resilience.

Resilience, however, is not a trait that resides within the child. Rather, both the development of protective attributes such as IQ and the expression of such attributes depend on the environments that children encounter as they develop. A second general factor, therefore, is the community or communities within which development takes place. Is the community safe, or is it wracked with violence? Is adequate day care available, and what is the quality of the school system? Are peers positive and prosocial, or do they also push development in a negative direction? All of these environmental forces, as well as many others, can make a difference.

The third general determinant—and the one weighted most heavily by most theorists—is the quality of the relationships with the important adults in the child's life. For most children, of course, these adults are the parents.

Clearly, children who have been maltreated by a parent may lack an important resource available to most children. Even here, however, a positive, supportive relationship with a caring adult—perhaps a grandparent, perhaps a foster parent, perhaps a parent who did not maltreat—can be crucial. And, in the more common cases in which the parent was not the source of the problem, parents can be the key elements in the child's ability to cope with and to recover from the adversity. There may be no clearer example of one of this book's central themes: the importance of parents.

# References

Aassve, A., Goisis, A., & Sironi, M. (2012). Happiness and childbearing across Europe. *Social Indicators Research, 108*, 65–86. doi: 10.1007/s11205-011-9866-x

Abar, C. C., Jackson, K. M., Colby, S. M., & Barnett, N. P. (2015). Parent-child discrepancies in reports of parental monitoring and their relationship to adolescent alcohol-related behaviors. *Journal of Youth and Adolescence, 44*, 1688–1701. doi: 10.1007/s10964-014-0143-6

Achenbach, T. M. (2001). *Manual for the Child Behavior Checklist for ages 6–18*. Burlington, VT: Research Center for Children, Youth, and Families.

Achenbach, T. M., McConaughy, S. H., & Howell, C. T. (1987). Child/adolescent behavioral and emotional problems: Implications of cross-informant correlations for situational specificity. *Psychological Bulletin, 101*, 213–232. doi: 10.1037/0033-2909.101.2.213

Achim, A. M., Guitton, M. J., Jackson, P. L., Boutin, A., & Monetta, L. (2013). On what ground do we mentalize? Characteristics of current tasks and sources of information that contribute to mentalizing judgments. *Psychological Assessment, 25*, 117–126. doi: 10.1037/a0029137

Adolph, K. E., & Robinson, S. R. (2015). Motor development. In R. M. Lerner (Series Ed.) & L. S. Liben & U. Muller (Vol. Eds.), *Handbook of child psychology and developmental science: Vol. 2. Cognitive processes* (7th ed., pp. 113–157). Hoboken, NJ: Wiley.

Adrian, J. E., Clemente, R. A., Villanueva, L., & Rieffe, C. (2005). Parent-child picture-book reading, mothers' mental state language and children's theory of mind. *Journal of Child Language, 32*, 673–686. doi: 10.1017/S0305000905006963

Adrian, M., Zeman, J., & Veits, G. (2011). Methodological implications of the affect revolution: A 35-year review of emotion regulation assessment in children. *Journal of Experimental Child Psychology, 110*, 171–197. doi: 10.1016/j.jecp.2011.03.009

Ainsworth, M. D. S., Blehar, M. C., Waters, E., & Wall, S. (1978). *Patterns of attachment: A psychological study of the Strange Situation*. Hillsdale, NJ: Erlbaum.

Aitken, M. E., Rose, A., Mullins, S. H., Miller, B. K., Nick, T., Rettiganti, M., . . . Whiteside-Mansell, L. (2016). Grandmothers' beliefs and practices in infant safe sleep. *Maternal Child Health Journal, 20*, 1464–1471. doi: 10.1007/s10995-016-1945-9

Ajzen, I., & Fishbein, M. (2005). The influence of attitudes on behavior. In D. Albarracín, B. T. Johnson, & M. P. Zanna (Eds.), *The handbook of attitudes* (pp. 173–221). Mahwah, NJ: Erlbaum.

Albarran, A. S., & Reich, S. M. (2014). Using baby books to increase new mothers' self-efficacy and improve toddler language development. *Infant and Child Development, 23*, 374–387. doi: 10.1002/icd.1832

Albertos, A., Osorio, A., Lopez-del Burgo, C., Carlos, S., Beltramo, C., & Trullois, F. (2016). Parental knowledge and adolescents' risk behaviors. *Journal of Adolescence, 53*, 231–236. doi: 10.1016/j.adolescence.2016.10.010

Al-Maadadi, F., & Ikhief, A. (2015). What mothers know about child development and parenting in Qatar: Parenting cognitions and practices. *The Family Journal, 23*, 65–73. doi: 10.1177/1066480714555669

American Psychiatric Association. (2013). *Diagnostic and statistical manual of mental disorders* (5th ed.). Washington, DC: American Psychiatric Association.

Antill, J. K., Goodnow, J. J., Russell, G., & Cotton, S. (1996). The influence of parents and family context on children's involvement in household tasks. *Sex Roles, 34,* 215–236. doi: 10.1007/BF01544297

Antshel, K. M., Brewster, S., & Waisbren, S. E. (2004). Child and parent attributions in chronic pediatric conditions: Phenylketonuria (PKU) as an exemplar. *Journal of Child Psychology and Psychiatry. 45,* 622–630. doi: 10.1111/j.1469-7610.2004. 00251.x

Ardelt, M. A., & Eccles, J. S. (2001). Effects of mothers' parental efficacy beliefs and promotive parenting strategies on inner-city youth. *Journal of Family Issues, 22,* 944–972. doi: 10.1177/019251301022008001

Arnold, D. S., O'Leary, S. C., Wolff, L. S., & Acker, M. M. (1993). The Parenting Scale: A measure of dysfunctional parenting in discipline situations. *Psychological Assessment, 5,* 137–144. doi: 10.1037/1040-3590.5.2.137

Arnold, F., Bulatoa, R. A., Buripakdi, C., Chung, R. J., Fawcett, J. T., Iritani, T., . . . Wu, T. S. (1975). *The value of children: Vol 1. Introduction and comparative analysis.* Honolulu, HI: East-West Population Institute.

Arts, M., Taqi, I., & Begin, F. (2017). Improving the early initiation of breastfeeding: The WHO-UNICEF Breastfeeding Advocacy Initiative. *Breastfeeding Medicine, 12,* 326–337. doi: 10.1089/bfm.2017.0047

Assadi, S. M., Smetana, J. G., Shahmansouri, N., & Mohannadi, M. (2011). Beliefs about parental authority, parenting styles, and parent-adolescent conflict among Iranian mothers of middle adolescents. *International Journal of Behavioral Development, 35,* 424–431. doi: 10.1177/01650254114091

Assink, M., Spruit, A., Schuts, M., Lindauer, R., van der Put, C. E., & Stams, G. J. M. (2018). The intergenerational nature of child maltreatment: A three-level meta-analysis. *Child Abuse and Neglect, 84,* 131–145. doi: 10.1016/j.chiabu.2018.07.037

Astrachan-Fletcher, E., Veldhuis, C., Lively, N., Fowler, C., & Marcks B. (2008). The reciprocal effects of eating disorders and the postpartum period: A review of the literature and recommendations for clinical care. *Journal of Women's Health, 17,* 227–239. doi: 10.1089/jwh.2007.0550

Astuto, J., & Ruck, M. D. (2015). Early childhood as a foundation for civic engagement. In L. R. Sherrod, J. Torney-Purta, & C. A. Flanagan (Eds.), *Handbook of research on civic engagement in youth* (pp. 249–276). Hoboken, NJ: Wiley.

Augenstein, T. M., Thomas, S. A., Ehrlich, K. B., Daruwala, S., Reyes, S. M., Chrabaszcz, J. S., & De Los Reyes, A. (2016). Comparing multi-informant measures of parental monitoring and their links with adolescent delinquent behavior. *Parenting: Science and Practice, 16,* 164–186. doi: 10.1080/15295192.2016.1158600

Aunola, K., Nurmi, J., Lerkkanen, M., & Rasku-Puttonen, H. (2003). The roles of achievement-related behaviours and parental beliefs in children's mathematical performance. *Educational Psychology, 23,* 403–421. doi: 10.1080/01443410303212

Azar, S. T. (2002). Parenting and child maltreatment. In M. H. Bornstein (Ed.), *Handbook of parenting: Vol. 4. Social conditions and applied parenting* (2nd ed., pp. 361–388). Mahwah, NJ: Erlbaum.

Azar S. T., McGuier, D. J., Miller, E. A., Hernandez-Mekonnen, R., & Johnson, D. R. (2017). Child neglect and maternal cross-relational social cognitive and neurocognitive disturbances. *Journal of Family Psychology, 31,* 8–18. doi: 10.1037/fam0000268

Azar, S. T. Miller, E. A., McGuier, D. J., Stevenson, M. T., O'Donnell E., Olsen, N., & Spence, N. C. (2016). Maternal social information processing and the frequency and severity of mother perpetuated physical abuse. *Child Maltreatment, 21*, 308–316. doi: 10.1177%2F1077559516668047

Azar, S. T., Okado, Y., Stevenson, M. T., & Robinson, L. R. (2013). A preliminary test of a social information processing model of parenting risk in adolescent males at risk for later physical child abuse in adulthood. *Child Abuse Review, 22*, 268–286. doi: 10.1002/car.2244

Azar, S. T., Reitz, E. B., & Goslin, M. C. (2008). Mothering: Thinking is part of the job description: Application of cognitive views to understanding maladaptive parenting and doing intervention and prevention work. *Journal of Applied Developmental Psychology, 29*, 295–304. doi: 10.1016/j.appdev.2008.04.009

Azar, S. T., Robinson, D. R., Hekimian, E., & Twentyman, C. T. (1984). Unrealistic expectations and problem solving ability in maltreating and comparison mothers. *Journal of Consulting and Clinical Psychology, 52*, 687–691. doi: 10.1037/0022-006X.52.4.687

Azar, S. T., & Rohrbeck, C. A. (1986). Child abuse and unrealistic expectations: Further validation of the Parent Opinion Questionnaire. *Journal of Consulting and Clinical Psychology, 54*, 867–868. doi: 10.1037/0022-006X.54.6.867

Babcok Fenerci, R. L., & Allen, B. (2018). From mother to child: Maternal betrayal trauma and risk for maltreatment and psychopathology in the next generation. *Child Abuse and Neglect, 82*, 1–11. doi: 10.1016/j.chiabu.2018.05.014

Bader, L. R., & Fouts, H. N. (2019). Parents' perceptions about infant emotions: A narrative cross-disciplinary systematic literature review. *Developmental Review. 51*, 1–30. doi: 10.1016/j.dr.2018.11.003

Bahena, S., Schueler, B. E., McIntyre, J., & Gehlbach, H. (2016). Assessing parent perceptions of school fit: The development and measurement qualities of a survey scale. *Applied Developmental Science, 20*, 121–134. doi: 10.1080/10888691.2015.108530

Bailey, D. B., Skinner, D., & Sparkman, K. L. (2003). Discovering Fragile X syndrome: Family experiences and perceptions. *Pediatrics, 111*, 407–416. doi: 10.1542/peds.111.2.407

Baker, M., Schafer, G., Alcock, K. J., & Bartlett, S. (2013). A parentally administered developmental assessment for children from 10 to 24 months. *Infant Behavior and Development, 36*, 279–287. doi: 10.1016/j.infbeh.2013.01.007

Bandura, A. (1986). *Social foundations of thought and action: A social cognitive theory*. Englewood Cliffs, NJ: Prentice-Hall.

Bandura, A. (1997). *Self-efficacy: The exercise of control*. New York: W. H. Freeman.

Bandura, A., Barbaranelli, C., Caprara, G. V., & Pastorelli, C. (1996). Multifaceted impact of self-efficacy beliefs on academic functioning. *Child Development, 67*, 1206–1222. doi: 10.1111/1467-8624.ep9704150192

Bar, M. A., Shelef, L., & Bart, O. (2016). Do participation and self-efficacy of mothers to children with ASD predict their children's participation? *Research in Autism Spectrum Disorders, 24*, 1–10. doi: 10.1016/j.rasd.2016.01.002

Barbarin, O. A., Early, D., Clifford, R., Bryant, D., Frome, P., Burchinal, M., . . . Pianta, R. (2008). Parental conceptions of school readiness: Relations to ethnicity, socioeconomic status, and children's skills. *Early Education and Development, 19*, 671–701. doi: 10.1080/10409280802375257

Barfoot, J., Meredith, P., Ziviani, J., & Whittingham, K. (2017). Parent-child interactions and children with cerebral palsy: An exploratory studying investigating emotional availability, functional ability, and parent stress. *Child: Care, Health and Human Development, 43*, 812–822. doi: 10.1111/cch.12493

Barr, R. G. (2011). Mother and child: Preparing for a life. In D. P. Keating (Ed.), *Nature and nurture in early child development* (pp. 70–96). New York, NY: Cambridge University Press.

Bar-Tal, D., & Guttmann, J. A. (1981). A comparison of teachers', pupils', and parents' attributions regarding pupils' academic achievement. *British Journal of Educational Psychology, 51*, 301–311. doi: 10.1111/j.2044-8279.1981.tb02488.x

Bartholomew, M. K., Schoppe-Sullivan, S. J., Glassman, M., & Kamp Dush, C. M. (2012). New parents' Facebook use at the transition to parenthood. *Family Relations, 61*, 455–469. doi: 10.1111/j.1741-3729.2012.00708

Bartle, N. C., & Harvey, K. (2017). Explaining infant feeding: The role of previous personal and vicarious experience on attitudes, subjective norms, self-efficacy, and breastfeeding outcomes. *British Journal of Health Psychology, 22*, 763–785. doi: 10.1111/bjhp.12254

Bates, J. E., & Pettit, G. S. (2015). Temperament, parenting, and social development. In J. E. Grusec & P. D. Hastings (Eds.), *Handbook of socialization: Theory and research* (2nd ed., pp. 153–177). New York, NY: Guilford Press.

Baumrind, D. (1971). Current patterns of parental authority. *Developmental Psychology Monographs, 4*, 1–103. doi: 10.1037/h0030372

Bayley, N. (2006). *Bayley Scales of Infant and Toddler Development* (3rd ed.). San Antonio, TX: Harcourt Assessment. doi: 10.1002/978047047 9216.corpsy0111

Bayram Ozdemir, S. B., & Cheah, C. S. L. (2015). Turkish mothers' parenting beliefs in response to preschoolers' aggressive and socially withdrawn behaviors. *Journal of Child and Family Studies, 24*, 687–702. doi: 10.1007/s10826-013-9879-y

Bayram Ozdemir, S. B., & Cheah, C. S. L. (2017). Mothers' reactions to preschoolers' proactive and reactive aggressive behaviors. *Infant and Child Development, 26* doi: 10.1002/icd.1972

Beaver, K. M., Schwartz, J. A., Connolly, E. J., Al-Ghamdi, M., & Kobeisy, A. N. (2015). The role of parenting in the prediction of criminal involvement: Findings from a nationally representative sample of youth and a sample of adopted youth. *Developmental Psychology, 51*, 301–308. doi: 10.1037/a0038672

Becker, J. A., & Hall, M. S. (1989). Adult beliefs about pragmatic development. *Journal of Applied Developmental Psychology, 10*, 1–17. doi: 10.1016/0193-3973(89)90011-7

Becker-Haimes, E. M., Jensen-Doss, A., Birmaher, B., Kendall, P. C., & Ginsburg, G. S. (2018). Parent-youth informant disagreement: Implications for youth anxiety treatment. *Clinical Child Psychology, 23*, 42–56. doi: 10.1177/1359104516689586

Beckman, L. J. (1976). Causal attributions of teachers and parents regarding children's performance. *Psychology in the Schools, 13*, 212–218. doi: 10.1002/1520-6807(197604

Beer, J. S. (2002). Implicit self-theories of shyness. *Journal of Personality and Social Psychology, 83*, 1009–1024. doi: 10.1037/0022-3514.83.4.1009

Bein, L. A., Petrik, M. L., Saunders, S. M., & Wojcik, J. V. (2015). Discrepancy between parents and children in reporting of distress and impairment: Association with critical symptoms. *Clinical Child Psychology and Psychiatry, 20*, 515–524. doi: 10.1177/1359104514532185

Belenky, M. F., Clinchy, B. M., Goldberger, N. R., & Tarule, J. M. (1986). *Women's ways of knowing: The development of self, voice and mind.* New York, NY: Basic Books.

Belfield, C., & Garcia, E. (2014). Parental notions of school readiness: How have they changed and has preschool made a difference? *Journal of Educational Research, 107*, 138–151. doi: 10.1080/00220671.2012.753863

Bell, R. Q. (1968). A reinterpretation of the direction of effects in studies of socialization. *Psychological Review, 75*, 81–95. doi: 10.1037/h0025583

Belsky, J., Ward, M. J., & Rovine, M. (1986). Prenatal expectations, postnatal experiences, and the transition to parenthood. In R. D. Ashmore & D. M. Brodzinsky (Eds.), *Thinking about the family: Views of parents and children* (pp. 119–145). Hillsdale, NJ: Erlbaum.

Benasich, A. A., & Brooks-Gunn, J. (1996). Maternal attitudes and knowledge of child-rearing: Associations with family and child outcomes. *Child Development, 67*, 1186–1205. doi: 10.1111/1467-8624.ep9704150191

Berger, L. M., & Brooks-Gunn, J. (2005). Socioeconomic status, parenting knowledge and behaviors, and perceived maltreatment of young low-birth-weight children. *Social Service Review, 79*, 237–267. doi: 10.1086/428957

Bergeron, N., & Schneider, B. H. (2005). Explaining cross-national differences in peer-directed aggression: A quantitative synthesis. *Aggressive Behavior, 31*, 116–137. doi: 10.1002/ab.20049

Bergmuller, S. (2013). The relationship between cultural individualism-collectivism and student aggression across 62 countries. *Aggressive Behavior, 39*, 182–200. doi: 10.1002/ab.21472

Berlin, L. J., Cassidy, J., & Appleyard, K. (2008). The influence of early attachment on other relationships. In J. Cassidy & P. R. Shaver (Eds.), *Handbook of attachment* (2nd ed., pp. 333–347). New York, NY: Guilford Press.

Bernard, K., Nissim, G., Vaccaro, S., Harris, J. L., & Lindhiem, O. (2018). Association between maternal depression and maternal sensitivity from birth to 12 months: A meta-analysis. *Attachment and Human Development, 20*, 578–599. doi: 10.1080/14616734.2018.1430839

Bernier, A., Carlson, S. M., Deschenes, M., & Matte-Gagne, C. (2012). Social factors in the development of early executive functioning: A closer look at the caregiving environment. *Developmental Science, 15*, 12–24. doi: 10.1111/j.1467-7687.2011.01093.x

Bernier, R., & Dawson, G. (2016). Autism spectrum disorders. In D. Chicchetti (Ed.), *Developmental psychopathology: Vol. 3. Maladaptation and psychopathology* (3rd ed., pp. 81–115). Hoboken, NJ: Wiley.

Bernstein, D. M., Thornton, W. L., & Sommerville, J. A. (2011). Theory of mind through the ages: Older and middle-aged adults exhibit more errors than do younger adults on a continuous false belief task. *Experimental Aging Research, 37*, 481–502. doi: 10.1080/0361073X.2011.619466.:

Bernstein, R. E., Laurent, H. K., Measelle, J. R., Hailey, B. C., & Ablow, J. C. (2013). Little tyrants or just plain tired: Evaluating attributions for caregiving outcomes across the transition to parenthood. *Journal of Family Psychology, 27*, 851–861. doi: 10.1037/a0034651

stetBernstein, D., Rubin, D. C., & Siegler, I. C. (2011). Two versions of life: Emotionally negative and positive life events have different roles in the organization of life story and identity. *Emotion, 11*, 1190–1201. doi: 10.1037/a0024940

Bessey, M., Coulombe, J. A., Smith, I. M., & Corkum, P. (2013). Assessing parental sleep attitudes and beliefs in typically developing children and children with ADHD and ASD. *Children's Health Care, 42*, 116–133. doi: 10.1080/02739615.2013.766096

Best, D. L. (2010). Gender. In M. H. Bornstein (Ed.), *Handbook of cultural developmental science* (pp. 209–222). New York, NY: Psychology Press.

Bettleheim, B. (1962). Dialogues with mothers. New York, NY: Free Press of Glencoe.

Bhavnagri, N. P., & Parke, R. D. (1991). Parents as direct facilitators of children's peer relationships: Effects of age of child and sex of parent. *Journal of Social and Personal Relationships, 8*, 423–440. doi: 10.1177/0265407591083007

Bibok, M. B., Carpendale, J. I. M., & Muller, U. (2009). Parental scaffolding and the development of executive function. *New Directions for Child and Adolescent Development, 123*, 17–34.

Biddle, S. J. H., Wang, C. K. J., Chatzisarantis, N. L. D., & Spray, C. M. (2003). Motivation for physical activity in young people: Entity and incremental beliefs about athletic ability. *Journal of Sport Sciences, 21*, 973–979. doi: 10.1080/02640410310001641377

Biehle, S. N., & Mickelson, K. D. (2011). Personal and co-parent predictors of parenting efficacy across the transition to parenthood. *Journal of Social and Clinical Psychology, 30*, 985–1010. doi: 10.1521/jscp.2011.30.9.985

Biehle, S. N., & Mickelson, K. D. (2012). First-time parents' expectations about the division of childcare and play. *Journal of Family Psychology, 26*, 36–45. doi: 10.1037/a0026608

Bird, J. E., & Berman, L. S. (1985). Differing perceptions on mothers, fathers, and children concerning children's academic performance. *Journal of Psychology, 119*, 113–124. doi: 10.1080/00223980.1985.10542877

Bjorklund, D. F. (2007). *Why youth is not wasted on the young: Immaturity in human development*. Malden, MA: Blackwell Publishing.

Blacher, J., Baker, B. L., & Kaladjian, A. (2013). Syndrome specificity and mother-child interactions: Examining positive and negative parenting across contexts and time. *Journal of Autism and Developmental Disorders, 43*, 761–774. doi: 10.1007/s10803-012-1605-x

Black, M. M., Baqui, A. H., Zeman, K., McNary, S. W., Le, K., Arifeen, S. E., . . . Black, R. E. (2007). Depressive symptoms among rural Bangladeshi mothers: Implications for infant development. *Journal of Child Psychology and Psychiatry, 48*, 764–772. doi: 10.1111/j.1469-7610.2007.01752.x.

Blake, J. J., Lease, A. M., Olejnik, S. P., & Turner, T. L. (2010). Ethnic differences in parents' attitudes toward girls' use of aggression. *Journal of Aggression, Maltreatment, and Trauma, 19*, 393–413. doi: 10.1080/10926771003781362

Blocklin, M. K., Crouter, A. C., Updegraff, K. A., & McHale, S. M. (2011). Sources of parental knowledge in Mexican American families. *Family Relations, 60*, 30–44. doi: 10.1111/j.1741-3729.2010.00631.x

Blumberg, F. C., & Brooks, P. J. (Eds.). (2017). *Cognitive development in digital contexts*. San Diego, CA: Academic Press.

Bogdan, R. J. (Ed.). (1986). *Belief: Form, content and function*. Oxfordstet: Oxford University Press.

Bogenschneider, K., Small, S. A., & Tsay, J. C. (1997). Child, parent, and contextual influences on perceived parenting competence among parents of adolescents. *Journal of Marriage and Family, 59*, 345–362. doi: 10.2307/353475

Bolton, C., Calam, R., Barrowclough, C., Peters, S., Roberts, J., Wearden, A., & Morris, J. (2003). Expressed emotion, attributions and depression in mothers of children with problem behaviour. *Journal of Child Psychology and Psychiatry, 44*, 242–254. doi: 10.1111/1469-7610.00117

Bond, L. A., Belenky, M. F., Weinstock, J. S., & Cook, T. (1996). Imagining and engaging one's children: Lessons from poor, rural, New England mothers. In S. Harkness & C. M. Super (Eds.), *Parents' cultural belief systems: Their origins, expressions, and consequences* (pp. 467–495). New York, NY: Guilford Press.

Booth-LaForce, C., & Groh, A. M. (2018). Parent-child attachment and peer relations. In W. M. Bukowski, B. Laursen, & K. H. Rubin (Eds.), *Handbook of peer interactions, relationships, and groups* (2nd ed., pp. 349–370). New York, NY: Guilford Press.

Bora, E., Yucel, M., & Pantelis, C. (2009). Theory of mind impairment in schizophrenia: Meta-analysis. *Schizophrenia Research, 109*, 1–9. doi: 10.1016/j.schres.2008.12.020

Bornstein, M. H. (2014). Human infancy … and the rest of the lifespan. *Annual Review of Psychology, 65*, 121–158. doi: 10.1146/annurev-psych-120710-100359

Bornstein, M. H. (2015). Children's parents. In R. M. Lerner (Series Ed.) & M. H. Bornstein & T. Leventhal (Vol. Eds.), *Handbook of child psychology and developmental science: Vol. 4. Ecological settings* (7th ed., pp. 55–132). Hoboken, NJ: Wiley. doi: 10.1002/9781118963418.childpsy403

Bornstein, M. H., & Cote, L. R. (2004). "Who is sitting across from me?" Immigrant mothers' knowledge of parenting and children's development. *Pediatrics, 114*, 557–564. doi: 10.1542/peds.2004-0713

Bornstein, M. H., Cote, L. R., Haynes, O. M., Hahn, C. S., & Park, Y. (2010). Parenting knowledge: Experiential and sociodemographic factors in European American mothers of young children. *Developmental Psychology, 46*, 1667–1693. doi: 10.1037/a0020677

Bornstein, M. H., Haynes, O. M., Azuma, H., Galperin, C., Maital, S., Ogino, M., … Wright, B. (1998). A cross-national study of self-evaluations and attributions in parenting: Argentina, Belgium, France, Israel, Italy, Japan, and the United States. *Developmental Psychology, 34*, 662–676. doi: 10.1037/0012-1649.34.4.662

Bornstein, M. H., Hendricks, C., Hahn, C., Haynes, M., Painter, K. M., & Tamis-LeMonda, C. S. (2003). Contributors to self-perceived competence, satisfaction, investment, and role balance in maternal parenting: A multivariate ecological analysis. *Parenting: Science and Practice, 3*, 285–326. doi: 10.1207/s15327922par0304_2

Bornstein, M. H., Putnick, D. L., & Esposito, G. (2017). Continuity and stability in development. *Child Development Perspectives, 11*, 113–119. doi: 10.1111/cdep.12 221

Bornstein, M. H., Putnick, D. L., & Lansford, J. E. (2011). Parenting attributions and attitudes in cross-cultural perspective. *Parenting: Science and Practice, 11*, 214–237. doi: 10.1080/15295192.2011.585568

Boutwell, B. B., Young, J. N. Young, & Meldrum, R. C. (2018). On the positive relationship between breastfeeding & intelligence. *Developmental Psychology, 54*, 1426–1433. doi: 10.1037/dev0000537

Bowes, J. M., Chen, M., San, L. Q., & Yuan, L. (2004). Reasoning and negotiating about child responsibility in urban Chinese families: Reports from mothers, fathers and children. *International Journal of Behavioral Development, 28*, 48–58. doi: 10.1080/01650250344000262

Bowes, J. M., Flanagan, C., & Taylor, A. J. (2001). Adolescents' ideas about individual and social responsibility in relation to children's household work: Some international comparisons. *International Journal of Behavioral Development, 25*, 60–68. doi: 10.1080/016502500420000

Bowlby, J. (1969). *Attachment and loss: Vol. 1. Attachment.* New York, NY: Basic Books.

Bowlby, J. (1973). *Attachment and loss: Vol. 2. Separation.* New York, NY: Basic Books.

Boyd, M. J., Zaff, J. F., Phelps, E., Weiner, M. B., & Lerner, R. M. (2011). The relationship between adolescents' media use and civic engagement: The indirect effect of interpersonal communication with parents. *Journal of Adolescence, 34,* 1167–1179. doi: 10.1016/j.adolescence.2011.07.004

Boyd, R. C., & Gillham, J. E. (2009). Review of interventions for parental depression from toddlerhood to adolescence. *Current Psychiatry Reviews, 5,* 226–235. doi: 10.2174/157340009789542123

Boyd-Ball, A. J. Veronneau, M., Dishion, T. J., & Kavanagh, K. (2014). Monitoring and peer influence as predictors of increases in alcohol use among American Indian youth. *Prevention Science, 15,* 526–535. doi: 10.1007/s11121-013-0399-1

Boynton-Jarrett, R., Wright, R. J., Putnam, F. W., Hibert, E. L., Michels, K. B., Forman, M. R., & Rich-Edwards, J. (2013). Childhood abuse and age of menarche. *Journal of Adolescent Health, 52,* 241–247. doi: 10.1016/j.jadohealth.2012.06.006

Brackbill, Y., Kitch, D., & Noffsinger, W. B. (1988). The perfect child (from an elderly parent's point of view). *Journal of Aging Studies, 2,* 243–254. doi: 10.1016/0890-4065(88)90004-7

Bradford, V. A., Walkinshaw, L. P., Steinman, L., Otten, J. J., Fisher, K., Ellings, A., . . . Johnson, D. B. (2017). Creating environments to support breastfeeding: The challenges and facilitators of policy development in hospitals, clinics, early care and education, and worksites. *Maternal and Child Health Journal, 21,* 2188–2198. doi: 10.1007/s10995-017-2338-4

Bradshaw, C. P. (2015). Translating research to practice in bullying prevention. *American Psychologist, 70,* 322–332. doi: 10.1037/a0039114

Branje, S. (2018), Development of parent-adolescent relationships: Conflict interactions as a mechanism of change. *Child Development Perspectives, 12,* 171–176. doi: 10.1111/cdep.12278

Branstetter, S. A., & Furman, W. (2013). Buffering effect of parental monitoring knowledge and parent-adolescent relationships on consequences of adolescent substance use. *Journal of Child and Family Studies, 22,* 192–198. doi: 10.1007/s10826-012-9568-2

Bretherton, I., Lambert, J. D., & Golby, B. (2006). Modeling and reworking childhood experiences: Involved fathers' representations of being parenting and of parenting a preschool child. In O. Mayseless (Ed.), *Parenting representations: Theory, research, and clinical implications* (pp. 177–207). New York, NY: Cambridge University Press.

Bridgett, D. J., Burt, N. M., Edwards, E. S., & Deater-Deckard, K. (2015). Intergenerational transmission of self-regulation: A multidisciplinary review and integrative conceptual framework. *Psychological Bulletin, 141,* 602–654. doi: 10.1037/a0038662

Briggs-Gowan, M. J., Godoy, L., Heberle, A., & Carter, A. S. (2016). Assessment of psychopathology in young children. In D. Cicchetti (Ed.), *Developmental psychopathology: Vol 1. Theory and method* (3rd ed., pp. 1–45). Hoboken, NJ: Wiley.

Briley, D. A., Harden, K. P., & Tucker-Drob, E. M. (2014). Child characteristics and parental educational expectations: Evidence for transmission with transaction. *Developmental Psychology, 50,* 2614–2632. doi: 10.1037/a0038094

Bronfenbrenner, U. (1979). *The ecology of human development.* Cambridge, MA: Harvard University Press.

Bronfenbrenner, U. (1989). Ecological systems theory. In R. Vasta (Ed.), *Annals of child development: Vol. 6. Six theories of child development: Revised formulations and current issues* (pp. 187–249). Greenwich, CT: JAI Press.

Bronfenbrenner, U. (1993). The ecology of cognitive development: Research models and fugitive findings. In R. H. Wozniak & K. W. Fischer (Eds.), *Development in context* (pp. 3–44). Hillsdale, NJ: Erlbaum.

Bronfenbrenner, U. (2005). The bioecological theory of human development. In U. Bronfenbrenner (Ed.), *Making humans human: Bioecological perspectives on human development* (pp. 3–15). Thousand Oaks, CA: Sage. doi: 10.1002/9780470147 658. chpsy0114

Brown, C. S., & Stone, E. A. (2018). Environmental and social contributions to children's gender-typed toy play: The role of family, peers, and media. In E. S. Weigram & L. M. Dinalla (Eds.), *Gender typing of children's toys: How early play experiences impact development* (pp. 121–140). Washington, DC: American Psychological Association.

Brown, R. (1973). *A first language.* Cambridge, MA: Harvard University Press.

Brune, M. (2005). "Theory of mind" in schizophrenia: A review of the literature. *Schizophrenia Bulletin, 31*, 21–42. doi: 10.1093/schbul/sbi002

Buchanan, C. M. (2003). Mothers' generalized beliefs about adolescents: Links to expectations for a specific child. *Journal of Early Adolescence, 23*, 29–50. doi: 10.1177/0272431602239129

Buchanan, C. M., Eccles, J. S., Flanagan, C., Midgley, C., Feldlaufer, H., & Harold, R. N. (1990). Parents' and teachers' beliefs about adolescents: Effects of sex and experience. *Journal of Youth and Adolescence, 19*, 363–394. doi: 10.1007/BF01537078

Buchanan, C. M., & G. N. Holmbeck, G. N. (1998). Measuring beliefs about adolescent personality and behavior. *Journal of Youth and Adolescence, 27*, 607–627. doi: 10.1023/A:1022835107795

Buchanan, C. S., & Hughes, J. L. (2009). Construction of social reality during early adolescence: Can expecting storm and stress increase real or perceived storm and stress? *Journal of Research on Adolescence, 19*, 261–285. doi: 10.1111/j.1532-7795.2009.00596

Bugental, D. B. (1992). Affective and cognitive processes within threat-oriented family systems. In I. E. Sigel, A. McGillicuddy-DeLisi, & J. Goodnow (Eds.), *Parental belief systems* (2nd ed., pp. 219–248). Hillsdale, NJ:: Erlbaum.

Bugental, D. B. (2009). Predicting and preventing child maltreatment: A biocognitive transactional approach. In A. Sameroff (Ed.), *The transactional model of development: How children and contexts shape each other* (pp. 97–115). Washington, DC: American Psychological Association.

Bugental, D. B., Blue, J. B., Cortez, V., Fleck, K., Kopeikin, H., Lewis, H., Lewis, J. C., & Lyon, J. (1993). Social cognitions as organizers of automatic and affective responses to social challenges. *Journal of Personality and Social Psychology, 64*, 94–103. doi: 10.1037/0022-3514.64.1.94

Bugental, D. B., Blue, J. B., & Cruzcosa, M. (1989). Perceived control over caregiving outcomes: Implications for child abuse. *Developmental Psychology, 25*, 532–539. doi: 10.1037/0012-1649.25.4.532

Bugental, D. B., Brown, M., & Reiss, C. (1996). Cognitive representations of power in caregiving relationships: Biasing effects on interpersonal interaction and information processing. *Journal of Family Psychology, 10*, 397–407. doi: 10.1037/0893-3200.10.4.397

Bugental, D. B., & Cortez, V. L. (1988). Physiological reactivity to responsive and unresponsive children as moderated by perceived control. *Child Development, 59*, 686–693. doi: 10.1111/1467-8624.ep8589245

Bugental, D. B., Ellerson, P. C., Lin, E. K., Rainey, B., Kokotovic, A., & O'Hara, N. (2002). A cognitive approach to child abuse prevention. *Journal of Family Psychology, 16,* 243–258. doi: 10.1037/0893-3200.16.3.243

Bugental, D. B., & Happaney, K. (2000). Parent-child interaction as a power contest. *Journal of Applied Developmental Psychology, 21,* 267–282. doi: 10.1016/S0193-3973(99)00038-6

Bugental, D. B., & Happaney, K. (2002). Parental attributions. In M. H. Bornstein (Ed.), *Handbook of parenting: Vol 3. Being and becoming a parent* (2nd ed., pp. 509–535). Hillsdale, NJ: Erlbaum.

Bugental, D. B., & Happaney, K. (2004). Predicting infant maltreatment in low-income families: The interactive effects of maternal attributions and child status at birth. *Developmental Psychology, 40,* 234–243. doi: 10.1037/0012-1649.40.2.234

Bugental, D. B., & Johnston, C. (2000). Parental and child cognitions in the context of the family. *Annual Review of Psychology, 51,* 314–344. doi: 1146/annurev.psych.51.1.315

Bugental, D. B., &, Shennum, W. (1984). "Difficult" children as elicitors and targets of adult communication patterns: An attributional-behavioral transactional analysis. *Monographs of the Society for Research in Child Development, 49*(1). doi: 10.2307/1165910

Bugental, D. B., &, Shennum, W. (2002). Gender, power, and violence in the family. *Child Maltreatment, 7,* 56–64. doi: 10.1177/1077559502007001005

Burack, J. A., Russo, N., Green, C. G., Landry, O., & Iarocci, G. (2016). Developments in the developmental approach to intellectual disability. In D. Chicchetti (Ed.), *Developmental psychopathology: Vol. 3. Maladaptation and psychopathology* (3rd ed., pp. 1–67). Hoboken, NJ: Wiley.

Burnette, J. L. (2010). Implicit theories of body weight: Entity beliefs can weigh you down. *Personality and Social Psychology Bulletin, 36,* 410–422. doi: 10.1177/0146167209359768

Burnette J. L., O'Boyle E. H., VanEpps E. M., Pollack J. M., & Finkel, E. J. (2013). Mind-sets matter: A meta-analytic review of implicit theories and self-regulation. *Psychological Bulletin, 139,* 655–701. doi: 10.1037/a0029531

Byers, E. S., & Sears, H. A. (2012). Mothers who do and do not intend to discuss sexual health with their young adolescents. *Family Relations, 61,* 851–863. doi: 10.1111/j.1741-3729.2012.00740.x

Byers, E. S., Sears, H. A., & Weaver, E. D. (2008). Parents' reports of sexual communication with children in kindergarten to grade 8. *Journal of Marriage and Family, 70,* 86–96. doi: 10.1111/j.1741-3737.2007.00463.x

Byrne, S., Katz, S. J., Lee, T., Linz, D., & Mcllrath, M. (2014). Peers, predators, and porn: Predicting parental underestimation of children's risky online experiences. *Journal of Computer-Mediated Communication, 19,* 215–231. doi: 10.1111/jcc4.12040.

Cabrerra, N. J., Volling, B. L., & Barr, R. (2018). Fathers are parents, too! Widening the lens on parenting for children's development. *Child Development Perspectives, 12,* 152–157. doi: 10.1111/cdep.12275

Cadman, T., Diamond, P. R., & Fearon, P. (2018). Reassessing the validity of the Attachment Q-Sort: An updated meta-analysis. *Infant and Child Development, 27.* doi: 10.1002/icd.2034

Caldwell, B. M., & Bradley, R. (1979). *Home Observation for Measurement of the Environment.* Unpublished manuscript, University of Arkansas.

Caldwell, E. (1996). *Teenagers! A bewildered parents' guide*. San Diego, CA: Silvercat Publications.

Cannon, J., & Ginsburg, H. P. (2008). "Doing the math": Maternal beliefs about early mathematics versus language learning. *Early Education and Development, 19,* 238–260. doi: 10.1080/10409280801963913

Carlson, W., & Rose, S. J. (2007). The role of reciprocity in romantic relationships in middle childhood and early adolescence. *Merrill-Palmer Quarterly, 53,* 262–290. doi: 10.1353/mpq.2007.0008

Carter, A. S., Little, C., Briggs-Gowan, M. J., & Kogan, N. (1999). The Infant-Toddler Social and Emotional Assessment (ITSEA): Comparing parent ratings to laboratory observations of task mastery, emotion regulation, coping behaviors, and attachment status. *Infant Mental Health Journal, 20,* 375–392. doi: 10.1002/(SICI)1097-0355(199924)20:4%3C375::AID-IMHJ2%3E3.0.CO;2-P

Cashmore, J. A., & Goodnow, J. J. (1985). Agreement between generations: A two-process approach. *Child Development, 56,* 493–501. doi: 1111/1467-8624.ep7251661

Castro, V. L., Halberstadt, A. G., Lozada, F. T., & Craig, A. B. (2015). Parents' emotion-related beliefs, behaviours, and skills predict children's recognition of emotion. *Infant and Child Development, 24,* 1–22. doi: 10.1002/icd.1868

Cavanaugh, C., & Cauffman, E. (2015). Viewing law and order: Mothers' and sons' justice system legitimacy attitudes and juvenile recidivism. *Psychology, Public Policy, and Law, 21,* 432–441. doi: 10.1037/law0000054

Caye, A., Machado, J. D., & Rohde, L. A. (2017). Evaluating parental disagreement in ADHD diagnosis: Can we rely on a single report from home? *Journal of Attention Disorders, 21,* 561–566. doi: 10.1177%2F1087054713504134

Centers for Disease Control and Prevention (2017). *2016 Sexually Transmitted Diseases Survey*. Retrieved from https://www.cdc.gov/std/stats16/adolescents.htm

Centers for Disease Control and Prevention (2018a). *Autism prevalence slightly higher in CDC's ADDM Network*. Retrieved from https://www.cdc.gov/media/releases/2018/p0426-autism-prevalence.html

Centers for Disease Control and Prevention (2018b). *Sudden unexpected infant death and sudden infant death syndrome*. Retrieved from https://www.cdc.gov/sids/data.htm

Centers for Disease Control and Prevention (2018c). *Youth Risk Behavior Surveillance— United States, 2017*. Retrieved from https://www.cdc.gov/healthyyouth/data/yrbs/pdf/2017/ss6708.pdf

Chaidez, V., Garcia, E. F. Y., Wang, L. W., Angkustsiri, K., Krakowiak, P., Hertz-Picciotto, I., & Hansen, R. L. (2018). Comparison of maternal beliefs about causes of autism spectrum disorder and association with utilization of services and treatments. *Child: Care, Health and Human Development, 44,* 916–925. doi: 10.1111/cch.12612

Chandler, S., Howlin, P., Simonoff, E., Kennedy, J., & Baird, G. (2016). Comparison of parental estimate of developmental age with measured IQ in children with neurodevelopmental disorders. *Child: Care, Health and Development, 42,* 486–493. doi: 10.1111/cch.12346

Chandra, P. S., Bhargavaraman, R. P., Raghunandan, V. N. G. P., & Shaligram, D. (2006). Delusions related to infant and their association with mother–infant interactions in postpartum psychotic disorders. *Archives of Women's Mental Health, 9,* 285–288. doi: 10.1007/s00737-006-0147-7

Chang, F., Lee, C., Miao, N., Lin, S., Lee, S., Lung, C., & Liao, H. (2013). Parent-adolescent discrepancies in reports of adolescent tobacco and alcohol use associated with family relationships in Taiwan. *Journal of Substance Use, 18,* 288–301. doi: 10.3109/14659891.2012.674624

Chang, F., Lee, C., Miao, N., Lin, S., Lung, C., Liao, H., . . . Zeng, W. (2015). Parental efficacy and adolescence competence skills associated with adolescent substance use. *Journal of Substance Use, 20,* 85–92. doi: 10.3109/14659891.2013.859752

Chau, V., & Giallo, R. (2015). The relationship between parental fatigue, parenting self-efficacy, and behaviour: Implications for supporting parents in the early parenting period. *Child: Care, Health and Development, 41,* 626–633. doi: 10.1111/cch.12205

Cheah, S. L., & Park, S. (2006). South Korean mothers' beliefs regarding aggression and social withdrawal in preschoolers. *Early Childhood Research Quarterly, 21,* 61–75. doi: 10.1016/j.ecresq.2006.01.004

Cheah, S. L., & Rubin, K. H. (2004). European American and mainline Chinese mothers' responses to aggression and social withdrawal in preschoolers. *International Journal of Behavioral Development, 28,* 83–94. doi: 10.1080/01650250344000299

Cheah, C. S. L., & Sheperd, K. A. (2011). A cross-cultural examination of Aboriginal and European Canadian mothers' beliefs regarding proactive and reactive aggression. *Infant and Child Development, 20,* 330–346. doi 10.1002/icd.701

Chen, H. (2001). Parents' attitudes and expectations regarding science education: Comparisons among American, Chinese-American, and Chinese families. *Adolescence, 36,* 305–313.

Chen, M., Johnston, C., Sheeber, L., & Leve, C. (2009). Parent and adolescent depressive symptoms: The role of parental attributions. *Journal of Abnormal Child Psychology, 37,* 119–130. doi: 10.1007/s10802-008-9264-2

Chen, R. J., Flores, G., & Shetgiri, R. (2016). African-American and Latino parents' attitudes and beliefs regarding adolescent fighting and its prevention. *Journal of Child and Family Studies, 25,* 1746–1754. doi: 10.1007/s10826-015-0355-8

Chen, X., & Chen, H. (2010). Children's social functioning and adjustment in the changing Chinese society. In R. K. Silbereisen & X. Chen (Eds.), *Social change and human development: Concepts and results* (pp. 209–226). London, England: Sage.

Chen, X., Chung, J., Lechcier-Kimel, R., & French, D. (2011). Culture and social development. In P. K. Smith & C. H. Hart (Eds.), *Wiley-Blackwell handbook of childhood social development* (2nd ed., pp. 141–160). Hoboken, NJ: Wiley.

Chen, X., & French, D. C. (2008). Children's social competence in cultural context. *Annual Review of Psychology, 59,* 591–616. doi: 10.1146/annurev.psych.59.103006.093606

Chen, X., & Schmidt, F. A. (2015). Temperament and personality. In R. M. Lerner (Series Ed.) & M. E. Lamb (Vol. Ed.), *Handbook of child psychology and developmental science: Vol. 3. Socioemotional processes* (7th ed., pp. 152–200). Hoboken, NJ: Wiley.

Chi, T. C., & Hinshaw, S. P. (2002). Mother-child relationships of children with ADHD: The role of maternal depressive symptoms and depression-related distortions. *Journal of Abnormal Child Psychology, 30,* 387–400. doi: 10.1023/A:1015770025043

Chiang, T., Barrett, K. C., & Nunez, N. N. (2000). Maternal attributions of Taiwanese and American toddlers' misdeeds and accomplishments. *Journal of Cross-Cultural Psychology, 31,* 349–368. doi: 10.1177/0022022100031003004

Child Trends (2015a). *Attitudes toward spanking.* Retrieved from https://www.childtrends.org/indicators/attitudes-toward-spanking/

Child Trends. (2015b). *Early school readiness.* Retrieved from https://www.childtrends.org/indicators/early-school-readiness/

Child Trends. (2015c). *Parental expectations for their children's academic attainment.* Retrieved from http://www.childtrends.org/wp-content/ uploads/2012/07/115_Parental_Expectations.pdf

Child Trends (2018). *Teen births.* Retrieved from https://www.childtrends.org/indicators/teen-births

Chiocca, E. M. (2016). American parents' attitudes and beliefs about corporal punishment: An integrative literature review. *Journal of Pediatric Health Care, 31,* 372–383. doi: 10.1016/j.pedhc.2017.01.002

Chisholm, V., Atkinson, L., Donaldson, C., Noyes, K., Payne, A., & Kelnar, C. (2011). Maternal communication style, problem-solving and dietary adherence in young children with type 1 diabetes. *Clinical Child Psychology and Psychiatry, 16,* 443–458. doi: 10.1177/1359104510373312

Cho, C., & Cheon, H. J. (2005). Children's exposure to negative Internet content: Effects of family context. *Journal of Broadcasting and Electronic Media, 49,* 488–509. doi: 10.1207/s15506878jobem4904_8

Choi, K. Y. K., & Kovshoff, H. (2013). Do maternal attributions play a role in the acceptability of behavioural interventions for problem behaviour in children with autism spectrum disorders? *Research in Autism Spectrum Disorders, 7,* 984–996. doi: 10.1016/j.rasd.2013.04.010

Chung, E. K., Mathew, L., Rothkopk, A. C., Elo, I. T., Coyne, J. G., & Culhane, J. F. (2009). Parenting attitudes and infant spanking: The influence of childhood experiences. *Pediatrics, 124,* e278–286. doi: 10.1542/peds.2008-3247

Cicchetti, D. (2013). Annual research review: Resilient functioning in maltreated children—past, present, and future perspectives. *Journal of Child Psychology and Psychiatry, 54,* 402–422. doi: 10.1111/j.1469-7610.2012.02608.x

Cicchetti, D. (2016). Socioemotional, personality, and biological development: Illustrations from a multilevel developmental psychopathology perspective on child maltreatment. *Annual Review of Psychology, 67,* 187–211. doi: 10.1146/annurev-psych-122414-033259

Cicchetti, D., & Toth, S. (2015). Child maltreatment. In R. M. Lerner (Series Ed.) & M. E. Lamb (Vol. Ed.), *Handbook of child psychology and developmental science: Vol. 3. Socioemotional processes* (7th ed., pp. 513–563). Hoboken, NJ: Wiley.

Cicchetti, D., & Toth, S. (2016). Child maltreatment and developmental psychopathology: A multilevel perspective. In D. Chicchetti (Ed.), *Developmental psychopathology: Vol. 3. Maladaptation and psychopathology* (3rd ed., pp. 457–512). Hoboken, NJ: Wiley.

Cichy, K. E., Lefkowitz, E. S., Davis, E. M., & Fingerman, K L. (2013). "You are such a disappointment!": Negative emotions and parents' perceptions of adult children's lack of success. *Journal of Gerontology, 68B,* 893–901. doi: 10.1093/geronb/gbt053

Civitas Initiative, Zero to Three, & Brio Corporation. (2000). *What grown-ups understand about child development: A national benchmark survey.* Washington, DC: Zero to Three, National Center for Infants, Toddlers, and Families.

Clark, D. A., Donnellan, M. B., Robins, R. W., & Conger, R. D. (2015). Early adolescent temperament, parental monitoring, and substance use in Mexican-origin adolescents. *Journal of Adolescence, 41,* 121–130. doi: 10.1016/j.adolescence.2015.02.010

Cole, P. M., & Tan, P. Z. (2015). Emotion socialization from a cultural perspective. In J. E. Grusec & P. Hastings (Eds.), *Handbook of socialization* (2nd ed., pp. 637–660). New York, NY: Guilford Press.

Coleman, P. K., & Karraker, K. H. (1998). Self-efficacy and parenting quality: Findings and future applications. *Developmental Review, 18*, 47–85. doi: 10.1006/drev.1997.0448

Coleman, P. K., & Karraker, K. H. (2000). Parenting self-efficacy among mothers of school-aged children: Conceptualization, measurement, and correlates. *Family Relations, 49*, 13–24. doi: 10.1111/j.1741-3729.2000.00013.x

Coleman, P. K., & Karraker, K. H. (2003). Maternal self-efficacy beliefs, competence in parenting, and toddlers' behavior and developmental status. *Infant Mental Health Journal, 24*, 126–148. doi: 10.1002/imhj.10048

Collier, K. M., Coyne, S. M., Rasmussen, E. E., Hawkins, A. J., Padilla-Walker, L. M., Erikson, S. E., & Memmott-Elison, M. K. (2016). Does parental mediation of media influence child outcomes? A meta-analysis of media time, aggression, substance use, and sexual behavior. *Developmental Psychology, 52*, 798–812. doi: 10.1037/dev0000108

Collins, W. A. (1992). Parents' cognitions and developmental changes in relationships during adolescence. In I. E. Sigel, A. V. McGillicuddy-DeLisi, & J. J. Goodnow (Eds.), *Parental belief systems* (2nd ed., pp. 175–197). Hillsdale, NJ: Erlbaum.

Collins, W. A., & Luebker, C. (1994). Parent and adolescent expectancies: Individual and relational significance. In J. G. Smetana (Ed.), *Beliefs about parenting: Origins and developmental implications* (pp. 65–80). San Francisco, CA: Jossey-Bass.

Collins, W. A., Maccoby, E. E., Steinberg, L., Hetherington, E. M., & Bornstein, M. H. (2000). Contemporary research on parenting: The case for nature *and* nurture. *American Psychologist, 55*, 218–232. doi: 10.1037/0003-066X.55.2.218

Collins, W. A., & Steinberg, L. (2006). Adolescent development in interpersonal context. In W. Damon & R. M. Lerner (Series Eds.) & N. Eisenberg (Vol. Ed.), *Handbook of child psychology: Vol. 3. Social, emotional, and personality development* (6th ed., pp. 1003–1067). Hoboken, NJ: Wiley.

Collins, W. A., Welsh, D. P., & Furman, W. (2009). Adolescent romantic relationships. *Annual Review of Psychology, 60*, 631–652. doi: 10.1146/annurev.psych.60.110707.163459

Combs-Orme, T., Orme, J. G., & Lefmann, T. (2013). Early brain development: African American mothers' cognitions about the first three years. *Child and Adolescent Social Work Journal, 30*, 329–344. doi: 10.1007/s10560-012-0294-9

Connell, A. M., & Goodman, S. H. (2002). The association between psychopathology in fathers versus mothers and children's internalizing and externalizing behavior problems: A meta-analysis. *Psychological Bulletin, 128*, 746–773. doi: 10.1037//0033-2909.128.5.746

Connolly, J. A., & McIsaac C. (2009). Romantic relationships in adolescence. In R. M Lerner & L. Steinberg (Eds.), *Handbook of adolescent psychology: Vol. 2. Contextual influences on adolescent development* (3rd ed., pp. 104–151). Hoboken, NJ: Wiley.

Conrad, B., Gross, D., Fogg, L., & Ruchala, P. (1992). Maternal confidence, knowledge, and quality of mother-toddler interactions: A preliminary study. *Infant Mental Health Journal, 13*, 353–362.

Cook, R. C., Williams, K., R., Guerra, N. G., Kim, T., E., & Sadek, S. (2010). Predictors of bullying and victimization in childhood and adolescence: A meta-analytic investigation. *School Psychology Quarterly, 25*, 65–83. doi: 10.1037/a0020149

Cooper, H., Steenbergen-Hu, S., & Dent, A. L. (2012). Homework. In K. R. Harris, S. Graham, T. Urdan, A. G. Bus, S. Major, & H. L. Swanson (Eds.), *APA Educational psychology handbook: Vol. 3. Application to learning and teaching* (pp. 475–495). Washington, DC: American Psychological Association.

Corcoran, J., Schildt, B., Hochbrueckner, R., & Abell, J. (2017). Parents of children with attention deficit/hyperactivity disorder: A meta-synthesis, part II. *Child and Adolescent Social Work Journal, 34,* 337–348. doi: 10.1007/s10560-017-0497-1

Cote, L. R., & Azar, S. T. (1997). Child age, parent and child gender, and domain differences in parents' attributions and responses to children's outcomes. *Sex Roles, 36,* 23–50. doi: 10.1007/BF02766237

Cote, L. R., & Bornstein, M. H. (2003). Cultural and parenting cognitions in acculturating cultures. 1. Cultural comparisons and developmental continuity and stability. *Journal of Cross-Cultural Psychology, 34,* 324–349. doi: 10.1177/0022022103034003006

Cotler, S., & Shoemaker, D. J. (1969). The accuracy of mothers' reports. *Journal of Genetic Psychology, 114,* 97–107.

Cottone, E. A. (2012). Preschoolers' emergent literacy skills: The mediating role of maternal reading beliefs. *Early Education and Development, 23,* 351–372. doi: 10.1080/10409289.2010.527581

Crandall, A. A., Ghazarian, S. R., Deater-Deckard, K., Bell, M. A., & Riley, A. W. (2018). The interface of maternal cognitions and executive functioning in parenting and child conduct problems. *Family Relations, 67,* 339–353. doi: 10.1111/fare.12318

Crick, N. R., & Dodge, K. A. (1994). A review and reformulation of social-information processing mechanisms in children's social adjustment. *Psychological Bulletin, 115,* 74–101. doi: 10.1037/0033-2909.115.1.74

Crittenden, P. M. (1993). An information-processing perspective on the behavior of neglectful parents. *Criminal Justice and Behavior, 20,* 27–48. doi: 10.1177/0093854893020001004

Crittenden, P. M. (2016). *Raising parents: Attachment, representation, and treatment* (2nd ed.). New York, NY: Routledge.

Crouter, A. C., Bumpus, M. F., Davis, K. D., & McHale, S. M. (2005). How do parents learn about adolescents experiences? Implications for parental knowledge and adolescent risky behavior. *Child Development, 76,* 869–882. doi: 10.1111/j.1467-8624.2005.00883.x.

Crouter, A. C., & Head, M. R. (2002). Parental monitoring and knowledge of children. In M. H. Bornstein (Ed.), *Handbook of parenting: Vol. 3. Being and becoming a parent* (2nd ed., pp. 461–483). Mahwah, NJ: Erlbaum.

Crouter, A. C., Helms-Erikson, H., Updegraff, K., & McHale, S. M. (1999). Conditions underlying parents' knowledge about children's daily lives in middle childhood: Between- and within- family comparisons. *Child Development, 70,* 246–259. doi: 10.1111/1467-8624.00018

Crncec, R., Barnett, B., & Matthey, S. (2010). Review of scales of parenting confidence. *Journal of Nursing Measurement, 18,* 2010–2040. doi: 10.1891/1061-3749.18.3.210

Cruz, L. P., Camargos-Junior, W., & Rocha, F. L. (2013). The broad autism phenotype in parents of individuals with autism: A systematic review of the literature. *Trends in Psychiatry and Psychotherapy, 35,* 252–263.doi: 10.1590/2237-6089-2013-0019

Cummings, E. M., Cheung, R. Y. M., & Davies, P. T. (2013). Prospective relations between parental depression, negative expressiveness, emotional security, and children's internalizing symptoms. *Child Psychiatry and Human Development, 44,* 698–708. doi: 10.1007/s10578-013-0362-1

Cummings, E. M., Keller P. S., & Davies, P. T. (2005). Towards a family process model of maternal and paternal depressive symptoms: Exploring multiple relations with child and family functioning. *Journal of Child Psychology and Psychiatry, 46*, 479–489. doi: 10.1111/j.1469-7610.2004.00368.x

Daddis, C., & Smetana, J. G. (2014). Parenting from the social domain theory perspective: This time it's personal. In L. M. Scheier & W. B. Hansen (Eds.), *Parenting and teen drug use* (pp. 110–126). New York, NY: Oxford University Press.

Daga, S. S., Raval, V. V., & Raj, S. P. (2015). Maternal meta-emotion and child socioemotional functioning in immigrant Indian and White American families. *Asian American Journal of Psychology, 6*, 233–241. doi: 10.1037/aap0000014

Dahl, A., & Campos, J. J. (2013). Domain differences in early social interactions. *Child Development, 84*, 817–825. doi: 10.1111/cdev.12002

Dahl, A., Sherlock, B. R., Campos, J. J., & Theunissen, F. E. (2014). Mothers' tone of voice depends on the nature of infants' transgressions. *Emotion, 14*, 651–665. doi: 10.1037/a0036608

Dai, D. Y., & Schader, R. M. (2002). Decisions regarding music training: Parental beliefs and values. *Gifted Child Quarterly, 46*, 135–144. doi: 10.1177/001698620204600206

Damianova, M. K., & Sullivan, G. B. (2011). Rereading Vygotsky's theses on types of internalization and verbal mediation. *Review of General Psychology, 15*, 344–350. doi: 10.1037/a0025627

Danielson, M. L., Bitsko, R. H., Ghadour, R. M., Holbrook, J. R., Kogan, M. D., & Blumberg, S. J. (2018). Prevalence of parent-reported ADHD diagnosis and associated treatment among US children and adolescents, 2016. *Journal of Clinical Child and Adolescent Psychology, 47*, 199–212. doi: 10.1080/15374416.2017.1417860

Dardennes, R. M., Al Anbar, N. N., Prado-Netto, A., Kaye, K., Contejean, Y., & Al Anbar, N. (2011). Treating the cause of illness rather than the symptoms: Parental causal beliefs and treatment choices in autism spectrum disorder. *Research in Developmental Disabilities, 32*, 1137–1146. doi: 10.1016/j.ridd.2011.01.010

Darling, N., Cumsille, P., Caldwell, L. L., & Dowdy, B. (2006). Predictors of adolescents' disclosures to parents and perceived parental knowledge: Between- and within-person differences. *Journal of Youth and Adolescence, 35*, 667–678. doi: 10.1007/s10964-006-9058-1

Dasen, P. R. (1984). The cross-cultural study of intelligence: Piaget and the Baoule. *International Journal of Psychology, 19*, 407–434. doi: 10.1080/00207598408247539

Davidsen, K. A., Harder, S., MacBeth, A., Lundy, J., & Gumley, A. (2015). Mother-infant interaction in schizophrenia: Transmitting risk or resilience? A systematic review of the literature. *Social Psychiatry and Psychiatric Epidemiology, 50*, 1785–1798. doi: 10.1007/s00127-015-1127-x

DeBaryshe, B. D. (1995). Maternal belief systems: Linchpin in the home reading process. *Journal of Applied Developmental Psychology, 16*, 1–20. doi: 10.1016/0193-3973(95)90013-6

de Haan, A. D., Prinzie, P., & Dekovic, M. (2009). Mothers' and fathers' personality and parenting: The mediating role of sense of competence. *Developmental Psychology, 45*, 1695–1707. doi: 10.1037/a0016121

Dekovic, M., Noom, M. J., & Meeus, W. (1997). Expectations regarding development during adolescence: Parental and adolescent perceptions. *Journal of Youth and Adolescence, 26*, 253–272. doi: 10.1007/s10964-005-0001-7

Delgado-Hachey, M., & Miller, S. A. (1993). Mothers' accuracy in predicting their children's IQs: Its relationship to antecedent variables, mothers' academic achievement demands, and children's achievement. *Journal of Experimental Education, 62,* 43–59. doi 10.1080/00220973.1993.9943830

de Looze, M., Constantine, N. A., Jerman, P., Vermeulen-Smit, & Bogt, T. (2015). Parent-adolescent sexual communication and its association with adolescent sexual behavior: A nationally representative analysis in the Netherlands. *Journal of Sex Research, 52,* 257–268. doi: 10.1080/00224499.2013.858307

De Los Reyes, A., Goodman, K. L., Kliewer, W., & Reid-Quinones, K. (2010). The longitudinal consistency of mother-child reporting discrepancies of parental monitoring and their ability to predict child delinquent behaviors two years later. *Journal of Youth and Adolescence, 39,* 1417–1430. doi: 10.1007/s10964-009-9496-7

De Los Reyes, A., & Kazdin, A. E. (2005). Informant discrepancies in the assessment of childhood psychopathology: A critical review, theoretical framework, and recommendations for further study. *Psychological Bulletin, 131,* 483–509. doi: 10.1037/0033-2909.131.4.483

De Los Reyes, A., Wang, M., Thomas, S. A., Drabick, D. A. G., Burgers, D. E., & Rabinowitz, J. (2015). The validity of the multi-informant approach to assessing child and adolescent mental health. *Psychological Bulletin, 141,* 858–900. doi: 10.1037/a0038498

Del Vecchio, T., & O'Leary, S. G. (2008). Predicting maternal discipline responses to early child aggression. *Parenting: Science and Practice, 8,* 240–256. doi: 10.1080/15295190802204827

Demers, I., Bernier, A., Tarabulsy, G. M., & Provost, M. A. (2010). Mind-mindedness in adult and adolescent mothers: Relations to maternal sensitivity and infant attachment. *International Journal of Behavioral Development, 34,* 529–537. doi: 10.1177/0165025410365802

De Montigny, F., & Lacharite, C. (2005). Perceived parental efficacy: Concept analysis. *Journal of Advanced Nursing, 49,* 387–396. doi: 10.1111/j.1365-2648.2004.03302.x

Denham, S., Caal, S., Bassett, H. H., Benga, O., & Geangu, E. (2004). Listening to parents: Cultural variations in the meaning of emotions and emotion socialization. *Cognitie Creier Comportament, 8,* 321–349.

Dennis, C., & McQueen, K. (2009). The relationship between infant-feeding outcomes and postpartum depression: A qualitative systematic review. *Pediatrics, 123,* e736–e751. doi: 10.1542/peds.2008-1629

de Rosnay, M., Pons, F., Harris, P. L., & Morrell, J. M. B. (2004). A lag between understanding false belief and emotion attribution in young children: Relationships with linguistic ability and mothers' mental-state language. *British Journal of Developmental Psychology, 22,* 197–218. doi: 10.1348/026151004323044573

Diamond, L. M., & Savin-Williams, R. C. (2009). Adolescent sexuality. In R. M Lerner & L. Steinberg (Eds.), *Handbook of adolescent psychology: Vol. 1. Individual bases of adolescent development* (3rd ed., pp. 479–523). Hoboken, NJ: Wiley.

Dickens, C. (1859). *A tale of two cities.* London, England: Chapman and Hall.

DiPietro, J., Voegtline, K. M., Pater, H. A., & Costigan, K. A. (2018). Predicting child temperament and behavior from the fetus. *Development and Psychopathology, 30,* 855–870. doi: 10.1017/S0954579418000482

Dishion, T. J., & McMahon, R. J. (1998). Parental monitoring and the prevention of child and adolescent problem behavior: A conceptual and empirical reformulation. *Clinical Child and Family Psychology Review, 1,* 61–75. doi: 10.1023/A:1021800432380

Dishion, T. J., Nelson, S. E., & Kavanagh, K. (2003). The Family Check-Up with high-risk young adolescents: Preventing early-onset substance use by parent monitoring. *Behavior Therapy, 34,* 553–571. doi: 10.1016/S0005-7894(03)80035-7

Dittus, P. J., Michael, S. L., Becasen, J. S., Gloppen, K. M., McCarthy, K., & Guilamo-Ramos, V. (2015). Parental monitoring and its associations with adolescent sexual risk behavior: A meta-analysis. *Pediatrics, 136,* e1587–e1599. doi: 10.1542/peds.2015-0305

Dix, T., & Grusec, J. (1985). Parent attribution processes in the socialization of children. In I. E. Sigel (Ed.), *Parental belief systems* (pp. 201–233). Hillsdale, NJ: Erlbaum.

Dix, T., & Lochman, J. E. (1990). Social cognition and negative reactions to children: A comparison of mothers of aggressive and nonaggressive boys. *Journal of Social and Clinical Psychology, 9,* 418–438. doi: 10.1521/jscp.1990.9.4.418

Dix, T., & Meunier, L. (2009). Depressive symptoms and parenting competence: An analysis of 13 regulatory processes. *Developmental Review, 29,* 45–68. doi: 10.1016/j.dr.2008.11.002

Dix, T., Reinhold, D. P., & Zambarano, R. J. (1990). Mothers' judgment in moments of anger. *Merrill-Palmer Quarterly, 36,* 465–486.

Dix, T., Ruble, D., Grusec, J. E., & Nixon, S. (1986). Social cognition in parents: Inferential and affective reactions to children of three age levels. *Child Development, 57,* 879–894. doi: 10.2307/1130365

Dix, T., Ruble, D., & Zambarano, R. J. (1989). Mothers' implicit theories of discipline: Child effects, parent effects, and the attribution process. *Child Development, 60,* 1373–1391. doi: 10.1111/1467-8624.ep9772432

Dodge, K. A. (1986). A social information processing model of social competence in children. In M. Perlmutter (Ed.), *The Minnesota Symposium on Child Psychology* (Vol. 18, pp. 77–125). Hillsdale, NJ: Erlbaum.

Dodge, K. A., Coie, J. D., & Lynam, D. (2006). Aggression and antisocial behavior in youth. In W. Damon & R. M. Lerner (Series Eds.) & N. Eisenberg (Vol. Ed.), *Handbook of child psychology: Vol. 3. Social, emotional, and personality development* (6th ed., pp. 719–788). Hoboken, NJ: Wiley.

Dotterer, A. M., & Wehrspann, E. (2016). Parental knowledge: Examining reporter discrepancies and links to school engagement among middle school students. *Journal of Youth and Adolescence, 45,* 2431–2443. doi: 10.1007/s10964-016-0550-y

Doyle, A. C., & Le Grange, D. (2015). Family-based treatment for anorexia in adolescents. In H. Thompson-Brenner (Ed.), *Casebook of evidence-based therapy for eating disorders* (pp. 43–70). New York, NY: Guilford Press.

Drysdale, K., Shores, A., & Levick, W. R. (2004). Use of the Everyday Memory Questionnaire with children. *Child Neuropsychology, 10,* 67–75. doi: 10.1080/09297040490911087

Duell, N., Steinberg, L., Icenogle, G., Chein, J. Chaudhary, N., Di Giunta, L., . . . Chang, L. (2018). Age patterns in risk taking across the world. *Journal of Youth and Adolescence, 47,* 1052–1072. doi: 10.1007/s10964-017-0752-y

Dumka, L. E., Gonzales, N. A., Wheeler, L. A., & Millsap, R. E. (2010). Parenting self-efficacy and parenting practices over time in Mexican American families. *Issues in Comprehensive Pediatric Nursing, 24,* 522–531. doi: 10.1037/a0020833

Dunn, J. (2014). Moral development in early childhood and social interaction in the family. In M. Killen & J. G. Smetana (Eds.), *Handbook of moral development* (2nd ed., pp. 135–159). New York, NY: Psychology Press.

Dunn, J. (2015). Siblings. In J. E. Grusec & P. D. Hastings (Eds.), *Handbook of socialization: Theory and research* (2nd ed., pp. 182–201. New York, NY: Guilford Press.

Dunsmore, J. C., Her, P., Halberstadt, A. G., & Perez-Rivera, M. B. (2009). Parents' beliefs about emotions and children's recognition of parents' emotions. *Journal of Nonverbal Behavior, 33*, 121–140. doi: 10.1007/s10919-008-0066-6

Dunsmore, J. C., & Karn, M. A. (2001). Mothers' beliefs about feelings and children's emotional understanding. *Early Education and Development, 12*, 117–138. doi: 10.1207/s15566935eed1201_7

Dunsmore, J. C., & Karn, M. A. (2004). The influence of peer relationships and maternal socialization on kindergartners' developing emotion knowledge. *Early Education and Development, 15*, 39–56. doi: 10.1207/s15566935eed1501_3

DuPaul, G. J., Power, T. J., Anastopoulos, A. D., & Reid, R. (2016). *ADHD Rating Scale-5 for children and adolescents: Checklists, norms, and clinical interpretation.* New York, NY: Guilford Press.

DuPaul, G. J., Reid, R., Anastopoulos, A. D., Lambert, M. C., Watkins, M. W., & Power, T. J. (2016). Parent and teacher ratings of attention-deficit/hyperactivity disorder symptoms: Factor structure and normative data. *Psychological Assessment, 28*, 214–225. doi: 10.1037/pas0000166

Durgel, E. S., van de Vijver, F. J. R., & Yagmurlu, B. (2013). Self-reported maternal expectations and child-rearing practices: Disentangling the associations with ethnicity, immigration, and educational background. *International Journal of Behavioral Development, 37*, 35–43. doi: 10.1177/0165025412456145

Dweck, C. S. (1999). *Self-theories: Their role in motivation, personality, and development.* New York, NY: Psychology Press.

Dweck, C. S. (2006). *Mindset: The new psychology of success.* New York, NY: Random House.

Dweck, C. S. (2017). The journey to children's mindsets—and beyond. *Child Development Perspectives, 11*, 139–144. doi: 10.1111/cdep.1222 5

Dweck, C. S., Chiu, C., & Hong, Y. (1995). Implicit theories and their role in judgments and reactions: A world from two perspectives. *Psychological Inquiry, 6*, 267–285. doi: 10.1207/s15327965pli0604_

Eisenberg, N. (1986). *Altruistic emotion, cognition, and behavior.* Hillsdale, NJ: Erlbaum.

Eisenberg, N. (2000). Emotion, regulation, and moral development. *Annual Review of Psychology, 51*, 665–697. doi: 10.1146/annurev.psych.51.1.665

Eisenberg, N., Spinrad, T. L., & Knafo-Noam, A. (2015). Prosocial development. In R. M. Lerner (Series Ed.) & M. E. Lamb (Vol. Ed.), *Handbook of child psychology and developmental science: Vol. 3. Socioemotional processes* (7th ed., pp. 610–656). Hoboken, NJ: Wiley.

Eisenberg-Berg, N. (1979). Development of children's prosocial moral judgment. *Developmental Psychology, 15*, 128–137. doi: 10.1037/0012-1649.15.2.128

Eisner, M. P., & Malti, T. (2015). Aggressive and violent behavior. In R. M. Lerner (Series Ed.) & M. E. Lamb (Vol. Ed.), *Handbook of child psychology and developmental science: Vol. 3. Socioemotional processes* (7th ed., pp. 794–841). Hoboken, NJ: Wiley.

Elder, G. H., Jr. (1999). *Children of the great depression* (25th anniversary ed.). Boulder, CO: Westview Press.

Elliott, L., & Bachman, H. J. (2018). SES disparities in early math abilities: The contribution of parents' math cognitions, practices to support math, and math talk. *Developmental Review, 49*, 1–15. doi: 10.1016/j.dr.2018.08.001

Elsaesser, C., Russell, B., Ohanessian, C. M., & Patton, D. (2017). Parenting in a digital age: A review of parents' role in preventing adolescent cyberbullying. *Aggression and Violent Behavior, 35*, 62–72. doi: 10.1016/j.avb.2017.06.004

Else-Quest, N. M., & Morse, E. (2015). Ethnic variations in parental socialization and adolescent ethnic identity: A longitudinal study. *Cultural Diversity and Ethnic Minority Psychology, 21*, 54–64. doi: 10.1037/a0037820

Engels, R. C. M. E., Van der Vorst, H., Dekovic, M., & Meeus, W. (2007). Correspondence in collateral and self-reports on alcohol consumption: A within family analysis. *Addictive Behaviors, 32*, 1016–1030. doi: 10.1016/j.addbeh.2006.07.006

Enlund, E., Aunola, K., & Nurmi, J. (2015). Stability in parents' causal attributions for their children's academic performance: A nine-year follow-up. *Merrill-Palmer Quarterly, 61*, 509–536. doi: 10.13110/merrpalmquar1982.61.4.0509

Enlund, E., Aunola, K., Tolvanen, A., Lerkkanen, M., & Nurmi, J. (2017). Parental ability attributions regarding children's academic performance: Person-oriented approach on longitudinal data. *Journal of Applied Developmental Psychology, 52*, 12–23. doi: 10.1016/j.appdev.2017.06.003

Enlund, E., Aunola, K., Tolvanen, A., & Nurmi, J. (2015). Parental causal attributions and emotions in daily learning situations with the child. *Journal of Family Psychology, 20*, 568–575. doi: 10.1037/fam0000130

Ennett, S. T., Jackson, C., Cole, V. T., Haws, S., Foshee, V. A., Reyes, H. L. M., . . . Cai, L. (2016). A multidimensional model of mothers' perceptions of parent alcohol socialization and adolescent alcohol misuse. *Psychology of Addictive Behaviors, 30*, 19–28. doi: 10.1037/adb0000119

Entwisle, D. R., & Hayduk, L. A. (1978). *Too great expectations: The academic outlook of young children.* Baltimore, MD: John Hopkins University Press.

Epkins, C. C., & Harper, S. L. (2016). Mothers' and fathers' parental warmth, hostility/ rejection/neglect, and behavioral control: Specific and unique relations with parents' depression versus anxiety symptoms. *Parenting: Science and Practice, 16*, 125–145. doi: 10.1080/15295192.2016.1134991

Epley, N., Morewedge, C. K., & Keysar, B. (2004). Perspective taking in children and adults: Equivalent egocentrism but differential correction. *Journal of Experimental Social Psychology, 40*, 760–768. doi: 10.1016/j.jesp.2004.02.002

Erdley, C. A., Cain, K. M., Loomis, C. C., Dumas-Hines, F., & Dweck, C. S. (1997). Relations among children's social goals, implicit personality theories, and responses to social failure. *Developmental Psychology, 33*, 263–272. doi: 10.1037/0012-1649.33.2.263

Ereky-Stevens, K. (2008). Associations between mothers' sensitivity to infants' internal states and children's later understanding of mind and emotion. *Infant and Child Development, 17*, 527–543. doi: 10.1002/icd.572

Erel, O., & Burman, B. (1995). Interrelatedness of marital relations and parent-child relations: A meta-analytic review. *Psychological Bulletin, 118*, 108–132. doi: 10.1037/ 0033-2909.118.1.108

Erikson, E. (1968). *Identity: Youth and crisis.* New York, NY: Norton.

Ertem, I. O., Atay, G., Dogan, D. G., Bayhan, A., Bingoler, B. E., Gok, C. G., . . . Isikli, S. (2007). Mothers' knowledge of young child development in a developing country. *Child: Care, Health and Development, 33*, 728–737. doi: 10.1111/j.1365-2214.2007.00751.x

Esposito, G., Nakazawa, J., Venuti, P., & Bornstein, M. H. (2015). Judgment of infant cry: The roles of acoustic characteristics and sociodemographic characteristics. *Japanese Psychological Research, 57*, 126–134. doi: 10.1111/jpr.12072

Ewart, J. C., & Green, M. C. (1957). Conditions associated with the mother's esti-mate of the ability of her retarded child. *American Journal of Mental Deficiency, 62,* 521–533.

Fairbairn, C. E., Briley, D. E., Kang, D., Fraley, R. C., Hankin, B. L., & Ariss, T. (2018). A meta-analysis of longitudinal associations between substance use and interpersonal at-tachment security. *Psychological Bulletin, 144,* 532–555. doi: 10.1037/bul0000141

Families Special Interest Research Group. (2014). Families supporting a child with intel-lectual or developmental disabilities: The current state of knowledge. *Journal of Applied Research in Intellectual Disabilities, 27,* 420–430. doi: 10.1111/jar.12078

Farrington, D. P., Jolliffe, D., Loeber, R., Stouthamer-Loeber, M., & Kalb, L. M. (2001). The concentration of offenders in families, and family criminality in the prediction of boys' delinquency. *Journal of Adolescence, 24,* 579–596. doi: 10.1006/jado.2001.0424

Farris, J., Lefever, J. E. B., Borkowski, J. G., & Whitman, T. L. (2013). Two are better than one: The joint influence of maternal preparedness for parenting and children's self-esteem on academic achievement and adjustment. *Early Education and Development, 24,* 346–365. doi: 10.1080/10409289.2012.658551

Farrow, C., & Blissett, J. (2014). Maternal mind-mindedness during infancy, general par-enting sensitivity and observed child feeding behavior: A longitudinal study. *Attachment and Human Development, 16,* 230–241. doi: 10.1080/14616734.2014.898158

Farver, J. A. M., & Howes, C. (1993). Cultural differences in American and Mexican mother–child pretend play. *Merrill-Palmer Quarterly, 39,* 344–358.

Farver, J. A. M., Kim, Y. K., & Lee, Y. (1995). Cultural differences in Korean- and Anglo-American preschoolers' social interaction and play behaviors. *Child Development, 66,* 1088–1099. doi: 10.1111/1467-8624.ep9509180276

Favez, N., Tissot, H., Frascarolo, F., Stiefel, F., & Despland, J. (2016). Sense of competence and beliefs about parental roles in mothers and fathers as predictors of coparenting and child engagement in mother-father-infant triadic interactions. *Infant and Child Development, 25,* 283–301. doi: 10.1002/icd.1934

Fawcett, J. T. (1972). *The satisfactions and costs of children: Theories, concepts, methods.* Honolulu, HI: East-West Center.

Fay-Stammbach, T., Hawes, D. J., & Meredith, P. (2014). Parenting influences on execu-tive function in early childhood: A review. *Child Development Perspectives, 8,* 258–264. doi: 10.1111/cdep.12095

Fearon, R. P., Bakersman-Kranenburg, M. J., IJzendoorn, M. H., Lapsley, A., & Roisman, G. I. (2010). The significance of insecure attachment and disorganization in the devel-opment of children's externalizing behavior: A meta-analytic study. *Child Development, 81,* 435–456. doi: 10.1111/j.1467-8624.2009.01405.x.

Feldman, S. S., & Quatman, T. (1988). Factors influencing age expectations for adolescent autonomy: A study of early adolescents and parents. *Journal of Early Adolescence, 8,* 325–343. doi: 10.1177/0272431688084002

Fenson, L., Dale, P. S., Reznick, J. S., Bates, E., Thal, D. J., & Pethick, S. J. (1994). Variability in early communicative development. *Monographs of the Society for Research in Children, 59*(5). doi: 10.1111/1540-5834.ep9502141733

Fenson, L., Marchman, V. A., Thal, D., Dale, P., Reznick, J. S., & Bates, E. (2007). *MacArthur-Bates Communicative Development Inventories: User's guide and technical manual* (2nd ed.). Baltimore, MD: Brookes Publishing Company.

Fernandez-Alcantara, M., Correa-Delgado, C., Munoz, A., Salvatierra, M. T., Fuentes-Helices, T., & Laynez-Rubio, C. (2017). Parenting a child with a learning disability: A qualitative approach. *International Journal of Disability, Development and Education, 64,* 526–543. doi: 10.1080/1034912X.2017.1296938

Fernandez-Hermida, J., Calafat, A., Secades-Villa, R., Juan, M., & Sumnall, H. (2013). Cross-national study of factors that influence parents' knowledge about their children's alcohol use. *Journal of Drug Education, 43,* 155–172. doi: 10.2190/DE.43.2.d

Fernyhough, C. (2008). Getting Vygotskian about theory of mind: Mediation, dialogue, and the development of social understanding. *Developmental Review, 28,* 225–262. doi: 10.1016/j.dr.2007.03.001

Fidler, D. J., Hodapp, R. M., & Dykens, E. M. (2002). Behavioral phenotypes and special education: Parent report of educational issues for children with Down syndrome, Prader-Willi syndrome, and Williams syndrome. *Journal of Special Education, 36,* 80–88. doi: 10.1177/00224669020360020301

Field, T. M. (2010). Postpartum depression effects on early interactions, parenting, and safety practices: A review. *Infant Behavior and Development, 33,* 1–6. doi: 10.1016/j.infbeh.2009.10.005

Field, T. M. (2017). Infant sleep problems and interventions: A review. *Infant Behavior and Development, 47,* 40–53. doi: 10.1016/j.infbeh.2017.02.002

Fikkers, K. M., Piotrowski, J. T., & Valkenburg, P. M. (2017). A matter of style? Exploring the effects of parental mediation styles on early adolescents' media violence exposure and aggression. *Computers in Human Behavior, 70,* 407–415. doi: 10.1016/j.chb.2017.01.029

Fincham, F. D., & Grynch, J. H. (1991). Explanations for family events in distressed and nondistressed couples: Is one type of explanation used consistently? *Journal of Family Psychology, 4,* 341–353. doi: 10.1037/0893-3200.4.3.341

Fincham, F. D., & Hall, J. H. (2005). Parenting and the marital relationship. In T. Luster & L. Okagaki (Eds.), *Parenting: An ecological perspective* (2nd ed., pp. 205–233). Mahwah, NJ: Erlbaum.

Fingerman, K. L., Cheng, Y., Birditt, K., & Zarit, S. (2012). Only as happy as the least happy child: Multiple grown children's problems and successes and middle-age parents' well-being. *Journal of Gerontology, 67B,* 184–193. doi: 10.1093/geronb/gbr086

Fischbach, R. L., Harris, M. J., Ballan, M. S., Fischbach, G. D., & Link, B. G. (2016). Is there concordance in attitudes and beliefs between parents and scientists about autism spectrum disorder? *Autism, 20,* 353–363. doi: 10.1177%2F1362361315585310

Fisher, K. R., Hirsh-Pasek, K., Golinkoff, R., & Gryfe, S. G. (2008). Conceptual split? Parents' and experts' perceptions of play in the 21st century. *Journal of Applied Developmental Psychology, 29,* 305–316. doi: 10.1016/j.appdev.2008.04.006

Fisher, S. L., Bucholz. K. K., Reich, W., Fox, L., Kuperman, S., Kramer, J., . . . Bierut, L. J. (2006). Teenagers are right—Parents do not know much: An analysis of adolescent-parent agreement on reports of adolescent substance use, abuse, and dependence. *Alcoholism: Clinical and Experimental Research, 30,* 1699–1710. doi: 10.1111/j.1530-0277.2006.00205.x

Fivush, R., Brotman, M. A., Buckner, J. P., & Goodman, S. H. (2000). Gender differences in parent-child emotion narratives. *Sex Roles, 42,* 233–254. doi: 10.1023/A:1007091207068

Fletcher, A. C., Steinberg, L., & Williams-Wheeler, M. (2004). Parental influences on adolescent problem behavior: Revisiting Stattin and Kerr. *Child Development, 75,* 781–796. doi: 10.1111/j.1467-8624.2004.00706.x

Fogle, L. M., & Mendez, J. L. (2006). Assessing the play beliefs of African American mothers with preschool children. *Early Childhood Research Quarterly, 21*, 507–518. doi: 10.1016/j.ecresq.2006.08.002

Foley, S., & Hughes, C. (2018). Great expectations? Do mothers' and fathers' prenatal thoughts and feelings about the infant predict parent-infant interaction quality? A meta-analytic review. *Developmental Review, 48*, 40–54. doi: 10.1016/j.dr.2018.03.007

Fonagy, P., & Target, M. (1997). Attachment and reflective function: Their role in self-organization. *Development and Psychopathology, 9*, 679–700. doi: 10.1017/S0954579497001399

Frank, M. C., Braginsky, M., Yurovsky, D., & Marchman, V. A. (2017). Wordbank: An open repository for developmental vocabulary data. *Journal of Child Language, 44*, 677–694. doi: 10.1017/S0305000916000209

Frick, P. J. (2004). *The Inventory of Callous-Unemotional Traits*. Unpublished rating scale, University of New Orleans, New Orleans, LA.

Friedlmeier, W., Corapci, F., & Cole, P. M. (2011). Emotion socialization in cross-cultural perspective. *Social and Personality Psychology Compass, 5*, 410–427. doi: 10.1111/j.1751-9004.2011.00362.x

Friedman, N. P., Miyake, A., Young, S. E., DeFries, J. C., Corley, R. P., & Hewitt, J. K. (2008). Individual differences in executive function are almost entirely genetic in origin. *Journal of Experimental Psychology: General, 137*, 201–225. doi: 10.1037/0096-3445.137.2.201

Frith, C. D. (1992). *The cognitive neuropsychology of schizophrenia*. New York, NY: Psychology Press.

Frome, P. M., & Eccles, J. S. (1998). Parents' influence on children's achievement-related perceptions. *Journal of Personality and Social Psychology, 74*, 435–452. doi: 10.1037/0022-3514.74.2.435

Fry, P. S. (1985). Relations between teenagers' age, knowledge, expectations and maternal behaviour. *British Journal of Developmental Psychology, 3*, 47–55.

Fujiwara, T., Yamada, F., Okuyama, M., Kamimaki, I., Shikoro, N., & Barr, R. G. (2012). Effectiveness of educational materials designed to change knowledge and behavior about crying and shaken baby syndrome: A replication of a randomized control trial in Japan. *Child Abuse and Neglect, 36*, 613–620. doi: 10.1016/j.chiabu.2012.07.003

Fung, H., & Chen, E. C. (2001). Across time and beyond skin: Self and transgression in the everyday socialization among Taiwanese preschool children. *Social Development, 10*, 419–437. doi: 10.1111/1467-9507.00173

Furman, W. (2018). The romantic relationships of youth. In W. M. Bukowski, B. Laursen, & K. H. Rubin (Eds.), *Handbook of peer interactions, relationships, and groups* (2nd ed., pp. 410–428). New York, NY: Guilford Press.

Furman, W., & Lanthier, R. (2002). Parenting siblings. In M. H. Bornstein (Ed.), *Handbook of parenting: Vol. 1. Children and parenting* (2nd ed., pp. 165–188). Mahwah, NJ: Erlbaum

Furman, W., & Rose, A. J. (2015). Friendships, romantic relationships, and peer relationships. In R. M. Lerner (Series Ed.) & M. E. Lamb (Vol. Ed.), *Handbook of child psychology and developmental science: Vol. 3. Socioemotional processes* (7th ed., pp. 932–974). Hoboken, NJ: Wiley.

Furnham, A. (2000). Parents' estimates of their own and their children's multiple intelligences. *British Journal of Developmental Psychology, 18*, 583–594. doi: 10.1348/026151000165869

Furnham, A., & Bunclark, K. (2006). Sex differences in parents' estimations of their own and their children's intelligence. *Intelligence, 34,* 1–14. doi: 10.1016/j.intell.2005.05.005

Furnham, A., & Fukumoto, S. (2008). Japanese parents' estimates of their own and their children's multiple intelligences: Cultural modesty and moderate differentiation. *Japanese Psychological Research, 50,* 63–76. doi: 10.1111/j.1468-5884.2008.00362.x

Furnham, A., & Mkhize, N. (2003). Zulu mothers' beliefs about their own and their children's intelligence. *Journal of Social Psychology, 143,* 83–94. doi: 10.1080/00224540309598432

Furnham, A., & Valgeirsson, H. (2007). Parents' estimations of their own intelligence and that of their children: A comparison between English and Icelandic parents. *Scandinavian Journal of Psychology, 48,* 289–298. doi: 10.1111/j.1467-9450.2007.00587.x

Furnham, A., & Wu, C. (2014). The little emperor: Chinese parents' assessments of their own, their partner's and their only child's intelligence. *High Ability Studies, 25,* 121–141. doi: 10.1080/13598139.2014.966065

Gartstein, M. A., Bridgett, D. J., Dishion, T. J., & Kaufman, N. K. (2009). Depressed mood and maternal report of child behavior problems: Another look at the depression-distortion hypothesis. *Journal of Applied Developmental Psychology, 30,* 149–160. doi: 10.1016/j.appdev.2008.12.001

Gaskins, S. (2015). Childhood practices across cultures: Play and household work. In L. A. Jensen (Ed.), *The Oxford handbook of human development and culture* (pp. 185–197). New York, NY: Oxford University Press.

Gaydos, L. M., Blake, S. C., Gazmararian, J. C., Woodruff, W., Thompson, W. W., & Dalmida, S. G. (2015). Revisiting safe sleep recommendations for African-American infants: Why current counseling is inefficient. *Maternal and Child Health Journal, 19,* 496–503. doi: 10.1007/s10995-014-1530-z

George, C., Kaplan, N., & Main, M. (1985). *Adult Attachment Interview.* Unpublished manuscript: University of California at Berkeley, Berkeley, CA.

Georgiou, S. N. (1999). Achievement attributions of sixth grade children and their parents. *Educational Psychology, 19,* 399–412. doi: 10.1080/0144341990190402

Gershoff, E. T. (2002). Corporal punishment by parents and associated child behaviors and experiences: A meta-analysis and theoretical review. *Psychological Bulletin, 128,* 539–579. doi: 10.1037/0033-2909.128.4.539

Gershoff, E. T., & Grogan-Kaylor, A. (2016). Spanking and child outcomes: Old controversies and new meta-analyses. *Journal of Family Psychology, 30,* 453–469. doi: 10.1037/fam0000191

Gesell, A., & Ilg, F. L. (1949). *Child development, an introduction to the study of human growth.* Oxfordstet: Harper.

Giallo, R., Wood, C. E., Jellett, R., & Porter, R. (2013). Fatigue, wellbeing, and parental self-efficacy in mothers of children with an Autism Spectrum disorder. *Autism, 17,* 465–480. doi: 10.1177/1362361311416830

Ginsburg, K. R. (2007). The importance of play in promoting healthy child development and maintaining strong parent-child bonds. *Pediatrics, 119,* 182–191. doi: 10.1542/peds.2006-2697

Girard, L., Doyle, O., & Tremblay, R. E. (2017). Breastfeeding: Cognitive and noncognitive development in early childhood: A population study. *Pediatrics, 139,* 1–9. doi: 10.1542/peds.2016-1848

Glascoe, F. P. (1997). *Parents' evaluation of developmental status (PEDS)*. Nolensville, TN: Ellsworth & Vandermeer Press, Ltd.

Glatz, T., & Buchanan, C. M. (2015). Over-time associations among parental self-efficacy, promotive parenting practices, and adolescents' externalizing behaviors. *Journal of Family Psychology*, *29*, 427–437. doi: 10.1037/fam0000076

Gleason, T. R. (2005). Mothers' and fathers' attitudes regarding pretend play in the context of imaginary companions and of child gender. *Merrill-Palmer Quarterly*, *51*, 412–436. doi: 10.1353/mpq.2005.0022

Glidden, L. M. (2012). Family well-being and children with intellectual disability. In J. A. Burrack, R. M. Hodapp, G. Iarocci, G., & E. Zigler (Eds.), *Oxford handbook of intellectual disability and development* (pp. 303–317). New York, NY: Oxford University Press.

Gluck, B., & Rosenfeld, J. (2005). *How to survive your teenager*. Atlanta, GA: Hundreds of Heads Books, Inc.

Goldsmith, H. H., & Rothbart, M. K. (1991). Contemporary instruments for assessing early temperament by questionnaire and in the laboratory. In J. Strelan & A. Angleitner (Eds.), *Explorations in temperament: International perspectives on theory and measurement* (pp. 249–272). New York, NY: Plenum Press.

Golinkoff, R. M., & Hirsh-Pasek, K. (2016). *Becoming brilliant: What science tells us about raising successful children*. Washington, DC: American Psychological Association.

Gondoli, D. M., & Silverberg, S. B. (1997). Maternal emotional distress and diminished responsiveness: The mediating role of parenting efficacy and parental perspective taking. *Developmental Psychology*, *33*, 861–868. doi: 10.1037/0012-1649.33.5.861

Gonzalez, L. M., Anderson, V. A., Wood, S. J., Mitchell, L. A., Heinrich, L., & Harvey, A. S. (2008). The Observer-Memory Questionnaire—Parent Form: Introducing a new measure of everyday memory in children. *Journal of the International Neuropsychological Society*, *14*, 337–342. doi: 10.1017/S135561770808020X

Goodman, R. (1997). The Strengths and Difficulties Questionnaire: A research note. *Journal of Child Psychology and Psychiatry*, *38*, 581–586. doi: 10.1111/j.1469-7610.1997.tb01545.x

Goodman, S. H., & Brumley, H. E. (1990). Schizophrenic and depressed mothers: Relational deficits in parenting. *Developmental Psychology*, *26*, 31–39. doi: 10.1037/0012-1649.26.1.31

Goodman S. H., Rouse, M. H., Connell, A. M., Broth, M. R., Hall, C. M., & Heyward, D. (2011). Maternal depression and child psychopathology: A meta-analytic review. *Clinical Child and Family Psychological Review*, *14*, 1–27. doi: 10.1007/s10567-010-0080-1

Goodnow, J. J. (1988). Parents' ideas, actions, and feelings: Models and methods from developmental and social psychology. *Child Development*, *59*, 286–320. doi: 10.1111/1467-8624.ep8588523

Goodnow, J. J. (1996). Collaborative rules: How are people supposed to work with one another? In P. B. Baltes & U. M. Staudinger (Eds.), *Interactive minds: Life-span perspectives on the social foundation of cognition* (pp. 163–197). New York, NY: Cambridge University Press.

Goodnow, J. J. (2004). The domain of work in households: A relational models approach. In N. Haslam (Ed.), *Relational models theory: A contemporary overview* (pp. 167–196). Mahwah, NJ: Erlbaum.

Goodnow, J. J. (2006). Cultural perspectives and parents' views of parenting and development: Research directions. In K. H. Rubin & O. B. Chung (Eds.), *Parenting beliefs, behavior, and parent-child relations: A cross-cultural perspective* (pp. 35–57). New York, NY: Psychology Press.

Goodnow, J. J., Cashmore, J., Cotton, S., & Knight, R. (1984). Mothers' developmental timetables in two cultural groups. *International Journal of Psychology, 19,* 193–205. doi: 10.1080/00207598408247526

Goodnow, J. J., & Collins, W. A. (1990). *Development according to parents.* Hillsdale, NJ: Erlbaum.

Goodnow, J. J., & Delaney, S. (1989). Children' household work: Task differences, styles of assignment, and links to family relationships. *Journal of Applied Developmental Psychology, 10,* 209–226. doi: 10.1016/0193-3973(89)90005-1

Goodvin, R., & Rolfson, J. (2014). Mothers' attributions in reminiscing conversations about children's successes and failures: Connections with children's self-evaluations. *Merrill-Palmer Quarterly, 60,* 24–52. doi: 10.13110/merrpalmquar1982.60.1.0024

Gottman, J. M., Katz, L. F., & Hooven, C. (1996). Parental meta-emotion philosophy and the emotional life of families: Theoretical models and preliminary data. *Journal of Family Psychology, 10,* 243–268. doi: 10.1037/0893-3200.10.3.243

Gottman, J. M., Katz, L. F., & Hooven, C. (1997). *Meta-emotion: How families communicate emotionally.* Mahwah, NJ: Erlbaum.

Green, A. E., Bekman, N. M., Miller, E. A., Perrott, J. A., Brown, S. A., & Aarons, G. A. (2011). Parental awareness of substance use among youths in public service sectors. *Journal of Studies on Alcohol and Drugs, 72,* 44–52. doi: 10.15288/jsad.2011.72.44

Green, C. L., Walker, J. M. T., Hoover-Dempsey, K. V., & Sandler, H. M. (2007). Parents' motivation for involvement in children's education: An empirical test of a theoretical model of parental involvement. *Journal of Educational Psychology, 99,* 532–544. doi: 10.1037/0022-0663.99.3.532

Green, J. M., & KaftersioKaftersios, K. (1997). Positive experiences of early motherhood: Predictive variables from a longitudinal study. *Journal of Reproductive and Infant Psychology, 15,* 141–157. doi: 10.1080/02646839708404540

Green, S., Caplan, B., & Baker, B. (2014). Maternal supportive and interfering control as predictors of adaptive and social development in children with and without developmental delays. *Journal of Intellectual Disability Research, 58,* 691–703. doi: 10.1111/jir.1206410.1111/jir.12064

Gretarsson, S. J., & Gelfand, D. M. (1988). Mothers' attributions regarding their children's social behavior and personality characteristics. *Developmental Psychology, 24,* 264–269. doi: 10.1037/0012-1649.24.2.264

Grigorenko, E. L., Meier, E., Lipka, J., Mohatt, G., & Sternberg, R. J. (2004). Academic and practical intelligence: A case study of the Yup'ik in Alaska. *Learning and Individual Differences, 14,* 183–207. doi: 10.1016/j.lindif.2004.02.002

Groh, A. M., Roisman, G. I., Booth-LaForce, C., Fraley, R. C., Owen, M. T., Cox, M. J., & Burchinal, M. R. (2014). The Adult Attachment Interview: Psychometrics, stability and change from infancy, and developmental origins. *Monographs of the Society for Research in Child Development, 79*(3).

Gruhn, M. A., Dunbar J. P., Watson, K. H., Reising, M. M., McKee, L., Cole, D. A., & Compass, B. E. (2016). Testing specificity among parents' depressive symptoms, parenting, and child internalizing and externalizing symptoms. *Journal of Family Psychology, 30,* 309–319. doi: 10.1037/fam0000183

Grusec, J. E., Chaparro, M. P., Johnston, M., & Sherman, A. (2014). The development of moral behavior from a socialization perspective. In M. Killen & J. G.

Smetana (Eds.), *Handbook of moral development* (2nd ed., pp. 113–134). New York, NY: Psychology Press.

Grusec, J. E., & Goodnow, J. J. (1994). Impact of parental discipline methods on the child's internalization of values: A reconceptualization of current points of view. *Developmental Psychology, 30,* 4–19. doi: 10.1037/0012-1649.30.1.4

Grusec, J. E., Hastings, P., & Mammone, N. (1994). Parenting cognitions and relationship schemas. In J. G. Smetana (Ed.), *Beliefs about parenting: Origins and developmental implications* (pp. 5–19). San Francisco, CA: Jossey-Bass.

Grych, J. H. (2002). Marital relationships and parenting. In M. H. Bornstein (Ed.), *Handbook of parenting: Vol. 4: Social conditions and applied parenting* (2nd ed., pp. 203–225). Mahwah, NJ: Erlbaum.

Guajardo, N. R., & Watson, A. C. (2002). Narrative discourse and theory of mind development. *Journal of Genetic Psychology, 163,* 305–325. doi: 10.1080/00221320 209598686

Guilamo-Ramos, V., Bouris, A., Lee, J., McCarthy, K., Michael, S. L., Pitt-Barnes, S., & Dittus, P. (2012). Paternal influences on adolescent sexual risk behaviors: A structured literature review. *Pediatrics, 130,* e1313–e1325. doi: 10.1542/peds.2011-2066

Gustafson, G. E., Wood, R. M., & Green, J. A. (2000). Can we hear the causes of infants' cries? In R. G. Barr, B. Hopkins, & J. A. Green (Eds.), *Crying as a sign, symptom, and a signal* (pp. 8–22). New York, NY: Cambridge University Press.

Gutierrez, J., & Sameroff, A. (1990). Determinants of complexity in Mexican-American and Anglo-American mothers' conceptions of child development. *Child Development, 61,* 384–394. doi: 10.1111/1467-8624.ep5878987

Gutierrez, J., Sameroff, A., & Karrer, B. M. (1988). Acculturation and SES effects on Mexican-American parents' concepts of development. *Child Development, 59,* 250–255. doi: 10.1111/1467-8624.ep10514970

Gutman, L. M., Peck S. C., Malanchuk, O., Sameroff, A. J., & Eccles, J. S. (2017). Moving through adolescence: Developmental trajectories of African American and European American youth. *Monographs of the Society for Research in Child Development, 82*(4). doi: 10.1111/mono.12327

Ha, C., Sharp, C., & Goodyear, I. (2011). The role of child and parent mentalizing for the development of conduct problems over time. *European Child and Adolescent Psychiatry, 20,* 291–300. doi: 10.1007/s00787-011-0174-4

Haidt, J. (2007). The new synthesis in moral psychology. *Science, 316,* 998–1002. doi: 10.1126/science.1137651

Haight, W. L., Parke, R. D., & Black, J. E. (1997). Mothers' and fathers' beliefs about and spontaneous participation in their toddlers' pretend play. *Merrill-Palmer Quarterly, 43,* 271–290.

Haimovitz, K., & Dweck C. S. (2016). Parents' views of failure predict children's fixed and growth intelligence mind-sets. *Psychological Science, 27,* 859–869. doi: 10.1177/0956797616639727

Hakim-Larson, J., Parker, A., Lee, C., Goodwin, J., & Voelker, S. (2006). Measuring parental meta-emotion: Psychometric properties of the Emotion-Related Styles Self-Test. *Early Education and Development, 17,* 229–251. doi: 10.1207/s15566935eed1702_2

Halberstadt, A. G., Dunsmore, J. C., Bryant, A. Jr., Parker, A. E., Beale, K. S., & Thompson, J. A. (2013). Development and validation of the Parents' Beliefs about Children's Emotions Questionnaire. *Psychological Assessment, 25,* 1195–1210. doi: 10.1037/a0033695

Halberstadt, A. G., Dunsmore, J. C., McElwain, N., Eaton, K. L., & McCool, A. (2001). *Parents' beliefs about negative emotions.* Unpublished manuscript, North Carolina State University.

Halberstadt, A. G., Thompson, J. A., Parker, A. E., & Dunsmore, J. C. (2008). Parents' emotion-related beliefs and behaviours in relation to children's coping with the 11 September 2001 terrorist attacks. *Infant and Child Development, 17,* 557–580. doi: 10.1002/icd.569

Halle, T. G., & Darling-Churchill, K. E. (2016). Review of measures of social and emotional development. *Journal of Applied Developmental Psychology, 45,* 8–18. doi: 10.1016/j.appdev.2016.02.003

Halperin, E., Russell, A. G., Trzesniewski, K. H., Gross, J. J., & Dweck, C. S. (2011). Promoting the Middle East peace process by changing beliefs about group malleability. *Science, 333,* 1767–1769. doi: 10.1126/science.1202925

Haltigan, J. D., Lerkes, E. M., Burney, R. V., O'Brien, M., Supple, A., & Calkins, S. D. (2012). The Infant Crying Questionnaire: Initial factor structure and validation. *Infant Behavior and Development, 35,* 876–883. doi: 10.1016/j.infbeh.2012.06.001

Hammond, S. I., Muller, U., Carpendale, J. I. M., Bibok, M. B., & Liebermann-Finestone, D. P. (2012). The effects of parental scaffolding on preschoolers' executive function. *Developmental Psychology, 48,* 271–281. doi: 10.1037/a0025519

Hansen, T. (2012). Parenthood and happiness: A review of folk theories versus empirical evidence. *Social Indicators Research, 108,* 29–64. doi: 10.1007/s11205-011-9865-y

Harkness, S., Mavridis, C. J., Liu, J. J., & Super, C. M. (2015). Parental ethnotheories and the development of family relationships in early and middle childhood. In L. A. Jensen (Ed.), *The Oxford handbook of human development and culture: An interdisciplinary perspective* (pp. 271–291). New York, NY: Oxford University Press.

Harkness, S., Moscardino, U., Bermudez, M. R., Zylicz, P. O., Welles-Nystrom, B., Blom, M., ... Super, C. M. (2006). Mixed methods in international collaborative research: The experiences of the International Study of Parents, Children, and Schools. *Cross-Cultural Research, 40,* 65–82. doi: 10.1177/1069397105283179

Harkness, S., & Super, C. M. (1986). The developmental niche: A conceptualization at the interface of child and culture. *International Journal of Behavioral Development, 9,* 545–569. doi: 10.1177%2F016502548600900409

Harkness, S., & Super, C. M. (1992). Parental ethnotheories in action. In I. E. Sigel, A. V. McGillicuddy-DeLisi, & J. J. Goodnow (Eds.), *Parental belief systems* (2nd ed., pp. 373–391). Hillsdale, NJ: Erlbaum.

Harkness, S., & Super, C. M. (Eds.). (1996). *Parents' cultural belief systems: Their origins, expressions, and consequences.* New York, NY: Guilford Press.

Harkness, S., & Super, C. M. (2002). Culture and parenting. In M. H. Bornstein (Ed.), *Handbook of parenting: Vol. 2, Biology and ecology of parenting* (2nd ed., pp. 253–280). Mahwah, NJ: Erlbaum.

Harkness, S., & Super, C. M. (2006). Harkness, S., & Super, C. M. (2006). Themes and variations: Parental ethnotheories in Western cultures. In K. H. Rubin & O. B. Chung (Eds.), *Parenting beliefs, behavior, and parent-child relations: A cross-cultural perspective* (pp. 61–79). New York, NY: Psychology Press.

Harkness, S., Super, C. M., Bermudez, M. R., Moscardino, U., Rha, J., Mavridis, C., ... Zlyicz, P. O. (2010). Parental ethnotheories of children's learning. In D. F. Lancy, J. Bock, & S. Gaskins (Eds.), *The anthropology of learning in childhood* (pp. 65–81). Lanham, MD: AltaMira Press.

Harkness, S., Super, C. M., Bermudez, M. R., Zylicz, P. O., Welles-Nystrom, B., Bonichi, S., . . . Mavridis, C. J. (2011). Children's activities and their meanings for parents: A mixed-methods study in six Western countries. *Journal of Family Psychology, 25,* 799–813. doi: 10.1037/a0026204

Harkness, S., Super, C. M., & van Tijen, N. (2000). Individualism and the "Western mind" reconsidered: American and Dutch parents' ethnotheories of the child. In S. Harkness, C. Raeff, & C. M. Super (Eds.), *Variability in the social construction of the child* (pp. 23–39). San Francisco, CA: Jossey-Bass.

Hart, B. M., & Risley, T. R. (1995). *Meaningful differences in the everyday experience of young American children.* Baltimore, MD: Brookes.

Hart, K. C., Ros, R., Gonzalez, V., & Graziano, P. A. (2018). Parent perceptions of medication treatment for preschool children with ADHD. *Child Psychiatry and Human Development, 49,* 155–162. doi: 10.1007/s10578-017-0737-9

Harter, S. (1982). The Perceived Competence Scale for Children. *Child Development, 53,* 87–97. doi: 10.1111/1467-8624.ep8587568

Hartley, S. L., Schaidie, E. M., & Burson, C. F. (2013). Parental attributions for the behavior problems of children and adolescents with autism spectrum disorders. *Journal of Developmental and Behavioral Pediatrics, 34,* 651–660. doi: 10.1097/01.DBP.0000437725.39459.a0

Haskett, M. E., Scott, S. S., Grant, R., Ward, C. S., & Robinson, C. (2003). Child-related cognitions and affective functioning of physically abusive and comparison parents. *Child Abuse & Neglect, 27,* 663–686. doi: 10.1016/S0145-2134(03)00103-0

Haskett, M. E., Scott, S. S., Willoughby, M., Ahern, L., & Nears, K. (2006). The Parenting Opinion Questionnaire and child vignettes for use with abusive parents: Assessment of psychometric properties. *Journal of Family Violence, 21,* 137–151. doi: 10.1007/s10896-005-9010-2

Hassall, R., & Rose, J. (2005). Parental cognitions and adaptation to the demands of caring for a child with an intellectual disability: A review of the literature and implications for clinical interventions. *Behavioural and Cognitive Psychotherapy, 33,* 71–88. doi: 10.1017/S135246580400178X

Hastings, P., & Grusec, J. E. (1997). Conflict outcome as a function of parental accuracy in perceiving child cognitions and affect. *Social Development, 6,* 67–90. doi: 10.1111/j.1467-9507.1997.tb00095.x

Hastings, P. Miller, J. G., & Troxel, N. R. (2015). Making good: The socialization of children's prosocial development. In J. E. Grusec & P. Hastings (Eds.), *Handbook of socialization* (2nd ed., pp. 637–660). New York, NY: Guilford Press.

Hastings, R. P., & Taunt, H. M. (2002). Positive perceptions in families of children with developmental disabilities. *American Journal on Mental Retardation, 107,* 116–127. doi: 10.1352/0895-8017(2002)107%3C0116:PPIFOC%3E2.0.CO;2

Hauser-Cram, P., Warfield, M. E., Shonkoff, J. P., & Krauss, M. W. (2001). Children with disabilities: A longitudinal study of child development and parent well-being. *Monographs of the Society for Research in Child Development, 66*(3). doi: 10.1111/1540-5834.00151

Hauser-Cram, P., Warfield, M. E., Shonkoff, J. P., Krauss, M. W., Upshur, C. C., & Sayer, A. (1999). Family influences on adaptive development in young children with Down syndrome. *Child Development, 70,* 979–989. doi: 10.1111/1467-8624.00071

Havighurst, S. S., Wilson, K. R., Harley, A. E., Kehoe, C., Efron, D., & Prior, M. R. (2013). "Tuning into Kids": Reducing young children's behavior problems using an emotion coaching program. *Child Psychiatry and Human Development, 44,* 247–264. doi: 10.1007/s10578-012-0322-1

Havighurst, S. S., Wilson, K. R., Harley, A. E., Prior, M. R., & Kehoe, C. (2010). *Tuning into Kids*: Improving emotion socialization practices in parents of preschool children— findings from a community trial. *Journal of Child Psychology and Psychiatry, 51,* 1342–1350. doi: 1111/j.1469-7610.2010.02303.x

Hawk, C. K., & Holden, G. W. (2006). Meta-parenting: An initial investigation into a new social cognition construct. *Parenting: Science and Practice, 6,* 321–342. doi: 10.1207/s15327922par0604_3

Hawk, S. T., Keijsers, L., Frijas, T., Hale III, W. W., Branje, S., & Meeus, W. (2013). "I still haven't found what I'm looking for": Parental privacy invasion predicts reduced parental knowledge. *Developmental Psychology, 49,* 1286–1298. doi: 10.1037/a0029484

Hawkins, E., Madigan, S., Moran, G., & Pederson, D. R. (2015). Mediating and moderating processes underlying the association between maternal cognition and infant attachment. *Journal of Applied Developmental Psychology, 39,* 24–33. doi: 10.1016/j.appdev.2015.04.001

Hayes, S. A., & Watson, S. L. (2013). The impact of parenting stress: A meta-analysis of studies comparing the experience of parenting stress in parents of children with and without autism spectrum disorder. *Journal of Autism and Developmental Disorders 43,* 629–642. doi: 10.1007/s10803-012-1604-y

Heatherington, L., Tolejko, N., McDonald, M., & Funk, J. (2007). Now why'd he do that? The nature and correlates of mothers' attributions about negative teen behavior. *Journal of Family Psychology, 21,* 315–319. doi: 10.1037/0893-3200.21.2.315

Heerman, W. J., Taylor, J. L., Wallstaon, K. A., & Barkin, S. L. (2017). Parenting self-efficacy, parent depression, and healthy childhood behaviors in a low-income minority population: A cross-sectional analysis. *Maternal and Child Health Journal, 21,* 1156–1165. doi: 10.1007/s10995-016-2214-7

Heider, F. (1958). *The psychology of interpersonal relations.* New York, NY: Wiley.

Heinicke, C. (2002). The transition to parenting. In M. H. Bornstein (Ed.), *Handbook of parenting: Vol 3. Being and becoming a parent* (2nd ed., pp. 363–388). Hillsdale, NJ: Erlbaum.

Heriot, J. T., & Schmickel, G. A. (1967). Maternal estimates of IQ in children evaluated for learning potential. *American Journal of Mental Deficiency, 71,* 920–924.

Herman, S., Adkins, M., & Moon, R. Y. (2015). Knowledge and beliefs of African-American and American Indian parents and supporters about infant safe sleep. *Journal of Community Health, 40,* 12–19. doi: 10.1007/s10900-014-9886-y

Hess, C. R., Teti, D. M., & Hussey-Gardner, B. (2004). Self-efficacy and parenting of high-risk infants: The moderating role of parent knowledge of infant development. *Journal of Applied Developmental Psychology, 25,* 423–437. doi: 10.1016/j.appdev.2004.06.002

Hess, R. D., Kashiwagi, K., Azuma, H., Price, G. G., & Dickson, W. P. (1980). Maternal expectations for mastery of developmental tasks in Japan and the United States. *International Journal of Psychology, 15,* 259–271. doi: 10.1080/00207598008246996:

Hewstone, M. (1989). *Causal attribution.* Cambridge, MA: Blackwell.

Hibbs, R., Rhind, C., Salerno, L., Lo Coco, G., Goddard, E., Schmidt, U., . . . Treasure, J. (2015). Development and validation of a scale to measure caregiving skills in eating disorders. *International Journal of Eating Disorders, 48,* 290–297. doi: 10.1002/eat.22362

Hiebert-Murphy, D., Williams, E. A., Mills, R. S. L., Walker, J. R., Feldgaier, S., Warren, M., . . . Cox, B. J. (2012). Listening to parents: The challenges of parenting kindergarten-aged children who are anxious. *Clinical Child Psychology and Psychiatry, 17*, 384–399. doi: 10.1177/135910451141549

Higgins, E. T. (1981). Role taking and social judgment: Alternative developmental perspectives and processes. In J. H. Flavell & L. Ross (Eds.), *Social cognitive development* (pp. 119–153). Cambridge, UK: Cambridge University Press.

Hill, N. E., & Bush, K. R. (2001). Relationships between parenting environment and children's mental health among African American and European American mothers and children. *Journal of Marriage and Family, 63*, 954–966. doi: 10.1111/j.1741-3737.2001.00954.x

Hinduja, S. K., & Patchin, J. W. (2015). *Bullying beyond the schoolyard: Preventing and responding to cyberbullying* (2nd ed.) Thousand Oaks, CA: Corwin.

Hines, M. (2015). Gendered development. In R. M. Lerner (Series Ed.) & M. E. Lamb (Vol. Ed.), *Handbook of child psychology and developmental science: Vol. 3. Socioemotional processes* (7th ed., pp. 842–887). Hoboken, NJ: Wiley.

Hirsh-Pasek, K., Golinkoff, R. M., Berk, L., & Singer, D. G. (2009). *A mandate for playful learning in preschool: Presenting the evidence.* New York, NY: Oxford University Press.

Hirsjarvi, S., & Perala-Littunen, S. (2001). Parental beliefs and their role in child-rearing. *European Journal of Psychology of Education, 16*, 87–116. doi: 10.1007/BF03172996

Hobbs, S. A., Schweitzer, J. B., & Cohen, L. L. (2003). Maternal attributions related to compliance with cystic fibrosis treatment. *Journal of Clinical Psychology in Medical Settings, 10*, 273–277. doi: 10.1023/A:1026349303930

Hodapp, R. M. (2002). Parenting children with mental retardation. In M. H. Bornstein (Ed.), *Handbook of parenting: Vol. 1. Children and parenting* (2nd ed., pp. 355–382). Mahwah, NJ: Erlbaum.

Hodapp, R. M., & Dykens, E. M. (2006). Mental retardation. In W. Damon & R. M. Lerner (Series Eds.) & K. A. Renninger & I. E. Sigel (Vol. Eds.), *Handbook of child psychology: Vol. 4. Child psychology in practice* (6th ed., pp. 453–496). Hoboken, NJ: Wiley.

Hoeve, M., Dubas, J. S., Eichelsteim, V. I., van der Laan, P. H., Smeenk, W., & Gerris, J. R. M. (2009). The relationship between parenting and delinquency: A meta-analysis. *Journal of Abnormal Child Psychology, 37*, 749–775. doi: 10.1007/s10802-009-9310-8

Hoeve, M., Stams, G. J. J. M., van der Put, C. E., Dubas, J. S., van de Laan, P. H., & Gerris, J. R. M. (2012). A meta-analysis of attachment to parents and delinquency. *Journal of Abnormal Child Psychology, 40*, 771–785. doi: 10.1007/s10802-011-9608-1

Hoffman, M. L. (2000). *Empathy and moral development: Implications for caring and justice.* Cambridge, England: Cambridge University Press.

Holden, G. W., & Edwards, L. A. (1989). Parental attitudes toward child rearing: Instruments, issues, and implications. *Psychological Bulletin, 106*, 29–58. doi: 10.1037/0033-2909.106.1.29

Holden, G. W., & Hawk, C. K. (2003). Meta-parenting in the journey of child rearing: A cognitive mechanism for change. In L. Kuczynski (Ed.), *Handbook of dynamics in parent-child relations* (pp. 189–210). Thousand Oaks, CA: Sage.

Holden, G. W., Hawk, C. K., Smith, M. M., Singh, J. P., & Ashraf, R. (2017). Disciplinary practices, metaparenting, and the quality of parent-child relationships in African-American, Mexican-American, and European-American mothers. *International Journal of Behavioral Development, 41*, 482–490. doi: 10.1177/0165025416687414

Holloway, S. D., & Hess, R. D. (1985). Mothers' and teachers' attributions about children's mathematics performance. In I. E. Sigel (Ed.), *Parental belief systems* (pp. 177–199). Hillsdale, NJ: Erlbaum.

Holloway, S. D., Kashiwagi, K., Hess, R. D., & Azuma, H. (1986). Causal attributions by Japanese and American mothers and children about performance in mathematics. *International Journal of Psychology, 21,* 269–286. doi: 10.1080/00207598608247590

Holmes, T. R., Bond, L. A., & Byrne, C. (2008). Mothers' beliefs about knowledge and mother-adolescent conflict. *Journal of Social and Personal Relationships, 25,* 561–586. doi: 10.1177/0265407508090873

Hoover-Dempsey, K. V., Bassler, O. C., & Brissie, J. S. (1992). Explorations in parent-school relations. *Journal of Educational Research, 85,* 287–294. doi: 10.1080/00220671.1992.9941128

Hoover-Dempsey, K. V., Bassler, O. C., & Burow, R. (1995). Parents' reported involvement in students' homework: Strategies and practices. *Elementary School Journal, 95,* 435–450. doi: 10.1086/461854

Hourigan, S. E., Goodman, K. L., & Southam-Gerow, M. A. (2011). Discrepancies in parents' and children's reports of child emotion regulation. *Journal of Experimental Child Psychology, 110,* 198–212. doi: 10.1016/j.jecp.2011.03.002

Huang, C. (2017). Cross-informant agreement of the Child Behavior Checklist for Youths: A meta-analysis. *Psychological Reports, 120,* 1096–1116. doi: 10.1177/0033294117717733#SG-PRXJ170041_1096_0_400662

Huang, H. L., Li, S. S., Cheng, C. P., Lin, C. Y., Yang, Y. K., & Huang, J. H. (2014). The negative attribution processes of mothers of children with attention deficit/hyper-activity disorder. *Research in Developmental Disabilities, 35,* 87–98. doi: 10.1016/j.ridd.2013.09.037

Huang, K., O'Brien Caughy, M., Genevro, J. L., & Miller, T. L (2005). Maternal knowledge of child development and quality of parenting among White, African-American and Hispanic mothers. *Journal of Applied Developmental Psychology, 26,* 149–170. doi: 10.1016/j.appdev.2004.12.001

Hubert, J. (2011). 'My heart is always where he is.' Perspectives of mothers of young people with severe intellectual disabilities and challenging behaviour living at home. *British Journal of Learning Disabilities, 39,* 216–224. doi: 10.1111/j.1468-3156.2010.00658.x

Hudson, D. B., Campbell-Grossman, C., Fleck, M. O., Elek, S. M., & Shipman, A. (2003). Effects of the New Fathers Network on first-time fathers' parenting self-efficiency and parenting satisfaction during the transition to parenthood. *Issues in Comprehensive Pediatric Nursing, 26,* 217–229. doi: 10.1080/01460860390246687

Hudson, D. B., Elek, S. M., & Fleck, M. O. (2001). First-time mothers' and fathers' transition to parenthood: Infant care self-efficacy, parenting satisfaction, and infant sex. *Issues in Comprehensive Pediatric Nursing, 24,* 31–43. doi: 10.1080/014608601300035580

Hughes, C., Devine, R. T., & Wang, Z. (2018). Does parental mind-mindedness account for cross-cultural differences in preschoolers' theory of mind? *Child Development, 89,* 1296–1310. doi: 10.1111/cdev.12746

Hughes, C., Roman, G., Hart, M. J., & Ensor, R. (2013). Does maternal depression predict young children's executive function?—a 4-year longitudinal study. *Journal of Child Psychology and Psychiatry, 54,* 169–177. doi: 10.1111/jcpp.12014.

Hughes, D., & Chen, L. (1997). When and what parents tell children about race: An examination of race-related socialization among African American families. *Applied Developmental Science, 1,* 200–214. doi: 10.1207/s1532480xads0104_4

Hughes, D., Rodriguez, J., Smith, E. P., Johnson, D. J., Stevenson, H. C., & Spicer, P. (2006). Parents' ethnic-racial socialization practices: A review of research and directions for future study. *Developmental Psychology, 42,* 747–770. doi: 10.1037/0012-1649.42.5.747

Hunt, J. McV., & Paraskevopoulos, J. (1980). Children's psychological development as a function of the inaccuracy of their mothers' knowledge of their abilities. *Journal of Genetic Psychology, 136,* 285–298. doi: 10.1080/00221325.1980.10534123

Hunter, S. B., Barber, B. K., Olsen, J. A., McNeely, C. A., & Bose, K. (2011). Adolescents' self-disclosure to parents across cultures: Who discloses and why. *Journal of Adolescent Research, 26,* 447–478. doi: 10.1177/0743558411402334

Hurd, H. D., & Gettinger, M. (2011). Mothers' and teachers' perceptions of relational and physical aggression in pre-school children. *Early Child Development and Care, 181,* 1343–1359. doi: 10.1080/03004430.2010.527336

Hutchins, T. L., Bond, L. A., Silliman, E. R., & Bryant, J. B. (2009). Maternal epistemological perspectives and variations in mental state talk. *Journal of Speech, Language, and Hearing Research, 52,* 61–80. doi: 10.1044/1092-4388(2008/07-0161)

Hutchins, T. L., Prelock, P. A., & Bonazinga, L. (2012). Psychometric evaluation of the Theory of Mind Inventory (ToMI): A study of typically developing children and children with autism spectrum disorder. *Journal of Autism and Developmental Disorders, 42,* 327–342. doi: 10.1007/s10803-011-1244-7

Hutman, T., Siller, M., & Sigman, M. (2009). Mothers' narratives regarding their child with autism predict maternal synchronous behavior during play. *Journal of Child Psychology and Psychiatry, 50,* 1255–1263. doi: 10.1111/j.1469-7610.2009.02109.x.

Hyde, J. S. (2005). The gender similarities hypothesis. *American Psychologist, 60,* 581–592. doi: 10.1037/0003-066X.60.6.581

Hyde, J. S. (2014). Gender similarities and differences. *Annual Review of Psychology, 65,* 373–398. doi: 10.1146/annurev-psych-010213-115057

Hymel, S., & Swearer, S. M. (2015). Four decades of research on school bullying. *American Psychologist, 70,* 293–299. doi: 10.1037/a0038928

Ingersoll, B., & Wainer, A. (2014). The broader autism phenotype. In F. R. Volkmar, S. J. Rogers, R. Peal, & K. A. Pelphrey (Eds.), *Handbook of autism and pervasive developmental disorders. Vol. 1. Diagnosis, development, and brain mechanisms* (2nd ed., pp. 28–56). Hoboken, NJ: Wiley.

Ireton, H. (1992). *Child Development Inventory Manual.* Retrieved from file:///C:/Users/Owner/Downloads/cdi+manual(10).pdf

Ireton, H. (1994). *Infant Development Inventory.* Minneapolis, MN: Behavior Science Systems, Inc.

Isquith, P. K., Roth, R M., Kenworthy, L., & Gioia, G. (2014). Contribution of rating scales to intervention for executive dysfunction. *Applied Neuropsychology: Child, 3,* 197–204. doi: 10.1080/21622965.2013.870014

Ivrendi, A., & Isikoglu, N. (2010). A Turkish view of fathers' involvement in children's play. *Early Childhood Education Journal, 37,* 519–526. doi: 10.1007/s10643-010-0376-2

Izzo, C., Weiss, L., Shanahan, T., & Rodriguez-Brown, F. (2000). Parental self-efficacy and social support as predictors of parenting practices and children's socio-emotional adjustment in Mexican immigrant families. *Journal of Prevention and Intervention in the Community, 20,* 197–213. doi: 10.1300/J005v20n01_13

Jaccard, J., Dittus, P. J., & Gordon, V. V. (1998), Parent-adolescent congruency in reports of adolescent sexual behavior and in communications about sexual behavior. *Child Development, 69,* 247–261. doi: 10.2307/1132083

Jahromi, L. B., Guimond, A. B., Umana-Taylor, A. J., Updegraff, K. A., & Toomey, R. B. (2014). Family context, Mexican-origin adolescent mothers' parenting knowledge, and children's subsequent developmental outcomes. *Child Development, 85,* 593–609. doi: 10.1111/cdev.12160

Jahromi, L. B., Umana-Taylor, A. J., Updegraff, K. A., & Lara, E. E. (2012). Birth characteristics and developmental outcomes of infants of Mexican-origin adolescent mothers: Risk and promotive factors. *International Journal of Behavioral Development, 36,* 145–156. doi: 10.1177/0165025411430777

Jain, A., Sherman, S. N., Chamberlin, L. A., Carter, Y., Powers, S. W., & Whitaker, R. C. (2001). Why don't low-income mothers worry about their preschoolers being overweight? *Pediatrics, 107,* 1138–1146. doi: 10.1542/peds.107.5.1138

Jessee, A., Mangelsdorf, S. C., Shigeto, A., & Wong, M. S. (2012). Temperament as a moderator of the effects of parental depressive symptoms on child behavior problems. *Social Development, 21,* 610–627. doi: 10.1111/j.1467-9507.2011.00639.x

Jeynes, W. H. (2005). A meta-analysis of the relation of parental involvement to urban elementary school student academic achievement. *Urban Education, 40,* 237–269. doi: 10.1177/0042085905274540

Jiang, S., & Myse, H. (2016). Parental beliefs on children's play: Comparisons among mainline Chinese, Chinese immigrants in the USA, and European-Americans. *Early Child Development and Care, 186,* 341–352. doi: 10.1080/03004430.2015.1030633

Jimerson, T. L., & Bond, L. A. (2001). Mothers' epistemologies, turn-taking, and contingent interaction with preschoolers. *Journal of Applied Developmental Psychology, 22,* 379–396. doi: 10.1016/S0193-3973(01)00079-X

Job, V. Dweck, C. S., &Walton, G. M. (2010). Ego depletion—Is it all in your head? Implicit theories about willpower affect self-regulation. *Psychological Science, 21,* 1686–1693. doi: 10.1177/0956797610384745

Johnson, J. E., & Martin, C. (1983, October). *Family environments and kindergarten children's academic knowledge.* Paper presented at the meeting of the Northeast Educational Research Association, Ellesville, NY.

Johnston, C. (2011). Mothers' predictions of their sons' executive functioning skills: Relations to child behavior problems. *Child Psychiatry and Human Development, 42,* 482–494. doi: 10.1007/s10578-011-0221-x

Johnston, C., & Chronis-Tuscano, A. (2015). Families and ADHD. In R. A. Barkley (Ed.), *Attention-deficit hyperactivity disorder: A handbook for diagnosis and treatment* (pp. 191–209. New York, NY: Guilford Press.

Johnston, C., Fine, S., Weiss, M., Weiss, J., Weiss, G., & Freeman, W. S. (2000). Effects of stimulus medication treatment on mothers' and children's attributions for the behavior of children with attention deficit hyperactivity disorder. *Journal of Abnormal Child Psychology, 28,* 371–382. doi: 10.1023/A:1005121110278

Johnston, C., & Freeman, W. (1997). Attributions for child behavior in parents of children without behavior disorders and children with attention-deficit-hyperactivity disorder. *Journal of Consulting and Clinical Psychology, 65,* 636–645. doi: 10.1037/0022-006X.65.4.636

Johnston, C., Hommersen, P., & Seipp, C. M. (2009). Maternal attributions and child oppositional behavior: A longitudinal study of boys with and without attention-deficit/hyperactivity disorder. *Journal of Consulting and Clinical Psychology, 77,* 189–195. doi: 10.1037/a0014065

Johnston, C., Mah, J. W. T., & Regambal, M. (2010). Parenting cognitions and treatment beliefs as predictors of experience using behavioral parenting strategies in families of children with attention-deficit/hyperactivity disorder. *Behavior Therapy, 41*, 491–504. doi: 10.1016/j.beth.2010.02.001

Johnston, C., & Mash, E. J. (1989). A measure of parenting satisfaction and efficacy. *Journal of Clinical Child Psychology, 18*, 167–175. doi: 10.1207/s15374424jccp1802_8

Johnston, L. D., Miech, R. A., O'Malley, P. M., Bachman, J. G., Schulenberg, J. E., & Patrick, M. E. (2018). *Monitoring the Future national survey results on drug use: 1975–2017: Overview, key findings on adolescent drug use.* Ann Arbor, MI: Institute for Social Research, University of Michigan.

Jones, E. E., & Davis, K. E. (1965). From acts to dispositions: The attribution process in person perception. In L. Berkowitz (Ed.), *Advances in experimental social psychology* (Vol. 2, pp. 219–266). New York, NY: Academic Press.

Jones, J. D., Brett, B. E., Ehrlich, K. B., Lejuez, C. W., & Cassidy, J. (2014). Maternal attachment style and responses to adolescents' negative emotions: The mediating role of maternal emotion regulation. *Parenting: Science and Practice, 14*, 235–257. doi: 10.1080/15295192.2014.972760

Jones, T. L., & Prinz, R. J. (2005). Potential roles of parental self-efficacy in parent and child adjustment: A review. *Clinical Psychology Review, 25*, 341–363. doi: 10.1016/j.cpr.2004.12.004

Juntilla, N., Aromaa, M., Rautava, P., Piha, J., & Raiha, H. (2015). Measuring multidimensional parental self-efficacy of mothers and fathers of children age 1.5 and 3 years. *Family Relations, 64*, 665–680. doi: 10.1111/fare.12161

Juntilla, N., & Vauras, M. (2014). Latent profiles of parental self-efficacy and children's multisource-evaluated social competence. *British Journal of Developmental Psychology, 84*, 397–414. doi: 10.1111/bjep.12040

Juvonen, J., & Graham, S. (2014). Bullying in schools: The power of bullies and the plight of victims. *Annual Review of Psychology, 65*, 159–185. doi: 10.1146/annurev-psych-010213-115030

Kagitcibasi, C., & Ataca, B. (2015). Value of children, family change, and implications for the care of the elderly. *Cross-Cultural Research, 49*, 374–392. doi: 10.1177/1069397115598139

Kahng, S. K., Oyserman, D., Bybee, D., & Mowbray, C. (2008). Mothers with serious mental illness: When symptoms decline does parenting improve? *Journal of Family Psychology, 22*, 162–166. doi: 10.1037/0893-3200.22.1.162

Kaitz M., & Maytal, H. (2005). Interactions between anxious mothers and their infants: An integration of theory and research findings. *Infant Mental Health Journal, 26*, 570–597. doi: 1002/imhj.20069

Kaley, F., Reid, V., & Flynn, E. (2011). The psychology of infant colic: A review of current research. *Infant Mental Health, 32*, 526–541. doi: 10.1002/imhj.20308

Kalmijn, M., & de Graff, P. M. (2012). Life course changes of children and well-being of parents. *Journal of Marriage and Family, 74*, 269–280. doi: 10.1111/j.1741-3737.2012.00961.x

Kan, M. L., McHale, S., & Crouter, A. C. (2008). Parental involvement in adolescent romantic relationships: Patterns and correlates. *Journal of Youth and Adolescence, 37*, 168–179. doi: 10.1007/s10964-007-9185-3

Kanazawa, S. (2015). Breastfeeding is positively associated with child intelligence even net of parental IQ. *Developmental Psychology, 51*, 1683–1689. doi: 10.1037/dev0000060

Karing, C., Dorfler, T., & Artelt, C. (2015). How accurate are teacher and parent judgments of lower secondary school children's test anxiety? *Educational Psychology, 35*, 909–925. doi: 10.1080/01443410.2013.814200

Karkkainen, R., Raty, H., & Kasanen, K. (2010). How are children's perceptions of the malleability of their academic competencies related to their teachers' and parents' views? *Social Psychology of Education, 13*, 557–573. doi: 10.1007/s11218-010-9126-y

Karraker, K. H., & Coleman, P. K. (2005). The effects of child characteristics on parenting. In T. Luster & L. Okagaki (Eds.), *Parenting: An ecological perspective* (2nd ed., pp. 147–176). Mahwah, NJ: Erlbaum.

Karraker, K. H., & Evans, S. L. (1996). Adolescent mothers' knowledge of child development and expectations for their own infants. *Journal of Youth and Adolescence, 25*, 651–666. doi: 10.1007/BF01537359

Karstad, S. B., Kvello, O., Wichstom, L., & Berg-Nielsen, T. S. (2014). What do parents know about their children's comprehension of emotions? Accuracy of parental estimates in a community sample of pre-schoolers. *Child: Care, Health and Development, 40*, 346–353. doi: 10.1111/cch.12071

Karstad, S. B., Wichstom, L., Reinfjell, T., Belsky, J., & Berg-Nielsen, T. S. (2015). What enhances the development of emotion understanding in young children? A longitudinal study of interpersonal predictors. *British Journal of Developmental Psychology, 33*, 340–354. doi: 10.1111/bjdp.12095

Katz, L. F., & Gottman, J. M. (1986). *The Meta-Emotion Interview.* Unpublished manuscript, University of Washington.

Katz, L. F., Maliken, A. C., & Stettler, N. M. (2012). Parental meta-emotion philosophy: A review of research and theoretical framework. *Child Development Perspectives, 6*, 417–422. doi: 1111/j.1750-8606.2012.00244.x

Kawabata. Y., Alink, L. R. A., Tseng, W., van IJzendoorn, M. H., & Crick, N. R. (2011). Maternal and paternal parenting styles associated with relational aggression in children and adolescents: A conceptual analysis and meta-analytic review. *Developmental Review, 31*, 240–278. doi: 10.1016/j.dr.2011.08.001

Keijsers, L., Voelkle, M. C., Maciejewski, D., Branje, S., Koot, H., & Hiemstra, M. (2016). What drives developmental change in adolescent disclosure and maternal knowledge? Heterogeneity in within-family processes. *Developmental Psychology, 52*, 2057–2070. doi: 10.1037/dev0000220

Keller, H., Miranda, D., & Gauda, G. (1984). The naïve theory of the infant and some maternal attitudes. *Journal of Cross-Cultural Psychology, 15*, 165–179. doi: 10.1177/0022002184015002005

Kelley, H. H. (1967). Attribution theory in social psychology. In D. Levine (Ed.), *Nebraska Symposium on Motivation* (Vol. 15, pp. 192–241). Lincoln: University of Nebraska Press.

Kerr, M., & Stattin, H. (2000). What parents know, how they know it, and several forms of adolescent adjustment: Further support for a reinterpretation of monitoring. *Developmental Psychology, 36*, 366–380. doi: 10.1037/0012-1649.36.3.366

Kerr, M., Stattin, H., & Burk, W. J. (2010). A reinterpretation of parental monitoring in longitudinal perspective. *Journal of Research on Adolescence, 20*, 39–64. doi: 10.1111/j.1532-7795.2009.00623.x

Kerr, M., Stattin, H., & Ozdemir, M. (2012). Perceived parenting style and adolescent adjustment: Revisiting direction of effects and the role of parental knowledge. *Developmental Psychology, 48*, 1540–1553. doi: 10.1037/a0027720

Khazan, I., McHale, J. P., & Decourcey, W. (2008). Violated wishes about division of childcare labor predict early coparenting process during stressful and nonstressful family evaluations. *Infant Mental Health Journal, 29,* 342–361. doi: 10.1002/imhj.20183

Khodayarifard, M., Brinthaupt, T. M., & Anshel, M. H. (2010). Relationship of parents' and children's general attributional styles to academic performance. *Social Psychology of Education, 13,* 351–365. doi: 10.1007/s11218-010-9114-2

Kijakovic, M., & Hunt, C. (2016). A meta-analysis of predictors of bullying and victimization in adolescence. *Journal of Adolescence, 49,* 134–145. doi: 10.1016/j.adolescence.2016.03.002

Kil, H., Grusec, J. E., & Chaparro, M. P. (2018). Maternal disclosure and adolescent prosocial behavior: The mediating roles of adolescent disclosure and coping. *Social Development, 27,* 652–664. doi: 10.1111/sode.12287

Killen, M., & Smetana, J. G. (2015). Origins and development of morality. In R. M. Lerner (Series Ed.) & M. E. Lamb (Vol. Ed.), *Handbook of child psychology and developmental science: Vol. 3. Socioemotional processes* (7th ed., pp. 701–749). Hoboken, NJ: Wiley.

Kim, J. I., Kim, B., Kim, J., Hong, S., Shin, M., Yoo, H., & Cho, S. (2017). Breastfeeding is associated with enhanced learning abilities in school-aged children. *Child and Adolescent Psychiatry and Mental Health, 11,* Article 11. doi: 10.1186/s13034-017-0169-0

Kincaid, C., Jones, D. J., Sterret, E., & McKee, L. (2012). A review of parenting and adolescent sexual behavior: The moderating role of gender. *Clinical Psychology Review, 32,* 177–188. doi: 10.1016/j.cpr.2012.01.002

Kinlaw, C. R., Kurtz-Coster, B., & Goldman-Fraser, J. (2001). Mothers' achievement beliefs and behaviors and their children's school readiness: A cultural comparison. *Journal of Applied Developmental Psychology, 22,* 493–506. doi: 10.1016/S0193-3973(01)00090-9

Kirk, E., & Sharma, S. (2017). Mind-mindedness in mothers of children with autism spectrum disorder. *Research in Autism Spectrum Disorders, 43-44,* 18–26. doi: 10.1016/j.rasd.2017.08.005

Kirkman, J. J. L., Dadds, M. R., & Hawes, D. J. (2018). Development and validation of the Knowledge of Parenting Strategies Scale: Measuring effective parenting strategies. *Journal of Child and Family Studies, 27,* 3200–3217. doi: 10.1007/s10826-018-1165-6

Kish, A. M., & Newcombe, P. A. (2015). "Smacking never hurt me!" Identifying myths surrounding the use of corporal punishment. *Personality and Individual Differences, 87,* 121–129. doi: 10.1016/j.paid.2015.07.035

Klein-Tasman, B. P., Lira, E. N., Li-Barber, K. T., Gallo, F. J., & Brei, N. G. (2015). Parent and teacher perspectives about problem behavior in children with Williams syndrome. *American Journal on Intellectual and Developmental Disabilities, 120,* 72–86. doi: 10.1352/1944-7558-120.1.72

Kliegel, M., & Jager, T. (2007). The effects of age and cue-action reminders on event-based prospective memory performance in preschoolers. *Cognitive Development, 23,* 33–46. doi: 10.1016/j.cogdev.2006.08.003

Kliman, D. S., & Vukelich, C. (1985). Mothers and fathers: Expectations for infants. *Family Relations, 34,* 305–313. doi: 10.2307/583567

Knee, C. R. (1998). Implicit theories of relationships: Assessment and prediction of romantic relationship initiation, coping, and longevity. *Journal of Personality and Social Psychology, 74,* 360–370. doi: 10.1037/0022-3514.74.2.360

Knight, R. (1986). Parents' satisfaction with progress and beliefs about stability of traits. In C. Pratt, A. F. Garton, W. E. Tummer, & A. R. Nesdale (Eds.), *Research issues in child development* (pp. 188–195). Sydney, Australia: Allen & Unwin.

Knight, R., & Goodnow, J. J. (1988). Parents' beliefs about influence over cognitive and social development. *International Journal of Behavioral Development, 11*, 517–527. doi: 10.1177/016502548801100409

Kochanska, G. (1995). Children's temperament, mother's discipline, and security of attachment: Multiple pathways to emerging internalization. *Child Development, 66*, 597–615. doi: 10.2307/1131937

Kochanska, G. S. (2002). Mutually responsive orientation between mothers and their young children: A context for the early development of conscience. *Current Directions in Psychological Science, 11*, 191–195. doi: 10.1111/1467-8721.00198

Kochanska, G., S., DeVet, K., Goldman, M., Murray, K., & Putnam, S. P. (1994). Maternal reports of conscience development and temperament in young children. *Child Development, 65*, 852–868. doi: 10.1111/1467-8624.ep9408220885

Kochanska, G., S., Radke-Yarrow, M., Kucyniski, L., & Friedman, S. L. (1987). Normal and affectively ill mothers' beliefs about their children. *American Journal of Orthopsychiatry, 57*, 345–350. doi: 10.1111/j.1939-0025.1987.tb03543.x

Kohlberg, L. (1969). Stage and sequence: The cognitive-developmental approach to socialization. In D. Goslin (Ed.), *Handbook of socialization theory and research* (pp. 347–480). Skokie, IL: Rand McNally.

Kohlhoff, J., & Barnett, B. (2013). Parenting self-efficacy: Links with maternal depression, infant behaviour and adult attachment. *Early Human Development, 89*, 249–256. doi: 10.1016/j.earlhumdev.2013.01.008

Kondo-Ikemura, K., Behrens, K. Y., Umemura, T., & Nakona, S. (2018). Japanese mothers' prebirth Adult Attachment Interview predicts their infants' response to the Strange Situation Procedure: The Strange Situation in Japan revisited three decades later. *Developmental Psychology, 54*, 2007–2015. doi: 10.1037/dev0000577

Korat, O. (2011). Mothers' and teachers' estimations of first graders' literacy level and their relation to the children's actual performance in different SES groups. *Education and Treatment of Children, 34*, 347–371. doi: 10.1353/etc.2011.0021

Kowal, M. K., Krull, J. L., & Kramer, L. (2006). Shared understanding of parental differential treatment in families. *Social Development, 15*, 276–295. doi: 10.1111/j.1467-9507.2006.00341.x.

Ksinan, A. J., & Vazsonyi, A. T. (2016). Longitudinal associations between parental monitoring discrepancy and delinquency: An application of the latent congruency model. *Journal of Youth and Adolescence, 45*, 2369–2386. doi: 10.1007/s10964-016-0512-4

Kuhn, D. (1991). *The skills of argument.* Cambridge, England: Cambridge University Press.

Kuhn, J. C., & Carter, A. S. (2006). Maternal self-efficacy and associated parenting cognitions among mothers of children with autism. *American Journal of Orthopsychiatry, 76*, 564–575. doi: 10.1037/0002-9432.76.4.564

Kulkofsky, S., Wang, Q., & Koh, J. B. K. (2009). Functions of memory sharing and mother-child reminiscing behaviors: Individual and cultural variations. *Journal of Cognition and Development, 10*, 92–114. doi: 10.1080/15248370903041231

Kunseler, F. C., Willemen, A. M., Oosterman, M., & Schuengel, C. (2014). Changes in parenting self-efficacy and mood symptoms in the transition to parenthood: A bidirectional association. *Parenting: Science and Practice, 14*, 215–234. doi: 10.1080/15295192.2014.972758

Kurt, A. N. C. (in press). Characteristics of the knowledge and attitudes of parents about epilepsy. *Epilepsy and Behavior.* doi: 10.1016/j.yebeh.2018.04.004

Ladd, G. W. (2005). *Children's peer relationships and social competence*. New Haven, CT: Yale University Press.

Ladd, G. W., & Hart, C. H. (1992). Creating informal play opportunities: Are parents' and preschoolers' initiations related to children's competence with peers? *Developmental Psychology, 28*, 1179–1187. doi: 10.1037/0012-1649.28.6.1179

Ladd, G. W., & Pettit, G. S. (2002). Parenting and the development of children's peer relationships. In M. H. Bornstein (Ed.), *Handbook of parenting: Vol. 5. Practical issues in parenting* (2nd ed., pp. 269–309). Mahwah, NJ: Erlbaum.

Ladd, G. W., Profilet, S. M., & Hart, C. H. (1992). Parents' management of children's peer relations: Facilitating and supervising children's activities in the peer culture. In R. D. Parke & G. W. Ladd (Eds.), *Family-peer relationships: Modes of linkage* (pp. 215–253). Hillsdale, NJ: Erlbaum.

LaFleur, L. K., Zhao, Y., & Zeringue, M. M. (2016). Warmth and legitimacy beliefs contextualize adolescents' negative reactions to parental monitoring. *Journal of Adolescence, 51*, 58–67. doi: 10.1016/j.adolescence.2016.05.013

LaForett. D. R., & Mendez, J. L. (2017a). Children's engagement in play at home: A parent's role in supporting play opportunities during early childhood. *Early Child Development and Care, 187*, 910–923. doi: 10.1080/03004430.2016.1223061

LaForett. D. R., & Mendez, J. L. (2017b). Play beliefs and responsive parenting among low-income mothers of preschoolers in the United States. *Early Child Development and Care, 187*, 1359–1371. doi: 10.1080/03004430.2016.1169180

Lagace-Seguin, D. G., & Coplan, R. J. (2005). Maternal emotional styles and child social adjustment: Assessment, correlates, outcomes and goodness of fit in early childhood. *Social Development, 14*, 613–636. doi: 10.1111/j.1467-9507.2005.00320.x

Lagattuta, K. H., Sayfan, K., & Bamford, C. (2012). Do you know how I feel? Parents underestimate worry and overestimate optimism compared to child self-report. *Journal of Experimental Child Psychology, 113*, 211–232. doi: 10.1016/j.jecp.2012.04.001

Laird, R. D., Pettit, G. S., Bates, J. E., & Dodge, K. A. (2003). Parents' monitoring-relevant knowledge and adolescents' delinquent behavior: Evidence of correlated developmental changes and reciprocal influences. *Child Development, 74*, 752–768. doi: 10.1111/1467-8624.00566.

Lamb, C. S., & Crano, W. D. (2014). Parents' beliefs and children's marijuana use: Evidence for a self-fulfilling prophecy. *Addictive Behaviors, 39*, 127–132. doi: 10.1016/j.addbeh.2013.09.009

Lansford, J. E., & Bornstein, M. H. (2011). Parenting attributions and attitudes in diverse cultural contexts: Introduction to the special issue. *Parenting: Science and Practice, 11*, 87–101. doi: 10.1080/15295192.2011.585552

Lansford, J. E., Godwin, J., Alampay, L. P., Uribe Tirado, L. M., Zelli, A., Al-Hassan, S. M., . . . Tapanya, S. (2016). Mothers', fathers', and children's perceptions of parents' expectations about children's family obligations in nine countries. *International Journal of Psychology, 51*, 366–374. doi: 10.1002/ijop.12185

Larsen, J. J., & Juhasz, A. M. (1986). The Knowledge of Child Development Inventory. *Adolescence, 21*, 39–54.

Larzelere, R. E., Morris, A. S., & Harrist, A. W. (Eds.). (2013) *Authoritative parenting: Synthesizing nurturance and discipline for optimal child development* Washington, DC: American Psychological Association.

Laursen, B., & Collins, W. A. (1994). Interpersonal conflict during adolescence. *Psychological Bulletin, 115*, 197–209. doi: 10.1037/0033-2909.115.2.197

Laursen, B., Coy, K. C., & Collins, W. A. (1998). Reconsidering changes in parent-child conflict across adolescence: A meta-analysis. *Child Development, 69,* 817–832. doi: 10.2307/1132206

Law, D. M., Shapka, J. D., & Olson, B. F. (2010). To control or not control? Parenting behaviours and adolescent online aggression. *Computers in Human Behavior, 25,* 1651–1656. doi: 10.1016/j.chb.2010.06.013

Leahy-Warren, P., & McCarthy, G. (2011). Maternal parental self-efficacy in the post-partum period. *Midwifery, 27,* 802–810. doi: 10.1016/j.midw.2010.07.008

Leaper, C. (2002). Parenting girls and boys. In M. H. Bornstein (Ed.), *Handbook of parenting: Vol. 1. Children and parenting* (2nd ed., pp. 189–226). Mahwah, NJ: Erlbaum.

Leaper, C., Anderson, K. J., & Sanders, P. (1998). Moderators of gender effects on parents' talk to their children: A meta-analysis. *Developmental Psychology, 34,* 3–27. doi: 10.1037/0012-1649.34.1.3

Leaper, C., & Farkas, T. (2015). The socialization of gender during childhood and adolescence. In J. E. Grusec & P. Hastings (Eds.), *Handbook of socialization* (2nd ed., pp. 541–565). New York, NY: Guilford Press.

Leavell, A. S. (2013). *The freedom to move: Gender differences in infants' movement opportunities and longitudinal outcomes.* (Unpublished doctoral dissertation). New York University, New York, NY.

Leerkes, E., & Burney, R. V. (2007). The development of parenting efficacy among new mothers and fathers. *Infancy, 12,* 45–67. doi: 10.1080/15250000701298964

Leerkes, E. M., Parade, S. H., & Burney, R. V. (2010). Origins of mothers' and fathers' beliefs about infant crying. *Journal of Applied Developmental Psychology, 31,* 467–474. doi: 10.1016/j.appdev.2010.09.003

Leman, K. (2011). *Have a new teenager by Friday.* Grand Rapids, MI: Revell.

Lench, H. C., Levine, L. J., & Whalen, C. K. (2013). Exasperating or exceptional? Parents' interpretations of their child's ADHD behavior. *Journal of Attention Disorders, 17,* 141–151. doi: 10.1177%2F1087054711427401

Lennon, J. M., Murray, C. B., Bechtel, C. F., & Holmbeck, G. N. (2015). Resilience and disruption in observed family interactions in youth with and without spina bifida: An eight-year, five-way longitudinal study. *Journal of Pediatric Psychology, 40,* 943–955. doi: 10.1093/jpepsy/jsv033

Lereya, S. T., Samara, M., & Wolke, D. (2013). Parenting behavior and the risk of becoming a victim and a bully/victim: A meta-analysis study. *Child Abuse and Neglect, 37,* 1091–1108. doi: 10.1016/j.chiabu.2013.03.001

Lerner, J. V., Phelps, E., Forman, Y., & Bowers, E. P. (2009). Positive youth development. In R. M. Lerner & L. Steinberg (Eds.), *Handbook of adolescent psychology: Vol. 1. Individual bases of adolescent development* (3rd ed., pp. 524–558). Hoboken, NJ: Wiley.

Lesane-Brown, C. L. (2006). A review of race socialization within Black families. *Developmental Review, 26,* 400–426. doi: 10.1016/j.dr.2006.02.001

Leung, D. W., & Slep Smith. A. M. (2006). Predicting inept discipline: The role of parental depressive symptoms, anger, and attributions. *Journal of Consulting and Clinical Psychology, 74,* 524–534. doi: 10.1037/0022-006X.74.3.524

Levick, W. R. (2010). Observer rating of memory in children: A review. *Brain Impairment, 11,* 144–151. doi: 10.1375/brim.11.2.144

Levine, K. G. (2013). *When good kids do bad things: A survival guide for parents of teenagers.* Melbourne, Australia: MetaPlume Corporation.

Liau, A. K., Khoo, A., & Ang, P. H. (2008). Parental awareness and monitoring of adolescent Internet use. *Current Psychology, 27,* 217–233. doi: 10.1007/s12144-008-9038-6

Liben, L. S., Schroeder, K. M., Borriello, G. A., & Weisgram, E. S. (2018). Cognitive consequences of gendered toy play. In E. S. Weigram & L. M. Dinalla (Eds.), *Gender typing of children's toys: How early play experiences impact development* (pp. 213–255). Washington, DC: American Psychological Association.

Licata, M., Paulus, M., Thoermer, C., Kristen, S., Woodward, A. L., & Sodian, B. (2014). Mother-infant interaction quality and infants' ability to encode actions as goal-directed. *Social Development, 23,* 340–356. doi: 10.1111/sode.12057

Lightfoot, E., Hill, K., & LaLiberte, T. (2011). Prevalence of children with disabilities in the child welfare system and out of home placement: An examination of administrative records. *Child and Youth Services Review, 33,* 2069–2075. doi: 10.1016/j.childyouth.2011.02.019

Lillard, A. S. (2015). The development of play. In R. M. Lerner (Series Ed.) & L. S. Liben & U. Muller (Vol. Eds.), *Handbook of child psychology and developmental science: Vol. 2. Cognitive processes* (7th ed., pp. 425–468). Hoboken, NJ: Wiley. doi: 10.1002/9781118963418.childpsy209

Limber, S. P., Olweus, D., Wang, W., & Masiello, M. (2018). Evaluation of the Olweus Bullying Prevention Program: A large scale study of US students in grades 3–11. *Journal of School Psychology, 69,* 56–72. doi: 10.1016/j.jsp.2018.04.004

Lin, A. (2015). Citizenship education in American schools and its role in developing civic engagement: A review of the research. *Educational Review, 67,* 35–63. doi: 10.1080/00131911.2013.813440

Lin, Y., & Yawkey, T. D. (2013). Does play matter to parents? Taiwanese parents' perceptions of child' play. *Education, 134,* 244–254.

Lin, Y., & Yawkey, T. D. (2014). Parents' play beliefs and the relationship to children's social competence. *Education, 135,* 107–114.

Livingstone, S. (2009). *Children and the Internet.* Cambridge, UK: Polity Press.

Livingstone, S., & Bober, M. (2004). *UK children go online: Surveying the experiences of young people and their parents.* London: LSE Research Online.

Livingstone, S., & Haddon, L. (2008). Risky experiences for children online: Charting European research on children and the internet. *Children and Society, 22,* 314–323. doi: 10.1111/j.1099-0860.2008.00157x

Lo, S. L., Vroman, L. N., & Durbin, C. E. (2015). Ecological validity of laboratory assessments of child temperament: Evidence from parent perspectives. *Psychological Assessment, 27,* 280–290. doi: 10.1037/pas0000033

Lok, S. M., & McMahon, C. A. (2006). Mothers' thoughts about their children: Links between mind-mindedness and emotional availability. *British Journal of Developmental Psychology, 24,* 477–488. doi: 10.1348/026151005X49854

Lopez-Perez, B., & Wilson, E. L. (2015). Parent-child discrepancies in the assessment of children's and adolescents' happiness. *Journal of Experimental Child Psychology, 139,* 249–255. doi: 10.1016/j.jecp.2015.06.006

Loughlin-Presnal, J. E., & Bierman, K. L. (2017). Promoting parent academic expectations predicts improved school outcomes for low-income children entering kindergarten. *Journal of School Psychology, 62,* 67–80. doi: 10.1016/j.jsp.2017.03.007

Low, J., Apperly, I. A., Butterfill, S. A., & Rakoczy, H. (2016). Cognitive architecture of belief reasoning in children and adults: A primer on the two-systems account. *Child Development Perspectives, 10,* 184–198. doi: 10.1111/cdep.12183

Loyd, A. B., & Gaither, S. E. (2018). Racial/ethnic socialization for White youth: What we know and future directions. *Journal of Applied Developmental Psychology, 59,* 54–64. doi: 10.1016/j.appdev.2018.05.004

Luke, N., & Banerjee, R. (2013). Differentiated associations between childhood maltreatment experiences and social understanding: A meta-analysis and systematic review. *Developmental Review, 33,* 1–28. doi: 10.1016/j.dr.2012.10.001

Lundell, L. J., Grusec, J. E., McShane, K. E., & Davidod, M. (2008). Mother-adolescent conflict: Adolescent goals, maternal perspective-taking, and conflict intensity. *Journal of Research on Adolescence, 18,* 555–571. doi: 10.1111/j.1532-7795.2008.00571.x.

Lundy, B. L. (2013). Paternal and maternal mind-mindedness and preschoolers' theory of mind: The mediating role of interactional attunement. *Social Development, 22,* 58–74. doi: 10.1111/sode.12009

Luthar, S. S., & Ciciolla, L. (2015). Who mothers Mommy? Factors that contribute to mothers' well-being. *Developmental Psychology, 51,* 1812–1823. doi: 10.1037/dev0000051

Luthar, S. S., & Ciciolla, L. (2016). What it feels like to be a mother: Variations by children's developmental stages. *Developmental Psychology, 52,* 143–154. doi 10.1037/dev0000062

Luthar, S. S., Grossman, E. J., & Small, P. J. (2015). Resilience and adversity. In R. M. Lerner (Series Ed.) & M. E. Lamb (Vol. Ed.), *Handbook of child psychology and developmental science: Vol. 3. Socioemotional processes* (7th ed., pp. 932–974). Hoboken, NJ: Wiley.

Ly, T. M. (2008). Asian American parents' attributions of children with Down syndrome: Connections with child characteristics and culture. *Intellectual and Developmental Disabilities, 46,* 129–140. doi: 10.1352/0047-6765(2008)46[129:AAPAOC]2.0.CO;2

Ly, T. M., & Hodapp, R. M. (2005). Parents' attributions of their child's jigsaw-puzzle performance: Comparing two genetic syndromes. *Mental Retardation, 43,* 135–144. doi: 10.1352/0047-6765(2005)43%3C135:PAOTCJ%3E2.0.CO;2

Lytton, H., & Romney, D. M. (1991). Parents' differential socialization of boys and girls: A meta-analysis. *Psychological Bulletin, 109,* 267–296. doi: 10.1037/0033-2909.109.2.267

Maccoby, E. E., & Jacklin, C. N. (1974). *The psychology of sex differences.* Stanford, CA: Stanford University Press.

MacKinnon-Lewis, C., Castellino, D. R., Brody, G. H., & Fincham, F. D. (2001). A longitudinal examination of the associations between fathers' and children's attributions and negative interactions. *Social Development, 10,* 473–487. doi: 10.1111/1467-9507.00176

MacPhee D. (1981). *Knowledge of Infant Development Inventory.* Princeton, NJ: Educational Testing Service.

MacPhee, D (1983, April). *The nature of parents' experiences with and knowledge about infant development.* Paper presented at the meeting of the Society for Research m Child Development, Detroit, MI.

MacPhee, D., Benson, J. B., & Bullock, D. (1986, April). *Influences on maternal self-perceptions.* Paper presented at the biennial International Conference on Infant Studies, Los Angeles.

MacPhee, D., Fritz, J., & Miller-Heyl, J. (1996). Ethnic variations in personal social networks and parenting. *Child Development, 67,* 3278–3295. doi: 10.1111/1467-8624.ep9706244860.

MacPhee, D., Miller-Heyl, J., & Carroll, J. (2014). Impact of the Dare To Be You Family Support Program: Collaborative replication in rural counties. *Journal of Community Psychology, 42,* 707–722. doi: 10.1002/jcop.21647

Macy, M. (2012). The evidence behind developmental screening instruments. *Infancy and Young Children, 25*, 19–61. doi: 10.1097/IYC.0b013e31823d37dd

Madon, S., Guyll, M., Spoth, R., Cross, S. E., & Hilbert, S. J. (2003). The self-fulfilling influence of mother expectations on children's underage drinking. *Journal of Personality and Social Psychology, 84*, 1188–1205. doi: 10.1037/0022-3514.84.6.1188

Madon, S., Willard, J., Guyll, M., Trudeau, L., & Spoth, R. (2006). Self-fulfilling prophecy effects of mothers' beliefs on children's alcohol use: Accumulation, dissipation, and stability over time. *Journal of Personality and Social Psychology, 90*, 911–926. doi: 10.1037/0022-3514.90.6.911

Madsen, S. D. (2008). Parents' management of adolescents' romantic relationships through dating rules: Gender variations and correlates of relationship qualities. *Journal of Youth and Adolescence, 37*, 1044–1058. doi: 10.1007/s10964-008-9313-8

Mah, J. W. T., & Johnston, C. (2008). Parental social cognitions: Considerations in the acceptability of and engagement in behavioral parent training. *Clinical Child and Family Psychological Review, 11*, 218–236. doi: 10.1007/s10567-008-0038-8

Majorano, M., & Lavelli, M. (2014). Maternal input to children with specific language impairment during shared book reading: Is mothers' language in tune with their children's production? *International Journal of Language Communication Disorders, 49*, 204–214. doi: 10.1111/1460-6984.12062.

Malle, B. F. (2011). Attribution theories: How people make sense of behavior. In D. Chadee (Ed.), *Theories in social psychology* (pp. 72–95). Malden, MA: Wiley-Blackwell.

Malti, T., & Ongley, S. E. (2014). The development of moral emotions and moral reasoning. In M. Killen & J. G. Smetana (Eds.), *Handbook of moral development* (2nd ed., pp. 163–183). New York, NY: Psychology Press.

Mansbach, I. K., & Greenbaum, C. W. (1999). Developmental maturity expectations of Israeli fathers and mothers: Effects of education, ethnic origin, and religiosity. *International Journal of Behavioral Development, 23*, 771–797. doi: 10.1080/016502599383793

Mansfield, A. F., & Clinchy, B. (2002). Toward the integration of objectivity and subjectivity: Epistemological development from 10 to 16. *New Ideas in Psychology, 20*, 225–262. doi: 10.1016/S0732-118X(02)00008-9

Mantz, P. H., & Bracaliello, C. B. (2016). Expanding home visiting outcomes: Collaborative measurement of parental play beliefs and examination of their association with parents' involvement in toddler's learning. *Early Childhood Research Quarterly, 36*, 157–167. doi: 10.1016/j.ecresq.2015.12.015

March, J. S. (2013). *Multidimensional Anxiety Scale for Children 2*. Toronto, Canada: Multi-Health Systems.

Marcia, J. (1980). Identity in adolescence. In J. Adelson (Ed.), *Handbook of adolescent psychology* (pp. 159–187). New York, NY: Wiley.

Markham, C. M., Lormand, D., Gloppen, K. M., Peskin, M. F., Flores, B., Low, B., & House, L. D. (2010). Connectedness as a predictor of sexual and reproductive health outcomes for youth. *Journal of Adolescent Health, 46*, S23–S41. doi: 10.1016/j.jadohealth.2009.11.214

Martin, A. J., Darlow, B. A., Salt, A., Hague, W., Sebastian, L., Mann, K., & Tarnow-Mordi, W. (2012). Identification of infants with major cognitive delay using parental report. *Developmental Medicine and Child Neurology, 54*, 254–259. doi: 10.1111/j.1469-8749.2011.04161.x

Martin, C. L., Ruble, D. N., & Szkrybalo, J. (2002). Cognitive theories of early gender development. *Psychological Bulletin, 128*, 903–933. doi: 10.1037/0033-2909.128.6.903

Martin, J. L., & Ross, H. S. (2005). Sibling aggression: Sex differences and parents' reactions. *International Journal of Behavioral Development, 29*, 129–138. doi: 10.1080/01650250444000469

Martinez, G. M., Chandra, A., Abma, J. C., Jones, J., & Mosher, W. D. (2006). Fertility, contraception, and fatherhood: Data on men and women from Cycle 6 (2002) of the 2002 National Survey of Family Growth. *National Center for Health Statistics Vital and Health Statistics, 26*, 1–142.

Martinez-Brockman, J. L., Shebl, F. M., Harari, N., & Perez-Escamilla, R. (2017). An assessment of the social cognitive predictors of exclusive breastfeeding using the Health Action Process Approach. *Social Science and Medicine, 182*, 106–116. doi: 10.1016/j.socscimed.2017.04.014

Martins, C., & Gaffan, E. A. (2000). Effects of early mental depression on patterns of infant-mother attachment: A meta-analytic investigation. *Journal of Child Psychology and Psychiatry, 41*, 737–746. doi: 10.1111/1469-7610.00661

Martorell, G. A., & Bugental, D. B. (2006). Maternal variation in stress reactivity: Implications for harsh parenting practices with very young children. *Journal of Family Psychology, 20*, 641–647. doi: 10.1037/0893-3200.20.4.641

Masche, J. G. (2010). Explanation of normative declines in parents' knowledge about their adolescent children. *Journal of Adolescence, 33*, 271–284. doi: 10.1016/j.adolescence.2009.08.002

Mash, E. J., Johnston, C., & Kovitz, K. (1983). A comparison of the mother–child interactions of physically abused and non-abused children during play and task situations. *Journal of Clinical Child Psychology, 12*, 337–346. doi: 10.1080/15374418309533154

Masten, A. S. (2014). *Ordinary magic: Resilience in development*. New York, NY: Guilford Press. BF 723 R46 M37

Masten, A. S., & Cicchetti, D. (2016). Resilience in development: Progress and transformation. In D. Cicchetti (Ed.), *Developmental psychopathology* (3rd ed., Vol. 4, pp. 271–333). Hoboken, NJ: Wiley.

Mayes, S. D., & Lockridge, R. (2018). Brief report: How accurate are teacher reports of autism symptoms compared to parent report? *Journal of Autism and Developmental Disorders, 48*, 1833–1840. doi: 10.1007/s10803-017-3325-8

McCloskey, G., & Perkins, L. A. (2013). *Essentials of executive functions assessment*. New York, NY: Wiley.

McConnell, D., Savage, A., Sobsey, D., & Uditsky, B. (2015). Benefit-finding or finding benefits? The positive impact of having a disabled child. *Disability and Society, 30*, 29–45. doi: 10.1080/09687599.2014.984803

McCord, B. L., & Raval, V. V. (2016). Asian Indian immigrant and White American maternal emotion socialization and child socio-emotional functioning. *Journal of Child and Family Studies, 25*, 464–474. doi: 10.1007/s10826-015-0227-2

McCullough, C., & Shaffer, A. (2014). Maternal depressive symptoms and child externalizing problems: Moderating effects of emotionally maltreating parenting behaviors. *Journal of Child and Family Studies, 23*, 389–398. doi: 10.1007/s10826-013-9804-4

McDonald, S. E., Ma, L., Green, K. E., Hitti, S. A., Cody, A. M., Donovan, C., . . . Ascione, F. R. (2018). Evaluation of the Parent-Report Inventory of Callous-Unemotional Traits in a sample of children recruited from intimate partner violence services: A multidimensional Rasch analysis. *Journal of Clinical Psychology, 74*, 418–441. doi: 10.1002/jclp.22497

McGillicuddy, N. B., Rychtarik, R. G., Morsheimer, E. T., & Burke-Storer, M. R. (2007). Agreement between parent and adolescent reports of adolescent substance use. *Journal of Child and Adolescent Substance Use, 16*, 59–78. doi: 10.1300/J029v16n04_04

McGillicuddy-DeLisi, A. V. (1982a). Parental beliefs about developmental processes. *Human Development, 25*, 192–200. doi: 10.1159/000272796

McGillicuddy-DeLisi, A. V. (1982b). The relationship between parents' beliefs about development and family constellation, socioeconomic status, and parents' teaching strategies. In L. M. Laosa & I. E. Sigel (Eds.), *Families as learning environments for children* (pp. 262–299). New York, NY: Plenum Press.

McGillicuddy-DeLisi, A. V. (1985). The relationship between parental beliefs and children's cognitive level. In I. E. Sigel (Ed.), *Parental belief systems* (pp. 7–24) Hillsdale, NJ Erlbaum.

McGillicuddy-DeLisi, A. V. (1992). Parents' beliefs and children's personal-social development. In I. E. Sigel, A. V. McGillicuddy-DeLisi, & J. J. Goodnow (Eds.), *Parental belief systems* (2nd ed., pp. 115–142). Hillsdale, NJ: Erlbaum.

McGillicuddy-DeLisi, A. V., & Subramanian, S. (1994). Tanzanian and United States mothers' beliefs about parents' and teachers' roles in children's knowledge acquisition. *International Journal of Behavioral Development, 17*, 209–237. doi: 10.1177/016502549401700201

McGillicuddy-DeLisi, A. V., & Subramanian, S. (1996). How do children develop knowledge: Beliefs of Tanzanian and American mothers. In S. Harkness & C. M. Super (Eds.), *Parents' cultural belief systems* (pp. 143–168). New York, NY: Guilford Press.

McIntosh, H., Hart, D., & Youniss, J. (2007). The influence of family political discussion on youth civic development: Which parent qualities matter? *Political Science and Politics, 40*, 495–499. doi: 10.1017/S1049096507070758

McKenna, J. J., & Gettler, L. T. (2016). There is no such thing as infant sleep, there is no such thing as breastfeeding, there is only *breastsleeping. Acta Paedetrica, 105*, 17–21. doi: 10.1111/apa.13161

McKenna, J. J., & Gettler, L. T. (2017). Supporting a 'bottom-up,' new, no-holds-barred, psycho-anthro-pediatrics: Making room (scientifically) for bedsharing families. *Sleep Medicine Reviews, 32*, 1–3. doi10.1111/apa.13139

McMahon. C. A., & Meins, E. (2012). Mind-mindedness, parenting stress, and emotional availability in mothers of preschoolers. *Early Childhood Research Quarterly, 27*, 245–252. doi: 10.1016/j.ecresq.2011.08.002

Mehta, U. M., Bhagyavathi, M. D., Kumar, C. N., Thirthalli, J., & Gangadhar, B. N. (2014). Cognitive deconstruction of parenting in schizophrenia: The role of theory of mind. *Australian and New Zealand Journal of Psychiatry, 48*, 249–258. doi10.1177%2F0004867413500350

Meins, E. (1997). *Security of attachment and the social development of cognition.* New York, NY Psychology Press.

Meins, E. (2012). Social relationships and children's understanding of mind: Attachment, internal states, and mind-mindedness. In M. Siegal & L. Surian (Eds.), *Access to language and cognitive development* (pp. 23–43). New York, NY: Oxford University Press.

Meins, E. (2013). Sensitive attunement to infants' internal states: Operationalizing the construct of mind-mindedness. *Attachment and Human Development, 15*, 524–544. doi: 10.1080/14616734.2013.830388

Meins, E., Fernyhough, C., Arnott, B., Leekam, S. R., & de Rosnay, M. (2013). Mind-mindedness and theory of mind: Mediating roles of language and perspectival symbolic play. *Child Development, 84,* 1777–1790. doi: 10.1111/cdev.12061

Meins, E., Fernyhough, C., de Rosnay, M., Arnott, B., Leekam, S. R., & Turner, M. (2012). Mind-mindedness as a multidimensional construct: Appropriate and nonattuned mind-related comments independently predict infant-mother attachment in a socially diverse sample. *Infancy, 17,* 393–415. doi: 10.1111/j.1532-7078.2011.00087.x NA

Meins, E., Fernyhough, C., Wainwright, R., Clark-Carter, D., Gupta, M. D., Fradley, E., & Tuckey, M. (2003). Pathways to understanding mind: Construct validity and predictive validity of maternal mind-mindedness. *Child Development, 74,* 1194–1211. doi: 10.1111/1467-8624.00601

Meins, E., Fernyhough, C., Wainwright, R., Gupta, M. D., Fradley, E., & Tuckey, M. (2002). Maternal mind-mindedness and attachment security as predictors of theory of mind understanding. *Child Development, 73,* 1715–1726. doi: 10.1111/1467-8624.00501

Meirsschaut, M., Roeyers, H., & Warreyn, P. (2010). Parenting in families with a child with autism spectrum disorder and a typically developing child: Mothers' experiences and cognitions. *Research in Autism Spectrum Disorders, 4,* 661–669. doi: 10.1016/j.rasd.2010.01.002

Melson, G. F., Ladd, G. W., & Hsu, H. (1993). Maternal support networks, maternal cognitions, and young children's social and cognitive development. *Child Development, 64,* 1401–1417. doi: 10.1111/1467-8624.ep9402220351

Merrifield, K. A., & Gamble, W. C. (2013). Associations among marital qualities, supportive and undermining coparenting, and parenting self-efficacy: Testing spillover and stress-buffering processes. *Journal of Family Issues, 34,* 510–533. doi: 10.1177/0192513X12445561

Merrifield, K. A., Gamble, W. C., & Yu, J. J. (2015). Using social cognitive theory to understand meta-parenting in parents of young children. *Family Science, 6,* 362–369. doi: 10.1080/19424620.2015.1076495

Mesman, J., & Groeneveld, M. G. (2018). Gendered parenting in early childhood: Subtle but unmistakable if you know where to look. *Child Development Perspectives, 12,* 22–27. doi: 10.1111/cdep.12250

Messina, I., Cattaneo, L., Venuti, P., de Pisapia, N. Serra, M., Esposita, G., . . . Bornstein, M. H. (2015). Sex-specific automatic responses to infant cries: TMS reveals greater excitability in females than males in motor evoked potentials. *Frontiers in Psychology, 6,* 1909. doi: 10.3389/fpsyg.2015.01909

Mezulis, A. H., Hyde, J. S., & Clark, R. (2004). Father involvement moderates the effect of maternal depression during a child's infancy on child behavior problems in kindergarten. *Journal of Family Psychology, 18,* 575–588. doi: 10.1037/0893-3200.18.4.575

Michels, N., Vanaelst, B., Stoppie, E., Huybrechts, I., Bamman, K., De Henauw, S., & Sloen, I. (2013). Parental and children's report of emotional problems: Agreement, explanatory factors, and event-emotion correlation. *Child and Adolescent Mental Health, 18,* 180–186. doi: 10.1111/j.1475-3588.2012.00672.x

Mileva-Seitz, V. R., Bakermans-Kranenburg, M. J., Battaini, C., & Luijk, M. P. C. M. (2017). Parent-child bed-sharing: The good, the bad, and the burden of evidence. *Sleep Medicine Reviews, 32,* 4–17. doi: 10.1016/j.smrv.2016.03.003

Milkie, M. A., Norris, D. R., & Bierman, A. (2011). The long arm of offspring: Adult children's troubles as teenagers and elderly parents' mental health. *Research on Aging, 33,* 327–355. doi: 10.1177/0164027511400632

Miller, C. L., Miceli, P. J., Whitman, T. L., & Borkowski, J. G. (1996). Cognitive readiness to parent and intellectual-emotional development in children of adolescent mothers. *Developmental Psychology*, *32*, 533–541. doi: 10.1037/0012-1649.32.3.533

Miller, E., & Almon, J. (2009). *Crisis in the kindergarten: Why children need to play in school.* College Park, MD: Alliance for Childhood.

Miller, L. E., Perkins, K. A., Dai, Y. G., & Fein, D. A. (2017). Comparison of parent report and direct assessment of child skills in toddlers. *Research in Autism Spectrum Disorders*, *41–42*, 57–65. doi: 10.1016/j.rasd.2017.08.002

Miller, P., Henry, D., & Votruba-Drzal, E. (2016). Strengthening causal inferences in developmental research. *Child Development Perspectives*, *10*, 275–280. doi: 10.1111/cdep.12202

Miller, P. J., Fung, H., Lin, S., Chen, E. C., & Boldt, B. R. (2012). How socialization happens on the ground: Narrative practices as alternate socializing pathways in Taiwanese and European families. *Monographs of the Society for Research in Child Development*, *77*(1). doi: 10.1111/j.1540-5834.2011.00641.x

Miller, S. A. (1986). Parents' beliefs about their children's cognitive abilities. *Developmental Psychology*, *22*, 276–284. doi: 10.1037/0012-1649.22.2.276

Miller, S. A. (1988). Parents' beliefs about cognitive development. *Child Development*, *59*, 259–285. doi: 10.1111/1467-8624.ep8588509

Miller, S. A. (1995). Parents' attributions for their children's behavior. *Child Development*, *66*, 1557–1584. doi: 10.1111/1467-8624.ep9601152089

Miller, S. A. (2000). Children's understanding of preexisting differences in knowledge and belief. *Developmental Review*, *20*, 227–282. doi: 10.1006/drev.1999.0501

Miller, S. A. (2012). *Theory of mind: Beyond the preschool years.* New York, NY: Psychology Press.

Miller, S. A. (2016). *Parenting and theory of mind.* New York, NY: Oxford University Press.

Miller S. A., & Davis, T. L. (1992). Beliefs about children: A comparative study of mothers, teachers, peers, and self. *Child Development*, *63*, 1251–1265. doi: 10.2307/1131531

Miller, S. A., Davis, T. L., Wilde, C. A., & Brown, J. (1993). Parents' knowledge of their children's preferences. *International Journal of Behavioral Development*, *16*, 35–60. doi: 10.1177/016502549301600103

Miller, S. A., Manhal, M., & Mee, L. (1991). Parental beliefs, parental accuracy, and children's cognitive performance: A search for causal relations. *Developmental Psychology*, *27*, 267–276. doi: 10.1037/0012-1649.27.2.267

Miller, S. A., White, N., & Delgado, M. (1980). Adults' conceptions of children's cognitive abilities. *Merrill-Palmer Quarterly*, *26*, 135–151.

Miller-Heyl, J., MacPhee, D., & Fritz, J. J. (1998). DARE to be you: A family-support, early prevention program. *Journal of Primary Prevention*, *18*, 257–285. doi: 10.1023/A:1024602927381

Miller-Loncar, C. L., Landry, S. H., Smith, K. E., & Swank, P. R. (1997). The role of child-centered perspectives in a model of parenting. *Journal of Experimental Child Psychology*, *66*, 341–361. doi: 10.1006/jecp.1997.2392

Miller-Loncar, C. L., Landry, S. H., Smith, K. E., & Swank, P. R. (2000). The influence of complexity of maternal thoughts on sensitive parenting and children's social responsiveness. *Journal of Applied Developmental Psychology*, *21*, 335–356. doi: 10.1016/S0193-3973(00)00044-7

Mills, R. S. L. (2005). Taking stock of the developmental literature on shame. *Developmental Review*, *25*, 26–63. doi: 10.1016/j.dr.2004.08.001

Mills, R. S. L., & Rubin, K. H. (1990). Parental beliefs about problematic social behaviors in early childhood. *Child Development, 61,* 138–151. doi: 10.1111/1467-8624. ep9102040549

Mills, R. S. L., & Rubin, K. H. (1993). Parental ideas as influences on children's social competence. In S. Duck (Ed.), *Learning about relationships* (pp. 98–117). Thousand Oaks, CA: Sage.

Milner, J. S. (1993). Social information processing and physical child abuse. *Clinical Psychology Review, 13,* 275–294. doi: 10.1016/0272-7358(93)90024-G

Milner, J. S. (2003). Social information-processing in high-risk and physically abusive parents. *Child Abuse and Neglect, 27,* 7–20. doi: 10.1016/S0145-2134(02)00506-9

Mindell, J. A., Leichman, E. S., Puzino, K., Walters, R., & Bhullar, B. (2015). Parental concerns about infant and toddler sleeps assessed by a mobile app. *Behavioral Sleep Medicine, 13,* 359–374. doi: 10.1080/15402002.2014.905475

Mize, J., Pettit, G. S., & Brown, E. G. (1995). Mothers' supervision of their children's peer play: Relations with beliefs, perceptions, and knowledge. *Developmental Psychology, 31,* 311–321. doi: 10.1037/0012-1649.31.2.311

Moffitt, T. E. (1993). Adolescence-limited and life-course-persistent antisocial behavior: A developmental taxonomy. *Psychological Review, 100,* 674–701. doi: 10.1037/0033-295X.100.4.674

Mollborn, S., & Everett, B. (2010). Correlates and consequence of parent-teen incongruence in reports of teens' sexual experience. *Journal of Sex Research, 47,* 314–329. doi: 10.1080/00224490902954315

Mondschein, E. R., Adolph, K. E., & Tamis-LeMonda, C. S. (2000). Gender bias in mothers' expectations about infant crawling. *Journal of Experimental Child Psychology, 77,* 304–316. doi: 10.1006/jecp.2000.2597

Moorman, E. A., & Pomerantz, E. M. (2010). Ability mindsets influence the quality of mothers' involvement in children's learning: An experimental investigation. *Developmental Psychology, 46,* 1354–1362. doi: 10.1037/a0020376

Morawska, A., Sanders, M. R., & Winter, L. (2007). *The Knowledge of Effective Parenting Scale.* Brisbane, QLD, Australia: The School of Psychology, The University of Queensland.

Morawska, A., Winter, L., & Sanders, M. R. (2009). Parenting knowledge and its role in the prediction of dysfunctional parenting and disruptive child behavior. *Child: Care, Health and Development, 35,* 217–226. doi: 10.1111/j.1365-2214.2008.00929.x

Morey, J. N., & Gentzley, A. L. (2017). Parents' perceptions of and responses to children's emotions: Relations with meta-emotion philosophy and adult attachment. *Parenting: Science and Practice, 17,* 73–103. doi: 10.1080/15295192.2017.1304782

Mori, Y., Downs, J., Wong, K., Heyworth, J., & Leonard, H. (2018). Comparing parental well-being and its determinants across three different genetic disorders causing intellectual disability. *Journal of Autism and Developmental Disorders, 48,* 1651–1665. doi: 10.1007/s10803-017-3420-x

Moroni, S. Dumont, H., Trautwein, U., Niggli, A., & Baeriswyl, F. (2015). The need to distinguish between quantity and quality in research on parent involvement: The example of parental help with homework. *Journal of Educational Research, 108,* 417–431. doi: 10.1080/00220671.2014.901283

Morrell, J. M. B. (1999). The role of maternal cognitions in infant sleep problems as assessed by a new instrument, the Maternal Cognitions about Infant Sleep

Questionnaire. *Journal of Child Psychology and Psychiatry, 40,* 247–258. doi: 10.1111/1469-7610.00438

Morris, A. S., Criss, M. M., Silk, J. S., & Houltber, B. J. (2017). The impact of parenting on emotion regulation during childhood and adolescence. *Child Development Perspectives, 11,* 233–238. doi: 10.1111/cdep.12238

Morris, A. S., Squeglia, L. M., Jacobus, J., & Silk, J. S. (2018). Adolescent brain development: Implications for understanding risk and resilience processes through neuroimaging research. *Journal of Research on Adolescence, 28,* 4–9. doi: 10.11111/jora.12379

Morris, L. B. (2013). Mothers' perceptions of their children's play: Scale development and validation. *Universal Journal of Psychology, 1,* 121–144. doi: 10.13189/ujp.2013.010306

Mounts, N. S., & Kim, H. (2009). Expectations for parental management of dating in an ethnically diverse sample of early adolescents. *Journal of Adolescent Research, 24,* 531–560. doi: 10.1177/0743558409338057

Moussaoui, N., & Braster, S. (2011). Perceptions and practices of stimulating children's cognitive development among Moroccan immigrant mothers. *Journal of Child and Family Studies, 29,* 370–383. doi: 10.1007/s10826-010-9401-8

Mowbray, C., Oyserman, D., Bybee, D., & MacFarlane, P. (2002). Parenting of mothers with a serious mental illness: Differential effects of diagnosis, clinical history, and other mental health variables. *Social Work Research, 26,* 225–240. doi: 10.1093/swr/26.4.225

Mowder, B. A., & Shamah, R. (2011). Parent Behavior Importance Questionnaire-Revised: Scale development and psychometric characteristics. *Journal of Child and Family Studies, 20,* 295–302. doi: 10.1007/s10826-010-9392-5

Muelenhard, C. L., & Peterson, Z. D. (2011). Distinguishing between *sex* and *gender*: History, current conceptualizations, and implications. *Sex Roles, 64,* 791–803. doi: 10.1007/s11199-011-9932-5

Muenks, K., Miele, D. B., Ramani, G. B., Stapleton, L. M., & Rowe, M. L. (2015). Parental beliefs about the fixedness of ability. *Journal of Applied Developmental Psychology, 41,* 78–89. doi: 10.1016/j.appdev.2015.08.002

Mugny, G., & Carugati, F. (1989). *Social representations of intelligence.* New York, NY: Cambridge University Press.

Murayama, K., Pekrun, R., Suzuki, M., Marsh, H. W., & Lichtenfeld, S. (2015). Don't aim too high for your kids: Parental overaspiration undermines students' learning in mathematics. *Journal of Personality and Social Psychology, 111,* 766–779. doi: 10.1037/pspp0000079

Murdoch, K. W. (2013). An examination of parental self-efficacy among mothers and fathers. *Psychology of Men and Masculinity, 14,* 314–323. doi: 10.1037/a0027009

Murphey, D. A. (1992). Constructing the child: Relations between parents' beliefs and child outcomes. *Developmental Review, 12,* 199–232. doi: 10.1016/0273-2297(92)90009-Q

Mynttinen, M., Pietila, A., & Kangasniemi, M. (2017). What does parental involvement mean in preventing adolescents' use of alcohol? An integrative review. *Journal of Child and Adolescent Substance Abuse, 26,* 338–351. doi: 10.1080/1067828X.2017.1306471

Nader-Grosbois, N., & Mazzone, S. (2015). Validation de la francophone de l' Emotion Regulation Checklist. *European Journal of Applied Psychology, 65,* 29–41. doi: 10.1016/j.erap.2014.10.002

Narad, M. E., Garner, A., Peugh, J. L., Tamm, L., Antonini, T. N., Kingery, K. M., . . . Epstein, J. N. (2015). Parent-teacher agreement on ADHD symptoms across development. *Psychological Assessment, 27,* 239–248. doi: 10.1037/a0037864

Natale, K., Aunola, K., & Nurmi, J. (2009). Children's school performance and their parents' causal attributions to ability and effort: A longitudinal study. *Journal of Applied Developmental Psychology, 30*, 14–22. doi: 10.1016/j.appdev.2008.10.002

National Vital Statistics Report (2018). Births: Final data for 2016. Retrieved from https://www.cdc.gov/nchs/data/nvsr/nvsr67/nvsr67_01.pdf

Neiderhiser, J. M., Reiss, D., Hetherington, E. M., & Plomin, R. (1999). Relationships between parenting and adolescent adjustment over time: Genetic and environmental contributions. *Developmental Psychology, 35*, 680–692.doi: 10.1037/0012-1649.35.3.680

Neisser, U., Boodoo, G., Bouchard, T. J., Jr., Boykin, A. W., Brody, N., Ceci, S. J., ... Urbina, S. (1996). Intelligence: Knowns and unknowns. *American Psychologist, 51*, 77–101. doi: 10.1037/0003-066X.51.2.77

Nelson, K. (2007). *Young minds in social worlds.* Cambridge, MA: Harvard University Press.

Nelson, S. K., Kushlev, K., English, T., Dunn, E. W., & Lyubomirsky, S. (2013). In defense of parenthood: Children are associated with more joy than misery. *Psychological Science, 24*, 3–10. doi: 10.1177/0956797612447798

Nelson, S. K., Kushlev, K., & Lyubomirsky, S. (2014). The pains and pleasure of parenting: When, why, and how is parenthood associated with more or less well-being? *Psychological Bulletin, 140*, 846–895. doi: 10.1037/a0035444

Neto, F., & Furnham, A. (2011). Sex differences in parents' estimations of their own and their children's multiple intelligences: A Portuguese replication. *The Spanish Journal of Psychology, 14*, 99–110. doi: 10.5209/rev_SJOP.2011.v14.n1.8

Nevo, B., & Khader, A. M. B. (1995). Cross-cultural, gender, and age differences in Singaporean mothers' conceptions of children's intelligence. *Journal of Social Psychology 135*, 509–517. doi: 10.1080/00224545.1995.9712219

Nevsimalova, S., & Bruni, O. (Eds.). (2017). *Sleep disorders in children.* Cham, Switzerland: Springer International Publishing.

Newman, L., Stevenson, C. S., Bergman, L. R., & Boyce, P. (2007). Borderline personality disorder, mother-infant interaction and parenting perceptions: Preliminary findings. *The Australian and New Zealand Journal of Psychiatry, 41*, 598–605. doi: 10.1080/00048670701392833

Nicholson, J. S., Howard, K. S., & Borkowski, J. G. (2008). Mental models for parenting: Correlates of metaparenting among fathers of young children. *Fathering, 6*, 39–61. doi: 10.3149/fth.0601.39

Niela-Vilen, H., Axelin, A., Salantera, S., & Melender, H. (2014). Internet-based peer support for parents: A systematic integrative review. *International Journal of Nursing Studies, 51*, 1524–1537. doi: 10.1016/j.ijnurstu.2014.06.009

Nigg, J. T. (2016). Attention and impulsivity. In D. Cicchetti (Ed.), *Developmental psychopathology: Vol. 3. Maladaptation and psychopathology* (3rd ed., pp. 591–646). Hoboken, NJ: Wiley.

Ninio, A. (1979). The naive theory of the infant and other maternal attitudes m two subgroups in Israel. *Child Development, 50*, 976–980. doi: 10.1111/1467-8624.ep7251687

Ninio, A. (1987). A comparison of mothers' and fathers' beliefs concerning the timetable of cognitive development in infancy. *Israel Social Science Research, 5*, 6–16.

Ninio, A. (1988). The effects of cultural background, sex, and parenthood on beliefs about the timetable of cognitive development in infancy. *Merrill-Palmer Quarterly, 34*, 369–388.

Ninio, A., & Rinott, N. (1988). Fathers' involvement in the care of their infants and their attributions of cognitive competence in infants. *Child Development, 59,* 652–663. doi: 10.1111/1467-8624.ep8589204

Nobre-Lima, L., da Luz Vale-Dias, M., Mendes, T. V., Monico, L., & MacPhee, D. (2014). The Portuguese version of the Knowledge of Infant Development Inventory-P (KIDI-P). *European Journal of Developmental Psychology, 11,* 740–745. doi: 10.1080/17405629.2014.929941

Notten, N., & Nikken, P. (2016). Boys and girls taking risks online: A gendered perspective on social context and adolescents' risky online behavior. *New Media and Society, 18,* 966–988. doi: 10.1177/1461444814552379

Nucci, L., & Smetana, J. G. (1996). Mothers' concepts of young children's areas of personal freedom. *Child Development, 67,* 1870–1886. doi: 10.1111/1467-8624. ep9704041069stop

Nuendorf, A., Niemi, R. G., & Smets, K. (2016). The compensation effect of civic education on political engagement: How civic classes make up for missing parental socialization. *Political Behavior, 38,* 923–939. doi: 10.1007/s11109-016-9341-0

Nuttall, A. K., Valentino, K., Wang, L., Lefever, J. B., & Borkowski, J. G. (2015). Maternal history of parentification and warm responsiveness: The mediating role of knowledge of infant development. *Journal of Family Psychology, 29,* 863–872. doi: 10.1037/fam0000112

Nylen, K. J., Moran, T. E., Franklin, C. L., & O'Hara, M. W. (2006). Maternal depression: A review of relevant treatment approaches for mothers and infants. *Infant Mental Health Journal, 27,* 327–343. doi: 10.1002/imhj.20095

O'Callaghan, M. F., Borkowski, J. G., Whitman, T. L., Maxwell, S. E., & Keogh, D. (1999). A model of adolescent parenting: The role of cognitive readiness to parent. *Journal of Research on Adolescence, 9,* 203–225. doi: 10.1207/s15327795jra0902_5

O'Donnell, L., Stueve, A., Duran, R., Myint-U., A., Agronick, C., Doval, A. S., & Wilson-Simmons, R. (2008). Parenting practices, parents' underestimation of daughters' risks, and alcohol and sexual behaviors of urban girls. *Journal of Adolescent Health, 42,* 496–502. doi: 10.1016/j.jadohealth.2007.10.008

O'Hara, M. W., & McCabe, J. E. (2013). Postpartum depression: Current status and future directions. *Annual Review of Clinical Psychology, 9,* 379–407. doi: 10.1146/annurev-clinpsy-050212-185612

Okagaki, l., & Bingham, G. E. (2005). Parents' social cognitions and their parenting behaviors. In T. Luster & L. Okagaki (Eds.), *Parenting: An ecological perspective* (2nd ed., pp. 3–33). Mahwah, NJ: Erlbaum.

6Okagaki, L., & Frensch, P. A. (1998). Parenting and children's school achievement: A multiethnic perspective. *American Educational Research Journal, 35,* 123–144. doi: 10.2307/1163454

Okagaki, L., & Sternberg, R. J. (1993). Parental beliefs and children's school performance. *Child Development, 64,* 36–56. doi: 10.1111/1467 8624.ep9309015106

Olweus, D. (1993). *Bullying at school: What we know and what we can do.* Oxford, UK/Cambridge, MA: Blackwell.

Olweus, D. (2013). School bullying: Development and some important challenges. *Annual Review of Clinical Psychology, 9,* 751–780. doi: 10.1146/annurev-clinpsy-050212-185516

Oosterhoff, B., & Metzger, A. (2016). Mother-adolescent civic messages: Associations with adolescent civic behavior and civic judgments. *Journal of Applied Developmental Psychology, 43,* 62–70. doi: 10.1016/j.appdev.2016.01.001

Oppenheim, D., Koren-Karie, N., Dolev, S., & Yirmiya, N. (2009). Maternal insight and resolution of the diagnosis are associated with secure attachment in preschoolers with autism spectrum disorders. *Child Development, 80,* 519–527. doi: 10.1111/j.1467-8624.2009.01276.x.

Orme, J. G., & Hamilton, M. (1987). Measuring parental knowledge of normative child development. *Social Service Review, 61,* 655–669.

Ornaghi, V., Brockmeier, J., & Gavazzi, I. G. (2011). The role of language games in children's understanding of mental states: A training study. *Journal of Cognition and Development, 12,* 239–259. doi: 10.1080/15248372.2011.563487

O'Sullivan, J. T., & Howe, M. L. (1996). Causal attributions and reading achievement: Individual differences in low-income families. *Contemporary Educational Psychology, 21,* 363–387. doi: 10.1006/ceps.1996.0027

O'Sullivan, L. F., & Thompson, A. E. (2014). Sexuality in adolescence. In D. L. Tolman & L. M. Diamond (Eds.), *APA handbook of sexuality and psychology: Vol. 1. Person-based approaches* (pp. 433–486). Washington, DC: American Psychological Association. doi: 10.1037/14193-015

Out, D., Pieper, S., Bakermans-Kranenburg, & van IJzendoorn, M. H. (2010). Physiological reactivity to infant crying: A behavioral genetic study. *Genes, Brain, and Behavior, 9,* 868–876. doi: 10.1111/j.1601-183X.2010.00624.x

Ozdemir, S. B., & Cheah, C. S. L. (2015). Turkish mothers' parenting beliefs in response to preschoolers' aggressive and socially withdrawn behaviors. *Journal of Child and Family Studies, 24,* 687–702. doi: 10.1007/s10826-013-9879-y

Pachter, L. M., & Dworkin, P. H. (1997). Maternal expectations about normal child development in 4 cultural groups. *Archives of Pediatrics and Adolescent Medicine, 151,* 1144–1150. doi: 10.1001/archpedi.1997.02170480074011

Padilla-Walker, L. M., Coyne, S. M., & Collier, K. M. (2016). Longitudinal relations between parental media monitoring and adolescent aggression, prosocial behavior, and externalizing problems. *Journal of Adolescence, 46,* 86–97. doi: 10.1016/j.adolescence.2015.11.002

Padilla-Walker, L. M., Coyne, S. M., Kroff, S. L., & Memmoff-Elison, M. K. (2018). The protective role of parental media monitoring style from early to late adolescence. *Journal of Youth and Adolescence, 47,* 445–459. doi: 10.1007/s10964-017-0722-4

Padilla-Walker L. M., Son, D., & Nelson, L. J. (2018). A longitudinal growth mixture model of child disclosure to parents across adolescence. *Journal of Family Psychology, 32,* 475–483. doi: 10.1037/fam0000369

Palacios, J. (1990). Parents' ideas about the development and education of their children: Answers to some questions. *International Journal of Behavioral Development, 13,* 137–155. doi: 10.1177/016502549001300201

Palacios, J., Gonzalez, M., & Moreno, M. (1992). Stimulating the child in the zone of proximal development: The role of parents' ideas. In I. E. Sigel, A. V. McGillicuddy-DeLisi, & J. J. Goodnow (Eds.), *Parental belief systems* (2nd ed., pp. 71–94). Hillsdale, NJ: Erlbaum.

Palacios, J., & Moreno, M. (1996). Parents' and adolescents' ideas on children: Origins and transmission of intracultural diversity. In S. Harkness & C. M. Super (Eds.), *Parents' cultural belief systems* (pp. 215–253). New York, NY: Guilford Press.

Pancer, S. M. (2015). *The psychology of citizenship and civic engagement.* New York, NY: Oxford University Press.

Pancer, S. M., Pratt, M., Hunsberger, B., & Alisar, S. (2007). Community and political involvement in adolescence: What distinguishes the activists from the uninvolved? *Journal of Community Psychology, 35*, 741–759. doi: 10.1002/jcop.20176

Park, J. L., Hudec, K. L., & Johnston, C. (2017). Parental ADHD symptoms and parenting behaviors: A meta-analytic review. *Clinical Psychology Review, 56*, 25–39. doi: 1016/j.cpr.2017.05.003

Parker, A. E., Halberstadt, A. G., Dunsmore, J. C., Townley, G., Bryant, A., Thompson, J. A., & Beale, K. S. (2012). "Emotions are windows into one's heart": A qualitative analysis of parental beliefs about children's emotions across three ethnic groups. *Monographs of the Society for Research in Child Development, 77*(3). doi: 10.1111/j.1540-5834.2012.00676.x

Parks, P. L., & Smeriglio, V. L. (1986). Relationships among parental knowledge, quality of stimulation in the home and infant development. *Family Relations, 35*, 411–416. doi: 10.2307/584369

Parmar, P., Harkness, S., & Super, C. M. (2004). Asian and Euro-American parents' ethnotheories of play and learning: Effects on preschool children's home routines and school behaviour. *International Journal of Behavioral Development, 28*, 97–104. doi: 10.1080/01650250344000307

Parsons, C. E., Young, K. S., Rochat, T. J., Kringelbach, L. K., & Stein, A. (2012). Postnatal depression and its effects on child development: A review of evidence from low- and middle-income countries. *British Medical Bulletin, 101*, 57–79. doi: 10.1093/bmb/ldr047

Paschall, K. W., & Mastergeorge, A. M. (2016). A review of 25 years of research in bidirectionality in parent-child relationships: An examination of methodological approaches. *International Journal of Behavioral Development, 40*, 442–451. doi: 10.1177/0165025415607379

Patall, E. A., Cooper, H., & Robinson, J. C. (2008). Parent involvement in homework: A research synthesis. *Review of Educational Research, 78*, 1039–1101. doi: 10.3102/0034654308325185

Paterson, A. D., Babb, K. A., Camodeca, A., Goodwin, J., Hakim-Larson, J., Voelker, S., & Gragg, M. (2012). Emotion-Related Parenting Styles (ERPS): A short form for measuring parental meta-emotion philosophy. *Early Education and Development, 23*, 583–602. doi: 10.1080/10409289.2011.569316

Pawlby, S., Fernyhough, C., Meins, E., Pariante, C. M., Seneviratne, G., & Bentall, R. P. (2010). Mind-mindedness and maternal responsiveness in infant-mother interactions in mothers with severe mental illness. *Psychological Medicine, 40*, 1861–1869. doi: 10.1017/S0033291709992340

Peck, S. C., Brodish, A. B., Malanchuk, O., Banerjee, M., & Eccles, J. S. (2014). Racial/ethnic socialization and identity development in Black families: The role of parent and youth reports. *Developmental Psychology, 50*, 1897–1909. doi: 10.1037/a0036800

Pena, J. V., Menendez, C. R., & Torio, S. (2010). Family and socialization processes: Parental perception and evaluation of their children's household labor. *Journal of Comparative Family Studies, 41*, 131–148.

Perez Rivera, M. B., & Dunsmore, J. C. (2011). Mothers' acculturation and beliefs about emotions, mother-child emotion discourse, and children's emotion understanding in Latino families. *Early Education and Development, 22*, 324–354. doi: 10.1080/10409281003702000

Perrigo, J. L., Berkovits, L. D., Cederbaum, J. A., Williams, M. E., & Hurlburt, M. S. (2018). Child abuse and neglect re-report rates for young children with developmental delays. *Child Abuse and Neglect, 83*, 1–9. doi: 10.1016/j.chiabu.2018.05.029

Perry, W. G. (1970). *Forms of intellectual and ethical development in the college years.* New York, NY: Holt, Rinehart, and Winston.

Pesu, L., Viljaranta, J., & Aunola, K. (2016). The role of parents' and teachers' beliefs in children's self-concept development. *Journal of Applied Developmental Psychology, 44*, 63–71. doi: 10.1016/j.appdev.2016.03.001

Peterson, C., Xu, L., Florence, C., Parks, S. E., Miller, T. R., Barr, R. G., . . . Steinbeigle, R. (2014). The medical cost of abusive trauma in the United States. *Pediatrics, 134*, 91–99. doi: 10.1542/peds.2014-0117

Peterson, C. C., Garnett, M., Kelly, A., & Attwood, T. (2009). Everyday social and conversation applications of theory-of-mind understanding by children with autism-spectrum disorders or typical development. *European Child and Adolescent Psychiatry, 18*, 105–115. doi: 10.1007/s00787-008-0711-y

Pezdek, K., Berry, T., & Renno, P. A. (2002). Children's mathematics achievement: The role of parents' perceptions and their involvement in homework. *Journal of Educational Psychology, 94*, 771–777. doi: 10.1037/0022-0663.94.4.771

Pharis, M. E., & Manosevitz, M. (1980). Parental models: A means for evaluating different prenatal contexts. In D. B. Sawin, R. C. Hawkins, L. O. Walker, & J. H. Penticuff (Eds.), *Exceptional infant* (Vol. 4, pp. 215–233). New York, NY: Bruner/Mazel.

Phelan, T. W. (1998). *Surviving your adolescents: How to manage and let go of your 13-18 year old* (2nd ed.).Glen Ellyn, IL: Child Management Press.

Phillips, B. A., Connors, F., & Curtner-Smith, M. E. (2017). Parenting children with Down syndrome: An analysis of parenting styles, parenting dimensions, and parental stress. *Research in Developmental Disabilities, 68*, 9–19. doi: 10.1016/j.ridd.2017.06.010

Phillipson, S. (2006). Cultural variability in parent and child achievement attributions: A study from Hong Kong. *Educational Psychology, 26*, 625–642. doi: 10.1080/01443410500390772

Phinney, J. S. (1992). The Multigroup Ethnic Identity Measure: A new scale for use with diverse groups. *Journal of Adolescent Research, 7*, 156–176. doi: 10.1177/074355489272003

Piaget, J. (1926). *The language and thought of the child.* New York, NY: Harcourt Brace.

Piaget, J. (1932). *The moral judgment of the child.* London, UK: Routledge & Kegan Paul.

Pickett, W., Marlenga, B., & Berg, R. L. (2003). Parental knowledge of child development and the assignment of tractor work to children. *Pediatrics, 112*, e11–16. doi: 10.1542/peds.112.1.e11

Pillay, D., Girdler, S., Collins, M., & Leonard, H. (2012). "It's not what you were expecting, but it's still a beautiful journey": The experience of mothers of children with Down syndrome. *Disability and Rehabilitation, 34*, 1501–1510. doi: 10.3109/09638288.2011.650313

Pillow, B. H. (2008). Development of children's understanding of cognitive activities. *Journal of Genetic Psychology, 169*, 297–321. doi: 10.3200/GNTP.169.4.297-321

Podsakoff, P. M., MacKenzie, S. B., & Podsakoff, N. P. (2012). Sources of method bias in social science research and recommendations on how to control it. *Annual Review of Psychology, 63*, 539–569. doi: 10.1146/annurev-psych-120710-100452

Pratt, M. W., Hunsberger, B., Pancer, S. M., Roth, D., & Santolupa, S. (1993). Thinking about parenting: Reasoning about developmental issues across the life span. *Developmental Psychology, 29*, 585–595. doi: 10.1037/0012-1649.29.3.585

Prendergast, S., & MacPhee, D. (2018). Parental contributions to children's persistence and school readiness. *Early Childhood Research Quarterly*, *45*, 31–44. doi: 10.1016/j.ecresq.2018.05.005

Price, G. G., & Gillingham, M. C. (1985). Effects of mothers' overestimations and underestimations of their children's intellectual ability: A reanalysis of Hunt and Paraskevopoulos. *Journal of Genetic Psychology*, *146*, 477–481. doi: 10.1080/00221325.1985.10532466

Priest, N., Walton, J., White, F., Kowal, E., Baker, A., & Paradies, Y. (2014). Understanding the complexities of ethnic-racial socialization processes for both minority and majority groups: A 30-year systematic review. *International Journal of Intercultural Relations*, *43*, 139–155. doi: 10.1016/j.ijintrel.2014.08.003

Prom-Wormley, E., & Maes, H. H. (2014). Parental influence on adolescent drug use. In L. M. Scheier & W. B. Hansen (Eds.), *Parenting and teen drug use* (pp. 15–36). New York, NY: Oxford University Press.

Pulsifer, M. B., Hoon, A. H., Palmer, F. B., Gopalan, R., & Capute, A. J. (1994). Maternal estimates of developmental age in preschool children. *Journal of Pediatrics*, *125*, S18–S24. doi: 10.1016/S0022-3476(94)70171-7

Punch, S. (2003). Childhoods in the majority world: Miniature adults or tribal children? *Sociology*, *37*, 277–295. doi: 10.1177/0038038503037002004

Putnam, S. P., Sanson, A. V., & Rothbart, M. K. (2002). Child temperament and parenting. In M. H. Bornstein (Ed.), *Handbook of parenting: Vol. 1. Children and parenting* (2nd ed., pp. 255–277). Mahwah, NJ: Erlbaum.

Quota, S., Punamaki, R., & Sarraj E. E. (2008). Child development and family mental health in war and military violence: The Palestinian experience. *International Journal of Behavioral Development*, *32*, 310–321. doi: 10.1177/0165025408090973

Racz, S. J., & McMahon, R. J. (2011). The relationship between parental knowledge and monitoring and child and adolescent conduct problems: A 10-year update. *Clinical Child and Family Psychology Review*, *14*, 377–398. doi: 10.1007/s10567-011-0099-y

Ramos, K. D. (2003). Intentional versus reactive bed co-sleeping. *Sleep Research Online*, *5*, 141–147.

Rangnathan, C., & Montemayor, R. (2014). Parental efficacy, parental monitoring efficacy, and monitoring among Asian-Indian parents of adolescents living in Chennai, India. *Journal of Adolescence*, *37*, 1363–1372. doi: 10.1016/j.adolescence.2014.10.002

Raty, H., & Kasanen, K. (2013). Parents' perceptions of their child's academic competencies construe their educational reality: Findings from a 9-year longitudinal study. *Journal of Applied Social Psychology*, *43*, 1110–1119. doi: 10.1111/jasp.12076

Raty, H., Vanska, J., Kasanen, K., & Karkkainen, R. (2002). Parents' explanations of their child's performance in mathematics and reading: A replication and extension of Yee and Eccles. *Sex Roles*, *46*, 121–128. doi: 10.1023/A:1016573627828

Rautianen, R., Raty, H., & Kasanen, K. (2016). Is children's intelligence malleable? Parental perspectives on implicit theories of intelligence. *Nordic Psychology*, *68*, 233–243. doi: 10.1080/19012276.2016.1149093

Reader, J. M., Teti, D. M., & Cleveland, M. J. (2017). Cognitions about infant sleep: Interparental differences, trajectories across the first year, and coparenting quality. *Journal of Family Psychology*, *31*, 453–463. doi: 10.1037/fam0000283

Reese, E., Haden, C. A., & Fivush, R. (1996). Mothers, fathers, daughters, sons: Gender differences in autobiographical reminiscing. *Research on Language and Social Interaction*, *29*, 27–56. doi: 10.1207/s15327973rlsi2901_3

Reich S. (2005). What do mothers know? Maternal knowledge of child development. *Infant Mental Health Journal, 26*, 143–156. doi: 10.1002/imhj.20

Reich, S. M., & Vandell, D. L. (2014). The interplay between parents and peers as socializing influences in children's development. In P. K. Smith & C. H. Hart (Eds.), *Wiley handbook of childhood social development* (2nd ed., pp. 263–280). Hoboken, NJ: Wiley.

Reis, A. H., de Oliveira, S. E. S., Bandeira, D. R., Andrade, N. C., Abreu, N., & Sperb, T. M. (2016). Emotion Regulation Checklist (ERC): Preliminary studies of cross-cultural adaptation and validation for use in Brazil. *Temas em Psicologia, 24*, 77–96. doi: 10.9788/TP2016.1-06

Reis, J. (1988). Child-rearing expectations and developmental knowledge according to maternal age and parity. *Infant Mental Health Journal, 9*, 287–304. doi: 10.1002/1097-0355(198824)9:4%3C287::AID-IMHJ2280090404%3E3.0.CO;2-3

Rescorla, L. A., Bochicchio, L., Achenbach, T. M., Ivanova, M. Y., Almquist, F., Begovac, I., . . . Verhulst, F. C. (2014). Parent-teacher agreement on children's problems in 21 societies. *Journal of Clinical Child and Adolescent Psychology, 43*, 627–642. doi: 10.1080/15374416.2014.900719

Rescorla, L. A., Ginzburg, S., Achenbach, T. M., Ivanova, M. Y., Almquist, F., Begovac, I., & Verhulst, F. C. (2013). Cross-informant agreement between parent-reported and adolescent self-reported problems in 25 societies. *Journal of Clinical Child and Adolescent Psychology, 42*, 262–273. doi: 10.1080/15374416.2012.717870

Rest, J. R. (1983). Morality. In P. H. Mussen (Ed.), *Handbook of child psychology: Vol. 3, Cognitive development* (4th ed., pp. 556–629). New York, NY: Wiley.

Reyes, N. M., Lindly, O. J., Chavez, A. E., Folan, A., Macias, K., Smith, K. A., . . . Zuckerman, K. (2018). Maternal beliefs about autism: A link between intervention services and autism severity in White and Latino mothers. *Research in Autism Spectrum Disorders, 51*, 38–48. doi: 10.1016/j.rasd.2018.04.001

Reynolds, E. K., MacPherson, L., Matusiewicz, A. K., Schreibers, W. M., & Lejuez, C. W. (2011). Discrepancy between mother and child reports of parental knowledge and the relation to risk behavior engagement. *Journal of Clinical Child and Adolescent Psychology, 40*, 67–79. doi: 10.1080/15374416.2011.533406

Reznick, J. S., Baranek, G. T., Reavis, S., Watson, L. R., & Crais, E. R. (2007). A parent-report instrument for identifying one-year-olds at risk for an eventual diagnosis of autism: The First Year Inventory. *Journal of Autism and Developmental Disorders, 37*, 1691–1710. doi: 10.1007/s10803-006-0303-y

Rice, C. E., Rosanoff, M., Dawson, G., Durkin, M. S., Croen, L. A., Singer, A., & Yeargin-Allsopp, M. (2012). Evaluating changes in the prevalence of autism spectrum disorders (ASDs). *Public Health Reviews, 34*(2), 1–22. doi: 10.1007/BF03391685

Richters, J. E. (1992). Depressed mothers as informants about their children: A critical review of the evidence for distortion. *Psychological Bulletin, 112*, 485–499. doi: 10.1037/0033-2909.112.3.485

Rieffe, C., Ketelaar, L., & Wiefferink, C. H. (2010). Assessing empathy in young children: Construction and validation of an empathy questionnaire *Personality and Individual Differences, 49*, 362–367. doi: 10.1016/j.paid.2010.03.046

Rigby, J., Conroy, S., Miele-Norton, M., Pawlby, S., & Happe, F. (2016). Theory of mind as a predictor of maternal sensitivity in women with severe mental illness. *Psychological Medicine, 46*, 1853–1863. doi: 10.1017/S0033291716000337

Rigo, P., De Pisapia, N., Bornstein, M. H., Putnick, D. L., Serra, M., Esposito, G., & Venuta, P. (2017). Brain processes in men and women in response to emotive sounds. *Social Neuroscience*, *12*, 150–162. doi: 10.1080/17470919.2016.1150341

Riordan, D., Appleby, L., & Faragher, B. (1999). Mother-infant interaction in postpartum women with schizophrenia and affective disorders. *Psychological Medicine*, *29*, 991–995. doi: 10.1017/S0033291798007727

Ritvo, E. R., Freeman, B. J., Pingree, C., Mason-Brothers, A., Jorde, L. B., Jenson, W. R., . . . Ritvo, A. (1989). The UCLA-University of Utah epidemiologic survey of autism: Prevalence. *American Journal of Psychiatry*, *146*, 194–199. doi: 10.1176/ajp.146.2194

Rivas-Drake, D., Urbana-Taylor, A. J., Schaefer, D. R., & Medina, M. (2017). Ethnic-racial identity and friendships in early adolescence. *Child Development*, *88*, 710–724. doi: 10.1111/cdev.12790.

Robins, D. L., Adamson, L. B., Barton, M., Connell, J. E., Jr., Dumont-Mathieu, T., Dworkin, P. H., . . . Vivanti, G. (2016). Universal autism screening for toddlers: Recommendations at odds. *Journal of Autism and Developmental Disorders*, *46*, 1880–1882. doi: 10.1007/s10803-016-2697-5

Robins, D. L., Casagrande, K., Barton, M., Chen, C. A., Dumont-Mathieu, T., & Fein, D. (2014). Validation of the Modified Checklist for Autism in Toddlers, Revised with Follow-up (M-CHAT-R/F). *Pediatrics*, *133*, 37–45. doi: 10.1542/peds.2013-1813

Rodriguez, A., & Adamsons, K. (2012). Parenting expectations: Younger and older first-time parents. *Marriage and Family Review*, *48*, 248–271. doi: 10.1080/01494929.2012.665014

Rogers, S. J., & Talbott, M. R. (2016). Early identification and early treatment of autism spectrum disorder. In R. M. Hodapp & D. J. Fidler (Eds.), *International review of research in developmental disabilities* (pp. 233–275). Cambridge, MA: Elsevier.

Roggman, L. A., Benson, B., & Boyce, L. (1999). Fathers with infants: Knowledge and involvement in relation to psychosocial functioning and religion. *Infant Mental Health Journal*, *20*, 257–277. doi: 10.1002/(SICI)1097-0355(199923)20:3%3C257::AID-IMHJ4%3E3.0.CO;2-S

Rogoff, B. (1990). *Apprenticeship in thinking: Cognitive development in social context.* New York, NY: Oxford University Press.

Rogoff, B. (2003). *The cultural nature of human development.* New York, NY: Oxford University Press.

Rogoff, B. (2014). Learning by observing and pitching in to family and community endeavors: An orientation. *Human Development*, *57*, 69–91. doi: 10.1159/000356757

Rollins, N. C., Bhandari, N., Hajeebhay, N., Horton, S., Lutter, C. K., Martinez, J. C., . . . Victora, C. J. (2016). Why invest, and what will it take to improve breastfeeding practices? *Lancet*, *387*, 491–504. doi: 10.1016/S0140-6736(15)01044-2

Rominov, H., Giallo, R., & Whelan, T. M. (2016). Fathers' postnatal distress, parenting self-efficacy, later parenting behavior, and children's emotional behavioral functioning: A longitudinal study. *Journal of Family Psychology*, *30*, 907–917. doi: 10.1037/fam0000216

Roopnarine, J. L. (2011). Cultural variations in beliefs about play, parent-child play, and children's play: Meaning for childhood development. In A. D. Pellegrini (Ed.), *The Oxford handbook of the development of play* (pp. 19–37). New York, NY: Oxford University Press.

Roopnarine, J. L., & Davidson, K. L. (2015). Parent-child play across cultures: Advancing play research. *American Journal of Play, 7*, 228–252.

Roopnarine, J. L., Logie, C., Davidson, K. L., Krishnakumar, A., & Narine, L. (2015). Caregivers' knowledge about children's development in three ethnic groups in Trinidad and Tobago. *Parenting: Science and Practice, 15*, 229–245. doi: 1080/15295192.2015.1053331

Rosenthal, D. A., & Bornholt, L. (1988). Expectations about development in Greek- and Anglo-Australian families. *Journal of Cross-Cultural Psychology, 19*, 19–34. doi: 10.1177/0022002188019001002

Rosenthal, D. A., & Gold, R. (1989). A comparison of Vietnamese-Australian and Anglo-Australian mothers' beliefs about intellectual development. *International Journal of Psychology, 24*, 179–193. doi: 10.1080/00207594.1989.10600041

Rosenthal, R. (2012). The Pygmalion Effect and its mediating mechanisms. In J. Aronson (Ed.), *Improving academic achievement: Impact of psychological factors on education* (pp. 25–36). San Diego, CA: Academic Press.

Roskam, I., Brassart, E., Loop, L., Mouton, B., & Schelstraete, M. (2015). Stimulating parents' self-efficacy beliefs or verbal responsiveness: Which is the best way to decrease children's externalizing behaviors? *Behaviour Research and Therapy, 72*, 38–48. doi: 10.1016/j.brat.2015.06.012

Ross, J. A. (2017). *How to hug a porcupine: Negotiating the prickly points of the tween years.* New York, NY: McGraw-Hill.

Rossi, G., Lenzi, M., Sharkey, J. D., Vieno, A., & Santinello, M. (2016). Factors associated with civic engagement in adolescence: The effects of neighborhood, school, family, and peer contexts. *Journal of Community Psychology, 44*, 1040–1058. doi: 10.1002/jcop.21826

Roth, R. M., Isquith, P. K., & Gioia, G. A. (2014). Assessment of executive functioning using the Behavior Rating Inventory of Executive Functioning (BRIEF). In S. Goldstein & J. A. Naglieri (Eds.), *Handbook of executive functioning* (pp. 301–331). New York, NY: Springer Science and Business Media. doi: 10.1007/978-1-4614-8106-5_18

Rothbart, M. K. (2011). *Becoming who we are: Temperament and personality in development.* New York, NY: Guilford Press.

Rothbart, M. K., & Bates, J. E. (2006). Temperament. In W. Damon & R. M. Lerner (Series Eds.) & N. Eisenberg (Vol. Ed.), *Handbook of child psychology: Vol. 3. Social, emotional, and personality development* (6th ed., pp. 99–166). Hoboken, NJ: Wiley.

Rowe, M. L. (2018). Understanding socioeconomic differences in parents' speech to children. *Child Development Perspectives, 12*, 122–127. doi: 10.1111/cdep.12271

Rowe, M. L., Denmark, N., Harden, B. J., & Stapleton, L. M. (2016). The role of parent education and parenting knowledge in children's language and literacy skills among White, Black, and Latino families. *Infant and Child Development, 25*, 198–220. doi: 10.1002/icd.1924

Roy, R. N., Schumm W. R., & Brit, S. L. (2014). *Transition to parenthood.* New York, NY: Springer.

Rubin, J. Z., Provenzano, F. J., & Luria, Z. (1974). The eye of the beholder: Parent' views on sex of newborns. *American Journal of Orthopsychiatry, 44*, 512–519. doi: 10.1111/j.1939-0025.1974.tb00905.x

Rubin, K. H., Cheah, C., & Menzer, M. M. (2010). Peers. In M. H. Bornstein (Ed.), *Handbook of cultural developmental science* (pp. 223–237). New York, NY: Psychology Press.

Rubin, K. H., Coplan, R. J., Bowker, J. C., & Menzer, M. (2014). Social withdrawal and shyness. In P. K. Smith & C. H. Hart (Eds.), *Wiley handbook of childhood social development* (2nd ed., pp. 434–452). Hoboken, NJ: Wiley.

Rubin, K. H., Hemphill, S. A., Chen, X., Hastings, P., Sanson, A., Lo Coco, A., . . . Cui, L. (2006). A cross-cultural study of behavioral inhibition in toddlers: East-West-North-South. *International Journal of Behavioral Development, 30*, 219–226. doi: 10.1177/0165025406066723

Rubin, K. H., & Mills, R. S. L. (1990). Maternal beliefs about adaptive and maladaptive social behaviors in normal, aggressive, and withdrawn preschoolers. *Journal of Abnormal Child Psychology, 18*, 419–435. doi: 10.1007/BF00917644

Rubin, K. H., & Mills R. S. L. (1992a). A longitudinal study of maternal beliefs about children's social behaviors. *Merrill-Palmer Quarterly, 38*, 494–512.

Rubin, K. H., & Mills R. S. L. (1992b). Parents' thoughts about children's socially adaptive and maladaptive behaviors: Stability, change, and individual differences. In I. E. Sigel, A. V. McGillicuddy-DeLisi, & J. J. Goodnow (Eds.), *Parental belief systems* (2nd ed., pp. 41–69). Hillsdale, NJ: Erlbaum.

Rubin, K. H., Mills, R. S. L., & Rose-Krasnor, L. (1989). Maternal beliefs and children's competence. In B. H. Schneider, G. Attili, J. Nadel, & R. P. Weissberg (Eds.), *Social competence in developmental perspective* (pp. 313–331. Dordrecht, Netherlands: Kluwer.

Ruble, D. N., Fleming, A. S., Hackel, L. S., & Stangor, C. (1988). Changes in the marital relationship during the transition to first time motherhood: Effects of violated expectations concerning division of household labor. *Journal of Personality and Social Psychology, 55*, 78–87. doi: 10.1037/0022-3514.55.1.78

Ruby, J. L., Belden, A. C., Whalen, D., Harms, M. P., & Barch, D. M. (2016). Breastfeeding and childhood IQ: The mediating role of gray matter volume. *Journal of the American Academy of Child and Adolescent Psychiatry, 55*, 367–375. doi: 10.1016/j.jaac.2016.02.009

Ruffman, T., Slade, L., Devitt, K., & Crowe, E. (2006). What mothers say and what they do: The relation between parenting, theory of mind, language, and conflict/cooperation. *British Journal of Developmental Psychology, 24*, 105–124. doi: 10.1348/026151005X82848

Russell, A., & Russell, G. (1982). Mother, father, and child beliefs about child development. *Journal of Psychology, 110*, 297–306. doi: 10.1080/00223980.1982.9915353

Russell, A., & Russell, G. (1988). Mothers' & fathers' explanations of observed interactions with their children. *Journal of Applied Developmental Psychology, 9*, 421–440. doi: 10.1016/0193-3973(88)90010-X

Russell, C. G., & Worsley, A. (2013). Why don't they like that? And can I do anything about it? The nature and correlates of parents' attributions and self-efficacy beliefs about preschool children's food preferences. *Appetite, 66*, 34–43. doi: 10.1016/j.appet.2013.02.020

Russell, S. T., Watson, R., & Muraco, J. A. (2012). The development of same-sex intimate relationships during adolescence. In B. Laursen & W. A. Collins (Eds.), *Relationship pathways: From adolescence to young adulthood* (pp. 215–234). Thousand Oaks, CA: Sage.

Ryan, S. M., Jorm, A. F., & Lubman, D. I. (2010). Parenting factors associated with reduced adolescent alcohol use: A systematic review of longitudinal studies. *Australian and New Zealand Journal of Psychiatry, 44*, 774–783. doi: 10.1080/00048674.2010.501759

Ryff, C. D., Lee, Y. H., Essex, M. J., & Schmutte, P. S. (1994). My children and me: Midlife evaluations of grown children and of self. *Psychology and Aging, 9*, 195–205. doi: 10.1037/0882-7974.9.2.195

Sacrey, L. R., Bryson, S., Zwaigenbaum, L., Brian, J., Smith, I. M., Roberts, W., . . . Garon, N. (2018). The Autism Parent Screen for Infants: Predicting risk of autism spectrum disorder based on parent-reported behavior observed at 6–24 months of age. *Autism, 22*, 322–334. doi: 10.1177%2F1362361316675120

Sadeh, A., Flint-Ofir, E., Tirosh, T., & Tikotzky, L. (2007). Infant sleep and parental sleep-related cognitions. *Journal of Family Psychology, 21*, 74–87. doi: 10.1037/0893-3200.21.1.74

Safer, D. J. (2018). Is ADHD really increasing in youth? *Journal of Attention Disorders, 22*, 107–115. doi: 10.1177%2F1087054715586571ttp

Salmivalli, C., & Peets, K. (2018). Bullying and victimization. In W. M. Bukowski, B. Laursen, & K. H. Rubin (Eds.), *Handbook of peer interactions, relationships, and groups* (2nd ed., pp. 302–321). New York, NY: Guilford Press.

Salmon, K., & Reese, E. (2016). The benefits of reminiscing with young children. *Current Directions in Psychology, 25*, 233–238. doi: 10.1177/0963721416655100

Sameroff, A. (Ed.). (2009). *The transactional model of development: How children and contexts shape each other.* Washington, DC: American Psychological Association.

Sameroff, A. J., & Feil, L. A. (1985). Parental concepts of development. In I. E. Sigel (Ed.), *Parental belief systems* (pp. 83–105). Hillsdale, NJ: Erlbaum.

Sameroff, A. J., & Fiese, B. H. (1992). Family representations of development. In I. E. Sigel, A. V. McGillicuddy-DeLisi, & J. J. Goodnow (Eds.), *Parental belief systems* (2nd ed., pp. 347–369). Hillsdale, NJ: Erlbaum.

Sameroff, A. J., Seifer, R., Baldwin, A., & Baldwin, C. (1993). Stability of intelligence from preschool to adolescence: The influence of social and family risk factors. *Child Development, 64*, 80–97. doi: 10.2307/1131438

Sameroff, A. J., Seifer, R., Barocas, R., Zax, M., & Greenspan, S. (1987). Intelligence quotient scores of 4-year-old children: Social-environmental risk factors. *Pediatrics, 79*, 343–350.

Sanders, M. R., & Woolley, M. L. (2005). The relationship between maternal self-efficacy and parenting practices: Implications for parent training. *Child: Care, Health and Development, 31*, 65–73. doi: 10.1111/j.1365-2214.2005.00487.x

Sanders, W., Parent, J., Forehand, R., Sullivan, A. D. W., & Jones, D. J. (2016). Parental perceptions of technology and technology-focused parenting: Association with youth screen time. *Journal of Applied Developmental Psychology, 44*, 28–38. doi: 10.1016/j.appdev.2016.02.005

Santini, P., & Williams, L. C. (2016). Parenting programs to prevent corporal punishment: A systematic review. *Paudeia, 26*, 121–129. doi: 10.1590/1982-43272663201614

Santos, C. E., Kornienko, O., & Rivas-Drake, D. (2017). Peer influence on ethnic-racial development: A multi-site investigation. *Child Development, 88*, 725–742. doi: 10.1111/cdev.12789

Sattler, J. M., Feldman, J., & Bohanan, A. L. (1985). Parental estimates of children's receptive vocabulary. *Psychology in the Schools, 22*, 303–307.doi: 10.1002/1520-6807(198507)22:3%3C303::AID-PITS2310220312%3E3.0.CO;2-J

Saudino, K. J., Dale, P. S., Oliver, B. Petrill, S. A., Richardson, V., Rutter, M., . . . Plomin, R. (1998). The validity of parent-based assessment of the cognitive abilities of 2-year-olds. *British Journal of Developmental Psychology, 16*, 349–363. doi: 10.1111/j.2044-835X.1998.tb00757.x

Savage, S. L., & Gauvain, M. (1998). Parental beliefs and children's everyday planning in European-American and Latino families. *Journal of Applied Developmental Psychology*, *19*, 319–340. doi: 10.1016/S0193-3973(99)80043-4

Scarzello, D., Arace, A., & Prino, L. E. (2016). Parental practices of Italian mothers and fathers during early infancy: The role of knowledge about parenting and child development. *Infant Behavior and Development*, *44*, 133–143. doi: 10.1016/j.infbeh.2016.06.006

Scheir, L. M., & Hensen, W. B. (2014). Parenting styles and adolescent drug use. In L. M. Scheier & W. B. Hansen (Eds.), *Parenting and teen drug use* (pp. 62–91). New York, NY: Oxford University Press.

Schlegel, A., & Barry, H. III. (1991). *Adolescence: An anthropological inquiry.* New York, NY: Free Press.

Schneider, W., Waldfogel, J., & Brooks-Gunn, J. (2015). The Great Recession and behavior problems in 9-year-old children. *Developmental Psychology*, *51*, 1615–1629. doi: 10.1037/dev000038

Schueler, B. E., Capotosto, L., Bahena, S., McIntyre, J., & Gehlbach, H. (2014). Measuring parent perceptions of school climate. *Psychological Assessment*, *26*, 314–320. doi: 10.1037/a0034830

Schuette, C., & Killen, M. (2009). Children's evaluations of gender-stereotypical household activities in the family context. *Early Education and Development*, *20*, 693–712. doi: 10.1080/10409280802206908

Schwartz, S. J., Syed, M., Yip, T., Knight, G. P., Umana-Taylor, A. J., Rivas-Drake, D., & Lee, R. M. (2014). Methodological issues in ethnic and racial identity research with ethnic minority populations: Theoretical precision, measurement issues, and research designs. *Child Development*, *85*, 58–76. doi: 10.1111/cdev.12201

Secer, Z., Ogelman, H. G., & Onder, A. (2013). The analysis of the relationship between fathers' parenting self-efficacy and the peer relations of preschool children. *Early Child Development and Care*, *183*, 63–74. doi: 10.1080/03004430.2011.653809

Seifert, K. L. (2000). Uniformity and diversity in everyday views of the child. In S. Harkness, C. Raeff, & C. M. Super (Eds.), *Variability in the social construction of the child* (pp. 75–92). San Francisco, CA: Jossey-Bass Publishers.

Seiffge-Krenke, I., Overbeek, G., & Vermulst, A. (2010). Parent-child relationship trajectories during adolescence: Longitudinal associations with romantic outcomes in emerging adulthood. *Journal of Adolescence*, *33*, 159–171. doi: 10.1016/j.1adolescence.2009.04.001

Seiler, S. J., & Navarro, J. N. (2014). Bullying on the pixel playground: Investigating risk factors of cyberbullying at the intersection of children's online-offline social lives. *Cyberpsychology: Journal of Psychosocial Research on Cyberspace*, *8*(4), article 6. doi: 10.5817/CP2014-4-6

Seng, A. C., & Prinz, R. J. (2008). Parents who abuse: What are they thinking? *Clinical Child and Family Psychological Review*, *11*, 163–175. doi: 10.1007/s10567-008-0035-y

Sevigny, P. R., & Loutzenhiser, L. (2010). Predictors of parenting self efficacy in mothers and fathers of toddlers. *Child: Care, Health and Development*, *36*, 179–189. doi: 10.1111/j.1365-2214.2009.00980.x.

Sevigny, P. R., Loutzenhiser, L., & McAuslan, P. (2016). Development and validation of the Fathering Self-Efficacy Scale. *Psychology of Men and Masculinity*, *17*, 92–102. doi: 10.1037/a0039659

Sexton, D., Thompson, B., Perez, J., & Rheams, T. (1990). Maternal versus professional estimates of developmental status for young children with handicaps: An ecological approach. *Topics in Early Childhood Special Education, 10*(3), 80–95. doi: 10.1177/027112149001000307

Seybold, J., Fritz, J., & MacPhee, D. (1991). Relation of social support to the self-perceptions of mothers with delayed children. *Journal of Community Psychology, 19*, 29–36. doi: 10.1002/1520-6629(199101)19:1%3C29::AID-JCOP2290190104%3E3.0.CO;2-4

Shai, D., & Belsky, J. (2017). Parental embodied mentalizing: How the nonverbal dance between parents and infants predicts children's socio-emotional functioning. *Attachment and Human Development, 19*, 191–209. doi: 10.1080/14616734.2016.1255653

Sharp, C., Fonagy, P., & Goodyer, I. N. (2006). Imagining your child's mind: Psychosocial adjustment and mothers' ability to predict their children's attributional response styles. *British Journal of Developmental Psychology, 24*, 197–214. doi: 10.1348/026151005X82569 10.1348/026151005X82569

Shaw, D. S., Hyde, L. W., & Brennan, L. M. (2012). Early predictors of boys' antisocial trajectories. *Development and Psychopathology, 24*, 871–888. doi: 10.1017/S0954579412000429

Sheeber, L. B., Johnston, C., Chen, M., Leve, C., Hops, H., & Davis, B. (2009). Mothers' and fathers' attributions for adolescent behavior: An examination of families of depressed, subdiagnostic, and nondepressed youth. *Journal of Family Psychology, 23*, 871–881. doi: 10.1037/a0016758

Shepperd, J. A., Lipsey, N. P., Pachur, T., & Waters, E. A. (2018). Understanding the cognitive and affective mechanisms that underlie proxy risk perceptions among caregivers of asthmatic children. *Medical Decision Making, 38*, 562–572. doi: 10.1177%2F0272989X18759933

Sherrod, L. R., Flanagan, C., & Youniss, J. (2002). Dimensions of citizenship and opportunities for youth development: The *what, why, when, where, and who* of citizenship development. *Applied Developmental Science, 6*, 264–272. doi: 10.1207/S1532480XADS0604_14

Sherrod, L. R., & Lauckhardt, J. (2009). The development of citizenship. In R. M Lerner & L. Steinberg (Eds.), *Handbook of adolescent psychology: Vol. 2. Contextual influences on adolescent development* (3rd ed., pp. 372–407). Hoboken, NJ: Wiley.

Sherrod, L. R., Torney-Purta, J., & Flanagan, C. A. (Eds.). (2010). *Handbook of research on civic engagement in youth*. Hoboken, NJ: Wiley.

Shiakou, M., & Belsky, J. (2013). Exploring parent attitudes toward children's play and learning in Cyprus. *Journal of Research in Childhood Education, 27*, 17–30. doi: 10.1080/02568543.2012.739592

Shields, A., & Cicchetti, D. (1997). Emotion regulation among school-age children: The development and validation of a new criterion Q-sort scale. *Developmental Psychology, 33*, 906–916. doi: 10.1037/0012-1649.33.6.906

Shields, A., & Cicchetti, D. (2001). Parental maltreatment and emotional dysregulation as risk factors for bullying and victimization in middle childhood. *Journal of Clinical Child Psychology, 30*, 349–363. doi: 10.1207/S15374424JCCP3003_7

Shipman, V. C., McKee, D. J., & Bridgeman, B. (1976). *Stability and change in family status, situational and process variables and their relationship to children's cognitive performance*. Princeton, NJ: Educational Testing Service.

Shorey, S., Chan, S., Chong, Y. S., & He, H. (2015). Predictors of maternal parental self-efficacy among primiparas in the early postnatal period. *Western Journal of Nursing Research, 37*, 1601–1622. doi: 10.1177/0193945914537724

Shulman, S., Scharf, M., & Shachar-Shapira, L. (2012). The intergenerational transmission of adolescent romantic relationships. In P. K. Kerig, M. S. Shulz, & S. T. Hauser (Eds.), *Adolescence and beyond: Family processes and development* (pp. 113–133). New York, NY: Oxford University Press.

Shumow, L., & Lomax, R. (2002). Parental efficacy: Predictor of parenting behavior and adolescent outcomes. *Parenting: Science and Practice, 2,* 127–150. doi: 10.1207/S15327922PAR0202_03

Shuster, M. M., Li, Y., & Shi, J. (2012). Maternal cultural values and parenting practices: Longitudinal associations with Chinese adolescents' aggression. *Journal of Adolescence, 35,* 345–355. doi: 10.1016/j.adolescence.2011.08.006

Shweder, R. A., Goodnow, J. J., Hatano, G., LeVine, R. A., Markus, H. R., & Miller, P. J. (2006). The cultural psychology of development: One mind, many mentalities. In W. Damon & R. M. Lerner (Series Eds.) & R. M. Lerner (Vol. Ed.), *Handbook of child psychology: Vol. 1. Theoretical models of human development* (6th ed., pp. 716–792). Hoboken, NJ: Wiley.

Siegel, D. M., Aten, M. J., & Roghmann, K J. (1998). Self-reported honesty among middle and high school students responding to a sexual behavior questionnaire. *Journal of Adolescent Health, 23,* 20–28. doi: 10.1016/S1054-139X(97)00274-7

Sigel, I. E. (1982). The relationship between parental distancing strategies and the child's cognitive behavior. In L. M. Laosa & I. E. Sigel (Eds.), *Families as learning environments for children* (pp. 47–86). New York, NY: Plenum.

Sigel, I. E. (1985a). A conceptual analysis of beliefs. In I. E. Sigel (Ed.), *Parental belief systems* (pp. 347–371). Hillsdale, NJ: Erlbaum.

Sigel, I. E. (Ed.). (1985b). *Parental belief systems.* Hillsdale, NJ: Erlbaum.

Sigel, I. E. (1986). Reflections on the belief-behavior connection: Lessons learned from a research program on parental belief systems and teaching strategies. In R. D. Ashmore & D. M. Brodzinsky (Eds.), *Thinking about the family: Views of parents and children* (pp. 35–65). Hillsdale, NJ: Erlbaum.

Sigel, I. E. (1992). The belief-behavior connection: A resolvable dilemma? In I. E. Sigel, A. V. McGillicuddy-DeLisi, & J. J. Goodnow (Eds.), *Parental belief systems* (2nd ed., pp. 433–456). Hillsdale, NJ: Erlbaum.

Sigel, I. E., & Kim, M. (1996). The answer depends on the question: A conceptual and methodological analysis of a parent belief–behavior interview regarding children's learning. In S. Harkness & C. M. Super (Eds.), *Parents' cultural belief systems: Their origins, expressions, and consequences* (pp. 83–120). New York, NY: Guilford Press.

Sigel, I. E., & McGillicuddy-DeLisi, A. V. (2002). Parent beliefs are cognitions: The dynamic belief systems model. In M. H. Bornstein (Ed.), *Handbook of parenting: Vol. 3. Being and becoming a parent* (2nd ed., pp. 485–508). Mahwah, NJ: Erlbaum.

Silinskas, G., Kiuru, N., Aunola, K., Lerkkanen, M., & Nurmi, J. (2015). The developmental dynamics of children's academic performance and mother' homework-related affect and practices. *Developmental Psychology, 51,* 419  433. doi: 10.1037/a0038908

Siller, M., Reyes, N., Hotez, E., Hutman, T., & Sigman, M. (2014). Longitudinal change in the use of services in autism spectrum disorder: Understanding the role of child characteristics, family demographics, and parent cognitions. *Autism, 18,* 433–446. doi: 10.1177/1362361313476766

Silverman, C., & Brosco, J. P. (2007). Understanding autism: Parents and pediatricians in historical perspective. *Archives of Pediatrics and Adolescent Medicine 161,* 392–398. doi: 10.1001/archpedi.161.4.392

Simons-Morton, B. G. (2004). The protective effect of parental expectations against early adolescent smoking initiation. *Health Education Research, 19*, 561–569. doi: 10.1093/her/cyg071

Simpkins, S. D., Fredricks, J. A., & Eccles, J. S. (2015). The role of parents in the ontogeny of achievement-related motivation and behavioral choices. *Monographs of the Society for Research in Child Development, 80*(2). doi: 10.1111/mono.12157

Simpson, J. A., Collins, W. A., & Salvatore, J. E. (2011). The impact of early interpersonal experience on adult romantic relationship functioning: Recent findings from the Minnesota Longitudinal Study of Risk and Adaptation. *Current Directions in Psychological Science, 20*, 355–359. doi: 10.1177/0963721411418468

Sistler, A. K., & Gottfried, N. W. (1990). Shared child development knowledge between grandmother and mother. *Family Relations, 39*, 92–96. doi: 10.2307/584955

Skibbe, L. E., Justice, L. M., Zucker, T. A., & McGinty, A. S. (2008). Relations among maternal literacy beliefs, home literacy practices, and the emergent literacy skills of preschoolers with specific language impairment. *Early Education and Development, 19*, 68–88. doi: 10.1080/10409280701839015

Skoric, M. M., Zhu, Q., Goh, D., & Pang, N. (2016). Social media and citizen engagement: A meta-analytic review. *New Media and Society, 18*, 1817–1839. doi: 10.1177/1461444815616221

Slonims, V., Cox, A., & McConachie, H. (2006). Analysis of mother-infant interaction in infants with Down syndrome and typically developing infants. *American Journal on Mental Retardation, 111*, 273–289. doi: 10.1352/0895-8017(2006)111[273:AOMIII]2.0.CO;2

Smetana, J. G. (1988). Concepts of self and social convention: Adolescents' and parents' reasoning about hypothetical and actual family conflicts. In M. R. Gunnar & W. A. Collins (Eds.), *Minnesota Symposium on Child Psychology: Development during the transition to adolescence* (pp. 79–122). Hillsdale, NJ: Erlbaum.

Smetana, J. G. (1989). Toddlers' social interactions in the context of moral and conventional transgressions in the home. *Developmental Psychology, 25*, 499–508. doi: 10.1037/0012-1649.25.4.499

Smetana, J. G. (1995). Parenting styles and conceptions of parental authority during adolescence. *Child Development, 66*, 299–316. doi: 10.1111/1467-8624.ep9505240334

Smetana, J. G. (1999). The role of parents in moral development: A social domain analysis. *Journal of Moral Education, 28*, 311–321. doi: 10.1080/030572499103106

Smetana, J. G. (2000). Middle-class African American adolescents' and parents' conceptions of parental authority and parenting practices: A longitudinal investigation. *Child Development, 71*, 1672–1686. doi: 10.1111/1467-8624.00257

Smetana, J. G. (2011a). *Adolescents, families, and social development: How teens construct their worlds.* Malden, MA: Wiley-Blackwell.

Smetana, J. G. (2011b). Parenting beliefs, parenting, and parent-adolescent communication in African American families. In N. E. Hill, T. L. Mann, & H. E. Fitzgerald (Eds.), *African American youth and mental health: Vols. 1 and 2. Development and context, prevention and social policy* (pp. 173–197). Santa Barbara, CA: Prager.

Smetana, J. G., Ahmad, I., & Wray-Lake, L. (2015). Iraqi, Syrian, and Palestinian refugee adolescents' beliefs about parental authority legitimacy and its correlates. *Child Development, 86*, 2017–2033. doi: 10.1111/cdev.12457

Smetana, J. G., Ahmad, I., & Wray-Lake, L. (2016). Beliefs about parental authority legitimacy among refugee youth in Jordan: Between- and within-person variations. *Developmental Psychology, 52*, 484–495. doi: 10.1037/dev0000084

Smetana, J. G., & Asquith, P. (1994). Adolescents' and parents' conceptions of parental authority and personal autonomy. *Child Development, 65*, 1147–1162. doi: 10.1111/1467-8624.ep7252861

Smetana, J. G., Robinson, J., & Rote, W. M. (2015). Socialization in adolescence. In J. E. Grusec & P. Hastings (Eds.), *Handbook of socialization* (2nd ed., pp. 60–84). New York, NY: Guilford Press.

Smetana, J. G., & Rote, W. M. (2015). What do mothers want to know about teens' activities? Levels, trajectories, and correlates. *Journal of Adolescence, 38*, 5–15. doi: 10.1016/j.adolescence.2014.10.006

Smetana, J. G., Villalobos, M., Tasopoulous-Chan, M., Gettman, D. C., & Campione-Barr, N. (2009). Early and middle adolescents' disclosure to parents about activities in different domains. *Journal of Adolescence, 32*, 693–713. doi: 10.1016/j.adolescence.2008.06.010

Smith, N., Sheldrick, R. C., & Perrin, E. C. (2013). An abbreviated screening instrument for autism spectrum disorders. *Infant Mental Health Journal, 34*, 149–155. doi: 10.1002/imhj.21356

Smith Leavell, A., & Tamis-LeMonda, C. S. (2013). Parenting in infancy and early childhood: A focus on gender socialization. In M. A. Fine & F. D. Fincham (Eds.), *Handbook of family theories: A content-based approach* (pp. 11–27). New York, NY: Routledge.

Snellen, M., Mack, K., & Trauer, T. (1999). Schizophrenia, mental state, and mother-infant interaction: Examining the relationship. *Australian and New Zealand Journal of Psychiatry, 33*, 902–911. doi10.1046%2Fj.1440–1614.1999.00641.x

Sobol, M. P., Ashbourne, D. T., Earn, B. M., & Cunningham, C. E. (1989). Parents' attributions for achieving compliance from attention-deficit-disordered children. *Journal of Abnormal Child Psychology, 17*, 359–369. doi: 10.1007/BF00917405

Sobring, E., & Lundin, L. (2012). Mothers' and fathers' insights into their teenagers' use of the internet. *New Media and Society, 14*, 1181–1197. doi: 10.1177/1461444812440160

Soenens, B., Vansteenkiste, M., Luyckx, K., & Goossens, L. (2006). Parenting and adolescent problem behavior: An integrated model with adolescent self-disclosure and perceived parental knowledge as intervening variables. *Developmental Psychology, 42*, 305–318. doi: 10.1037/0012-1649.42.2.305

Sola-Carmona, J. J., Lopez-Liria, R., Padilla-Gongora, E., Daza. M. T., Aguilar-Parra, J. M., & Salido-Campos, M. A. (2016). Factors associated with the anxiety, subjective psychological well-being and self-esteem of parents of blind children. *PLOS One, 11*(9), e0162294. doi: 10.1371/journal.pone.0162294

Solomon, B. S., Bradshaw, C. P., Wright, J., & Cheng, T. L. (2008). Youth and parental attitudes toward fighting. *Journal of Interpersonal Violence, 23*, 544–560. doi: 10.1177/0886260507312947

Soltis, J. (2004). The signal functions of early infant crying. *Behavioral and Brain Sciences, 27*, 443–458. doi: 10.1017/S0140525X0400010X

Sommer, K., Whitman, T. L., Borkowski, J. G., Gondoli, D. M., Burke, J., Maxwell, S. E., & Weed, K. (2000). Prenatal maternal predictors of cognitive and emotional delays in children of adolescent mothers. *Adolescence, 35*, 87–112.

Sommer, K., Whitman, T. L., Borkowski, J. G., Schellenbach, C., Maxwell, S., & Keogh, D. (1993). Cognitive readiness and adolescent parenting. *Developmental Psychology*, *29*, 389–398. doi: 10.1037/0012-1649.29.2.389

Sonnenschein, S., Metzger, S. R., & Stapleton, L. M. (2014). What parents know about how well their children are doing in school. *Journal of Educational Research*, *107*, 152–162. doi: 10.1080/00220671.2013.788987

Sood, E. D., Mendez, J. L., & Kendall, P. C. (2012). Acculturation, religiosity, and ethnicity predict mothers' causal beliefs about separation anxiety disorder and preferences for help-seeking. *Journal of Cross-Cultural Psychology*, *43*, 393–409. doi: 10.1177/0022022110389492

Spittler, G. (1998). *Hirtenarbreit.* Cologne, Germany: Rudiger Koppe.

Sprong, M., Schothorst, P., Vos, E., Hox, J., & Van Egeland, H. (2007). Theory of mind in schizophrenia. *British Journal of Psychiatry*, *191*, 5–13. doi: 10.1192/bjp.bp.107.035899

Squires, J., Twombley, E., Bricker, D., & Potter, L. (2009). *Ages and stages questionnaires (ASQ): A parent-completed child monitoring system* (3rd ed.). Baltimore, MD: Brookes.

Sroufe, L. A., Egeland, B., Carlson, E. A., & Collins, W. A. (2005). *The development of the person: The Minnesota Study of Risk and Adaptation from Birth to Adulthood.* New York. NY: Guilford Press. doi: 10.1111/j.1469-7610.2007.01794.x

Stallings, J., Fleming, A S., Corter, C., Worthman, C., & Steiner, M. (2001). The effects of infant cries and odors on sympathy, cortisol, and autonomic responses in new mothers and nonpostpartum women. *Parenting: Science and Practice*, *1*, 71–100. doi: 10.1080/15295192.2001.9681212

Stattin, H., & Kerr, M. (2000). Parental monitoring: A reinterpretation. *Child Development*, *71*, 1072–1085. doi: 10.1111/1467-8624.00210

Stattin, H., Kerr M., & Tilton-Weaver, L. (2010). Parental monitoring: A critical evaluation of the research. In V. Guilamo-Ramos, J. Jaccord, & P. Dittus (Eds.), *Parental monitoring of adolescents* (pp. 3–38). New York, NY: Columbia University Press.

Stein, A., Craske, M. G., Lehtonen, A., Harvey, A., Savage-McGynn, E., Davies, B., . . . Counsell, N. (2012). Maternal cognitions and mother-infant interaction in postnatal depression and generalized anxiety disorder. *Journal of Abnormal Psychology*, *121*, 795–809. doi: 10.1037/a0026847

Steinberg, L. (2014). *Age of opportunity: Lessons from the new science of adolescence.* New York, NY: Houghton Mifflin.

Steinberg, L., & Silk, J. S. (2002). Parenting adolescents. In M. H. Bornstein (Ed.), *Handbook of parenting: Vol. 1. Children and parenting* (2nd ed., pp. 103–134). Mahwah, NJ: Erlbaum.

Sterling, A. M., Warren, S. F., Brady, N., & Fleming, K. (2013). Influences on maternal responsivity in mothers of children with Fragile X syndrome. *American Journal on Intellectual and Developmental Disabilities*, *118*, 310–326. doi: 10.1352/1944-7558-188.4.310

Stern, J. A., & Cassidy, J. (2018). Empathy from infancy to adolescence: An attachment perspective on the development of individual differences. *Developmental Review*, *47*, 1–22. doi: 10.1016/j.dr.2017.09.002

Stern, M., Karraker, K. H., Sopko, A. M., & Norman, S. (2000). The prematurity stereotype revisited: Impact on mothers' interactions with premature and full-term infants. *Infant Mental Health Journal*, *21*, 495–509. doi: 10.1002/1097-0355(200011/12)21:6%3C495::AID-IMHJ7%3E3.0.CO;2-F

Sternberg, R. J. (2004). Culture and intelligence. *American Psychologist, 59*, 325–338. doi: 10.1037/0003-066X.59.5.325

Sternberg, R. J. (2007). Who are the bright children? The cultural context of being and acting intelligent. *Educational Researcher 36*, 148–155. doi: 10.3102/ 0013189X07299881

Sternberg, R. J. (2014). The development of adaptive competence: Why cultural psychology is necessary and not just nice. *Developmental Review, 34*, 208–224. doi: 10.1016/j.dr.2014.05.004

Sternberg, R. J., Nokes, C., Geissler, P W. Prince, R., Okatcha, F., Bundy, D. A., & Grigorenko, E. L. (2001). The relationship between academic and practical intelligence: A case study in Kenya. *Intelligence, 29*, 401–418. doi: 10.1016/S0160-2896(01)00065-4

Stettler, N., & Katz, L. F. (2014). Changes in parents' meta-emotion philosophy from preschool to early adolescence. *Parenting: Science and Practice, 14*, 162–174. doi: 10.1080/ 15295192.2014.945584

Stevens, J. H., Jr. (1984a). Black grandmothers' and black adolescent mothers' knowledge about parenting. *Developmental Psychology, 20*, 1017–1025. doi: 10.1037/ 0012-1649.20.6.1017

Stevens, J. H., Jr. (1984b). Child development knowledge and parenting skills. *Family Relations, 33*, 237–244. doi: 10.2307/583789

Stevens, J. H., Jr. (1988). Shared knowledge about infants among fathers and mothers. *Journal of Genetic Psychology, 149*, 515–525. doi: 10.1080/00221325.1988.10532177

Stevenson, H. W., & Lee, S. (1990). Contexts for achievement. *Monographs of the Society for Research in Child Development, 55*(1–2, Serial No. 221). doi: 10.1111/1540-5834. ep11891953

St. George, J., Wroe, J. K., & Cashin, M. E. (2018). The concept and measurement of fathers' stimulating play: A review. *Attachment and Human Development, 20*, 634–658. doi: 10.1080/14616734.2018.1465106

Stoiber, K. C. (1992). Parents' beliefs about their children's cognitive, social, and motor functioning. *Early Education and Development, 3*, 244–259. doi: 10.1207/ s15566935eed0303_4

Stolz, L. (1967). *Influences on parent behavior.* Stanford, CA: Stanford University Press.

Storeba, O. J., Rasmussen, P. D., & Simonsen, E. (2016). Association between insecure attachment and ADHD: Environmental mediating factors. *Journal of Attention Disorders, 20*, 187–196. doi: 10.1177%2F1087054713501079

Stratton, P. (1997). Attributional coding of interview data: Meeting the needs of long-haul passengers. In N. Hayes (Ed.), *Doing qualitative analysis in psychology* (pp. 115–142). Hove, England: Psychology Press.

Super, C., Axia, G., Harkness, S., Welles-Nystrom, B., Zylic, P. O., Parmar, P., . . . McGurk, H. (2008). Culture, temperament, and the 'difficult child': A study of seven Western cultures. *European Journal of Developmental Science, 2*, 136–157.

Super, C., & Harkness, S. (2011). Charting infant development: Milestones along the way. In L. A. Jensen (Ed.), *The Oxford handbook of human development and culture* (pp. 79–93). New York, NY: Oxford University Press.

Suskind, D. L., Leffel, K. R., Graf, E., Hernandez, M. W., Gunderson, E. A., Sapolich, S. G., . . . Levine, S. C. (2016). A parent-directed language intervention for children of low socioeconomic status: A randomized controlled pilot study. *Journal of Child Language, 43*, 366–406. doi: 10.1017/S0305000915000033

Suskind, D. L., Leung, C. Y. Y., Webber, R. J., Hundertmark, A. C., Leffel, K. R., Suskind, E., ... Graf, E. (2018). Development of the Survey of Parent/Provider Expectations and Knowledge (SPEAK). *First Language, 38*, 312–331. doi: 10.1177%2F0142723717737691

Swit, C. S., McMaugh, A. L., & Warburton, W. A. (2017). Teacher and parent perceptions of relational and physical aggression during early childhood. *Journal of Child and Family Studies, 27*, 118–130. doi: 10.1007/s10826-017-0861-y

Symons, K., Ponnet, K., Emmery, K., Walrave, M., & Heirman, W. (2017). Parental knowledge of adolescents' online content and contact risks. *Journal of Youth and Adolescence, 46*, 401–416. doi: 10.1007/s10964-016-0599-7

Tahiroglu, D., Moses, L. J., Carlson, S. M., Mahy, C. E. V., Olofson, E. L., & Sabbagh, M. A. (2014). The Children's Social Understanding Scale: Construction and validation of a parent-report measure for assessing individual differences in children's theories of mind. *Developmental Psychology, 50*, 2485–2497. doi: 10.1037/a0037914

Tamis-LeMonda, C. S., Chen, L. A., & Bornstein, M. H. (1998). Mothers' knowledge about children's play and language development: Short-term stability and interrelations. *Developmental Psychology, 34*, 115–124. doi: 10.1037/0012-1649.34.1.115

Tamis-LeMonda, C. S., Shannon, J., & Spellman, M. (2002). Low-income adolescent mothers' knowledge about domains of child development. *Infant Mental Health Journal, 23*, 88–103. doi: 10.1002/imhj.10006

Tamis-LeMonda, C. S., Uzgiris, I., & Bornstein, M. H. (2002). Play in parent-child interactions. In M. H. Bornstein (Ed.), *Handbook of parenting: Vol. 5. Practical issues in parenting* (2nd ed., pp. 221–241). Mahwah, NJ: Erlbaum.

Task Force on Sudden Infant Death Syndrome (2016). SIDS and other sleep-related infant deaths: Updated 2016 recommendations for a safe infant sleeping environment. *Pediatrics, 138*, e20162938. doi: 10.1542/peds.2016-2938

Tazouti, Y., Malarde, A., & Michea, A. (2010). Parental beliefs concerning development and education, family educational practices and children's intellectual and academic performances. *European Journal of Psychology of Education, 25*, 19–35. doi: 10.1007/s10212-009-0002-0

Temcheff, C. E., Letarte, M., Boutin, S., & Marcil, K. (2018). Common components of evidence-based parenting programs for preventing maltreatment of school-age children. *Child Abuse and Neglect, 80*, 226–237. doi: 10.1016/j.chiabu.2018.02.004

Tennenbaum, H. R., & Leaper, C. (2002). Are parents' gender schemas related to their children's gender-related cognitions? A meta-analysis. *Developmental Psychology, 38*, 615–630. doi: 10.1037/0012-1649.38.4.615

Thomas, A., & Chess, S. (1977). *Temperament and development.* New York, NY: Brunner/Mazel.

Thomas, A., Chess, S., & Birch, H. (1968). *Temperament and behavior disorders in children.* New York, NY: New York University Press.

Thomas, R., Sanders, S., Doust, J., Beller, E., & Glasziou, P. (2015). Prevalence of attention-deficit/hyperactivity disorder: A systematic review and meta-analysis. *Pediatrics, 135*, e994–e1001. doi: 10.1542/peds.2014-3482

Thompson, R. A. (2013). Attachment theory and research: Precis and prospect. In P. Zelazo (Ed.), *The Oxford handbook of developmental psychology: Vol 2. Self and other* (pp. 191–216). New York, NY: Oxford University Press.

Thompson, R. A. (2014). Conscience development in early childhood. In M. Killen & J. G. Smetana (Eds.), *Handbook of moral development* (2nd ed., pp. 73–92). New York, NY: Psychology Press.

Tikotzky, L., & Sadeh, A. (2009). Maternal sleep-related cognitions and infant sleep: A longitudinal study from pregnancy through the 1st year. *Child Development, 80,* 860–874. doi: 10.1111/j.1467-8624.2009.01302.x

Tomasello, M. (1999). *The cultural origins of human cognition.* Cambridge, MA: Harvard University Press.

Torney-Purta, J., Lehmen, R., Oswald, H., & Scholz, W. (2001). *Citizenship and education in twenty-eight countries: Civic knowledge and engagement at age fourteen.* Amsterdam, the Netherlands: IEA.

Toth, S. L., Petrenko, C. L. M., Gravener-Davis, J. A., & Handley, E. D. (2016). Advances in prevention science: A developmental psychology perspective. In D. Cicchetti (Ed.), *Developmental psychopathology* (3rd ed., Vol. 4, pp. 815–873). Hoboken, NJ: Wiley.

Trommsdorff, G., & Nauck, B. (2010). Introduction to special section for *Journal of Cross-Cultural Psychology*: Value of children: A concept for better understanding cross-cultural variations in fertility behavior and intergenerational relationships. *Journal of Cross-Cultural Psychology, 41,* 637–651. doi: 10.1177/0022022110373335

Turiel, E. (1979). Distinct conceptual and developmental domains: Social convention and morality. In C. B. Keasey (Ed.), *Nebraska Symposium on Motivation* (Vol. *27,* pp. 77–116). Lincoln: University of Nebraska Press.

Turiel, E. (2002). *The culture of morality: Social development, context, and conflict.* Cambridge, England: Cambridge University Press.

Twomey, J. E., High, P., & Lester, B. M. (2012). Colic: What's maternal health got to do with it? *Infant Mental Health Journal, 33,* 543–552. doi: 10.1002/imhj.21344

Umberson, D. (1992). Relationships between adult children and their parents: Psychological consequences for both generations. *Journal of Marriage and Family, 54,* 664–674. doi: 10.2307/353252

Urmana-Taylor, A. J. (2015). Ethnic identity research: How far have we come? In C. F. Santos & A. J. Urmana-Taylor (Eds.), *Studying ethnic identity: Methodological and conceptual approaches across disciplines* (pp. 11–26). Washington, DC: American Psychological Association.

Urmana-Taylor, A. J., Quintana, S. M., Lee, R. M., Cross, Jr., W. E., Rivas-Drake, D., Schwartz, S. J., . . . Seaton, E. (2014). Ethnic and racial identity during adolescence and into young adulthood: An integrated conceptualization. *Child Development, 85,* 21–39. doi: 10.1111/cdev.12196

US Department of Health & Human Services, Administration for Children and Families, Administration on Children, Youth and Families, Children's Bureau. (2018). Child maltreatment 2016. Available from https://www.acf.hhs.gov/cb/research-data-technology/statistics-research/child-maltreatment.

van Beek, Y., Genta, M. L., Constabile, A., & Sansavini, A. (2006). Maternal expectations about infant development of pre-term and full-term infants: A cross-national comparison. *Infant and Child Development, 15,* 41–58. doi: 10.1002/icd.428

Van Egeren, L. A. (2004). The development of the coparenting relationship over the transition to parenthood. *Infant Mental Health Journal, 25,* 453–477. doi: 10.1002/imhj.20019

van IJzendoorn, M. H. (1995). Adult attachment representations, parental responsiveness, and infant attachment: A meta-analysis on the predictive validity of the Adult Attachment Interview. *Psychological Bulletin, 117,* 387–403. doi: 10.1037/0033-2909.117.3.387

van IJzendoorn, M. H., Vereijken, C. M. J. L., Bakermanns-Kraneburg, J., & Riksen-Walraven, J. M. (2004). Assessing attachment security with the Attachment

Q-Set: Meta-analytic evidence for the validity of the observer AQS. *Child Development,* *75,* 1188–1213. doi: 10.1111/j.1467-8624.2004.00733.x

Van Ryzin, M. J., Roseth, G. J., Fosco, G. M., Lee, Y., & Chen, I. (2016). A component-centered meta-analysis of family-based prevention programs for adolescent substance use. *Clinical Psychology Review, 45,* 72–80. doi: 10.1016/j.cpr.2016.03.007

Vaughn, B. E., Coppola, G., Verissimo, M., Monteiro, L., Santos, A. J., Posada, G., . . . Korth, B. (2007). The quality of secure-base scripts predicts children's secure-base behavior at home in three sociocultural groups. *International Journal of Behavioral Development,* *31,* 65–76. doi: 10.1177/0165025407073574

Vaughn, B. E., Waters, H. S., Coppola, G., Cassidy, J., Bost, K. K., & Verissimo, M. (2006). Script-like attachment representations and behavior in families and across cultures: Studies of parental secure base narratives. *Attachment and Human Development, 8,* 179–184. doi: 10.1080/14616730600856008

Verhage, M. L., Oosterman, M., & Schuengel, C. (2013). Parenting self-efficacy predicts perceptions of infant negative temperament characteristics, not vice versa. *Journal of Family Psychology, 27,* 844–849. doi: 10.1037/a0034263

Verhage, M. L., Schuengel, C., Madigan, S., Fearon, R. M. P., Oosterman, M., Cassibba, R., . . . van IJzendoorn, M. H. (2016). Narrowing the transmission gap: A synthesis of three decades of research on intergenerational transmission of attachment. *Psychological Bulletin, 142,* 337–366. doi: 10.1037/bul0000038

Victora, C. G., Bahl, R., Barros, A. J. D., Franca, G. V. A., Horton, S., Krasevec, J., . . . Rollins, N. C. (2016). Breastfeeding in the 21st century: Epidemiology, mechanisms, and life-long effect. *Lancet, 387,* 475–490. doi: 10.1016/S0140-6736(15)01024-7

Vinik, J., Almas, A., & Grusec, J. (2011). Mothers' knowledge of what distresses and what comforts their children predicts children's coping, empathy, and prosocial behavior. *Parenting: Science and Practice, 11,* 56–71. doi: 10.1080/15295192.2011.539508

Vollink, T., Dehue, F., & Mc Gunkin, C. (Eds.). (2016). *Cyberbullying: From theory to intervention.* New York, NY: Routledge Press.

Von Stumm, S., & Plomin, R. (2015). Breastfeeding and IQ growth from toddlerhood through adolescence. *PLOS ONE, 10,* ArtID: e01338676.

Vukelich, C., & Kliman, D. S. (1985). Mature and teenage mothers' infant growth expectations and use of child development information sources. *Family Relations, 34,* 189–196. doi: 10.2307/583891

Vygotsky, L. S. (1962). *Thought and language.* Cambridge, MA: MIT Press.

Vygotsky, L. S. (1978). *Mind in society.* Cambridge, MA: Harvard University Press.

Wachs, T. D., Black, M. M., & Engle, P. L. (2009). Maternal depression: A global threat to children's health, development, and behavior and to human rights. *Child Development Perspectives, 3,* 51–59. doi: 10.1111/j.1750-8606.2008.00077.x

Waizenhofer, R. N., Buchanan, C. M., & Jackson-Newsom, J. (2004). Mothers' and fathers' knowledge of adolescents' daily activities: Its sources and its links with adolescent adjustment. *Journal of Family Psychology, 18,* 348–360. doi: 10.1037/0893-3200.18.2.348

Walker, L. J., Henning, K. H., & Krettenauer, T. (2000). Parent and peer contexts for children's moral reasoning development. *Child Development, 71,* 1033–1048. doi: 10.1111/1467-8624.00207

Walker, L. J., & Taylor, J. H. (1991). Family interactions and the development of moral reasoning. *Child Development, 62,* 264–283. doi: 10.2307/1131002

Wallat-Petre, H. (2001). Learning how to make the right pots: Apprenticeship strategies and maternal culture, a case study in handmade pottery from Cameroon. *Journal of Anthropological Research, 57,* 471–493.

Walper, S., & Wendt, E. (2015). Adolescents' relationships with mother and father and their links to the quality of romantic relationships: A classification approach. *European Journal of Developmental Psychology, 12,* 516–532. doi: 10.1080/17405629.2015.1065727

Walters, G. D. (2015). Parental attitude toward deviance as a predictor of delinquency: Making the connection via perception and cognition. *Journal of Adolescence, 39,* 27–35. doi: 10.1016/j.adolescence.2014.12.002

Wan, M. W., Abel, K. M., & Green, J. (2008). The transmission of risk to children from mothers with schizophrenia: A developmental psychopathology model. *Clinical Psychology Review, 28,* 613–637. doi: 10.1016/j.cpr.2007.09.001

Wan, W. M., Salmon, M. P., Riordan, D. M., Appleby, L., Webb, R., & Abel, K. M. (2007). What predicts poor infant-mother interaction in schizophrenia? *Psychological Medicine, 37,* 537–546. doi: 10.1017/S0033291706009172

Wan, M. W., Warren, K., Salmon, M. P., & Abel, K. M. (2008). Patterns of maternal responding in postpartum mothers with schizophrenia. *Infant Behavior and Development, 31,* 532–538. doi: 10.1016/j.infbeh.2008.04.003

Wang, Q. (2013). *The autobiographical self in time and culture.* New York, NY: Oxford University Press.

Wang, Y., & Dix, T. (2013). Patterns of depressive parenting: Why they occur and their role in early developmental risk. *Journal of Family Psychology, 27,* 884–895. doi: 10.1037/a0034829

Wang, Y., & Dix, T. (2015). Mothers' early depressive symptoms predict children's low social competence in first grade: Mediation by children's social cognition. *Journal of Child Psychology and Psychiatry, 56,* 183–192. doi: 10.1111/jcpp.12297

Warash, B. G., Root, A. E., & Doris, M. D. (2017). Parents' perceptions of play: A comparative study of spousal perspectives. *Early Child Development and Care, 187,* 958–966. doi: 10.1080/03004430.2016.1237511

Ward, T. C. S. (2015). Reasons for mother-infant bed-sharing: A systematic narrative synthesis of the literature and implications for future research. *Maternal and Child Health Journal, 19,* 675–690. doi: 10.1007/s10995-014-1557-1

Warton, P. M., & Goodnow, J. J. (1995). Money and children's household jobs: Parents' views of their interconnections. *International Journal of Behavioral Development, 18,* 335–350. doi: 10.2307/1130711

Waters, E. (1995). The Attachment Q-Set (Version 3.0). *Monographs of the Society for Research in Child Development, 60*(2–3, Serial No. 244). doi: 10.1111/1540-5834.ep11935598

Waters, E., & Deane, K. E. (1985). Defining and assessing individual differences in attachment relationships: Q-methodology and the organization of behavior in infancy and early childhood. *Monographs of the Society for Research in Child Development, 50*(1–2, Serial No. 209). doi: 10.2307/3333826

Waters, H. S., & Waters, E. (2006). The attachment working models concept: Among other things, we build script-like representations of secure base experiences. *Attachment and Human Development, 8,* 185–197. doi: 10.1080/14616730600856016

Waters, T., Ruiz, S. K., & Roisman, G. J. (2017). Origins of secure base script knowledge and the developmental construction of attachment representations. *Child Development, 88,* 198–209. doi: 10.1111/cdev.12571

Weary, G., Stanley, M. A., & Harvey, J. H. (1989). *Attribution.* New York, NY: Springer-Verlag.

Weiner, B. (1986). *An attributional theory of motivation and emotion.* New York, NY: Springer-Verlag.

Wellman, H. M. (2014). *Making minds: How theory of mind develops.* New York, NY: Oxford University Press.

Wernand, J. J., Kunseler, F. C., Oosterman, M., Beekman, A. T. F., & Schuengel, C. (2014). Prenatal changes in parenting self-efficacy: Linkages with anxiety and depressive symptoms in primiparous women. *Infant Mental Health Journal, 35,* 42–50. doi: 10.1002/imhj.21425

Wessel, M. A., Cobb, J. C., Jackson, E. B., Harris, G. S., & Detwiler, A. C. (1954). Paroxysmal fussing in infancy, sometimes called "colic." *Pediatrics, 14,* 421–434.

White, C., & Barrowclough, C. (1998). Depressed and non-depressed mothers with problematic preschoolers: Attributions for child behaviours. *British Journal of Clinical Psychology, 37,* 385–398. doi: 10.1111/j.2044-8260.1998.tb01396.x

Whiteman, S. D., McHale, S. M., & Crouter, A. C. (2003). What parents learn from experience: The first child as first draft? *Journal of Marriage and Family, 65,* 608–621. doi: 10.1111/j.1741-3737.2003.00608.x

Whittingham, K., Sofronoff, K., Sheffield, J., & Sanders, M. R. (2008). An exploration of parental attributions within the autism spectrum disorders population. *Behaviour Change, 25,* 201–214. doi: 10.1375/bech.25.4.201

Widom, C. S., & White, H. R. (1997). Problem behaviours in abused and neglected children grown up: Prevalence and co-occurrence of substance abuse, crime and violence. *Criminal Behaviour and Mental Health, 7,* 287–310. doi: 10.1002/cbm.191

Wilder, S. (2014). Effects of parental involvement on academic achievement: A meta-synthesis. *Educational Review, 66,* 377–397. doi:10.1080/00131911.2013.780009

Williams, R. J., McDermitt, D. R., Bertrand, L. D., & Davis, R. M. (2003). Parental awareness of adolescent substance use. *Addictive Behaviors, 28,* 803–809. doi: 10.1016/S0306-4603(01)00275-1

Williamsen, M. E., & van de Fons, J. R. (1997). Developmental expectations of Dutch, Turkish-Dutch, and Zambian mothers: Towards an explanation of cross-cultural differences. *International Journal of Behavioral Development, 21,* 837–854. doi: 1080/016502597384695

Wilson, K. R., Havighurst, S. S., Kehoe, C., & Harley, A. E. (2016). Dads tuning in to kids: Preliminary evaluation of a fathers' parenting program. *Family Relations, 65,* 535–549. doi: 10.1111/fare.12216

Wilson, S., & Durbin, C. E. (2010). Effects of paternal depression on parenting behaviors: A meta-analytic review. *Clinical Psychology Review, 30,* 167–180. doi: 10.1016/j.cpr.2009.10.007

Winter, L., Morawska, A., & Sanders, M. W. (2012a). The effect of behavioral family intervention on knowledge of effective parenting strategies. *Journal of Child and Family Studies, 21,* 881–890. doi: 10.1007/s10826-011-9548-y

Winter, L., Morwska, A., & Sanders, M. (2012b). The Knowledge of Effecting Parenting Scale (KEPS): A tool for public health approaches to universal parenting programs. *Journal of Primary Prevention, 33,* 85–97. doi: 10.1007/s10935-012-0268-x

Wittkowski, A., Dowling, H., & Smith, D. M. (2016). Does engaging in a group-based intervention increase parental self-efficacy in parents of preschool children? A systematic review of the current literature. *Journal of Child and Family Studies, 25,* 3173–3191. doi: 10.1007/s10826-016-0464-z

Wolf, A. E. (2002). *Get out of my life—but first would you drive Cheryl and me to the mall?* New York, NY: Farrar Strauss Giroux.

Wong, M. S., McElwain, N. L., & Halberstadt, A. G. (2009). Parent, family, and child characteristics: Associations with mother-and father-reported emotion socialization practices. *Journal of Family Psychology, 23,* 452–463. doi: 10.1037/a0015552

Yasui, M. (2015). A review of the empirical assessment of processes in ethnic-racial socialization: Examining methodological advances and future areas of development. *Developmental Review, 37,* 1–40. doi: 10.1016/j.dr.2015.03.001

Yau, J., & Smetana, J. G. (1996). Adolescent-parent conflict among Chinese adolescents in Hong Kong. *Child Development, 67,* 1262–1275. doi: 10.1111/1467-8624.ep9704150195

Yau, J., & Smetana, J. G. (2003). Adolescent-parent conflict in Hong Kong and Shenzhen: A comparison of youth in two cultural contexts. *International Journal of Behavioral Development, 27,* 201–211. doi: 10.1080/01650250244000209

Yeager, D. S., Trzesniewski, K. H., & Dweck, C. S. (2013). An implicit theories of personality intervention reduces adolescent aggression in response to victimization and exclusion. *Child Development, 84,* 970–988. doi: 10.1111/cdev.12003

Young, A., Pierce, M. C., Kaczor, K., Lorenz, D. J., Hickey, S., Berger, S. P., . . . Thompson, R. (2018). Are negative/unrealistic parent descriptors of infant attributes associated with physical abuse? *Child Abuse and Neglect, 80,* 41–51. doi: 10.1016/j.chiabu.2018.03.020

Young, A., & Tattersall, H. (2007). Universal Newborn Hearing Screening and early identification of deafness: Parents' responses to knowing early and their expectations for child communication development. *Journal of Deaf Studies and Deaf Education, 12,* 209–220. doi: 10.1093/deafed/enl033

Youngstrom, E., Izard, C., & Ackerman, B. (1999). Dysphoria-related bias in maternal ratings of children. *Journal of Consulting and Clinical Psychology, 67,* 905–916. doi: 10.1037/0022-006X.67.6.905

Youniss, J. (2014). Civic-political engagement: Developmental science comes of age. *International Journal of Developmental Science, 8,* 149–153. doi: 10.3233/DEV-000078

Zablotsky, B., Colpe, L. J., Pringle, B. A., Kogan, M. D., Rice, C., & Blumberg, S. J. (2017). Age of parental concern, diagnosis, and service initiation among children with autism spectrum disorder. *American Journal on Intellectual and Developmental Disabilities, 122,* 49–61. doi: 10.1352/1944-7558-122.1.49

Zahn-Waxler, C., Duggal, S., & Gruber, R. (2002). Parental psychopathology. In M. H. Bornstein (Ed.), *Handbook of parenting: Vol. 4. Social conditions and applied parenting* (2nd ed., pp. 295–328). Mahwah, NJ: Erlbaum.

Zahn-Waxler, C., & Kochanska, G. (1990). The origins of guilt. In R. A. Thompson (Ed.), *Nebraska symposium on motivation, 1988: Socioemotional development* (pp. 183 258). Lincoln: University of Nebraska Press.

Zajicek-Farber, M. L. (2009). Postnatal depression and infant health practices among high-risk women. *Journal of Child and Family Studies, 18,* 236–245. doi: 10.1007/s10826-008-9224-z

Zajicek-Farber, M. L. (2010). The contributions of parenting and postnatal depression on emergent language of children in low-income families. *Journal of Child and Family Studies, 19,* 257–269. doi: 10.1007/s10826-009-9293-7

Zand, D. H., Pierce, K. J., Bultas, M. W., McMillin, S. E., Gott, R. M., & Wilmott, J. (2015). Accuracy of knowledge of child development in mothers and children receiving early intervention services. *Journal of Early Intervention, 37,* 226–240. doi: 10.1177/1053815115610633

Zeifman, D. M. (2003). Predicting adult responses to infant distress: Adult characteristics associated with perceptions, emotional reactions, and timing of intervention. *Infant Mental Health Journal, 24,* 597–612. doi: 10.1002/imhj.10077

Zell, E., Krizan, Z., & Teeter, S. R. (2015). Evaluating gender similarities and differences using metasynthesis. *American Psychologist, 70,* 10–20. doi: 10.103.1037/a0038208

Zevenbergen, A. A., Haman, E., & Olszariska, A. A. (2012). Middle-class Polish and American mothers' belief regarding parent-child narratives. *Journal of Cross-Cultural Psychology, 43,* 979–988. doi: 10.1177/0165025406066723

Zukow-Goldring, P. (2002). Sibling caregiving. In M. H. Bornstein (Ed.), *Handbook of parenting: Vol 3. Being and becoming a parent* (2nd ed., pp. 253–286). Hillsdale, NJ: Erlbaum.

Zych, I., Ortega-Ruiz, R., & Del Rey, R. (2015). Systematic review of theoretical studies on bullying and cyberbullying: Facts, knowledge, prevention, and intervention. *Aggression and Violent Behavior, 23,* 1–21. doi: 10.1016/j.avb.2015.10.001

# Name Index

Note: Page references followed by an italicized *f* or *t* indicate a figure or table on the page.

*For the benefit of digital users, indexed terms that span two pages (e.g., 52–53) may, on occasion, appear on only one of those pages.*

Aassve, G., 125–26
Abar, C. C., 252–53
Abel, K. M., 302, 303, 304
Abell, J., 290–91
Ablow, J. C., 112–13
Abma, J. C., 126
Achenbach, T. M., 279–80
Achim, A. M., 34
Acker, M. M., 94
Ackerman, B., 298–99
Adamsons, K., 113
Adkins, M., 150–51
Adrian, J. E., 188
Adrian, M., 208–9
Ahern, L., 306–7
Ahmad, I., 122
Ainsworth, M. D. S., 24–25, 27, 157, 159
Aitken, M. E., 150–51
Ajzen, I., 6, 64–65
Albarran, A. S., 100*t*
Albertos, A., 251–52
Alcock, K. J., 140
Al-Ghamdi, M., 260
Al-Hiyari, R., 216*t*
Alink, L. R. A., 216–17
Alisar, S., 272
Allen, B., 305–6
Al-Maadadi, F., 92–93
Almas, A., 209
Almon, J., 73
Anastopoulos, A. D., 279–80
Anderson, K. J., 237
Ang, P. H., 265–66
Anshel, M. H., 169
Antill, J. K., 116

Antshel, K. M., 278*t*
Apperly, I. A., 34
Appleby, L., 302
Appleyard, K., 162–63
Arace, A., 92, 136–37
Ardelt, M. A., 100*t*
Arnold, D. S., 94
Arnold, F., 124
Arnott, B., 161–62, 187
Aromaa, M., 98–99
Artelt, C., 167*t*
Arts, M., 153
Ashbourne, D. T., 78
Ashraf, R., 108–10
Asquith, P., 120–21
Assadi, S. M., 122
Assink, M., 305–6
Astrachan-Fletcher, E., 296–97
Astuto, J., 273
Ataca, B., 124
Aten, M. J., 257
Atkins, M., 246*t*
Attwood, T., 189
Augenstein, T. M., 260–61
Aunola, K., 39–40, 42–43, 50, 169,
    171, 173–74
Axelin, A., 46–47
Azar, S. T., 19–22, 20*f*, 172, 305–7, 308
Azuma, H., 166, 199

Babcok Fenerci, R. L., 305–6
Bachman, H. J., 174
Bader, L. R., 210
Baeriswyl, F., 177
Bahena, S., 167*t*

Bailey, D. B., 278*t*
Baird, G., 284
Baker, B., 285–86
Baker, M., 140
Bakermans-Kranenburg, M. J., 145, 148, 159, 216–17
Baldwin, A., 69–70
Baldwin, C., 69–70
Bales, A., 216*t*
Ballan, M. S., 295–96
Bamford, C., 209
Bandura, A., 27–28, 29, 89, 96, 100*t*
Banerjee, M., 275
Banerjee, R., 306
Bar, M. A., 294
Baranek, G. T., 293
Barbaranelli, C., 100*t*
Barbarin, O. A., 178
Barber, B. K., 245
Barch, D. M., 152
Barfoot, J., 278*t*
Barkin, S. L., 299
Barnett, B., 96, 299
Barnett, N. P., 252
Barocas, R., 68
Barr, R., 38, 151
Barrett, K. C., 78
Barrowclough, C., 299
Barry, H. III., 259
Bart, O., 294
Bar-Tal, D., 169
Bartholomew, M. K., 46–47
Bartle, N. C., 153
Bartlett, S., 140
Bassett, H. H., 207–8
Bassler, O. C., 100*t*, 176
Bates, J. E., 154, 156, 260, 288–89
Battaini, C., 148
Baumrind, D., 110, 122–23
Bayley, N., 143
Beale, K. S., 205*t*
Beaver, K. M., 260
Bechtel, C. F., 278*t*
Becker, J. A., 58, 78, 80
Becker-Haimes, E. M., 281
Beckman, L. J., 169
Beekman, A. T. F., 112

Beer, J. S., 84*t*
Begin, F., 153
Behrens, K. Y., 160
Bein, L. A., 281
Belden, A. C., 152
Belenky, M. F., 2, 71–72
Belfield, C., 167*t*, 178
Bell, M. A., 216
Bell, R. Q., 51
Beller, E., 287–88
Belsky, J., 74–75, 110, 161, 209
Benasich, A. A., 68–69, 92, 93–94
Benga, O., 207–8
Benson, J. B., 92, 106
Berg, R. L., 13
Berger, L. M., 92
Bergeron, N., 214–15
Bergman, L. R., 296–97
Bergmuller, S., 214–15
Berg-Nielsen, T. S., 42, 209
Berk, L., 73
Berkovits, L. D., 305
Berlin, L. J., 162–63
Berman, L. S., 170, 191
Bernard, K., 298*t*
Bernier, A., 188, 193
Bernier, R., 283, 291, 292*t*, 293–94
Bernstein, D. M., 34, 126
Bernstein, R. E., 112–13
Berry, T., 173–74
Bertrand, L. D., 254
Bessey, M., 147
Best, D. L., 235–36
Bettelheim, B., 128
Bhagyavathi, M. D., 304
Bhargavaraman, R. P., 303
Bhavnagri, N. P., 231
Bhullar, B., 147
Bibok, M. B., 193
Biddle, S. J. H., 84*t*
Biehle, S. N., 111–12, 113–14
Bierman, A., 127
Bierman, K. L., 174
Bingham, G. E., 3
Birch, H., 153–54
Bird, J. E., 170, 191
Birditt, K., 127

Birmaher, B., 281
Bjorklund, D. F., 53–54
Blacher, J., 285–86
Black, J. E., 74–75
Black, M. M., 298t, 301
Blake, J. J., 215
Blehar, M. C., 24–25, 157
Blissett, J., 188
Blocklin, M. K., 247
Blue, J. B., 41, 102
Blumberg, F. C., 265
Bober, M., 265–66
Bogdan, R. J., 3, 4
Bogenschneider, K., 99
Bogt, T., 257
Bohanan, A. L., 179–80
Boldt, B. R., 192
Bolton, C., 299
Bonazinga, L., 189
Bond, L. A., 2, 71–73, 264
Booth-LaForce, C., 229
Bora, E., 303–4
Borkowski, J. G., 93–94, 108–10, 139–40
Bornholt, L., 247–48
Bornstein, M. H., 31f, 45, 49–50, 56, 64–
    65, 81, 91–92, 105, 107–8, 112–13,
    125, 136, 145, 162–63, 199–200, 231
Borriello, G. A., 238
Bose, K., 245
Boutin, A., 34
Boutin, S., 308
Boutwell, B. B., 152
Bowers, E. P, 268
Bowes, J. M., 117
Bowker, J. C., 230
Bowlby, J., 24, 25–26
Boyce, L., 92
Boyce, P., 296–97
Boyd, M. J., 272
Boyd, R. C., 300
Boyd-Ball, A. J., 251–52
Boynton-Jarrett, R., 306
Bracaliello, C. B., 73–74, 75
Brackbill, Y., 126
Bradford, V. A., 153
Bradley, R., 69
Bradshaw, C. P., 215, 218

Brady, N., 286
Braginsky, M., 196
Branje, S., 261–62
Branstetter, S. A., 251–52
Brassart, E., 100t
Braster, S., 52, 164
Brei, N. G., 278t
Brennan, L. M., 278t
Bretherton, I., 88
Brett, B. E., 207
Brewster, S., 278t
Bricker, D., 140
Bridgeman, B., 172–73
Bridgett, D. J., 210, 297–98
Briggs-Gowan, M. J., 278–80
Briley, D. A., 172–73, 174
Brinthaupt, T. M., 169
Brio Corporation, 39, 55t, 56, 73–75, 134
Brissie, J. S., 100t, 176
Brit, S. L., 88
Brockmeier, J., 188
Brodish, A. B., 275
Brody, G. H., 264
Bronfenbrenner, U., 30, 31f, 32–33, 37
Brooks, P. J., 265
Brooks-Gunn, J., 32, 68–69, 92, 93–94
Brosco, J. P., 296
Brotman, M. A., 211–12
Brown, C. S., 236–37
Brown, E. G., 232
Brown, J., 181
Brown, M., 104–5
Brown, R., 195
Brumley, H. E., 302
Brune, M., 303–4
Bruni, O., 151
Bryant, A. Jr., 205t
Bryant, J. B., 72–73
Buchanan, C. M., 99, 243, 248, 249t
Buckner, J. P., 211–12
Bugental, D. B., 15, 41, 102, 103t, 104–6,
    112–13, 307, 308
Bullock, D., 106
Bumpus, M. F., 247
Bunclark, K., 179
Bunn, P., 225t
Burack, J. A., 284, 285

Burk, W. J., 243
Burke-Storer, M. R., 254
Burman, B., 125–26
Burnette, J. L., 83, 84t
Burney, R. V., 111–12, 145
Burson, C. F., 294
Burt, N. M., 210
Bush, K. R., 100t
Butterfill, S. A., 34
Bybee, D., 296–97, 303
Byers, E. S., 257
Byrne, C., 264
Byrne, S., 265–66

Caal, S., 207–8
Cabrerra, N. J., 38
Cadman, T., 159
Cain, K. M., 84t
Calafat, A., 254
Caldwell, B. M., 69, 240t
Caldwell, L. L., 245–46
Camargos-Junior, W., 295
Campbell-Grossman, C., 98
Campione-Barr, N., 245–46
Campos, J. J., 220
Cannon, J., 164
Caplan, B., 285–86
Capotosto, L., 167t
Caprara, G. V., 100t
Capute, A. J., 284–85
Carlson, E. A., 27, 269–70
Carlson, S. M., 193
Carlson, W., 268–69
Carpendale, J. I. M., 193
Carroll, J., 107
Carter, A. S., 278–80, 294, 295–96
Carugati, F., 41, 55t
Cashin, M. E., 73
Cashmore, J., 40, 78, 117, 200
Cassidy, J., 162–63, 207, 227
Castellino, D. R., 264
Castro, V. L., 211
Cauffman, E., 261
Cavanaugh, C., 261
Caye, A., 288
Cederbaum, J. A., 305
Centers for Disease Control and
    Prevention, 150, 255–56, 293

Chaidez, V., 295–96
Chandler, S., 284–85
Chandra, A., 126
Chandra, P. S., 303
Chang, F., 100t, 254
Chaparro, M. P., 227, 245–46
Chatzisarantis, N. L. D., 84t
Chau, V., 98
Cheah, S. L., 31f, 78, 80, 212, 213–14, 230
Chen, E. C., 192, 226
Chen, H., 167t, 170–71, 230
Chen, I., 253
Chen, L., 199–200, 275
Chen, M., 117, 298t
Chen, R. J., Flores, G., & Shetgiri, R., 41
Chen, X., 154, 157, 230
Cheng, T. L., 215
Cheng, Y., 127
Cheon, H. J., 265–66
Chess, S., 153–54
Cheung, R. Y. M., 298t, 300
Chi, T. C., 298–99
Chiang, T., 78
Child Trends, 174, 178, 215, 216, 256
Chiocca, E. M., 216
Chisholm, V, 278t
Chiu, C., 84t
Cho, C., 265–66
Choi, K. Y. K., 294
Chong, Y. S., 98
Chronis-Tuscano, A., 289
Chung, E. K., 216
Chung, J., 230
Chung, O. B., 31f
Cicchetti, D., 208–9, 292t, 305, 306, 309
Cichy, K. E., 126, 127
Ciciolla, L., 125
Civitas Initiative, 39, 55t, 56, 73–75, 134
Clark, D. A., 252–53
Clark, R., 297–98
Clarke-Stewart, A., 25t
Clemente, R. A., 188
Cleveland, M. J., 148
Clinchy, B. M., 71–72
Cobb, J. C., 146
Cohen, L. L., 278t
Coie, J. D., 214
Colby, S. M., 252

Cole, P. M., 207
Coleman, P. K., 96, 97*t*, 98, 100*t*, 157
Collier, K. M., 266, 267
Collins, M., 276
Collins, W. A., 3–4, 5–6, 8–9, 27, 44, 45*t*,
    49–50, 114–15, 247–48, 262–63,
    268, 269–70
Combs-Orme, T., 134
Conger, R. D., 252–53
Connell, A. M., 297–98
Connolly, E. J., 260
Connolly, J. A., 269
Connors, F., 285–86
Conrad, B., 101–2
Conroy, S., 304
Constabile, A., 134
Constantine, N. A., 257
Cook, R. C., 218
Cook, T., 2, 71–72
Cooper, H., 177
Coplan, R. J., 204, 230
Corapci, F., 207
Corcoran, J., 290–91
Corkum, P, 147
Corter, C., 145
Cortez, V. L., 104
Costigan, K. A., 154
Cote, L. R., 45, 91–92, 136, 172
Cotler, S., 179–80
Cotton, S., 78, 116, 117, 200
Cottone, E. A., 178
Cottrell, L., 246*t*
Coulombe, J. A., 147
Cox, A., 285–86
Coy, K. C., 262
Coyne, S. M., 266–67
Craig, A. B., 211
Crais, E. R., 293
Crandall, A. A., 216
Crano, W. D., 254–55
Crick, N. R., 20, 216–17
Criss, M. M., 210
Crittenden, P. M., 19
Crncec, R., 96
Cross, S. E., 254–55
Crouter, A. C., 243–44, 247, 270–71
Crowe, E., 188
Cruz, L. P., 295

Cruzcosa, M., 41, 102
Cummings, E. M., 298*t*, 300
Cumsille, P., 245–46
Cunningham, C. E., 78
Curtner-Smith, M. E., 285–86

Daddis, C., 251–52
Dadds, M. R., 90, 225*t*
Daga, S. S., 207–8
Dahl, A., 220
Dai, D. Y., 13
Dai, Y. G., 295
da Luz Vale-Dias, M., 92
Damianova, M. K., 22
Danielson, M. L., 287–88
Dardennes, R. M., 295–96
Darling, N., 245–46
Darling-Churchill, K. E., 228
Dasen, P. R., 183–84
D'Assessandri, D., 246*t*
Davidod, M., 263–64
Davidsen, K. A., 302
Davidson, K. L., 41, 76–77, 198*t*, 198
Davies, P. T., 298*t*, 300
Davis, E. M., 126
Davis, K. D., 247
Davis, K. E., 15
Davis, R. M., 254
Davis, T. L., 179–80, 181, 191
Dawson, G., 283, 291, 292*t*, 293–94
Deane, K. E., 157, 158–59
Deater-Deckard, K., 210, 216
DeBaryshe, B. D., 178
Decourcey, W., 113
de Graff, P. M., 127
de Haan, A. D., 99, 101
Dehue, F., 217
Dekovic, M., 99, 247–48, 254
Delaney, S., 116
Delgado, M., 57, 185
Delgado-Hachey, M., 179–80
de Looze, M., 257, 258–59
De Los Reyes, A., 260–61, 280–82, 298–99
Del Rey, R., 217
Del Vecchio, T., 213
Demers, I., 188
De Montigny, F., 97
Denham, S., 207–8

Denmark, N., 196–97
Dennis, C., 301
Dent, A. L., 177
de Rosnay, M., 161–62, 187–88
Deschenes, M., 193
Despland, J., 58–59
Detwiler, A. C., 146
DeVet, K., 224–25
Devine, R. T., 187–88
Devitt, K., 188
Diamond, L. M., 257, 259
Diamond, P. R., 159
Dickens, Charles, 239
Dickson, W. P., 199
DiPietro, J., 154
Dishion, T. J., 244, 251–52, 253, 297–98
Dittus, P. J., 256–58
Dix, T., 15, 43, 47–48, 78, 79, 80, 216, 227,
    297, 298t, 299–300
Dodge, K. A., 20, 214, 215–16, 260
Dolev, S., 294–95
Donnellan, M. B., 252–53
Dorfler, T., 167t
Doris, M. D., 73
Dotterer, A. M., 243
Doust, J., 287–88
Dowdy, B., 245–46
Dowling, H., 100–1
Downs, J., 285
Doyle, A. C., 151
Doyle, O., 152
Drysdale, K., 190t, 190–91
Duell, N., 250–51
Duggal, S., 300
Dumas-Hines, F., 84t
Dumka, L. E., 100t, 100–1
Dumont, H., 177
Dunn, E. W., 125–26
Dunn, J., 227, 233
Dunsmore, J. C., 204, 205t, 206,
    207–8, 210–11
DuPaul, G. J., 278t, 279–80, 288
Durbin, C. E., 154, 297–98
Durgel, E. S., 200
Dweck, C. S., 17, 77–78, 82, 83, 84t, 84–85
Dworkin, P. H., 200
Dykens, E. M., 284, 285–86, 287

Earn, B. M., 78
Eaton, K. L., 204
Eccles, J. S., 50, 100t, 172, 174–75, 240, 275
Edwards, E. S., 210
Edwards, L. A., 3
Egeland, B., 27, 269–70
Ehrlich, K. B., 207
Eisenberg, N., 222, 224, 226–27
Eisner, M. P., 214, 216–17
Elder, G. H., Jr., 32
Elek, S. M., 98–99
Elliott, L., 174
Elsaesser, C., 218–19, 267
Else-Quest, N. M., 273–74
Emmery, K., 265–66
Engels, R. C. M. E., 254
Engle, P. L., 301
English, T., 125–26
Enlund, E., 42–43, 169, 171–72
Ennett, S. T., 255
Ensor, R., 298t
Entwisle, D. R., 172–73, 175
Epkins, C. C., 298t
Epley, N., 263
Erdley, C. A., 84t
Ereky-Stevens, K., 187–88
Erel, O., 125–26
Erikson, E., 73, 273
Ertem, I. O., 90, 134
Esposito, G., 81, 145
Essex, M. J., 126
Evans, S. L., 135
Everett, B., 256–57
Ewart, J. C., 284

Fairbairn, C. E., 255
Families Special Interest Research
    Group, 285
Faragher, B., 302
Farkas, T., 236
Farrington, D. P., 261
Farris, J., 139–40
Farrow, C., 188
Farver, J. A. M., 74–75, 76
Favez, N., 58–59
Fawcett, J. T., 124
Fay-Stammbach, T., 193, 288–89

Fearon, R. P., 159, 216–17
Feil, L. A., 59, 67t, 67–68
Fein, D. A., 295
Feldman, J., 179–80
Feldman, S. S., 247–48
Fenson, L., 195, 196
Fernandez-Alcantara, M., 278t
Fernandez-Hermida, J., 254
Fernyhough, C., 22, 161–62, 187
Fidler, D. J., 287
Field, T. M., 147, 300–1
Fiese, B. H., 59, 69–70
Fikkers, K. M., 267–68
Fincham, F. D., 79, 114, 264
Fingerman, K. L., 126, 127
Finkel, E. J., 83
Fischbach, G. D., 295–96
Fischbach, R. L., 295–96
Fishbein, M., 6, 64–65
Fisher, K. R., 74
Fisher, S. L., 254
Fivush, R., 211–12
Flanagan, C., 117, 271, 272
Fleck, M. O., 98–99
Fleming, A. S., 113, 145
Fleming, K., 286
Fletcher, A. C., 252, 253
Flint-Ofir, E., 147
Flynn, E., 146
Fogg, L., 101–2
Fogle, L. M., 74t, 75
Foley, S., 162
Fonagy, P., 161, 188–89
Forehand, R., 267
Forman, Y., 268
Fosco, G. M., 253
Fouts, H. N., 210
Fowler, C., 296–97
Frank, M. C., 196
Franklin, C. L., 300
Frascarolo, F., 58–59
Fredericks, J. A., 50, 172
Freeman, W., 42–43
French, D. C., 157, 230
Frensch, P. A., 172–73
Frick, P. J., 279–80
Friedlmeier, W., 207

Friedman, N. P., 193
Friedman, S. L., 58
Frith, C. D., 303–4
Fritz, J., 101, 107–8
Frome, P. M., 174–75
Frost, A. D. J., 225t
Fry, P. S., 136, 139
Fujiwara, T., 146
Fukumoto, S., 182
Fung, H., 192, 226
Funk, J., 264
Furman, W., 231, 233, 251–52, 268, 269,
    270, 271
Furnham, A., 179, 182

Gaffan, E. A., 298t
Gaither, S. E., 273–74
Gallo, F. J., 278t
Gamble, W. C., 99, 108–10
Gangadhar, B. N., 304
Garcia, E., 167t, 178
Garnett, M., 189
Gartstein, M. A., 297–99
Gaskins, S., 76–77, 117–18
Gauda, G., 130
Gauvain, M., 200
Gavazzi, I. G., 188
Gaydos, L. M., 150–51
Geangu, E., 207–8
Gehlbach, H., 167t
Gelfand, D. M., 42–43, 78, 79–80
Genevro, J. L., 92
Genta, M. L., 134
Gentzley, A. L., 207
George, C., 26
Georgiou, S. N., 170
Gershoff, E. T., 215
Gesell, A., 130
Gettinger, M., 214
Gettler, L. T., 150
Gettman, D. C., 245–46
Ghazarian, S. R., 216
Giallo, R., 98, 99, 101
Gillham, J. E., 300
Gillingham, M. C., 180
Ginsburg, G. S., 281
Ginsburg, H. P., 73, 164

Gioia, G. A., 194*t*, 194, 279–80
Girard, L., 152
Girdler, S., 276
Glascoe, F. P., 140
Glassman, M., 46–47
Glasziou, P., 287–88
Glatz, T., 99
Gleason, T. R., 74–75
Glidden, L. M., 285
Gluck, B., 240*t*
Godoy, L., 278–79
Goh, D., 272
Goisis, A., 125–26
Golby, B., 88
Gold, R., 200
Goldberger, N. R., 71–72
Goldman, M., 224–25
Goldman-Fraser, J., 169–70
Goldsmith, H. H., 154, 155*t*
Golinkoff, R. M., 73, 74
Golombok, R., 235*t*
Gondoli, D. M., 100*t*, 101
Gonzales, N. A., 100*t*, 100–1
Gonzalez, L. M., 190
Gonzalez, M., 70
Gonzalez, V., 290–91
Goodman, K. L., 206, 260–61
Goodman, R., 279*t*, 279–80
Goodman, S. H., 211–12, 297–98,
    298*t*, 302
Goodnow, J. J., 3–4, 5–6, 8–9, 40, 44, 45*t*,
    51, 57, 58, 64–65, 78, 80, 114–15, 116,
    117, 200
Goodvin, R., 43
Goodwin, J., 204
Goodyear, I., 188–89
Goossens, L., 252
Gopalan, R., 284–85
Gordon, V. V., 256–57
Goslin, M. C., 19, 20*f*, 308
Gottfried, N. W., 39
Gottman, J. M., 204–6
Graham, S., 217
Grant, R., 307
Gravener-Davis, J. A., 308
Graziano, P. A., 290–91
Green, A. E., 254
Green, C. G., 284

Green, C. L., 176*f*, 176
Green, J., 302
Green, J. A., 145
Green, J. M., 113–14
Green, M. C., 284
Green, S., 285–86
Greenbaum, C. W., 136
Greenspan, S., 68
Gretarsson, S. J., 42–43, 78, 79–80
Grigorenko, E. L., 183–84
Groeneveld, M. G., 236
Grogan-Kaylor, A., 215
Groh, A. M., 27, 229
Gross, D., 101–2
Gross, J. J., 84*t*
Grossman, E. J., 309
Gruber, R., 300
Gruhn, M. A., 297–98, 298*t*
Grusec, J. E., 15, 64–65, 78, 105–6, 209,
    227, 245–46, 263–64
Grych, J. H., 114
Gryfe, S. G., 74
Grynch, J. H., 79
Guajardo, N. R., 188
Guerra, N. G., 218
Guerrero, L. W., 216*t*
Guilamo-Ramos, V., 257–58
Guimond, A. B., 92
Guitton, M. J., 34
Gumley, A., 302
Gustafson, G. E., 145
Gutierrez, J., 68
Gutman, L. M., 240
Guttmann, J. A., 169
Guyll, M., 254–55

Ha, C., 188–89
Hackel, L. S., 113
Haddon, L., 265
Haden, C. A., 211–12
Hahn, C. S., 45, 91–92, 136
Haidt, J., 219
Haight, W. L., 74–75
Hailey, B. C., 112–13
Haimovitz, K., 85
Hakim-Larson, J., 204
Halberstadt, A. G., 204, 205*t*, 206, 210–11
Hall, J. H., 114

Hall, M. S., 58, 78, 80
Halle, T. G., 228
Halperin, E., 84t
Haltigan, J. D., 145
Haman, E., 192
Hamilton, M., 130
Hammond, S. I., 193
Handley, E. D., 308
Hansen, T., 125, 126
Happaney, K., 15, 104, 105, 106, 307
Happe, F., 304
Harari, N., 153
Harden, B. J., 196–97
Harden, K. P., 172–73
Harder, S., 302
Harkness, S., 1, 9, 35–36, 37, 76, 128, 130,
    148, 164, 202
Harley, A. E., 211
Harms, M. P., 152
Harper, S. L., 298t
Harris, C., 246t
Harris, G. S., 146
Harris, J. L., 298t
Harris, M. J., 295–96
Harris, P. L., 187–88
Harrist, A. W., 123
Hart, B. M., 197
Hart, C. H., 231–32
Hart, D., 272
Hart, K. C., 290–91
Hart, M. J., 298t
Harter, S., 106
Hartley, S. L., 294
Harvey, J. H., 51
Harvey, K., 153
Haskett, M. E., 306–7, 308
Hassall, R., 285
Hastings, P., 105–6, 227, 263
Hastings, R. P., 283–84
Hauser-Cram, P., 286
Havighurst, S. S., 211
Hawes, D. J., 90, 193, 225t, 288–89
Hawk, C. K., 106, 108–10, 109t
Hawk, S. T., 245–46
Hawkins, E., 160–61
Hayduk, L. A., 172–73, 175
Hayes, S. A., 294
Haynes, O. M., 45, 91–92, 136

He, H., 98
Head, M. R., 243–44
Heatherington, L., 264
Heberle, A., 278–79
Hedges, R., 190t
Heerman, W. J., 299
Heider, F., 15
Heinicke, C., 110–11
Heirman, W., 265–66
Hekimian, E., 306–7
Helms-Erikson, H., 243
Henning, K. H., 222–23
Henry, D., 49–50
Hensen, W. B., 255
Her, P., 206
Heriot, J. T., 284
Herman, S., 150–51
Hernandez-Mekonnen, R., 306–7
Hess, C. R., 101–2
Hess, R. D., 166, 169, 199, 200–1
Hetherington, E. M., 49–50, 253
Hewstone, M., 19
Heyworth, J., 285
Hibbs, R., 278t
Hiebert-Murphy, D., 202, 276, 278t
Higgins, T., 34
High, P., 146
Hilbert, S. J., 254–55
Hill, K., 305
Hill, N. E., 100t
Hinduja, S. K., 217
Hines, M., 234, 236–37
Hinshaw, S. P, 298–99
Hirsh-Pasek, K., 73, 74
Hirsjarvi, S., 3
Hobbs, S. A., 278t
Hochbrueckner, R., 290–91
Hodapp, R. M., 278t, 284, 285–86, 287
Hoeve, M., 260
Hoffman, M. L., 224
Holden, G. W., 3, 106, 108 10, 109t
Holloway, S. D., 166, 169
Holmbeck, G. N., 248, 249t, 278t
Holmes, T. R., 264
Hommersen, P., 290
Hong, Y., 84t
Hoon, A. H., 284–85
Hooven, C., 204

Hoover-Dempsey, K. V., 100*t*, 176*f*, 176
Hotez, E., 67–68, 294
Houltber, B. J., 210
Hourigan, S. E., 206, 209
Howard, K. S., 108–10
Howe, M. L., 170
Howell, C. T., 280
Howes, C., 74–75, 76
Howlin, P., 284
Hox, J., 303–4
Hsu, H., 80
Huang, C., 280
Huang, H. L., 93–94, 290
Huang, K., 92, 93–94
Hubert, J., 276
Hudec, K. L., 289
Hudson, D. B., 98–99
Hughes, C., 108–10, 162, 187–88, 298*t*
Hughes, D., 275
Hughes, J. L., 248
Hunsberger, B., 69, 272
Hunt, C., 218
Hunt, J., 42, 179–80
Hunter, K., 225*t*
Hunter, S. B., 245
Hurd, H. D., 214
Hurlburt, M. S., 305
Hussey-Gardner, B., 101–2
Hutchins, T. L., 72–73, 189
Hutman, T., 67–68, 294–95
Hyde, J. S., 234, 237, 297–98
Hyde, L. W., 278*t*
Hymel, S., 217

Iarocci, G., 284
Ikhief, A., 92–93
Ilg, F. L., 130
Ingersoll, B., 295
Ireton, H., 140–41
Isikoglu, N., 74, 75
Isquith, P. K., 194*t*, 194, 279–80
Ivrendi, A., 74, 75
Izard, C., 298–99
Izzo, C., 100*t*

Jaccard, J., 256–57, 258–59
Jacklin, C. N., 237
Jackson, E. B., 146

Jackson, K. M., 252
Jackson, P. L., 34
Jackson-Newsom, J., 243
Jacobus, J., 250–51
Jager, T., 190
Jahromi, L. B., 92, 93–94, 98, 133, 136, 137, 139–40
Jain, A., 278*t*
Jellett, R., 99
Jensen-Doss, A., 281
Jerman, P., 257
Jessee, A., 297–98
Jeynes, W. H., 177
Jiang, S., 76
Job, V., 84*t*
Johnson, D. R., 306–7
Johnson, J. E., 56
Johnston, C., 42–43, 100*t*, 104, 193–94, 289–90, 298*t*
Johnston, L. D., 250
Johnston, M., 227
Jolliffe, D., 261
Jones, D. J., 257–58, 267
Jones, E. E., 15
Jones, J., 126
Jones, J. D., 207
Jones, T. L., 96
Jorm, A. F., 251–52
Juan, M., 254
Juhasz, A. M., 90
Juntilla, N., 98–99, 100*t*
Justice, L. M., 167*t*
Juvonen, J., 217

Kafetsios, K., 113–14
Kagitcibasi, C., 124
Kahng, S. K., 303
Kaitz M., 296–97
Kaladjian, A., 285–86
Kalb, L. M., 261
Kaley, F., 146
Kalmijn, M., 127
Kamp Dush, C. M., 46–47
Kan, M. L., 270–71
Kanazawa, S., 152
Kangasniemi, M., 255
Kaplan, N., 26
Karing, C., 167*t*

Karkkainen, R., 84*t*, 172
Karn, M. A., 204, 210
Karraker, K. H., 96, 97*t*, 98, 100*t*, 135, 157, 278*t*
Karrer, B. M., 68
Karstad, S. B., 42, 209–10
Kasanen, K., 84*t*, 84–85, 172, 173–74
Kashiwagi, K., 166, 199
Katz, L. F., 204, 205*t*, 206, 210
Katz, S. J., 265
Kaufman, N. K., 297–98
Kavanagh, K., 251–52, 253
Kawabata. Y., 216–17
Kazdin, A. E., 280, 281
Kehoe, C., 211
Keijsers, L., 245
Keller, H., 130, 133
Keller P. S., 298*t*
Kelley, H. H., 15–16
Kelly, A., 189
Kendall, P. C., 278*t*, 281
Kennedy, J., 284
Kenworthy, L., 194*t*
Keogh, D., 139
Kerr, M., 242*t*, 242, 243, 244–45, 255, 260, 268
Ketelaar, L., 224–25
Keysar, B., 263
Khader, A. M. B., 184–85
Khazan, I., 113, 114
Khodayarifard, M., 169
Khoo, A., 265–66
Kijakovic, M., 218
Kil, H., 245–46
Killen, M., 116, 219, 223, 226–27
Kim, H., 270–71
Kim, J. I., 152
Kim, M., 3, 63, 64–65
Kim, T., E., 218
Kim, Y. K., 76
Kincaid, C., 257–58
Kinlaw, C. R., 169–70
Kirk, E., 294–95
Kirkman, J. J. L., 90, 94
Kish, A. M., 216
Kitch, D., 126
Kiuru, N., 39–40
Klein-Tasman, B. P., 278*t*

Kliegel, M., 190
Kliewer, W., 260–61
Kliman, D. S., 136, 137
Knafo-Noam, A., 226–27
Knee, C. R., 84*t*
Knight, R., 57, 58, 78, 80, 81, 117, 200
Kobeisy, A. N., 260
Kochanska, G. S., 58, 224–25, 226, 227, 233
Kogan, N., 279–80
Koh, J. B. K., 192
Kohlberg, L., 222–23
Kohlhoff, J., 299
Kondo-Ikemura, K., 160
Korat, O., 173–74
Koren-Karie, N., 294–95
Kornienko, O., 275
Kovitz, K., 100*t*
Kovshoff, H., 294
Kowal, M. K., 233
Kramer, L., 233
Krauss, M. W., 286
Krettenauer, T., 222–23
Kringelbach, L. K., 301
Krishnakumar, A., 41, 198*t*, 198
Krizan, Z., 234
Kroff, S. L., 266–67
Krull, J. L., 233
Ksinan, A. J., 260–61
Kucyniski, L., 58
Kuhn, D., 71–72
Kuhn, J. C., 294, 295–96
Kulkofsky, S., 192
Kumar, C. N., 304
Kunseler, F. C., 112
Kurt, A. N. C., 278*t*
Kurtz-Coster, B., 169–70
Kushlev, K., 124, 125–26
Kvello, O., 42, 209

Lacharite, C., 97
Ladd, G. W., 80, 231–32
LaFleur, L. K., 245–46
LaForett, D. R., 74, 75, 76
Lagace-Seguin, D. G., 204
Lagattuta, K. H., 209
Laird, R. D., 260
LaLiberte, T., 305
Lamb, C. S., 254–55

Lambert, J. D., 88
Landry, O., 284
Landry, S. H., 68–69
Lansford, J. E., 105, 117
Lanthier, R., 233
Lapsley, A., 216–17
Lara, E. E., 98
Larsen, J. J., 90
Larzelee, R. E., 123
Lauckhardt, J., 271–72
Laurent, H. K., 112–13
Laursen, B., 262
Lavelli, M., 278t
Law, D. M., 266
Leahy-Warren, P., 98
Leaper, C., 235–36, 237
Lease, A. M., 215
Lechcier-Kimel, R., 230
Lee, C., 204
Lee, S., 166
Lee, S. J., 216t
Lee, T., 265
Lee, Y., 76, 253
Lee, Y. H., 126
Leekam, S. R., 161–62, 187
Leerkes, E. M., 111–12, 145–46
Lefever, J. B., 93–94, 139–40
Lefkowitz, E. S., 126
Lefmann, T., 134
Le Grange, D., 151
Lehmen, R., 271–72
Leichman, E. S., 147
Lejuez, C. W., 207, 252
Leman, K., 240t
Lench, H. C., 290–91
Lennon, J. M., 278t
Lenzi, M., 272
Leonard, H., 276, 285
Lereya, S. T., 218
Lerkkanen, M., 39–40, 50, 169, 173–74
Lerner, J. V., 268
Lerner, R. M., 272
Lesane-Brown, C. L., 275
Lester, B. M., 146
Letarte, M., 308
Leung, D. W., 299
Leve, C., 298t
Levick, W. R., 190t, 190–91

Levine, K. G., 240t
Levine, L. J., 290–91
Li, X., 246t
Li, Y., 214–15
Liau, A. K., 265–66
Li-Barber, K. T., 278t
Liben, L. S., 238
Licata, M., 188
Lichtenfeld, S., 173
Liebermann-Finestone, D. P., 193
Lightfoot, E., 305
Lillard, A. S., 73
Limber, S. P., 218
Lin, A., 272
Lin, S., 192
Lin, Y., 73–74, 75, 231
Lindhiem, O., 298t
Link, B. G., 295–96
Linz, D., 265
Lipka, J., 183–84
Lipsey, N. P., 278t
Lira, E. N., 278t
Little, C., 279–80
Liu, J. J., 35
Lively, N., 296–97
Livingstone, S., 265–66
Lo, S. L., 154–56
Lochman, J. E., 216
Lockridge, R., 295
Loeber, R., 261
Logie, C., 41, 198t, 198
Lok, S. M., 188
Lomax, R., 100t
Loomis, C. C., 84t
Loop, L., 100t
Lopez-Perez, B., 209
Loughlin-Presnal, J. E., 174
Loutzenhiser, L., 98, 99
Low, J., 34
Loyd, A. B., 273–74
Lozada, F. T., 211
Lubman, D. I., 251–52
Luebker, C., 262
Luijk, M. P. C. M., 148
Luke, N., 306
Lundell, L. J., 263–64
Lundin, L., 266
Lundy, B. L., 187–88

Lundy, J., 302
Luria, Z., 236
Luthar, S. S., 125, 309
Luyckx, K., 252
Ly, T. M., 278*t*, 287
Lynam, D., 214
Lytton, H., 238
Lyubomirsky, S., 124, 125–26

MacBeth, A., 302
Maccoby, E. E., 49–50, 237
MacFarlane, P., 296–97
Machado, J. D., 288
Mack, K., 303
MacKenzie, S. B., 48–49
MacKinnon-Lewis, C., 264
MacPhee, D., 46*t*, 46–47, 69, 90*t*, 90, 92–
    93, 101, 106, 107–8, 178
MacPherson, L., 252
Macy, M., 143
Madigan, S., 160–61
Madon, S., 254–55
Madsen, S. D., 270–71
Maes, H. H., 253, 255
Mah, J. W. T., 290
Main, M., 26
Majorano, M., 278*t*
Malanchuk, O., 240, 275
Malarde, A., 55*t*
Maliken, A. C., 205*t*, 210
Malle, B. F., 15
Malti, T., 214, 216–17, 219
Mammone, N., 105–6
Mangelsdorf, S. C., 297–98
Manhal, M., 179–80
Manosevitz, M., 135
Mansbach, I. K., 136
Mansfield, A. F., 71–72
Mantz, P. H., 73–74, 75
March, J. S., 279–80
Marchman, V. A., 196
Marcia, J., 273
Marcil, K., 308
Marcks B., 296–97
Markham, C. M., 257–58
Marlenga, B., 13
Marsh, H. W., 173
Martin, A. J., 284

Martin, C., 56
Martin, C. L., 237
Martin, J. L., 236–37
Martinez, G. M., 126
Martinez-Brockman, J. L., 153
Martins, C., 298*t*
Martorell, G. A., 104
Masche, J. G., 245
Mash, E. J., 100*t*, 290
Masiello, M., 218
Masry, Y. E., 225*t*
Masten, A. S., 309
Mastergeorge, A. M., 50
Matte-Gagne, C., 193
Matthey, S., 96
Matusiewicz, A. K., 252
Mavridis, C. J., 35
Maxwell, S. E., 139
Mayes, S. D., 295
Maytal, H., 296–97
Mazzone, S., 208–9
McAuslan, P., 98
McCabe, J. E., 300–1
McCarthy, G., 98
McCloskey, G., 194
McConachie, H., 285–86
McConaughy, S. H., 280
McConnell, D., 283–84
McCool, A., 204
McCord, B. L., 207–8
McCullough, C., 298*t*
McDermitt, D. R., 254
McDonald, M., 264
McDonald, S. E., 278*t*
McElwain, N. L., 204, 206
McGillicuddy, N. B., 254
McGillicuddy-DeLisi, A. V., 41, 55*t*, 56,
    57–58, 59–62, 63, 64, 65, 94
McGinty, A. S., 167*t*
McGuier, D. J., 306–7
Mc Gunkin, C., 217
McHale, J. P., 113
McHale, S. M., 243–44, 247, 270–71
McIntosh, H., 272
McIntyre, J., 167*t*
McIsaac C., 269
McKee, D. J., 172–73
McKee, L., 257–58

McKenna, J. J., 150
McIlrath, M., 265
McMahon, C. A., 188
McMahon, R. J., 244, 245, 251–52, 255
McMaugh, A. L., 214
McNeely, C. A., 245
McQueen, K., 301
McShane, K. E., 263–64
Measelle, J. R., 112–13
Medina, M., 275
Mee, L., 179–80
Meeus, W., 247–48, 254
Mehta, U. M., 304
Meier, E., 183–84
Meins, E., 33, 161–62, 187–88
Meirsschaut, M., 294
Meldrum, R. C., 152
Melender, H., 46–47
Melson, G. F., 80
Memmoff-Elison, M. K., 266–67
Mendes, T. V., 92
Mendez, J. L., 74t, 74, 75, 76, 278t
Menendez, C. R., 88–89
Menzer, M., 230
Meredith, P., 193, 278t, 288–89
Merrifield, K. A., 99, 108–10
Merz, S., 225t
Mesman, J., 236
Messina, I., 145
Metzger, A., 272
Metzger, S. R., 173–74
Meunier, L., 297, 299–300
Mezulis, A. H., 297–98
Miceli, P. J., 139
Michea, A., 55t
Michels, N., 209
Mickelson, K. D., 111–12, 113–14
Miele, D. B., 55t
Miele-Norton, M., 304
Mileva-Seitz, V. R., 148–50
Milkie, M. A., 127
Miller, C. L., 139–40
Miller, E., 73
Miller, E. A., 306–7
Miller, J. G., 227
Miller, L. E., 295
Miller, P., 49–50
Miller, P. J., 192

Miller, S. A., 15, 34, 40, 57, 65, 168, 170–
    72, 179–80, 181, 185, 186, 187, 191,
    196–97, 284–85
Miller, T. L, 92
Miller-Heyl, J., 101, 107
Miller-Loncar, C. L., 68–69
Mills, R. S. L., 19, 43, 78, 80, 212, 213,
    226, 229
Millsap, R. E., 100t, 100–1
Milner, J. S., 19
Mindell, J. A., 147
Miranda, D., 130
Mize, J., 232
Mkhize, N., 182
Moffitt, T. E., 260
Mohannadi, M., 122
Mohatt, G., 183–84
Mollborn, S., 256–57
Monetta, L., 34
Monico, L., 92
Montemayor, R., 100t
Moon, R. Y., 150–51
Moorman, E. A., 51, 83–84
Moran, G., 160–61
Moran, T. E., 300
Morawska, A., 90, 94–96, 95t, 101–2
Moreno, M., 70
Morewedge, C. K., 263
Morey, J. N., 207
Mori, Y., 285
Moroni, S., 177
Morrell, J. M. B., 147t, 147–48, 187–88
Morris, A. S., 123, 210, 250–51
Morris, L. B., 73, 75–76
Morse, E., 273–74
Morsheimer, E. T., 254
Mosher, W. D., 126
Mounts, N. S., 270–71
Moussaoui, N., 52, 164
Mouton, B., 100t
Mowbray, C., 296–97, 303
Mowder, B. A., 90, 94
Muelenhard, C. L., 234
Muenks, K., 55t, 83–84
Mugny, G., 41, 55t
Muller, U., 193
Muraco, J. A., 268–69
Murayama, K., 173, 175

Murdoch, K. W, 98–99
Murphey, D. A., 51, 65
Murray, C. B., 278t
Murray, K., 224–25
Mynttinen, M., 255
Myse, H., 76

Nader-Grosbois, N., 208–9
Nakazawa, J., 145
Nakona, S., 160
Nakonezny, P. A., 108–10
Narad, M. E., 288
Narine, L., 41, 198t, 198
National Vital Statistics Report, 255–56
Nauck, B., 124
Navarro, J. N., 218–19
Nears, K., 306–7
Neiderhiser, J. M., 253
Neisser, U., 54–55
Nelson, K., 22
Nelson, L. J., 245
Nelson, S. E., 253
Nelson, S. K., 124–26
Neto, F., 182
Nevo, B., 184–85
Nevsimalova, S., 151
Newcombe, P. A., 216
Newman, L., 296–97
Nicholson, J. S., 108–10
Niela-Vilen, H., 46–47
Niemi, R. G., 272
Nigg, J. T., 287, 288
Niggli, A., 177
Nikken, P., 266
Ninio, A., 130, 134, 136–37
Nissim, G., 298t
Nixon, S., 78
Nobre-Lima, L., 92
Noffsinger, W. B., 126
Noom, M. J., 247–48
Norman, S., 278t
Norris, D. R., 127
Notten, N., 266
Nucci, L., 120, 220, 221t
Nuendorf, A., 272
Nunez, N. N., 78
Nurmi, J., 39–40, 42–43, 50, 169, 171, 173–74

Nuttal, A. K., 93–94
Nylen, K. J., 300

O'Boyle E. H., 83
O'Brien Caughy, M., 92
O'Callaghan, M. F., 139
O'Donnell, L., 256–57, 258–59
Ogelman, H. G., 98
Ohanessian, C. M., 218–19
O'Hara, M. W., 300–1
Okado, Y., 19
Okagaki, L., 3, 172–73, 184
O'Leary, S. G., 94, 213
Olejnik, S. P., 215
Olsen, J. A., 245
Olson, B. F., 266
Olszariska, A. A., 192
Olweus, D., 217, 218
Onder, A., 98
Ongley, S. E., 219
Oosterhoff, B., 272
Oosterman, M., 112
Oppenheim, D., 294–95
Orme, J. G., 130, 134
Ornaghi, V., 188
Ortega-Ruiz, R., 217
O'Sullivan, J. T., 170
O'Sullivan, L. F., 257
Oswald, H., 271–72
Out, D., 145
Overbeek, G., 270
Oyserman, D., 296–97, 303
Ozdemir, M., 255
Ozdemir, S. B., 78, 80, 212, 213–14

Pachter, L. M., 200
Pachur, T., 278t
Padilla-Walker, L. M., 245, 266–68
Palacios, J., 55t, 70, 71
Palmer, F. B., 284–85
Pancer, S. M., 69, 272
Pang, N., 272
Pantelis, C., 303–4
Parade, S. H., 145
Paraskevopoulos, J., 42, 179–80
Parent, J., 267
Park, J. L., 289
Park, S., 78, 80, 212

Park, Y., 45, 91–92, 136
Parke, R. D., 25t, 74–75, 231
Parker, A. E., 202, 204, 205t, 207–8, 210, 239
Parks, P. L., 139
Parmar, P., 76
Parsons, C. E., 301
Paschall, K. W., 50
Pastorelli, C., 100t
Patall, E. A., 177
Patchin, J. W., 217
Pater, H. A., 154
Paterson, A. D., 204
Patton, D., 218–19
Pawlby, S., 303, 304
Peck, S. C., 240, 275
Pederson, D. R., 160–61
Peets, K., 217
Pekrun, R., 173
Pena, J. V., 88–89
Perala-Littunen, S., 3
Perez, J., 284–85
Perez-Escamilla, R., 153
Perez-Rivera, M. B., 206, 207–8
Perkins, K. A., 295
Perkins, L. A., 194
Perrigo, J. L., 305
Perrin, E. C., 293
Perry, W. G., 71–72
Pesu, L., 39–40
Peterson, C., 146, 189
Peterson, Z. D., 234
Petrenko, C. L. M., 308
Petrik, M. L., 281
Pettit, G. S., 156, 231, 232, 260, 288–89
Pezdek, K., 173–74
Pharis, M. E., 135
Phelan, T. W., 240t
Phelps, E., 268, 272
Phillips, B. A., 285–86
Phillipson, S., 169–71
Phinney, J. S., 274t
Piaget, J., 23, 66–67, 73, 86, 180, 185–86, 222–23, 263
Pickett, W., 13
Pieper, S., 145
Pietila, A., 255
Piha, J., 98–99

Pillay, D., 276
Pillow, B. H., 71–72
Piotrowski, J. T., 267–68
Plomin, R., 152, 253
Podsakoff, N. P., 48–49
Podsakoff, P. M., 48–49
Pollack J. M., 83
Pomerantz, E. M., 51, 83–84
Ponnet, K., 265–66
Pons, F., 187–88
Porter, R., 99
Potter, L., 140
Power, T. J., 279–80
Pratt, M., 69, 272
Prelock, P. A., 189
Prendergast, S., 178
Price, G. G., 180, 199
Priebe, A., 216t
Priest, N., 275
Prino, L. E., 92, 136–37
Prinz, R. J., 96, 306, 307–8
Prinzie, P., 99
Prior, M. R., 211
Profilet, S. M., 231–32
Prom-Wormley, E., 253, 255
Provenzano, F. J., 236
Provost, M. A., 188
Pulsifer, M. B., 284–85
Punamaki, R., 278t
Punch, S., 117–18
Putnam, S. P., 156, 224–25
Putnick, D. L., 81, 105
Puzino, K., 147

Quatman, T., 247–48
Quota, S., 278t

Racz, S. J., 245, 251–52, 255
Radke-Yarrow, M., 58
Raghunandan, V. N. G. P., 303
Raiha, H., 98–99
Raj, S. P., 207–8
Rakoczy, H., 34
Ramani, G. B., 55t
Ramos, K. D., 149
Rangnathan, C., 100t
Rasku-Puttonen, H., 50, 173–74
Rasmussen, P. D., 289

Raty, H., 84*t*, 84–85, 172, 173–74
Rautava, P., 98–99
Rautianen, R., 84–85
Raval, V. V., 207–8
Reader, J. M., 148
Reavis, S., 293
Reese, E., 191–92, 211–12
Regambal, M., 290
Reich, S. M., 90, 100*t*, 232
Reid, R., 278*t*, 279–80
Reid, V., 146
Reid-Quinones, K., 260–61
Reinfjell, T., 209
Reinhold, D. P., 47–48
Reis, A. H., 208–9
Reis, J., 136
Reiss, C., 104–5
Reiss, D., 253
Reitz, E. B., 19, 20*f*, 308
Renno, P. A., 173–74
Rescorla, L. A., 280, 281
Rest, J. R., 222–23
Reyes, N., 67–68, 278*t*, 294
Reynolds, E. K., 252
Reznick, J. S., 293
Rheams, T., 284–85
Rice, C. E., 293
Richardson, B., 246*t*
Richters, J. E., 298–99
Rieffe, C., 188, 224–25
Rigby, J., 304
Rigo, P., 145
Riksen-Walraven, J. M., 159
Riley, A. W., 216
Rinott, N., 136–37
Riordan, D., 302
Risley, T. R., 197
Ritvo, E. R., 293
Rivas-Drake, D., 275
Robins, D. L., 293
Robins, R. W., 252–53
Robinson, C., 307
Robinson, D. R., 306–7
Robinson, J. C., 177
Robinson, L. R., 19
Rocha, F. L., 295
Rochat, T. J., 301
Rodriguez, A., 113

Rodriguez-Brown, F., 100*t*
Roeyers, H., 294
Rogers, S. J., 293
Roggman, L. A., 92
Roghmann, K J., 257
Rogoff, B., 22, 118
Rohde, L. A., 288
Rohrbeck, C. A., 306–7
Roisman, G., 160–61, 216–17
Rolfson, J., 43
Rollins, N. C., 152–53
Roman, G., 298*t*
Rominov, H., 98, 100*t*, 100–1
Romney, D. M., 238
Roopnarine, J. L., 41, 76–77, 198*t*, 198, 199
Root, A. E., 73
Ros, R., 290–91
Rose, A. J., 231, 269, 271
Rose, J., 285
Rose, S. J., 268–69
Rose-Krasnor, L., 229
Rosenfeld, J., 240*t*
Rosenthal, D. A., 175, 200, 247–48
Roseth, G. J., 253
Roskam, I., 100*t*
Ross, H. S., 236–37
Ross, J. A., 240*t*
Rossi, G., 272
Rote, W. M., 251
Roth, D., 69
Roth, R. M., 194*t*, 194–95, 279–80
Rothbart, M. K., 154, 155*t*, 156
Rovine, M., 110
Rowe, M. L., 55*t*, 196–97
Roy, R. N., 88, 110–11, 113–14
Rubin, D. C., 126
Rubin, J. Z., 236
Rubin, K. H., 19, 31*f*, 43, 78, 80, 157, 212,
    213, 229, 230–31
Ruble, D., 43, 78, 113, 227, 237
Ruby, J. L., 152
Ruchala, P., 101–2
Ruck, M. D., 273
Ruffman, T., 188
Ruiz, S. K., 160–61
Russell, A., 42–43, 58, 84*t*
Russell, B., 218–19
Russell, C. G., 13

Russell, G., 42–43, 58, 116
Russell, S. T., 268–69
Russo, N., 284
Rust, J., 235*t*
Ryan, S. M., 251–52, 255
Rychtarik, R. G., 254
Ryff, C. D., 126

Sacrey, L. R., 293
Sadeh, A., 147–48
Sadek, S., 218
Safer, D. J., 287–88
Salantera, S., 46–47
Salmivalli, C., 217
Salmon, K., 191–92
Salmon, M. P., 303
Salvatore, J. E., 269–70
Samara, M., 218
Sameroff, A. J., 49, 59, 66, 67*t*, 67–68,
    69–70, 240
San, L. Q., 117
Sanders, M. R., 90, 94, 95*t*, 100*t*, 294
Sanders, M. W., 94
Sanders, P., 237
Sanders, S., 287–88
Sanders, W., 267
Sandler, H. M., 176*f*, 176
Sansavini, A., 134
Sanson, A. V., 156
Santinello, M., 272
Santini, P., 215–16
Santolupa, S., 69
Santos, C. E., 275
Sarraj E. E., 278*t*
Sattler, J. M., 179–80, 196–97
Saudino, K. J., 140
Saunders, S. M., 281
Savage, A., 283–84
Savage, S. L., 200
Savin-Williams, R. C., 257, 259
Sayfan, K., 209
Scarzello, D., 92, 94, 136–37
Schader, R. M., 13
Schaefer, D. R., 275
Schafer, G., 140
Schaidie, E. M., 294
Scharf, M., 271
Scheir, L. M., 255

Schelstraete, M., 100*t*
Schildt, B., 290–91
Schlegel, A., 259
Schmickel, G. A., 284
Schmidt, F. A., 154, 157
Schmutte, P. S., 126
Schneider, B. H., 214–15
Schneider, W., 32
Scholz, W., 271–72
Schoppe-Sullivan, S. J., 46–47
Schothorst, P., 303–4
Schreibers, W. M., 252
Schroeder, K. M., 238
Schueler, B. E., 167*t*
Schuengel, C., 112
Schuette, C., 116
Schumm, W. R., 88
Schwartz, J. A., 260
Schwartz, S. J., 275
Schweitzer, J. B., 278*t*
Scott, S. S., 306–7
Sears, H. A., 257
Secades-Villa, R., 254
Secer, Z., 98, 100*t*
Seifer, R., 68, 69–70
Seifert, K. L., 52
Seiffge-Krenke, I., 270
Seiler, S. J., 218–19
Seipp, C. M., 290
Seng, A. C., 306, 307–8
Sevigny, P. R., 98–99
Sexton, D., 284–85
Seybold, J., 107–8
Shachar-Shapira, L., 271
Shaffer, A., 298*t*
Shahmansouri, N., 122
Shai, D., 161
Shaligram, D., 303
Shamah, R., 90, 94
Shanahan, T., 100*t*
Shannon, J., 130, 131*t*
Shapka, J. D., 266
Sharkey, J. D., 272
Sharma, S., 294–95
Sharp, C., 188–89
Shaw, D. S., 278*t*
Shebl, F. M., 153
Sheeber, L., 278*t*, 298*t*

Sheffield, J., 294
Sheldrick, R. C., 293
Shelef, L., 294
Shennum, W., 104–6
Sheperd, K. A., 213–14
Shepperd, J. A., 278*t*
Sherlock, B. R., 220
Sherman, A., 227
Sherrod, L. R., 271–72
Shi, J., 214–15
Shiakou, M., 74–75
Shields, A., 208–9, 306
Shigeto, A., 297–98
Shipman, A., 98
Shipman, V. C., 172–73
Shoemaker, D. J., 179–80
Shonkoff, J. P., 286
Shores, A., 190–91
Shorey, S., 98
Shulman, S., 271
Shumow, L., 100*t*
Shuster, M. M., 214–15
Shweder, R. A., 37
Siegel, D. M., 257
Siegler, I. C., 126
Sigel, I. E., 3, 4, 59, 61*t*, 62, 63, 64–65, 67*t*
Sigman, M., 67–68, 294–95
Silinskas, G., 39–40
Silk, J. S., 210, 243–44, 250–51, 262–63
Siller, M., 67–68, 294–95
Silliman, E. R., 72–73
Silverberg, S. B., 100*t*, 101
Silverman, C., 296
Simonoff, E., 284
Simonsen, E., 289
Simons-Morton, B. G., 254–55
Simpkins, S. D., 50, 172, 174–75
Simpson, J. A., 269–70
Singer, D. G., 73
Singh, J. P., 108–10
Sironi, M., 125–26
Sistler, A. K., 39
Skibbe, L. E., 167*t*
Skinner, D., 278*t*
Skoric, M. M., 272
Slade, L., 188
Slep Smith. A. M., 299
Slonims, V., 285–86

Small, P. J., 309
Small, S. A., 99
Smeriglio, V. L., 139
Smetana, J. G., 88, 119, 120–23, 219, 220–21, 221*t*, 223, 226–27, 239, 240, 245–46, 251–52
Smets, K., 272
Smith, D. M., 100–1
Smith, I. M., 147
Smith, K. E., 68–69
Smith, M. M., 108–10
Smith, N., 293
Smith Leavell, A., 236
Snellen, M., 303
Sobol, M. P., 78
Sobring, E., 266
Sobsey, D., 283–84
Soenens, B., 252
Sofronoff, K., 294
Sola-Carmona, J. J., 278*t*
Solomon, B. S., 215
Soltis, J., 145
Sommer, K., 90, 136, 138, 139–40
Sommerville, J. A., 34
Son, D., 245
Sonnenschein, S., 173–74
Sood, E. D., 278*t*
Sopko, A. M., 278*t*
Southam-Gerow, M. A., 206
Sparkman, K. L., 278*t*
Spellman, M., 130, 131*t*
Spinrad, T. L., 226–27
Spittler, G., 117–18
Spoth, R., 254–55
Spray, C. M., 84*t*
Sprong, M., 303–4
Squeglia, L. M., 250–51
Squires, J., 140
Sroufe, L. A., 27, 269–70
Stallings, J., 145
Stangor, C., 113
Stanley, M. A., 51
Stanton, B., 246*t*
Stapleton, L. M., 55*t*, 173–74, 196–97
Stattin, H., 242*t*, 242, 243, 244–45, 255, 260, 268
Steenbergen-Hu, S., 177
Stein, A., 51, 301

Steinberg, L., 49–50, 243–44, 247–48, 250–51, 252, 262–63
Steiner, M., 145
Sterling, A. M., 286
Stern, J. A., 227
Stern, M., 278t
Sternberg, R. J., 183–84, 185
Sterret, E., 257–58
Stettler, N. M., 205t, 206, 210
Stevens, J. H., Jr., 136–37, 139
Stevenson, C. S., 296–97
Stevenson, H. W., 166
Stevenson, M. T., 19
St. George, J., 73
Stiefel, F., 58–59
Stoiber, K. C., 179–80
Stolz, L., 1, 52, 202
Stone, E. A., 236–37
Storeba, O. J., 289
Stouthamer-Loeber, M., 261
Stratton, P., 43
Subramanian, S., 41, 55t, 56, 57–58, 60–62
Sullivan, A. D. W., 267
Sullivan, G. B., 22
Sumnall, H., 254
Super, C., 1, 9, 35–36, 37, 76, 128, 130, 148, 157, 202
Super, C. M., 76
Suskind, D. L., 196–97
Suzuki, M., 173
Swank, P. R., 68–69
Swart, S., 108–10
Swearer, S. M., 217
Swit, C. S., 214
Symons, K., 265–66
Szkrybalo, J., 237

Tahiroglu, D., 189
Talbott, M. R., 293
Tamis-LeMonda, C. S., 130–34, 131t, 141, 199–200, 231, 236
Tamm, L., 108–10
Tan, P. Z., 207
Taqi, I., 153
Tarabulsy, G. M., 188
Target, M., 161

Tarule, J. M., 71–72
Task Force on Sudden Infant Death Syndrome, 149–50
Tasopoulous-Chan, M., 245–46
Tattersall, H., 278t
Taunt, H. M., 283–84
Taylor, A. J., 117
Taylor, C. A., 216t
Taylor, J. H., 222–23
Taylor, J. L., 299
Tazouti, Y., 55t
Teeter, S. R., 234
Temcheff, C. E., 308
Tennenbaum, H. R., 237
Teti, D. M., 101–2, 148
Theunissen, F. E., 220
Thirthalli, J., 304
Thomas, A., 153–54
Thomas, R., 287–88
Thompson, A. E., 257
Thompson, B., 284–85
Thompson, J. A., 205t, 210
Thompson, R. A., 162–63, 227
Thornton, W. L., 34
Tikotzky, L., 147–48
Tilton-Weaver, L., 244–45
Tirosh, T., 147
Tissot, H., 58–59
Tolejko, N., 264
Tolvanen, A., 42–43, 169
Tomasello, M., 22
Toomey, R. B., 92
Torio, S., 88–89
Torney-Purta, J., 271–72
Toth, S. L., 305, 306, 308
Trauer, T., 303
Trautwein, U., 177
Tremblay, R. E., 152
Trommsdorff, G., 124
Troxel, N. R., 227
Trudeau, L., 254–55
Trzesniewski, K. H., 84t
Tsay, J. C., 99
Tseng, W., 216–17
Tucker-Drob, E. M., 172–73
Turiel, E., 119–20
Turner, T. L., 215

Twentyman, C. T., 306–7
Twombley, E., 140
Twomey, J. E., 146

Uditsky, B., 283–84
Umana-Taylor, A. J., 92, 98, 273, 275
Umberson, D., 127
Umemura, T., 160
Updegraff, K. A., 92, 98, 243, 247
US Department of Health & Human
    Services, 305–6
Uzgiris, I., 231

Vaccaro, S., 298t
Valentino, K., 93–94
Valgeirsson, H., 182
Valkenburg, P. M., 267–68
van Beek, Y., 134
van de Fons, J. R., 200
Vandell, D. L., 232
Van der Vorst, H., 254
van de Vijver, F. J. R., 200
Van Egeland, H., 303–4
Van Egeren, L. A., 114
VanEpps E. M., 83
van IJzendoorn, M. H., 145, 159,
    160, 216–17
Van Ryzin, M. J., 253
Vanska, J., 172
Vansteenkiste, M., 252
van Tijen, N., 1, 35, 128, 202
Vassalio, S., 225t
Vaughn, B. E., 160–61
Vauras, M., 100t
Vazsonyi, A. T., 260–61
Veitz, G., 208–9
Veldhuis, C., 296–97
Venuti, P., 145
Vereijken, C. M. J. L., 159
Verhage, M. L., 27, 112, 160
Vermeulen-Smit, E., 257
Vermulst, A., 270
Veronneau, M., 251–52
Victora, C. G., 152
Vieno, A., 272
Viljaranta, J., 39–40

Villalobos, M., 245–46
Villanueva, L., 188
Vinik, J., 209, 210
Voegtline, K. M., 154
Voelker, S., 204
Volling, B. L., 38
Vollink, T., 217
Von Stumm, S., 152
Vos, E., 303–4
Votruba-Drzal, E., 49–50
Vroman, L. N., 154
Vukelich, C., 136, 137
Vygotsky, L. S., 22–23, 24, 71, 73,
    118, 180

Wachs, T. D., 301
Wai-Chi Chan, S., 98
Wainer, A., 295
Waisbren, S. E., 278t
Waizenhofer, R. N., 243–44
Waldfogel, J., 32
Walker, J. M. T., 176f, 176
Walker, L. J., 222–23
Wall, S., 24–25, 157
Wallat-Petre, H., 117–18
Wallstaon, K. A., 299
Walper, S., 270
Walrave, M., 265–66
Walters, G. D., 261
Walters, R., 147
Walton, G. M., 84t
Wan, M. W., 302, 303, 304
Wang, C. K. J., 84t
Wang, L., 93–94
Wang, Q., 191–92
Wang, W., 218
Wang, Y., 298t, 300
Wang, Z., 187–88
Warash, B. G., 73, 74
Warburton, W. A., 214
Ward, C. S., 307
Ward, M. J., 110
Ward, T. C. S., 149, 150
Warfield, M. E., 286
Warren, K., 303
Warren, S. F., 286

Warreyn, P., 294
Warton, P M., 116
Waters, E., 24–25, 157, 158*t*, 158–59, 160, 161*t*, 278*t*
Waters, H. S., 160, 161*t*
Waters, T., 160–61
Watson, A. C., 188
Watson, L. R., 293
Watson, R., 268–69
Watson, S. L., 294
Weary, G., 51
Weaver, E. D., 257
Wehrspann, E., 243
Weiner, B., 15–16, 77–78
Weiner, M. B., 272
Weinstock, J. S., 71–72
Weisgram, E. S., 238
Weiss, L., 100*t*
Wellman, H. M., 33
Welsh, D. P., 268
Wendt, E., 270
Wernand, J. J., 112
Wessel, M. A., 146
Whalen, C. K., 290–91
Whalen, D., 152
Wheeler, L. A., 100*t*, 100–1
Whelan, T. M., 98
White, C., 299
White, H. R., 306
White, N., 57, 185
Whiteman, S. D., 243–44
Whitman, T. L., 139–40
Whittingham, K., 278*t*, 294
Wichstom, L., 42, 209
Widom, C. S., 306
Wiefferink, C. H., 224–25
Wilde, C. A., 181
Wilder, S., 177
Willard, J., 254–55
Willemen, A. M., 112
Williams, K., R., 218
Williams, L. C., 215–16
Williams, M. E., 305
Williams, R. J., 254
Williamsen, M. E., 200
Williams-Wheeler, M., 252
Willoughby, M., 306–7

Wilson, E. L., 209
Wilson, K. R., 211
Wilson, S., 297–98
Winter, L., 90, 94–96, 95*t*
Wittkowski, A., 100–1
Wojcik, J. V., 281
Wolf, A. E., 240*t*
Wolff, L. S., 94
Wolke, D., 218
Wong, K., 285
Wong, M. S., 206, 210, 297–98
Wood, C. E., 99
Wood, R. M., 145
Woolley, M. L., 100*t*
Worsley, A., 13
Worthman, C., 145
Wray-Lake, L., 122
Wright, J., 215
Wroe, J. K., 73
Wu, C., 182

Yagmurlu, B., 200
Yasui, M., 275
Yau, J., 120–21, 122
Yawkey, T. D., 73–74, 75, 231
Yeager, D. S., 84*t*
Yirmiya, N., 294–95
Young, A., 278*t*, 307
Young, J. N., 152
Young, K. S., 301
Youngstrom, E., 298–99
Youniss, J., 271–72
Yu, J. J., 108–10
Yuan, L., 117
Yucel, M., 303–4
Yurovsky, D., 196

Zablotsky, B., 293
Zaff, J. F., 272
Zahn-Waxler, C., 226, 300
Zajicek-Farber, M. L., 196–97, 301
Zambarano, R. J., 43, 47–48, 227
Zand, D. H., 92
Zarit, S., 127
Zax, M., 68
Zeifman, D. M., 145–46
Zell, E., 234, 237

Zeman, J., 208–9
Zeringue, M. M., 245–46
Zero to Three, 39, 55*t*, 56, 73–75, 134
Zevenbergen, A. A., 192
Zhao, Y., 245–46

Zhu, Q., 272
Ziviani, J., 278*t*
Zucker, T. A., 167*t*
Zukow-Goldring, P., 117–18
Zych, I., 217

# Subject Index

Tables and figures are indicated by *t* and *f* following the page number

*For the benefit of digital users, indexed terms that span two pages (e.g., 52–53) may, on occasion, appear on only one of those pages.*

AAI *See* Adult Attachment Interview
abuse and neglect, 13, 22, 218, 277, 305–10
  capacity for resilience and
    recovery, 309–10
  child-oriented cognitions, 306–7, 308
  defined, 305
  effects of, 306
  heightened risk, 305–6
  interventions, 308–9
  low perceived control among parents
    who experienced, 104, 105
  parental attributions, 307
  parental expectations, 306–7
  parental self-efficacy, 307–8
  parent-oriented cognitions, 307–8
  parents' own childhood experiences, 92,
    105, 305–6, 307
  prevalence of, 305
academic performance, 165–78, 167*t*
  attribution theory, 17–19
  cross-cultural comparisons, 166
  feedback about, 165
  gender differences, 166
  parental attributions, 166, 167–72
    causality *vs.* correlation, 171
    concordance between parents, 169
    cross-cultural comparisons, 169–71
    effects of, 170–71
    gender differences, 172
    mother-father comparisons, 168
    parental beliefs as predictive
      of, 62–63
    parent-teacher comparisons, 169
    specific causes *vs.* underlying
      dimensions, 167–68
    stability of parental beliefs, 171–72

  parental involvement and support,
    167, 175–78
    causality *vs.* correlation, 177–78
    homework, 177
    model of, 176*f*
    school readiness, 178
    variation in, 176–77
  parents' expectations and evaluation of
    child's ability, 165–67, 172–75
    accuracy of, 173–74
    belief-performance relation, 175
    effects on performance, 173–74
    gender differences, 174–75
accuracy of parents' beliefs and judgments,
    44–45, 45*t*, 79
adolescence, 243–44
  Internet and social media, 265–66
  parent-child conflict, 263
  sexual activity, 256–57
  substance use, 254
autism spectrum disorder, 295–96
cognitive development in childhood
  academic performance, 173–74
  executive function, 193–94
  IQ, 40, 179–80, 181–82
  language, 196–97
  memory, 190, 191
  milestones and timetables, 199–200
  Piagetian concepts, 186
  theory of mind, 188–89
emotional development in childhood,
    204–6, 208–10
infancy, 132–38, 140, 141–43, 154
intellectual disabilities, 284–85
ADHD. *See* attention-deficit hyperactivity
  disorder

ADHD Rating Scale-5, 279–80
adolescence, 12, 239–75
 challenge of, 239–40, 240t
 conflict, 261–64
 Internet, 265–68
 parental knowledge, 241–48, 246t
  adolescence in general, 247–48, 249t
  adolescents' activities, 241–47, 242t
 positive developments, 268–75
  civic engagement, 271–73
  ethnic identity, 273–75, 274t
  romantic relationships, 268–71
 risky behaviors, 249–61
  delinquency, 259–61
  sexual activity, 255–59
  substance use, 250t, 250–55
Adult Attachment Interview (AAI), 26t,
   26–27, 105–6, 159–60
adult social cognition, 5–6
age of children, 45, 78, 79
 accuracy of parents' beliefs and
   judgments, 284–85
 emotional development, 206
 life satisfaction of parents and, 125
 parental knowledge, 92
 self-disclosure, 245
age of parents
 life satisfaction of parents and, 125
 parental knowledge, 92, 136, 137, 138
aggression, 212–19
 age of children, 213
 bullying, 217–19
 cross-cultural comparisons,
   212, 214–15
 gender-role development, 236–37
 normative development, 212–17
 parents' emotional responses to, 213
 punishment-aggression relation,
   215–16, 216t
 stability of development, 80, 81
 types of aggression and parental
   response, 213–14
agreement or shared meaning of beliefs,
   39, 44–45, 45t
academic performance, 168–69
 adolescence, 243–44
 attributions, 105, 170
 atypical development, 280–81

crying, 145
developmental problems, 281
developmental processes, 62
emotional development, 206, 209
ethnic identity, 275
infancy, 136–37, 145
Internet and social media, 266
IQ, 180, 181
milestones and timetable studies, 136
nurture: processes issue, 62
parental success, perception of, 127
parent-child conflict, 263
play, 74
self-efficacy, 98–99
substance use, 252–53, 254
alcohol. See substance use
American Academy of
   Pediatricians, 149–50
AQS See Attachment Q-Set
ASD. See autism spectrum disorder
attachment, 24, 129, 157–63
 Adult Attachment Interview, 26t, 26–27
 attachment classifications, 25t
 Attachment Q-Set, 157–59, 158t
 attention-deficit hyperactivity
   disorder, 289
 consequences of, 162–63
 delinquency, 260
 low perceived control among parents in
   dismissive category, 105–6
 mind-mindedness, 161–62
 moral behavior, 227
 parent-report measures, 158, 159
 peer relationships, 231
 romantic relationships, 269–70
 secure base scripts, 160–61, 161t
 secure vs. insecure attachment,
   25–26t, 25–27
 sensitive responsiveness, 159–60
 Strange Situation procedure, 24–25, 25t,
   157, 159
 substance use, 255
 working models, 25–26
Attachment Q-Set (AQS), 157–59, 158t
attention-deficit hyperactivity disorder
   (ADHD), 13, 287–91
 causes of, 288
 diagnosis, 288

parental attributions, 290
parental practices, 288–89
parental self-efficacy, 290
parents with, 289
prevalence of, 287–88
treatment, 290–91
attribution theory and attributions, 15–19
abuse and neglect, 307
academic performance, 166, 167–72
actor-observer bias, 18–19
agreement or shared meaning of beliefs,
105, 170
attention-deficit hyperactivity
disorder, 290
attributional style, 18
attributions for parents' own
behavior, 18
autism spectrum disorder, 294
beliefs regarding parenting, 102–6, 103t
cross-cultural comparisons, 105
low perceived control over
failure, 102–6
mother-father comparisons, 105
continuity-discontinuity issue, 78–82
depression, 299
dimensions along which attributions
vary, 16t, 17–18
factors governing attributions,
16t, 16–17
factors heightening probability of
attributional activity, 19
fundamental attribution error, 18
self-efficacy and, 29
self-serving bias, 19
theory of mind, 188–89
atypical development, 12, 276–310
abuse and neglect, 305–10
assessment, 277–82
accuracy of parents' beliefs, 281–82
child-report measures, 280
concordance between parents and
children, 280–81
parent-report measures,
278–80, 279t
timing and certainty of eventual
diagnosis, 283
attention-deficit hyperactivity
disorder, 287–91

autism spectrum disorder, 291–96, 292t
clinical conditions, 296–97
depression, 297–301, 298t
schizophrenia, 301–4
cognitive-social division in
classification, 282
individual differences, 283
intellectual disabilities, 284–87
list of childhood conditions, 278t
augmenting principle, 16t, 17
authoritarian parenting style, 32,
122–23, 220–21
authoritative parenting style, 122–23, 220–
21, 231, 245–46, 255, 285–86
Autism Parent Screen for Infants, 293
Autism Speaks, 283
autism spectrum disorder (ASD), 13,
283, 291–96
accuracy of parents' beliefs, 295–96
broader autism phenotype, 295
characteristics of, 292t
diagnosis, 293
mind-mindedness, 294–95
parental attributions, 294
parental practices, 293–94
parental self-efficacy, 294
parents with, 295
variation in, 291
autonomy, 120–23, 261–62

Bayley Scales of Infant Development,
93–94, 143
Bayley Scales of Mental Development, 71
bed-sharing, 147, 148–49
breastfeeding, 149
cross-cultural comparisons, 148
quality of sleep, 149
sudden infant death syndrome, 149–50
Behavior Rating Inventory of Executive
Function (BRIEF), 194t,
194–95, 279–80
breastfeeding
bed-sharing and, 149
bottle feeding vs., 152–53
postpartum depression, 301
bullying, 217–19
cyberbullying, 217, 218–19, 265–66
features of, 217

bullying, (cont.)
    intervention programs, 218
    role of parents, 218
    self-report measures, 217

Caregiver Knowledge of Child
        Development Inventory
        (CKDI), 90
Catalog of Previous Experience with
        Infants (COPE), 46t, 46–47, 92–93
CDIs See Communicative Development
        Inventories
child abuse. See abuse and neglect
Child Abuse Prevention and Treatment
        Act, 305
Child Behavior Checklist, 139–40,
        193–94, 279–81
Child Development Questionnaire, 60, 62
Children's Memory Questionnaire-
        Revised, 190t, 190
child-report measures
    atypical development, 280
    delinquency, 260–61
    parental knowledge, 242–43, 246
    sexual activity, 257, 258–59
    substance use, 252–53
civic engagement, 271–73
    modeling, 272
    nonparental influences, 272
    parental contribution to, 272–73
    types of, 271
Civitas Initiative, 55t, 56, 74–75, 134
CKDI See Caregiver Knowledge of Child
        Development Inventory
closed-choice methods, 44, 168
cognitive development in childhood, 13,
        164–201
    academic performance, 165–78, 167t
        expectations, 172–75
        parental attributions, 167–72
        parental involvement and support,
            175–78, 176f
    executive function, 192–95, 194t
    intelligence, 178–85
        IQ, 179–81
        multiple forms of, 181–83
        parents' conceptions of, 183–85
    language, 195–98

memory, 190t, 190–92
    milestones, 198t, 198–201
    Piagetian concepts, 185–86
    theory of mind, 186–89
Communicative Development Inventories
        (CDIs), 195–96, 197–98
Concepts of Development Questionnaire,
        66–67, 67t, 69–70
conflict. See parent-child conflict
consensus information, 16t
consistency information, 16t
Construction of the Child Interview, 59
constructivist-nonconstructivist
        continuum, 60–62, 63, 66
continuity-discontinuity issue, 54t, 77–85
    attribution approaches, 78–82
    beliefs about stability of
        development, 79
    environmental stability, 81–82
    factors contributing to stability or
        change, 79–80
    failure mindsets, 85
    fixed (entity) vs. growth (incremental)
        mindset, 82–83
    fixedness of intelligence, 82–85, 84t
    focus on individual differences vs.
        similarities, 81
    mastery vs. performance orientation, 82
    nature-nurture issue and, 85
    valence effect, 80–81
COPE See Catalog of Previous Experience
        with Infants
covariation principle, 16t, 16
cross-cultural psychology, 9
crying, 129, 144–46
    infant colic, 146
    infant-directed vs. parent-oriented
        beliefs, 145–46
    mother-father comparisons, 145
    parent-nonparent comparisons, 145
cultural psychology, 9
culture and cross-cultural comparisons,
        9. See also ethnic identity;
        ethnotheories
    academic performance, 166,
        169–71, 173–74
    adolescence, 247–48
    aggression, 212, 214–15

attribution theory, 105
bed-sharing, 148
cultural transmission and cultural
    change, 9
decision-making power, 122
depression, 301
eating, 151–52
emotional development, 207–8
ethnic identity, 275
ethnotheories, 31–32
household responsibilities, 117–18
intelligence, 183–85
language as intellectual "tool" provided
    by culture, 23
low perceived control over failure, 105
memory talk, 192
milestones and timetable studies, 200–1
nurture: agents issue, 57–58
nurture: processes issue, 62
parental attributions, 105
parental beliefs and, 9, 67–68
play, 76–77
reasons for having children, 124
sexual activity, 259
social withdrawal, 230
substance use, 250–51
temperament, 157
variation in parental knowledge,
    92, 93–94
cyberbullying, 217, 218–19, 265–66

decision-making power, 115,
    119t, 119–23
autonomy, 120–23
conventional issues, 119t, 119–20
cross-cultural comparisons, 122
moral issues, 119t, 119–20
multifaceted issues, 119t, 120
parent-child conflict, 121–22
parenting styles, 122–23
personal issues, 119t, 120
prudential issues, 119t, 119–20
delinquency, 259–61
attachment, 260
categories of, 259
child-report measures, 260–61
gender differences, 260
overt vs. covert, 260

own children vs. general
    comparison, 261
parental practices, 260
parent-report measures, 260–61
depression, 13, 297–301
behavior-outcome relation, 297, 298t,
    299–300
belief-behavior relation, 299
cross-cultural comparisons, 301
depression distortion
    hypothesis, 298–99
gender differences, 297–98
parental attributions, 299
parental self-efficacy, 299
postpartum depression, 300–1
temperament, 297–98
Development According to Parents
    (Goodnow and Collins), 114
developmental processes, 12, 52–87, 54t
continuity-discontinuity issue,
    54t, 77–85
attribution approaches, 78–82
beliefs about stability of
    development, 79
environmental stability, 81–82
factors contributing to stability or
    change, 79–80
failure mindsets, 85
fixed (entity) vs. growth
    (incremental) mindset, 82–83
fixedness of intelligence, 82–85, 84t
focus on individual differences vs.
    similarities, 81
mastery vs. performance
    orientation, 82
nature-nurture issue and, 85
valence effect, 80–81
holistic-separate issue, 54t, 86–87
nature-nurture issue, 53–56, 54t
examples of items used in studies of,
    55t, 55–56
variation across different aspects of
    development, 53–54
variation in goal of
    explanation, 54–55
varied labels for, 53
nurture: agents issue, 54t, 57–59
belief of mothers vs. fathers, 58

developmental processes, (*cont.*)
  cross-cultural comparisons, 57–58
  depressed *vs.* normally functioning
    mothers, 58
  importance of parents *vs.*
    teachers, 57
  importance of self-discovery, 57
  judgment of other parent's
    importance, 58–59
  nurture: processes issue, 54*t*, 59–77
  behavior-development relation,
    65, 69
  belief-behavior relation, 63–64
  beliefs-development relation,
    62–63, 68
  categorical and compensating/
    perspectivist levels of thought,
    66–67, 67*t*
  concordance between parents, 62
  constructivist-nonconstructivist
    continuum, 60–62, 63, 66
  context and parental
    consistency, 64–65
  cross-cultural comparisons, 62
  level of parental knowledge, 69
  modern-traditional-paradoxical
    continuum, 70–71
  play, 73–77, 74*t*
  Sameroff approach, 66–70, 67*t*
  Sigel and McGillicuddy-DeLisi
    approach, 59–65, 61*t*
  stability of parental beliefs, 69–70
  variation in parental beliefs, 60–62
  women's beliefs of knowledge and
    knowing, 72
*Diagnostic and Statistical Manual of
    Mental Disorders*, 5th edition
    (DSM-5), 288
directionality issue, 49, 51
discounting principle, 16*t*, 17
distancing strategies, 64, 72–73
distinctiveness information, 16*t*
Down syndrome, 13, 284, 286–87
Down syndrome advantage, 285
drugs. *See* substance use
DSM-5 *See Diagnostic and Statistical
    Manual of Mental Disorders*, 5th
    edition

eating, 129, 151–53
  breastfeeding, 149, 152–53, 301
  cross-cultural comparisons, 151–52
  timing, 151–52
ecological systems theory, 30–33, 31*f*
  chronosystem, 32
  exosystem, 30, 32
  macrosystem, 31–32
  mesosystem, 30
  microsystem, 30, 32
economic/utilitarian reasons for having
    children, 124
Educational Testing Service (ETS),
    59–65, 61*t*
egocentrism, 263
emotional development, 203–12, 205*t*
  accuracy of parents' beliefs, 208–9
    concordance between parents and
      children, 209
    parent-report measures, 208
  belief-development relation, 210–11
  emotional component of morality, 219,
    224–26, 225*t*
    defining empathy, 224
    defining guilt, 224
    defining shame, 224
    inductive reasoning, 225–26
    love withdrawal techniques of
      discipline, 226
    parent-report measures,
      224–25, 225*t*
    self-report measures, 224–25
  intervention research, 211
  memory talk, 211–12
  origin of parents' beliefs, 206–8
    age of children, 206
    cross-cultural comparisons, 207–8
    mother-father comparisons, 206
    parents' own childhood
      experiences, 207
    parental meta-emotion philosophy,
      204–6, 205*f*, 205*t*
Emotion Regulation Checklist
    (ERC), 208–9
Emotion-Related Parenting Styles
    Self-Test, 204
Emotion-Related Parenting Styles Short
    Form, 204

empathy
  defined, 224
  inductive reasoning, 225–26
  parent-report measures, 224–25, 225*t*
epistemological beliefs, 71–73, 264
epistemology, 71–72
ERC *See* Emotion Regulation Checklist
ethnic identity, 273–75, 274*t*
  cultural socialization, 275
  developments that relate positively
    to, 273
  egalitarianism, 275
  parental contributions, 275
  peer relationships and, 275
  preparation for bias, 275
ethnotheories, 35–37
  defined, 35
  developmental niche, 36–37
  hierarchical organization, 35–36
  household responsibilities, 118
  intelligence, 183–84
  open-ended, nondirective
    questioning, 41
  pervasive themes, 36
  similarities in, 35–36
ETS *See* Educational Testing Service
executive function, 192–95
  accuracy of prediction, 193–94
  defined, 192–93
  individual differences among
    children, 193
  parent-report measures, 194*t*, 194
  scaffolding, 193
experimental studies, 49–50, 51

family, beliefs regarding, 12, 114–27
  decision-making power, 115,
    119*t*, 119–23
  autonomy, 120–23
  conventional issues, 119*t*, 119–20
  cross-cultural comparisons, 122
  moral issues, 119*t*, 119–20
  multifaceted issues, 119*t*, 120
  parent-child conflict, 121–22
  parenting styles, 122–23
  personal issues, 119*t*, 120
  prudential issues, 119*t*, 119–20
  household responsibilities, 114–18

cross-cultural comparisons, 117–18
  gender of child, 116
  goals and, 116–17
  guided participation, 117–18
  learning by observing and pitching
    in, 118
  nature of task, 115
  self-care *vs.* family-work tasks, 116
  willingness and, 116–17
value of children, 115, 123–27
  parental satisfaction during
    childhood, 123
  value of having children, 123
  view of how well their child/life has
    turned out, 123, 126–27
family size and number of children, 45,
  60–62, 107–8
First Year Inventory, 293
fixedness of intelligence, 82–85
  belief/behavior-development
    relation, 83–84
  failure mindsets, 85
  fixed (entity) *vs.* growth (incremental)
    mindset, 82–84
  mastery *vs.* performance orientation, 82
  targets for studies of, 83, 84*t*
Fragile X syndrome, 284

gender differences: children
  academic performance, 166,
    172, 174–75
  depression, 297–98
  sexual activity, 257
  stability of development, 80
gender differences: parents, 38–39. *See
    also* agreement or shared meaning
    of beliefs
  adolescence, 243–44, 245
  delinquency, 260
  Internet and social media, 266
  low perceived control over failure, 105
gender-role development, 234–38
  aggression, 236–37
  early differential treatment, 236
  gender schemas, 237
  "gender similarities" conclusion, 237–38
  parental contribution to, 235–36
  parental talk, 237

gender-role development, (*cont.*)
   parent-report measures, 234–35, 235*t*
   Preschool Activities Inventory, 235*t*
   toy and play preferences, 236–37
guilt
   defined, 224
   inductive reasoning, 226
   love withdrawal techniques of
     discipline, 226
   parent-report measures, 224–25

*Handbook of Research on Civic Engagement
   in Youth, The* (Sherrod, Torney-
   Purta, & Flanagan), 272
holistic-separate issue, 54*t*, 86–87
Home Observation for Measurement of
   the Environment (HOME), 69, 71,
   93–94, 139
household responsibilities, 114–18
   cross-cultural comparisons, 117–18
   gender of child, 116
   goals and, 116–17
   guided participation, 117–18
   learning by observing and pitching
     in, 118
   nature of task, 115
   self-care *vs.* family-work tasks, 116
   willingness and, 116–17

infancy, 12, 128–63
   attachment, 129, 157–63
     consequences of, 162–63
     mind-mindedness, 161–62
     parent-report measures, 158, 159
     secure base scripts, 160–61, 161*t*
     sensitive responsiveness, 159–60
     Strange Situation procedure, 157, 159
   crying, 129, 144–46
     infant colic, 146
     infant-directed *vs.* parent-oriented
      beliefs, 145–46
     mother-father comparisons, 145
     parent-nonparent comparisons, 145
   eating, 129, 151–53
     breastfeeding *vs.* bottle feeding and,
      149, 152–53
     cross-cultural comparisons, 151–52
     timing, 151–52

parental knowledge, 90–96, 129,
   130, 131*t*
   accuracy and its
     determinants, 132–38
   age of mother, 136, 137, 138
   effects on child development, 139–40
   effects on parental behavior, 139
   mother-father comparisons, 136–37
   own children *vs.* general
     comparison, 134–35
   parent-report measures, 140–44, 142*t*
   sources of belief, 137
   transition to parenting, 138
sleeping, 129, 146–51
   bed-sharing, 147, 148–50
   night waking and sleep schedule,
     147*t*, 147–48
   sleep position, 147, 150–51
temperament, 129, 153–57
   behavioral measures, 154
   cross-cultural comparisons, 157
   defined, 153
   dimensions of, 153
   effect on parenting, 156
   parental behavior and, 156
   parental characteristics
     affecting, 154–56
   parent-report measures, 153–56, 155*t*
   physiological measures, 154
transition to parenting, 110–14
   as determinant of beliefs, 111
   egalitarian division of child
     care, 113–14
   perceived control over failure, 112–13
   self-efficacy, 111–12
Infant Behavior Questionnaire-Revised, 155*t*
Infant Crying Questionnaire, 145
Infant Development Inventory, 141,
   142*t*, 143
Infant-Toddler Social and Emotional
   Assessment, 279–80
information processing perspective, 15,
   19–22, 23
   executive function, 20*f*, 21
   individual differences, 22
   schemas, 20*f*, 21
   social information processing theory,
     20*f*, 20–22

insecure attachment, 25t, 25–26. *See also* attachment
intellectual disabilities, 284–87
  accuracy of parents' beliefs, 284–85
  causes of, 284
  cognitive differences among syndromes, 286–87
  defined, 284
  parental knowledge, 287
  parental reactions to diagnosis, 285
  parenting styles, 285–86
  parent-report measures, 284
intelligence, 178–85
  fixedness of, 82–85, 84t
  IQ, 179–81
    accuracy of prediction, 179
    belief-performance relation, 179–80
    causality *vs.* correlation, 180
    match hypothesis, 180, 181
    overestimation, 179, 181
  multiple forms of, 181–83
    comparison among, 182
    comparison of judges, 182
    cross-cultural comparisons, 182–83
    gender differences, 182–83
  parents' conceptions of, 183–85
    cross-cultural comparisons, 183–85
    origin of intelligence, 184
    underlying nature of intelligence, 184
    what constitutes intelligent behavior, 183–84
interfering interactional style, 223
Internet and social media, 265–68
  accuracy of parents' beliefs, 265–66
  categories of risk, 265
  gender differences, 266
  parental knowledge, 265–66, 268
  parental monitoring, 266–68
  self-disclosure, 266
IQ. *See* intelligence

justice reasoning, 222

Knowledge of Child Development Inventory (KCDI), 90
Knowledge of Effective Parenting Scale (KEPS), 90, 94–96

Knowledge of Infant Development Inventory (KIDI), 69, 90t, 90–96, 107–8, 125, 129, 130, 132, 135, 141–43, 196–97, 241
Knowledge of Parenting Strategies Scale (KOPSS), 90

language, 195–98, 200
  effects of parental knowledge, 197
  family talk
    gender-role development, 237
    moral behavior, 227
    romantic relationships, 270–71
    sex, 257–58
  infant-directed speech (motherese), 197
  as intellectual "tool" provided by culture, 23
  nature-nurture issue, 53–54
  parental response to child's language, 197
  parent-report measures, 195–96
  parents as models for language learning, 197
Leeds Attributional Coding System, 43
longitudinal studies, 49–51
low perceived control over failure, 102–6
  childhood attachment category of parent, 105–6
  cross-cultural comparisons, 105
  defined, 102–4
  gender differences, 105
  negative outcomes, 104
  parents who experienced abuse and neglect, 105
  transition to parenting, 106

marital satisfaction
  life satisfaction and, 125–26
  self-efficacy, 99
  transition to parenting, 113–14
match hypothesis, 180, 181
Maternal Emotional Styles Questionnaire, 204
MEIM (Multigroup Ethnic Identity Measure), 273, 274t
memory, 190–92
  autobiographical memory, 191–92
  importance and centrality of, 190

memory, (*cont.*)
  memory talk, 191–92, 211–12
  parent-report measures, 190*t*, 190–91
  standard laboratory tasks, 191
memory talk, 191–92, 211–12
meta-parenting, 108–10, 109*t*
  anticipating, 108, 109*t*
  assessing, 108–10, 109*t*
  problem solving, 108, 109*t*, 110
  reflecting, 108–10, 109*t*
Meta-Parenting Profile Questionnaire
      (MPQ), 106, 108–10, 109*t*
methodology in research, 12, 14, 37–51
  effects of parental beliefs, 48–51
    causality *vs.* correlation, 49, 51
    measurement challenges, 48–49
    techniques for overcoming
        challenges, 49–51
  flowchart of decisions, 38*t*, 38
  origins of beliefs, 45–48
    comparison of naturally occurring
        groups, 45
    measuring relevant experience
        directly, 46*t*, 46–47
    rational and emotional sources for
        parents' beliefs, 47–48
  what to study
    characteristics of beliefs, 44–45, 45*t*
    describe-your-child method, 41, 44
    explanations for child's status, 42
    focus of questioning, 38*t*, 41–44
    inferential approach, 43
    judgment of child's status, 42
    naturally occurring *vs.*
        experimentally elicited
        behavior, 42–43
    open-ended, nondirective
        questioning, 41, 44
    presentation of child's behavior or
        attribute, 42
    presentation of standardized
        vignettes, 43
    self-report measures, 43
  whom to study
    child assessments, 39–40
    concordance between parents, 39
    gender differences between
        parents, 38–39

  grandparents, 39
  inclusion of fathers in research, 38
  parent-nonparent comparisons, 39
  participants for research, 38–40
  targets for participants' beliefs, 40–41
milestones and timetables, 90*t*
  adolescence, 247–48
  cognitive development in childhood,
      198*t*, 198–201
    accuracy of parents' beliefs, 199–200
    cross-cultural comparisons, 200–1
  infancy, 129, 130–34, 131*t*, 138, 141–43
    mother-father comparisons, 136
    "overestimation" and
        "underestimation" of infant
        capabilities, 132–33
    own children *vs.* general
        comparison, 134–35
    timing *vs.* order of
        emergence, 133–34
mind-mindedness, 43, 161–62, 187–88
Modified Checklist for Autism in
      Toddlers, 293
Modified Prospective and Retrospective
      Memory Questionnaire, 190
monitoring, 244–46, 246*t*
  delinquency, 260
  Internet and social media, 266–68
  romantic relationships, 270–71
  sexual activity, 258
  substance use, 252, 253
Monitoring the Future Study, 250*t*, 250–51
morality, 219–27
  behavioral component, 219, 226–27
    contributors to, 227–28
    determinants of, 226–27
  cognitive component, 219, 220–24, 221*t*
    justifications for parenting practices,
        220, 221*t*
    moral reasoning, 221–23
    parenting styles, 220–21
    peer relationships, 222–23
    variation in parental response to
        transgressions, 220
  emotional component, 219,
      224–26, 225*t*
    defining empathy, 224
    defining guilt, 224

defining shame, 224
inductive reasoning, 225–26
love withdrawal techniques of
    discipline, 226
parent-report measures,
    224–25, 225t
self-report measures, 224–25
Mothers' Perceptions of Their Children's
    Play, 74t
MPQ *See* Meta-Parenting Profile
    Questionnaire
Multidimensional Anxiety Scale for
    Children 2, 279–80
Multigroup Ethnic Identity Measure
    (MEIM), 273, 274t

National Down Syndrome Society, 283
National Fragile X Foundation, 283
nature-nurture issue, 12, 53–56, 54t
    continuity-discontinuity issue and, 85
    examples of items used in studies of,
        55t, 55–56
    variation across different aspects of
        development, 53–54
    variation in goal of explanation, 54–55
    varied labels for, 53
neglect. *See* abuse and neglect
night waking and sleep schedule,
    147t, 147–48
nonparents, comparisons of parents and,
    2–3, 39, 45
    adolescence, 248
    crying, 145
    life satisfaction, 125
    nature-nurture issue, 56
    Piagetian concepts, 186
nurture: agents issue, 54t, 57–59
    cross-cultural comparisons, 57–58
    depressed *vs.* normally-functioning
        mothers, 58
    importance of parents *vs.* teachers, 57
    importance of self-discovery, 57
    judgment of other parent's
        importance, 58–59
    mother-father comparisons, 58
nurture: processes issue, 54t, 59–77, 61t
    behavior-development relation, 65, 69
    belief-behavior relation, 63–64

beliefs-development relation, 62–63, 68
categorical and compensating/
    perspectivist levels of thought,
    66–67, 67t
concordance between parents, 62
constructivist-nonconstructivist
    continuum, 60–62, 63, 66
context and parental consistency, 64–65
cross-cultural comparisons, 62
level of parental knowledge, 69
modern-traditional-paradoxical
    continuum, 70–71
play, 73–77, 74t
Sameroff approach, 66–70, 67t
Sigel and McGillicuddy-DeLisi
    approach, 59–65, 61t
stability of parental beliefs, 69–70
variation in parental beliefs, 60–62
women's beliefs of knowledge and
    knowing, 72

Observer-Memory Questionnaire-Parent
    Form, 190
Olweus Bullying Prevention Program
    (OBPP), 218
open-ended, nondirective questioning,
    38t, 41, 44, 135, 168, 192, 248
overestimation bias, 181, 186

parental beliefs. *See also* adolescence;
        atypical development; cognitive
        development in childhood;
        infancy; social development in
        childhood
    about wide variety of topics, 2
    "beliefs" *vs.* other labels, 3–4
    "beliefs" *vs.* values and goals, 4
    characteristics of, 44–45, 45t
    effects of, 2
    marked differences among, 2
    origins of, 45–48
    parental competence and, 8
    parental expectations and, 7–8
    parent-child comparisons, 12
    reasons for studying, 5–11
        belief-behavior relation, 6–7
        belief-development relation, 7
        effects of beliefs on parents, 7–8

parental beliefs. (*cont.*)
    multidisciplinary interest, 8–9
    parent-report measures of child
        characteristics, 10
    pragmatic importance, 10–11
    study of adult social cognition, 5–6
    study of culture and cultural
        differences, 9
   scope of, 3
   terminology, 2–4
Parental Knowledge Scale, 242*t*,
    242–43, 251
parental meta-emotion philosophy (PMEP)
    approach, 204–6, 205*f*, 205*t*, 210
Parental Monitoring Scale, 246*t*
parental success, perception of, 126–27
    causality *vs.* correlation, 127
    educational/occupational success of
        child, 126
    long-term effects, 127
    mixed outcomes among children, 127
    mother-father comparisons, 127
    quality of the relationship with parent
        and, 126
    social/interpersonal success of
        child, 126
Parent Attribution Test (PAT), 102, 103*t*,
    105–6, 112–13
Parent Behavior Importance
    Questionnaire-R (PBIQ-R), 90
parent-child conflict
    adolescence, 247–48, 261–64
       accuracy of parents' beliefs, 263
       autonomy, 261–62
       biological and social changes, 262–63
       epistemological beliefs, 264
       mother-father comparisons, 263
       parental attributions, 264
       parental expectations, 262–63
       perspective-taking ability, 263–64
    decision-making power, 121–22
parentification, 93–94
parenting, beliefs regarding, 12, 89–114
    attributions, 102–6, 103*t*
       cross-cultural comparisons, 105
       low perceived control over
         failure, 102–6
       mother-father comparisons, 105

investment and balance, 106–8
meta-parenting, 108–10, 109*t*
parental knowledge, 90*t*, 90–96
    judgments about children and
        parenting, 91–92
    knowledge-behavior and knowledge-
        development relation, 93
    knowledge of parenting
        practices, 94–96
    sources of individual differences
        in, 92
    standardized instruments, 90
parental self-efficacy, 95*t*, 96–102,
    97*t*, 100*t*
    in conjunction with other
        variables, 101–2
    defined, 96
    domain-specific nature of, 96
    effects of, 99–101
    factors influencing success or
        failure, 98
    mother-father comparisons, 98–99
    sources of, 96–97
    specificity in study of, 96
    transition to parenting, 110–14
       as determinant of beliefs, 111
       egalitarian division of child
         care, 113–14
       perceived control over failure, 112–13
       self-efficacy, 111–12
Parent Meta-Emotion Interview, 204
Parent Play Beliefs Scale, 73, 74*t*
Parent-Reported Inventory of Callous-
    Unemotional Traits, 279–80
parent-report measures, 10–11
    attachment, 158, 159
    atypical development, 278–80, 279*t*
    delinquency, 260–61
    emotional development, 208,
        224–25, 225*t*
    empathy, 224–25, 225*t*
    error and validity, 143
    executive function, 194*t*, 194
    gender-role development, 234–35, 235*t*
    guilt, 224–25
    infancy, 140–44, 142*t*
    intellectual disabilities, 284
    language, 195–96

memory, 190*t*, 190–91
morality, 224–25, 225*t*
other measures *vs.*, 141–43
parental knowledge, 140–44, 142*t*
sexual activity, 258–59
substance use, 252–53
temperament, 153–56, 155*t*
theory of mind, 189
variation in purpose, 140–41
variation in scope, 140
Parents' Beliefs About Children's Emotions Questionnaire, 204, 205*t*
Parents' Beliefs About Feelings Questionnaire, 204
Parents' Beliefs About Negative Emotions Questionnaire, 204
Parents' Ideas Questionnaire, 70–71
Parent's Observations of Social Interactions, 293
Parents' Perception of Child's Play, 74*t*
PAT *See* Parent Attribution Test
PBIQ-R (Parent Behavior Importance Questionnaire-R), 90
Peabody Picture Vocabulary Test, 196–97
peer relationships, 230–33
  attachment, 231
  effect on parent-child relationship, 232–33
  ethnic identity, 275
  friendships, 230–31
  morality, 222–23
  parental contribution to, 231–32
  parental management of, 231–32, 232*t*
  play, 231
  romantic relationships, 270
  sociometric status, 230–31
Perceived Competence Scale for Children (Self-Perception Profile for Children), 106
permissive parenting style, 122–23, 220–21
perspective-taking ability, 263–64
physical punishment, 215–16, 216*t*
Piagetian concepts, 185–86
play, 73–77, 74*t*, 200
  belief-behavior relation, 75
  belief-development relation, 75
  children's awareness of parental beliefs, 75–76

concordance between parents, 74
cross-cultural comparisons, 76–77
gender-role development, 236–37
nurture: processes issue, 73–77, 74*t*
outcomes related to, 74–75
peer relationships, 231
postpartum depression, 301
psychologists' beliefs, 73
variation in parental beliefs, 73–75
PMEP *See* parental meta-emotion philosophy approach 204–6, 205*f*, 205*t*, 210
postpartum depression, 301
Prader-Willi syndrome, 284, 286–87
proactive aggression, 213–14
prompt-word method, 160, 161*t*
prosocial reasoning, 222
psychological reasons for having children, 124

reactive aggression, 213–14
reading, 53–54
relational aggression, 214
Rochester Longitudinal Study, 59, 66–70, 67*t*
romantic relationships, 268–71
  attachment, 269–70
  defined, 268–69
  family talk, 270–71
  parental monitoring, 270–71
  parenting styles, 270
  parents' own childhood experiences, 271
  peer relationships and, 270
  variation in, 269

scaffolding, 193
schizophrenia, 301–4
  degrees of parenting deficits, 303
  effects of, 302
  theory of mind, 303–4
  variation in, 301–2
secure attachment, 25–26*t*, 25–27, 159–60. *See also* attachment
secure base scripts, 160–61, 161*t*
self-efficacy, 95*t*, 28–29, 96–102, 97*t*, 100*t*
  academic performance, 175, 176

self-efficacy, (cont.)
  agreement or shared meaning of
      beliefs, 98–99
  attention-deficit hyperactivity
      disorder, 290
  attribution theory and, 29
  autism spectrum disorder, 294
  breastfeeding, 153
  in conjunction with other
      variables, 101–2
  contributing sources, 28–29
  contribution to performance, 29
  defined, 28, 96
  depression, 299
  domain-specific nature of, 28, 96
  effects of, 99–101
  factors influencing success or failure, 98
  family talk about sex, 257
  Internet and social media, 267
  marital satisfaction, 99
  mother-father comparisons, 98–99
  parental characteristics and life
      circumstances, 98
  sources of, 96–97
  specificity in study of, 96
  transition to parenting, 111–12
Self-Perception Profile for Children See
      Perceived Competence Scale for
      Children
Self-Perceptions of the Parental
      Role (SPPR)
  balance-investment, 106–8
  competence, 107
  cross-cultural comparisons, 107–8
self-serving bias, 81, 84–85, 170
SES. See socioeconomic status
sexual activity, 255–59
  accuracy of parents' beliefs, 256–57
  child-report measures, 257, 258–59
  cross-cultural comparisons, 259
  family talk about sex, 257–58
  gender differences, 257
  parental knowledge, 256–57
  parental monitoring, 258
  parent-report measures, 258–59
  parents' own childhood
      experiences, 257
  quality of parent-child relationship, 258

reciprocal parent-child
      influences, 258–59
  trends among US adolescents, 255–56
shame
  defined, 224
  inductive reasoning, 226
  parental inducement of, 226
shared methods variance, 48–49
sibling relations, 233
  moral behavior, 227
  parents' differential treatment of
      siblings, 233
  siblings' perceptions of differential
      treatment, 233
SIDS See sudden infant death syndrome
single-reporter bias, 48–49, 63
SIP See social information
      processing theory
sleeping, 129, 146–51
  bed-sharing, 147, 148–50
  night waking and sleep schedule,
      147t, 147–48
  sleep position, 147, 150–51
social cognitive theory, 28
social competence, 228–33
  defined, 228
  peer relationships, 230–33
      effect on parent-child
          relationship, 232–33
      friendships, 230–31
      parental contribution to, 231–32
      parental management of,
          231–32, 232t
      sociometric status, 230–31
  sibling relations, 233
      parents' differential treatment of
          siblings, 233
      siblings' perceptions of differential
          treatment, 233
  social withdrawal, 228–30
      cross-cultural comparisons, 230
      nurturing of social skills, 229
      parents' emotional responses to, 229
      shyness/timidity vs., 230
social development in childhood,
      13, 202–38
  aggression, 212–19
      bullying, 217–19

normative development,
212–17, 216*t*
emotional development, 203–12, 205*t*
gender-role development, 234–38, 235*t*
morality, 219–27
behavioral component, 226–27
cognitive component, 220–24, 221*t*
emotional component, 224–26, 225*t*
social competence, 228–33
peer relationships, 230–33, 232*t*
sibling relations, 233
social withdrawal, 228–30
social information processing (SIP)
theory, 20*f*, 20–22
social learning theory, 27–28
social/traditional reasons for having
children, 124
social withdrawal, 228–30
cross-cultural comparisons, 230
nurturing of social skills, 229
parents' emotional responses to, 229
shyness/timidity *vs.*, 230
stability of development, 80
sociocultural theory, 22–24
household responsibilities, 118
importance of social experience for
development, 22–23
intellectual "tools," 23–24
Piagetian theory *vs.*, 23
relevance to parents, 23–24
zone of proximal development, 24,
71, 118
socioeconomic status (SES)
abuse and neglect, 305–6
language, 197
play, 74
variation in parental beliefs,
60–62, 67–68
speech-for-self, 23
SPPR. *See* Self-Perceptions of the
Parental Role
stability of development
environmental stability, 81–82
factors contributing to, 79–80
parental beliefs, 79
stability of parental beliefs, 50–51, 69–70,
120–21, 122, 171–72
statistical controls, 49–50

Stereotypes of Adolescence Scale, 249*t*
Strange Situation procedure, 24–25, 25*t*,
157, 159
Strengths and Difficulties Questionnaire,
279*t*, 279–80
Study of Beliefs About Developmental
Milestones (Tamis-LeMonda et
al.), 130–34, 131*t*, 141
substance use, 250–55
accuracy of parents' beliefs, 254
adolescents' self-disclosure, 252, 253
causality *vs.* correlation, 253
child-report measures, 252–53
concordance between parents and
children, 252–53, 254
cross-cultural comparisons, 250–51
modeling, 255
parental expectations, 254–55
parental knowledge, 251–52, 253–54
parental monitoring, 252, 253
parental practices, 255
parent-report measures, 252–53
reciprocal parent-child
influences, 253
trends among US adolescents,
250*t*, 250
sudden infant death syndrome
(SIDS), 149–50
sudden unexpected death in infancy
(SUDI), 149–50

temperament, 98, 129, 153–57
behavioral measures, 154
cross-cultural comparisons, 157
defined, 153
dimensions of, 153
effect on parenting, 156
parental behavior and, 156
parental characteristics
affecting, 154–56
parent-report measures, 153–56, 155*t*
physiological measures, 154
theories, 12, 14–37
attribution theory, 15–19
actor-observer bias, 18–19
attributional style, 18
attributions for parents' own
behavior, 18

theories, (*cont.*)
  dimensions along which attributions
    vary, 16*t*, 17–18
  factors governing attributions,
    16*t*, 16–17
  factors heightening probability of
    attributional activity, 19
  fundamental attribution error, 18
  self-efficacy and, 29
  self-serving bias, 19
  complementary nature of, 15
  ecological systems theory, 30–33, 31*f*
    chronosystem, 32
    exosystem, 30, 32
    macrosystem, 31–32
    mesosystem, 30
    microsystem, 30, 32
  ethnotheories, 35–37
    defined, 35
    developmental niche, 36–37
    hierarchical organization, 35–36
    pervasive themes, 36
    similarities in, 35–36
  general theoretical framework for
    research, 14
  incorporating elements of one approach
    into another, 15
  information processing perspective,
    15, 19–22
    executive function, 20*f*, 21
    individual differences, 22
    schemas, 20*f*, 21
    social information processing theory,
      20*f*, 20–22
  reciprocal relation between theories and
    research, 12, 15
  self-efficacy, 28–29
    contributing sources, 28–29
    contribution to performance, 29
    defined, 28
    domain-specific nature of, 28
  sociocultural theory, 22–24
    importance of social experience for
      development, 22–23
    intellectual "tools," 23–24
    Piagetian theory *vs.*, 23
    relevance to parents, 23–24
    zone of proximal development, 24

theory of mind, 33–35
  individual differences, 34
  lack of prominence in parents' beliefs
    research, 33–34
  situational differences, 34
  which beliefs fall under heading
    of, 33
  working models, 15, 24–27
    Adult Attachment Interview,
      26*t*, 26–27
    attachment classifications, 25*t*
    of childhood attachment
      relationships, 25–26
    Strange Situation procedure, 24–25, 25*t*
theory of mind, 33–35, 186–89
  individual differences, 34
  lack of prominence in parents' beliefs
    research, 33–34
  mind-mindedness, 187–88
  parent-report measures, 189
  situational differences, 34
  which beliefs fall under heading of, 33
tobacco. *See* substance use
Toddler and Play Scale, 74*t*
*Too Great Expectations?* (Entwisle and
  Alexander), 175
transactional model of development, 49,
  169–70, 171
transition to parenting, 110–14
  as determinant of beliefs, 111
  egalitarian division of child care, 113–14
  perceived control over failure,
    106, 112–13
  self-efficacy, 111–12

value of children, 115, 123–27
  parental satisfaction during
    childhood, 123
  value of having children, 123
  view of how well their child/life has
    turned out, 123, 126–27
Vineland Scales, 139–40
Williams syndrome, 284, 286–87
*Women's Ways of Knowing* (Belenky
  et al.), 72
working models, 15, 24–27, 25–26*t*
  Adult Attachment Interview,
    26*t*, 26–27

attachment, 159–60, 161
attachment classifications, 25*t*
of childhood attachment
    relationships, 25–26
Strange Situation procedure, 24–25, 25*t*

Youth Risk Behavior
    Surveillance, 255–56

zone of proximal development, 24, 71, 118,
    223–24